Scott Foresman
Science

The Diamond Edition

PEARSON
Scott
Foresman

Editorial Offices: Glenview, Illinois • Parsippany, New Jersey • New York, New York
Sales Offices: Boston, Massachusetts • Duluth, Georgia • Glenview, Illinois •
Coppell, Texas • Sacramento, California • Mesa, Arizona
www.pearsonsuccessnet.com

Series Authors

Dr. Timothy Cooney
Professor of Earth Science and Science Education
University of Northern Iowa (UNI)
Cedar Falls, Iowa

Dr. Jim Cummins
Professor
Department of Curriculum, Teaching, and Learning
The University of Toronto
Toronto, Canada

Dr. James Flood
Distinguished Professor of Literacy and Language
School of Teacher Education
San Diego State University
San Diego, California

Barbara Kay Foots, M.Ed
Science Education Consultant
Houston, Texas

Dr. M. Jenice Goldston
Associate Professor of Science Education
Department of Elementary Education Programs
University of Alabama
Tuscaloosa, Alabama

Dr. Shirley Gholston Key
Associate Professor of Science Education
Instruction and Curriculum Leadership Department
College of Education
University of Memphis
Memphis, Tennessee

Dr. Diane Lapp
Distinguished Professor of Reading and Language Arts in Teacher Education
San Diego State University
San Diego, California

Sheryl A. Mercier
Classroom Teacher
Dunlap Elementary School
Dunlap, California

Karen L. Ostlund, Ph.D.
UTeach Specialist
College of Natural Sciences
The University of Texas at Austin
Austin, Texas

Dr. Nancy Romance
Professor of Science Education & Principal Investigator
NSF/IERI Science IDEAS Project
Charles E. Schmidt College of Science
Florida Atlantic University
Boca Raton, Florida

Dr. William Tate
Chair and Professor of Education and Applied Statistics
Department of Education
Washington University
St. Louis, Missouri

Dr. Kathryn C. Thornton
Former NASA Astronaut Professor
School of Engineering and Applied Science
University of Virginia
Charlottesville, Virginia

Dr. Leon Ukens
Professor Emeritus
Department of Physics, Astronomy, and Geosciences
Towson University
Towson, Maryland

Steve Weinberg
Consultant
Connecticut Center for Advanced Technology
East Hartford, Connecticut

ISBN: 978-0-328-28962-2; 0-328-28962-0 (SVE); 978-0-328-30450-9;
0-328-30450-6 (A); 978-0-328-30451-6; 0-328-30451-4 (B); 978-0-328-30452-3;
0-328-30452-2 (C); 978-0-328-30453-0; 0-328-30453-0 (D)

2 3 4 5 6 7 8 9 10 V063 15 14 13 12 11 10 09 08 07
CC: N1

Consulting Author

Dr. Michael P. Klentschy
Superintendent
El Centro Elementary School
District
El Centro, California

Science Content Consultants

Dr. Frederick W. Taylor
Senior Research Scientist
Institute for Geophysics
Jackson School of Geosciences
The University of Texas at Austin
Austin, Texas

Dr. Ruth E. Buskirk
Senior Lecturer
School of Biological Sciences
The University of Texas at Austin
Austin, Texas

Dr. Cliff Frohlich
Senior Research Scientist
Institute for Geophysics
Jackson School of Geosciences
The University of Texas at Austin
Austin, Texas

Brad Armosky
McDonald Observatory
The University of Texas at Austin
Austin, Texas

Content Consultants

Adena Williams Loston, Ph.D.
Chief Education Officer
Office of the Chief Education
Officer

Clifford W. Houston, Ph.D.
*Deputy Chief Education Officer
for Education Programs*
Office of the Chief Education
Officer

Frank C. Owens
Senior Policy Advisor
Office of the Chief Education
Officer

Deborah Brown Biggs
*Manager, Education Flight
Projects Office*
Space Operations Mission
Directorate, Education Lead

Erika G. Vick
*NASA Liaison to
Pearson Scott Foresman*
Education Flight Projects Office

William E. Anderson
*Partnership Manager
for Education*
Aeronautics Research Mission
Directorate

Anita Krishnamurthi
Program Planning Specialist
Space Science Education and
Outreach Program

Bonnie J. McClain
Chief of Education
Exploration Systems
Mission Directorate

Diane Clayton, Ph.D.
Program Scientist
Earth Science Education

Deborah Rivera
Strategic Alliances Manager
Office of Public Affairs
NASA Headquarters

Douglas D. Peterson
*Public Affairs Officer
Astronaut Office*
Office of Public Affairs
NASA Johnson Space Center

Nicole Cloutier
*Public Affairs Officer
Astronaut Office*
Office of Public Affairs
NASA Johnson Space Center

Reviewers

iv

Science

See learning in a whole new light

Unit A Life Science

How are the
living things
around us alike
and different?

What are the
parts of a cell?

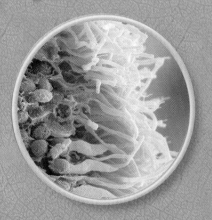

Chapter 3 • Reproduction

How do living things reproduce?

Chapter 4 • Body Systems

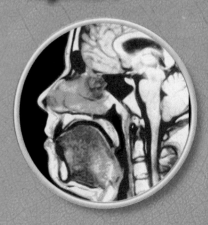

How do body parts work together?

Unit A Life Science

Chapter 5 • Plants

What processes take place in plants?

Chapter 6 • Biomes

How do organisms live together in ecosystems?

Chapter 7 • Ecosystems

How do energy, organisms, and the environment interact?

Unit B Earth Science

How does the theory of plate tectonics explain Earth's landforms?

How do rocks and minerals form soils?

Chapter 10 • Reshaping Earth's Surface

What processes change Earth's landforms?

Unit B   Earth Science

How can we use Earth's resources wisely?

Chapter 11 • Earth's Resources

Chapter 12 • Climate and Weather

What causes Earth's weather and climate?

Unit C Physical Science

Chapter 13 • Matter

How can the properties of matter change?

Chapter 14 • Building Blocks of Matter

What do the many types of matter have in common?

Chapter 15 • Forces and Motion

How are motion and forces related?

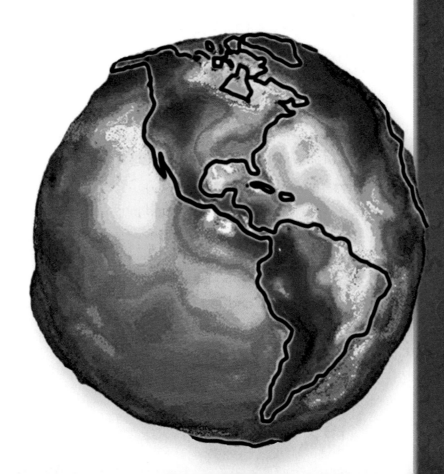

Unit C Physical Science

How do machines make work easier?

How can energy change from one form to another?

Chapter 18 • Thermal and Light Energy

How are thermal energy and light energy transferred?

Unit D Space and Technology

Chapter 19 • Earth, Sun, and Moon

What are the effects of the movements of Earth and the Moon?

Chapter 20 • The Universe

What is Earth's place in the universe?

Chapter 21 • Impacts of Technology

How can
robots help us
now and in
the future?

How to Read Science

A page like this one is toward the beginning of each chapter. It shows you how to use a reading skill that will help you understand what you read.

Before Reading

Before you read the chapter, read the Build Background page and think about how to answer the question. Recall what you already know as you answer the question. Work with a partner to make a list of what you already know. Then read the How to Read Science page.

Target Reading Skill

Each page has one target reading skill. The reading skill corresponds with a process skill in the Directed Inquiry activity on the facing page. The reading skill will be useful as you read science.

Real-World Connection

Each page has an example of something you might read. It also connects with the Directed Inquiry activity.

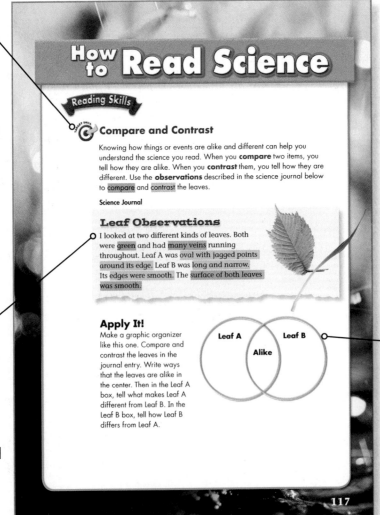

Graphic Organizer

A useful strategy for understanding anything you read is to create a graphic organizer. A graphic organizer can help you think about the information and relate parts of it to each other. Each reading skill has a certain graphic organizer.

Both plants and animals give off carbon dioxide during cellular respiration.

Carbon Dioxide–Oxygen Cycle

You may have noticed that the equations for photosynthesis and cellular respiration look a lot alike. In fact, look at these two equations again.

$$\text{carbon dioxide} + \text{water} \xrightarrow[\text{chlorophyll}]{\text{light energy}} \text{glucose} + \text{oxygen}$$

$$\text{glucose} + \text{oxygen} \longrightarrow \text{carbon dioxide} + \text{water} + \text{energy}$$

The processes are almost the reverse of each other. The materials produced during one process are the same materials that are needed for the other process. In other words, they form a cycle. Together, photosynthesis and cellular respiration form the carbon dioxide–oxygen cycle.

The carbon dioxide–oxygen cycle can be summarized in this way: Day and night, animals breathe oxygen from the air. Plants take in oxygen and carbon dioxide through their leaves. During respiration, both plants and animals use oxygen to change energy in food to energy they can use. They give off carbon dioxide. Plants use some of the energy and carbon dioxide to produce more food and oxygen in the process of photosynthesis. The carbon dioxide–oxygen cycle assures that living things do not run out of the oxygen and carbon they need.

✓ Lesson Checkpoint

1. What do plants need to carry on photosynthesis?
2. Why do most leaves have more stomata on the lower epidermis than on the upper epidermis?
3. **Compare and Contrast** How does the role of energy differ in photosynthesis and cellular respiration?

125

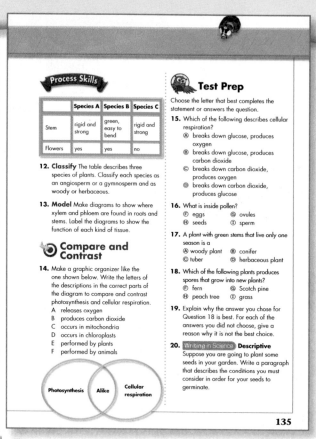

Process Skills

	Species A	Species B	Species C
Stem	rigid and strong	green, easy to bend	rigid and strong
Flowers	yes	yes	no

12. **Classify** The table describes three species of plants. Classify each species as an angiosperm or a gymnosperm and as woody or herbaceous.

13. **Model** Make diagrams to show where xylem and phloem are found in roots and stems. Label the diagrams to show the function of each kind of tissue.

Compare and Contrast

14. Make a graphic organizer like the one shown below. Write the letters of the descriptions in the correct parts of the diagram to compare and contrast photosynthesis and cellular respiration.
   A   releases oxygen
   B   produces carbon dioxide
   C   occurs in mitochondria
   D   occurs in chloroplasts
   E   performed by plants
   F   performed by animals

Photosynthesis   Alike   Cellular respiration

Test Prep

Choose the letter that best completes the statement or answers the question.

15. Which of the following describes cellular respiration?
   Ⓐ breaks down glucose, produces oxygen
   Ⓑ breaks down glucose, produces carbon dioxide
   Ⓒ breaks down carbon dioxide, produces oxygen
   Ⓓ breaks down carbon dioxide, produces glucose

16. What is inside pollen?
   Ⓕ eggs   Ⓖ ovules
   Ⓗ seeds   Ⓘ sperm

17. A plant with green stems that live only one season is a
   Ⓐ woody plant   Ⓑ conifer
   Ⓒ tuber   Ⓓ herbaceous plant

18. Which of the following plants produces spores that grow into new plants?
   Ⓕ fern   Ⓖ Scotch pine
   Ⓗ peach tree   Ⓘ grass

19. Explain why the answer you chose for Question 18 is best. For each of the answers you did not choose, give a reason why it is not the best choice.

20. Writing in Science **Descriptive** Suppose you are going to plant some seeds in your garden. Write a paragraph that describes the conditions you must consider in order for your seeds to germinate.

135

During Reading

As you read the lesson, use the Checkpoint to check your understanding. Some Checkpoints ask you to use the reading target skill.

After Reading

After you have read the chapter, think about what you found out. Exchange ideas with your partner. Compare the list you made before you read the chapter with what you learned by reading it. Answer the questions in the Chapter Review. One question uses the reading target skill.

Graphic Organizers

These are the target reading skills with their graphic organizers.

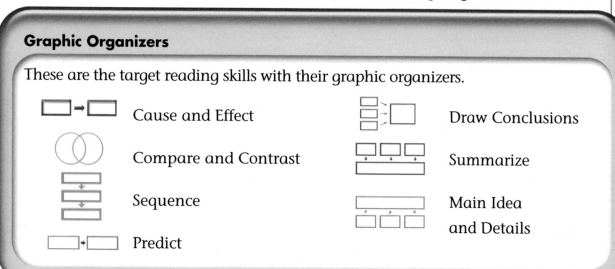

Cause and Effect

Compare and Contrast

Sequence

Predict

Draw Conclusions

Summarize

Main Idea and Details

Science Process Skills

Exploring a Rain Forest

Scientists use process skills when they explore places or investigate events. You will use these skills when you do the activities in this book. Which process skills might scientists use when they explore a tropical rain forest?

Observe

A scientist exploring a rain forest observes many things. You use your senses too to find out about other objects, events, or living things.

Classify

Scientists classify living and nonliving things in a rain forest according to their properties. When you classify, you arrange or sort objects, events, or living things.

Estimate and Measure

Scientists might estimate the size of an organism in a rain forest. When they estimate, they tell what they think an object's size, mass, or temperature will measure. Then they measure these factors in units.

Infer
During an investigation, scientists infer what they think is happening, based on what they already know.

Predict
Before they go into a rain forest, scientists tell what they think they will find.

Make and Use Models
Scientists might make and use models, such as maps, to help plan where to go during an investigation.

Make Operational Definitions
When scientists make operational definitions, they describe objects or events based on their experiences.

Science Process Skills

Form Questions and Hypotheses

Think of a statement that you can test to solve a problem or answer a question about a python or other organism in a tropical rain forest.

Collect Data

Scientists collect data from their observations in rain forests. They put the data into charts or tables.

Interpret Data

Scientists use the information they collected to solve problems or answer questions.

If you were a scientist, you might explore a tropical rain forest or other area. What questions might you have about the things you see? How would you use process skills in your investigation?

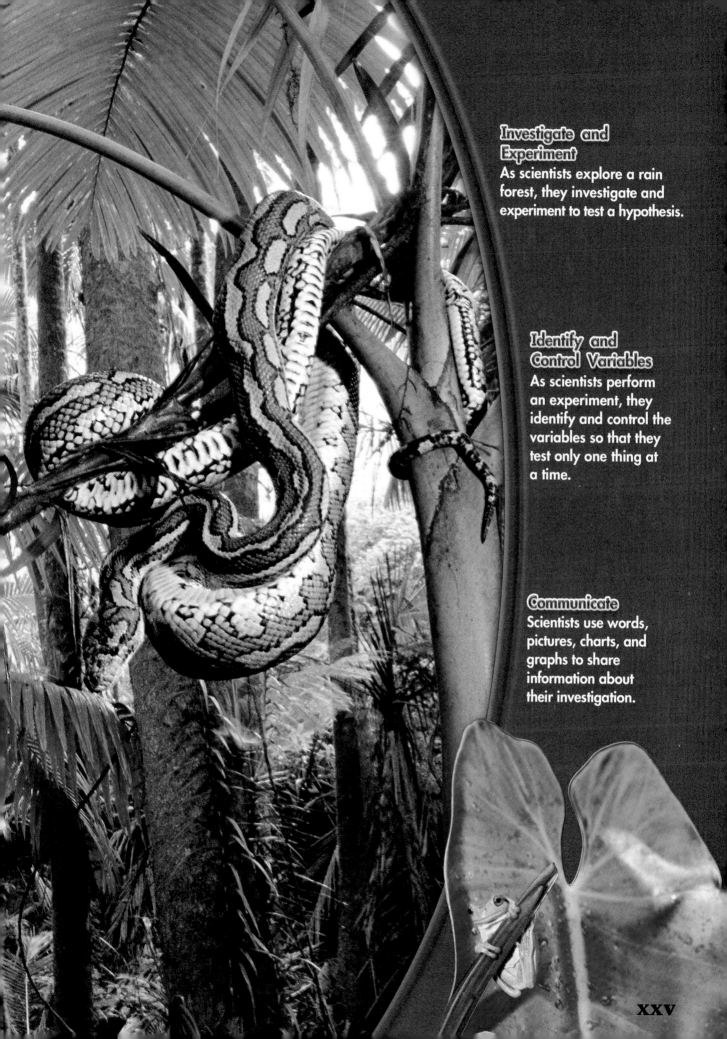

Investigate and Experiment

As scientists explore a rain forest, they investigate and experiment to test a hypothesis.

Identify and Control Variables

As scientists perform an experiment, they identify and control the variables so that they test only one thing at a time.

Communicate

Scientists use words, pictures, charts, and graphs to share information about their investigation.

Using Scientific Methods for Science Inquiry

Scientists use scientific methods as they work. Scientific methods are organized ways to answer questions and solve problems. Scientific methods include the steps shown here. Scientists might not use all the steps. They might not use the steps in this order. You will use scientific methods when you do the **Full Inquiry** activity at the end of each unit. You also will use scientific methods when you do **Science Fair Projects.**

Ask a question.
You might have a question about something you observe.

What material is best for keeping heat in water?

State your hypothesis.
A hypothesis is a possible answer to your question.

If I wrap the jar in fake fur, then the water will stay warmer longer.

Identify and control variables.
Variables are things that can change. For a fair test, you choose just one variable to change. Keep all other variables the same.

Test other materials. Put the same amount of warm water in other jars that are the same size and shape.

Test your hypothesis.
Make a plan to test your hypothesis. Collect materials and tools. Then follow your plan.

Collect and record your data.
Keep good records of what you do and find out. Use tables and pictures to help.

Interpret your data.
Organize your notes and records to make them clear. Make diagrams, charts, or graphs to help.

State your conclusion.
Your conclusion is a decision you make based on your data. Communicate what you found out. Tell whether or not your data supported your hypothesis.

Fake fur did the best job of keeping the water warm.

Go further.
Use what you learn. Think of new questions to test or better ways to do a test.

Ask a Question

State Your Hypothesis

Identify and Control Variables

Test Your Hypothesis

Collect and Record Your Data

Interpret Your Data

State Your Conclusion

Go Further

Science Tools

Graduated cylinders and beakers can be used to measure volume, or the amount of space an object takes up.

Scientists use many different kinds of tools. Tools can make objects appear larger. They can help you measure volume, temperature, length, distance, and mass. Tools can help you figure out amounts and analyze your data. Tools can also help you find the latest scientific information.

A **hand lens** makes objects appear larger. A hand lens, or magnifying glass, doesn't enlarge things as much as a microscope does, but you can easily carry a hand lens.

A **microscope** uses a series of lenses that make objects appear larger. When you change the combination and position of lenses, you magnify objects by different amounts.

A **stopwatch** is a watch with a hand that can be stopped or started. It can be used for timing experiments.

A meterstick or **metric ruler** is used to measure length. A meterstick is one meter long. The stick is divided into smaller units—usually centimeters and millimeters.

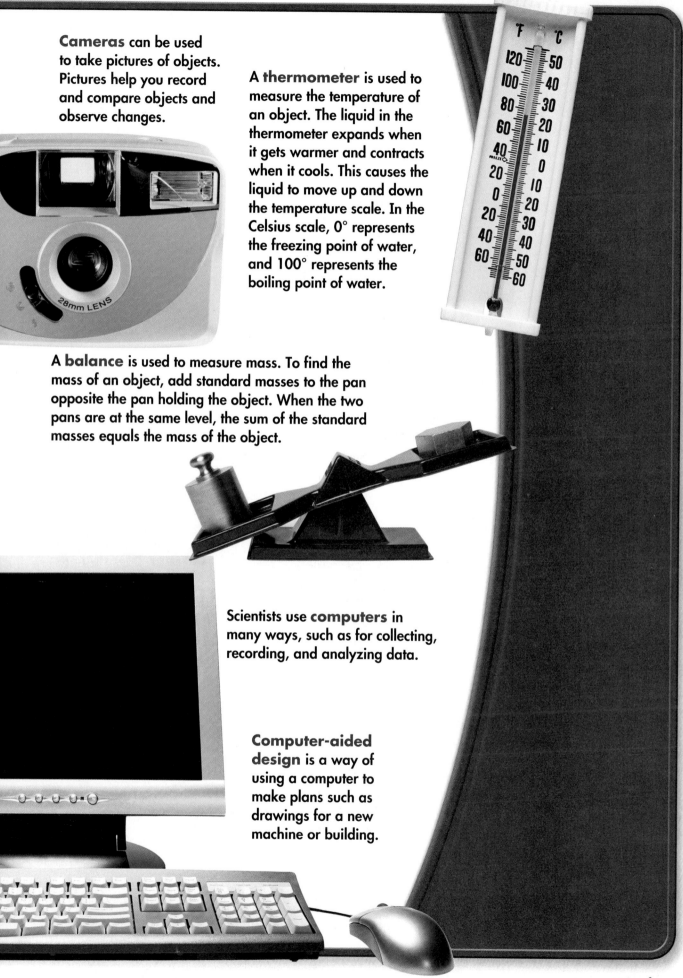

Cameras can be used to take pictures of objects. Pictures help you record and compare objects and observe changes.

A **thermometer** is used to measure the temperature of an object. The liquid in the thermometer expands when it gets warmer and contracts when it cools. This causes the liquid to move up and down the temperature scale. In the Celsius scale, 0° represents the freezing point of water, and 100° represents the boiling point of water.

A **balance** is used to measure mass. To find the mass of an object, add standard masses to the pan opposite the pan holding the object. When the two pans are at the same level, the sum of the standard masses equals the mass of the object.

Scientists use **computers** in many ways, such as for collecting, recording, and analyzing data.

Computer-aided design is a way of using a computer to make plans such as drawings for a new machine or building.

Science Tools

Scientists use **barometers** to measure the air pressure, which can be a good indicator of weather patterns.

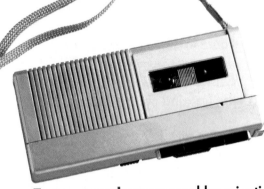

Tape recorders are used by scientists to record and learn about sounds made by organisms or objects.

Field guides are books that you might take into the field to learn the details of objects that you are observing, such as plants, animals, or stars.

Calculators make analyzing data easier and faster.

A **spring scale** is used to measure force. Because the weight of an object is a measure of the force of gravity on the object, you can use a spring scale to measure weight in grams.

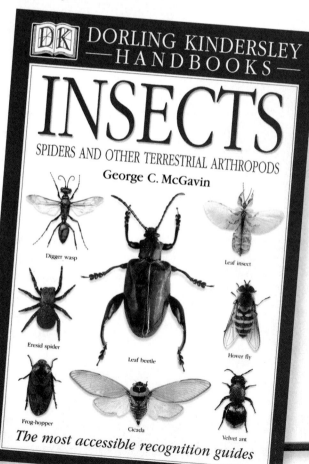

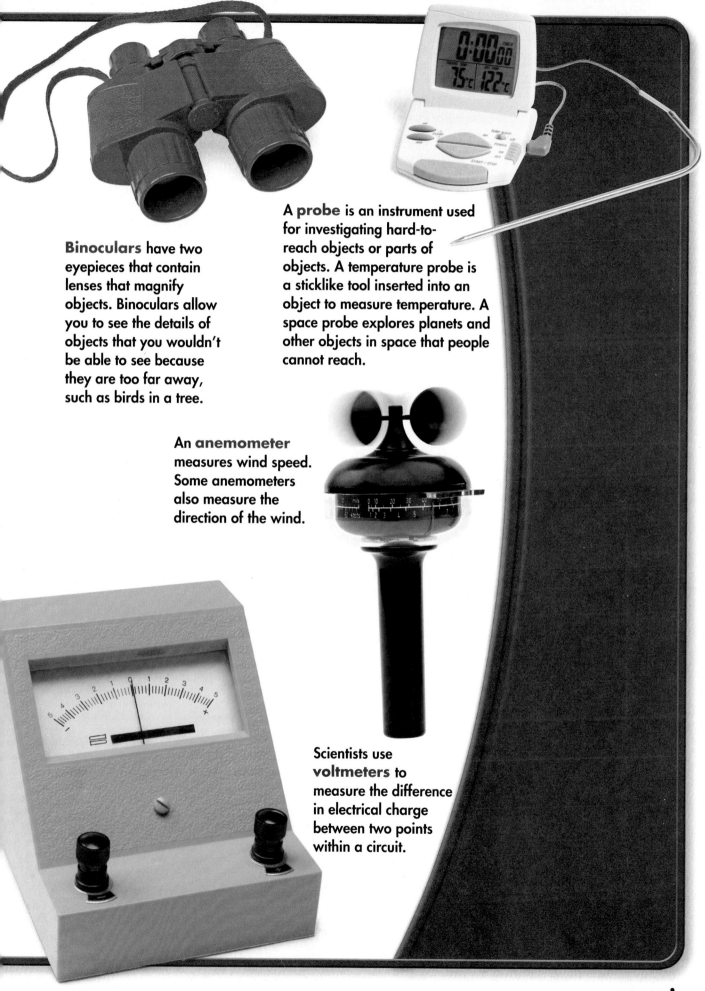

Binoculars have two eyepieces that contain lenses that magnify objects. Binoculars allow you to see the details of objects that you wouldn't be able to see because they are too far away, such as birds in a tree.

A **probe** is an instrument used for investigating hard-to-reach objects or parts of objects. A temperature probe is a sticklike tool inserted into an object to measure temperature. A space probe explores planets and other objects in space that people cannot reach.

An **anemometer** measures wind speed. Some anemometers also measure the direction of the wind.

Scientists use **voltmeters** to measure the difference in electrical charge between two points within a circuit.

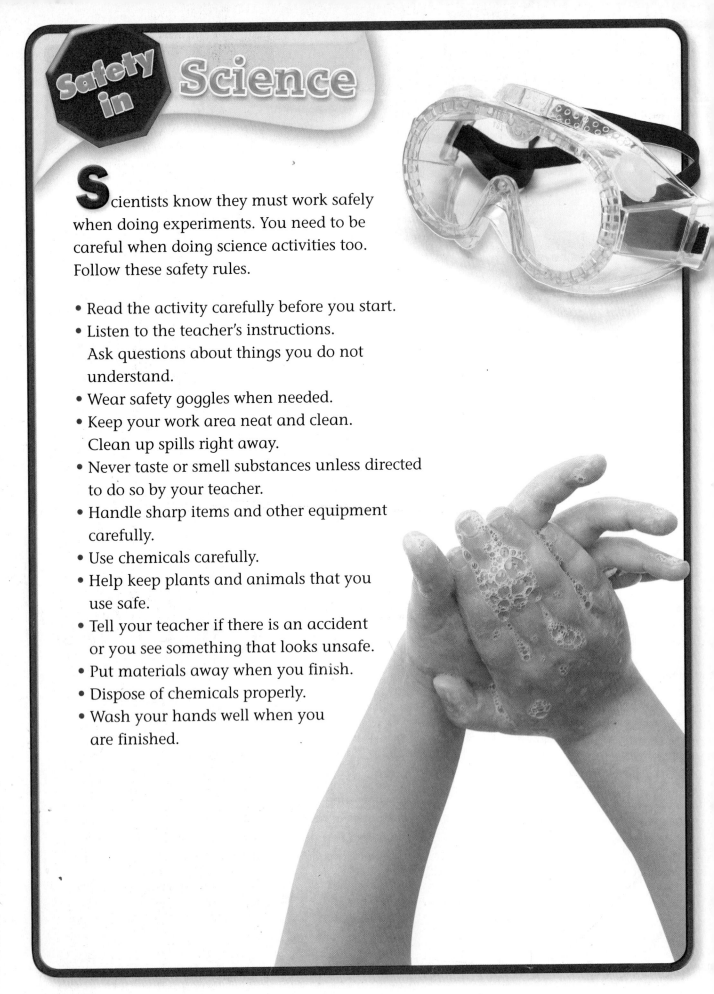

Safety in Science

Scientists know they must work safely when doing experiments. You need to be careful when doing science activities too. Follow these safety rules.

- Read the activity carefully before you start.
- Listen to the teacher's instructions. Ask questions about things you do not understand.
- Wear safety goggles when needed.
- Keep your work area neat and clean. Clean up spills right away.
- Never taste or smell substances unless directed to do so by your teacher.
- Handle sharp items and other equipment carefully.
- Use chemicals carefully.
- Help keep plants and animals that you use safe.
- Tell your teacher if there is an accident or you see something that looks unsafe.
- Put materials away when you finish.
- Dispose of chemicals properly.
- Wash your hands well when you are finished.

Unit A

Life Science

Chapter 1
Classification

You Will Discover

- where living things on Earth live.
- how Earth's living things are classified.

online
Student Edition
pearsonsuccessnet.com

How are living things alike and different?

adaptation

biosphere

The part of Earth that can support living things

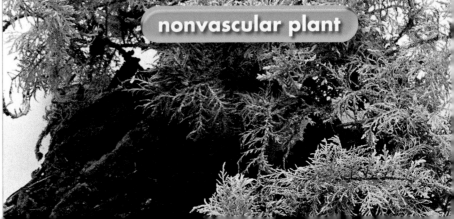

nonvascular plant

2

Chapter 1 Vocabulary

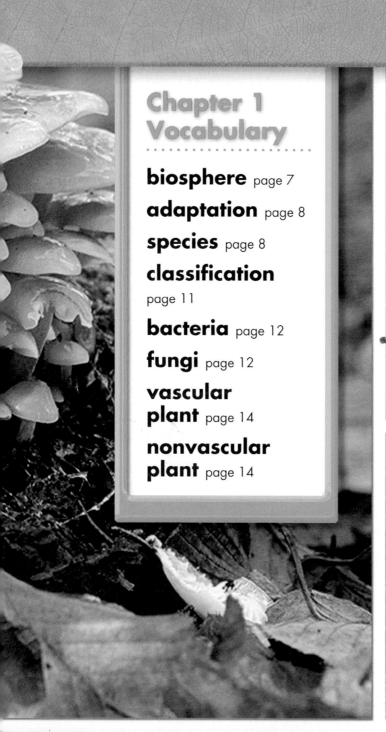

classification

species

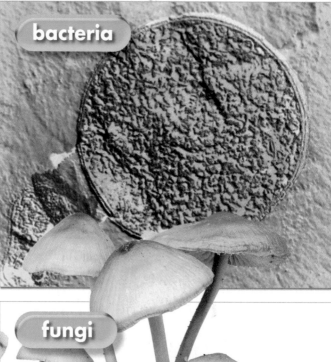

bacteria

vascular plant

fungi

3

Explore How are mushrooms different?

Scientists can tell one type of mushroom from another by studying spore prints, the patterns and colors made by mushroom spores.

Materials

3 kinds of mushrooms

plastic knife

white and black paper

3 cups

What to Do

1 Cut off the stem so the mushroom lies flat. Place the mushroom on the paper.

2 Cover the mushroom with a cup and leave it for 2 days.

3 Repeat steps 1 and 2 with 2 other kinds of mushrooms.

4 After 2 days, remove the cups. Carefully remove the mushrooms. **Observe** the spore prints on the paper.

Your teacher will tell you which color of paper to use for each mushroom.

Process Skills

Spore prints can help you **classify** mushrooms.

Explain Your Results

1. How are the spore prints alike and different? Are the prints a useful way to tell mushrooms apart? Explain.

2. How can you use a spore print to **classify** mushrooms?

How to Read Science

TARGET SKILL Compare and Contrast

When you look at how things are alike and different, you are **comparing** and **contrasting.** When comparing two items, tell how they are alike. When contrasting, tell how items are different.

- Clue words and phrases such as *similar, like, all, both, in the same way,* and *as well as* signal comparisons.

- Clue words such as *different, unlike, in a different way,* and *in contrast* signal contrasts.

Clue words are marked in the article below.

Science Article

Fungi

Molds and mushrooms are two kinds of fungi. Molds, such as the black, fuzzy mold that grows on bread, are threadlike fungi. In contrast, mushrooms are club fungi, fungi that are somewhat umbrella shaped. Both molds and mushrooms grow rootlike structures that often are hidden underneath the ground. All fungi get their food from other organisms.

Apply It!

Make a graphic organizer like the one shown to **compare** and **contrast** molds and mushrooms. Then tell how you would use the graphic organizer to **classify** molds and mushrooms.

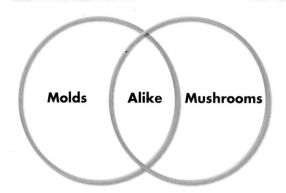

Molds   Alike   Mushrooms

5

🔊 You Are There!

You are trudging along in the hot desert, and a flash of bright yellow catches your attention. A closer look reveals bright cactus flowers. Suddenly you hear a rustling noise. What is this shocking beauty among the blossoms? A snake! What kind of snake is this? How can you find out? Perhaps no one has ever seen this type of snake before—you may have discovered a new organism!

AudioText 🔊

Where on Earth do organisms live?

Earth is home to millions of different living things. A large number of living things have not yet been discovered.

These colorful fungi are well suited to grow on the damp forest floor.

The Biosphere

You probably know that living things are on almost every type of land, and also deep in the oceans and high in Earth's atmosphere. You may think that the area where things live is large. But if you could shrink Earth to the size of an apple, the area in which things can live would be less than the thickness of the apple's skin.

The part of Earth that can support living things is called the **biosphere.** Living things and their environments make up the biosphere. The biosphere has many environments, such as deserts, oceans, fields, beaches, backyards, and the sidewalks of the busiest streets.

Determined dandelions poke through this sidewalk. Your neighborhood is also part of the biosphere.

Organisms in the Biosphere

Scientists have discovered and named nearly two million different organisms in Earth's biosphere. Even so, scientists think that millions more organisms have not been discovered.

Why are so many living things still unknown? Some parts of Earth have not been well studied. Earth's deep oceans, polar areas, dense rain forests, and vast deserts are just some of the areas about which we still have a lot to learn. Also, many of Earth's organisms are very tiny and hard to find.

Each organism in the biosphere interacts with other organisms and the environment to produce a web of interactions. Humans, too, play an important part in this changing web. Because all parts of the web are connected, a small change in one part can produce a large change in another part.

1. ✔**Checkpoint** What is the biosphere?
2. **Writing in Science** **Descriptive** Write a paragraph that describes an environment in your area. Name the types of organisms that live there.

This blackside hawkfish spends much of its time motionless among the coral. Coral are living organisms. What you usually see are coral shells. The soft, living body of the coral grows inside holes in the shell.

Variety Among Living Things

If your class wrote the names of all the different organisms each student knows, imagine how long the list would be! But your list would be very small compared to all the known organisms on our planet.

Earth has an amazing variety of living things. These organisms have many different body plans and structures. These differences make it possible for organisms to live in almost every place on Earth.

Look at the plants and animals pictured on these pages. They all are alike in some ways. For example, they are made of cells, they require a source of energy, and they reproduce. But these organisms are also very different. The differences enable each kind of organism to survive in its particular environment.

A characteristic that enables an organism to survive and reproduce in its environment is called an **adaptation.** For example, the spines of the cactus are actually modified leaves. Their shape helps stop water loss from the plant. They also protect the cactus from being eaten. The thick, fleshy stems of a cactus can store a lot of water—an important adaptation for a plant that grows in such a dry environment. As you look at the other pictures on these pages, think about how each organism's adaptations help it survive in its environment.

How do the adaptations of this cactus help it survive?

The hard shells of these snails help protect their soft bodies, much the same as your skull protects your brain.

Groups of Organisms

Although there is great variety among organisms, some groups of organisms share many of the same characteristics. These organisms may be members of the same species. A **species** is a group of very similar organisms whose members can mate with one another and produce offspring that are able to produce offspring. For example, the horses in the photo are members of the same species. Each species has a two-part scientific name. The scientific name for the horse is *Equus caballus*.

Each type of fish has a mouth designed for its own style of feeding. This parrotfish scrapes algae off the surrounding coral. Can you see how it gets its name?

SciLinks Take It to the Net
pearsonsuccessnet.com
keyword: adaptation
code: g6p8

Like the horses below, individuals in the same species often don't look exactly alike. In fact, they can be different in many ways, including size, color, and shape. But they do share similar body plans and structures.

As you can see from the chart, the number of species for different kinds of organisms is very large. The chart, however, only includes the species that have been identified and live today. Some scientists think that 99 percent of all species that have ever lived on Earth no longer exist. Most of them have left no fossil evidence that they lived.

Group	Number of Living Species
Vertebrates	**42,000**
Mammals	4,000
Birds	9,000
Reptiles	6,000
Amphibians	4,000
Fish	19,000
Invertebrates	**980,000**
Plants	**248,000**

What characteristics do these horses share?

✓ **Lesson Checkpoint**

1. Why haven't scientists identified all species that live today or lived in the past?
2. What is a species? What are some ways members of a species differ?
3. **Writing in Science** **Expository** Choose an organism that you are familiar with. Describe its environment and some of its adaptations. Tell how the organism's adaptations help it survive in its environment.

How do scientists group organisms?

Scientists sort organisms into groups with similar characteristics. Grouping organisms makes studying them easier. Many scientists today divide all Earth's organisms into six main groups called kingdoms.

Kingdom

How Organisms Are Grouped

With so many kinds of organisms, how can scientists study them? Think about how a music store organizes the CDs it sells. Most music stores group together musicians that share certain characteristics.

Phylum

Class

Animals
The organisms shown here are all members of the animal kingdom. Animals are multicellular organisms that must obtain their food by eating other organisms.

Arthropods
Animals that belong to the arthropod phylum share these characteristics: jointed legs, a body divided into segments, and a hard outer skeleton.

Insects
The insect class contains only arthropods with bodies that are divided into three sections and that usually have three pairs of legs at the middle section.

A music store may sort the musicians by the type of music they play. In a similar way, scientists group Earth's many organisms by the similarities of their characteristics. These similarities may or may not be easily seen. The grouping of things according to their similarities is called **classification.**

Throughout history, scientists have used different classification systems. Even today, scientists do not agree on a single system. However, most scientists today use a system similar to the one developed by Carolus Linnaeus in the 1700s.

Linnaeus first grouped all organisms into two very large groups, called kingdoms. These were the plant kingdom and the animal kingdom. Then Linnaeus divided each kingdom into smaller groups based on the features of the organisms. The most common classification system scientists use today is based on six kingdoms, which are divided into smaller and smaller groups. Study the pictures below to see how many scientists today divide the animal kingdom.

1. ✓Checkpoint Why do scientists classify organisms?
2. Math in Science Scientists have discovered about 800,000 species of insects. But scientists think that there may be as many as 10,000,000 insect species. What percentage of the total number of insect species have been discovered?

Order

Family

Genus

Species

Coleoptera
This order contains only insects with two pairs of wings that meet in a straight line along the back. The longer back wings are under the front wings.

Coccinellidae
This family contains only ladybug beetles. All members are dome-shaped, usually brightly colored and spotted, have short legs, and are less than one centimeter long.

Coccinella novemnotata
Members of different species in the same genus are very similar but cannot mate with one another. The red spotted ladybug beetle belongs to the genus *Coccinella* and the species *novemnotata*.

Organisms in The Six Kingdoms

Linnaeus did not have the scientific tools that scientists have today, such as powerful microscopes to study an organism's cells. As scientists developed new tools for studying organisms, they recognized living things that didn't fit into Linnaeus's two kingdoms—plants and animals. For example, scientists discovered **bacteria,** single-celled organisms that do not have a nucleus. Both plant and animal cells contain a nucleus. This important difference caused many scientists to think that bacteria should be grouped separately from plants or animals. Today most scientists classify organisms according to their cell structure and how they get food and reproduce.

Many scientists put organisms into six kingdoms. Kingdom Archaebacteria includes bacteria that live where most other organisms cannot—in water that has a lot of salt or is very hot. The kingdom Eubacteria includes all other bacteria. They live in almost every environment, including your body. In fact, there are more bacteria in your mouth than there are people on Earth!

Protists and Fungi

The more than 200,000 known species of protists are mostly one-celled organisms. Some scientists think that this kingdom should be broken into smaller kingdoms. The cells of all protists contain a nucleus.

Some protists are like animals. They get energy by eating other organisms. The ameba is an example. Plantlike protists contain chlorophyll that they use to make their own food during photosynthesis. Algae are plantlike protists. Some protists are like fungi. They grow in damp, nutrient-rich environments, where they absorb food through their cell membranes.

Fungi are mostly many-celled organisms that often grow in moist, dark places. Many give off chemicals that break down the organisms on which they grow. In the process, fungi get the nutrients they need. In two types of fungi, mushrooms and molds, cells form threadlike strands called hyphae. The hyphae take in the nutrients for the organism. Hyphae can form thick, large mats. One single mushroom in Oregon has a web of underground hyphae that spreads 2,200 acres. That's the size of 1,665 football fields! Yeast cells, another kind of fungus that you can see in the picture, are not connected by hyphae.

Many fungi look like plants and have cells similar to plants. But plant cells contain chlorophyll, which plants use as they make food. Fungi do not have chlorophyll. Instead they take in nutrients from other organisms.

Like most fungi, this mold absorbs nutrients from other organisms—in this case a strawberry.

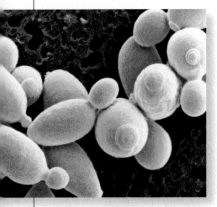

Yeasts are important fungi used in the process of making bread.

The Six Kingdoms

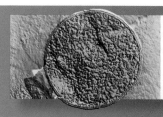

Archaebacteria
Archaebacteria have been on Earth for billions of years. Some can live in hot springs where water temperatures can reach 110°C. Archaebacteria can grow in water that is ten times saltier than seawater.

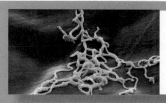

Eubacteria
Eubacteria can cause disease, but many are helpful. They make soil fertile and are necessary for making foods such as yogurts and cheeses. Some eubacteria make vitamins in the human body.

Protists
Protists formed much of the gas and oil we use today. Although some protists are harmful, most are helpful. Many are food for other organisms, including Earth's largest organisms—whales.

Fungi
Fungi are used to make foods and medicines such as penicillin. Some fungi can cause human diseases, such as athlete's foot and ringworm. They also cause plant diseases called rusts.

Plants
Without plants, life on Earth would not exist. These trout lilies have roots, stems, and leaves—characteristics of all plants. Like all plants, they can trap the Sun's energy to produce glucose.

Animals
Animals get energy by eating other organisms or their remains. Topi, such as this one, live in Africa. Like all organisms, a topi has special adaptations that make it able to find and eat the type of food it needs.

✓ Lesson Checkpoint

1. What are the six kingdoms of organisms? Give an example of each.
2. **Compare and Contrast** How do fungi differ from plants?
3. Writing in Science **Descriptive** Collect leaves from local trees and write descriptions of them. Use your descriptions and a field guide for trees from your local library or other sources to identify the trees the leaves came from.

Lesson 3

How are plants and animals classified?

Plants can make their own food. Animals get energy from other living things. Organisms in the plant and animal kingdoms can be classified into smaller groups.

Plant Classification

Look around. How many different kinds of plants do you see? Plants come in many colors, sizes, and shapes. Some are as tall as the coast redwoods in California, which can rise 112 meters. Others, like the duckweed that covers many ponds, are tiny—as little as 0.6 millimeters tall. But whether big or small, plants are important to all other living organisms on Earth. Most living things gain energy directly or indirectly from plants. Besides being a source of food, plants also help make Earth's climate stable.

Notice in the diagram on the next page that all plants can be divided into two groups—vascular plants and nonvascular plants. **Vascular plants** have cells that form tubes for carrying water and nutrients throughout the plants. These tubes can carry materials long distances, such as up the trunk of a 112-meter redwood.

Vascular plants can be divided into two groups—plants that make seeds and plants that do not. You probably are most familiar with plants that produce seeds. Some examples of seed plants are tulips, grasses, maple trees, and tomato plants. Some seed plants are gymnosperms, seed plants that do not produce flowers. They include plants that you might call "evergreens," such as pine or fir. Angiosperms are seed plants that produce flowers. Horsetails and ferns are two kinds of seedless plants.

Other plants, called **nonvascular plants,** do not have tubes to carry materials. Instead materials must pass slowly from one cell to another. For this reason, most nonvascular plants, such as mosses, are small. There are at least 232,000 species of vascular plants and about 16,000 species of nonvascular plants.

Nonvascular

Materials cannot travel quickly through nonvascular plants, so nonvascular plants such as this moss live in damp places, where water is plentiful.

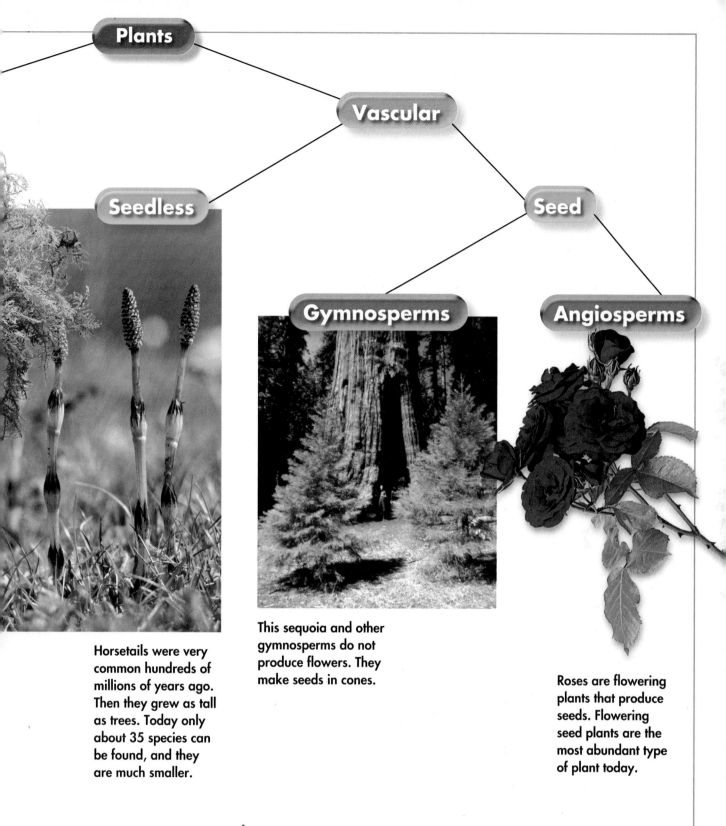

Plants

Vascular

Seedless

Seed

Gymnosperms

Angiosperms

Horsetails were very common hundreds of millions of years ago. Then they grew as tall as trees. Today only about 35 species can be found, and they are much smaller.

This sequoia and other gymnosperms do not produce flowers. They make seeds in cones.

Roses are flowering plants that produce seeds. Flowering seed plants are the most abundant type of plant today.

1. ✓**Checkpoint** Name the two groups of vascular plants and give examples of each.
2. **Social Studies in Science** The first person to develop a way to classify living things was Aristotle, a Greek scholar. Research Aristotle's classification system. Summarize Aristotle's system in a graphic organizer.

Animal Classification

You probably recognize some of the organisms pictured on these two pages as animals. But you might think that some, such as the peacock worms or sea fans, are plants. The animal kingdom is divided into about 35 different phyla. You can read about six of these phyla on the next page.

Although animals can be very different, they all share certain characteristics. Animals are multicellular organisms, and they cannot make their own food. They get food by eating other organisms. The cells of animals contain a nucleus but do not have a cell wall.

About 95 percent of all animal species on Earth are invertebrates. Invertebrates are animals that do not have a backbone. They range in size from microscopic mites that cover your body to the giant squid, which can be 20 meters long.

Only the phylum Chordates contains animals that are vertebrates, or animals with backbones. Fishes, amphibians, reptiles, birds, and mammals are vertebrates.

How is this squid similar to other mollusks?

The segmented body, jointed legs, and hard outer skeleton make this centipede a member of what phylum?

✓ **Lesson Checkpoint**

1. Use the information on page 17 to identify one characteristic of each phylum.
2. Give at least three details to support this statement: The plant kingdom includes species with a variety of characteristics.
3. **Compare and Contrast** Use a compare and contrast graphic organizer to show how plants and animals are alike and different.

Animal Phyla

Cnidarians

These beauties on the coral reef are animals, not exotic plants. The fan-shaped creatures are corals called sea fans. The phylum Cnidarians also includes jellyfish and anemones. Cnidarians have a single body opening that is usually surrounded by a ring of stinging cells.

Mollusks

It's hard to believe, but this graceful animal is related to a clam. This nautilus belongs to the invertebrate phylum Mollusks, which includes clams, squid, octopuses, snails, and slugs. All mollusks have soft bodies, and most have hard shells.

Segmented Worms

These feathers are actually the tentacles of peacock worms that live on the ocean floor. The worm uses its tentacles to catch food. Other animals in this phylum are the common earthworm and leeches.

Arthropods

This tarantula spider is not an insect, but it belongs to the same phylum as insects—Arthropods. Other spiders, crabs, millipedes, and centipedes are also arthropods. All arthropods have segmented bodies, jointed appendages, and hard skeletons on the outside of their bodies. Arthropods include almost 85 percent of Earth's animal species.

Echinoderms

Sea stars are echinoderms, animals that live in the ocean and have tough, spiny skins. This phylum also includes brittle stars, sea lilies, sea urchins, and sea cucumbers. Echinoderm bodies have a unique five-part balanced arrangement of parts that makes these animals easy to recognize. They have skeletons made of hard calcium plates inside their bodies.

Chordates

This impressive gorilla belongs to a group of animals called vertebrates, which is one kind of animal in the Chordate phylum. Most vertebrates have a spinal cord and brain. The gorilla is warm-blooded, which means that its body can keep a certain temperature no matter what the outside temperature is. Other vertebrates, such as reptiles, are cold-blooded. Their body temperature changes with that of their environments.

Lab zone Guided Inquiry

Investigate How can you identify and classify organisms?

An identification key is a tool that helps a user to identify an organism based on its characteristics.

Materials

watermelon

Fuji apple

orange

lemon

banana

How to Read and Construct Keys

Process Skills

Following the steps in an identification key can help you identify and **classify** organisms.

What to Do

1. Study the steps in the first part of How to Read and Construct Keys. Then follow the steps to learn how to use a key to identify the insects below.

Ladybug
flight wings: protected
shape: round

Dragonfly
flight wings: unprotected
wings: stick out from body

June Beetle
flight wings: protected
shape: oblong

Housefly
flight wings: unprotected
wings: point to back end of body

Sample Identification Key

1. a. If the flight wings are protected by a hard covering, go to step 2.
   b. If the flight wings are not protected by a hard covering, go to step 3.
2. a. If the body has a round shape, it is a ladybug.
   b. If the body has an oblong shape, it is a June beetle.
3. a. If the wings stick out from the side of the body, it is a dragonfly.
   b. If the wings point to the back end of the body, it is a housefly.

2 First, think of ways to **classify** the fruits based on their characteristics. Then, study the second part of How to Read and Construct Keys. Use what you learn to help you complete the Fruit Identification Key.

shape: oval

skin: smooth

color: 2-tone, striped

shape: round

skin: smooth

color: solid, red

shape: round

skin: bumpy

color: solid, orange

shape: oval

skin: bumpy

color: solid, yellow

shape: long, narrow

skin: smooth

color: solid, yellow

Fruit Identification Key	
1	**a.** If the skin is bumpy, go to step 2.
	b. If the skin is smooth, go to step 3.
2	**a.** If the fruit is round, it is an _____.
	b. If the fruit is oval, it is a _____.
3	**a.** If the color is solid, go to step 4.
	b. If the color is striped, it is a _____.
4	**a.** If the shape is long and narrow, it is a _____.
	b. If the shape is round, it is a _____.

Explain Your Results

1. The key lists one special characteristic for each fruit. How does this help you identify a fruit?

2. **Infer** What other characteristics of fruits could be used in an identification key?

Go Further

How would you classify another group of things, such as seashells? Design a key that identifies 6 different things in 5 steps.

Analyzing Data About Species

Have you ever seen an ungulate? You have probably seen many of them, even different kinds of ungulates. Ungulates are animals with toes that end in hooves.

Among ungulates there are two orders—those that have an even number of toes and those that have an odd number of toes. The circle graph below shows the number of species within each family of odd-toed ungulates.

Odd-Toed Ungulates

Rhinoceroses

Horses/Zebras

Tapirs

© Tools Take It to the Net
pearsonsuccessnet.com

Use the circle graph to answer the questions.

1. Are there more species of rhinoceroses or tapirs?

2. Which group has about 25% of the species?

3. If the total number of species is 16, which most likely gives the number of species in each family?
    A. 8 species of horses and zebras
        4 species of rhinoceroses
        4 species of tapirs
    B. 5 species of horses and zebras
        5 species of rhinoceroses
        6 species of tapirs
    C. 7 species of horses and zebras
        5 species of rhinoceroses
        4 species of tapirs
    D. 9 species of horses and zebras
        4 species of rhinoceroses
        3 species of tapirs

Lab zone Take-Home Activity

Choose one of the ungulate families shown on the circle graph. Research to find estimates of how many animals for each species in that family are alive today. Write a report or make a bar graph showing what you learned.

21

Chapter 1 Review and Test Prep

Use Vocabulary

adaptation (p. 8)

bacteria (p. 12)

biosphere (p. 7)

classification (p. 11)

fungi (p. 12)

nonvascular plant (p. 14)

species (p. 8)

vascular plant (p. 14)

Write the word from the list above that best matches each description.

_____ **1.** A group of similar organisms that can mate and reproduce

_____ **2.** The grouping of things according to their similarities

_____ **3.** Plant with tubes for carrying water and nutrients

_____ **4.** The part of Earth that can support living things

_____ **5.** Plant that does not have tubes for carrying water and nutrients

_____ **6.** Usually many-celled organisms that often grow in moist, dark places

_____ **7.** Single-celled organisms that do not have a nucleus

_____ **8.** A characteristic that enables an organism to survive and reproduce in its environment

Explain Concepts

9. Why do scientists classify organisms?

10. Explain how mushrooms, molds, and yeasts are alike and different.

11. What percentage of all vertebrate species are mammals? Use the table below to help you answer the question.

Vertebrate Species	
Group	**Number of species**
Fish	19,000
Amphibians	4,000
Reptiles	6,000
Birds	9,000
Mammals	4,000

Process Skills

12. Predict You find an unknown organism that you think is a plant. You decide to look at some of its cells under the microscope. Predict what substance you will find in the cells if the organism is a plant.

13. Questions and Hypotheses You want to grow some mushrooms in the classroom, but you aren't sure what conditions are best for growth. Use what you learned about fungi in this chapter to write a testable hypothesis for finding out.

MindPoint Quiz Show

14. **Classify** An organism has the following characteristics: It is made of a single cell with a nucleus, it lives in a pond, and it can make its own food as well as take in nutrients from other organisms. Into what kingdom would you classify this organism? Why?

Compare and Contrast

15. Make a graphic organizer like the one shown below. Fill in the circles to compare and contrast vascular and nonvascular plants.

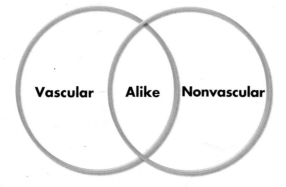

Vascular   Alike   Nonvascular

Test Prep

Choose the letter that best completes the statement or answers the question.

16. Which feature is probably not the same for all organisms in the same species?

  Ⓐ how they obtain nutrients
  Ⓑ their size
  Ⓒ how they reproduce
  Ⓓ their body structure

17. Which is an example of a kingdom?

  Ⓕ Arthropod
  Ⓖ Archaebacteria
  Ⓗ Angiosperm
  Ⓘ Vertebrate

18. Which is NOT a characteristic of bacteria?

  Ⓐ single-celled organisms
  Ⓑ cells without a nucleus
  Ⓒ found almost everywhere on Earth
  Ⓓ cells containing chlorophyll

19. Explain why the answer you chose for Question 18 is the best. For each of the answers that you did not choose, give a reason why it is not the best choice.

20. **Writing in Science** **Descriptive**
Write a paragraph that explains why most nonvascular plants are small.

YNES MEXIA

Plants have been used to treat illnesses for hundreds of years. What treatments and cures are locked in the thousands of plants yet to be discovered? That's one of the questions Ynes Mexia wanted to explore.

Mexia's interest in plants began in 1920 when Mexia was 50 years old. She started taking field trips with the Sierra Club to explore the variety of flowers growing in the hills around San Francisco. To learn more, she entered the University of California to study botany—the science of plants.

Armed with greater knowledge and endless curiosity, Mexia made her first major expedition in 1925 to western Mexico. Over the next 13 years, she explored many different environments in search of new plant species. She climbed the slopes of Mt. McKinley in Alaska. She trekked through the deserts of the American Southwest. She even rafted and canoed thousands of kilometers up the Amazon River to explore the rain forests of South America.

Mexia collected thousands of specimens, including some that were important sources of medicines. She also discovered new species. Because of her work, we know more about the amazing variety and uses of plants.

Lab zone Take-Home Activity

Ynes Mexia carefully drew and photographed her specimens for others to study. Are you a keen observer? Take a field trip near your home or in a park. Draw, photograph, or describe several kinds of plants. Display your work for others to enjoy.

online
Student Edition
pearsonsuccessnet.com

Chapter 2
Cells

You Will Discover

- how scientists learned about cells.
- what the function is of some common cell parts.
- how cells make new cells.

25

What are the parts of a cell?

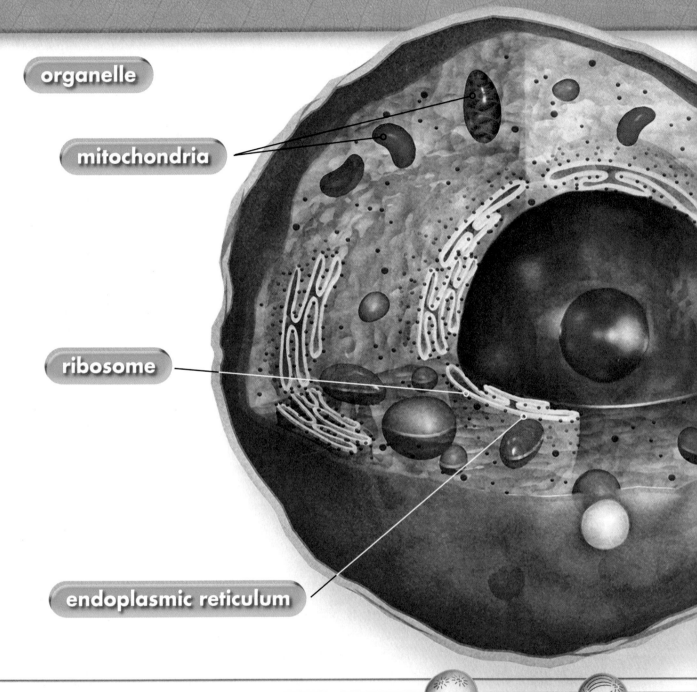

organelle

mitochondria

ribosome

endoplasmic reticulum

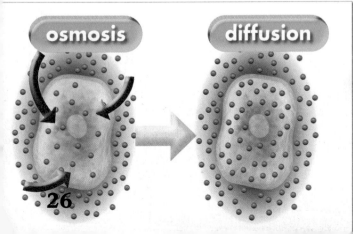

osmosis

diffusion

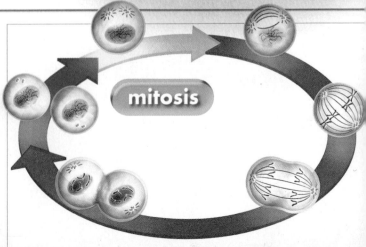

mitosis

26

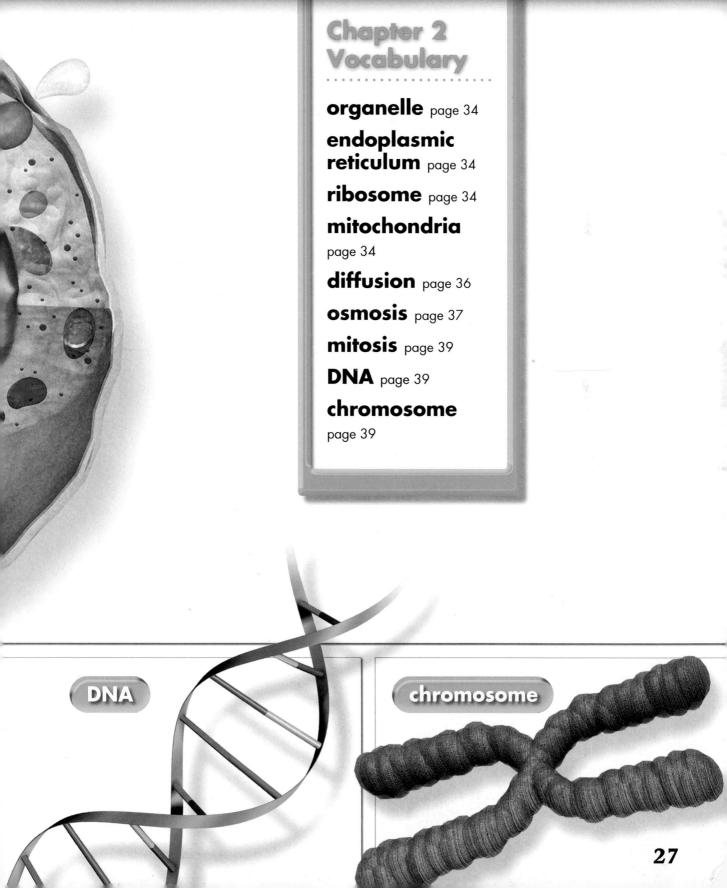

Chapter 2 Vocabulary

DNA

chromosome

Explore How can you make a water-drop lens?

Materials

safety pin
(taped shut)

dropper

water

newspaper

What to Do

1 Place one drop of water in the loop at the end of the safety pin.

2 Hold the safety pin loop over the newspaper and look at the letter *e*.

3 **Observe** the letter. Move the pin closer and farther from the *e*. Draw what you see.

Explain Your Results

1. Is the *e* you see through the "lens" larger than or smaller than the printed *e*? How does moving the pin closer and farther from the *e* affect what you see?

2. **Infer** How could you use a water-drop lens to study an object?

How to Read Science

 TARGET SKILL

Make Inferences

Sometimes writers do not directly tell you everything they mean. Instead, they hint at ideas by the way they write. When you make an **inference,** you use facts you have read to make a guess about what the writer is trying to say.

• Try to make an inference from the facts you read.

• Use what you already know to help you make inferences.

Science Article

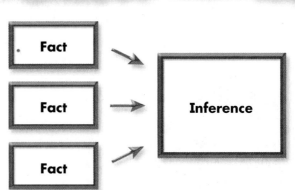

Seeing Cell Parts

In 1683, Anton van Leeuwenhoek used a simple light microscope to see very small cells. Later in 1857, scientists used more powerful microscopes to see the mitochondria of a cell. But it wasn't until after the invention of the electron microscope in 1931 that scientists were able to see the structure of some of the cell's smaller organelles, such as the endoplasmic reticulum. Why can parts of a cell that can't be seen with a light microscope be viewed with an electron microscope?

Apply It!
Make a graphic organizer like this one. List the facts from the science article in your graphic organizer. Then write your **inference.**

Fact	→	
Fact	→	Inference
Fact	→	

29

You Are There!

The summer sun warms your face as you gaze into the pond. You see plenty of plant life— giant water lilies, grasses, and tiny duckweed plants. But is there anything else? Nothing appears to be moving. Could it be that only these plants live here? Now look closer— through a microscope. What are all those things zooming through the water?

AudioText

Algae

Paramecium

Spirogyra

What is a cell?

What do plants, earthworms, dogs, and people have in common? All living things, no matter how large or how small, are made of cells.

Jobs of Cells

In what ways are the organisms in the pictures alike? They all live in pond water, and like all living things, they are made of cells. A cell is the smallest unit that can carry out the activities of life.

Some organisms are made of only a single cell. The single-celled organisms shown on this page look very different. Yet each must perform the same tasks to stay alive. They must obtain nutrients and energy, remove waste products, grow, and reproduce.

Most single-celled organisms are too small to be seen without a microscope. Even though they are tiny, each cell is made of many parts that do a variety of jobs. For example, single-celled green algae absorb sunlight. They use the energy of sunlight to make food. The paramecium has hairlike structures that help it swim. In these one-celled organisms, each part of the cell performs a different task.

Larger organisms are made of many cells. Another way to say this is that larger organisms are multicellular. In multicellular organisms, different cells can do special tasks. In your body, for example, muscle cells are specialized for movement. Your skin cells, however, are specialized for protection. Since each type of cell does a different job, a multicellular organism can do many tasks efficiently.

1. **✓Checkpoint** How are cells in single-celled and multicellular organisms similar? How are they different?

2. **Math** in Science Because cells and their parts are so small, scientists measure them in micrometers, μm. Find out how large a micrometer is.

Using Microscopes to See Cells

Today scientists know a lot about cells. But for much of history, people didn't even know that cells existed. Because they are so small, cells were not discovered until the invention of the microscope.

The first person to describe cells was Robert Hooke. Born in England in 1635, Hooke made a simple microscope with a series of lenses within a tube. Hooke used his microscope to examine thin layers of cork. Cork is the bark of the cork tree and is made of cells that are no longer alive. When Hooke looked at the cork through his microscope, what he saw looked like tiny rectangular rooms. Hooke called these structures "cells." Hooke wrote that in a cubic inch of the cork were more than 12 hundred million cells, which he described as "incredible."

About the same time Hooke was making his discovery, Dutch scientist Anton van Leeuwenhoek was building small, hand-held microscopes, each containing a single lens. He used his microscopes to look at pond water. In the water, he observed single-celled organisms, which he called "very little animalcules." Although his microscopes were small, they were powerful enough to see individual blood cells and bacteria.

Hooke saw dead cork cells through his microscope.

The Cell Theory

Over hundreds of years, scientists learned more about cells. In 1838, Matthias Schleiden, a German scientist, concluded that all plants are made of cells. The next year, Theodore Schwann said that all animals are made of cells. Soon these scientists announced that all living things are made of cells.

Although the discoveries of Schleiden and Schwann added important knowledge to the field of science, scientists still didn't know where cells came from. Then in 1855, Rudolf Virchow, a German doctor, stated that all new cells come only from already existing cells. The observations of these and other scientists form the cell theory. You can read the three parts of the cell theory in the time line. Today scientists continue to learn more about cells as their microscopes become more powerful.

✓ Lesson Checkpoint

1. Why was the development of the microscope important to the discovery of cells?
2. What are the three parts of the cell theory?
3. Writing in Science **Narrative** Write a journal entry as Hooke might have written it on the day he discovered cells. Be sure to use words that show Hooke's excitement.

Learning About Cells

1663   Robert Hooke (English) discovers cells.

1683   Anton von Leeuwenhoek (Dutch) reports observations of "very little animalcules."

Antique microscope

Cell Theory
- All living things are made of one or more cells.
- Cells are the basic units of living things.
- All cells come from existing cells.

1831   Robert Brown (Scottish) discovers the cell nucleus.

1838   Matthias Schleiden and Theodor Schwann (German) propose the cell theory.

1855   Rudolf Virchow (German) states that cells
1857   could come only from other living cells.   Albrecht von Kölliker (Swiss) finds mitochondria in muscle cells.

1865   Julius von Sachs (German) shows that chlorophyll is located in chloroplasts.

1875   Microscopes similar to those used today are in common use.

1931   Ernst Ruska and Max Knoll (German) invent the electron microscope

1953   George E. Palade (Romanian-American) describes ribosomes.

What are the functions of organelles?

Cells share common features, but they also show striking differences. Each cell part performs a different job.

Parts of a Cell

To stay alive, all cells must perform certain life functions. For example, a cell must get, store, and release energy. It must also make proteins, release wastes, and recycle materials. A cell needs to control what enters and exits it. Finally, a cell needs a "control center" to direct cell activities and store information.

These life tasks are performed by cell organelles. **Organelles** are structures that perform specific functions within the cell. As you read and study the diagram of an animal cell, notice the function of each organelle.

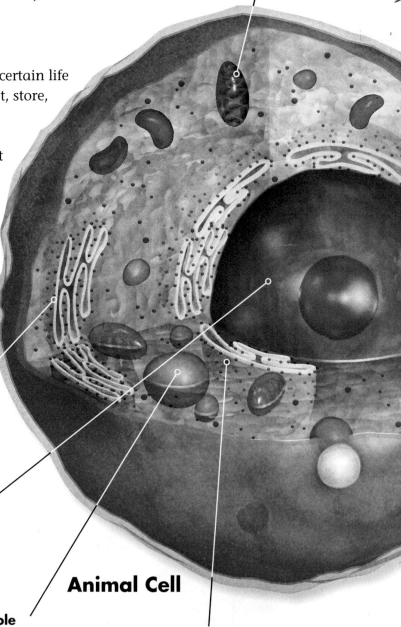

Mitochondrion
Mitochondria convert the chemical energy of food into a form that the cell can use.

Animal Cell

Endoplasmic reticulum (ER)
The **endoplasmic reticulum** is a network of folded membranes. It serves as the cell's transportation system. It also helps make proteins and other substances needed by the cell.

Nucleus
The nucleus directs the cell's activities. It contains the cell's operating instructions and stores information that will be passed along to new cells.

Vacuole
A vacuole contains fluid and is surrounded by a membrane. Vacuoles store water and nutrients, and help the cell digest food.

Ribosome
Ribosomes begin the process of making proteins.

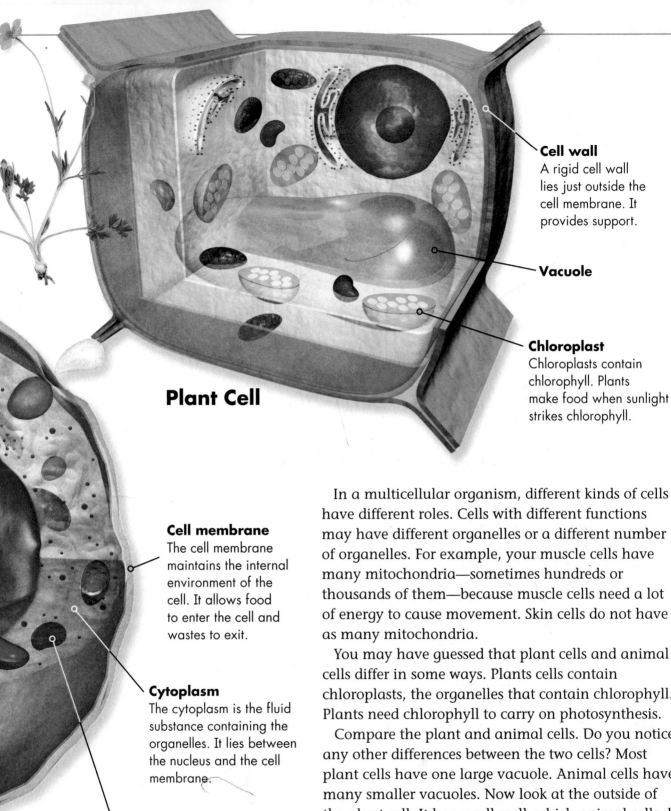

Cell wall
A rigid cell wall lies just outside the cell membrane. It provides support.

Vacuole

Chloroplast
Chloroplasts contain chlorophyll. Plants make food when sunlight strikes chlorophyll.

Plant Cell

Cell membrane
The cell membrane maintains the internal environment of the cell. It allows food to enter the cell and wastes to exit.

Cytoplasm
The cytoplasm is the fluid substance containing the organelles. It lies between the nucleus and the cell membrane.

Lysosome
Lysosomes contain powerful chemicals that break down harmful molecules and recycle worn-out cell parts.

In a multicellular organism, different kinds of cells have different roles. Cells with different functions may have different organelles or a different number of organelles. For example, your muscle cells have many mitochondria—sometimes hundreds or thousands of them—because muscle cells need a lot of energy to cause movement. Skin cells do not have as many mitochondria.

You may have guessed that plant cells and animal cells differ in some ways. Plants cells contain chloroplasts, the organelles that contain chlorophyll. Plants need chlorophyll to carry on photosynthesis.

Compare the plant and animal cells. Do you notice any other differences between the two cells? Most plant cells have one large vacuole. Animal cells have many smaller vacuoles. Now look at the outside of the plant cell. It has a cell wall, which animal cells do not have.

1. **✓Checkpoint** How are animal cells and plant cells similar? How are they different?
2. **⟳ Make Inferences** A brain cell contains thousands of mitochondria. What can you infer from this information about the brain's need for energy?

35

Diffusion

You already know that a cell has many organelles. But did you know that a cell—especially its cytoplasm—is mostly water? In fact, about two-thirds of the mass of a cell is water. Substances needed by the cell, such as nutrients or salts, are dissolved in the water. Where do these dissolved substances come from?

In most cases, a substance moves from an area where it is plentiful to other areas where it is less plentiful. For example, think about dropping a sugar cube into a glass of iced tea. What happens? Even if you don't stir it, individual particles of sugar slowly move away from those in the cube. Eventually, all of the sugar particles will diffuse, or spread, throughout the iced tea. The movement of a substance from an area of its higher concentration to an area of its lower concentration is called **diffusion.** Some substances enter and leave a cell through this process. The diagram below shows what happens during diffusion.

Diffusion occurs because the particles that make up matter are always moving. As they move, the particles bump into each other and move apart. Over time, the particles will spread out until they are evenly spread throughout the area.

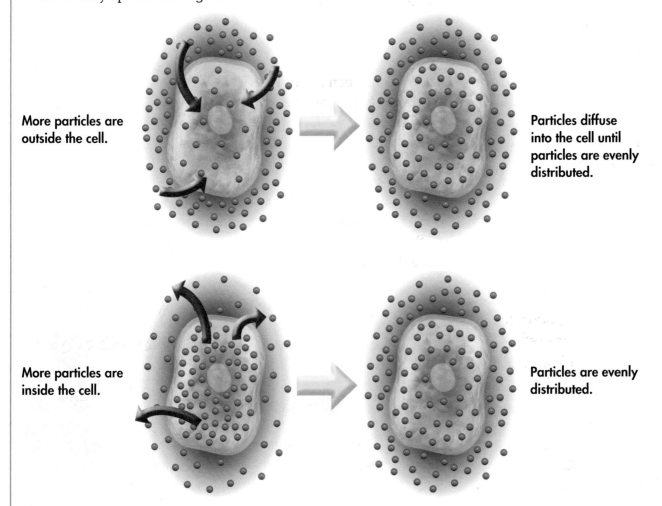

More particles are outside the cell.

Particles diffuse into the cell until particles are evenly distributed.

More particles are inside the cell.

Particles are evenly distributed.

The Cell Membrane

The cell needs many substances. The cell membrane controls the environment inside the cell. Only some substances can pass through a cell membrane by diffusion. Many substances that are made of small particles, such as oxygen, water, and carbon dioxide, can diffuse through the cell membrane. Larger particles, such as salts and proteins, cannot.

Here's how diffusion works in a cell. Cells of living things are surrounded by water, and they contain a lot of water. The water both inside and outside the cell contains many dissolved substances, including oxygen. The cell constantly uses oxygen, so more oxygen particles usually are in the water surrounding a cell than inside the cell. The particles of oxygen move through the cell membrane from outside the cell—where there are more of them—into the cell—where there are less.

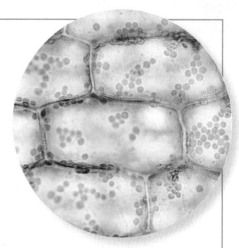

Normal plant cells

Diffusion of Water

Because cells can't function without water, the movement of water through the cell membrane is very important. The diffusion of water across the cell membrane is called **osmosis.**

You can see in the pictures what can happen if a cell doesn't have enough water. It will shrink. Can you see in the photos how the cytoplasm has pulled away from the cell wall? When that happens, the pressure on the cell wall is reduced. The result is that the cell walls of the plant can't support the plant, and the plant wilts.

Too much water can be a problem—especially for animal cells. If too much water moves into the cell, it can burst. The cell membrane helps the cell keep a proper balance of all the materials inside the cell.

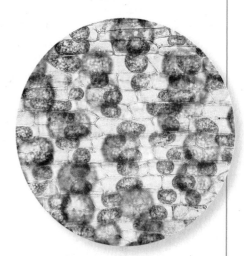

Cells in a wilted plant

A plant wilts when its cells lose water.

✓ Lesson Checkpoint

1. What important function does the cell membrane have in the cell?
2. Use the following words in a sentence: *water, osmosis, cell, cell membrane.*
3. Writing in Science **Descriptive** Write a paragraph to describe the parts and processes in a cell by comparing them to a factory. For example, the nucleus might be the supervisor of the factory, who makes important decisions.

Surface Area

As a cell gets larger, it needs more food and produces more wastes. During growth, both the cell membrane and the organelles within it get larger. But the volume of the materials inside the cell grows faster than the surface area—the area of the cell membrane. Sooner or later there isn't enough cell membrane to allow enough materials into and out of the cell.

To see how this works, look at the diagram. The total amount of material inside the eight smaller cells is equal to the amount in the large cell. But which has more surface area—the eight smaller cells or the larger one?

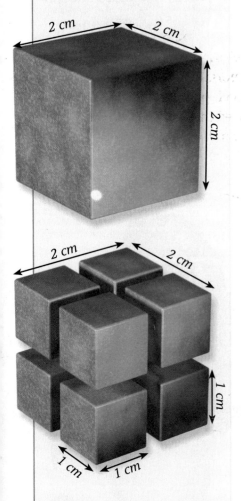

2 cm
2 cm
2 cm

2 cm
2 cm
1 cm
1 cm
1 cm

How do cells grow and divide?

As multicellular organisms grow in size, their cells increase in number. New cells also form to replace old or damaged cells. Cells make new cells through the processes of mitosis and cell division.

Cell Size and Growth

All living things—no matter how large or how small—are made of cells. Some cells are long and narrow, some are thin and flat, and others are round. Some cells, such as red blood cells, are even donut-shaped. But when it comes to size, all cells are similar—they are small.

To understand why cells are small, think about a cell's needs. To stay alive, a cell must take in oxygen, absorb food, and release wastes. These materials and others must move through all parts of the cell. Throughout the cells, materials constantly move between the cell membrane and organelles. Materials also move from organelle to organelle.

As a cell gets larger, the trip from the cell membrane to other cell parts gets longer. A particle of sugar would have to travel farther in a large cell than in a small cell. Wastes, too, would have to travel farther to exit the cell. If a cell grew too large, materials would not be able to move fast enough throughout the cell for life functions to continue. If that happened, the cell would die.

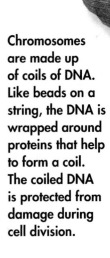

Chromosomes are made up of coils of DNA. Like beads on a string, the DNA is wrapped around proteins that help to form a coil. The coiled DNA is protected from damage during cell division.

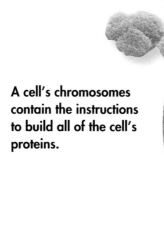

A cell's chromosomes contain the instructions to build all of the cell's proteins.

Cell Division

If cells can only get so large, how do organisms grow? Single-celled organisms divide into two new cells when they get too large. For a multicellular organism to grow, its cells must also divide into two new cells. Each cell will be a copy of the old cell. As new cells form, the organism grows larger. Cell division also makes new cells to replace old cells that are damaged or worn out.

Cell division begins with **mitosis,** the process in which the cell nucleus divides. The cell's nucleus contains **DNA,** a material that stores coded information about how an organism will grow and develop. The cell needs this information to make proteins, which control chemical reactions in the cell. Usually you don't see the DNA in cells. But when mitosis begins, DNA coils tightly to form bodies called **chromosomes.** You can see the cell's chromosomes as rod-shaped structures like those in the photo above.

DNA is often compared to a ladder.

1. ✓**Checkpoint** Why can a cell get only so large?
2. 🔵 **Make Inferences** The roots of a tree are growing. What process is going on in the root cells to make this happen?

Mitosis

Every species has a specific number of chromosomes, which are found in pairs inside the cell. Chromosomes contain a cell's operating instructions. So it's no surprise that a cell must have a full set of chromosomes to function properly. Mitosis ensures that each new cell gets the right chromosomes in the right number. Each nucleus in the resulting cells will receive a complete set of chromosomes.

Mitosis is often described in stages, but mitosis is really a continuous process. Each stage moves smoothly into the next. When mitosis is finished, the cell cytoplasm divides.

1 The cell gets ready to divide. First, the cell copies its DNA. Then the DNA becomes threadlike strands called chromatin.

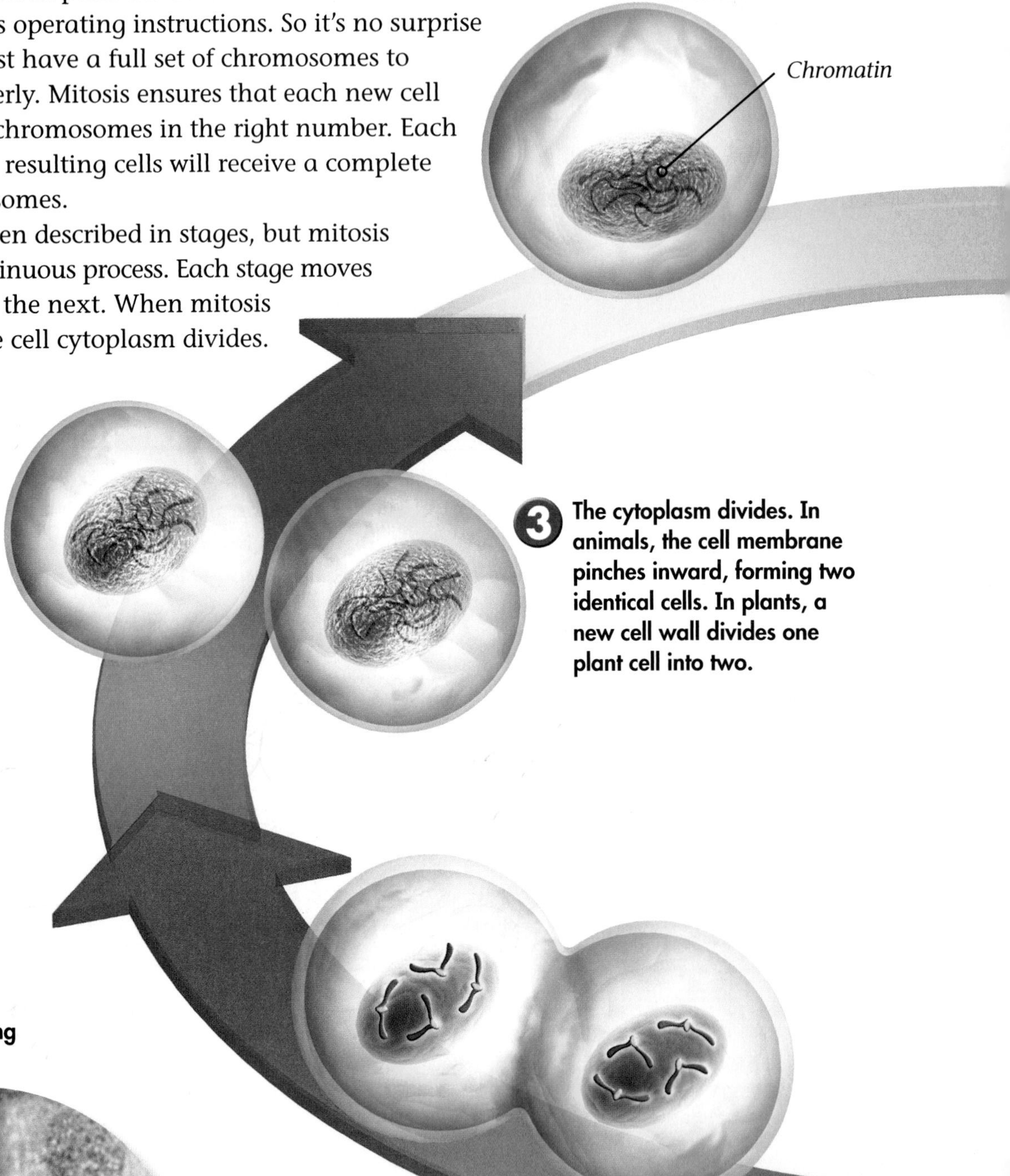

Chromatin

3 The cytoplasm divides. In animals, the cell membrane pinches inward, forming two identical cells. In plants, a new cell wall divides one plant cell into two.

Cell wall forming in plant cell

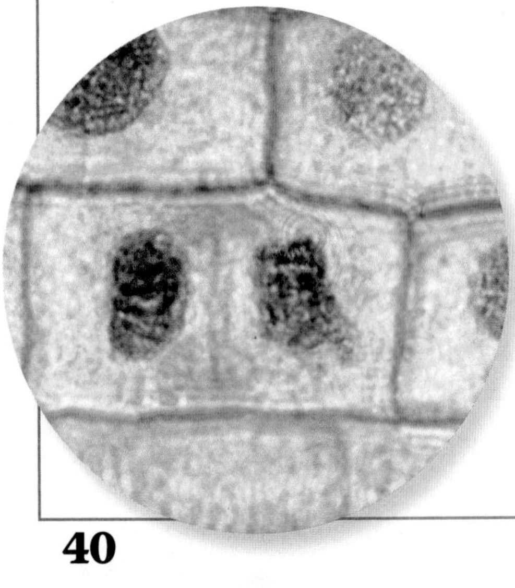

2 The chromosomes uncoil and become chromatin. A new membrane forms around each nucleus. Mitosis is complete.

40

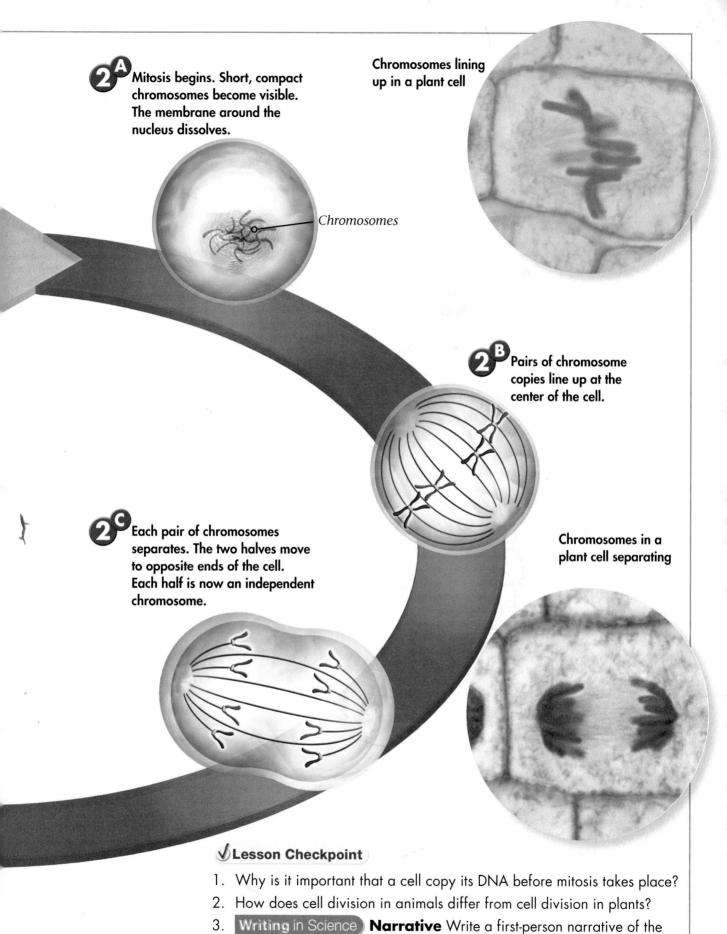

2A Mitosis begins. Short, compact chromosomes become visible. The membrane around the nucleus dissolves.

Chromosomes

Chromosomes lining up in a plant cell

2B Pairs of chromosome copies line up at the center of the cell.

2C Each pair of chromosomes separates. The two halves move to opposite ends of the cell. Each half is now an independent chromosome.

Chromosomes in a plant cell separating

✓ **Lesson Checkpoint**

1. Why is it important that a cell copy its DNA before mitosis takes place?
2. How does cell division in animals differ from cell division in plants?
3. **Writing in Science** **Narrative** Write a first-person narrative of the events of cell division from the viewpoint of a cell undergoing mitosis.

41

Guided Inquiry

Investigate How can you make a model of the way a cell membrane works?

Some substances can move through a cell membrane. Some cannot.

Materials

safety goggles and plastic gloves

cup and water

dropper and iodine

plastic spoon and cornstarch

plastic sandwich bag and twist tie

Process Skills

Making a model can help you understand how something works.

What to Do

1. Fill a cup half full with water. Add 10 drops of iodine.

Water with iodine

Be careful!

Be careful handling iodine. It could stain your skin and clothes.

2. Place a spoonful of cornstarch in the plastic bag. Add 3 spoonfuls of water.

Close the bag with a twist tie.

This bag is a model of a cell membrane.

3 Place the bag in the cup.

4 **Observe** your **model** at the times listed in the chart. Record your observations.

Movement Through a Membrane		
Time (minutes)	**Color**	
	Solution in Cup	Solution in Bag
0 (start)		
5		
10		
15		
60		

The water with iodine should cover the bag.

5 Sketch the cup and the bag. Use an arrow to show the direction a substance must have moved in the activity.

Explain Your Results

1. Which substance moved—the iodine or the starch? How do you know?
2. **Infer** The plastic bag is a **model** of a cell membrane. What does the mixture of cornstarch and water represent?

Go Further

What might happen if the water with iodine were placed in the bag and the mixture of starch and water were placed in the cup? Develop a plan to answer this or any other questions you may have.

43

Measuring Cells

Most cells are very small—too small to be seen without any scientific instrument. A bacteria cell is about 0.000001 m (1 millionth of a meter) long. A human white blood cell is only about 0.000012 m in diameter.

Rather than writing small numbers with so many zeros, scientists use prefixes to make more appropriate units for discussing cell sizes. You have already worked with some of these prefixes, such as *milli-, centi-,* and *deci-.* You have also worked with the unit kilometer for measuring longer lengths or distances.

The most common unit used for the size of cells is the micrometer. The prefix *micro-* is abbreviated µ (µ is the Greek letter *mu*). The prefix *micro-* means "one millionth." You already know how large a meter is. A micrometer is one millionth of a meter or one thousandth of a millimeter.

Instead of writing the size of a bacteria cell as 0.000001 m or 0.001 mm, we can write it as 1 µm. A white blood cell is about 12 µm in diameter. Frog eggs are cells that are nearly 1,000 times as long as bacteria cells, so they measure about 1,000 µm, or 1 mm.

ORGANISM	SIZE
Average animal cell	10 µm
Euglena	50 µm
Volvox colony	100 µm
Ceratium	500 µm

1. The largest known cell is the yolk of an ostrich egg. It is about the size of a baseball. Which unit would be most appropriate and convenient to use to measure an ostrich egg yolk?

   A. kilometer
   B. centimeter
   C. millimeter
   D. micrometer

2. Use the chart on page 44 to list these microscopic organisms in order from smallest to largest: Volvox colony, average animal cell, Euglena, Ceratium.

3. Red blood cells carry oxygen. Look at the chart of red blood cell sizes of some mammals.

Enlarged frog egg

Mammal	Size of Red Blood Cell
Human	7.5 µm
Elephant	9.2 µm
Gerbil	6.1 µm
Zebra	5.1 µm
Orca	6.8 µm

Write the data in sequential order, starting with the smallest red blood cell. Can you conclude that the larger the animal, the larger their red blood cells will be? Explain.

4. Flea egg cells are about 0.5 mm long. Human platelet cells, which help blood clot, are about 2 µm long. Which is longer? Explain how you know.

Enlarged white blood cell

Lab zone Take-Home Activity

Measure the length of five or more objects at home. Use each of the following units at least once: meter, centimeter, millimeter. Be sure to use an appropriate unit for the object being measured. Make a list of the objects and the length of each.

Chapter 2 Review and Test Prep

Use Vocabulary

chromosome (p. 39)	**mitochondria** (p. 34)
diffusion (p. 36)	**mitosis** (p. 39)
DNA (p. 39)	**organelle** (p. 34)
endoplasmic reticulum (p. 34)	**osmosis** (p. 37)
	ribosome (p. 34)

Match each definition with a term from the box.

1. The diffusion of water across a cell membrane

2. Cell organelle that begins the process of making proteins

3. Structure in the nucleus made up of long, threadlike DNA coils

4. The process in which the cell nucleus divides during the production of two cells with identical DNA

5. The movement of a substance from an area of its higher concentration to an area of its lower concentration

6. Cell organelles that convert the chemical energy of food into a form the cell can use

7. The material that stores coded information about how an organism will grow and develop

8. A network of folded membranes in the cell's cytoplasm that transports materials and assembles proteins and other substances needed by the cell

9. Structure that performs a specific function within a cell

Explain Concepts

10. What are the three parts of the cell theory?

11. Explain how organelles are specialized to perform various tasks in a cell.

Process Skills

12. **Classify** You look at a cell under the microscope and note that it has a nucleus, a large vacuole, a cell wall, and chloroplasts. Does this cell belong to a plant or animal? How do you know?

13. **Predict** A new cell forms. The cell continues to grow but does not divide. Predict what will happen to the cell and explain why.

14. **Model** Make a diagram to show the process of osmosis.

 Make Inferences

15. Read the paragraph. Then complete the graphic organizer to make an inference to answer this question: Where does photosynthesis take place in a plant?

Plants have many kinds of cells, and each kind of cell has a different job. Leaf cells are packed with chloroplasts. The chloroplasts contain chlorophyll, which absorbs sunlight. Plants use the energy in sunlight to make glucose during photosynthesis. Root cells, however, usually do not have chloroplasts.

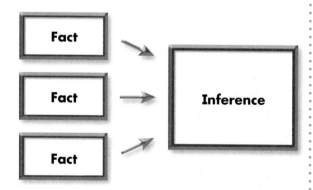

Test Prep

Choose the letter that best completes the statement or answers the question.

16. A cell with chloroplasts is probably specialized for
Ⓐ transmitting nerve impulses.
Ⓑ storing food.
Ⓒ absorbing sunlight.
Ⓓ movement.

17. Which organelle provides support to help plants stand upright?
Ⓕ cell membrane
Ⓖ chloroplast
Ⓗ nucleus
Ⓘ cell wall

18. Which activity occurs in a mitochondrion?
Ⓐ Energy the cell can use is released.
Ⓑ Water and nutrients are stored.
Ⓒ Proteins are made.
Ⓓ Worn-out cell parts are recycled.

19. Explain why the answer you chose for Question 16 is best. For each of the answers you did not choose, give a reason why it is not the best choice.

20. Writing in Science **Descriptive**
Suppose that you are a travel agent. You are planning a tour of a cell. Write a brochure describing some of the features that travelers will see on their tour.

Rosalind Franklin

Rosalind Franklin was a key figure in what many call the most important discovery of the 20th century. She helped unlock the secrets of DNA!

Franklin had made a name for herself in the 1940s. This English scientist was one of the world's top experts on X-ray diffraction. In this technique, a powerful X-ray beam is aimed at a crystal, producing an image on film. Franklin perfected the technique when studying the structure of coal.

Then in 1951, Franklin turned her attention to DNA. In the early 1950s, scientists knew that DNA was the substance that carries traits from parents to offspring. But how did DNA actually pass on this genetic information? To answer that, scientists needed to know what DNA looked like. What was its structure?

The breakthrough came in 1953. Franklin produced her best X-ray photo of DNA. It showed clues to the DNA structure. A co-worker showed the photo to James Watson, who was trying to figure out DNA's structure by building models with his partner, Francis Crick. The photo gave Watson and Crick the clues they needed to finish their model correctly. They discovered the structure of DNA and were able to explain how it works. But Franklin's work was the key part to the puzzle.

Lab zone Take-Home Activity

The quest to figure out DNA's structure was an intense competition in the early 1950s. Make a poster that shows the role each of these scientists played in that quest: Rosalind Franklin, Maurice Wilkins, Linus Pauling, James Watson, and Francis Crick.

EC CRU 10 9 8 7 6 5 4 3 2 1

Chapter 3
Reproduction

You Will Discover

- how traits are passed from parent to offspring.
- how organisms reproduce.
- the differences between organisms produced by asexual reproduction and those produced by sexual reproduction.

online
Student Edition
pearsonsuccessnet.com

How do living things reproduce?

heredity

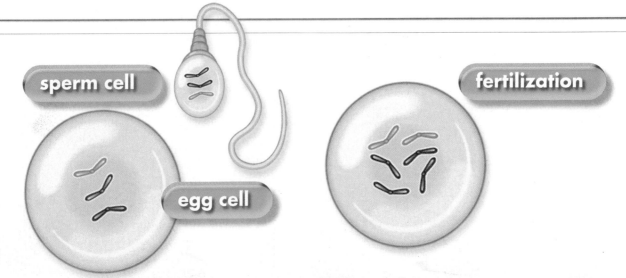

sperm cell

egg cell

fertilization

Chapter 3 Vocabulary

asexual reproduction

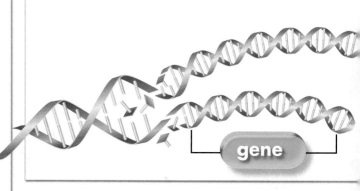

gene

sexual reproduction

selective breeding

meiosis

51

Explore How do sunflower seeds vary?

Materials

sunflower seeds

toothpick

Seed Stripe Chart
and Graph

What to Do

1 First, count 100 sunflower seeds.

2 Then, **observe** each seed. Count the stripes on one side of the seeds. Include the side stripes.

3 Next, record your data.

Wash your hands after
handling the seeds.

4 Finally, make a bar graph of your results.

Process Skills
You **infer** when you make a careful guess based on **observations** or past experiences.

Explain Your Results

1. Based on your **observations,** how did the number of stripes per seed vary?

2. **Infer** What other characteristics could you use to describe how the seeds were alike and different?

How to Read Science

TARGET SKILL

Sequence

An important part of understanding the science you read is understanding the order in which events happen. The step-by-step ordering of events is called **sequence.** Sequence may be used to determine the steps in an activity or the stages of a process.

- When you sequence events, you decide which events happened first, second, third, and so on.

- Clue words, such as *begin, first, then, after, when, before,* and *now,* can help you place events in the correct order.

Clue words have been marked in the article below.

Science Article

A Seed Forms

The first step in forming a seed happens when pollen is moved from the male part of a flower to the female part. Then a tube grows out of the pollen to the ovule, the part of the flower that has the female sex cell. After fertilization, the fertilized egg grows into a young organism. The ovule grows into the seed covering. A fruit covers the seed.

Apply It!

Make a graphic organizer like the one shown. Fill in the boxes to show the **sequence** of events in the formation of a seed. Use enough boxes in your graphic organizer to show all the steps. Then add another box and **infer** what happens as the seed sprouts.

1

⬇

2

⬇

3

You Are There!

Hiding behind a tree, you scan the landscape with your binoculars. There! At the edge of a wooded area you see a pair of baboons—and they have a baby! The baby looks so small and helpless. Still, you know that this baby will grow up and have babies of its own someday. Will those babies look just like this little fellow?

AudioText

What is asexual reproduction?

The colors of these snapdragons are traits that were inherited from the parent plants.

During asexual reproduction, a parent passes inherited traits to its offspring. An organism's inherited traits and environment work together to develop its characteristics. Learned traits are not passed from parent to offspring.

Heredity

If the baboons in the picture were grouped with other kinds of animals, you could easily tell which parents belonged with which offspring. **Heredity** is the passing of traits from parents to their offspring. Because parents and offspring share traits, they resemble each other. An organism may grow to be bigger, smaller, lighter, or darker than its parent, but the basic pattern is the same. Oak trees make acorns, which grow to become oak trees, not maple trees.

All organisms inherit traits. Heredity is the reason bacteria have a certain shape or absorb certain chemicals. Heredity gives a tiger stripes and a leopard spots—and never the other way around. Do you have dimples? What color are your eyes? These are just a few of the traits that humans inherit.

Inherited traits do not act alone to give an organism its traits. Environment also affects characteristics. Heredity and environment work together to produce a tree's height. For example, a tree may inherit the ability to grow 12 meters tall. However, if the tree doesn't get the nutrients it needs, it probably will not grow to 12 meters.

Organisms also have traits that they didn't inherit. Perhaps you are good at basketball. Heredity may have given you athletic ability. Even so, you still had to practice playing the game. Playing basketball well is a learned trait. Learned traits cannot pass from parent to offspring through heredity.

1. ✓**Checkpoint** What factors influence an organism's characteristics?
2. **Writing in Science** **Descriptive** Describe yourself as if you were writing to a pen pal you have never met. Tell about some inherited traits, such as your eye color, as well as some learned traits.

This bacterium cell is splitting into two cells. The red areas show the cells' DNA.

Buds have formed on this hydra's side. These buds will break free of the parent.

Conditions around the bread were right for mold spores to reproduce.

Asexual Reproduction

Individual organisms do not live forever. For that reason, the passing of traits from parents to offspring is necessary in order for a species to survive. A parent might have traits that help it survive in its environment. These traits can be passed to offspring so that they too can live successfully and reproduce.

The organisms shown on these pages are producing new individuals. Although the processes they use may seem different, each is doing so by asexual reproduction. In **asexual reproduction,** offspring come from a single parent. Organisms reproduce asexually by mitosis. The offspring will have the same DNA as the parent.

Kinds of Asexual Reproduction

Some organisms, such as the bacterium on this page, reproduce when a parent cell splits to produce two offspring cells of the same size. Each offspring cell has the same traits as the parent cell. This kind of asexual reproduction, called fission, often is a fast way to reproduce. Think about it—the number of offspring keeps doubling. Some bacteria can reproduce in as little as 20 minutes if they have the right conditions. Within 20 minutes, one cell becomes two. In 40 minutes, four cells result, and so on. In only eight hours, the original cell will have multiplied to nearly 17 million new bacteria! Of course, conditions usually do not remain right for reproduction to continue at that rate.

Yeasts, some plants, and the hydra on the left reproduce asexually by a process called budding. During this process, a cell in the parent's body produces a small version of the parent. Many buds can form on a single parent, and each bud has DNA identical to the parent.

Forming spores is another kind of asexual reproduction. A spore is a reproductive cell that has a nucleus and a little bit of cytoplasm. A hard coat covers most spores. This coat protects the spore when conditions in the environment might be harmful.

When conditions are right, a spore develops into a new individual with the same DNA as the parent. Most organisms that reproduce by spores produce many spores at the same time. Molds reproduce by forming spores. Spores are light, so they are easily spread by wind.

Some sea stars can reproduce asexually by forming new individuals from body parts. In the past, oyster fishers tried to protect their oyster beds from sea stars that ate the oysters. The fishers captured the sea stars, chopped them into pieces, and then threw them back into the water. The problem only got worse. Many of the chopped-up parts of the sea stars grew into new individuals. Soon there were many more sea stars than before the fishers began chopping them up!

In a similar way, new plants can grow from pieces of a plant. Did you ever see a potato that has begun to grow sprouts like the one shown on this page? The buds form on the plant through the process of mitosis. Each bud can be cut from the plant and planted. It will grow into a new potato plant. In a similar way, many weeds can grow a whole new plant from a small bit of root that a gardener misses. Anyone who has tried to get rid of dandelions by pulling them out soon learns that!

This northern sea star is growing four new arms from the one remaining arm.

The potato is an underground stem.

✓ Lesson Checkpoint

1. What are four ways that organisms reproduce asexually?

2. Why does asexual reproduction produce offspring with identical DNA?

3. **Health** in Science The bacteria that produce tetanus produce spores that infect the human body. Find out what the symptoms of tetanus are, how a person gets a tetanus infection, and why getting vaccinated against it is important.

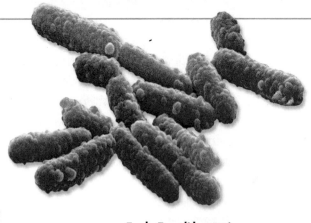

Lesson 2

How are traits passed on?

The instructions for an organism's traits can be found in its DNA. The structure of DNA makes it possible for organisms to pass traits to their offspring.

Each *E. coli* bacterium has 1 chromosome, which contains 3,000 genes that are made of 4 million base pairs.

Structure of DNA

When new organisms result from asexual reproduction, why do the two new cells share the same traits? The answer is in the nucleus of the parent cell.

For most organisms, a cell nucleus contains its chromosomes. The chromosomes contain a set of instructions that control all the activities of a cell. These instructions tell individual cell parts what to do. They also tell cells of multicellular organisms how to work together to form an individual organism. For example, the chromosomes in each cell of a gorilla contain all the instructions to make a gorilla.

Chromosomes are made up of proteins and DNA, which is short for deoxyribonucleic acid. The DNA strands in chromosomes are tightly coiled. If you were able to stretch out the 46 chromosomes in a single human cell and lay them end to end, the strand would be about two meters long. Although the strands are long, they are very thin.

Even under a microscope, you cannot see the chromosomes in most cells except during cell division. Other times, the DNA and proteins that make up chromosomes are spread throughout the nucleus.

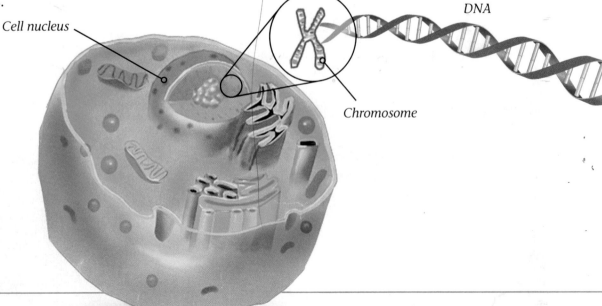

Cell nucleus

Chromosome

DNA

Scientists have been able to see chromosomes for more than 100 years. But until the 1950s, no one understood the importance of DNA. Around that time, the works of several scientists were used to show that DNA carries all the instructions for a cell. Their works also showed that DNA is passed from a parent cell to its offspring.

In 1953 two scientists, James Watson and Francis Crick, described the structure of DNA. To do this, they used X-ray photographs made by Rosalind Franklin, an English chemist. If you looked at a strand of DNA, you would see that it looks like a twisted ladder. This "ladder" contains millions of "rungs." These rungs are made up of just four kinds of materials, called bases. The bases are known by the letters *A, T, C,* and *G.* Each rung is made up of two bases, called base pairs.

The DNA of a chromosome is divided into sections called genes. A **gene** is a series of base pairs, or rungs. The number of rungs varies from gene to gene. One known gene has over 2 million rungs. Each gene controls what substances the cell makes and when it makes them. These substances determine an organism's traits. For example, the genes in the cells of a rose determine the plant's flower color by telling the flower cells what pigments to make.

1. ✓**Checkpoint** What is a gene?
2. **Technology** in Science Use the Internet to find out how Watson and Crick used Franklin's X rays to figure out the structure of DNA.

A gene is a series of base pairs, or rungs. The number of rungs varies from gene to gene, but at least one known gene has over 2 million rungs.

Base pair

How Many Chromosomes?

Members of the same species have the same number of chromosomes. That's because each species has its own unique number of chromosomes. As you can see from the pictures, the number of chromosomes each cell of a species has tells you nothing about the size of the individuals.

Gorilla: 48 chromosomes, two more than each human cell

Crayfish: 200 chromosomes

Horsetail: 216 chromosomes

59

Copying DNA

The DNA of all living things is made up of pairs of the same four bases. Notice in the diagram that the order of the base pairs varies from place to place on the DNA ladder. The order determines exactly what instructions each gene gives to an organism's cells. For example, an arrangement of TA-CG-GC-TA will give different instructions than an arrangement of TA-AT-GC-TA. Different organisms have different arrangements of base pairs. That's what makes organisms different.

Two bases fit together to form each rung, but they fit together only in certain ways. Base T can only pair with base A, and bases G and C can only pair with each other. This pairing allows DNA to make an exact copy of itself when a cell divides through mitosis.

This baby camel has a condition called albinism. Its white coloring is caused by a change in the gene that is responsible for making the substances that produce pigments.

DNA Bases

Base A
Base T
Base G
Base C

1 Before a cell divides, the base pairs pull apart. One base stays attached to each side of the ladder.

2 Extra bases float around inside the nucleus.

3 The extra bases join the bases still attached to the DNA strands.

Base pairs are always AT, TA, GC, or CG.

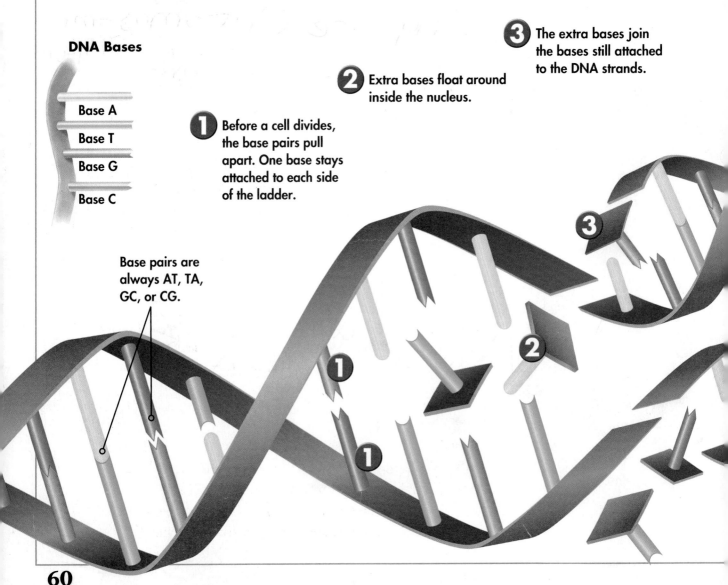

When a cell undergoes mitosis, its DNA "unzips," and the base pairs come apart. Free-floating bases within the cell's nucleus pair with the separated bases on the DNA strand. The process continues until two complete double strands of DNA are formed. The two strands are identical to the original DNA. In this way, an organism that reproduces asexually gives exact copies of its genes to each new cell.

Sometimes an error occurs, and a strand of DNA does not make an exact copy of itself. A base might be added or deleted, or one base may replace another. This change is called a mutation. A mutation can change the instructions a gene sends. Sometimes a changed gene is passed to an organism's offspring.

The Human Genome Project

In 1990 a group of scientists set out to map all the genes that make up the human chromosomes. A map of the full set of genes that make up a species is called a genome. By 2003 this team had charted the more than three billion base pairs that make up more than 30,000 genes in human DNA.

The computer screen display above shows part of a human DNA strand that was mapped during the Human Genome Project. Notice the different colors of the bands. Each of the four colors represents a different base.

Using the information learned through the Human Genome Project, scientists have found thousands of genes that cause diseases. They hope to use this information to gain a better understanding of how diseases are passed from parent to offspring. They also use the information to develop new treatments for diseases.

Tools from this project have helped scientists map the genomes of other species too. These studies can help us learn how to raise healthier crops and livestock.

4 Because each base pairs only with one other kind of base, the two new complete strands of DNA are identical.

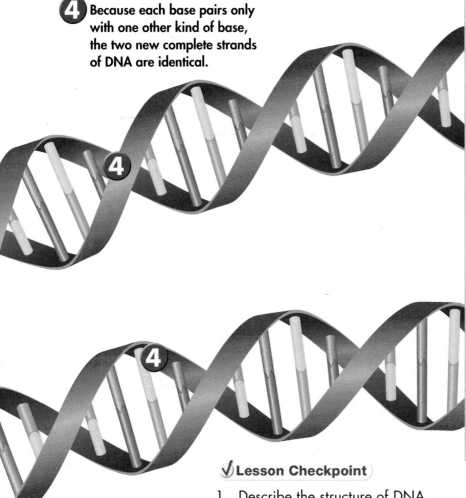

✓ Lesson Checkpoint

1. Describe the structure of DNA.
2. Why is it important that base A can pair only with base T and base G can pair only with base C?
3. 🔁 **Sequence** How does DNA make an exact copy of itself? Use a graphic organizer to show the process.

61

Lesson 3

What is sexual reproduction?

During sexual reproduction, organisms get genes from two different parents. When that happens, the organism shares some traits with each parent.

Reproduction by Two Parents

You know that asexual reproduction results in two cells with the same DNA as the parent cell. Have you ever seen a mother cat and her kitten? You probably noticed that the kitten didn't look exactly like its mother. That is because cats produce offspring by **sexual reproduction,** or reproduction by two parents. The kitten gets half its DNA from one parent and half from the other. How does that work?

Living things that reproduce sexually have special cells called sex cells. The sex cells of the female parent are called **egg cells.** The sex cells of the male parent are called **sperm cells.** Sex cells have only half as many chromosomes as other cells in the organism's body. For example, the body cells of a house cat each have 38 chromosomes. But a cat's sex cells each have only 19 chromosomes.

Sex cells form by a process called **meiosis.** In meiosis, one cell divides into four new cells. Each new cell has only half the number of chromosomes as the parent cell. Study the diagram on the next page to see how this happens.

During sexual reproduction, the male cell and the female cell join in a process called **fertilization.** During fertilization, an egg cell and a sperm cell unite to form a new cell. This cell, called a zygote, is the first cell of a new organism. Since each sex cell has only half the usual number of chromosomes, the new organism receives a complete set. The zygote will divide by mitosis to form the many cells that make up the adult body of the organism.

Only one of these sperm cells can fertilize this egg.

These offspring were produced by sexual reproduction.

1. ✓**Checkpoint** How are sex cells different from other cells in an organism?

2. Math in Science A dog has 78 chromosomes. How many chromosomes would you expect to find in a dog's sex cells?

62

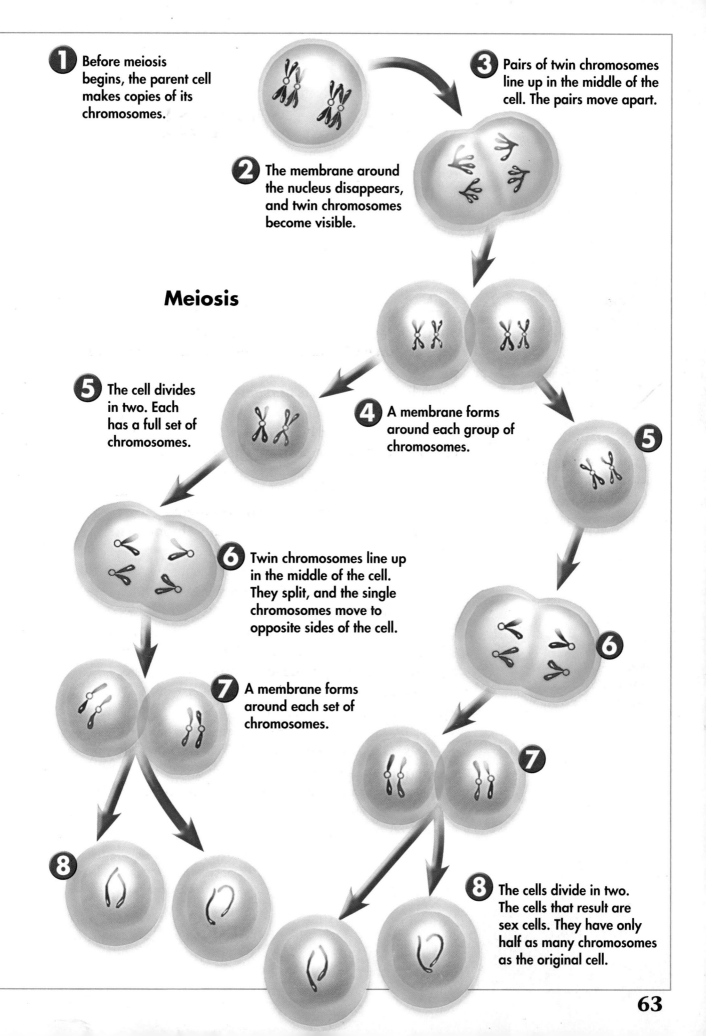

1 Before meiosis begins, the parent cell makes copies of its chromosomes.

2 The membrane around the nucleus disappears, and twin chromosomes become visible.

3 Pairs of twin chromosomes line up in the middle of the cell. The pairs move apart.

Meiosis

4 A membrane forms around each group of chromosomes.

5 The cell divides in two. Each has a full set of chromosomes.

5

6 Twin chromosomes line up in the middle of the cell. They split, and the single chromosomes move to opposite sides of the cell.

6

7 A membrane forms around each set of chromosomes.

7

8

8 The cells divide in two. The cells that result are sex cells. They have only half as many chromosomes as the original cell.

Fertilization in Flowering Plants

Red, blue, yellow, pink—these are just a few of the many colors that flowers come in. They come in a seemingly endless variety of shapes and sizes too. Why do flowers have so much variety?

A flower is an adaptation that allows a plant to reproduce sexually. In flowering plants, fertilization takes place within the flower. The male sex cells of flowering plants are in pollen—the powdery substance found on many flowers. Pollen is produced by the flower's stamen. The female egg is produced at the bottom of the female part of the flower—the pistil. For a flowering plant to reproduce, pollen must get from a stamen to a pistil. This process is called pollination. Look at the diagram to see how pollen gets from the top of the pistil to the egg of the flower.

A plant's flower is adapted for the way that pollination occurs. For example, some plants depend on insects to transfer pollen from a stamen to a pistil—either on the same plant or on different plants. These kinds of plants have flower adaptations that attract insects. The adaptations might be brightly colored petals or strong fragrances that appeal to insects. When an insect visits a plant, pollen can rub off onto the insect and be carried to other flowers. Birds and mammals can carry pollen too. Plants that depend on wind, water, or other sources to carry pollen would have different flower adaptations.

Compare the pollen from a goldenrod flower at the top with that of the lily on the bottom.

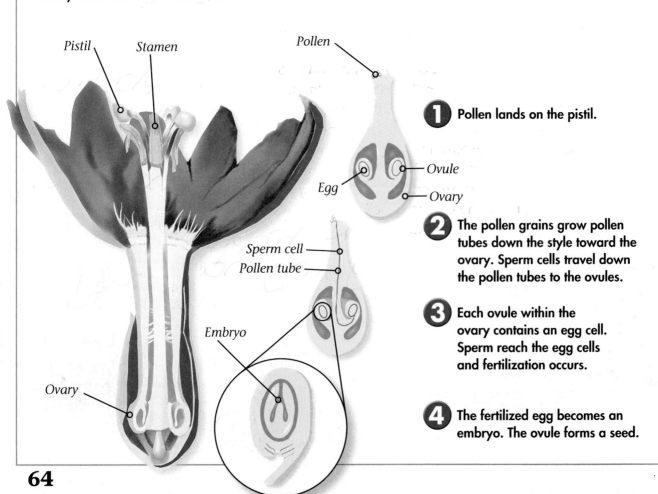

Pistil   Stamen   Pollen

1 Pollen lands on the pistil.

Ovule

Egg

Ovary

2 The pollen grains grow pollen tubes down the style toward the ovary. Sperm cells travel down the pollen tubes to the ovules.

Sperm cell

Pollen tube

Embryo

3 Each ovule within the ovary contains an egg cell. Sperm reach the egg cells and fertilization occurs.

Ovary

4 The fertilized egg becomes an embryo. The ovule forms a seed.

Fertilization in Animals

When animals reproduce sexually, they too must join a sperm cell and an egg cell. Fertilization can take place inside or outside the body of the female.

Many animals that live in or near water use fertilization that takes place outside the female's body. This type of fertilization is called external fertilization. During external fertilization, animals release sperm and eggs into the water. The sperm swim to the eggs, and fertilization takes place. Each time a sperm and egg unite, a zygote forms and a new individual starts to develop.

The staghorn corals shown in the picture are animals that use external fertilization. They live in the waters around the Florida Keys, the Bahamas, the Caribbean Islands, and other areas of the world. In August or September of each year, they release sperm and eggs into the water at the same time. Billions of sperm and eggs can be released at one time.

Staghorn coral

Animals like the staghorn coral that use external fertilization usually produce large numbers of sperm and eggs. But only a few of the fertilized eggs will survive to become adults. Many will die because of environmental conditions, such as severe weather or pollution. Others will be eaten by predators.

External fertilization would be difficult for land animals because the sperm and eggs would dry out too quickly. For most species of animals that live on land, fertilization takes place inside the female's body.

These dark gray eggs will protect the developing bird until it hatches.

Fertilized eggs also need moisture. In some animals, the zygote develops in the female's body where it is moist. Other animals, such as birds and turtles, have eggs with shells that protect the animals developing within the eggs from drying out. The shells also provide protection from other damage.

1. **✓Checkpoint** What is the difference between internal fertilization and external fertilization?

2. **◎ Sequence** Draw and label a picture of the parts of a flower. Then write the steps that happen between pollination and fertilization.

Individuals Differ

Unlike individuals produced by asexual reproduction, offspring produced by sexual reproduction share characteristics of both parents. Each individual has its own set of traits. The individuals may look very similar to their parents, but each has a unique set of DNA. Meiosis is the reason.

Recall that when male and female sex cells form by meiosis, each cell receives only half the DNA that is found in other cells of the individual's body. During fertilization, the sperm cell and egg cell unite, and the DNA of the two cells combines. The zygote that forms has a combination of DNA from the mother and the father. For example, the puppies in the picture have the same mother and father. How many differences can you see among the four puppies? Each puppy is unique because each formed from the combination of a different sperm and egg. That means that each puppy inherited a different combination of DNA. Those different combinations give the puppies different characteristics.

Comparing Sexual and Asexual Reproduction

You might wonder which type of reproduction is better—sexual or asexual. The answer is that each type has both advantages and disadvantages.

Asexual reproduction is the simpler form of reproduction. It often can occur very quickly, producing many offspring in a short time. And one lone organism can reproduce even if the closest individual of its species is hundreds of kilometers away.

Asexual reproduction takes less energy than sexual reproduction. The reason is that in asexual reproduction, organisms do not have to use energy to make sex cells. This can be an advantage when energy-supplying food is scarce.

Egg cell

Sperm cell

Fertilization

Zygote

Puppies inherit some DNA from each parent. Notice that no two of the puppies look exactly alike.

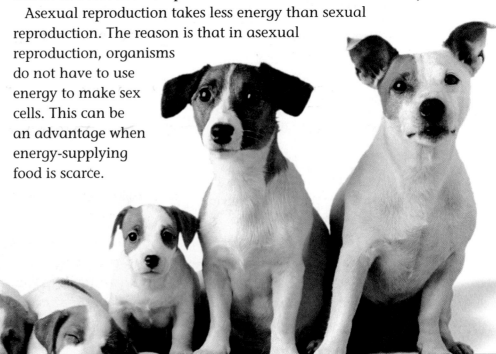

Because all organisms produced by asexual reproduction have the same DNA as the parent cell, their survival in an environment may be threatened if conditions change. Think about a group of amebas living in a pond. Suppose most of the amebas are offspring of the same parent ameba. Those amebas will have identical DNA and, therefore, the same traits. The traits enable them to survive in their environment. What would happen if the water the amebas lived in suddenly became warmer?

Since the amebas are alike, all can only live within a similar temperature range. If the water becomes warmer than that range, all the amebas probably will die.

Now think about another group of organisms living in the same environment. The difference is that those individuals resulted from sexual reproduction. Each individual has traits that are slightly different from those of other individuals. Some may be able to survive in water that is a little warmer or a little cooler. When a temperature change happens, some individuals have a better chance to survive and reproduce. They will be able to pass on this trait to their offspring, who also will be able to live in the warmer water. In other words, individuals who have traits that make them most suited to the environment survive to pass the traits on to offspring.

Paramecia can reproduce very quickly through asexual reproduction.

Asexual Reproduction	Sexual Reproduction
• Can happen quickly	• Is a slow process
• Requires less energy	• Requires more energy
• Needs just one parent cell	• Must have two parent cells
• Produces offspring with DNA identical to parent	• Produces offspring with unique DNA

✓ **Lesson Checkpoint**

1. Why is each individual produced by sexual reproduction unique?
2. What are some advantages of asexual reproduction?
3. Writing in Science **Expository** Some species, such as sponges, can reproduce both sexually and asexually. Write a paragraph that explains how being able to reproduce both ways might help these species' survival. Use the terms *DNA*, *traits*, and *environment*.

How do genes determine traits?

Genes work together to determine individual traits. Scientists can use what they know about how genes work to produce organisms that are more useful.

Dominant and Recessive Traits

An individual formed by sexual reproduction gets traits from both parents. What determines which trait will show up in offspring? For example, the parent guinea pigs shown on the left have two different types of fur. One parent has smooth fur. The other has rough fur. What kind of fur will their offspring have?

The offspring of the mother and father are hybrids.

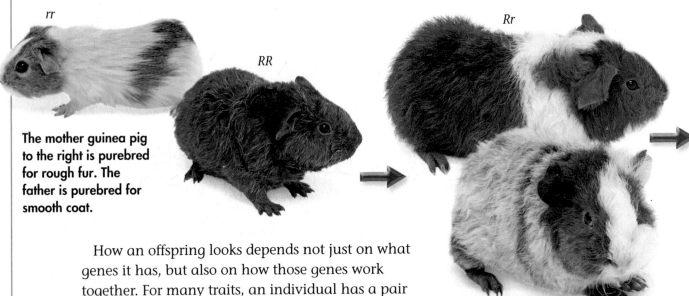

rr

RR

Rr

Rr

The mother guinea pig to the right is purebred for rough fur. The father is purebred for smooth coat.

How an offspring looks depends not just on what genes it has, but also on how those genes work together. For many traits, an individual has a pair of genes, one gene from each parent. But genes have different versions. For example, one version of the gene that determines the type of coat in guinea pigs is for smooth coat. The other version is for rough coat. When the two different versions of a gene occur together, one version may show up. The other may not.

A version of a gene that masks the effect of another version is called a dominant trait. The trait that is hidden is called a recessive trait. In guinea pigs, rough fur is a dominant trait. Smooth fur is a recessive trait. That means an offspring with a version of the gene for rough fur and a version for smooth fur will have rough fur. The only way a guinea pig can have smooth fur is if both versions of the gene are for smooth fur.

Both versions of the gene for fur type in the mother guinea pig in the picture are dominant. These versions are represented by *RR*. Each *R* represents a gene for rough coat. The father's genes are both for smooth fur, which is shown as *rr*. An organism with two versions of a dominant trait or two versions of a recessive trait is called purebred for that trait.

Because guinea pigs reproduce sexually, each of their babies will get one dominant version of the gene, *R*, from the mother and one recessive version, *r*, from the father. The offspring's genes will be *Rr*, and they will have rough fur. An organism with one dominant and one recessive version of a trait is called a hybrid.

However, if two *Rr* guinea pigs mate, each baby can receive an *R* or an *r* from each parent. The offspring can have one of three possible gene combinations: *RR*, *Rr*, and *rr*. Only the *rr* combination will show up as a smooth coat.

When two hybrids produce offspring, there is only a 1-in-4 chance that offspring will have smooth fur.

RR

Rr

Rr

rr

1. ✓**Checkpoint** What is a dominant trait?
2. **Art** in Science Gregor Mendel experimented with thousands of pea plants to study heredity. Find out about Mendel's famous pea plant experiments. Summarize your findings in a visual display.

Sharing Dominance

Not all gene pairs follow the dominant-recessive pattern. Some traits, such as the color of the Erminette chicken pictured below, show both versions of a gene at work. The chicken has genes for both black and white feathers. But neither color is dominant. Instead the colors share dominance.

As you can see in the diagram, the Erminette chicken was produced by a parent with white feathers and a parent with black feathers. The diagram is called a Punnett square. It is used to show all the possible offspring with a particular trait that can result when two individuals mate. In this Punnett square, one parent chicken was purebred for black feathers, which is represented by two genes for black feathers—*bb*. The other parent was purebred for white feathers—*ww*. The possible offspring from these two parents would all be hybrids. Each would have one gene for white feathers and one for black feathers—*bw*. Offspring with those two versions of the gene would have both black and white feathers like the Erminette chicken.

Black chicken

	b	*b*
w	*bw* Erminette	*bw* Erminette
w	*bw* Erminette	*bw* Erminette

White chicken

What would happen if two Erminette chickens mated and produced offspring? Study the second Punnett square to find out.

Erminette

	b	*w*
b	*bb* Black chicken	*bw* Erminette
w	*bw* Erminette	*ww* White chicken

Erminette

Now look at the Punnett square for color in four o'clock plants. One parent has red flowers, and the other has white. You probably would expect the offspring to have red or white flowers. But in this case, neither color is present in the offspring. Instead of red or white, the offspring are pink. Four o'clock plants do not follow the dominant–recessive pattern

With some traits, such as color in four o'clock plants, the effects of two genes appear to blend. The red four o'clock parent and the white four o'clock parent produced pink offspring—a blending of the red and white colors of the parent plants.

But what would happen if the pink offspring reproduced? As you can see, the possible offspring could be red, white, or pink! Look at the second Punnett square to see how that could happen.

You can see a similar example in humans. A child of a straight-haired parent and a curly-haired parent will have wavy hair. Two parents with wavy hair can have children with wavy hair, straight hair, or curly hair.

Erminette chicken

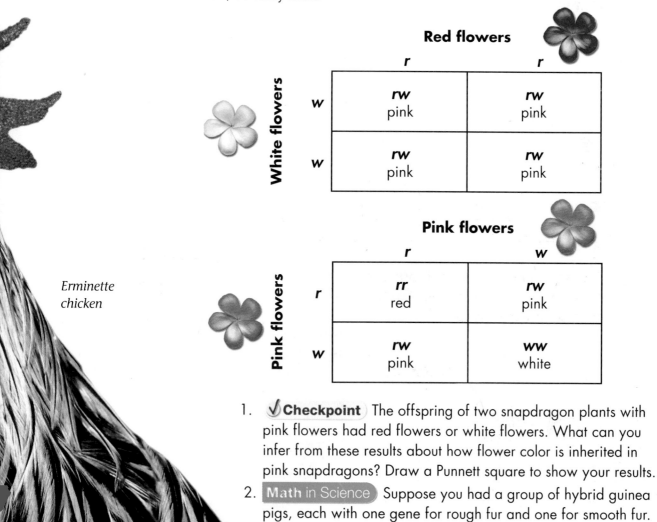

Red flowers

	r	r
w	rw pink	rw pink
w	rw pink	rw pink

White flowers

Pink flowers

	r	w
r	rr red	rw pink
w	rw pink	ww white

Pink flowers

1. ✓**Checkpoint** The offspring of two snapdragon plants with pink flowers had red flowers or white flowers. What can you infer from these results about how flower color is inherited in pink snapdragons? Draw a Punnett square to show your results.

2. **Math in Science** Suppose you had a group of hybrid guinea pigs, each with one gene for rough fur and one for smooth fur. If together they had 100 offspring, about how many of the offspring would you expect to have smooth fur?

71

The corn we eat today is the result of selective breeding.

Choosing Traits

The familiar ear of corn shown to the left is probably not much like its wild ancestor. Around 8,000 to 10,000 years ago, people in what is now Mexico began to change a grass-like plant they had been gathering in nature for food. They did this by choosing and planting seeds from plants that had traits they liked. When the new plants produced seeds, the people again chose the best seeds. This process continued for many generations of plants. Over time, a plant that served as better food resulted—an early version of the corn we eat today. Selecting a few organisms with desired traits to serve as parents of offspring is called **selective breeding.**

People around the world use selective breeding to produce plants and animals with traits that are valuable to humans. Cows have not always produced as much milk as they do now. In the early 1800s, most dairy cows made only about 1,500 liters of milk a year. Today, some kinds of cows can make as much as 10,000 liters a year! Other kinds produce milk with certain traits, such as a high amount of fat. How did these changes happen? The traits were produced through selective breeding and better nutrition.

Selective breeding also helps produce crops with more food per plant. Many varieties of fruits and vegetables are bred to resist diseases, insect pests, and drought. People have raised chickens that lay more eggs. Selective breeding has been used to produce dogs that are smarter, stronger, healthier, or friendlier.

What traits of this cow do you think were produced by selective breeding?

Writings and sculptures of the Afghan hound date back to 3500 B.C. The Afghans of the deserts of Egypt were bred to hunt gazelle, deer, and leopards. In the mountains of Afghanistan, the Afghan hound was used to guard sheep and cattle. It also was a hunter of small game.

The Shetland sheepdog was developed in the Shetland Islands to help herd sheep. The winters on the Shetland Isles are long, and little plant life grows. The farmers of the area developed the Shetland sheepdog to herd sheep and to keep the gardens safe from the flocks.

Luther Burbank

In the history of selective breeding, perhaps no one has been more successful than Luther Burbank, who was born in Massachusetts in 1849. Luther Burbank developed more than 800 varieties of plants. You may have eaten some of the new varieties of plums, pineapples, walnuts, and almonds that he developed.

One of Burbank's most important successes was the development of the Burbank potato. At the time, the potato was an important food for many people in Ireland. When a disease called potato blight killed potato crops in Ireland for several years, these people did not have enough to eat. Eventually as many as one million people in Ireland died because of this potato disease. The Burbank potato was resistant to potato blight. It was shipped to Ireland to be planted in place of the diseased potatoes. The potato helped prevent even more deaths.

Today's dogs come in many shapes and sizes—from the tiny Chihuahua to the large Saint Bernard. But they are also some of humans' oldest friends. Ancient clues in cave paintings and burials reveal that dogs and people have lived together for thousands of years. Dogs of many sizes and shapes appear in the archaeological records of almost all human cultures from thousands of years ago. Selected for hunting, herding, protection, companionship, or looks, dogs were welcomed into many homes.

Over the years, people have used selective breeding to produce the characteristics they choose. Most of today's almost 400 different dog breeds were produced after 1850.

✓ Lesson Checkpoint

1. Explain how offspring can have traits that show both versions of a gene.
2. Why do people use selective breeding?
3. 🔵 **Sequence** Explain the process of selective breeding.

Investigate How can a coin toss model heredity?

In some ways the process of inheriting traits is like a game of chance. It can be modeled by coin tosses.

Materials

coins

dot labels

What to Do

1 Use coins to **model** how the genes for height are inherited in a pea plant.

2 Label the "head" of both coins with a **T**. Label the "tail" of both coins with a **t**.

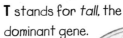

T stands for *tall*, the dominant gene.

t stands for *short*, the recessive gene.

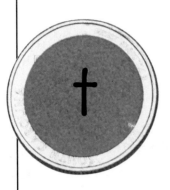

Process Skills

Modeling the process of inheritance and **interpreting** your **data** can help you understand how the genes for a particular trait are inherited.

3 Shake the 2 coins, and then toss them gently onto your work surface.

4 Record the letters showing on the coins. These letters stand for the genes inherited by one pea plant offspring.

Use a chart like this one.

Coin Toss	Inherited Genes	Offspring Appearance
1	Tt	tall
2		
3		

5 Repeat steps 3 and 4 until you have 16 trials.

6 Draw a Punnett square, showing all the possible different offspring of the parents used for steps 3–5.

Explain Your Results

1. **Interpret Data** Based on what you learned **modeling** the process of inheritance, which combination appeared most often— **TT, tt,** or **Tt?**

2. Which combinations produce tall offspring? Explain.

Go Further

How can you model the inherited traits of offspring whose parents have the genes **TT** and **Tt**? Make a plan to investigate.

Math in Science

Probability of INHERITING TRAITS

You have learned how Punnett squares can be used to show the possible combinations of genes in the offspring of two organisms. They can help us answer questions about heredity in terms of probability or ratios. Remember, probabilities and ratios can be expressed as fractions or as percents.

The following Punnett square represents the possible offspring of two four o'clock plants, discussed earlier in this chapter. The Punnett square below shows the possible offspring of a red plant and a white plant. Remember, neither red nor white flowers are dominant.

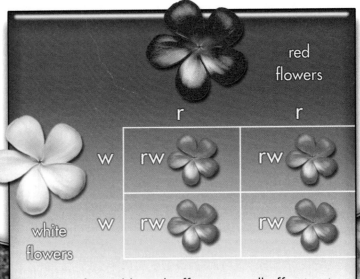

The ratio of possible pink offspring to all offspring is 4:4, or $\frac{4}{4}$. We can also say that the probability of an offspring being pink is $\frac{4}{4}$, or 1. In other words, 100% of the offspring will be pink. The only possible gene combination for offspring of these two plants is *rw*.

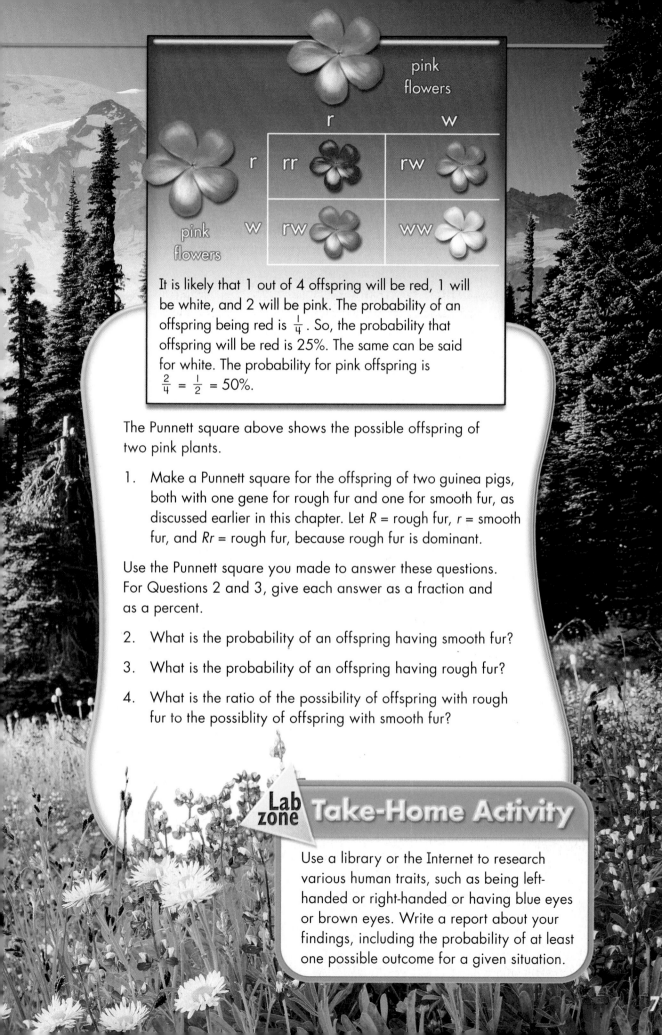

pink
flowers

	r	w
r	rr	rw
w	rw	ww

pink
flowers

It is likely that 1 out of 4 offspring will be red, 1 will be white, and 2 will be pink. The probability of an offspring being red is $\frac{1}{4}$. So, the probability that offspring will be red is 25%. The same can be said for white. The probability for pink offspring is $\frac{2}{4} = \frac{1}{2} = 50\%$.

The Punnett square above shows the possible offspring of two pink plants.

1. Make a Punnett square for the offspring of two guinea pigs, both with one gene for rough fur and one for smooth fur, as discussed earlier in this chapter. Let *R* = rough fur, *r* = smooth fur, and *Rr* = rough fur, because rough fur is dominant.

Use the Punnett square you made to answer these questions. For Questions 2 and 3, give each answer as a fraction and as a percent.

2. What is the probability of an offspring having smooth fur?

3. What is the probability of an offspring having rough fur?

4. What is the ratio of the possibility of offspring with rough fur to the possiblity of offspring with smooth fur?

Lab zone Take-Home Activity

Use a library or the Internet to research various human traits, such as being left-handed or right-handed or having blue eyes or brown eyes. Write a report about your findings, including the probability of at least one possible outcome for a given situation.

Use Vocabulary

asexual reproduction (p. 56)	meiosis (p. 62)
	selective breeding (p. 72)
egg cell (p. 62)	
fertilization (p. 62)	sexual reproduction (p. 62)
genes (p. 59)	
heredity (p. 55)	sperm cell (p.62)

Write the vocabulary word from the list above that best completes each sentence.

1. During _____, a sperm cell joins with an egg cell.

2. The process of selecting a few organisms with desired traits to serve as parents of offspring is called _____.

3. An organism uses _____ to produce offspring by itself.

4. Sex cells are created by a process called _____.

5. A male's sex cell is called a(n) _____.

6. Offspring receive DNA from two parents through _____.

7. The passing of traits from parent to offspring is called _____.

8. A(n) _____ is a female's sex cell.

9. Chromosomes are divided into sections of DNA called _____.

Explain Concepts

10. Explain why sex cells have only half as many chromosomes as the other cells in an organism's body.

11. Why don't offspring of two parents look exactly like either parent?

12. The Punnett square below shows the possible offspring for two parent guinea pigs. Parent A is hybrid for rough fur. Parent B has smooth fur. What percentage of the possible offspring are likely to have smooth fur?

Parent A

	R	r
r	Rr	rr
r	Rr	rr

Parent B

Process Skills

13. Predict Species A lives successfully in a cornfield. It reproduces asexually. Species B, which reproduces sexually, also lives in the cornfield. Which species would be more likely to survive in that cornfield if a drought hit the area one season? Explain your answer.

14. Infer What kind of reproduction—sexual or asexual—is happening in the bacterium in the picture? How do you know?

🎯 Sequence

15. Make a graphic organizer like the one below. Fill in the steps to show what happens when DNA copies itself.

> **First,** base pairs pull apart. One base stays attached to each side of ladder

⬇

> **Next,**

⬇

> **Finally,**

Test Prep

Choose the letter that best completes the statement or answers the question.

16. All living things share the same
- Ⓐ dominant genes.
- Ⓑ way of producing offspring.
- Ⓒ number of chromosomes.
- Ⓓ four bases in their DNA.

17. A dog may inherit the potential to grow to 22 kg but may not reach that weight because of its
- Ⓕ genes.
- Ⓖ environment.
- Ⓗ learning.
- Ⓘ parents.

18. One advantage of sexual reproduction is
- Ⓐ speed of reproduction.
- Ⓑ variation among offspring.
- Ⓒ identical DNA.
- Ⓓ better base pairs.

19. Explain why the answer you chose for Question 16 is best. For each of the answers you did not choose, give a reason why it is not the best choice.

20. Writing in Science **Expository**
Write a summary of what happens when the genes that determine the color of flowers share dominance. Explain how you could prove that the flowers' traits are determined by two different genes.

Daniel Barta
BOTANIST

Would you guess that a love for plants could lead a scientist to outer space? It did for Daniel J. Barta. Along with scientists from many different areas of study, he works every day to solve problems that people will face in space.

Barta earned his Ph.D. in Botany/Horticulture (the science of plant reproduction) in 1991 from the University of Wisconsin in Madison. He then went to work at the Wisconsin Center for Space Automation and Robotics. This may seem like an odd workplace for a man who works with plants. But it made perfect sense. The Center was trying to learn if plants could be grown in space. Dr. Barta was trying to find out if plants could reproduce in space.

NASA was interested in Dr. Barta's work because plants can be the solution to many problems in human space travel. For example, astronauts in space need a constant supply of food, water, and oxygen. Dr. Barta grew sweet potatoes in conditions identical to those in a spaceship. The experiment showed that growing plants on spacecraft can provide astronauts with food, clean water, and oxygen. When humans someday build stations on the Moon or travel to Mars, they will have people like Daniel Barta to thank.

Lab zone Take-Home Activity

Write a short story about astronauts on a spaceship who depend on plants for food and oxygen. Think about what crises the astronauts might face if the plants begin to die. What steps would they have to take? How do they solve their problem?

EC CRU 10 9 8 7 6 5 4 3 2 1

Chapter 4

Body Systems

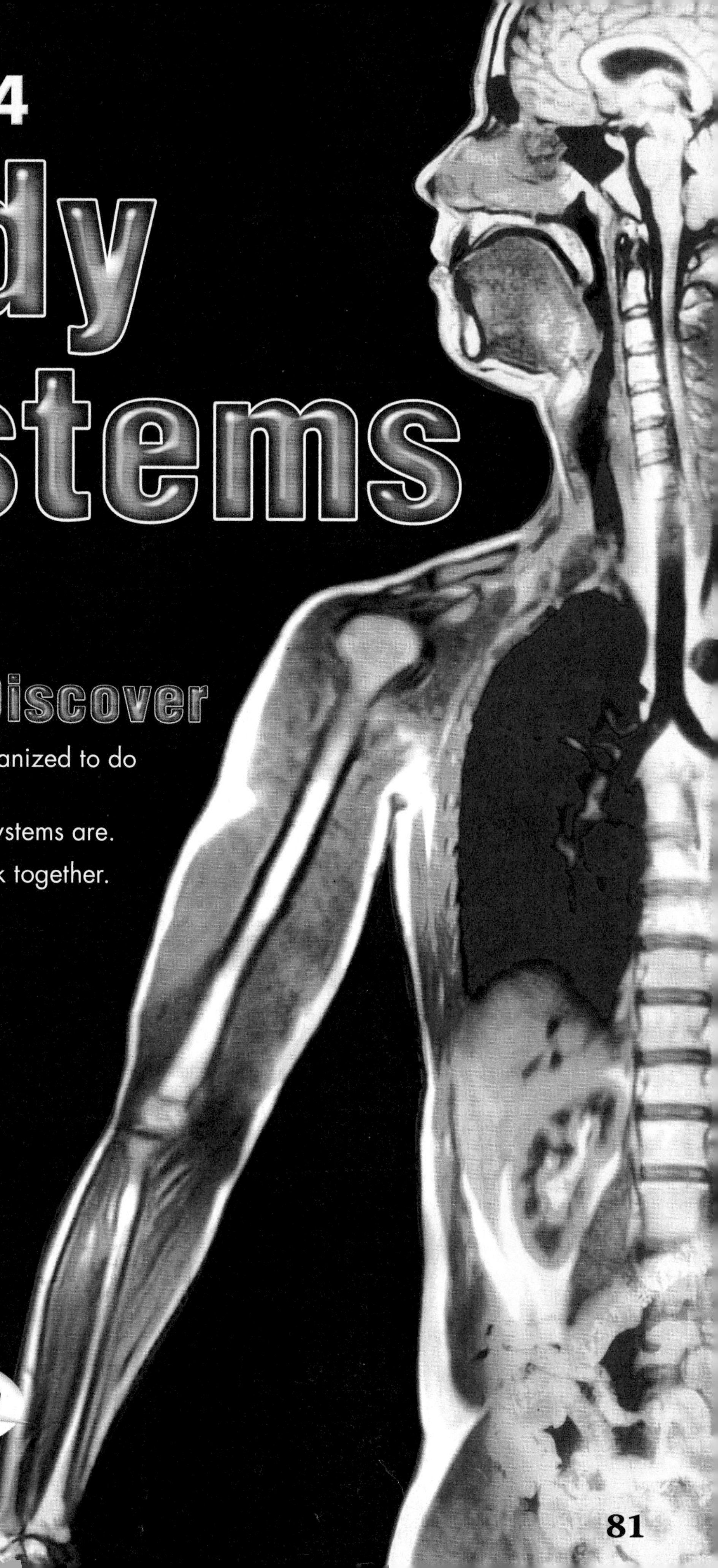

You Will Discover

- how body cells are organized to do certain tasks.
- what the major body systems are.
- how body systems work together.

online
Student Edition
pearsonsuccessnet.com

How do body parts work together?

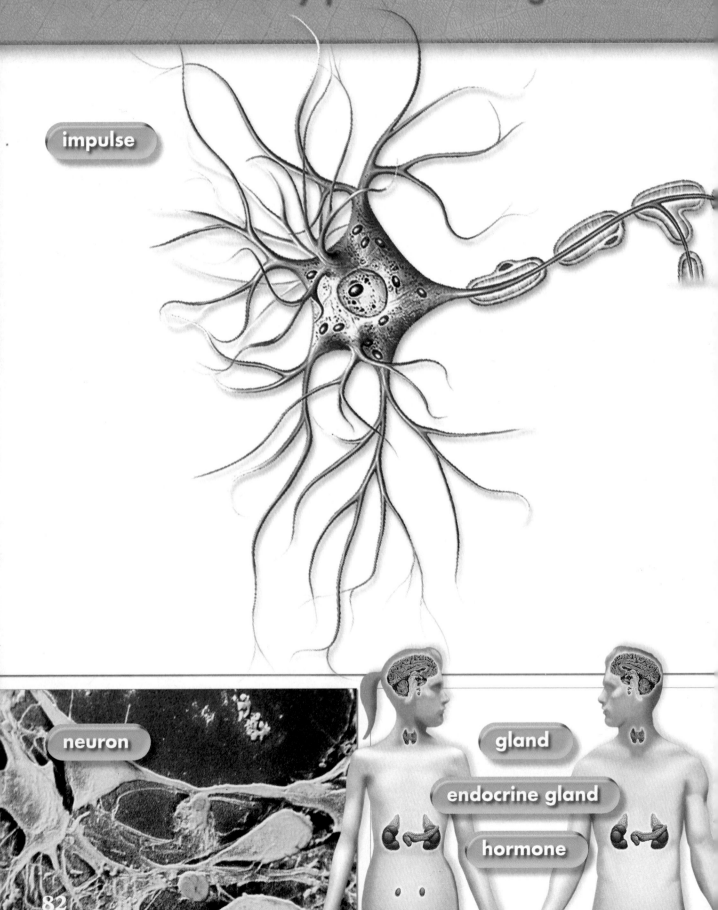

impulse

neuron

gland

endocrine gland

hormone

82

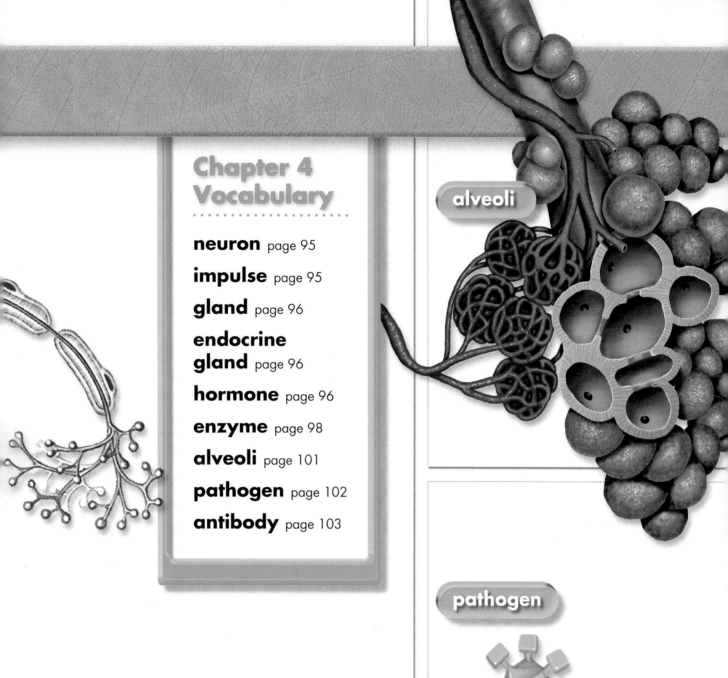

Chapter 4 Vocabulary

alveoli

pathogen

enzyme

chemicals that help break down food into nutrients

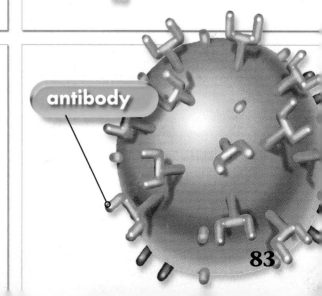

antibody

83

Explore What are some differences between two types of cells?

Materials

prepared slide of cheek cells and prepared slide of blood cells

Note: Commercially prepared slides are safe.

microscope

What to Do

1 Place Slide A (cheek cells) on the microscope. Draw a picture of what you **observe.**

2 Replace Slide A with Slide B (blood cells). Draw a picture of what you observe.

	Drawing
Slide A: Cheek Cells	
	human cheek cells
Slide B: Blood Cells	
	human blood cells

Process Skills

Careful **observations** can help you find cause-and-effect relationships.

Explain Your Results

Compare and contrast the cells you **observed.** **Communicate** how they are alike and different.

How to Read Science

Cause and Effect

In science, you often **observe** and read about events that happen. Understanding what causes these events is important. A **cause** is the reason something happens. What happens is the **effect.** Read the article below to see how causes result in effects.

- Look for clue words that signal cause-and-effect relationships. Some clue words are *result, cause, because of, so, since,* and *thus.*

- The effect of one event can become the cause of another event.

Science Article

Muscle Cells

The cells that make up muscles have an important characteristic. Muscles cells can contract. When a group of cells make a muscle contract, they cause the muscle to become shorter and thicker. When that happens, the muscle pulls on the bone that it is attached to. The pull results in movement of the bone.

Apply It!

Make a graphic organizer like the one shown. For each **cause-and-effect** relationship in the article, write the cause in the Cause box. Then write the effect.

| **Cause** | ➡ | **Effect** |

🔊 You Are There!

Faster, faster, faster! Your body pushes itself to be first at the finish line. You can feel your heart pounding harder and faster. Your muscles burn. Your breathing is deep and quick. What is going on in your body to cause these things to happen?

AudioText 🔊

How is the body organized?

Cells are the building blocks of your body. Specialized cells make up different body parts, which work together to meet all of the needs of your body.

Cells Working Together

Your body is able to do some pretty amazing things. You can run and catch a ball. You can write and read. You can dance, play an instrument, or even create your own music. No one body part is responsible for any of these activities. Instead, each part involved contributes in its own way.

The human body is an amazing system made up of more than 75,000,000,000,000 cells. These cells are so small that a sheet of about 10,000 of them would only cover the head of a pin. Every one of those cells is a living unit. At the same time, each cell is part of a larger living unit—your body.

Millions of chemical processes go on in your body every minute. Those chemical processes take place in cells. Cells depend on each other to keep all the body's internal conditions in balance so that all cells can work properly. For example, the important processes that go on in your body cells can only happen within a particular temperature range—around 37°C (98.6° F). Cells in different parts of your body work together to make sure the body's temperature stays in that range. Your body depends on its cells to make it run smoothly.

The surprising thing about cells is that they do so many important tasks but they are so small. The largest cell, the human egg cell, is about the diameter of a human hair. Most human cells are much smaller. How can so many tiny, individual cells in the body work together so efficiently? The answer is in the way cells are organized.

1. **✓Checkpoint** Why is keeping the body in balance important?

2. **Health** in Science Use Internet resources to find out three things you can do each day to help your body perform at its best.

Levels of Organization

Although all cells are made of the same basic parts, each type of cell is adapted to perform certain activities or functions. Keeping the body in balance requires many different activities, but each cell does not have to do them all. Cells are organized by the activities they do.

Similar cells that work together to perform a particular function in the body make up tissues. Cells that can contract, or shorten, make up muscle tissue. When the cells that make up muscle tissue contract, some part of your body moves. You use muscle tissue when your eyes move to read this page or when you move in your chair.

Although muscle tissue contracts to move your body, nerve tissue tells the muscle tissue to do so. The cells that make up nerve tissue are alike in that they can carry messages from one cell to another. Your brain is made of mostly nerve tissue. Other types of tissue hold together body parts, support the body, cushion organs, or release substances.

When two or more tissues work together to do a job, they form an organ. The job of an organ is usually not as simple as the job of a tissue. For example, your heart must pump blood all over your body. To do so, it must have different kinds of tissues—muscle tissue that contracts, nerve tissue that directs its activities, and other tissues to hold it together and carry blood.

Each organ in your body is part of an organ system. Different organ systems work together and depend on each other. Read the chart on the next page to see the important jobs each body system does.

Cells
The heart must beat without stopping so that the body has a constant supply of blood. Heart muscle cells have many mitochondria (red) to provide energy for this task.

Tissues
The arrangement of muscle cells in this heart tissue allows the muscles to shorten and then relax, causing the heart to beat.

The Body's Major Systems

System	Function
Circulatory	Transports oxygen, nutrients, and cell wastes
Digestive	Breaks down foods into a form the body can use
Endocrine	Controls internal conditions, growth, development, and reproduction
Excretory	Removes wastes from the blood
Immune	Defends the body against pathogens
Muscular	Allows body movement and movement of substances within the body
Nervous	Controls body movement, thought, and behavior
Reproductive	Produces sex cells and offspring
Respiratory	Provides the body with oxygen and removes gas wastes from the blood
Skeletal	Provides body protection and support; interacts with muscles to allow movement

Blood Cells

These blood cells are only two of the many kinds of cells that make up your body. Red blood cells carry oxygen throughout the body so that all cells can carry out life functions. White blood cells help to fight off disease-causing invaders that attack the body.

Although each person is unique, the cells of everyone's body are similar in some ways. This similarity makes it possible for individuals to donate their blood to others. Other cell similarities enable people to donate entire organs.

Organs

The heart itself is an organ. In addition to muscle tissue, the heart is made of tissues that provide support and protection and that form its blood vessels.

✓ Lesson Checkpoint

1. What is the basic unit of structure in the human body?
2. Identify and give an example of each level of organization in the human body.
3. **Health** in Science There are four basic types of blood. Usually, only individuals with the same type can exchange blood. Use reference sources to find out the four basic types of blood and which one can be donated to anyone.

What systems help move body parts?

Your skeleton provides support, protects organs, makes new blood cells, and stores important minerals. Its 206 bones work with skeletal muscles to allow your body to move.

Skeletal System

When you look at a bone, like the one in the picture, you might think that it is dead. But the bones of your body are very alive. Bones are made of living tissues, as well as nonliving minerals that are deposited by bone cells. Blood flows through every part of a bone.

Parts of a Bone

A The thin, tough, outer covering on the surface of a bone is living tissue.

B Blood vessels in the bone carry blood, which supplies materials that bone cells need. Blood also removes wastes that bone cells produce.

C Compact bone is the hardest material in the human body, except for tooth enamel. It is made up of "bony tubes." This structure is very strong.

D Spongy bone tissue makes the bone lightweight. It is thickest near joints.

E Red marrow in the spongy bone of the long arm and leg bones makes new red blood cells. Yellow marrow in the center cavity of long bones stores fat.

Living bone cells are found in tiny spaces in compact bone. They secrete minerals and other materials that harden to form bone.

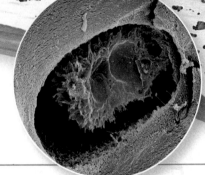

When you were a baby, some of your bones were made of a flexible material called cartilage. Much of the cartilage is replaced by hard bone as a person ages. But you still have cartilage. Move the tip of your nose or the tops of your ears. The flexible tissue in those places is cartilage. Bones and cartilage make up your skeletal system.

Bones have several functions. They support your body and give you height. Bones of the skull, rib cage, and back protect important organs. Some bones form new blood cells. Bones also store minerals, such as calcium and phosphorus. Small amounts of stored minerals are released when the body needs them. These same minerals make bones hard and strong.

Calcium in the bony material that makes up much of your body's long bones helps make the bones hard and heavy. The network of spaces in this normal bone below helps make the bone lighter.

As people grow older, they lose calcium in their bones. The result can be seen in the bone below. This is a bone of a person who has a disease called osteoporosis. Bones that are weakened like this can break easily.

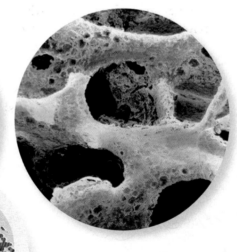

1. ✓**Checkpoint** What are three functions of bones?

2. ○ **Cause and Effect** What is osteoporosis? What is its cause?

Joints

A joint is a place where two bones meet. Flexible cartilage covers and protects the ends of bones at joints. The shape of cartilage surfaces and the way they fit together determine the directions a joint can move. Strong cords of tissue called ligaments connect the bones in each joint.

Ball-and-Socket

The shoulder joint allows the arm to swing freely in a circle. This type of joint allows the most movement.

Hinge

The knee joint works like the hinges of a door. It allows the leg to bend and straighten.

Pivot

The joint at your elbow allows bones to rotate around one another. This allows your arm to twist.

Muscular System

Your bones support your body, but without your muscles you would not be able to move. In fact, you wouldn't be able to stand, breathe, or swallow food. The more than 600 muscles of your body make up 40 to 50 percent of your body weight. The muscles and the tissues that attach them to bones make up the muscular system.

Your body has three types of muscle tissue. The muscle tissue in your heart, called cardiac muscle, is found nowhere else in the body. This kind of muscle tissue can contract time after time without getting tired. Another kind of muscle, called smooth muscle, can be found in organs of the digestive system and blood vessels. Cardiac and smooth muscles are involuntary muscles—they work automatically to control movements inside your body. For example, the smooth muscles lining your stomach cause it to twist and turn to mix food with digestive juices.

The third kind of muscle—skeletal muscle—is voluntary muscle. You can control voluntary muscles. The muscles that move your arms and legs are voluntary muscles.

All muscles can contract, but only skeletal muscles are responsible for the body's movement. Your bones and skeletal muscles work together to make your body move. Pairs of muscles attach to opposite sides of a bone near a joint. When one muscle contracts and pulls the bone, the opposite muscle relaxes. Movement results in the direction of the pulling muscle. Muscles never push on bones to cause movement.

The muscle on the top of the leg is relaxing. This allows the lower leg to be pulled backward. To straighten the leg, the muscle on the top of the leg would contract and the muscle on the back of the leg would relax.

The hinge joint of the knee allows the lower leg to move freely.

Tough bands, called tendons, attach muscles to bones.

The lower leg is pulled back because the muscle on the back of the leg is contracting, pulling on the bones of the lower leg.

Keeping Muscles and Bones Healthy

Although your muscles are very strong, they can become injured or develop other problems. Overworking or stretching your muscles too far may result in a muscle strain or an irritation of the tendons, the tough tissue that connects muscle to bone. Muscular dystrophy is a condition in which the muscles become weaker and weaker as the muscles are slowly destroyed. It is an inherited condition, and the most common form occurs mostly in males.

Disorders of the skeletal system include arthritis and osteoporosis. Arthritis is a condition in which the joints become painful and swollen. It is the most common disease in the United States not caused by germs. Arthritis can affect children or adults. Osteoporosis is a condition in which bones become weak and break easily. Although symptoms of osteoporosis do not show up until people become older, getting enough calcium during childhood and adolescence and being physically active can help prevent this condition.

You can keep your skeletal and muscular systems strong and healthy by eating healthful foods. Get plenty of rest and exercise. Some people warm up before beginning exercise. Warming up loosens muscles, tendons, and ligaments.

✓ Lesson Checkpoint

1. What are the three types of muscles?
2. What are three things you can do to keep your skeletal and muscle systems healthy?
3. 🎯 **Cause and Effect** How do muscles and bones work together to cause movement?

Milk products are rich in vitamin D, calcium, and phosphorus.

Carrots are good sources of vitamin A, which helps the body use calcium and phosphorus to form bone.

Fruits and pasta provide energy to muscles. Bananas provide potassium, which the muscles need to do their work.

How do systems control the body?

Your nervous and endocrine systems extend out to all parts of the body. They communicate with and control all body systems.

Nervous System

Muscles contract to move the bones of your body, but they can't do that without receiving messages from the nervous system. Your nervous system includes the brain, the spinal cord, nerves, and sense organs. The nervous system is constantly collecting information both inside and outside your body. It allows you to speak, think, taste, hear, and see. It helps the body stay balanced by processing and responding to the information it receives.

Parts of the Brain

A Brain stem
Maintains blood pressure, heartbeat, respiration, and digestion

B Cerebellum
Controls balance and posture; helps fine-tune movements

C Cerebrum
Interprets information that senses gather; controls muscle movement, thinking, and language

1 A racer's body is set to explode from the starting line. His eyes are trained on the starter. He waits for the wave of the flag to begin the race.

2 When the start flag is waved, the racer's eyes see the movement. They send a message through the spinal cord to the brain: "It's time to begin!"

3 The brain interprets the messages and responds by sending nerve impulses back through the spinal cord to the muscles in the legs and arms of the racer. The impulses tell muscles to contract, and the racer's body drives forward.

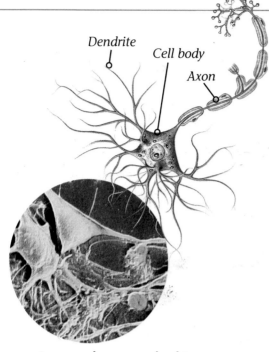

Dendrite

Cell body

Axon

A neuron has many dendrites, but only one axon. The cell body of a neuron is small, but the axon can be very long. The axon of neurons in an adult leg can be a meter long.

Nerve cells, called **neurons,** pass messages throughout your body. Each neuron has a cell body with many thin branches. Short branches, called dendrites, carry messages from other neurons to the cell body. A long branch, the axon, carries messages away from the cell body to other nerve cells.

When the dendrite of a neuron receives a message, the chemical makeup of the neuron changes. This chemical change causes an **impulse,** or message, to travel along the neuron and from one neuron to the next. These impulses can travel in only one direction— from the axon of one neuron to the dendrite of another neuron.

Most impulses travel along neurons to the brain, which controls almost everything you experience and do. Much of the information that your nervous system collects is processed by the brain. The brain interprets the information and responds by sending messages to different parts of the body telling them to act.

Impulses received and sent by the brain pass through the spinal cord. This long bundle of nerves runs down your back and is protected by your backbone. Some neurons in the spinal cord carry messages to the brain. Others carry them away.

Reflexes

Some messages that the body receives do not pass to the brain. One example is the response of your body when you touch your hand to a hot surface. The response to that action is a reflex, a response that happens automatically without the brain "thinking" about it. Reflexes happen very fast. They help protect the body from dangerous situations.

Without the nervous system, the many parts of your body would not be able to work together. You can help protect your nervous system by avoiding alcohol and other illegal drugs. Wear protective gear when playing sports or doing any activity in which the brain may be injured. Wear seat belts when riding in a car. Never dive into a shallow pool.

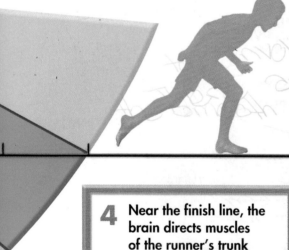

4 Near the finish line, the brain directs muscles of the runner's trunk to lean forward. This movement improves the racer's time.

1.   ✓**Checkpoint** What are the two kinds of branches that extend from the cell body of a neuron? What does each do?

2.   **Math** in Science If a nerve signal travels to and from the brain at a speed of 30 meters per second, how long would it take the signal to travel 3 meters? Use this equation: time = distance/speed.

Endocrine System

Your nervous system helps maintain balance in the body's processes by interpreting information about the environment and then telling parts of the body to act. Your endocrine system also helps balance your body's processes. But it controls slower processes, such as growth and sugar levels in the blood.

The endocrine system is made up of glands. A **gland** is an organ that produces a chemical. Some glands release their chemicals into tiny tubes called ducts. The endocrine glands do not release chemicals into ducts. Each **endocrine gland** is an organ that releases chemical substances directly into the blood. The substances they release are called **hormones.** Hormones control many of your body's functions.

The endocrine system continually checks your body's condition. It releases hormones when needed to maintain your body's internal balance. Each kind of hormone travels in the blood to particular target cells throughout the body. Each hormone causes target cells to perform certain tasks. For example, a hormone may cause bones to grow or muscles to store sugar.

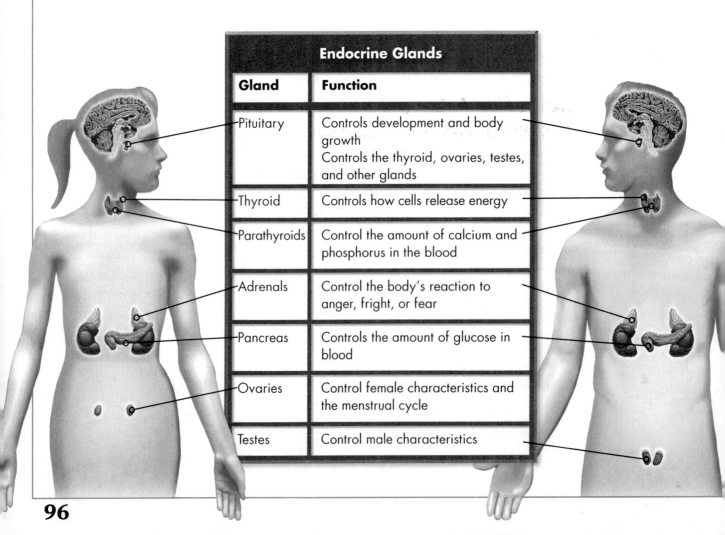

Endocrine Glands

Gland	Function
Pituitary	Controls development and body growth Controls the thyroid, ovaries, testes, and other glands
Thyroid	Controls how cells release energy
Parathyroids	Control the amount of calcium and phosphorus in the blood
Adrenals	Control the body's reaction to anger, fright, or fear
Pancreas	Controls the amount of glucose in blood
Ovaries	Control female characteristics and the menstrual cycle
Testes	Control male characteristics

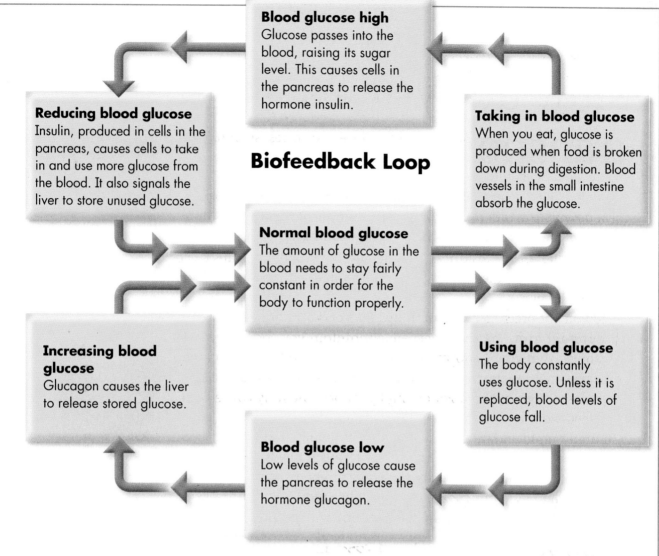

Biofeedback Loop

Blood glucose high
Glucose passes into the blood, raising its sugar level. This causes cells in the pancreas to release the hormone insulin.

Reducing blood glucose
Insulin, produced in cells in the pancreas, causes cells to take in and use more glucose from the blood. It also signals the liver to store unused glucose.

Taking in blood glucose
When you eat, glucose is produced when food is broken down during digestion. Blood vessels in the small intestine absorb the glucose.

Normal blood glucose
The amount of glucose in the blood needs to stay fairly constant in order for the body to function properly.

Increasing blood glucose
Glucagon causes the liver to release stored glucose.

Using blood glucose
The body constantly uses glucose. Unless it is replaced, blood levels of glucose fall.

Blood glucose low
Low levels of glucose cause the pancreas to release the hormone glucagon.

Biofeedback Loop

Endocrine glands keep important body substances in balance. They do this by releasing fewer or more hormones. This allows glands to turn on, turn off, speed up, or slow down the activities of organs and tissues.

An example of the way the endocrine glands help maintain balance in the body is the way hormones control blood sugar, or glucose, in the blood. All the body's cells need glucose to carry on life functions. The process is summarized in the diagram of a biofeedback loop. A biofeedback loop is a circular pathway that sends information back and forth from one part of the body to another. If the biofeedback loop doesn't work properly, problems including diabetes, can result.

✓ Lesson Checkpoint

1. How do impulses travel throughout the nervous system? Use the terms *axon* and *dendrite* in your answer.

2. Both the nervous system and the endocrine system control the body's processes. How do their functions differ?

3. 🔄 **Cause and Effect** What causes the pancreas to release insulin?

How do systems transport materials?

The digestive system takes in materials needed by the body. It breaks them down into a form that body cells can use. The respiratory system takes in oxygen that cells need and gets rid of carbon dioxide wastes that cells produce.

Digestive System

Did you eat breakfast this morning? Do you know why it is important to do so? The foods you eat contain important substances that your body needs to grow, repair itself, and carry on other life processes. Your body can't function properly without a constant supply of these substances. When you sleep, your body continues to use those substances, but you aren't replacing those that are used. A good breakfast can restore your body's supply of the materials it needs.

After you eat, getting important nutrients to body cells can take some time. Body cells can't use most foods until they are broken down into simpler substances. Organs of the digestive system work together to break down food into a useable form. Some foods break down during mechanical digestion—the tearing, crushing, and mashing of food. In chemical digestion, chemicals called **enzymes** help break down food into nutrients.

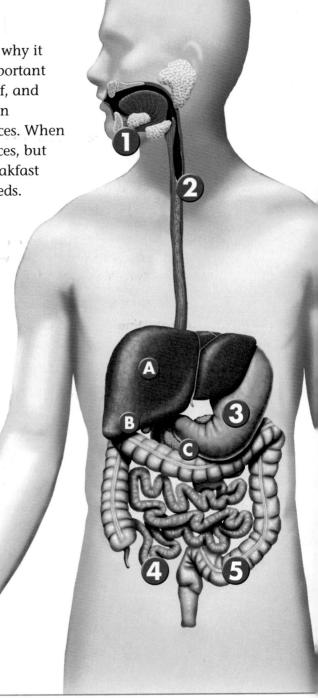

A Liver
The liver produces bile, which helps digest fat. The liver also stores some nutrients and breaks down harmful substances in the blood.

B Gallbladder
Bile produced by the liver is stored in the gallbladder until it is released to the small intestine when it is needed.

C Pancreas
The pancreas produces enzymes that flow into the small intestine. These enzymes and other substances neutralize stomach acid that is mixed with the food that enters the small intestine.

Process of Digestion

1 Mouth

Mechanical digestion begins in the mouth where teeth shred food. The tongue mixes the food with saliva, which is a mixture of water and enzymes produced by the salivary glands. Saliva begins the process of chemical digestion. It starts the breakdown of starch into simple sugars.

2 Esophagus

After the food becomes soft and moist, the tongue pushes it to the esophagus. Rhythmic contractions of the smooth muscles in the esophagus push the food toward the opening to the stomach.

3 Stomach

The stomach continues the mechanical digestion by squeezing its contents with muscular contractions. Glands in the stomach produce enzymes and acid that begin the breakdown of proteins. The acid also kills bacteria that have been swallowed with food. After several hours in the stomach the food has become a soupy mixture.

4 Small Intestine

Most digestion takes place in the small intestine. Tiny fingerlike projections, called villi, line the small intestine. Digested food passes into the blood through the walls of the villi. These structures increase the surface area, where digested materials can be absorbed into the blood. The villi absorb about 7.5 liters of fluid a day.

5 Large Intestine

Materials that cannot be absorbed into the bloodstream pass into the large intestine. Little digestion takes place here. The large intestine absorbs water from the undigested material and stores solid wastes until they leave the body.

1. ✓ Checkpoint How does each part of the digestive system contribute to digestion?
2. Social Studies in Science Find out what people in another country eat. Write a paragraph describing the foods they eat.

A Closer View

Tongue
The large, red structures in this electron microscope image of the surface of the tongue are small taste buds. The smaller fingerlike projections form a rough surface on the tongue that helps in the chewing and movement of food.

Stomach
The oval cells in this electron microscope image of the stomach lining produce mucus that protects the stomach from digestive substances. Pits in the lining contain glands that produce digestive juices.

Small Intestine
As many as 40 villi per square millimeter cover the surface of the small intestine. There are more at the beginning of the intestine than toward the end.

Circulatory System

As you just read, the many villi lining the small intestine contain blood vessels that pick up nutrients and pass them into the blood. These vessels carry the blood and nutrients to cells in all parts of your body. The task of transporting nutrients is done by your circulatory system, which also carries other materials throughout the body. The circulatory system is made up of blood, the heart, and blood vessels.

The liquid part of the blood is called plasma. Although plasma is mostly water, it contains many other substances too. Among them are nutrients that blood picks up from the small intestine. Plasma also carries waste products produced by cells. Red blood cells, white blood cells, and platelets also float in the plasma.

When blood picks up nutrients from the small intestine, the blood is traveling in tiny blood vessels called capillaries. Capillaries are the smallest blood vessels in your body. They are so narrow that red blood cells must travel through them one cell at a time. The capillary walls are very thin, so materials can pass through them. Materials are exchanged between the blood in the capillaries and the cells they pass among. Blood flows from capillaries into larger vessels called veins. Veins carry blood to the heart.

Your heart is a muscular organ that is about the size of your fist. It beats about 70 times a minute in adults, a little faster in children and teens. The pumping of your heart moves blood through all parts of your body. Blood travels away from the heart in thick, muscular tubes called arteries. As arteries move farther from your heart, they branch and become smaller and smaller until they form capillaries.

Many capillaries surround each alveolus.

Oxygen in an alveolus moves across the alveolus and capillary walls. There red blood cells pick up the oxygen and carry it throughout the body. Carbon dioxide moves from capillaries to the alveolus.

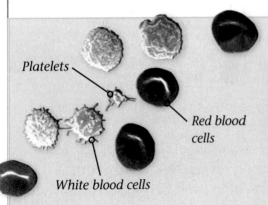

Platelets

Red blood cells

White blood cells

Blood Cells

Red blood cells carry oxygen to your cells. White blood cells attack and destroy bacteria, viruses, and other disease-causing particles. Platelets are pieces of cells formed in bone marrow. When you are cut or bleeding, platelets cause tiny fibers to form in the blood. These fibers cause the blood to clot, which helps stop bleeding.

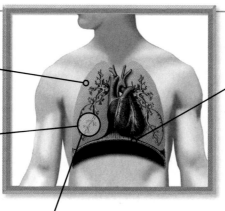

Lungs
Lungs are made of a spongy material that contains many branching tubes, air sacs, and blood vessels.

Diaphragm
Lungs do not contain muscle tissue. Air enters your lungs when the muscular diaphragm contracts, pulling your ribs up and out. The diaphragm relaxes when you exhale.

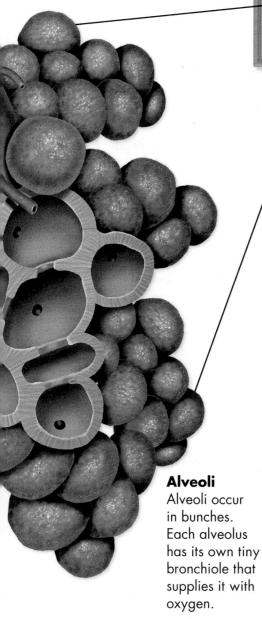

Alveoli
Alveoli occur in bunches. Each alveolus has its own tiny bronchiole that supplies it with oxygen.

Respiratory System

As cells in your body receive nutrients from the blood, they also need oxygen. Cells use oxygen to release energy from nutrients. In the process, carbon dioxide is produced. This gas is a waste that must be removed from cells. Blood is the substance that delivers the oxygen and removes the carbon dioxide. Blood picks up oxygen and releases carbon dioxide as it travels through your lungs.

Your lungs are part of the respiratory system. The respiratory system also includes your nose, trachea, and bronchial tubes. The function of the respiratory system is to take in oxygen from the air and release carbon dioxide from the body.

When you breathe in, air enters your nose. From your nose, air moves to the lungs through the trachea. The trachea branches into bronchial tubes, which continue to branch into smaller and smaller tubes. The smallest of these tubes are called bronchioles. In the lungs bronchioles end at tiny sacs, called **alveoli.** Capillaries cover the alveoli. It is in the alveoli that oxygen enters the blood and carbon dioxide is removed. This gas exchange occurs quickly and at all times. When you breathe out, the carbon dioxide leaves the lungs and exits the body.

✓ **Lesson Checkpoint**

1. How does the exchange of carbon dioxide and oxygen take place?
2. How do the digestive and circulatory systems work together to provide body cells with the materials they need?
3. **Writing** in Science **Expository** Find out what simple steps everyone can take to keep his or her respiratory system healthy. Then write a two-minute radio announcement that informs the public of what you found.

Lesson 5

How do systems keep the body healthy?

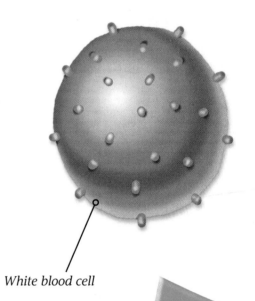

Pathogen

White blood cell

Fighting off disease is the job of the immune system, but other systems contribute to the task. In fact, everything the body does requires the work of several systems.

Immune System

You may not know it, but a war is going on in your body every day. Your body must constantly defend itself against pathogens that are trying to attack it. **Pathogens** are organisms such as bacteria, viruses, and fungi that cause disease.

Pathogens can be found everywhere, but most never get a chance to make you sick. A healthy body is able to defend itself against pathogens. Your body has several ways to defend itself from pathogen invaders.

Many pathogens enter the body through its openings. Your body's first line of defense is to prevent pathogens from entering. It does this in several ways. Your skin is an effective barrier that stops many pathogens. The tears that your eyes produce wash pathogens away. Tears also contain chemicals that kill bacteria. The linings of your nose, mouth, and throat secrete mucus that traps pathogens. Your saliva and the juices produced in your stomach contain pathogen-killing chemicals.

Your body's reflexes also help fight pathogens. Sneezing and coughing rid your lungs and throat of pathogens. Your stomach may expel food that contains pathogens.

After a pathogen enters the body, a white blood cell recognizes it. The white blood cell reproduces many times, producing many more white blood cells.

How Pathogens Are Spread

- Direct contact with an infected person, such as kissing or touching
- Breathing in tiny droplets of moisture from an infected person who sneezes or coughs
- Using eating utensils that an infected person has used
- Contact with an organism, such as an insect, that carries the pathogen
- Eating or drinking contaminated food or water

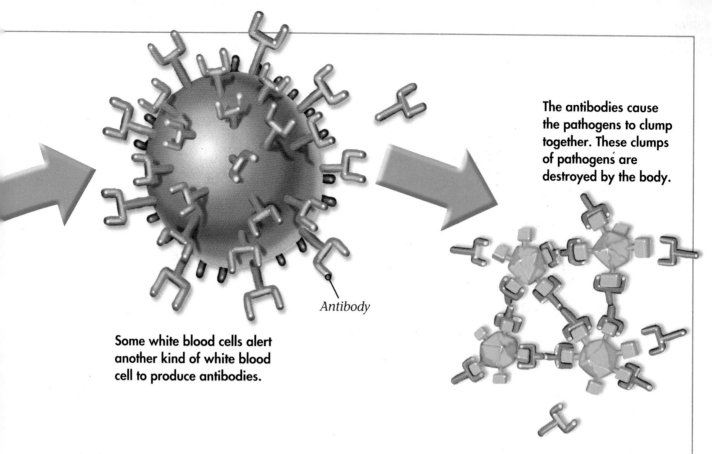

The antibodies cause the pathogens to clump together. These clumps of pathogens are destroyed by the body.

Antibody

Some white blood cells alert another kind of white blood cell to produce antibodies.

Fighting Pathogens

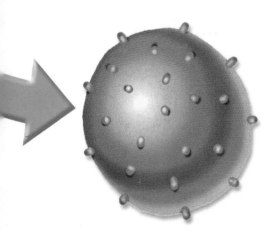

Other white blood cells attack body cells that contain the pathogens. They kill the infected cells and the pathogens.

Even with these defenses, pathogens sometimes enter your body. When that happens, your immune system springs into action to fight the invaders. First, it increases blood flow to the area of the pathogens. That's why an infected cut becomes red and swollen. The increased blood supply signals one type of white blood cell to attack and kill pathogens. This type of white blood cell will attack any kind of invader.

Other types of white blood cells are more specialized. They can tell the difference between various pathogens. These white blood cells produce **antibodies,** chemicals that kill specific pathogens. This response also allows the body to recognize and fight the same pathogen if it enters the body again. Study the diagram to see how white blood cells target and fight specific pathogens.

Your body responds in the same way to vaccinations. A vaccine is made of dead or weakened pathogens that can no longer cause the disease. The vaccine triggers your immune system to produce white blood cells that continue to fight pathogens when they enter the body.

1. ✓Checkpoint What are four barriers to pathogens entering the body? Why are they important?
2. Writing in Science **Narrative** Write a story about a war between pathogens and white blood cells in a person's body.

Systems Working Together

Look at the people in the picture. What is going on in their bodies as they ride their bikes? Many systems are working hard to enable them to be successful at their tasks. Read the information on these pages to see how some of those systems are contributing.

Your amazing body sometimes runs so smoothly that you may forget that, like any machine, you need to take care of it on a daily basis. Everything you do—running, reading a book, eating, brushing your teeth, or getting upset with a friend—affects your health.

You might think that at your age there isn't much you can or need to do to stay healthy. Developing good health habits now can help you stay healthy now and for many years in the future. Many adult health problems start when a person is young. You just don't notice them until later. It's never too soon to take responsibility for your own health. Read the list on the next page to learn about some simple habits you can develop to stay healthy.

Respiratory and Circulatory Systems

These systems begin to work harder with activity. Breathing rate increases. This provides more oxygen to the working muscles. It helps get rid of their carbon dioxide waste. The heart pumps faster. This delivers more nutrients and oxygen to muscles.

Endocrine System

Endocrine glands check the body's condition. Their hormones make sure the muscles have enough energy. They maintain stability.

Digestive System

The digestive system has already begun its work before activity begins. Its role is to prepare the body for activity. Some nutrients are in the blood, ready to supply energy. Some nutrients are stored in tissue to be used as needed.

Nervous System

Nerves in the eyes, ears, nose, and skin gather information about the environment. This information is sent to the brain as impulses, which travel to the brain through the spinal cord. The brain interprets and tells different parts of the body what to do.

Muscular and Skeletal Systems

Muscles in the legs receive messages from the brain telling them to contract. As they contract, the muscles pull on the leg bones. This results in movement. To continue the activity, the contracting muscles relax. Muscles opposite them then contract. This moves the bones in the opposite direction.

Staying-Healthy Habits

- Eat well-balanced meals.
- Get regular physical activity.
- Sleep at least eight hours every night.
- Avoid using alcohol, drugs, or tobacco.
- Keep your body clean. Wash your hands often.
- Wear protective gear when participating in sports that require it.
- Wear a safety belt when riding in an automobile.
- Drink plenty of water.

✓ Lesson Checkpoint

1. What is a pathogen?
2. Explain how your body systems work together when you are reading a book.
3. **Cause and Effect** What causes the body to produce antibodies?

The Amazing Machine

Your body isn't working hard only when you are very active. Here's what happens each day.

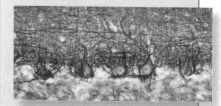

Brain cells
You use about 7,000,000 brain cells.

Heart tissue
Your heart beats 100,000 times.

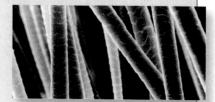

Hair cells
Your hair grows almost a half millimeter.

Red blood cells
Each red blood cell, the most common type of cell in your body, will pass through the heart 14,000 times.

Guided Inquiry

Investigate How do air sacs affect the surface area of a lung?

In your lungs are thousands of air sacs called alveoli. Because of these alveoli, the surface area of your lungs is huge.

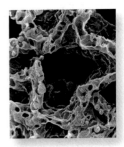

Materials

red construction paper

yellow construction paper

tape

meterstick

scissors

What to Do

1 Roll the red paper into a cylinder.

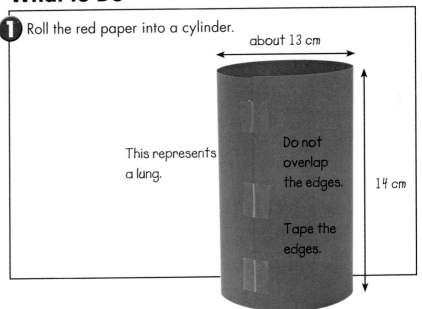

about 13 cm

This represents a lung.

Do not overlap the edges.

Tape the edges.

14 cm

2 Roll the yellow papers into tubes. These are **models** of the alveoli in the lung. Tape the edges.

Do not overlap the edges.

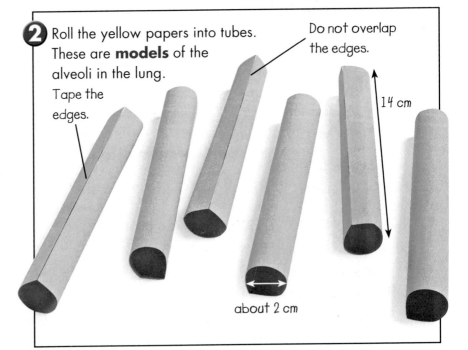

14 cm

about 2 cm

Process Skills

Making a model can help you understand how alveoli increase the surface area of a lung.

3 Fill the red cylinder with yellow tubes. Count the yellow tubes that fit inside.

4 Remove the yellow tubes. Unroll them and place them flat, side-by-side, as shown.

5 Remove the tape from the red cylinder. Place the red paper next to the yellow sheets.

6 **Measure** the area of the red sheet. Measure the total area of the yellow sheets. Compare the areas.

	Total Area (cm²)
Red cylinder	
Yellow tubes	

Explain Your Results

1. What was the total area of the yellow tubes?
2. How did adding the yellow tubes affect the surface area inside the red cylinder?
3. What part of the **model** represents the outer part of the lung? What part represents the alveoli?

Go Further

What materials could you use to make a model of a bone? Develop a plan to answer this or any other questions you may have.

EQUATIONS and HEART RATES

A person's heart rate (or pulse) is usually expressed in beats per minute. An easy way to find your heart rate is to count the beats for 10 seconds and then multiply by 6. This will give an accurate heart rate, because there are 60 seconds in a minute, and 10 × 6 = 60.

If your doctor told you that your heart rate was 72 beats per minute, how many heartbeats did the doctor count in 10 seconds?

Let b equal the number of beats in 10 seconds.

$6b = 72$ Write a multiplication equation.

$\dfrac{6b}{6} = \dfrac{72}{6}$ Multiplication and division are inverses, so divide both sides by 6.

$b = 12$

The doctor counted 12 beats in 10 seconds.

If you are healthy, it is a good idea to increase your heart rate by exercising, but there are limits to how high it should go. One guideline is that an adult's maximum heart rate plus age should equal 220. What is the safe maximum heart rate for a healthy 30-year-old?

Let R equal an adult's maximum heart rate.

$R + 30 = 220$ Write an addition equation.

$R + 30 - 30 = 220 - 30$ Addition and subtraction are inverses,

$R = 190$ so subtract 30 from both sides.

The safe maximum heart rate for a healthy 30-year-old is 190 beats per minute.

Write and solve an equation to answer
the questions.

1. If you count 28 heartbeats in 10
seconds after exercising, what is
your heart rate in beats per minute?

2. If the doctor tells you that your heart rate
is 84 beats per minute, how many beats
did the doctor count in 10 seconds?

For Questions 3 and 4, use the information
about maximum safe heart rates on page 108.

3. Find the safe maximum heart rate for a
person who is 25 years old.

4. At what age would a person's maximum
heart rate be 180 beats per minute?

Lab zone Take-Home Activity

Count the beats of your heart for 10
seconds. Then multiply by 6 to find your
heart rate in beats per minute. Do it
first after sitting still for 10 minutes. Then
do it again immediately after exercising,
1 minute later, and 5 minutes later.
Compare the results.

Use Vocabulary

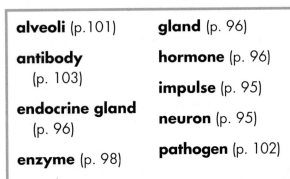

alveoli (p.101)	**gland** (p. 96)
antibody (p. 103)	**hormone** (p. 96)
endocrine gland (p. 96)	**impulse** (p. 95)
	neuron (p. 95)
enzyme (p. 98)	**pathogen** (p. 102)

Use the vocabulary word from the list above that best completes each sentence.

1. A nerve cell is also called a(n) _____.

2. A chemical released by endocrine glands is called a(n) _____.

3. A(n) _____ is an organ that produces a chemical.

4. A message in a nerve cell is a(n) _____.

5. Oxygen enters the blood in tiny sacs called _____.

6. A(n) _____ is a chemical that breaks down food.

7. A chemical that destroys a specific kind of pathogen is a(n) _____.

8. An organism that causes disease is called a(n) _____.

9. A tissue or organ that releases a chemical into the bloodstream is a(n) _____.

Explain Concepts

10. Explain how muscles and bones work together to cause movement.

11. The body's systems work together to keep all its life processes balanced. Why do you think balance is important?

12. The graph shows the level of glucose in a person's body before and after she drank some juice. Use the information in the graph to explain how the body systems work together to keep the body's processes balanced.

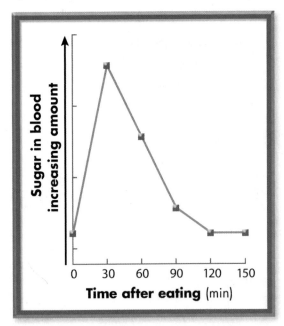

13. **Infer** Suppose the small intestine did not have villi. What could you infer about the body's ability to supply nutrients to its cells.

14. **Model** Draw a diagram to show how oxygen and carbon dioxide are exchanged in the alveoli of the lungs.

Cause and Effect

15. Make a graphic organizer like the one below. Fill in the correct cause and effect.

Cause	Effect
High glucose level in blood	
	Glucagon is released.

Test Prep

Choose the letter that best completes the statement or answers the question.

16. Which describes two or more tissues working together to perform a function?
Ⓐ organelles Ⓑ cells
Ⓒ system Ⓓ organ

17. Which system takes in oxygen from the air and delivers it to the blood?
Ⓕ circulatory system
Ⓖ digestive system
Ⓗ respiratory system
Ⓘ endocrine system

18. Which is the most common disease in the United States that is not caused by a pathogen?
Ⓐ arthritis
Ⓑ osteoporosis
Ⓒ muscular dystrophy
Ⓓ virus

19. Explain why the answer you chose for Question 17 is best. For each of the answers you did not choose, give a reason why it is not the best choice.

20. Writing in Science **Descriptive**
Explain how your body's systems work together when you use a computer.

Pharmacologist

A pharmacologist is a scientist who studies and develops new drugs that help people and animals. These medical researchers are concerned with every part of the human body. They use scientific methods to try to find new ways to prevent and cure disease. They test new drugs to make sure they work and are safe. For example, some new drugs have helped treat cancer and heart disease.

As a pharmacologist you might work in a medical school, a pharmaceutical (drug) company, a research laboratory, a government agency, or a university. In any of these places, you might spend the day working with other researchers and doing experiments. You might also spend a lot of time in the library looking for information about a particular disease or drug. If you like studying about the human body and animals and how chemicals can affect them, then you might like being a pharmacologist. Becoming a pharmacologist takes a lot of work, though. Most pharmacologists go to college for at least six years. You can begin preparing to be a pharmacologist now by studying science and math.

Emily M. Holton, Ph.D., is a pharmacologist who works at NASA's Ames Research Center. She is studying the effect of gravity on human bone growth and development. Her study is important because in the weightlessness of space, astronauts might lose bone strength.

Lab zone **Take-Home Activity**

Suppose you are a pharmacologist developing a drug to cure a disease. What disease would you choose to find a cure for? Why?

Chapter 5

Plants

Discovery Channel School
Student DVD
DISCOVERY CHANNEL SCHOOL

online
Student Edition
pearsonsuccessnet.com

You Will Discover

- what the parts of a vascular plant are.
- how photosynthesis and respiration are related.
- how plants grow.

What processes take place in plants?

photosynthesis

xylem

epidermis

phloem

Chapter 5 Vocabulary

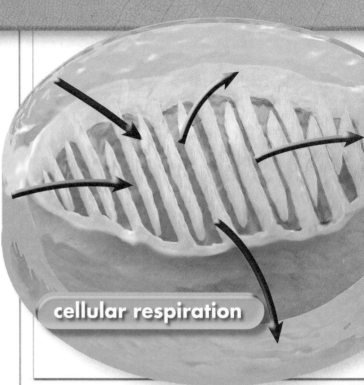

cellular respiration

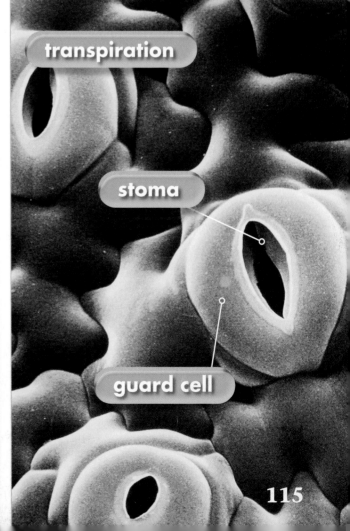

transpiration

stoma

guard cell

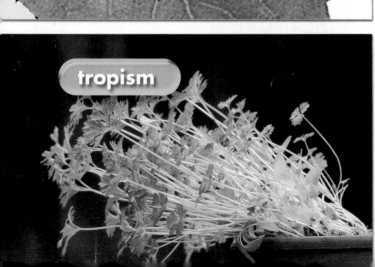

tropism

115

Explore How does a plant get the gases it needs?

Gases a plant needs enter through its leaves. In this activity, you will try to discover if the gases enter through the top side of the leaf, the bottom side, or both sides.

Materials

plant

petroleum jelly

cotton swab

What to Do

1 Coat the top side of 2 leaves with petroleum jelly. Coat the bottom side of 2 other leaves. Handle the leaves gently.

2 Place the plant in a sunny window. **Observe** it every day for 1 week.

Process Skills

You **infer** when you make a careful guess based on your **observations** and past experience.

Explain Your Results

1. After 1 week, **compare** the leaves coated on the top with the leaves coated on the bottom.

2. Where do gases enter a leaf? Make an **inference** based on your **observations.**

How to Read Science

 Compare and Contrast

Knowing how things or events are alike and different can help you understand the science you read. When you **compare** two items, you tell how they are alike. When you **contrast** them, you tell how they are different. Use the **observations** described in the science journal below to compare and contrast the leaves.

Science Journal

Leaf Observations

I looked at two different kinds of leaves. Both were green and had many veins running throughout. Leaf A was oval with jagged points around its edge. Leaf B was long and narrow. Its edges were smooth. The surface of both leaves was smooth.

Apply It!

Make a graphic organizer like this one. Compare and contrast the leaves in the journal entry. Write ways that the leaves are alike in the center. Then in the Leaf A box, tell what makes Leaf A different from Leaf B. In the Leaf B box, tell how Leaf B differs from Leaf A.

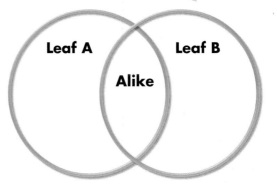

Leaf A   Leaf B

Alike

🔊 You Are There!

As you walk by the farmer's field, you can feel the warmth of the sunlight. The songs of birds fill the air. You glance down. What's that? You take a closer look. Small seedlings are beginning to break through the soil. How do these small plants grow into such large sunflowers? What will happen inside these plants as they grow?

AudioText 🔊

Lesson 1

What are the parts of a vascular plant?

Roots anchor a plant and absorb water and minerals from the soil. Leaves use the water to make food in the form of glucose for the plant. Stems provide support and transport water, minerals, and the glucose the plant makes.

Roots

Colorful flowers swaying back and forth in a garden on a windy day are beautiful. But why don't the plants blow away? The answer is found underground—the roots. A plant's roots spread throughout the soil and anchor the plant in the ground, even on a windy day. Some plants have one large root, called a taproot, with many smaller roots growing out from it. Carrots are taproots. Other plants, such as sunflowers, have a system of smaller roots that spread outward like the branches of a tree. A plant's root system may be as large as the part of the plant you see above ground.

Roots take in water and minerals from the soil. These materials enter the root through its **epidermis,** the thin outer layer of cells. The many tiny root hairs on the epidermis make it possible for the roots to take in more water from the soil than if the roots were smooth. From the epidermis, water and minerals move through a layer of cells to the xylem. **Xylem** moves water and minerals from the roots to other parts of a plant. It is part of the vascular system in all plants.

Another type of vascular tissue is phloem. **Phloem** carries sugars made in the leaves throughout the plant. Roots store some of these materials, usually in the form of starch. Carrots and sweet potatoes are roots that store food.

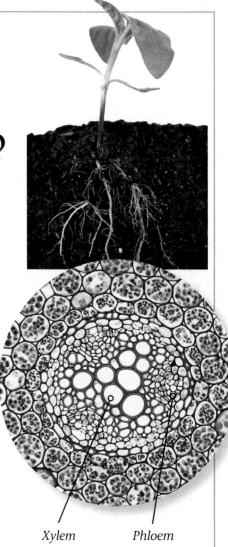

Xylem   Phloem

The xylem of this plant root is made of long, narrow cells that are connected end to end. As the cells get older, only their cell walls remain, forming tubes throughout the plant. Phloem is made of living cells.

1. ✓**Checkpoint** Name three functions of roots.
2. ⟳ **Compare and Contrast** How are the functions of xylem and phloem alike and different?

Stems

Stems can be straight or curved, short or tall, smooth or rough. But no matter what they look like, all stems help give the plant support. Like roots, stems have xylem and phloem, which move water, minerals, and glucose between the roots and leaves of the plant.

Plants with stems that are green and easy to bend are called herbaceous plants. The stems of herbaceous plants often die in cold weather, but their roots continue to live. Herbaceous plants grow new stems each year. Clover, grasses, and poppies are just a few of the many kinds of herbaceous plants.

Some stems, such as a tree trunk, are rigid and strong. Plants with this kind of stem are called woody plants. Woody plants often grow tall and may last many years. Trees, shrubs, and most vines are woody plants. Some woody plants may lose their leaves for part of the year, but their stems do not die.

Some stems grow underground. A white potato is an underground stem called a tuber. Food stored in tubers helps the plants survive times that are cold or have little rain—times when plants cannot make the sugar they need.

Phloem

Xylem

Cut Across a Stem

In many herbaceous plants, such as this sunflower, the xylem and phloem are found in bundles. These bundles form a ring. The xylem and phloem of other plants may be arranged differently, but xylem is always closer to the center of the stem.

Leaves

When you look at a plant, what is the first thing you notice? Often it is the leaves. Most leaves vary in shape and size, but all have one function in common—to make food in the form of glucose for a plant. During this process, water and gases pass in and out of the plant through small holes in the epidermis of the leaf. Each small hole is called a **stoma** (plural, stomata). Surrounding each stoma is a pair of guard cells. The two **guard cells** work together to open and close a leaf's stoma.

Sunlight can cause guard cells to take in water. The increased amount of water puts more pressure on the walls of the guard cells. This pressure forces the guard cells into a curved shape. When this happens, the stomata open. Most stomata are open in the daytime and closed at night.

When stomata open, gases from the air enter the leaf and water passes out of the leaf. This loss of water from the leaf is called **transpiration.** Air temperature, wind, and the amount of water in the air and the soil affect how much water is lost through transpiration.

As water moves out of a leaf, more water moves up through the xylem. Like drinking with a straw, transpiration pulls more water up through the xylem. Plants need most of the water their roots take in to replace the water lost during transpiration. When more water is being lost to transpiration than is being taken in by a plant's roots, the plant may wilt.

When the stomata are open, carbon dioxide from the air moves into the leaf. At the same time, water and the oxygen that is produced when plants make glucose pass out of the plant.

Guard cell

Stoma

Modified Leaves
Plants such as this Venus's flytrap usually live in areas where the soil contains few nutrients. The plant's leaves can catch insects such as this damselfly. Chemicals produced by the plant digest the insect. In this way, the plant gets the nutrients it needs.

✓ Lesson Checkpoint

1. How do guard cells open and close stomata?
2. What causes water to move upward through xylem?
3. Math in Science A single corn plant can lose 245 liters of water in one growing season. How much water must be available in the soil during the growing season to replace that water in a field of 10,000 corn plants?

Lesson 2

How do plants get and use energy?

The leaves of a plant make glucose that contains energy, which the plant can use for life functions. Cells break down the glucose to release the energy stored in them.

Photosynthesis

If you walk through the forest in the spring, you might see many colors of flowers. But if you look at the leaves of many different plants, they are mostly green. What is so special about the color green?

Leaves and other parts of plants are green because of chlorophyll, which is a green substance in the chloroplasts of plant cells. Chlorophyll enables a plant to make its own food in the form of glucose. Animal cells don't contain chlorophyll, so animals cannot make their own food.

The process in which plants make glucose is called **photosynthesis.** During photosynthesis, plants use light energy from the Sun, carbon dioxide from the air, and water to make glucose and oxygen. In the process, energy is stored in the glucose. Plants and organisms that eat plants can use the glucose as a source of energy for life processes.

Photosynthesis can only take place in the presence of chlorophyll. The process of photosynthesis can be summarized in an equation.

$$\text{carbon dioxide} + \text{water} \xrightarrow[\text{chlorophyll}]{\text{light energy}} \text{glucose} + \text{oxygen}$$

Notice in the equation that plants use carbon dioxide and release oxygen during photosynthesis. Most organisms could not live without the oxygen plants produce.

The leaves of plants have many adaptations that enable the plant to carry on photosynthesis. Study the diagram to see how a leaf is adapted to carry on photosynthesis.

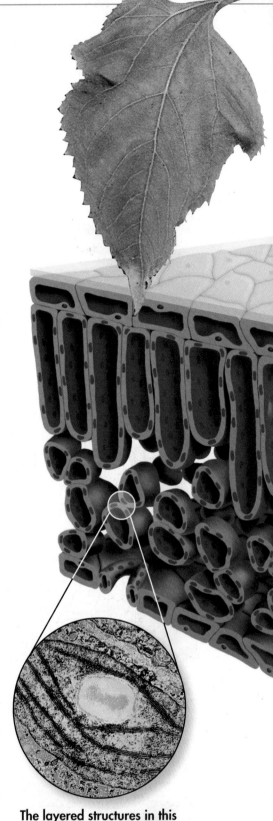

The layered structures in this chloroplast contain the chlorophyll. Glucose produced in chloroplasts by photosynthesis may then be converted into starch. The large light-colored structure in this chloroplast is stored starch.

Leaf Structure

A waxy layer called the cuticle may cover a leaf and slow water loss.

The top and bottom of the leaf are covered with a layer of cells called the epidermis. This thin layer allows light to easily pass into the middle of the leaf.

Photosynthesis takes place in the middle of the leaf. These tall, thin cells absorb much of the sunlight that enters the leaf. In these cells are many chloroplasts that a plant needs to make sugar.

The veins of a leaf contain its xylem and phloem. Water and minerals enter the leaf through the xylem. Sugar made by the leaf moves to the rest of the plant through the phloem.

Cells in this part of the leaf are spread apart farther than other cells in the leaf. The air spaces surrounding cells allow the carbon dioxide that is needed for photosynthesis to move freely throughout the leaf.

Most leaves have more stomata on the lower epidermis. Less light reaches under the leaf, so the lower part is cooler and less water is lost through transpiration.

1. **Checkpoint** Describe three ways a plant's leaf is adapted for photosynthesis.

2. **Writing in Science** **Expository** Write a paragraph that explains the process of photosynthesis. Use the terms *roots, chloroplasts, xylem, phloem, stomata, glucose,* and *oxygen*.

Energy from Food

On sunny days, plants can make more glucose than they need. What happens to this extra glucose? Plants change the extra glucose into other kinds of sugars and starches, which they can store. To use the stored food when they need it, plants must break it down to release the energy it contains. In fact, all organisms must break down food to release the stored energy. **Cellular respiration** is the process by which cells break down glucose with the release of energy.

Cellular respiration begins in the cytoplasm of cells. Here glucose is broken down into simpler substances. If the cell contains oxygen, these simpler substances move into the mitochondria of the cell. The mitochondria use oxygen to further break down the simpler substances. This process produces carbon dioxide and water, and energy is released. Because a mitochondrion releases energy, it sometimes is called the powerhouse of a cell. The process of cellular respiration can be summarized like this:

glucose + oxygen ⟶ carbon dioxide + water + energy

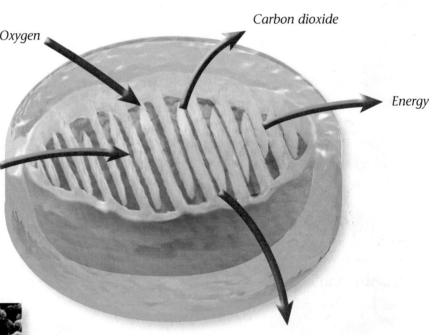

The blue structure in this electron microscope image is a mitochondrion. Chemical reactions take place on the many folds in the mitochondrion.

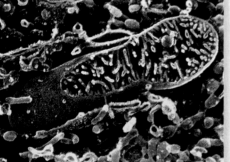

Cellular Respiration in a Mitochondrion

Both plants and animals give off carbon dioxide during cellular respiration.

Carbon Dioxide–Oxygen Cycle

You may have noticed that the equations for photosynthesis and cellular respiration look a lot alike. In fact, look at these two equations again.

$$\text{carbon dioxide} + \text{water} \xrightarrow[\text{chlorophyll}]{\text{light energy}} \text{glucose} + \text{oxygen}$$

$$\text{glucose} + \text{oxygen} \longrightarrow \text{carbon dioxide} + \text{water} + \text{energy}$$

The processes are almost the reverse of each other. The materials produced during one process are the same materials that are needed for the other process. In other words, they form a cycle. Together, photosynthesis and cellular respiration form the carbon dioxide–oxygen cycle.

The carbon dioxide–oxygen cycle can be summarized in this way: Day and night, animals breathe oxygen from the air. Plants take in oxygen and carbon dioxide through their leaves. During respiration, both plants and animals use oxygen to change energy in food to energy they can use. They give off carbon dioxide. Plants use some of the energy and carbon dioxide to produce more food and oxygen in the process of photosynthesis. The carbon dioxide–oxygen cycle assures that living things do not run out of the oxygen and carbon they need.

✓ Lesson Checkpoint

1. What do plants need to carry on photosynthesis?
2. Why do most leaves have more stomata on the lower epidermis than on the upper epidermis?
3. **Compare and Contrast** How does the role of energy differ in photosynthesis and cellular respiration?

Lesson 3

How do plants grow?

Some plants produce seeds in flowers. Other plants produce seeds in cones. The conditions that plants need to grow vary among species. Plants have behaviors that are responses to the environment.

Angiosperms

A tiny seedling just starting to emerge from a seed is the first step in the growth of a plant that may later produce seeds. Some seed plants, called angiosperms, produce flowers. Angiosperms can be found in almost every land environment. In fact, scientists have identified between 200,000 and 300,000 species of angiosperms. Only insects have more species than angiosperms. Some examples of angiosperms include the peach tree in the picture, as well as tulips, grasses, daylilies, orchids, oak trees, grapes, tomatoes, and apples.

All angiosperms are vascular plants. They have specialized tissues for transporting materials throughout the plant. You read about these tissues—xylem and phloem—earlier in this chapter. The seeds of angiosperms form after pollination and fertilization. Most seeds develop in a fruit, which protects the seeds until they can begin to grow.

Humans depend on angiosperms in many ways. We use them as food crops and to make medicines. Lumber, cloth, rubber, perfumes, and cork are other products made from angiosperms.

The fruit of this peach tree protects the seed. The seed is contained in a hard pit, which also protects it and keeps it from drying out.

Parts of a Seed

A The seed coat protects the embryo and cotyledon.

B The embryo is the part of a seed that grows into a new plant. In some seeds, the first true leaf is visible at the tip of the embryo.

C The cotyledon is sometimes called the seed leaf, but it isn't a true leaf. Cotyledons contain food that nourishes the plant until it can make its own food. This seed is called a dicot. It has two cotyledons. Some plants, called monocots, only have one cotyledon.

The cones on this Scotch pine are not yet fully grown.

Conifer cones, like this one, are covered with woody scales. The scales are modified leaves. The seeds are not protected by fruits.

Gymnosperms

You probably have seen cones like the one in the picture. Did you know that seeds develop in the cones? Plants that produce their seeds in cones are called gymnosperms. These plants do not produce flowers. Some of the oldest living organisms on Earth are gymnosperms. One type, the redwood, can live for thousands of years.

You probably are most familiar with one type of gymnosperm—the conifers. Conifers are woody plants with needles or scalelike leaves. The Scotch pine in the picture is a conifer.

Conifers have two types of cones—male and female. Female cones contain ovules with egg cells. Male cones make pollen that contains sperm. Pollen is carried, often by wind, from male cones to female cones. Sperm then fertilize the egg cells. After fertilization, the female cone closes up, and seeds grow within it. The cone remains closed until its seeds are mature. This process may take up to two years. When the seeds are mature, they are released and fall to the ground. Unlike angiosperms, the seeds of gymnosperms are not contained in fruits.

Gymnosperms are important as sources of wood and materials for paper products. Paints often are made with gymnosperm materials. Oils from gymnosperms are used as air fresheners, disinfectants, and scents in soaps and cosmetics. Gymnosperm seeds are a source of food.

1. ✓**Checkpoint** Name the three main parts of a seed and tell the function of each.
2. ⟳ **Compare and Contrast** Draw a graphic organizer that shows how angiosperms and gymnosperms are alike and different.

Germination and Growth

An embryo can only grow so large within the seed. Then the seed must wait until conditions in its environment are right for it to germinate. A plant germinates when it starts to grow from a seed. Each plant species needs certain conditions for germination and growth.

All seeds need a certain temperature to germinate. In colder climates seeds germinate in spring or early summer when the soil and air warm. Seeds also need water—to break open the seed coat. A plant that germinates in a tropical rain forest probably needs a higher temperature and more moisture than a plant that grows in a colder, drier climate.

Seeds need oxygen. When a seed coat opens, more oxygen can reach the cells of the embryo, and the cells get larger. Then they divide to make new cells. If the seeds get too much moisture, they may not get enough oxygen, and growth will not take place. Instead the seed will rot.

If conditions are not right, some seeds may become inactive—sometimes for long periods. This helps protect the embryo inside the seed. Some inactive seeds can survive conditions that would kill a growing plant. For example, some seeds can survive severe droughts, freezing temperatures, and forest fires.

The Growing Plant

When a seed germinates, a root begins to grow downward, and the stem begins to grow upward. A plant gets larger by producing new cells at the tips of its roots and stems. Branches on the plant's stem may grow from side buds. Some plants have growth that increases the plant's width. Cells also divide to repair damaged tissue in the plant.

Not all plants grow from seeds. Mosses and ferns produce spores from which plants grow. You can see in the table how spores and seeds differ. But spores, too, can only develop into plants if conditions are right. For most spore-producing plants, that means plenty of water is available.

Wheat seeds

Spores

Spore	Seed
Contains a single cell that grows into a new plant	Contains a multicellular embryo that develops into a new plant
Does not contain stored food	Contains stored food
Is usually very small	Can vary in size

Phototropism is a response to light. Growth chemicals cause stems to bend toward light. Roots, however, bend away from light.

The response of a plant to gravity is geotropism. Even though germination took place in darkness, the roots of this corn seedling grew downward and the stem grew upward.

Responding to the Environment

Have you ever wondered why roots grow down and stems grow up? The reason is that plants, like all living organisms, respond to their environments. You may not think that plants have behaviors because plant behavior is not easy to see. But plants bend, droop, twist, and turn.

Unlike animals, plants do not have nerves to control behaviors. Instead behaviors can result from chemicals the plants make. Chemicals cause the cells in different parts of the plant to grow at different rates. Cells on one side of a stem may grow faster than the cells on the opposite side. As you can see in the diagram, this uneven growth causes the stem to bend.

All the plants on this page are showing some kind of behavior. They are growing either toward or away from something in their environment. Plant behavior caused by growth toward or away from something in the environment is called a **tropism.** For example, the roots of many plants grow toward water. This response of plants to water is called hydrotropism.

Thigmotropism is a response to touch. A plant that has positive thigmotropism grows toward a surface that it touches. Plants with negative thigmotropism grow away from a surface.

During thigmotrophism cells on the side where the plant touches a surface grow more slowly.

✔ Lesson Checkpoint

1. At what three places does growth take place on a plant?
2. Why are tropisms important to a plant?
3. ⟳ **Compare and Contrast** How are seeds and spores alike and different?

129

Investigate How can you show how plants react to light?

Phototropism is one type of tropism. Phototropism is the tendency of plants to turn toward light or to grow toward light.

Materials

pinto bean seed

cup with soil and water

shoe box with a lid

2 index cards

scissors and tape

metric ruler

What to Do

1 Plant the bean seed in the cup and water it.

2 Cut an opening in one end of the shoe box.

3 Cut a 7-cm square hole in 2 index cards. Tape one card inside the shoe box.

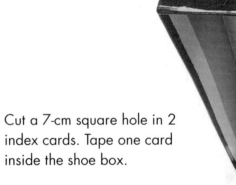

Process Skills

When you **investigate,** you design and carry out a procedure to answer a question.

opening

4 Place the cup in the shoe box. Put the cover on the box. Place the box in bright light.

Water your plant as needed. Do not overwater.

second index card

first index card

5 When the plant grows past the first index card layer, add the second index card.

6 **Predict** what will happen to the plant during your **investigation.** Record your prediction.

7 Record your observations. Day 1 is the day your plant sprouts.

	Plant Response to Light
Prediction	
Observations on Day 5	
Observations on Day 10	
Observations on Day 15	

Explain Your Results

1. How did the plant's growth change during this **investigation?** Explain.

2. What could you do to be certain the plant was responding to light and not to the barriers in the shoe box?

Go Further

Does a plant's stem grow away from the pull of gravity? Design and carry out an investigation to answer this or other questions you may have.

Math in Science

Number Patterns in Plants

Many different number patterns can be seen in plants. One number pattern is seen in the growth patterns of trees, the number of petals on a flower, the arrangement of leaves on a stem, and the pattern of seeds on the seed head of a flower.

One pattern is the Fibonacci sequence, discovered in the 13th century by an Italian mathematician, Leonardo Fibonacci. The diagram at the right shows how the Fibonacci sequence appears in the growth pattern of a tree.

In a sequence of numbers, each number in the pattern is called a term. Each term in the Fibonacci sequence is the sum of the previous two terms. If you start with 1, the first five terms of the sequence are 1, 1, 2, 3, 5.

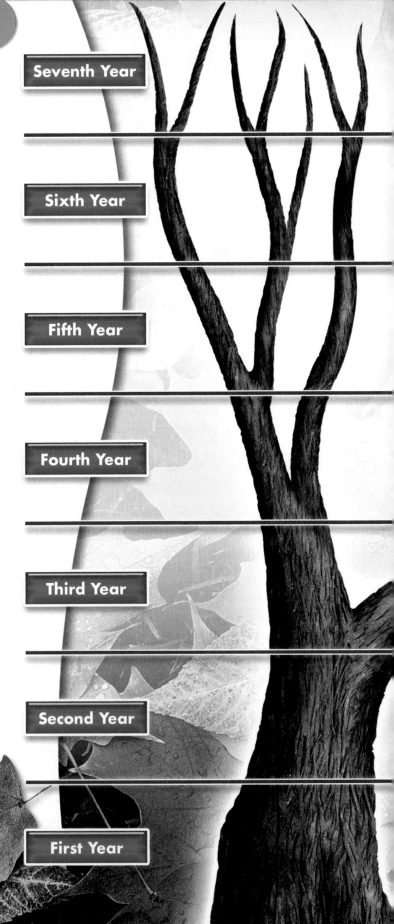

Seventh Year

Sixth Year

Fifth Year

Fourth Year

Third Year

Second Year

First Year

⊜ Tools Take It to the Net pearsonsuccessnet.com

Year	Number of Branches
First year	1 branch
Second year	1 branch
Third year	2 branches
Fourth year	
Fifth year	
Sixth year	
Seventh year	

Use the diagram to answer the questions.

1. Copy and complete the chart above.

2. If the tree shown in the diagram continued this growth pattern, what would be the number of branches for the eighth year?

3. Suppose a large tree grows for 15 years according to the pattern of the Fibonacci sequence. Make a table showing the number of branches in each year of growth. How many branches would there be in the 15th year?

Lab zone Take-Home Activity

Use library resources to find examples of the Fibonacci sequence in flowers, shells, or elsewhere in nature. Write a report including diagrams.

Chapter 5 Review and Test Prep

Use Vocabulary

cellular respiration (p. 124)	**photosynthesis** (p. 122)
epidermis (p. 119)	**stoma** (p. 121)
guard cell (p. 121)	**transpiration** (p. 121)
phloem (p. 119)	**tropism** (p. 129)
	xylem (p. 119)

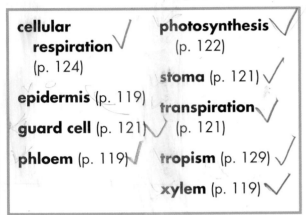

Choose the vocabulary term from the list above that matches each description.

1. This leaf part opens to allow water and gases to enter and leave a leaf.

2. Sugar made by the plant flows through this plant tissue.

3. This part of a leaf opens and closes a stoma.

4. During this process, cells of organisms release energy from food.

5. An example of this behavior is a plant growing toward sunlight.

6. During this process, water is lost from the leaf of a plant.

7. This plant structure carries water and minerals throughout a plant.

8. During this process, green plants make glucose.

Explain Concepts

9. Name and describe two plant tropisms.

10. Why is chlorophyll important to plants?

11. The picture below shows the inside of a leaf. Identify each part that is labeled with a letter. Also tell how each part is an adaptation that helps the plant carry on photosynthesis.

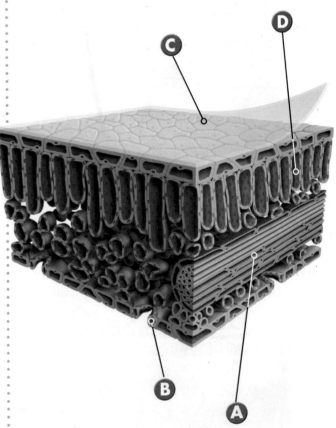

Process Skills

	Species A	Species B	Species C
Stem	rigid and strong	green, easy to bend	rigid and strong
Flowers	yes	yes	no

12. Classify The table describes three species of plants. Classify each species as an angiosperm or a gymnosperm and as woody or herbaceous.

13. Model Make diagrams to show where xylem and phloem are found in roots and stems. Label the diagrams to show the function of each kind of tissue.

Compare and Contrast

14. Make a graphic organizer like the one shown below. Write the letters of the descriptions in the correct parts of the diagram to compare and contrast photosynthesis and cellular respiration.

A   releases oxygen
B   produces carbon dioxide
C   occurs in mitochondria
D   occurs in chloroplasts
E   performed by plants
F   performed by animals

Photosynthesis   Alike   Cellular respiration

Test Prep

Choose the letter that best completes the statement or answers the question.

15. Which of the following describes cellular respiration?
Ⓐ breaks down glucose, produces oxygen
Ⓑ breaks down glucose, produces carbon dioxide
Ⓒ breaks down carbon dioxide, produces oxygen
Ⓓ breaks down carbon dioxide, produces glucose

16. What is inside pollen?
Ⓕ eggs   Ⓖ ovules
Ⓗ seeds   Ⓘ sperm

17. A plant with green stems that lives only one season is a
Ⓐ woody plant   Ⓑ conifer
Ⓒ tuber   Ⓓ herbaceous plant

18. Which of the following plants produces spores that grow into new plants?
Ⓕ fern   Ⓖ Scotch pine
Ⓗ peach tree   Ⓘ grass

19. Explain why the answer you chose for Question 18 is best. For each of the answers you did not choose, give a reason why it is not the best choice.

20. Writing in Science **Descriptive**
Suppose you are going to plant some seeds in your garden. Write a paragraph that describes the conditions you must consider in order for your seeds to germinate.

135

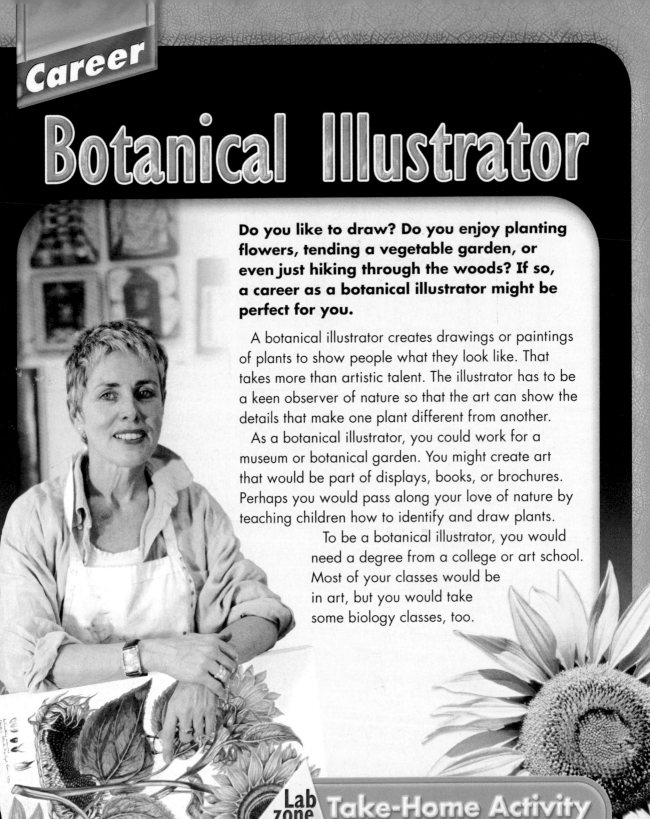

Botanical Illustrator

Do you like to draw? Do you enjoy planting flowers, tending a vegetable garden, or even just hiking through the woods? If so, a career as a botanical illustrator might be perfect for you.

A botanical illustrator creates drawings or paintings of plants to show people what they look like. That takes more than artistic talent. The illustrator has to be a keen observer of nature so that the art can show the details that make one plant different from another.

As a botanical illustrator, you could work for a museum or botanical garden. You might create art that would be part of displays, books, or brochures. Perhaps you would pass along your love of nature by teaching children how to identify and draw plants.

To be a botanical illustrator, you would need a degree from a college or art school. Most of your classes would be in art, but you would take some biology classes, too.

Lab zone Take-Home Activity

Find a flower, tree, or other plant. It could be outside or a houseplant. Make a drawing or painting of it. Focus on details, such as the edges of the leaves and the shades of color. Find out the name of your plant and label it. Display your work.

Chapter 6
Biomes

Web Games
Take It to the Net
pearsonsuccessnet.com

online
Student Edition
pearsonsuccessnet.com

You Will Discover

- how the biosphere is organized.
- what Earth's biomes are.
- how Earth's biomes differ.

How do organisms live together in ecosystems?

environment

ecosystem

abiotic factor

biotic factor

138

Chapter 6 Vocabulary

environment
page 144

population page 144

community page 144

ecosystem page 145

abiotic factor
page 146

biotic factor
page 146

biome page 148

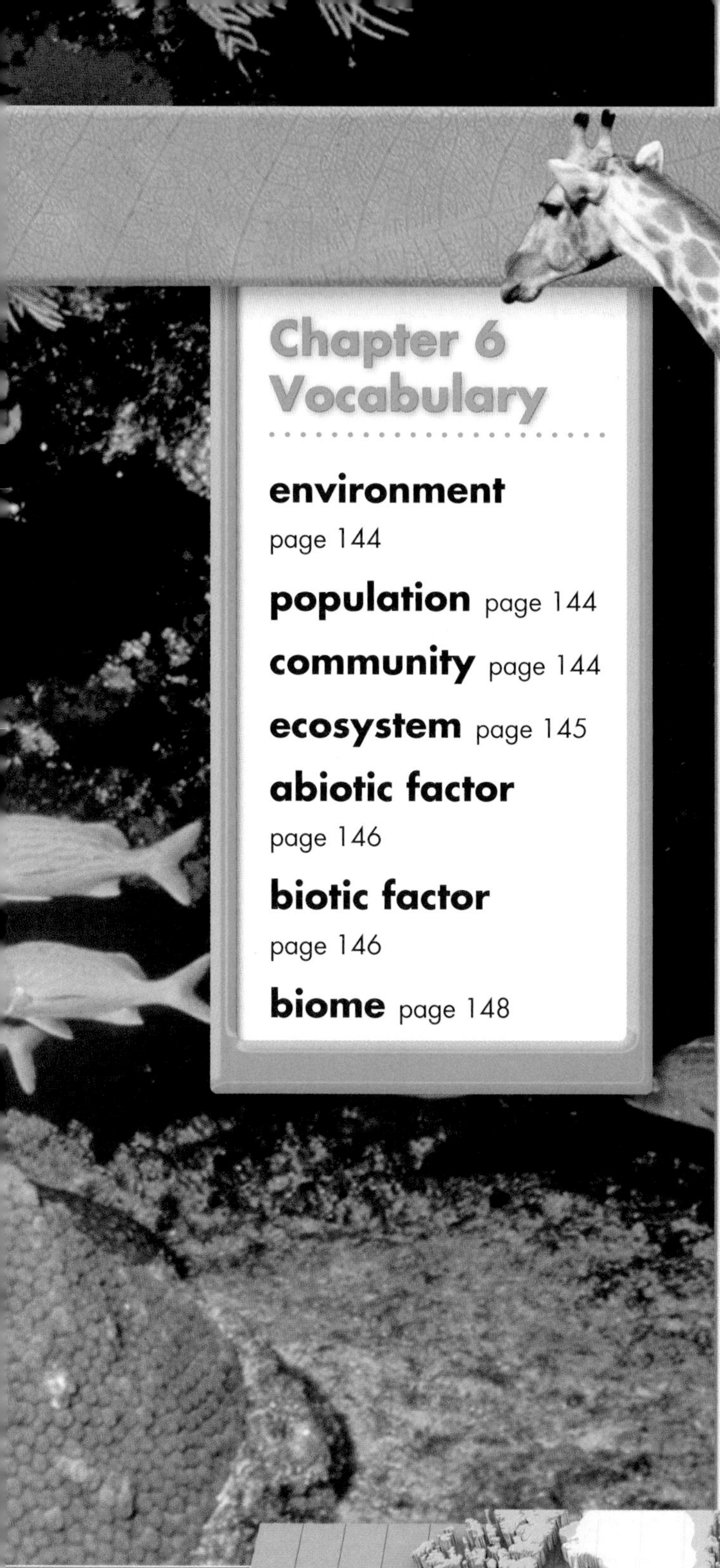

community

population

biome

Explore How can desert plants retain water?

Materials

paper towels

water

aluminum foil

waxed paper

paper clips

What to Do

1 Wet 3 paper towels.
Squeeze out the excess water.

2 Put 1 towel on the foil.
Roll up each of the 2 remaining
towels. Put 1 rolled towel on the foil.

3 Wrap the remaining rolled towel in
waxed paper. Use paper clips to keep the ends
closed. Put this towel on the foil.

rolled towel

flat towel

rolled towel
wrapped in
waxed paper

4 After 1 day, unroll the paper towels.
Observe the dampness of each towel.

Process Skills

You **infer** when
you make a
careful guess
based on your
observations
or experiences.

Explain Your Results

1. Compare how damp the towels were after 1 day.
2. Based on your **observations,** what can you **infer**
   about how the amount of surface exposed to the air
   affects how fast a leaf loses water?

How to Read Science

Main Idea and Details

The **main idea** tells what a reading selection is about. It is the most important idea in a passage. Quickly finding and understanding the main idea of a passage is an important reading skill. **Details** support the main idea.

- The main idea statement can appear anywhere in the passage, but often it is found in the topic sentence. The topic sentence often is the first sentence of a paragraph.

- Read the selection carefully. Note details that help make the main idea clearer.

Household Hint

Watering Your Houseplants

Although all plants need some water, the amount varies among houseplants. The soil in which African violets grow should always be kept moist. If you grow aloe, allow the soil to dry out before watering. A spider plant likes plenty of water, except during the months from October through January. Keep the soil dry then.

Apply It!

Make a graphic organizer like the one shown. Fill in the boxes to show the **details** of the passage. Then **infer** the **main idea** from the details.

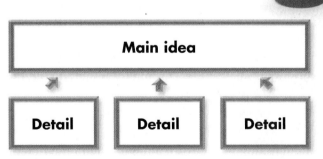

Main idea

Detail   Detail   Detail

You Are There!

The sizzling sun beats down on you. Sweat covers your body. You're hot and thirsty, but there is no shade in the desert. Wait! What's that sound? A rattlesnake lies coiled up on the path in front of you. You jump back. Ouch! You just brushed against the spiny thorns of a cactus. What other surprises will you find here?

AudioText

How are organisms on Earth connected?

All living things on Earth share resources, such as air, water, and light. Living things, including humans, are connected through the resources they share. The actions of humans can affect other parts of the biosphere.

Connections in the Biosphere

No matter where you go—the highest mountain, the deepest ocean, the hottest desert, or the coldest Arctic area—you will find living things. From microscopic bacteria to the largest whales, a variety of living things covers Earth. The biosphere is the part of Earth in which living things are found. It extends from about 10 kilometers above Earth's surface to about 10 kilometers below the surface of the ocean.

Although organisms may live in different parts of the biosphere, they all share Earth's resources, such as water, air, and light. Living things depend on and are connected to each other through the resources they share. If something happens to one organism, other organisms can be affected too. Humans—including you—are part of the relationships formed between living things in the biosphere. Human actions can affect the biosphere.

The study of how living things interact with each other and their environment is called ecology. The word *ecology* comes from the Greek words *oikos*, meaning "place where one lives," and *logos*, meaning "the study of." An ecologist is a scientist that studies the interactions of living things.

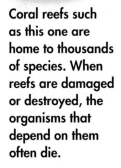

Coral reefs such as this one are home to thousands of species. When reefs are damaged or destroyed, the organisms that depend on them often die.

1. **✓Checkpoint** Explain how organisms in the biosphere are connected.
2. **Technology** in Science Organisms live deep in the ocean around vents that spew hot gases and other materials into the water. Find out what technology scientists use to study these deep areas and what they have discovered.

Interactions

How many people did you interact with today? What did you do? Do you have a pet? What do you and your pet do together? When you think about it, getting through the day without interacting with other living things is difficult. And what about the nonliving things around you? You breathe oxygen in and carbon dioxide out, drink water, and are warmed by sunshine. You couldn't live without any of those things.

Just like you, all organisms that live together in an area interact with each other and their environments. An organism's **environment** is anything that can affect the organism. An environment includes both living and nonliving parts.

Organization of the Biosphere

A **population** is a group of individuals that belong to the same species and live in the same area. All of the zebras in the pictures are a population living together. Each kind of grass growing there is also a population. But all the animals living there do not make up a population. That's because they are members of different species.

Each particular population lives in a certain area. For example, scientists may refer to a population living in a large area, such as the United States. Or they may only be interested in a particular population living in a very small area, such as the population of ticks on a dog.

Members within a population compete for resources in the environment. Each needs food, water, air, space, shelter, and other resources. If resources become limited, individuals can die, and the population gets smaller.

Individual populations do not live alone. Several populations live together and interact in an environment. A **community** is a group of populations that interact with each other in a particular area. The elephants, zebras, and giraffe are all part of the same community. If your family has pet dogs and cats, several populations live in your house—the human population, the dog population, and the cat population. Other populations live there too—bacteria, molds, and fleas on your pets.

Studying an individual species, such as zebras, helps scientists learn more about how organisms interact with their environment.

How would members of this population compete among themselves and with other populations?

Communities depend on the nonliving environment to meet many of their needs—water, shelter, and minerals are just a few. An **ecosystem** is a community of organisms living together along with the nonliving parts of the environment. An ecosystem can be as small as a crack in a sidewalk or as large as a forest. Earth's biosphere is made up of many ecosystems. Every ecosystem interacts with other ecosystems. Study the pictures to see how individuals, populations, and communities make up this ecosystem.

A community includes all organisms living together, not just the animals. What other organisms would be part of this community?

1. ✓ Checkpoint How are individuals, populations, communities, and ecosystems related?

2. Social Studies in Science Compare and contrast the community in the picture with the community in which you live. If possible, use a camera to take pictures of your community to show similarities and differences.

Meeting the Needs of Organisms

Although the organisms living in a community may differ in many ways, they all depend on their environment to meet their needs. **Abiotic factors** are the nonliving parts of an ecosystem. Water, sunlight, temperature, soil, and air are important abiotic factors that organisms depend on.

All living things need some water to survive. That's because many important chemical processes that take place in organisms need water. The amount of water in an ecosystem can limit the number of organisms it can support. If there isn't enough water for all the organisms in an ecosystem, some will die.

Because plants need sunlight for photosynthesis, sunlight is important to all living things. Most organisms that cannot make their own food by photosynthesis depend directly or indirectly on plants. The amount of sunlight an area receives determines the kinds of plants that grow there. That, in turn, determines the other organisms that live there.

Most organisms need air as a source of oxygen. Your own body cannot survive without oxygen for more than a few minutes. Organisms that live in water, such as fish, use oxygen that is dissolved in the water. Plants need another gas found in air, carbon dioxide, to carry on the process of photosynthesis.

The temperature of an area also helps determine which organisms live there. Each organism can live only in a particular temperature range. Your own body would not survive long without some protection in freezing temperatures. But the polar bear is at home in those temperatures.

Biotic factors are the living organisms in an ecosystem. Many biotic factors are too tiny to be seen. These include the billions of bacteria that can be found in the soil, microscopic mites that live on your skin, algae that fill the ocean, and protists that live in the digestive system of cattle.

This addax affects and is affected by other things in its environment.

How do the biotic and abiotic factors of these desert and arctic ecosystems differ?

Temperature is an important abiotic factor. Each organism can live only in a particular temperature range. This polar bear would not survive in the heat of a desert.

Adaptations

Biotic and abiotic factors shape the communities that live in an ecosystem. For example, the arctic environment is cold and windy. Most of the fresh water is frozen all year. The soil is frozen too. During the winter months, there is little or no daylight. How do these factors affect organisms that live there?

All organisms in a particular ecosystem have adaptations that help them survive there. An adaptation is a characteristic that helps an organism live and reproduce in a particular environment. Polar bears have thick fur to help keep their body warmth from escaping into the environment. They have black skin, which absorbs sunlight to warm the animal. Polar bears also have strong claws that help them walk on ice and capture animals for food. Their fur, which looks white, helps camouflage them in the snow.

The climate of the Arctic makes it difficult for trees and large plants to grow there. The plants that do grow in the Arctic are small. They are adapted to grow low to the ground to avoid damage from the strong winds. They need little sunlight for photosynthesis.

✓Lesson Checkpoint

1. List five things you need to stay alive. Tell how your environment helps you meet each need.
2. Identify each factor as biotic or abiotic: sunlight, grass, sand, bird, rock.
3. **Main Idea and Details** How do abiotic factors shape the communities that live in an ecosystem?

What are Earth's biomes?

Earth can be divided into biomes with similar climates and organisms. Temperature and amount of rainfall can be used to describe these biomes.

Climate and Biomes

If you traveled around the world and looked at the organisms living in different parts, you would notice that similar communities occur in places that have similar climates and landforms. A **biome** is a large group of ecosystems with similar climates and organisms. Grouping ecosystems into biomes helps ecologists describe the world.

Water, sunlight, and temperature are important abiotic factors that different organisms need in different amounts. For that reason, climate—the average yearly temperature and precipitation in an area—helps determine the characteristics of a biome. For example, the growing season of plants is mostly determined by temperature. Only plants that are adapted to the yearly temperatures of a particular biome can survive there. Because animals depend on plants for food, as plant populations get larger, so do the animal populations. More plants, more food.

Environments Within Biomes

Think about a tropical rain forest. Its wet, humid conditions and long periods of sunlight make it an ideal place for large trees and other plants to grow. Trees block some sunlight and help make different environments within the rain forest. The top layer gets plenty of sunlight, but lower toward the forest floor, conditions become darker. An amazing variety of species can survive in the many different environments of a rain forest. And, scientists estimate that at least two million species live in Earth's rain forests.

In cold climates, the growing season is short and the ground is frozen most of the year. Trees do not grow there, but you will find mosses and small shrubs. The number of species living in cold climates is much smaller than that of the rain forest.

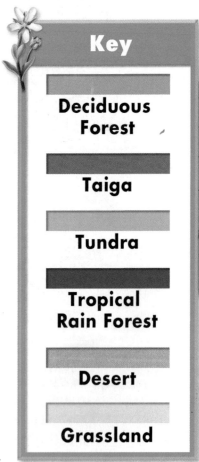

Key

Deciduous Forest

Taiga

Tundra

Tropical Rain Forest

Desert

Grassland

Taiga

Taiga covers the largest area of any type of biome on Earth. Its temperatures range from −40°C to 20°C. The amount of precipitation each year is about 60 cm.

Tundra

Tundra is found at the far northern parts of Earth. This biome is cold and dry. Temperatures are as low as −40°C during winter months. Only about 20 cm of precipitation falls each year.

Tropical Rain Forest

Tropical rain forests are found near the equator. They are warm and rainy all year with temperatures between 20°C and 25°C. The annual rainfall is about 200 cm.

Deciduous Forest

Deciduous forests are located in the areas halfway between the Arctic and the equator. They have an average precipitation of about 120 cm a year. These forests have four seasons.

Grassland

Grasslands get about 60 cm of precipitation a year. The summers are hot and winters are cold.

Desert

Deserts are dry. They get less than 25 cm of precipitation a year. But not all deserts are hot. Some areas of the world, such as the Antarctic continent, receive so little precipitation per year that they are considered deserts. In hot deserts, daytime temperatures can be as high as 38°C.

1. ✔ **Checkpoint** What are two ways that biomes differ?
2. **Math** in Science Find out how to change centimeters to inches. Then make a chart that shows the average precipitation in inches of each biome.

Characteristics of Biomes

Climate is an important factor in determining which organisms can live in an area. Another important factor influences biome communities too. Soil varies from place to place, and it plays an important role in what kinds of plants can survive in an ecosystem. A plant with roots that are adapted for absorbing water near the soil surface would not survive in areas where the only water is deep in the ground.

As you read about the different biomes on the next three pages, think about what you learn about each biome's soil. Then try to figure out how the organisms living in each biome are adapted to conditions there. Each biome is not a particular place, but different areas of the world that share similar characteristics. For example, the Mojave Desert of the southern United States has many characteristics similar to the Namib Desert in Africa. Keep in mind that although similar biomes in different parts of Earth will share similar climate and organisms, there are differences.

This porcupine doesn't have any hair on the bottom of its feet. The smooth skin there helps the animal climb deciduous forest trees, where it spends much of its time.

Tropical Rain Forest

The tropical rain forest contains more species than any other biome. These forests once covered 14 percent of Earth's land surface. More than half of those rain forests have been destroyed.

Dead organisms decay quickly in the hot, moist rain forest environment. Nutrients from the decaying plants are recycled quickly. Most of the nutrients are contained in the biome's plants, not in its soil. In fact, the soil is nutrient poor.

Rain forest trees can grow 75 meters tall. Their leafy tops form a dense covering called the canopy. Below are smaller trees, ferns, and vines. Few plants grow on the forest floor where little sunlight reaches. Many animals live in the canopy, where they eat fruits and insects. Bright colors, bold patterns, and loud sounds are common features of rain forest animals.

Deciduous Forest

The most common plants of the deciduous forests are deciduous trees—those that shed their leaves each year and then grow new ones. Examples include oak, maple, beech, and hickory. Gymnosperms also grow here. Shrubs and small plants grow on the forest floor. Songbirds, deer, bears, and raccoons are some common forest animals.

The winters in the deciduous forest are cold, so some animal species hibernate during the winter months. Many bird species migrate to warmer climates for the winter.

As the forest trees lose their leaves each year, they fall to the ground and decay. As a result, the soil of the deciduous forest is nutrient rich. The rich soil enables many species to live there. The trees themselves provide habitats for climbing plants, mosses, lichens, fungi, and algae.

Tree frogs such as these are common in tropical rain forests.

1. ✓ **Checkpoint** What are three factors that help determine the communities in an ecosystem?
2. **Art in Science** Design an organism that is adapted to live in a tropical rain forest or a deciduous forest. Use common art supplies to make your organism.

Taiga

Conifers, such as fir, spruce, and hemlock, are some of the plants that have adapted to the poor soil and long, cold winters of the taiga, also called the boreal forest or coniferous forest. A few deciduous trees and small shrubs also grow here.

Many animals, such as squirrels, birds, and insects, eat berries and seeds of the conifers. Large animals, such as elk, moose, and deer, eat tree bark and new plant shoots. Predators such as wolves, lynx, grizzly bears, and hawks eat other animals.

The long, thick hair of this caribou helps keep it warm during long taiga winters.

Grassland

Grasslands do not receive enough rain to support many large trees. But they have some of the most fertile soil on Earth, which makes them excellent for farming. Every year millions of tons of wheat, corn, and soybeans are produced on the grasslands of the United States. Lush tall grasses and other small plants cover the land.

Some of the largest animals on Earth live on grasslands—including bison, zebras, rhinoceros, and giraffes. Coyotes, prairie dogs and other rodents and insects such as grasshoppers, are common grassland animals too.

The many grasses of the grassland biome provide plentiful food for grasshoppers.

The dark feathers of this ptarmigan turn white in winter, which helps it hide from predators in the snow.

Tundra

An important feature of the tundra is its permafrost—a layer of permanently frozen soil just beneath the surface. In summer, the top layer of soil thaws. The resulting water cannot seep through the frozen layer of soil, so the top soil layer becomes soggy. The cold temperatures, high winds, and short growing season of the tundra limit plant growth to short shrubs, grasses, mosses, and a few very short trees.

Flies and mosquitoes are food for many birds, which migrate in winter. Foxes, lemmings, hares, and caribou are among the common animals.

This sonoran kingsnake lives in Utah, Arizona, New Mexico, and Nevada.

Desert

Although many people think that all deserts are hot, many deserts can be quite cool, especially at night. The common characteristic of all deserts is that they are dry. Some of the driest deserts of the world don't receive any rainfall at all! In areas where rain falls, most of the water evaporates.

Desert plants include cacti and other plants that have short growth cycles. Many animals are active at night when temperatures are cooler.

✓ Lesson Checkpoint

1. Explain how climate is important in determining what organisms live in an ecosystem.
2. Why do so many species live in tropical rain forests?
3. **Main Idea and Details** Write a main idea statement about one of the biomes in this lesson. Give three details to support your main idea.

Investigate Why are biomes near the Equator warmer?

Different regions of Earth tend to be warmer or cooler because the Sun's rays reach the Earth at different angles.

Materials

clay

3 thermometers

protractor and metric ruler

lamp

clock with a second hand

Process Skills

You **interpret data** when you use the information in a chart to explain your **observations**.

What to Do

1 Place the thermometers in the clay. Use the protractor to place one thermometer at a 90° angle, one at a 60° angle, and one at a 30° angle.

2 Place the lamp 20 cm from the thermometers.

3 Turn on the lamp. Wait 3 minutes.

4 **Observe** the temperature of each thermometer after 3 minutes. Record your data.

Thermometer	Angle	Starting Temperature (°C)	Temperature after 3 Minutes (°C)
1	90° angle	°C	°C
2	60° angle	°C	°C
3	30° angle	°C	°C

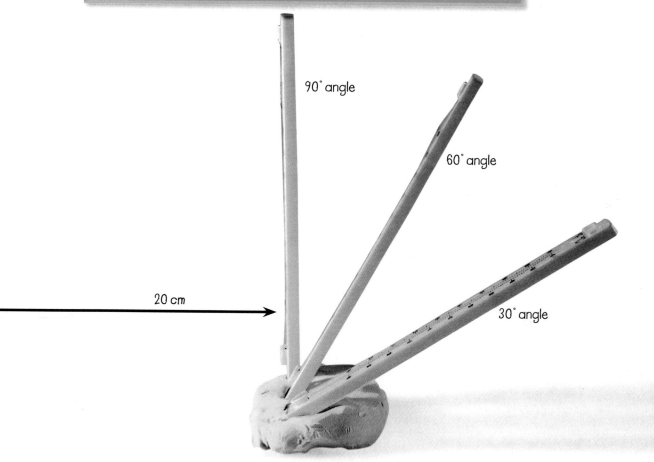

90° angle

60° angle

20 cm

30° angle

Explain Your Results

1. Which thermometer showed the highest temperature? Which showed the lowest?

2. **Interpret Data** Why are the temperatures different?

Go Further

Make a drawing of an organism living in a biome that receives direct sunlight all year long. Label your organism's adaptations.

Statistics About CLIMATES

Distance from the equator, which is 0° latitude, is often a good predictor of temperature; the farther from the equator, the colder the climate. The same is not true for distance from the prime meridian, which is 0° longitude.

The chart below gives information for three cities that are close to 28° E longitude, making them roughly equal distances from the prime meridian. Notice that their average annual temperatures vary as their distances from the equator vary.

City	Approximate Latitude	Average annual temperature	Average Monthly Precipitation (in mm) for selected months						Average annual precipitation
			January	March	May	July	September	November	
Helsinki, Finland	60° North	5°C	46	36	36	60	70	67	620 mm
Cairo, Egypt	30° North	21°C	5	3	0	0	0	3	25 mm
Johannesburg, South Africa	26° South	16°C	125	89	19	5	28	114	730 mm

Use the chart on page 156 to answer each question.

1. Find the mean monthly precipitation in Helsinki for the six months given. Look at the average annual precipitation. Would you expect the months not shown for Helsinki to have more or less precipitation than the months shown?

2. What is the mode for monthly precipitation in Cairo? What does this suggest about the climate in Cairo?

3. If Johannesburg has a wet season and a dry season, does the data indicate that the wet season occurs in winter or in summer? Remember, Johannesburg is in the Southern Hemisphere.

4. If an Egyptian travel company wanted to convince people that the climate in Cairo is not totally dry, should it report the mean, median, or mode of average monthly precipitation? Explain.

5. Based on what you have learned in this chapter, in which biome do you think each of the three cities lies? Compare the amounts of precipitation in the three locations on the chart. Can you infer any relationship between latitude and precipitation?

Lab zone Take-Home Activity

Make outdoor temperature recordings at three regular times during the day (possibly before school, after school, and at bedtime) for two weeks. Analyze your data. Can you draw any conclusions about temperature and time of day?

Use Vocabulary

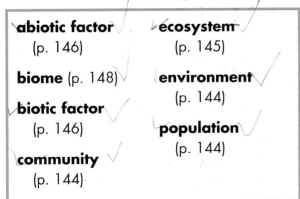

abiotic factor (p. 146)	**ecosystem** (p. 145)
biome (p. 148)	**environment** (p. 144)
biotic factor (p. 146)	**population** (p. 144)
community (p. 144)	

Choose the vocabulary term from the box that best matches each definition.

1. The nonliving parts of an ecosystem

2. A group of individuals that belong to the same species and live in the same area

3. Large group of ecosystems with similar climates and organisms

4. Group of populations living together in a particular area

5. Anything that can affect an organism

6. The living components in an ecosystem

7. Community of organisms living together along with the nonliving parts of the environment

Explain Concepts

8. Describe three adaptations of a polar bear and tell how each helps the animal survive in its environment.

9. Compare and contrast deciduous forests and tropical rain forests.

10. Write a description of the desert shown in the photograph. Use the terms *population*, *community*, and *ecosystem*.

11. The tundra biome gets about 20 cm of precipitation each year. The tropical rain forest gets about 200 cm of precipitation. What percentage of precipitation does the tundra get compared to the amount the tropical rain forest receives?

Process Skills

12. **Interpret Data** The graph shows climate information for two cities. City A is in the northeast part of the United States, where forests are common. City B is in the midwestern part of the United States, where forests seldom grow. Use the climate data to explain why forests do not grow near City B.

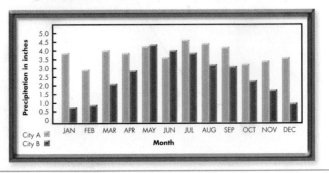

13. Infer Suppose a scientist discovers the remains of an unknown species. By examining the remains, scientists learn that the animal was adapted to conserve water. What can you infer about the environment the animal lived in?

 **Main Idea and Details**

14. Make a graphic organizer like the one shown below. Write details to support the main idea.

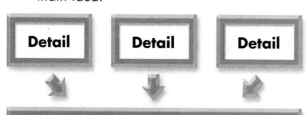

| Detail | Detail | Detail |

A biome is a group of ecosystems with similar characteristics.

 Test Prep

Choose the letter that best completes the statement or answers the question.

15. What two factors can be used to summarize the climate of a biome?
- Ⓐ wind and temperature
- Ⓑ wind and soil
- Ⓒ precipitation and temperature
- Ⓓ precipitation and soil

16. A group of tigers living together is an example of
- Ⓕ a community
- Ⓖ a population
- Ⓗ an ecosystem
- Ⓘ an environment

17. Which biome has soil that is frozen most of the year?
- Ⓐ deciduous forest
- Ⓑ tundra
- Ⓒ grassland
- Ⓓ tropical rain forest

18. Which is an example of a biotic factor of an ecosystem?
- Ⓕ amount of water
- Ⓖ number of living things
- Ⓗ amount of light
- Ⓘ daily temperatures

19. Explain why the answer you chose for Question 15 is best. For each of the answers you did not choose, give a reason why it is not the best choice.

20. Writing in Science **Persuasive** Write an advertisement to convince travelers to visit one of the biomes you learned about in this chapter. Include a description of the following: the biome's climate, three plants, three animals, and activities a visitor might do there.

PARK RANGER

While visiting a national park, you are likely to see a park ranger. Do you have any questions about wildlife? Do you want to find a nice trail? Do you need first aid for a bad scrape? Park rangers are there to help.

A park ranger helps people safely enjoy the many state and national parks. Rangers work in some urban parks, too, such as Central Park in New York City. Park rangers do many jobs. In the same day, a ranger might teach visitors about wildlife, clear a downed tree from a trail, and rescue a lost hiker. The rangers make sure that people are obeying the park rules and not disturbing the wildlife.

A love of the outdoors is one of the most important qualities of park rangers. They learn about biology, ecology, and other topics in college. Rangers should also have good communication skills so that they can help people understand the importance of a park's ecosystems.

Lab zone Take-Home Activity

One of a park ranger's jobs is to search for fires and to make sure visitors do not start illegal fires. Make a poster that would show visitors the importance of not being careless with fires in the park.

EC CRU 10 9 8 7 6 5 4 3 2 1

Chapter 7
Ecosystems

You Will Discover

- how adaptations help organisms survive in ecosystems.
- how energy and materials travel through ecosystems.
- the ways ecosystems can change.

How do energy, organisms, and the environment interact?

competition

symbiosis

host

parasite

162

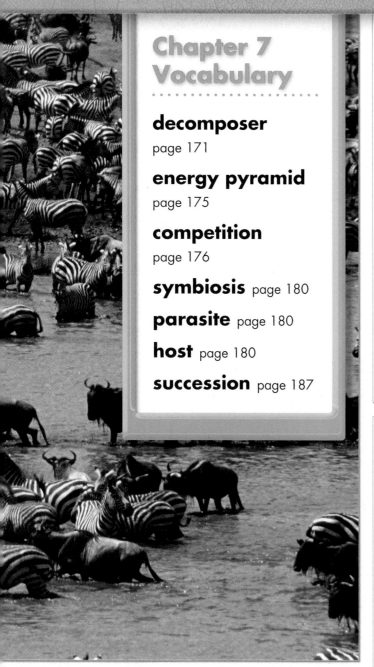

Chapter 7 Vocabulary

decomposer

succession

energy pyramid

Tawny owl

Baby weasel

Snake

Decreasing amount of energy

Increasing numbers of organisms

Small rodents

Bank Vole

Seed Grass seed
heads

Grasses Berries

163

Explore What does an owl eat?

Materials

safety goggles

paper

owl pellet and
bone sorting chart

forceps

wooden probe

hand lens

Process Skills

You **infer** when
you make a
careful guess
based on your
observations and
experiences.

What to Do

1 Place the owl pellet on paper.

2 Separate the bones from the fur and other material
in the pellet.

Be careful!

Be careful while
using sharp
objects.

3 Use the bone sorting chart that came with your owl
pellet to help identify the bones. Compare the bones
from the pellet to the bones in the chart. Make a list
of the type and number of bones you found.

Explain Your Results

1. What kinds of bones were the most common in
   your pellet?

2. What can you **infer** about the diet of an owl?

How to Read Science

Predict

A **prediction** is a guess about what may happen in the future. It is based on observations, facts, and what you already know. Being able to make predictions as you read science will help you put ideas together.

- When making a prediction, identify important facts.

- Use the facts and what you already know to decide what is likely to happen.

Some facts are marked in the article.

Science Article

Field Interactions

If you were to study the interaction among organisms in a field, you would easily see how one organism depends on another. The field is filled with grasses and other plants. The many crickets and grasshoppers there eat these plants. The shrew, in turn, eats the crickets and grasshoppers. Only the lone owl that eats the shrews is safe from being eaten. What would happen to all these organisms if most of the plants died?

Apply It!

Make a graphic organizer like this one. List the facts from the article in your graphic organizer. Also think about what you can **infer** from the information. Then write a **prediction.**

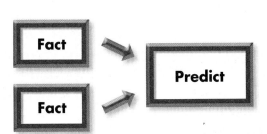

You Are There!

What's that? Over there! Do you see those big ears? It's a fox, but why does such a small animal need such large ears? How does this adaptation help the fox survive in the desert? What other adaptations help desert animals?

AudioText

Lesson 1

Why do adaptations vary among species?

Arctic fox

Organisms are adapted to the environment in which they live. Each species has its own unique set of adaptations.

Surviving in the Environment

Staying cool in a hot desert is not easy. The ears on the fennec fox may look too large for its head, but these ears are a useful adaptation. When the fennec fox becomes too hot, blood rushes to its ears. There body heat moves from the fox's blood into the air. Large ears help keep the fennec fox cool.

Can you guess why small ears are an important adaptation for the arctic fox? The arctic fox must have adaptations that help keep it warm in the extreme cold of its environment. Small ears help an arctic fox by reducing heat loss.

Because Earth's many species live in different environments, each has a unique set of adaptations that helps it meet its needs in different ways. The table shows some other adaptations of the fennec fox and the arctic fox. Compare their adaptations with those of the gray fox, which lives in the deciduous forest.

Gray fox

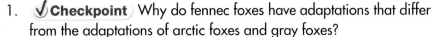
Fennec fox

Adaptations for Different Environments	
Fennec fox	• Pale fur reflects the Sun's rays. • Fur on feet protects against burning desert sand.
Arctic fox	• Thick fur changes from white in winter to brown in summer to help the fox blend in with its environment. • Thick fur covers bottom of feet to reduce heat loss.
Gray fox	• Small body and short legs make moving through the forest easy. • Curved claws are good for climbing up trees to avoid predators and find food.

1. ✓**Checkpoint** Why do fennec foxes have adaptations that differ from the adaptations of arctic foxes and gray foxes?
2. **Art** in Science Draw an organism that lives in your environment. Label its adaptations and tell how each enables it to live successfully.

167

This peacock displays the shimmering colors of his feathers to attract a female.

Structural Adaptations

The species shown on these pages have different living conditions, and their adaptations make them able to live successfully in their environments. Those adaptations developed over many generations, not during the lifetime of a single individual. A species changes over long periods as individuals are born with new characteristics that make them better suited to survive. These individuals survive and pass their new characteristics to offspring.

Adaptations enable organisms to get energy and to find mates and reproduce. They also protect organisms from their environments. Adaptations can include behaviors, structures, and body processes.

The mandrill shown on the next page has several important structural adaptations. His long jaw gives his mouth plenty of room for large teeth to grind the seeds and grasses he eats. His powerful hands dig other foods—roots and bulbs. Large pouches open in the cheeks beside the lower teeth and extend down the side of the neck. These pouches can hold as much food as a stomach. This storage frees the mandrill's hands and feet for running and climbing.

When rain hits these puffballs, spores spew from them and spread out. In the right conditions, the spores will grow into new organisms.

Behaviors and Body Processes

The mandrill's teeth have a function other than eating. When the male mandrill shows his large front teeth, the behavior serves as a warning to other males. Animal behaviors are adaptations that are just as important as structural adaptations. Many animal behaviors are inherited traits. You probably are familiar with many behavioral adaptations. Have you ever seen a spider's web or a bird's nest? These structures are a result of inherited behaviors.

The processes that go on in an organism's body also are adaptations that aid survival. When animals hibernate, their body processes slow down. Their temperature may become lower, and their heartbeat and breathing slow down. Hibernation protects animals from the cold months in their environment.

This dormouse is one of many organisms that hibernate.

The bright colors on the face of this mandrill make it easier for other members of the species to know he is one of their own.

Adaptations

Type	Examples
Structures	• Webbed feet of water birds • Backbone of vertebrates • Seeds of plants
Behaviors	• Caring for young • Building nests • Migrating to warmer climates in winter
Body processes	• Hibernation • Photosynthesis • Digestion

✓ Lesson Checkpoint

1. Give one example of each type of adaptation: behavior, structure, body process.

2. What adaptations do you have for getting energy and for protection from your environment?

3. 🔄 **Predict** What might happen to the species of puffball shown on page 168 if the area where it lives received little or no rain for several years? Explain your answer.

Extinction

Species that cannot adapt to changing conditions in their environment will become extinct. When a species becomes extinct, all individuals of the species have died.

Some people think that species became extinct only in the past. But species continue to become extinct even today. Some scientists estimate that one plant or animal species becomes extinct every 20 minutes. They point out that about 40 species of fishes out of 950 species have become extinct in the past century.

Some causes of extinction are natural, such as climate changes. Other species become extinct because of human causes, such as habitat destruction or pollution. The American bald eagle shown above almost became extinct—in part because of the use of DDT, a chemical used to kill insects.

169

How do organisms get energy?

All living things need energy to carry out life functions. A food web shows how energy can move through organisms in an ecosystem.

Energy Flow in Ecosystems

As the brown bear prowls the woods in search of food, it needs energy to stay alive and grow. All organisms need energy to carry on life functions, such as growth, movement, repair, and reproduction. Where does this energy come from?

Most living things on Earth depend on the energy of sunlight— either directly or indirectly. The berry bush gets energy directly from sunlight. The leaves of the bush use the energy of sunlight in the process of photosynthesis to produce glucose. Plants can use the chemical energy in glucose as a source of energy for life functions. Plants are producers, organisms that can make their own food.

Consumer

Decomposer

Not all organisms get their energy directly from the Sun. Bears and other animals do not have adaptations for capturing sunlight to make food. They are consumers, organisms that get energy by eating other organisms. When the bear eats the berries on the bush, it gets energy stored in the berries. The bear is indirectly using energy from sunlight.

The toadstools in the picture can't make their own food, and they don't eat other organisms. How do they get energy? When organisms die and fall to the ground, their bodies decay. Decay is caused by **decomposers,** organisms that get energy by breaking down the remains of dead organisms. Toadstools are decomposers. Decomposers release the materials from the dead organisms' bodies back into the environment, where they can be used by other organisms. Without decomposers, nothing would decay. That might sound good at first. But then remember—dead organisms would just pile up forever!

Producer

1. ✓Checkpoint Explain how most life on Earth depends on energy from sunlight.
2. **Health in Science** Humans depend indirectly on sunlight for energy. But the UV rays of sunlight can be harmful to the body. Find out how the human body is adapted to protect itself from these harmful rays. Also find out what you can do to get more protection.

Life Without Sunlight

More than a kilometer below the ocean's surface, chimney-like structures, called hydrothermal vents, spew water that can be hotter than boiling. Water pressure is so great that it would crush your lungs immediately. Sunlight never reaches these vents. You might think such conditions make life impossible, but a unique group of organisms thrive there.

Perhaps the most noticeable organisms are giant tubeworms. They have no mouth or digestive system. They get energy from billions of bacteria that live inside them. These bacteria are producers but they don't use sunlight. The bacteria change energy from chemicals in the vent water into food for the tubeworms.

Vent ecosystems are teeming with a variety of species. You can find giant clams, mussels, spiderlike crabs, and soft-bodied spaghetti worms. Blind shrimp, octopuses, and fishes swarm about. In all, you will find more than 500 different species. And scientists are discovering new species every few weeks. That's a lot of life—without any sunlight!

171

Food Chains

As organisms produce food or eat other organisms for food, energy travels from organism to organism throughout an ecosystem. A food chain shows one possible path along which energy can move through an ecosystem. The arrows on a food chain always point toward the organism that receives the energy. For example, the microscopic organisms, common mussel, and herring gull in the picture form a food chain. What other food chains can you find?

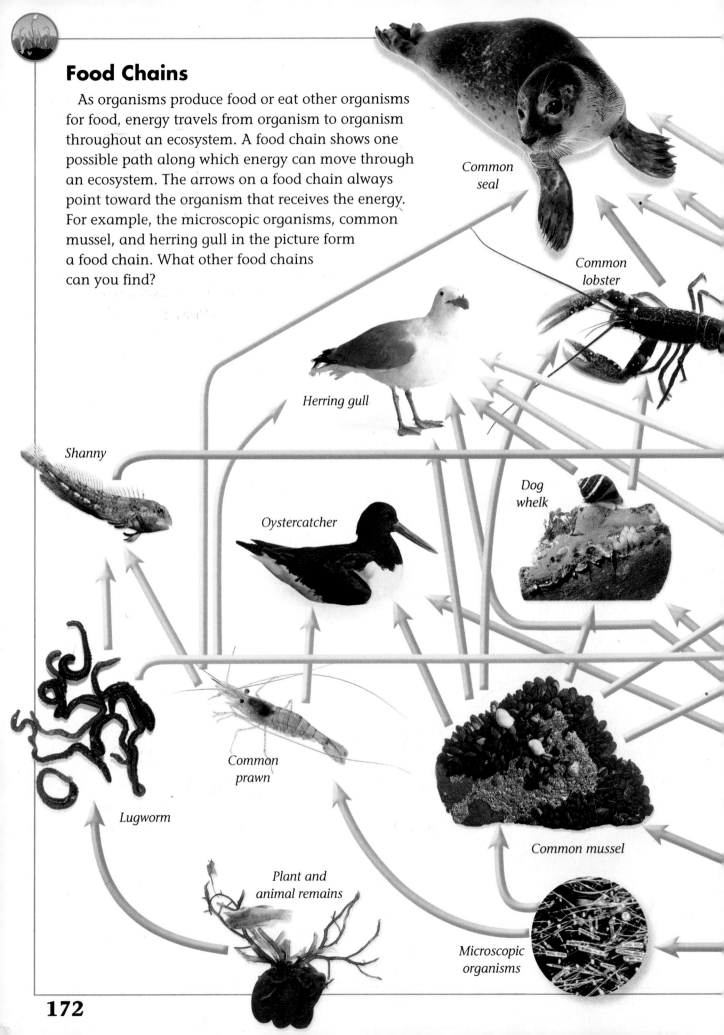

Common seal

Common lobster

Herring gull

Shanny

Dog whelk

Oystercatcher

Common prawn

Lugworm

Plant and animal remains

Common mussel

Microscopic organisms

An Ocean Food Web

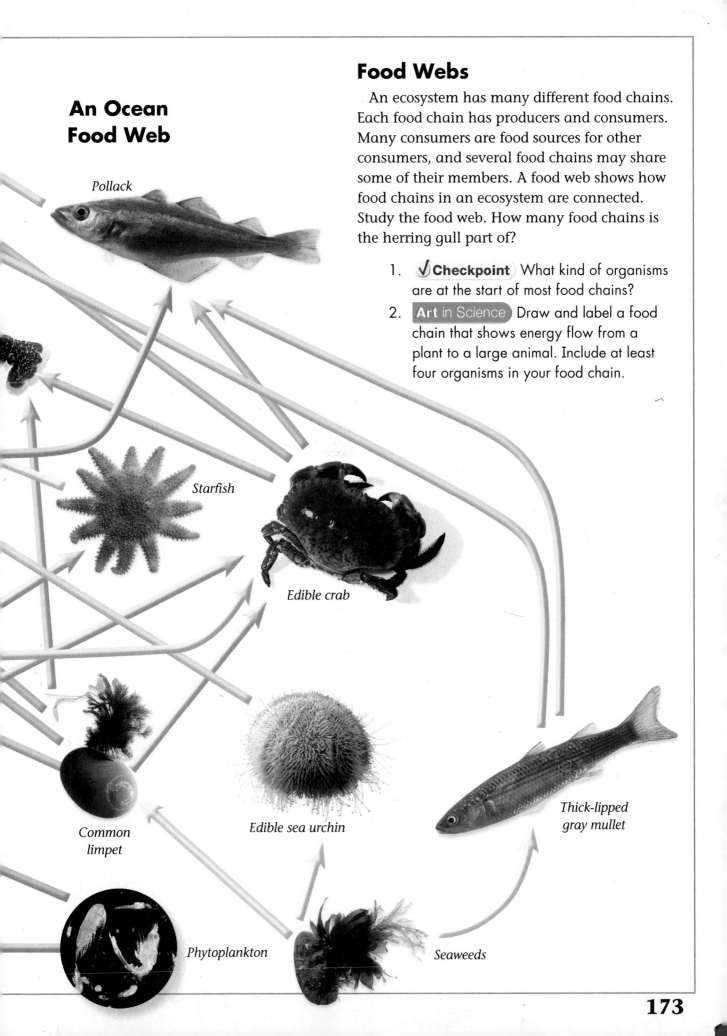

Pollack

Starfish

Edible crab

Common limpet

Edible sea urchin

Thick-lipped gray mullet

Phytoplankton

Seaweeds

Food Webs

An ecosystem has many different food chains. Each food chain has producers and consumers. Many consumers are food sources for other consumers, and several food chains may share some of their members. A food web shows how food chains in an ecosystem are connected. Study the food web. How many food chains is the herring gull part of?

1. ✓**Checkpoint** What kind of organisms are at the start of most food chains?
2. **Art** in Science Draw and label a food chain that shows energy flow from a plant to a large animal. Include at least four organisms in your food chain.

Energy Pyramid

When you study a food chain, you can see the path that energy takes from producers to the top consumer. But a food chain doesn't tell you anything about how much energy moves from link to link.

Not all of the energy a green plant captures from sunlight is passed to other organisms. The plant uses some of the energy for life processes, and some energy is lost as heat. This is true for all levels of a food chain. A snake uses energy as it slithers across the ground in search of prey. A wood mouse uses energy as it digs a burrow. Organisms must use energy to grow, move, and reproduce. As a result, only part of the energy is available to the next level of the food chain.

Decreasing amount of energy

Tawny owl

Baby weasel

Small rodents

Seed

Grass seed heads

Chemicals in the Food Chain

Energy isn't the only thing passed along in a food chain. Harmful substances can pass up through the food chain too. You can see in the energy pyramid that many organisms at the base of the pyramid support fewer organisms toward the top. When an organism eats harmful substances, they can be stored in the organism's tissues. As organisms higher up in the food chain eat the many organisms below, they also eat the harmful substances stored in tissues. As a result, the amount of harmful substances becomes more concentrated as you move up the pyramid. As the concentration increases, the effects of the substances can become more harmful—or even deadly.

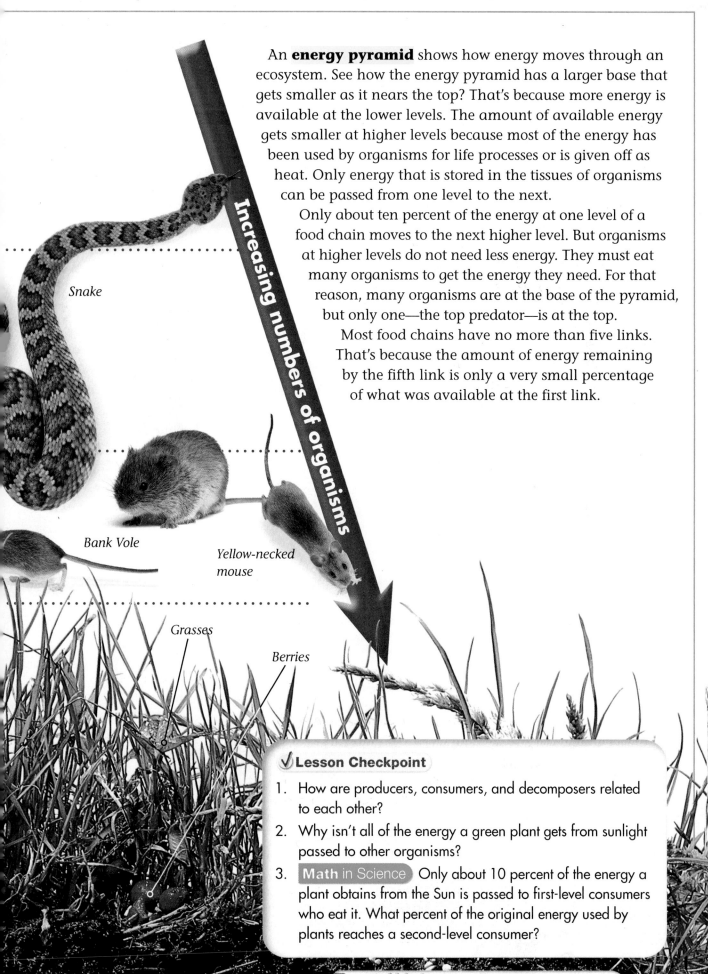

An **energy pyramid** shows how energy moves through an ecosystem. See how the energy pyramid has a larger base that gets smaller as it nears the top? That's because more energy is available at the lower levels. The amount of available energy gets smaller at higher levels because most of the energy has been used by organisms for life processes or is given off as heat. Only energy that is stored in the tissues of organisms can be passed from one level to the next.

Only about ten percent of the energy at one level of a food chain moves to the next higher level. But organisms at higher levels do not need less energy. They must eat many organisms to get the energy they need. For that reason, many organisms are at the base of the pyramid, but only one—the top predator—is at the top.

Most food chains have no more than five links. That's because the amount of energy remaining by the fifth link is only a very small percentage of what was available at the first link.

Increasing numbers of organisms

Snake

Bank Vole

Yellow-necked mouse

Grasses

Berries

✓**Lesson Checkpoint**

1. How are producers, consumers, and decomposers related to each other?

2. Why isn't all of the energy a green plant gets from sunlight passed to other organisms?

3. **Math** in Science Only about 10 percent of the energy a plant obtains from the Sun is passed to first-level consumers who eat it. What percent of the original energy used by plants reaches a second-level consumer?

How do organisms compete for resources?

Organisms compete for resources in an ecosystem. Predators survive by eating prey. Some organisms have symbiotic relationships.

Competition

A watering hole is a good place to see the animals on the African savannah. You might see zebras, giraffes, gazelles, wildebeests, and other animals. How can an ecosystem have enough resources for so many organisms?

Competition is the struggle among organisms to survive in a habitat with limited resources. Like all organisms, the animals on the savannah in the picture need food, water, and a place to live. The animals that survive compete successfully for these resources.

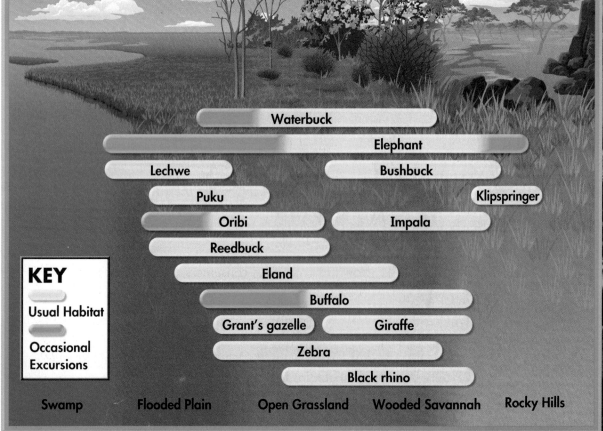

Waterbuck

Elephant

Lechwe

Bushbuck

Puku

Klipspringer

Oribi

Impala

Reedbuck

Eland

Buffalo

Grant's gazelle

Giraffe

Zebra

Black rhino

KEY

Usual Habitat

Occasional Excursions

Swamp   Flooded Plain   Open Grassland   Wooded Savannah   Rocky Hills

In what ways do these animals compete?

As you can see in the diagram on page 176, all the animals on the savannah do not live in the same area. Different species live in different places. Those that do live together have different needs. Organisms with different needs can live together with little competition. Zebras and wildebeests can graze together on the savannah because they have different diets. Zebras prefer the tall, coarse grasses. When zebras eat those grasses, they expose the shorter grasses, which wildebeests then eat.

Competition happens when organisms in an ecosystem have similar needs. An ecosystem can't always meet its organism's needs. Resources, including water, food, and shelter, are limited. Organisms with helpful adaptations will survive. Others will die.

When Resources Are Scarce

Sometimes members of the same species compete. This might happen if resources become scarce, for example by drought. If water in the savannah is scarce, zebras that can survive with less water might survive. Those that need more water might not.

Competition also occurs between different species. Like wildebeests, gazelles eat short, tender grass. If drought reduces the number of grass plants, wildebeests and gazelles will compete for the limited resource.

All organisms, not just animals, compete for resources. Plants compete for water, growing space, minerals, and sunlight. Some plants even have strategies for reducing competition. They release into the soil poisonous chemicals that kill other species around them.

1. ✓**Checkpoint** What causes competition?
2. ⊙ **Predict** Two species of birds live in the same tree. Species A eats ants that live in the tree. Species B eats ants and caterpillars. Which species is more likely to survive if the ant population decreases? Why?

177

Eye Placement

To survive, many animals need eyes that are located where they can see what is most important to them.

Predators often have eyes that are in front of the head. This placement helps the animals judge how far away something is.

The eyes of prey are often on the side of its head. This allows the prey to avoid predators by seeing a wide area.

How did the decrease in the number of wolves starting in 1980 affect the moose population?

Predators and Prey

Animals use different methods to get the food they need. Some animals, like the tapirs in the photo on the next page, eat plants. But these tapirs can be food for other animals, such as panthers. An animal that feeds on other animals is called a predator. The animal that a predator eats is called a prey.

The number of predators that an ecosystem can support depends on the number of prey. And the number of prey depends on how many predators there are. It's a balancing act. As you can see in the graph below, as the number of predators increases, more prey are eaten. The number of prey gets smaller. When that happens, the predators do not have enough food, and some will die. As a result, fewer prey are eaten, and more prey survive to become food for more predators. The number of predators increases again.

Adaptations

Both predators and prey have adaptations that help them survive. Many predators are adapted to hunt and kill. They may be fast or have a keen sense of smell, hearing, or sight to help them locate prey. Some predators have behaviors that help them catch prey. Pack animals, such as wolves, work as a group to attack individuals from a herd. An alligator floats with only its eyes and nostrils out of water. Its strong jaw muscles and sharp teeth help the alligator grab its meal.

Not all predators chase after their prey. A jellyfish has hundreds of stinging cells on its tentacles. Chemicals in these cells can paralyze the prey, which then can be eaten.

Prey are adapted to avoid predators. Some prey animals secrete a poison and are brightly colored to warn away predators. Others mimic, or look like, a dangerous animal. Some prey depend on camouflage to make them look like something else, such as a plant, stick, or rock.

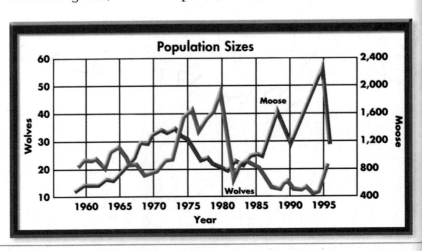

Prey animals also use behavioral adaptations to avoid being killed by predators. Did you ever hear someone say that they "were playing possum" when they pretended to be sleeping? When threatened, possums curl up and play dead. Predators that are only interested in live prey leave them alone. Sow bugs act in a similar way. When touched, they curl up into a ball. The hard outer covering on their backs acts as armor to protect the animals.

Protective coloration, a structural adaptation, makes a baby tapir hard to spot in the forest. Its spots and stripes look like sunlight shining through the trees.

Would you be able to easily find these insects? What structural adaptation helps them avoid predators?

The spikes of the sea urchin are brittle and sharp. Any predator that attacks the sea urchin will have to deal with the painful jabs it gets from the spikes.

1. **✓ Checkpoint** Give an example of a predator and a prey adaptation for each type: behavior, structure, body process.

2. **Writing in Science** **Expository** Write a paragraph explaining how the sizes of predator-prey populations depend on each other.

The bright color of this poison dart frog is a warning to predators. Glands in its skin release bad-tasting, poisonous

Symbiosis

Can you tell what's happening with the weevil beetle shown on this page? The long thin object growing on its back is a killer fungus. The fungus and beetle are an example of symbiosis. **Symbiosis** is a close, long-term relationship between organisms that benefits at least one of the organisms.

Parasitism is a type of symbiosis in which one organism is helped but the other is harmed. A **parasite** is the organism that benefits in the relationship. A **host** is the organism that is harmed. Parasites do not usually kill their hosts because they depend on the hosts for food. But the parasites often weaken their hosts. The weevil beetle and fungus have a parasite-host relationship. Which organism do you think benefits?

Like the fungus on the beetle, many parasites live on their hosts. Did you ever have a pet with fleas? Fleas are parasites that live off the blood of mammals. As the flea obtains the blood, it can cause itching and possibly disease in the host.

Parasites may also live inside the host. Horses, for example, sometimes take in parasites called tapeworms when they graze in a pasture. The tapeworms live and feed in the horse's intestines. The tapeworms "steal" nutrients from the horse. Tapeworms can cause poor digestion and slow growth for the horse.

Sometimes when two organisms live together, both organisms benefit. This kind of symbiotic relationship is called mutualism. The moray eel and the cleaner shrimp in the photo live together in a mutualistic relationship. The cleaner shrimp eats dead tissue and parasites from the mouth of the eel.

Commensalism is symbiosis that helps one organism, but neither helps nor harms the other. You may have seen photographs of a whale with barnacles on its sides. As the whale moves from place to place, the barnacles can get food from the water. The barnacles do not help or harm the whale.

You may not realize that you are part of many symbiotic relationships. Most are harmless, but some relationships can be harmful. Read about some of those relationships on the next page.

Parasitism
This fungus is a parasite on the weevil beetle.

Mutualism
How do the eel and the cleaner shrimp benefit in this symbiotic relationship?

Commensalism
This air plant gets a place to live. The tree is neither helped nor harmed.

Symbiosis in the Human Body

Mites that cover your skin and live at the base of your eyelashes get food by eating dead skin cells.

E. coli bacteria that live in the intestine take in nutrients from digested food. They help your body by making vitamin K, which helps your blood to clot.

Fleas and ticks get food by piercing the skin and sucking out blood.

Athlete's foot is caused by a fungus that lives on the skin of the foot. A foot infected with athlete's foot looks dry and cracked, and it itches.

✓ Lesson Checkpoint

1. Identify each example of symbiosis in the human body on this page as parasitism, mutualism, or commensalism.

2. **Predict** What do you think would happen to the fleas on a dog if they were unable to suck blood from their host?

3. **Writing in Science**
   Narrative Write a short, humorous story about two organisms living together in a mutualistic relationship.

181

How do materials cycle through ecosystems?

Nature depends on cycles so that resources can be used over and over. Earth would quickly run out of resources if they were not recycled. Some important cycles in nature are the nitrogen cycle, the carbon cycle, and the water cycle.

Recycling Matter

Chances are that your home and school recycle some of the materials they use. You might recycle papers, plastic, or glass. Nature too has a recycling system.

Like energy, the amount of matter on Earth is limited. But unlike energy that flows through ecosystems in only one direction, many of Earth's resources pass through ecosystems in a continuous cycle. If important materials that organisms need, such as nitrogen, water, carbon, and oxygen, were not cycled, they would soon run out. Because of Earth's cycles, organisms can use the same materials over and over. Three important cycles in nature are the nitrogen cycle, the carbon cycle, and the water cycle.

Nitrogen Cycle

One of the most important resources for all living things is nitrogen. It is a main component of protein, a building block of cells. Nitrogen is a common element in Earth's air. In fact, the air is about 78 percent nitrogen, but it is "free nitrogen." That means it is not combined with other elements. Most organisms need nitrogen that is "fixed," or combined with other elements.

Most free nitrogen is fixed by bacteria that live in the soil. Some bacteria live in nodules, or bumps, on certain plant roots. The bacteria get food from the plants, and plants absorb fixed nitrogen from the bacteria. Animals get nitrogen by eating plants or by eating prey that have eaten plants.

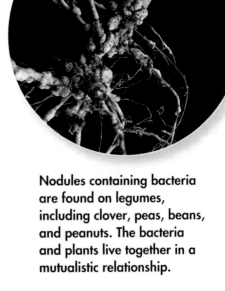

Soil bacteria change nitrogen to a gas.

Nodules containing bacteria are found on legumes, including clover, peas, beans, and peanuts. The bacteria and plants live together in a mutualistic relationship.

182

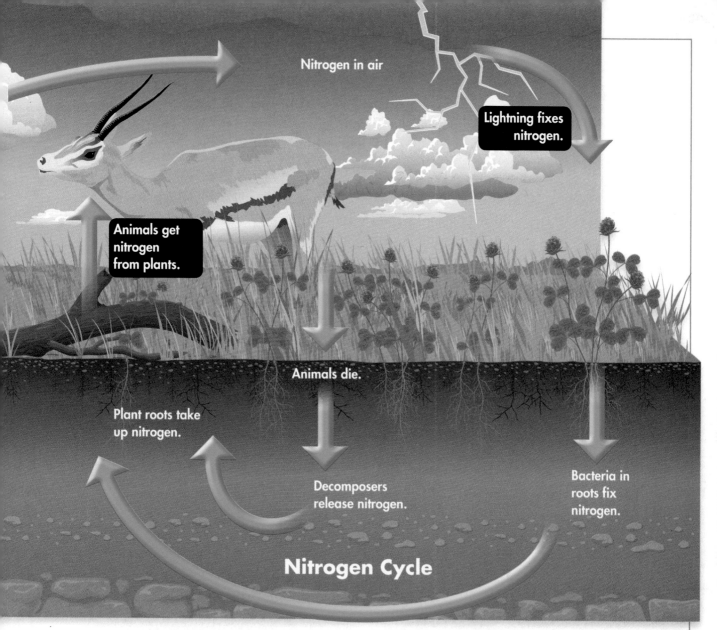

Nitrogen in air

Lightning fixes nitrogen.

Animals get nitrogen from plants.

Animals die.

Plant roots take up nitrogen.

Decomposers release nitrogen.

Bacteria in roots fix nitrogen.

Nitrogen Cycle

Fixed nitrogen may enter the soil in other ways too. A small amount of free nitrogen in the air is fixed by lightning. It is carried to the ground by rainfall. Fixed nitrogen also enters the soil because of decomposers. Decomposers break down dead organisms, and fixed nitrogen is released into the soil. This fixed nitrogen can be absorbed by plant roots.

How does nitrogen return to the air? Some bacteria live freely in the soil. These bacteria can break down fixed nitrogen into free nitrogen. This free nitrogen eventually enters the air, and the cycle continues. This movement of nitrogen through ecosystems is called the nitrogen cycle.

1. ✓**Checkpoint** What is the difference between fixed nitrogen and free nitrogen?

2. **Math in Science** Earth's air is made up of about 78 percent nitrogen, 20 percent oxygen, 1 percent argon, and smaller amounts of other gases. Draw a circle graph that shows the composition of air.

183

Carbon Cycle

The most common element in all living things is carbon. For example, about 18 percent of your body is carbon. Earth's atmosphere, rocks, and soil also contain carbon. Like nitrogen, carbon is cycled through ecosystems.

Carbon is cycled during photosynthesis and cellular respiration. It is cycled through the environment in other ways too. When decomposers, such as fungi and bacteria, break down wastes and the bodies of dead organisms, carbon is released into the soil to be used again by living organisms. Organisms that do not decompose can be buried and over time form fossil fuels, such as coal, oil, and natural gas. The carbon that was stored in these organisms when they were alive is released into the air when the fuels are burned. Carbon also is released into the air as carbon dioxide gas when volcanos erupt.

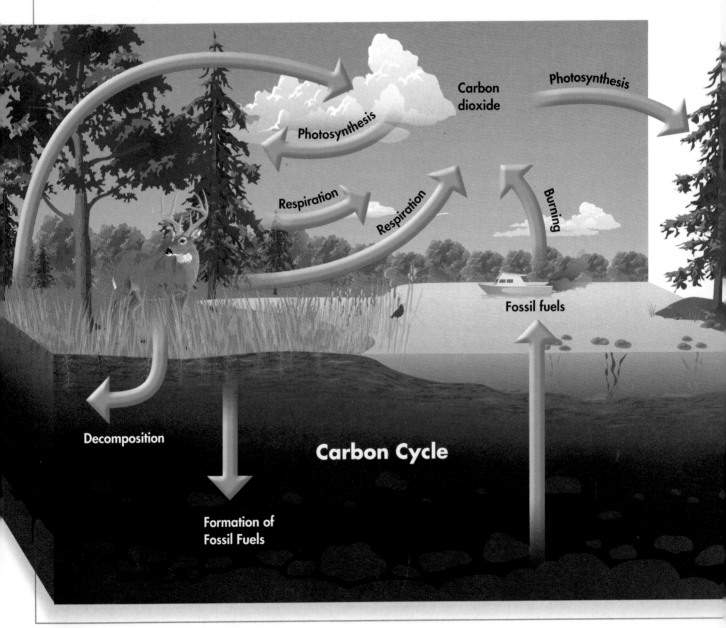

Carbon Cycle

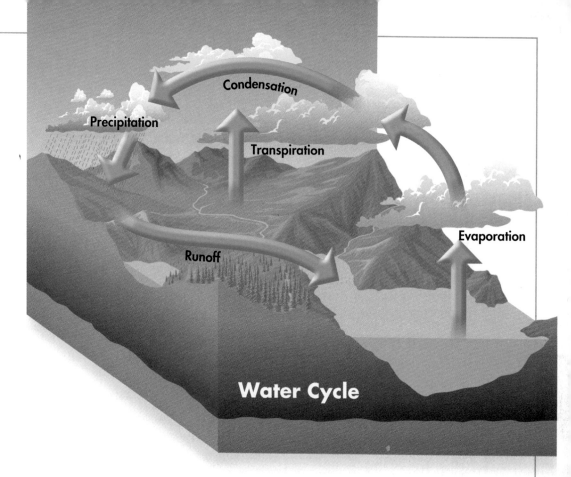

Condensation

Precipitation

Transpiration

Evaporation

Runoff

Water Cycle

Water Cycle

Can you imagine a day without water? Water is necessary for all life. Many chemical reactions that take place in organisms to keep them alive need water. The water cycle helps make water available to all parts of an ecosystem.

As the Sun heats lakes, streams, and other bodies of water, the water evaporates, or changes from a liquid to a gas. As water evaporates, the gas it forms, called water vapor, enters the air. Water also enters the air when the leaves of plants give off water vapor in the process of transpiration. Your breath and that of other animals also contain water.

Once water enters the air, it rises and cools. The cooler temperature causes the water to condense, or change back into tiny drops of water. Clouds form when water vapor condenses on dust or salt particles in the air. Water returns to Earth's surface as precipitation—rain, snow, or hail.

✔Lesson Checkpoint

1. Explain why each of the following is important to all living things: nitrogen, carbon, water.
2. What is the role of decomposers in the carbon cycle?
3. **Writing in Science** **Expository** Explain how the cycles of nature help provide Earth's organisms with an unlimited supply of some important resources.

How do ecosystems change?

Ecosystems change over time. Some changes are natural, and they may happen slowly or quickly. Humans also cause change to ecosystems.

Natural Changes

The morning of May 18, 1980, was bright and clear on Mount St. Helens in the state of Washington. The beautiful forestland around the mountain was filled with wild animals, towering trees, and wildflowers. But that morning everything changed. This volcanic mountain, which had long been quiet, violently erupted. The explosion spewed fiery rock and ash into the air. The hot blast, combined with mudflows, caused devastation for miles around. The land, which minutes before had been filled with life, was now bare and lifeless.

The eruption of Mount St. Helens sent clouds of smoke and ash more than 24 kilometers into the air. Within minutes of the eruption, the land, which had been heavily forested, was bare.

The land shown here is 11 kilometers from the volcano. Even at this distance, only burrowing animals survived. Some buried seeds also survived, allowing plants to slowly grow back.

A natural disaster like the explosion of Mount St. Helens changes ecosystems quickly. Ecosystems can also change quickly due to earthquakes, fires, landslides, or floods. Human activities, such as cutting down forests for lumber, can change ecosystems quickly too.

Slow Changes

Changes in the climate of an ecosystem can cause a slower change. As the climate becomes warmer or cooler, the kinds of organisms that can successfully live in the area change. Some species will die, but new species may begin to live there.

Ecosystems also change slowly through **succession,** a series of predictable changes that occur over time. These changes happen because organisms affect their environment. For example, land with no plants or animals, such as the land around Mount St. Helens after the eruption, will not remain bare. The first organisms to appear are called pioneer species. They can live in harsh conditions, such as poor soil or little water. Pioneer species may break down rocks. When these organisms die, their decayed bodies help make soil.

After soil forms, other organisms can live in the ecosystem. Seeds may blow in from another area. The seeds can take root and grow into new plants in the soil produced by the pioneer species. These plants, in turn, may change the environment so that other plants can live there. Over time, animals move into the area.

Succession also occurs when something happens to an ecosystem, but some plants and animals survive. A beaver may cut down trees to form a dam across a river. The flooded river changes the land ecosystem. Some plants and animals can live in the changed environment, while others die. Some organisms will move away, and others will take their place. Gradually, a new community develops with different kinds of organisms.

Fireweed was one of the first plants to grow after the volcano erupted.

Slowly, succession allows the ecosystem to recover. Plants make the soil more fertile. Animals gradually move into the area.

1. ✓**Checkpoint** Describe what might happen in an ecosystem after a volcano erupts.
2. **Technology** in Science Scientists have used GIS, geographical information systems, to study succession in the areas around Mount St. Helens after the eruption. Use the Internet to learn more about GIS.

Human Impacts

Humans are part of any ecosystem in which they live. Like other organisms living in an ecosystem, their activities can change the environment. Some organisms living in the changing environment cannot survive. The result can be fewer organisms or fewer species.

An action as simple as throwing away trash can affect ecosystems. Have you ever stopped to think about how much trash you throw away each day? Do you know where your trash ends up? Much of the household trash—product packaging, furniture, clothing, food scraps, yard trimming, and other items—ends up in landfills. In 2001, an average of more than four pounds of trash were produced by each person in the United States every day.

Using landfills has advantages. They reduce the odors and health hazards associated with open-air dumps. But they can cause problems too. Hazardous wastes can leak out of landfills and harm ecosystems. Paint, batteries, and other chemicals are a few examples of harmful wastes.

Even "safe" trash harms the environment. When landfills are built, the land changes, and some organisms will die. Another problem with landfills is that they become full. Then other areas must be used to dispose of wastes. As you can see in the map, many of the landfills in the United States are almost full.

The habitats of many organisms are destroyed when land is cleared for a housing development.

Years Before U.S. Landfills Are Full

Less than 5 years
5–10 years
More than 10 years
Unavailable

Dead fish show the effects that pollutants can have on an ocean ecosystem.

You might say that most people don't try to harm the environment. But people can harm the environment without realizing it. Every time someone burns fossil fuels, such as when driving a car, pollutants enter the air. Fossil fuels are burned to produce electricity too. The pollution that is produced when fossil fuels burn includes carbon dioxide. Carbon dioxide can cause changes in the environment.

Even ranching and farming can harm the environment. When livestock is allowed to overgraze, plants die and the soil can be easily eroded. The use of fertilizers on farms or on home gardens and lawns can enter the water cycle and pollute lakes, streams, and rivers.

Factories, such as this oil refinery, can pollute the air by releasing harmful gases. Scrubbers in the smokestacks can clean the smoke before it is released.

1. ✓**Checkpoint** What are some ways that humans change ecosystems?
2. Writing in Science **Persuasive** Choose a photo on this page. Use the photo to write an editorial about how humans can harm ecosystems. Persuade your readers to take action to save ecosystems.

Introduced Species

Zebra mussels, starling birds, and kudzu are aliens—they are living in parts of the world where they were not originally found. How did they get there? These and other organisms, called introduced species, were brought from their natural home to new places by people. Sometimes people moved the organisms on purpose, but other times the process wasn't planned. Introducing new species to an area causes changes in ecosystems. Often the process can create problems—some of them severe. How can that happen?

Introduced species can . . .

- use up nutrients, block sunlight, and cause other changes to the abiotic factors in an ecosystem.

- outcompete the native species that live in an ecosystem. If the number of plant species is reduced, the number of animal species that depend on them also will get smaller. About half of the endangered species in the United States are threatened by introduced species.

- cost the United States about $138 billion a year.

- cause disease, such as Dutch elm disease, which has killed many native elm trees.

Saving Ecosystems

The people in the picture are cleaning up oil along the coast of Prince William Sound in Alaska. In 1989 large areas of the coast were covered with millions of gallons of oil that leaked from an ocean oil tanker. Thousands of workers worked to help clean up the oil. For example, many of them scrubbed oil-covered animals, such as otters, with soap and water. Oil was cleaned from the water and rocks.

You might think that the effort of these people is a great way to help save the environment. But even with the help of all the scientists and volunteers who worked to clean up after the disaster, much of the damage could not be undone. As a result of the leak, 22 orca whales, 3,000 sea otters, 250,000 seabirds, 300 harbor seals, and 250 bald eagles were among the billions of animals that died. More than two billion dollars were spent to clean up the area. Today oil from that spill still seeps up through the beaches. Many populations of plants and animals have not recovered.

The top picture shows oil that leaked from a damaged oil tanker and covered the shoreline in Prince William Sound, Alaska. You can see in the image below it how clean-up efforts slowly made the ecosystem again habitable for plants and animals.

Cleaning up oil spills must be done quickly to prevent ecological disaster. A better plan is to avoid the disaster before it happens.

Preventing Problems

A better solution to problems such as this oil spill is to prevent them from happening in the first place. One way you can help save ecosystems is by understanding the effect that you have on the environment. Know that you can find ways to reduce the harm that you do.

One step in preserving Earth's ecosystems is to use resources wisely. Conserve, or save, resources by reusing, recycling, or reducing your use of them. You can see some examples of ways to do this in the photos on this page. Conserving resources also reduces the need for landfills.

Another way to help prevent harmful changes to ecosystems is to be informed. Remember that all organisms have needs that must be met in order to survive and reproduce. Know how ecosystems work. Understand how all parts of an ecosystem, including humans, affect other parts. Be aware that if you change ecosystems, some organisms may not survive. Some species might become extinct.

Explore ways that you as a citizen can become involved with keeping your environment healthy for all its organisms. For example, become a member of a local environmental group or start an environmental newsletter for your school or community. Know where to find accurate information about environmental issues.

As an adult, you will need to make decisions that affect your community and other environments in your state, country, or even the world. If you learn to be an informed citizen now, being a responsible adult will be easier later.

✓ Lesson Checkpoint

1. List three things you can do to help save ecosystems.
2. How can being informed help you protect ecosystems?
3. **Writing in Science** **Expository** Suppose a friend tells you that there is little she can do to protect ecosystems. How would you respond? Write a letter explaining your reasoning.

In 2001, more than 3 million tons of aluminum was thrown away in the United States. Recycling aluminum saves 95 percent of the energy needed to produce aluminum from natural resources.

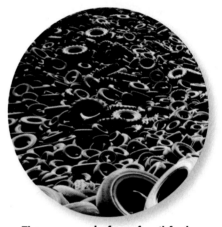

Tires are made from fossil fuels, a natural resource. Ground rubber from old tires can be used in asphalt and in highway noise barriers.

About 4 percent of the energy used in the United States is for making plastics. Recycling plastic products, such as these milk containers, decreases the use of natural resources.

Investigate How clean is the air?

Clean air is important to most living things.

Materials

4 index cards

metric ruler and hole punch

4 pieces of string

petroleum jelly and cotton swab

plastic bag

hand lens

Process Skills

Collecting data in a chart is one way to organize and **communicate** your **observations.**

What to Do

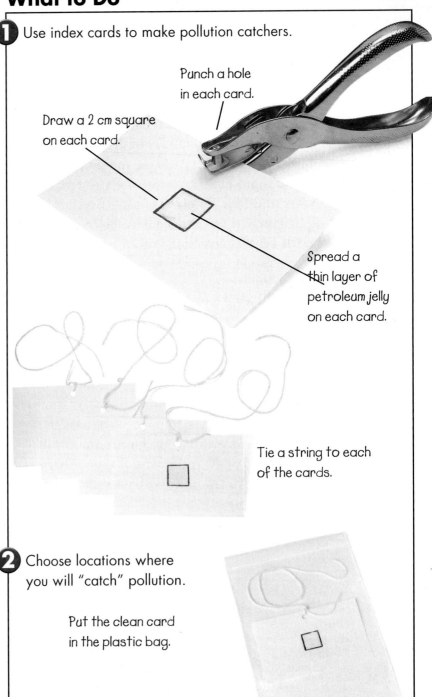

1 Use index cards to make pollution catchers.

Punch a hole in each card.

Draw a 2 cm square on each card.

Spread a thin layer of petroleum jelly on each card.

Tie a string to each of the cards.

2 Choose locations where you will "catch" pollution.

Put the clean card in the plastic bag.

3 Hang the 3 pollution catchers in locations you chose.

school entrance

4 After 3 days, remove the cards. Compare the 4 cards.

5 **Collect Data** by counting and describe the particles in the square on each card. Record your **observations.**

Location	Number of Particles in Square	Description (size, shape, color)
Clean card (in plastic bag)		

Explain Your Results

1. Compare your 4 cards. How are they alike and different?

2. **Communicate** Compare your results with the results of other groups. Discuss any similarities and differences you **observe.**

Go Further

How could you find out if the level of pollution differs between a weekday and the weekend at a specific location? Develop a plan to answer this or any other questions you may have.

Math in Science

Inactive Times for Animals

Some species have adapted to living through a cold season in their environment by hibernating. Hibernation is a period of inactivity when an organism needs much less energy. The organism's heart rate, temperature, and other body processes drop significantly.

Some people believe bears hibernate, but that is not accurate. Bears have periods of inactivity, called torpor, during which their bodies slow down—but not as much as a hibernating animal's body. Another difference between hibernation and torpor is that a bear can be quickly roused from its "sleep," while a hibernating animal cannot. A hummingbird's normal activity uses a lot of energy. In order to conserve energy while not gathering food, a hummingbird can become torpid overnight.

The chart below shows a comparison of heart rate and body temperature for some animals that hibernate and some that go into a state of torpor.

Organism	Normal Body Temperature (°F)	Reduced Activity Temperature (°F)	Normal Heart Rate (beats per min)	Reduced Activity Heart Rate (beats per min)
Hibernation				
Woodchuck	98	38	80	4
Ground squirrel	100	35	150	5
Torpor				
Black bear	96	88	55	10
Polar bear	98.6	95	46	27
Blue-throated hummingbird	105	66.2	250	50–180

e Tools Take It to the Net pearsonsuccessnet.com

Use the chart on page 194 to answer each question.

1. What is the difference between the normal and reduced activity temperatures for the blue-throated hummingbird? This difference is about what percent of the bird's normal body temperature?

2. The poorwill is the only bird known to truly hibernate. Would you expect its body temperature to drop by more than or less than 40 degrees? Explain.

3. If a human's body temperature drops by only 5%, medical care is needed. By what percent can a ground squirrel's temperature drop?

4. A heart rate of 6 beats per minute is equivalent to 1 beat every 10 seconds. What percent of the organisms on the chart can have a heart rate of less than 1 beat every 10 seconds?

5. Compare the bears with the other mammals on the chart What can you infer about body temperature and heart rate for organisms that are truly hibernating and those that are in a state of torpor?

Lab zone Take-Home Activity

Using a timepiece that marks seconds, record your heart rate (in beats per minute) during various activities. Also record it while resting. Compare the results with the animal data on page 194. Write a report about the comparisons.

Use Vocabulary

competition (p. 176)	**host** (p. 180)
	parasite (p. 180)
decomposer (p. 171)	**succession** (p. 187)
energy pyramid (p. 175)	**symbiosis** (p. 180)

Write the vocabulary term from the list above that best completes each sentence.

1. A(n) _____ is the organism that benefits in a relationship when another organism is harmed.

2. _____ is a series of predictable changes that occur in an ecosystem over time.

3. _____ is a close, long-term relationship between organisms that benefits at least one of the organisms.

4. The struggle among organisms to survive in a habitat with limited resources is _____ .

5. A(n) _____ is an organism that gets energy by breaking down the remains of dead organisms.

6. The organism that is harmed in a relationship when another organism benefits is the _____ .

7. A(n) _____ shows how energy moves through an ecosystem.

Explain Concepts

8. Why is sunlight such an important factor in an ecosystem?

9. Explain the mutualistic relationship that can provide plants with nitrogen.

10. Explain why the energy flow in an ecosystem can be shown as a pyramid.

11. The climate in a desert area is changing. Over several years, the area has received more rainfall. What effect will this change likely have on plants and animals in the ecosystem?

Process Skills

12. **Infer** What adaptations help this owl capture prey?

13. Forming Hypotheses A scientist studying an ecosystem notices that the numbers of red foxes and hares change in a cycle. A period with few foxes and many hares is followed by a period with many foxes and few hares. This is followed by a period with few foxes and many hares, and the cycle continues. Form a hypothesis about why the sizes of fox and hare populations show this pattern of change.

14. Making and Using Models Some chemicals that are used to kill insects can harm the birds that eat the insects and the consumers that eat the birds. Draw a diagram to model how harmful chemicals can move through a food chain.

Predict

15. The last few individuals of a species of mouse living in a field eat only a particular kind of grass. The town plans to convert the field into a baseball stadium. They will move the remaining mice to a new field about 30 kilometers away. The field does not have the kind of grass the mice eat. What might happen to this species if they are moved?

Test Prep

Choose the letter that best completes the statement or answers the question.

16. How do decomposers obtain energy?
Ⓐ eating animals
Ⓑ eating plants
Ⓒ breaking down plant remains
Ⓓ directly from the Sun

17. About what percent of the energy at one level of a food chain is transferred to the next higher level?
Ⓕ 10%   Ⓗ 30%
Ⓖ 70%   Ⓘ 90%

18. Which best describes why competition occurs among animals in an ecosystem if resources are scarce?
Ⓐ Different species of animals live in the same area.
Ⓑ Animals of similar species live in the same area.
Ⓒ Animals in an area have different needs.
Ⓓ Animals in an area have similar needs.

19. Explain why the answer you chose for Question 18 is best. For each of the answers you did not choose, give a reason why it is not the best choice.

20. Writing in Science **Description** Active volcanoes on the ocean floor can produce new islands. At first, the new islands will not have any living organisms. Describe the likely process of succession on a new island.

Tracking Migrations

SIGNALS OF SPRING™

Each year in many parts of the world, spring arrives and sends signals to many living things. Spring's signals include longer days and warmer temperatures. During this time, many species migrate from their winter homes in the warmer southern parts of the Northern Hemisphere to areas farther north.

The sandhill crane is just one of the many migrating bird species that cross the United States on their trip north. Some scientists are concerned about a loss of habitat for these birds in some areas along the migration routes. A critical factor for the birds along their route is food. The birds must be able to find enough food to complete their migration and reproduce. If certain habitats are harmed or destroyed, the cranes will have difficulty locating adequate food as they move to their summer homes.

Date	Latitude	Longitude
1/29	24.98°N	99.34°W
2/01	32.67°N	99.56°W
2/06	37.52°N	98.55°W
2/19	37.18°N	98.48°W
2/22	40.73°N	98.45°W
4/01	40.76°N	98.40°W
4/04	44.57°N	99.12°W
4/07	48.28°N	99.89°W
4/20	49.72°N	95.86°W
4/23	53.72°N	83.64°W
4/29	53.83°N	82.71°W

Migrating sandhill cranes in spring eventually reach their northern breeding sites in late April.

By using NASA satellite technology, scientists are able to track the migration of different sandhill crane populations. The scientists can combine this information with data they receive from NASA Earth imagery called NDVI (Normalized Difference Vegetation Index). These images allow scientists to see the growth of plants along the migratory path of the cranes as the spring temperatures warm. The green in the image shows where forested areas are and suggests areas where more food is available.

Scientists and the public can use the NASA information to explain the movement of migrating cranes. In the process, scientists learn about the critical migratory paths that the birds take. Efforts to preserve habitats can be made based on the animal track.

Ocean animals, such as the harbor porpoise, are always looking for food. Scientists can also use images from NASA to find the best sources of food for these animals. Scientists can track the migration patterns of ocean animals as they locate the sources of food.

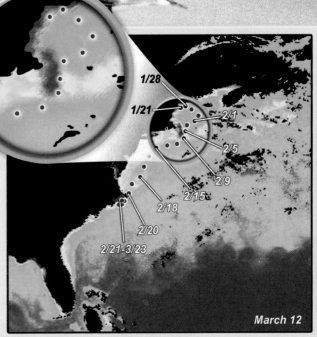

March 12

The harbor porpoise feeds on abundant marine life during its movement off the Eastern U.S. coast.

Lab zone Take-Home Activity

Find out what a sandhill crane eats. Then make a diagram to show the cranes' place in a food chain.

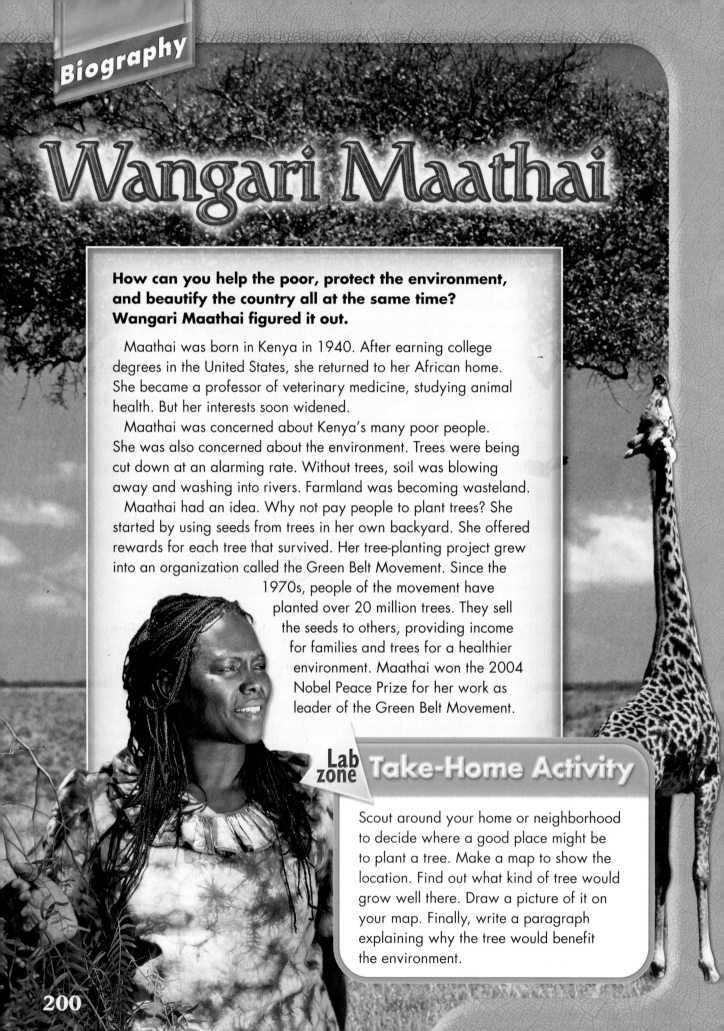

Wangari Maathai

How can you help the poor, protect the environment, and beautify the country all at the same time? Wangari Maathai figured it out.

Maathai was born in Kenya in 1940. After earning college degrees in the United States, she returned to her African home. She became a professor of veterinary medicine, studying animal health. But her interests soon widened.

Maathai was concerned about Kenya's many poor people. She was also concerned about the environment. Trees were being cut down at an alarming rate. Without trees, soil was blowing away and washing into rivers. Farmland was becoming wasteland.

Maathai had an idea. Why not pay people to plant trees? She started by using seeds from trees in her own backyard. She offered rewards for each tree that survived. Her tree-planting project grew into an organization called the Green Belt Movement. Since the 1970s, people of the movement have planted over 20 million trees. They sell the seeds to others, providing income for families and trees for a healthier environment. Maathai won the 2004 Nobel Peace Prize for her work as leader of the Green Belt Movement.

Lab zone Take-Home Activity

Scout around your home or neighborhood to decide where a good place might be to plant a tree. Make a map to show the location. Find out what kind of tree would grow well there. Draw a picture of it on your map. Finally, write a paragraph explaining why the tree would benefit the environment.

Unit A Test Talk

Find Important Words

When you take a test, finding important words can help answer questions about what you read. Read the passage and then answer the questions.

All living things are classified into one of six kingdoms. Members of each kingdom have characteristics that make them different from members of other kingdoms.

Members of the plants and animal kingdoms have many cells. Plants have chloroplasts in their cells, so they can make their own food by <u>photosynthesis</u>. Animals must get their food from other organisms.

Like plants, members of the <u>fungi</u> kingdom cannot move around, and most fungi are made of many cells. Unlike plants, however, fungi cannot make their own food.

Bacteria are organisms that have a single cell with no nucleus. They are divided into two kingdoms. Archaebacteria are found only in <u>extreme conditions</u>, such as hot springs. All other bacteria are <u>eubacteria</u>, which are found almost everywhere else.

All other organisms are in the protist kingdom. Like bacteria, most <u>protists</u> are made of only one cell. Unlike bacteria, however, the cells of protists have a nucleus.

When you read a test question, decide which word is most important. Look back at the passage to find where that word is used. The answer to the question will likely be nearby.

Use What You Know

1. What part of the cells of plants allows plants to make food by photosynthesis?
   Ⓐ chloroplasts
   Ⓑ mitochondria
   Ⓒ nucleus
   Ⓓ vacuole

2. How are plants different from fungi?
   Ⓐ They can live in hot springs.
   Ⓑ They can move around.
   Ⓒ They have only one cell.
   Ⓓ They make their own food

3. According to the passage, organisms in which kingdom live in extreme conditions?
   Ⓐ animals
   Ⓑ archaebacteria
   Ⓒ eubacteria
   Ⓓ protists

4. How are the cells of protists different from the cells of bacteria?
   Ⓐ They have chloroplasts.
   Ⓑ They have a nucleus.
   Ⓒ They have no cell wall.
   Ⓓ They have no cytoplasm.

201

Unit A Wrap-Up

Chapter 1

How are living things alike and different?
- All living things are made of cells, need energy, and reproduce.
- Organisms live in all kinds of environments that require specific adaptations.

Chapter 2

What are the parts of a cell?
- Each cell is made of organelles that perform life tasks.
- Different kinds of cells may have different organelles.

Chapter 3

How do living things reproduce?
- Living things reproduce asexually by mitosis or sexually by meiosis and mitosis.
- DNA, which contains the instructions for a cell's traits, passes from parent to offspring during reproduction.

Chapter 4

How do body parts work together?
- Cells that perform certain functions work together in groups called tissues, which combine to form organs.
- All body systems work together to keep the body in balance.

Chapter 5

What processes take place in plants?
- Plants carry on photosynthesis and respiration.
- Plant tropisms enable plants to respond to their environments.

Chapter 6

How do organisms live together in ecosystems?
- Organisms compete for biotic and abiotic resources.
- Temperature and amount of rainfall determine what organisms live in a biome.

Chapter 7

How do energy, organisms, and the environment interact?

- Energy flows through an ecosystem in a food chain of producers, consumers, and decomposers.
- Water, oxygen, carbon dioxide, and nitrogen cycle through ecosystems.

Performance Assessment

Model Plant and Animal Cells

How are plant and animal cells alike, and how are they different? Use construction paper, colored markers, and glue to make models of cells. Look back in your book to recall the different organelles found in plant cells. Which organelles are not found in animal cells? Use a circle of construction paper for an animal cell and a rectangle of construction paper for a plant cell. Glue cutouts of the different organelles to the cells. Use markers to add features to the organelles and the cells.

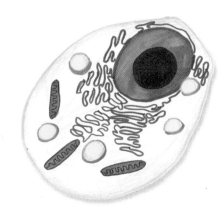

Read More About Life Science

Look for books like these in the library.

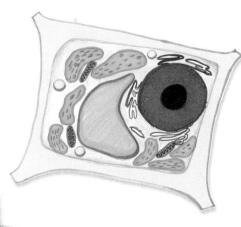

Experiment How can pollution affect plant growth?

Air pollution affects more than air. It can affect rain, which then falls on the land, harming organisms living there. In this experiment you will study how pollution can affect plants.

Materials

plastic Petri dishes with covers

potting soil and radish seeds

unpolluted water (control) and "polluted water"

graduated cylinder (or measuring cup)

metric ruler and tape

Process Skills

Every **experiment** must have a **hypothesis,** a testable statement. The hypothesis helps to guide the experiment.

Ask a question.
How does polluted water affect the growth of a plant?

State a hypothesis.
If you water radish seeds with polluted water instead of unpolluted water, will more, fewer, or the same number of seeds germinate? Write your **hypothesis.**

Identify and control variables.
The variable you change is the type of water. Remember to use the same amount of each type of water. Make sure everything else in the **experiment** stays the same too. The variable you observe is the number of seeds that germinate.

Test your hypothesis.

1 Label the side of each dish.

unpolluted water (control)

2 Fill each dish with potting soil. Do not pack the soil.

3 Scatter 10 seeds on the soil of each dish.

radish seeds

unpolluted water (control)

polluted water

4 Pour 10 mL of water in the "control" dish. Pour 10 mL of polluted water in the "polluted water" dish.

5 Cover each dish.

unpolluted water (control)

polluted water

6 Place the dishes where they will receive light.

7 **Observe** the seeds each day for the next 5 days.

polluted water

unpolluted water
(control)

Collect and record your data.

	Total Number of Seeds That Have Germinated	
Day	**Unpolluted Water** (Control)	**Polluted Water**
1	Seeds planted	Seeds planted
2		
3		
4		
5		

Interpret your data.
Use your data to make a bar graph like the one shown below. Look closely at your graph. Describe how the polluted water affected how many seeds germinated by day 5.

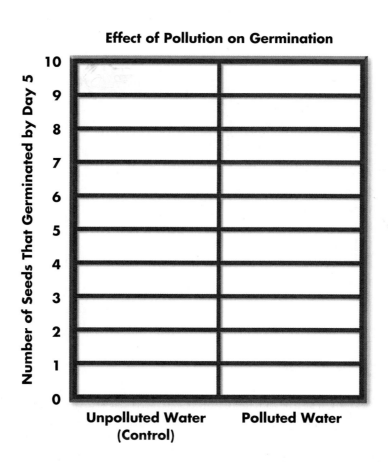

State your conclusion.
Explain how the polluted water affected the number of seeds that germinated and how the seedlings grew. Compare your hypothesis with your results.
Communicate your conclusion.

Go Further

What effect might the polluted water have on other types of plants? Design and carry out a plan to investigate this or other questions you may have.

Science Fair Projects

Full Inquiry

Using Scientific Methods

1. Ask a question.
2. State a hypothesis.
3. Identify and control variables.
4. Test your hypothesis.
5. Collect and record your data.
6. Interpret your data.
7. State your conclusions.
8. Go further.

Causes of Bread Mold

Mold is a type of fungus that sometimes forms on bread.

Idea: Design an experiment to test the effects of heat, cold, light, darkness, moisture, dryness, or another variable on mold formation and growth.

Desert Adaptations

Desert-dwelling organisms have adaptations that allow them to retain water.

Idea: Cover a small sponge with various materials to determine which material is best at preventing the sponge from losing water during a 24-hour period.

Biodegradable Materials

Which materials break down easily in a landfill, and which will likely remain unchanged for many years?

Idea: Design and construct an artificial landfill. Use your landfill to test the biodegradability of various materials such as food waste and packaging materials.

EC CRU 10 9 8 7 6 5 4 3 2

Unit B

Earth Science

You Will Discover

- what Earth's layers are made of.
- how Earth's moving plates create landforms.
- how the theory of plate tectonics explains Earth's features.
- what causes earthquakes and volcanoes.

Chapter 8

Plate Tectonics

How does the theory of plate tectonics explain Earth's landforms?

fault

plate tectonics

210

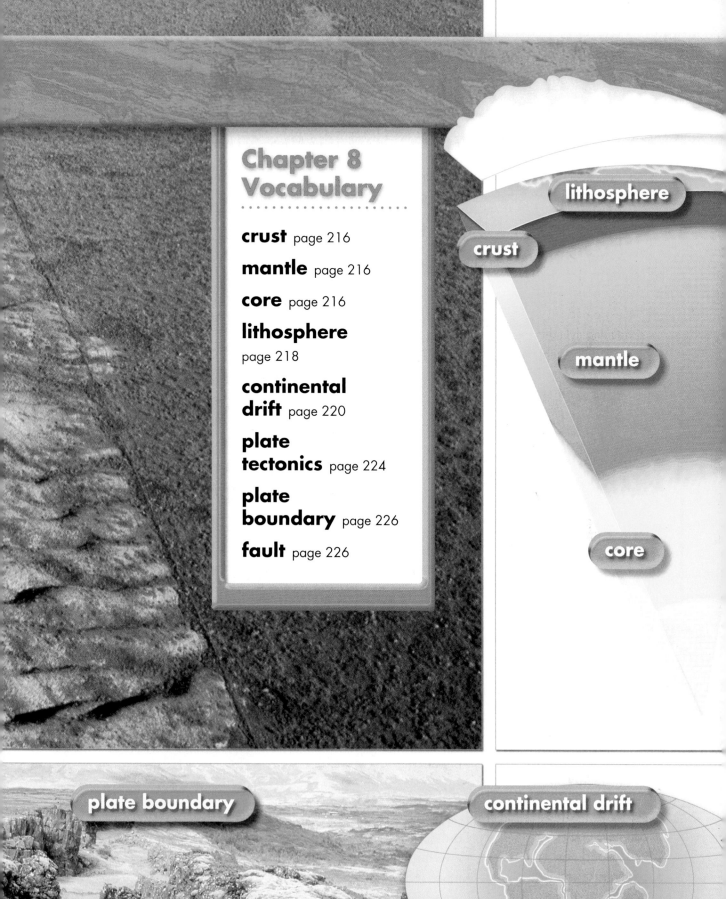

lithosphere

crust

mantle

core

plate boundary

continental drift

211

Explore How are Earth's layers studied?

Scientists study how earthquakes change speed and direction as they move through the Earth. They use their observations to draw conclusions about Earth's layers.

Materials

cup and graduated cylinder (or measuring cup)

water and dishwashing liquid

corn syrup

popcorn kernels

What to Do

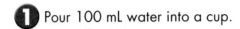

1 Pour 100 mL water into a cup.

2 Slowly add 50 mL dishwashing liquid.

3 Slowly add 50 mL corn syrup.

Scientists study how earthquakes travel to help learn about Earth's layers.

4 Look through the cup from the side at eye level. Drop in a kernel. **Observe** its path as it moves through the 3 liquids.

5 Repeat step 4 with a second kernel. This time observe the path of the kernel looking down from above your **model.**

The liquids represent Earth's layers.

water

dishwashing liquid

corn syrup

Process Skills

Using a model can help you understand how earthquakes might move through the layers of the Earth.

Explain Your Results

Earthquakes change speed and direction as they move through Earth's layers. How did the direction and speed of the kernels change as they moved through your **model?**

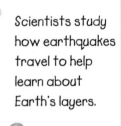

How to Read Science

Draw Conclusions

When you **draw conclusions,** you use your past experiences, previous knowledge, and current information to make a decision or form an opinion.

• Make a list of what you already know about the topic.

• If necessary, create **models** to help gather information.

• Then think about reasonable explanations for the facts.

Science Article

Mapping the Ocean Floor

Scientists can't see all the parts of Earth that they would like to study. Instead they use indirect evidence to get information about those places. One example is the ocean floor. Scientists bounce sound waves off the ocean floor. They record how long it takes for the sound waves to return to the surface. The longer it takes for a sound wave to bounce back, the deeper the ocean. Which do you think would take longer—a sound wave bouncing from a deep ocean valley or one from a shallow area near the coast?

Apply It!

Make a graphic organizer like this one. List the facts from the article. Then use the facts to **draw a conclusion** to answer the question.

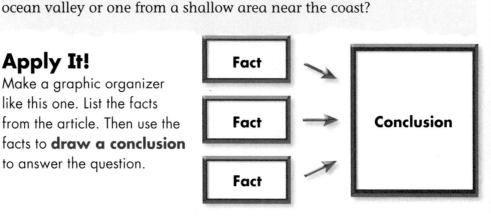

213

You Are There!

Listen! What's that? Do you hear that water roaring? Take a few steps around the path on this flat land. There it is—a waterfall! You are at Victoria Falls in Zimbabwe on the continent of Africa. Can you feel the spray of mist on your face? But how did the waterfall get here in the midst of this flat land? How did this waterfall and Earth's other land features form?

AudioText

What are Earth's layers made of?

Earth has a variety of surface features.
Beneath Earth's crust are the mantle and core.

The Naukluft Mountains
in Namib Desert, Africa

Earth's Variety

Victoria Falls is just one of Earth's many land features. The area around Victoria Falls is raised, flat land called a plateau. Water from the falls plunges into a gorge, or deep crack, in the plateau. In the United States, a very large plateau, the Colorado Plateau, covers areas of Utah, New Mexico, Arizona, and Colorado. At one time, this plateau was flat, but over thousands of years water has washed away some of the rock. Landforms such as the Grand Canyon are the result.

Depending on where you live, you might find other landforms, such as mountains, plains, and valleys. In the southern African desert of Namib, mountains rise high above the surrounding plains. Plains are flatlands with few trees. Valleys, such as the Napa Valley region in southern California, are found where mountains are close together.

Napa Valley,
California

Some of Earth's features are hidden by water. For example, beneath the Atlantic Ocean is a ridge, or long row, of towering mountains. Some of those mountains are volcanoes. Also below the ocean are trenches—long, narrow canyons in the ocean floor.

Although these features differ in many ways, they all formed from processes that began deep inside Earth. To understand the process, you need to understand what Earth is like inside.

1. **✓Checkpoint** What are trenches and ridges?
2. **Social Studies** in Science Choose a continent and research its most important land features. Draw a map that shows where the land features are located. Include brief descriptions of each feature on your map.

Earth's Layers

Sometimes Earth is described as a giant rock in space. In one way, that's true. Earth's surface is solid and is made of rock and soil. But Earth has different layers, and not all of them are solid.

Above Earth's surface is the atmosphere. Parts of the atmosphere constantly interact with Earth's land. This thin layer of gases is the air we breathe. Humans could not live on Earth without the atmosphere. In fact, Earth's atmosphere makes it the only planet we know of that can support life.

The outermost solid layer of Earth is the **crust,** the part of Earth we live on. It includes the soil and rock that covers Earth's surface. The thickness of the crust varies. The part of the crust covered by ocean water is about 6–11 kilometers thick. The part that is dry land is about 35–40 kilometers thick. When you think about high mountains, which are part of Earth's crust, you may think the crust is thick. Compared to the size of the Earth, the crust is just a thin shell.

The layer of Earth just below the crust is the **mantle.** This thick layer contains most of Earth's mass. The outer part of the mantle is solid, like the crust. The inner part is so hot that the rock can flow very slowly over time.

The **core** is the innermost layer of Earth. It is much denser, or compacted, than the mantle because of the weight of all the rock above it. The temperature of the core is thought to be about 7,000°C. That's as hot as the surface of the Sun. The outer core is so hot that it is a liquid. The inner core is solid.

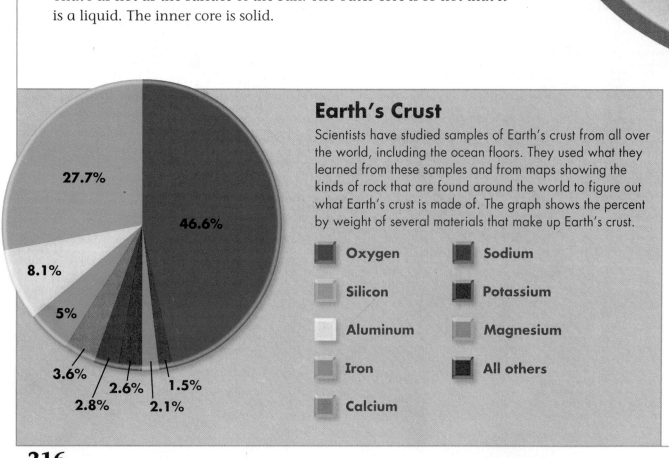

Earth's Crust

Scientists have studied samples of Earth's crust from all over the world, including the ocean floors. They used what they learned from these samples and from maps showing the kinds of rock that are found around the world to figure out what Earth's crust is made of. The graph shows the percent by weight of several materials that make up Earth's crust.

- Oxygen
- Silicon
- Aluminum
- Iron
- Calcium
- Sodium
- Potassium
- Magnesium
- All others

46.6%
27.7%
8.1%
5%
3.6%
2.8%
2.6%
2.1%
1.5%

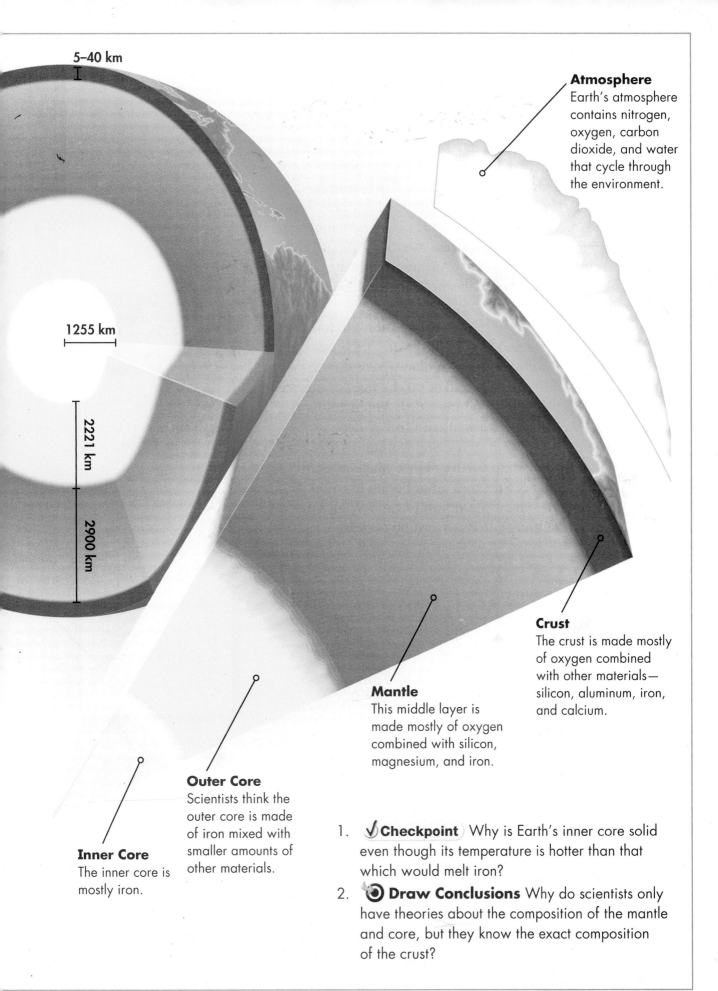

5–40 km

1255 km

2221 km

2900 km

Atmosphere
Earth's atmosphere
contains nitrogen,
oxygen, carbon
dioxide, and water
that cycle through
the environment.

Crust
The crust is made mostly
of oxygen combined
with other materials—
silicon, aluminum, iron,
and calcium.

Mantle
This middle layer is
made mostly of oxygen
combined with silicon,
magnesium, and iron.

Outer Core
Scientists think the
outer core is made
of iron mixed with
smaller amounts of
other materials.

Inner Core
The inner core is
mostly iron.

1. ✔️**Checkpoint** Why is Earth's inner core solid
even though its temperature is hotter than that
which would melt iron?

2. 🎯 **Draw Conclusions** Why do scientists only
have theories about the composition of the mantle
and core, but they know the exact composition
of the crust?

217

Earth's Plates

In some ways, the outer part of Earth is like an eggshell. If you boil an egg too long, the inner part becomes a soft solid, but the shell breaks into pieces. Earth's crust and the upper part of the mantle are called the **lithosphere.** Like a cracked eggshell, the lithosphere is not a continuous layer. It is broken into pieces called tectonic plates. The plates all have different shapes and sizes. Some, like the South American Plate, are the size of continents. Others, such as the Caribbean Plate, are much smaller. All the plates fit together like the pieces of a jigsaw puzzle.

You can see on the map that the plates don't follow the edges of the continents. Many of the plates are made of both continental crust—the crust that makes up continents—and oceanic crust—the crust that makes up the floor of the ocean. Most of the United States is on the North American Plate. Much of the Atlantic Ocean is also on this plate.

If you viewed Earth from space, you wouldn't see much of the land that makes up Earth's plates. Much of Earth's lithosphere is under oceans and other bodies of water. Look at the Pacific Plate. The western part of California is on this plate, but most of this plate is covered by ocean.

Major Tectonic Plates

A Pacific Plate

B North American Plate

C Cocos Plate

D Nazca Plate

E South American Plate

F African Plate

G Eurasian Plate

H Indian Plate

I Australian Plate

J Antarctic Plate

Deep cracks in the crust of Iceland show the edges of the North American Plate and the Eurasian Plate.

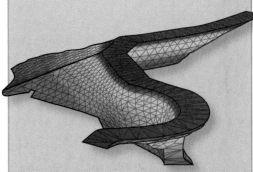

"Seeing" Inside Earth

You might wonder how scientists know so much about the inside of Earth if they can't go there. Earth's interior is just one of the many objects that scientists cannot observe directly. As with other objects they can't see, scientists use indirect evidence to study Earth's interior.

When earthquakes happen, they produce waves that travel through Earth's interior. The waves travel faster through certain kinds of materials than others, but they take only minutes to travel from one part of Earth to another. On their journey, they travel through the mantle.

Scientists can study the travel times of the waves to get clues about the kinds of materials inside Earth. Scientists also use the clues they gather to find out about Earth's plates.

Another way they learn about Earth's interior is to use a process called seismic tomography. Seismic tomography works this way. Scientific stations around the world detect earthquake waves and the collected data is used to make three-dimensional pictures like the one above.

Like the cracked shell of a boiled egg, Earth's plates rest on a soft solid. Recall that the lower part of the mantle can flow very slowly. The plates of the lithosphere float on top of this layer.

✔ Lesson Checkpoint

1. Describe the layers of Earth.

2. On which plate is most of the United States? On which plate is Hawaii?

3. Writing in Science **Descriptive** Earth's tectonic plates are often compared to a jigsaw puzzle. Write a paragraph describing how the plates and a jigsaw puzzle are alike and how they are different. Use the words *lithosphere*, *mantle*, and *crust*.

How do Earth's plates help create landforms?

Alfred Wegener introduced the idea that the continents drift slowly over Earth's surface. Evidence from fossils, rock types, ancient climates, and seafloor spreading supported this theory.

Continental Drift

Until the early 1600s, most people thought that Earth's continents were always in the same place. Then scientists began to notice that the coastlines of some continents looked as if they could fit together like a jigsaw puzzle. Many people wondered why.

Then in 1912 Alfred Wegener, a German scientist, suggested an explanation for the fit of the coastlines. Wegener thought that about 225 million years ago the continents were joined in one large continent he called Pangaea (meaning "all Earth"). Wegener suggested that long ago Pangaea broke apart.

Wegener also introduced the idea of **continental drift,** the theory that continents drifted apart in the past and continue to do so. A scientific theory is a well-tested concept that explains a wide range of observations. Wegener's theory stated that as Pangaea broke apart, its pieces moved to different parts of Earth to form today's continents.

The shape of continents was evidence for Wegener's ideas, but it wasn't proof. Other evidence supported Wegener's ideas. Plant and animal fossils found along the eastern coast of South America closely matched those found along the western coast of Africa. Wegener felt these similarities were impossible unless the species had once lived side-by-side when the continents were joined.

Further evidence for Wegener's ideas was found in rocks. Layers of rocks along the eastern coast of South America match layers of rocks along the western coast of Africa. Wegener said that the layers of rocks must have been joined at some time.

What forces could be strong enough to move whole continents? This is the question that Wegener could not answer. As a result, most scientists did not believe the idea of continental drift. They thought that the continents did not move, even over millions of years.

This is the last picture taken of Alfred Wegener before he left for Greenland in 1930. Wegener died in Greenland during a blizzard.

200 millon years ago

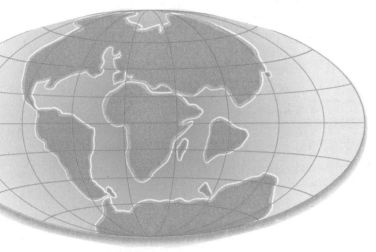

65 millon years ago

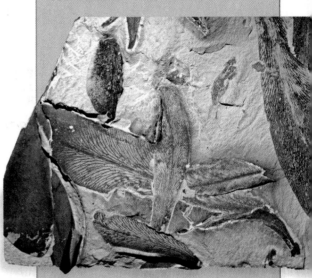

Today

1. **Checkpoint** What was the main reason most scientists did not accept the idea of continental drift?

2. **Writing in Science** **Expository** Wegener offered several types of evidence to support his idea of continental drift. Write a short paragraph that summarizes his evidence.

Fossil Evidence

Among the many bits of evidence for continental drift are two fossils.

Fossils of the ancient plant *Glossopteris* are found in South America, Africa, India, Antarctica, and Australia. These identical plants could only develop at places that were connected at some time in the past. In addition, *Glossopteris* fossils were also found in very cold regions of Earth. When the plants grew, these regions must have been located at warmer parts of Earth.

Fossils of this ancient reptile, called *Mesosaurus,* have also been found in both South America and Africa. This freshwater animal could not have survived a trip across a saltwater ocean. Wegener claimed the reptile must have walked from one area to the other when the continents were connected.

The Spreading Ocean Bottom

Not much other evidence supported Wegener's theory of continental drift. Later, better methods to map the ocean floor were developed. Scientists then collected data that showed long, deep ocean trenches. They also discovered a chain of mountains along the floor of the Atlantic Ocean. These mountains are now called the Mid-Atlantic Ridge.

In 1960 scientist Harry Hess offered an explanation for the trenches and ridges. He suggested that new crust forms at ocean ridges. He explained that magma, which is molten rock, pushes up through Earth's crust. As the magma cools, it forms new crust. More magma comes up and pushes the newly formed crust and the old crust aside. This process is known as seafloor spreading.

What causes the magma to rise? As Earth's plates move away from each other, the ocean floor spreads apart, and magma rises to fill the gap. But what causes the plates to move apart?

In the early 1930s, Arthur Holmes had developed ideas that scientists used in the 1960s to answer the question. When a liquid is heated, particles that make up the liquid move faster and spread apart. Hot liquids therefore weigh less and float above cooler liquids. As the hot liquid rises and cools, it becomes heavier and again sinks. More hot liquid can then rise above it. This process is called convection. The mantle is not a flowing liquid, but its rocks are so hot that they flow very slowly. The result is that currents in the mantle constantly rise, circle around, and fall. When the mantle moves, the plates floating on it also move. Convection is the force that moves Earth's plates.

This map shows the Atlantic Ocean floor. You can see the Mid-Atlantic Ridge.

Convection currents in the mantle cause the plates to move.

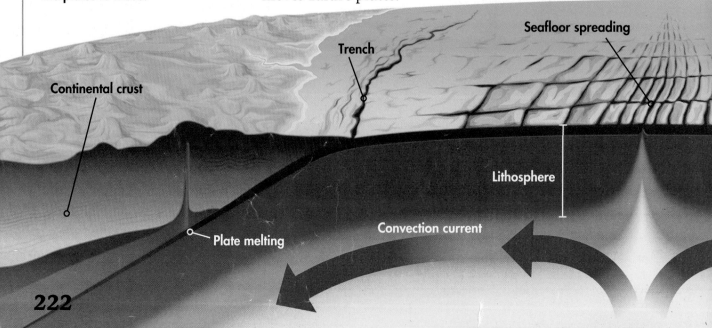

Continental crust

Trench

Seafloor spreading

Lithosphere

Plate melting

Convection current

Proof of Continental Drift

Although the explanation for sea floor spreading helped to support Wegener's ideas, scientists needed more proof of continental drift. In the early 1960s, scientists studying the magnetism of rocks near the Mid-Ocean Ridge noticed a pattern. In some places the magnetism faced north. In other places, it faced south. Scientists found alternating rows of north/south patterns spreading out from the Mid-Ocean Ridge. What did this evidence mean?

Earth's magnetism "flips" about every half million years. When rocks form from the cooling lava of volcanoes, the particular magnetic pattern at the time is "frozen" into the rocks. This was evidence that the alternating pattern of the rock has been slowly spreading out as new crust is formed.

✔ Lesson Checkpoint

1. Why do hot liquids float above cool liquids?
2. Math in Science A ship emits sound waves straight down toward the ocean floor. The waves take 2.1 seconds to reflect back to the ship. If the speed of sound in ocean water is about 1500 meters per second, how deep is the ocean at that point?
3. Writing in Science **Persuasive** Suppose you have a friend who doesn't believe that continental drift occurs. Write one or two paragraphs explaining the concept and why you believe it is true.

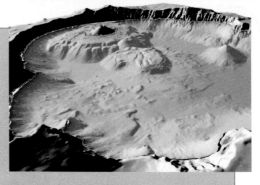

Sonar

Have you ever heard an echo? You might be surprised to know that scientists use echoes to map the ocean floor.

Beginning in the early 1900s, scientists began to use sound waves to learn about the ocean floor. Sonar, which stands for **SO**und **N**avigation **A**nd **R**anging, is a method of bouncing sound waves off objects and measuring the time it takes for the waves to return to where they started. Sonar is used mainly underwater, such as in the ocean.

Today scientists use different methods to send sounds and detect their return in the ocean. On their return, the sound waves enter a computer, where they produce electrical signals. The computer uses the information about time differences of the echoes to make an image of the ocean floor, similar to the picture above, which shows the floor of Crater Lake, Oregon.

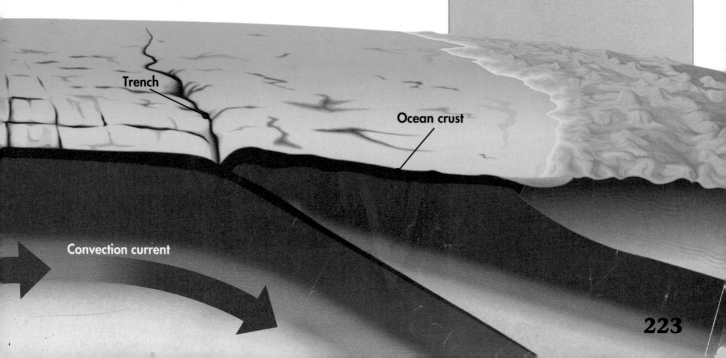

Trench

Ocean crust

Convection current

223

How do scientists explain Earth's features?

The theory of plate tectonics explains features such as mountains and volcanoes. Convection currents in the mantle cause Earth's plates to move. Plates can slide past each other, collide, or move away from each other.

Theory of Plate Tectonics

Wegener's idea of continental drift suggested that continents moved, but it did not explain many other parts of Earth's crust. Today scientists use the theory of **plate tectonics** to explain why Earth's features appear as they do.

According to the theory of plate tectonics, Earth's lithosphere is broken into about 20 moving plates. The continents and the ocean floor make up the surfaces of these moving plates.

Earth in the Future

The map shows how Earth will possibly look 50 million years from now.

A The Atlantic Ocean will widen.

B The part of California that lies on the Pacific Plate will move north.

C North America and South American will split apart.

D Africa and Asia will no longer be joined.

E Parts of eastern Africa may become an island.

F Australia will move northward and collide with Indonesia.

  SciLinks **Take It to the Net** pearsonsuccessnet.com keyword: plate tectonics code: g6p224

Earth's plates move in a continuous process in different directions—away from, alongside, or toward each other. How do scientists know how the plates move?

Scientists can figure out how the plates move by receiving radio signals from Global Positioning System (GPS) satellites in space to determine the precise distance between points on different plates and how the distances change over time. For example, they know from data they have collected that the North American Plate and the Eurasian Plate are moving about two centimeters a year away from each other.

The theory of plate tectonics explains many of Earth's features. Continents may break apart. Mountain chains may form where plates move together. As plates move apart, magma may rise to the surface, forming a volcano. Oceans may become larger or smaller. Throughout Earth's history, the positions of the land and the oceans have changed from the ancient Pangaea to the modern-day continents. Earth's plates will continue to move in the future.

The map shows where scientists predict the continents will be 50 million years from now. You might wonder how scientists can make this prediction. Evidence shows that plate movement has always taken place at about the same rate. And scientists predict that the plates will continue to move. They think it is possible that in the far distant future, the continents could come together once again to create another Pangaea-like continent.

Molten rock cools and hardens, forming new crust.

1. ✓**Checkpoint** How does the theory of plate tectonics differ from Wegener's idea of continental drift?

2. **Draw Conclusions** The map on page 224 shows where scientists think Earth's continents will be in 50 million years. What conclusion can you draw about the movement of North America after that?

Plate Boundaries

The pictures on this page show **plate boundaries**, areas where two plates meet. Plates move slowly in different directions. They may move apart, they may collide, or they may slide past each other. You can see the landforms that result as changes slowly happen at each kind of plate boundary.

At spreading boundaries, plates move away from each other and gaps form between the plates. Convection currents cause magma to rise from the mantle through these gaps. Huge valleys can form. This type of plate movement is responsible for seafloor spreading. The Mid-Atlantic Ridge formed at plate boundaries that were moving apart.

At fracture boundaries, plates slide past each other. This break in Earth's crust is called a **fault.** The movement of the plates past each other can cause strong earthquakes.

The area where two plates push against each other is called a colliding boundary. When plates collide, one plate might slide beneath the other. When plates carry continents into each other, towering mountains form. Other times, deep ocean trenches, earthquakes, and volcanoes can result.

Fracture Boundary
The San Andreas fault is a boundary between the North American Plate and the Pacific Plate. The two plates are sliding past each other.

Spreading Boundary
The Mid-Atlantic Ridge cuts across Iceland at the boundary between the Eurasian Plate and the North American Plate. These plates are moving away from each other.

Colliding Boundary

The Himalayan Mountains are still rising where the Eurasian Plate and the Indian Plate are colliding with each other.

GPS

How do scientists know how fast Earth's plates move? One method they use is the Global Positioning System (GPS).

The Global Positioning System is a group of 24 satellites, like the one above, in orbit over Earth. These satellites continually give off radio signals that can be picked up by GPS receiving units on Earth. By comparing signals from the GPS satellites, the position, speed, and direction of motion of a receiver can be figured out.

Scientists have placed GPS receivers at many different places on Earth to measure their precise position. By comparing measurements over time, scientists can determine the speed and direction of Earth's tectonic plates.

✔ Lesson Checkpoint

1. Seafloor spreading is found at which type of plate boundary?
2. Summarize the main points of the theory of plate tectonics.
3. 🔵 **Draw Conclusions** Suppose GPS satellites provide information that Tectonic Plate A has moved 1 centimeter to the west. Plate B, which lies directly east of Plate A, has moved about the same distance to the east. What kind of landform is most likely forming at this plate boundary? Explain your reasoning.

Lesson 4

What causes earthquakes and volcanoes?

Earthquakes are caused by the sudden shifting of rock as tectonic plates shift positions. Volcanoes occur where magma from the mantle either flows or explodes through the crust.

Scientists study the vibrations within Earth's crust to learn about earthquakes. This map shows the earthquake activity in California in a 24-hour period.

Earthquakes

Plate movement takes place so slowly that you can't see or feel it. In fact, some plates don't move for many years. Jagged rock edges in the lithosphere sometimes stop the movement. Over time, pressure builds up, until suddenly the pressure is too strong. The rocks lurch forward. Earth's crust shakes— an earthquake has happened!

Earthquakes cause damage when the pressure that builds up along a fault is suddenly released. The underground point where the earthquake occurs is called the focus. The point on Earth's surface directly over the focus is called the epicenter.

The energy from an earthquake is carried by waves. The waves spread out from the focus and from the epicenter. Some waves cause the ground to move back and forth. Other waves cause the ground to move up and down or in a circular motion.

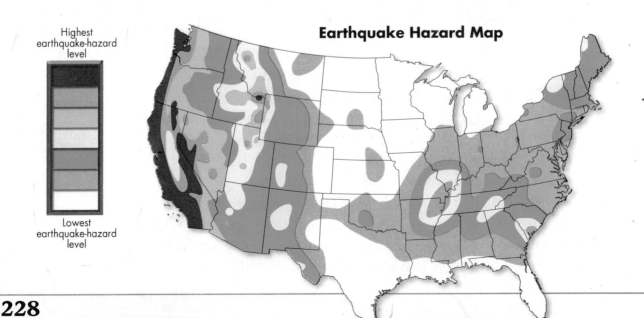

Highest earthquake-hazard level

Lowest earthquake-hazard level

Earthquake Hazard Map

Earthquake Magnitude

As the waves spread out, they lose energy. The possibility of earthquake damage, therefore, is greatest closest to the epicenter. Most damage often occurs to nearby construction, such as highways and buildings.

Almost all of the major earthquakes in the United States have occurred in California and Alaska. These states are on the plate boundary between the Pacific Plate and the North American Plate. Most earthquakes take place near the edges of plates.

The map on page 228 shows earthquake hazard—how likely an area is to have earthquakes—for different parts of the United States. As you can see, the highest levels are along the west coast.

The strength of an earthquake is given as its magnitude. An earthquake magnitude scale is a series of numbers. The number shows the total amount of energy released. The Richter scale is one such scale. Each increase of 1 on the scale indicates about 31 times more energy is released. The table shows the magnitude of some earthquakes and the number of people killed. Notice that the magnitude of an earthquake doesn't always indicate how much damage will result. The effect of an earthquake depends on many factors, including the size of the earthquake, its distance from the epicenter, the kind of rock in the area, and the types of buildings there.

The energy of an earthquake caused the damage to this freeway in Los Angeles, California.

The 1999 earthquake that caused this damage in Turkey caused many buildings to collapse.

Earthquakes

Date	Place	Magnitude	Total deaths
1/22/2003	Mexico	7.6	29
3/29/2003	Afghanistan	5.9	1
5/27/2003	Algeria	5.8	9
9/27/2003	Russia	7.3	3
12/26/2003	Iran	6.6	30,000

1. ✔Checkpoint How is an earthquake's epicenter related to its focus?
2. Art in Science When earthquakes occur, they produce two kinds of waves—S waves and P waves. Find out what these waves are. Make a visual display that describes these waves and how they travel.

Volcanoes

Picture a tall, cone-shaped mountain with thick, glowing matter spewing from it. The picture in your mind is of a volcano. A volcano is an opening in the surface of one of Earth's plates through which magma rises. Like earthquakes, most volcanoes occur near plate boundaries. The theory of plate tectonics explains why.

A **Ash Cloud**
Tiny bits of rock spew into the air during an eruption, forming a thick cloud of ash.

B **Crater**
A crater is a steep-sided depression at the top of a volcano. Craters can form during an eruption or if the rim of the volcano collapses.

Volcanic rock

C **Hot Spot**
Volcanoes are common in Hawaii, even though the islands are not near a plate boundary. Hawaii is on a hot spot—an area of on-going volcanic activity.

When one plate sinks beneath another at a plate boundary, the sinking crust melts into magma. Pressure can build up from gases trapped in the magma—somewhat like the pressure that builds when you shake a can of carbonated beverage. If the crust of the overlying plate can no longer withstand the pressure, magma explodes through it as a volcano. Magma that reaches the surface is called lava.

Volcanoes are more common than you might think. That's because you never hear about most volcanoes. They take place where plate boundaries are moving away from each other on the ocean floor. Magma quietly flows out onto the ocean floor. New crust forms from the cooled lava.

D Caldera
A caldera is a crater that is at least 1.6 km wide. A lake may form in a caldera. The 9.6 km wide Crater Lake in Oregon formed in a caldera of the Cascade Mountain Range.

E Basalt plain
Flows of lava spill out onto nearby ground forming new crust. Basalt is a dark volcanic rock.

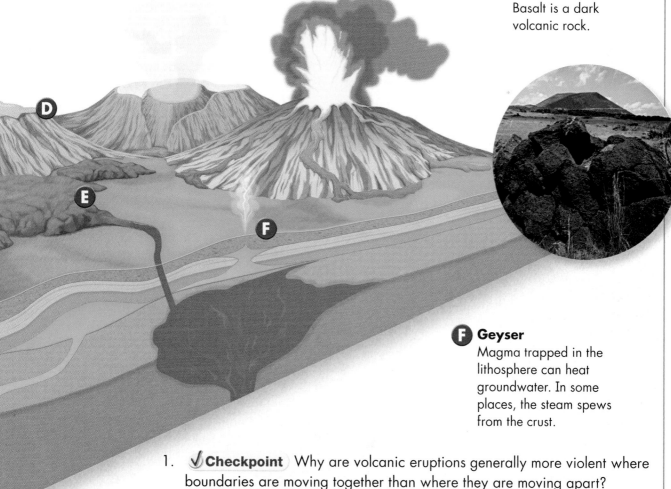

F Geyser
Magma trapped in the lithosphere can heat groundwater. In some places, the steam spews from the crust.

1. **✓Checkpoint** Why are volcanic eruptions generally more violent where boundaries are moving together than where they are moving apart?

2. **Writing in Science** **Narrative** Write a story about being a speck of magma inside a volcano. Explain what happens as pressure within the volcano builds up.

Predicting Volcanoes and Earthquakes

If an earthquake or volcano was threatening the area where you live, you'd want to know as soon as possible. Can scientists predict these potential disasters?

Scientists can use a variety of tools to make predictions about when and where volcanoes and earthquakes will happen. Seismometers, such as the ancient one below, detect tremors, or shaking movements in Earth's crust. The tremors may be a signal that magma is rising in a volcano or that Earth's plates are shifting. Another instrument, a tiltmeter, detects changes in the slope of the land. This change also tells scientists that magma is rising within a volcano.

Scientists can often predict where and when volcanoes will erupt. Maps show where past activity has occurred. They give clues to where future activity is likely to occur because volcanoes often have a pattern of eruption.

Predicting earthquakes isn't as easy as predicting volcanoes. Scientists can find the location of faults, but how can they know when plates will suddenly shift? Scientists listen for tremors, using an instrument called a seismograph. A free-moving part of the seismograph moves freely back and forth as the ground moves. The instrument records this movement.

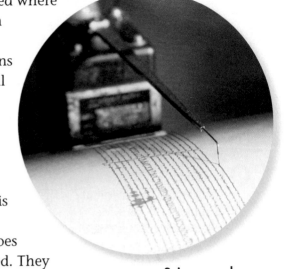

Seismograph

The first instrument used to predict earthquakes was invented in China in A.D. 132.

Small shifts in ground level would cause a ball in a dragon's mouth to fall into a frog's mouth. The frog that contained the ball would indicate the direction from which the earthquake occurred.

232

Preparing for Earthquakes

The best way to avoid earthquake damage and harm to your body is to be prepared. For example, people who live in an area at high risk for earthquakes can safeguard their home. The diagram shows some ways to do this. Be sure to read the other tips for earthquake safety on this page.

Earthquake Safety

Here are some tips to help keep you safe during an earthquake.

Before an earthquake:
- Make a family safety plan.

During an earthquake:
- If you are inside, get under a table or desk.

- Stay away from objects that might fall.

- If you are outside, stay away from buildings and move to an open area.

Reducing Earthquake Damage

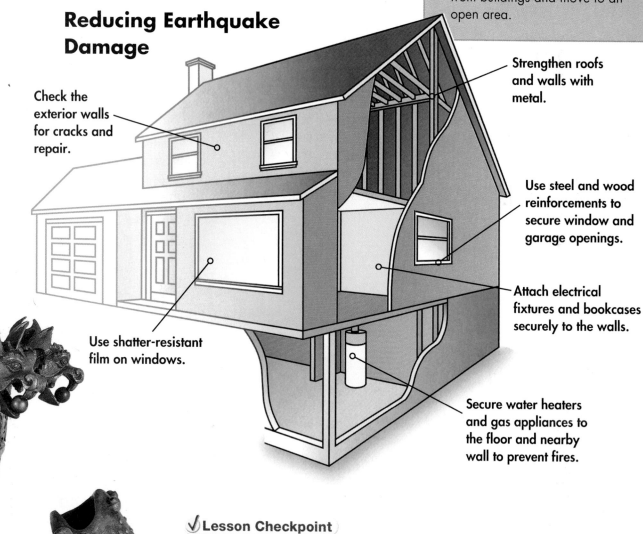

Check the exterior walls for cracks and repair.

Strengthen roofs and walls with metal.

Use steel and wood reinforcements to secure window and garage openings.

Attach electrical fixtures and bookcases securely to the walls.

Use shatter-resistant film on windows.

Secure water heaters and gas appliances to the floor and nearby wall to prevent fires.

✓ Lesson Checkpoint

1. What causes an earthquake?
2. What should you do during an earthquake?
3. **Writing** in Science **Descriptive** Go to a government Web site, such as FEMA or USGS, and find out how to prepare for an earthquake. Use the information to write a family safety plan for your own family or other families who live in earthquake areas.

233

Investigate How can you make convection currents?

Materials

4 foam cups

very warm water,
ice water,
room-temperature water

clear tub and red and
blue food coloring

clock or watch
(with a second hand)

red and blue markers
and ruler

Process Skills

Collecting data by making detailed drawings can help you form a mental picture of how convection currents work.

What to Do

1 Place the foam cups in 2 rows of 2.

2 Add very warm water to the 2 cups on the left. Add ice water to the 2 cups on the right.

Let the coloring slide down the side of the container.

5 cm

3 Fill a tub to a depth of about 5 cm with room-temperature water. Balance the tub on the cups. Wait 5 minutes.

very warm water

4 Add 4 drops of red coloring to the left end of the tub. Add 4 drops of blue coloring to the right end.

5 **Collect data.** Use red and blue markers to draw the convection currents you **observe**.

Convection Currents

Time	Side View	Top View
After 1 minute		
After 2 minutes		
After 3 minutes		

ice water

Explain Your Results

1. Examine the **data** you **collected**. What happened to the food coloring at the warm end of the tub? at the cold end?

2. How do your **observations** about convection currents relate to the motion of Earth's plates?

Go Further

What could you change to make 2 convection systems in the tub? Investigate further to find out.

Fishing with Sound

Fishermen like to know where the fish are. The problem is that people can't see far into the water. For us to see something, light must bounce off it and travel to our eyes. Light does not travel well through water, so we can't see clearly in water. Sonar equipment uses sound to let us "see" in places that light cannot easily travel, like underwater. Special sounds, called pings, are sent from the boat toward the bottom of the body of water. When these sound waves hit something, like the bottom or a school of fish, they reflect back to the boat, and a computer can turn the reflected waves it receives into a picture. The line graph below contains sonar data recorded in freshwater. Each point on the graph represents one ping.

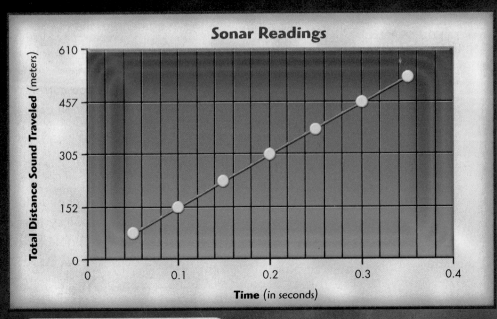

Sonar Readings

Total Distance Sound Traveled (meters)

610

457

305

152

0

0   0.1   0.2   0.3   0.4

Time (in seconds)

Use the graph on page 236 to answer each question.

1. For sound waves, what is the relationship between distance traveled and time?

2. How far did a ping travel in three tenths of a second?

3. A ping must travel down to an object and then back to the boat. If a ping travels 300 meters, how deep is the object from which it was reflected?

4. For what amount of time should a ping travel if you were looking for fish that swim at a depth of about 75 meters?

5. Sound travels through freshwater more slowly than through salt water. Predict how the sonar graph would change in salt water. Explain.

6. Predict how far a ping would travel in one half of a second. How did you make your prediction?

Lab zone Take-Home Activity

Make some measurements of distance as it relates to time. For example, measure the distance a model car travels in 10 seconds, 20 seconds, and so on. Make a line graph with your data. Is there a clear relationship between time and distance? If you think so, try making a prediction for another time period and see if your prediction holds true.

Chapter 8 Review and Test Prep

Use Vocabulary

continental drift (p. 220)	**lithosphere** (p. 218)
core (p. 216)	**mantle** (p. 216)
crust (p. 216)	**plate boundary** (p. 226)
fault (p. 226)	**plate tectonics** (p. 224)

Write the term from the list above that best completes each sentence.

1. The theory of _____ explains how the lithosphere is broken into moving plates that float on a layer of partly melted rock.

2. The place where two plates meet is called a _____.

3. Wegener proposed the idea of _____ to explain why continents seem to fit together like a jigsaw puzzle.

4. Most of Earth's mass is in the _____.

5. The part of Earth we live on is the _____.

6. Many earthquakes occur in southern California because of a large _____ in the crust.

7. Earth's crust and part of the upper mantle make up the _____.

8. The lower part of the _____ is under such pressure that it is solid, even though it is at an extremely high temperature.

Explain Concepts

9. Explain the process of convection.

10. How does plate tectonics explain the formation of mountains?

11. The pictures show two fossils—*Glossopteris,* an ancient plant, and *Mesosaurus,* an ancient reptile. Explain how these fossils can be used as evidence for continental drift.

12. Describe the sequence of events that led scientists to finally accept the idea of continental drift.

13. Infer what would happen if Earth's convection currents in Earth's mantle slowed down.

14. Observe Look around your home and school. What are some safety measures you could take to protect yourself if an earthquake happens?

Draw Conclusions

15. You are a scientist monitoring a series of instruments near a particular location. Your tiltmeter tells you that the slope of the land is changing. The seismometer indicates that tremors are getting larger. What would you conclude from this information? Use a graphic organizer like the one below to answer the questions.

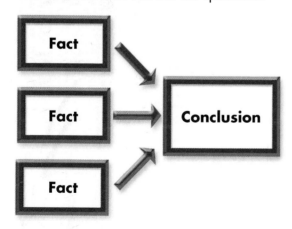

Test Prep

Choose the letter that best completes the statement or answers the question.

16. Which of Earth's layers contains convection currents that move the tectonic plates?
- Ⓐ upper mantle
- Ⓑ lower mantle
- Ⓒ outer core
- Ⓓ inner core

17. Which scientist proposed the idea of continental drift?
- Ⓕ Hess
- Ⓖ Holmes
- Ⓗ Matthews
- Ⓘ Wegener

18. Which of these is the best evidence of seafloor spreading?
- Ⓐ ocean ridges
- Ⓑ mid-ocean mountains
- Ⓒ volcanic islands
- Ⓓ ocean trenches

19. Explain why the answer you chose for Question 18 is best. For each of the answers you did not choose, give a reason why it is not the best choice.

20. Writing in Science **Expository** Explain what happens as Earth's plates move away from each other.

239

Biography

CAROL RAYMOND
Research Scientist

Dr. Carol Raymond is a research scientist working for NASA at its Jet Propulsion Laboratory. In 2003, Dr. Raymond led a team of scientists and researchers to find out if earthquakes can be predicted from space.

By using images from two satellites, scientists can study fault areas on Earth. They can detect tectonic plate movements as small as one millimeter per year. Dr. Raymond led development of a 20-year plan to place a system of satellites in space. These satellites will monitor fault zones and try to give warnings about places where earthquakes might be ready to occur.

Satellite image of Iran/Zagros Mountains, Canyon Fault

Dr. Raymond says that scientists eventually may be able to learn when stresses in the Earth's plates are at dangerous levels. She looks forward to a day when earthquake forecasters can give a monthly "hazard level" report, much like weather forecasters now predict approaching storms. This would give people and emergency services in the area time to prepare.

Dr. Raymond's research includes studying the movement of tectonic plates around the Earth and the history of ice sheets in Antarctica. She also studies the history of Mars and is currently the Project Scientist for the Dawn Discovery mission, which will study two large asteroids that were baby planets at the dawn of our solar system.

Lab zone Take-Home Activity

Make a poster warning people about an earthquake that is predicted for the coming months. In your poster, include instructions for how people can prepare and what they should do to keep themselves safe.

EC CRU 10 9 8 7 6 5 4 3 2 1

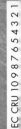

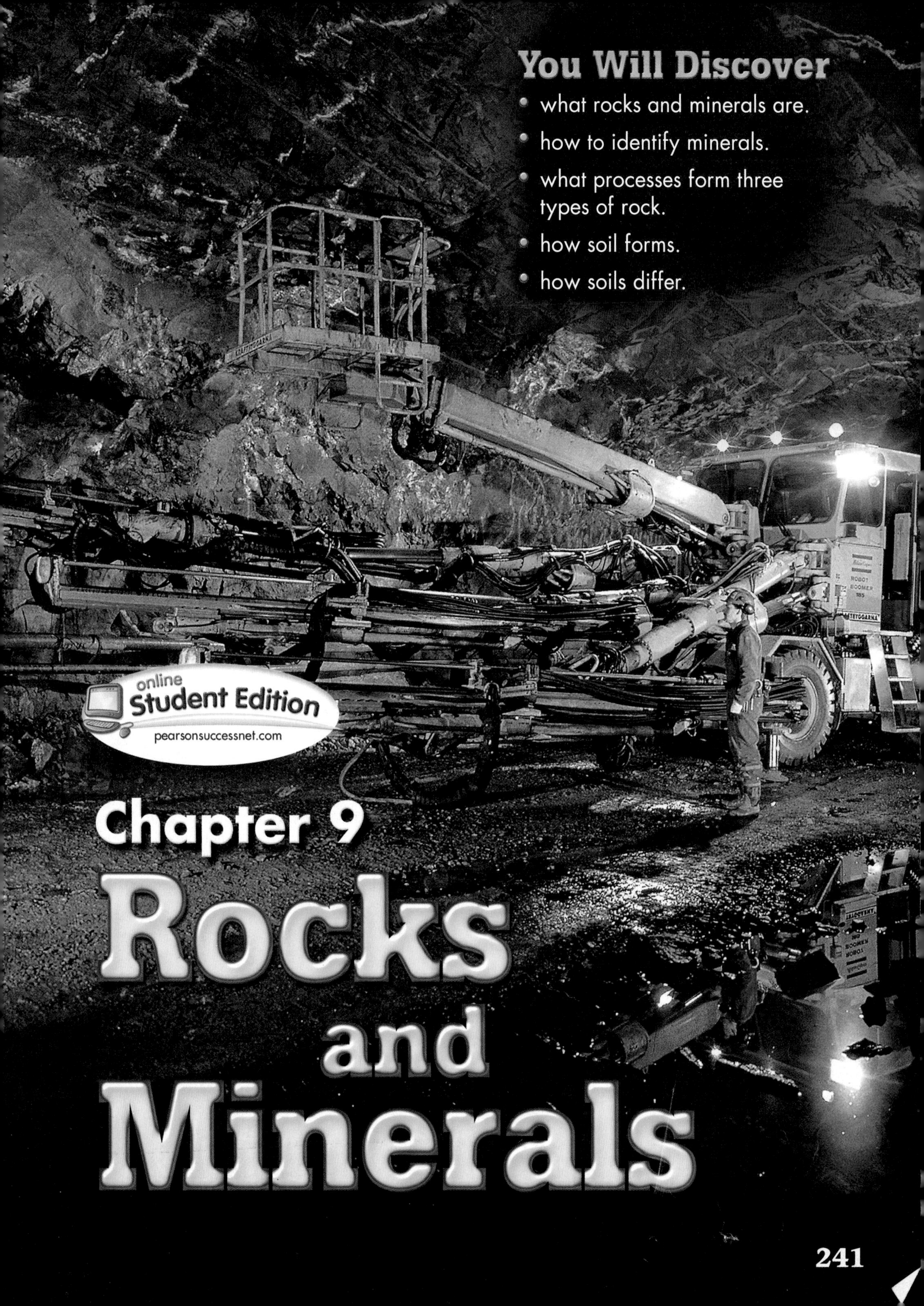

You Will Discover

- what rocks and minerals are.
- how to identify minerals.
- what processes form three types of rock.
- how soil forms.
- how soils differ.

online
Student Edition
pearsonsuccessnet.com

Chapter 9
Rocks
and
Minerals

How do rocks and minerals form soils?

sedimentary rock

organic matter

humus

Chapter 9 Vocabulary

igneous rock

crystal

mineral

metamorphic rock

Directed Inquiry

Explore What do mineral crystals look like?

Materials

mineral A

mineral B

2 toothpicks

microscope slide

microscope

What to Do

1 Use a toothpick to place a few crystals of mineral A on a microscope slide.

Wash your hands after handling the minerals.

2 Place the slide on the microscope stage and focus. Record your **observations** of the mineral in a chart. Include the mineral's color, a description, and a drawing.

3 Use a clean toothpick to replace mineral A with mineral B. Repeat step 2.

4 Compare your observations with the pictures. Identify the minerals you observed.

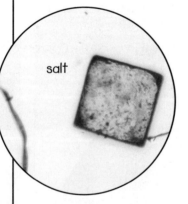

salt

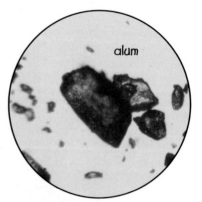

alum

Process Skills

Observing the physical characteristics of a mineral's crystals can help you identify the mineral.

Explain Your Results

1. Describe the crystals you **observed**.

2. Compare and contrast the crystals.

How to Read Science

TARGET SKILL

Compare and Contrast

Learning to find how things are alike and different can help you understand what you read. When you **compare** things, you tell how they are alike. When you **contrast** them, you tell how they are different.

- Sometimes writers use clue words such as *also, both,* and *like* to signal similarities.

- Clue words such as *although, but,* and *however* can signal differences.

- Remember to **observe** any pictures or diagrams that will help to compare and contrast things.

Some clue words are marked in the article below.

Science Article

Molten Rock

When molten rock cools and hardens, new rock forms. If the molten rock cools slowly, the new rock will have large crystals. However, if the molten rock cools quickly, there will not be time for large crystals to form. Granite and basalt are both formed from molten rock, although granite cooled slowly and basalt cooled quickly. Granite has large crystals, but basalt has small crystals.

Apply It!

Make a graphic organizer like the one shown. Use the graphic organizer to **compare** and **contrast** basalt and granite.

Granite   Alike   Basalt

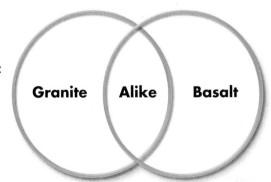

245

Gold! Dust and noise fill the cool Nevada air as gold mining trucks move tons of dirt. Searching for the precious metal is part of another day's work. Gold is too heavy to use for tools and too soft to be used for cutting. Yet no other mineral is as highly prized as gold. Its beauty has sparked wars, lured explorers to the New World, and made it a symbol of wealth. Exactly what is gold?

AudioText

What are rocks and minerals?

Each kind of mineral has its own unique chemical structure. Differences among minerals result from the way the particles of each mineral are arranged. Deep within Earth, newly formed rocks are exposed to heat and pressure. At Earth's surface, rocks are gradually broken down.

Pyrite

Beryl

Selenite

Minerals

Gold is only one of the many different minerals found on Earth. A **mineral** is a natural, nonliving solid with a definite chemical structure. To be a mineral, a substance must fit all parts of this definition. For example, coal is not a mineral because it is made from plants that lived long ago.

How many minerals can you name? You probably know more minerals than you think. For example, have you ever looked closely at grains of sand? If so, you were probably looking at a mineral called quartz. Earth's crust contains more than 4,000 kinds of minerals, yet only about two dozen are common. Other minerals you might be familiar with are diamond, quartz, emerald, copper, and ruby. Gemstones, such as emeralds and rubies, are minerals that are valued for their beauty and rarity.

Notice in the pictures that minerals have a geometric shape. The geometric shape is due to the way their particles are arranged. Minerals are made up of **crystals**. The particles of crystals are arranged in a particular, repeating pattern. This pattern is reflected in the shape of the crystal.

Crystals form when minerals are made in nature. Under perfect conditions, some crystals are large. But most crystals are so small that they cannot be seen without a microscope.

1. ✓**Checkpoint** Brass is made from zinc and copper, which are combined at high temperatures in furnaces. Is brass a mineral? Explain your answer.

2. **Math in Science** About what percentage of minerals are common?

Identifying Minerals

When you visit a zoo, you can identify many animals. You use characteristics such as size, color, and shape. Minerals also can be identified according to their characteristics, or properties. Scientists use hardness and other properties to identify minerals.

Talc, used in talcum powder, is a mineral. Talc is less hard than other minerals. Scientists use the Mohs hardness scale to tell the hardness of minerals. A mineral's hardness refers to how difficult it is to scratch its surface. A mineral can be scratched only by a harder mineral. The softest measure on the hardness scale is 1. The hardest is 10. Talc has a hardness of 1. Diamond is the hardest natural substance known. Its hardness is 10.

Mohs Hardness Scale

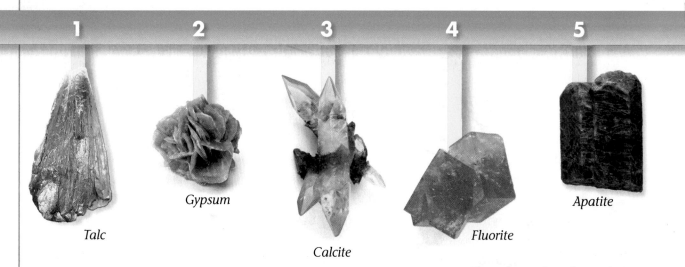

1   2   3   4   5

Talc   Gypsum   Calcite   Fluorite   Apatite

Other Properties of Minerals

A mineral may have different colors, depending on the kinds of materials in its crystals. For example, pure corundum is colorless. But when its crystals contain small amounts of chromium, it forms ruby, a red gemstone. A mineral's true color can be seen in its streak. The streak is the mark it makes when rubbed against an unglazed ceramic tile.

Just as a fingerprint can identify a crime suspect, the shape of its crystals can help identify a mineral. For example, fluorite crystals are shaped like cubes.

These four mineral samples may look different, but reddish-brown streaks show that all are the same.

Minerals also show particular patterns when they are broken. Many minerals tend to split, or cleave, along flat planes. This splitting is called cleavage. Other minerals do not split. Instead, they fracture, or break, into uneven pieces.

Luster is the appearance of a mineral in reflected light. A mineral may appear metallic or nonmetallic, greasy, glassy, or even waxy. Compare the luster of the quartz with that of corundum.

Some minerals have unusual properties. For example, fluorescent minerals show colors when viewed under ultraviolet (UV) light. A few minerals, such as magnetite, are magnetic.

Magnetite

Quartz

Topaz

Corundum

Diamond

Orthoclase

Several minerals are valuable because they are beautiful or have unique characteristics. Many of these minerals are also rare, which adds to their value. These minerals are often important natural resources. Since natural supplies are limited, scientists often seek ways to reuse minerals or replace them with less expensive materials. For example, aluminum and tin are two minerals that can be recycled. Scientists can make synthetic, or artificial, forms of gemstones such as diamonds, rubies, and emeralds.

1. ✓**Checkpoint** In the hardness scale, which minerals can be scratched by fluorite?

2. A streak plate is an unglazed ceramic tile. How can a streak plate help you identify a mineral?

3. **Social Studies in Science** Minerals are important natural resources. Find out where minerals are mined in the United States. Draw a map that shows these locations. Identify rare minerals.

Rocks

Most minerals are not found in pure form. Instead they are mixed together in rocks. A **rock** is a solid, natural material made up of one or more minerals. When studying rocks, scientists look at the rock's color and texture. Scientists can use a rock's characteristics to determine where and how it formed.

Rocks may not look very active, but they are always changing. As time passes, rocks break down, and the minerals in them are recycled. This pattern of change is called the rock cycle. The events of the rock cycle take place over millions of years. Study the diagram of the rock cycle to see how the three types of rock—metamorphic, igneous, and sedimentary—are formed.

Sedimentary rock is made from pieces of rocks and minerals. It forms in layers, with the oldest rock at the bottom. Because the layers are formed in sequence, sedimentary rock is like a "history book" with past events captured in each layer. Sometimes, the evidence of past events includes fossils, the remains of once-living animals or plants. Fossils are found only in sedimentary rock. An example of sedimentary rock is limestone. Limestone is made from the shells of tiny sea animals or from dissolved minerals that settle out of seawater.

Igneous rock forms when magma—the molten rock inside the Earth—cools and hardens. Some igneous rocks harden below Earth's surface and only appear after the rocks above them have worn away. Other igneous rocks form when lava cools at the Earth's surface. When lava cools quickly, fine-grained rock forms. Slowly cooling magma forms coarse-grained rock.

Metamorphic rock forms when heat, pressure, or chemical reactions change one type of rock into another type of rock. Metamorphic rock is made from sedimentary rock or igneous rock. For example, marble is a metamorphic rock that is formed from limestone, which is a sedimentary rock.

Sedimentary rock
The Vermilion Cliffs are multicolor sandstone formations in northern Arizona and southern Utah.

Rock Cycle

Sediments

Pressure

Erosion

Sedimentary rock

Heat and Pressure

Metamorphic rock

Igneous rock
Basalt is a fine-grained rock made from magma that cooled quickly when it reached the Earth's surface. The Devil's Postpile National Monument in California is named for its 18-meter-tall columns of basalt.

Igneous rock

Weathering and Erosion

Heat and Pressure

Cooling and Hardening

Melting

Magma

Melting

Metamorphic rock
Gneiss is formed from both igneous and sedimentary rock.

1. ✓ **Checkpoint**
   According to the picture, what causes igneous rock to change to magma?
2. ⟳ **Compare and Contrast** How are igneous rock, sedimentary rock, and metamorphic rock similar? How are they different?

The Grand Canyon

A desert was here long ago, and then a sandy beach. Deposits of sand and mud made the sandstones that are here today.

A layer of shale formed from silt deposited by a river.

A layer of sandstone formed when the area was a desert or a beach with deposits of mud and sand.

Layers of limestone and shale were formed when shallow seas covered the land more than 540 million years ago. Limestone layers contain fossils of marine organisms. The deepest limestone layers have the oldest fossils.

At the bottom of the canyon, granites and schists were deposited more than 2 billion years ago.

Clues to the Past

Did you know that every rock tells a story? Rocks have clues that tell us about past events. For example, a rock with tiny seashells reveals that the area where the rock formed was once an ancient sea. Large rocks may be evidence of a glacier, which left the rocks behind millions of years ago. By looking closely at rocks, scientists can learn a great deal about Earth's history.

Like detectives, scientists collect evidence, study it, and draw conclusions. A lot of evidence can be found in sedimentary rock. Because sedimentary rock forms in layers, scientists know that the oldest layers are at the bottom. Based on this fact, scientists can learn the relative age of each layer and the materials found in it. This method is called relative dating. Relative dating lets scientists place past events in sequential order. But it cannot reveal how long ago each event occurred.

Few places show Earth's story as dramatically as the Grand Canyon of Arizona. The canyon was formed five million years ago when the Colorado River cut through many layers of sedimentary rocks. Today visitors to the Grand Canyon can see more years of Earth's history than anywhere else on Earth. As you can see in the diagram, many layers of rock are exposed. Each layer has evidence of events that took place long ago.

Fossils

Fossils can form when an organism is buried in soft mud. Most fossils form from hard parts, such as bones, shells, or wood, that do not rot away. When fossils form underwater, minerals dissolved in the water may replace the animal's shell or skeleton and then harden. Burrows and footprints can also be fossilized.

Many fossils were made by species that are now extinct. Scientists have learned when many of these organisms lived. Finding these fossils in a rock can help scientists determine the rock's age. For example, trilobites were hard-shelled, ocean-dwelling animals. They were common about 500 million years ago. When scientists find a trilobite fossil, they know that the surrounding rock formed during this period.

Trilobites are extinct animals related to the ancestors of modern insects. Like insects, trilobites had three body segments and a hard outer skeleton.

Space Rocks

Some rocks are formed in outer space. When large rocks survive their trip through space and strike the Earth, they make a giant hole called a crater. Barringer Meteor Crater, a bowl-shaped pit found in the Arizona desert, is about 1.6 kilometers wide and about 180 meters deep. The crater formed when a meteorite hit the Earth 20,000 to 50,000 years ago.

A Petoskey stone is a fossil of marine animals known as corals. Petoskey stones are commonly found in Michigan's Lower Peninsula, which was covered with a shallow sea 350 million years ago.

✓ Lesson Checkpoint

1. Why do minerals have geometric shapes?
2. How can rocks help scientists learn about Earth's past?
3. **Compare and Contrast** How are gold, a mineral, and limestone, a sedimentary rock, alike and different? Use a graphic organizer to write your answer.

Why is soil important to living things?

Soil is made of weathered rock, air, water, and the remains of living organisms. Almost all land-dwelling organisms depend on soil for life. Plants obtain water and minerals from soil, and animals need plants for food. Insects and many other small animals live in soil. So do fungi and bacteria that are too small to see.

Forming Soil

The rock cycle isn't the only process that rocks are part of. They also are part of the process that forms soil. New soil begins when exposed rock begins to break down. This process, called weathering, can be due to physical factors, such as frost, drought, or changes in temperature. Rainwater and the substances dissolved in it also can break down rock. As weathering occurs, rock is broken down into smaller and smaller pieces. Air and water fill the spaces between the pieces of rock. The tiny particles of rock, along with the air and water, are the nonliving, or inorganic, part of soil.

2 As weathering continues, more soil forms. Larger plants appear. Dead plants and animals create humus, which provides nutrients for plants.

Young soil

Humus

1 As rock breaks down, small pieces collect at the surface. Mosses and lichens are the first plants to grow. They break down more rock, helping to release minerals. Soil begins to form.

Weathered rock

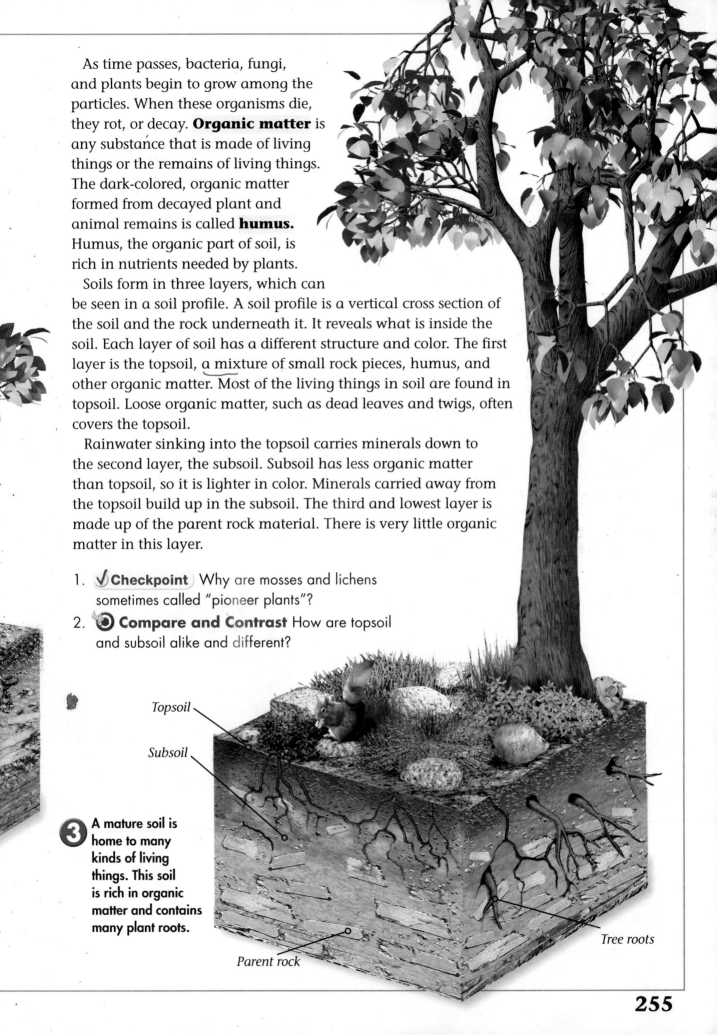

As time passes, bacteria, fungi, and plants begin to grow among the particles. When these organisms die, they rot, or decay. **Organic matter** is any substance that is made of living things or the remains of living things. The dark-colored, organic matter formed from decayed plant and animal remains is called **humus.** Humus, the organic part of soil, is rich in nutrients needed by plants.

Soils form in three layers, which can be seen in a soil profile. A soil profile is a vertical cross section of the soil and the rock underneath it. It reveals what is inside the soil. Each layer of soil has a different structure and color. The first layer is the topsoil, a mixture of small rock pieces, humus, and other organic matter. Most of the living things in soil are found in topsoil. Loose organic matter, such as dead leaves and twigs, often covers the topsoil.

Rainwater sinking into the topsoil carries minerals down to the second layer, the subsoil. Subsoil has less organic matter than topsoil, so it is lighter in color. Minerals carried away from the topsoil build up in the subsoil. The third and lowest layer is made up of the parent rock material. There is very little organic matter in this layer.

1. ✔Checkpoint Why are mosses and lichens sometimes called "pioneer plants"?

2. ⊙ **Compare and Contrast** How are topsoil and subsoil alike and different?

Topsoil

Subsoil

❸ A mature soil is home to many kinds of living things. This soil is rich in organic matter and contains many plant roots.

Tree roots

Parent rock

Kinds of Soils

Most of us think of soil as dark brown and crumbly, but there are many kinds of soils. Clay soils are fine grained and hold water extremely well. When rainfall is plentiful, clay soils can become waterlogged. Silt soils have medium-sized grains. Sandy soils are large grained and hold water poorly. Most soils are a mixture of clay, silt, and sand. Loam is a type of soil that contains silt and sand in roughly equal amounts.

Factors That Affect Soil

The climate of an area may be the most important factor that determines the type of soil that forms. The weathering that breaks down rock to form soil takes place more quickly in climates with a lot of rainfall and warm temperatures.

In tropical climates, the plentiful rainfall washes minerals out of the topsoil into the subsoil. The result is that tropical topsoil is very thin and not very fertile. In contrast, desert areas receive very little rain, so weathering is slow. The little rain that does fall evaporates quickly. Minerals that were dissolved in the water collect on the soil surface.

The type of soil that forms also depends on the kind of rock from which it forms. The kinds of minerals in the rock affect the characteristics of the soil. For example, reddish soils come from rock with iron-rich minerals. The minerals also can affect the weathering process.

Light-colored sandy soils have little organic matter. They are large grained and drain quickly.

Earthworms help soil formation by mixing the soil and breaking down organic matter.

Peat is partly decayed plant material that has been buried and compressed in a swamp. When dried, peat can be burned as fuel.

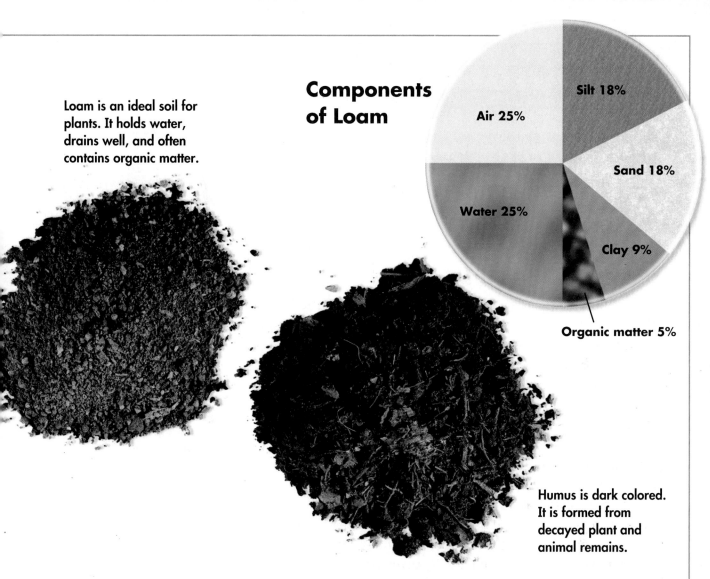

Loam is an ideal soil for plants. It holds water, drains well, and often contains organic matter.

Components of Loam

Silt 18%

Air 25%

Sand 18%

Water 25%

Clay 9%

Organic matter 5%

Humus is dark colored. It is formed from decayed plant and animal remains.

Soil color also is affected by the amount of organic matter in it. Soils with more organic matter are darker in color. Forest soils from the eastern United States have a lot of humus and are dark brown. The many leaves that fall from the forest trees every autumn help form the humus. The decaying leaves and plentiful rainfall form a thick, fertile soil. Tropical soils, which have little humus, are lighter in color.

Another factor that affects soil formation is the shape of the land. Mountains usually have thin layers of topsoil because much of the soil is eroded from their slopes. Land that is flat usually has a thick layer of topsoil.

✓ Lesson Checkpoint

1. How are humus and organic matter related?
2. **Compare and Contrast** How do clay soils differ from sandy soils?
3. **Writing in Science** **Persuasive** Write an advertisement for an ideal soil for growing plants.

Investigate How can you make a geologic time line?

A geologic time line is one way to show the events in Earth's history.

Materials

adding machine tape

meterstick

calculator (optional)

scissors

What to Do

1 To begin your **model** time line, complete the table below. Figure out the amount of time each distance represents. The scale for your time line is 1 millimeter = 1 million years.

Line Length	Time Interval (years)
1 mm	1 million years
5 mm	
10 mm (1 cm)	
100 mm (10 cm)	
1000 mm (1 meter)	

2 Look at the chart on p. 259 called Events in Earth's History. Calculate the distance each event should be from the end of the time line.

200 million
Dinosaurs become
dominant land animals

160 million
First birds

Process Skills

Making a model of a geologic time scale can help you form a mental image of amount of time involved.

3 Determine how much tape is needed to make a time line beginning when Earth forms to the present. **Measure** and cut this length of tape.

Events in Earth's History		
Event	**Years Ago**	**Distance from Right End of Time Line**
Current water level in Great Lakes	7,000	
Humans use fire as tool	110,000	
Ice Ages begin	1 million	
Earliest humans	2 million	
Rocky Mountains begin to form	40 million	40 mm
Dinosaurs become extinct	65 million	65 mm
First birds	160 million	160 mm
Dinosaurs become dominant land animals	200 million	200 mm
Pangaea begins to break up	245 million	
Appalachian Mountains formed	290 million	
First vertebrate animals	500 million	
Oxygen-rich atmosphere	2.5 billion	
Primitive life forms	3.5 billion	
Oldest rocks on Earth form	3.9 billion	
Earth forms	4.6 billion	

4 Place marks at equal lengths along the tape to show equal lengths of time.

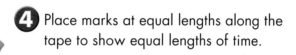

65 million
Dinosaurs become extinct

40 million
Rocky Mountains begin to form

5 Plot the events on your time line. Label each event you plot.

Explain Your Results

1. How are years represented in your **model**?

2. How useful was the scale you used? Could you clearly represent all the events?

Go Further

How would your model change if the scale you used was 1 cm = 1 million years? Find out.

Math in Science

FRACTIONAL PARTS of SOIL

Soil, which we often refer to as dirt, is one of our most important resources. Plants, which provide food, oxygen, and many other things for us, require soil for nutrients. Without soil, life on Earth would be impossible, yet soil is made up of common materials. The circle graph on this page represents the components of a typical sample of soil. Humus is the part of the soil that comes from decayed plant and animal remains.

SOIL COMPONENTS

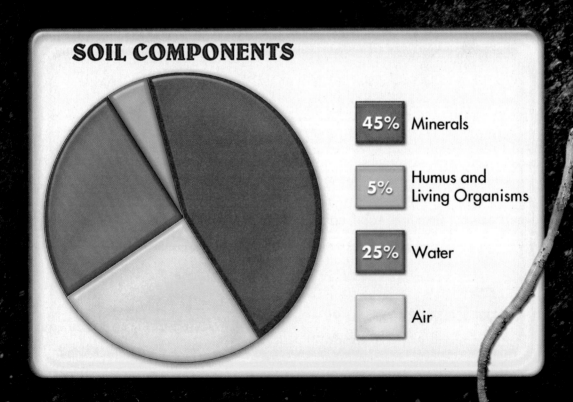

45% Minerals

5% Humus and Living Organisms

25% Water

Air

Tools Take It to the Net
pearsonsuccessnet.com

Use the circle graph to answer these questions.

1. It may surprise you that air is a major component of soil. What percent of the soil sample shown in the graph is air? What percent is not air?

2. What fraction of this soil is made up of air and water together? of minerals and water?

3. A square raised garden measures 2 m on each side and is 15 cm deep. About what volume of minerals would be in the soil needed to fill the raised bed if the soil matches the sample used in the circle graph? What volume of humus and living organisms would be in it?

4. It is estimated that more than 22 trillion, 727 billion kg of soil is lost per year, worldwide, due to erosion. Write this number in standard form and in scientific notation.

5. Minerals in the soil are sometimes classified by size. Silt particles are between 4×10^{-3} mm and 6×10^{-2} mm in diameter. Would a clay particle that is 0.003 mm in diameter be larger or smaller than a silt particle? Explain.

Lab zone Take-Home Activity

Find a potted plant or an empty pot. Estimate the volume of soil the pot would hold. Remember to include units. Potting soil is sometimes sold in cubic yards. Find out how many pots of this size you could fill with 1 cubic yard of potting soil.

Use Vocabulary

crystal (p. 247)	**mineral** (p. 247)
humus (p. 255)	**organic matter** (p. 255)
igneous rock (p. 250)	**rock** (p. 250)
metamorphic rock (p.250)	**sedimentary rock** (p. 250)

Write the term from the list above that best matches each phrase.

1. Any substance that is made of living things or the remains of living things

2. A nonliving, naturally occurring solid with a definite chemical structure

3. Rock that is made from pieces of rocks and minerals

4. Formed from one or more minerals combined

5. Rock that forms from molten rock that has cooled and hardened

6. The dark-colored matter formed from decayed plant and animal remains

7. A naturally formed solid with a definite internal pattern

8. Rock that forms when one type of rock changes into another type of rock

Explain Concepts

9. Describe four characteristics that can be used to identify minerals.

10. Describe the three layers found in a soil.

11. Use the information in the table to identify the mineral shown in the picture below.

	Hematite	Feldspar	Topaz
Hardness	6.5	6.0–6.5	8
Cleavage	none	breaks along two surfaces	breaks along all sides
Fracture	curved	uneven	brittle, uneven
Streak	brownish-red	white	white
Appearance	dull brown, brownish red, red, grey, or black	many colors	gold-yellow, green, or cream

12. Industrial diamonds are found in drills, rock-cutting saws, and metal-cutting tools. Explain why diamonds are used to make these items.

13. Predict Mosses and lichens begin growing on bare ground in pieces of weathered rock. Predict what will happen next and explain why.

14. Model Sedimentary rock forms in layers. Make a model to show why this is so.

🎯 Compare and Contrast

15. Make a graphic organizer like the one shown below. Fill in the correct information to show how sandy soils and clay soils are alike and different.

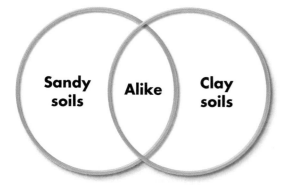

Sandy soils — Alike — Clay soils

 Test Prep

Choose the letter that best completes the statement or answers the question.

16. Marble is formed from limestone that is heated under pressure deep within the Earth. What kind of rock is marble?
Ⓐ metamorphic
Ⓑ sedimentary
Ⓒ volcanic
Ⓓ igneous

17. Which soil layer is least similar to the underlying rock?
Ⓕ subsoil
Ⓖ topsoil
Ⓗ humus
Ⓘ parent rock

18. In the Grand Canyon, the oldest fossils are found
Ⓐ on the surface of the ground.
Ⓑ in the uppermost layer of rock.
Ⓒ in the middle layers of rock.
Ⓓ in the lowest layers of rock.

19. Explain why the answer you chose for Question 16 is best. For each of the answers you did not choose, give a reason why it is not the best choice.

20. Writing in Science **Descriptive** Suppose that you have been given a sample of an unknown mineral. Write a paragraph describing the steps you would take to identify the mineral.

MICHAEL NOVACEK

Imagine getting dragged over the rocky ground by a spooked horse—or escaping from a cave full of poisonous snakes! It sounds like an episode from a TV reality show. But these are just some of the many adventures of paleontologist Michael Novacek.

Novacek grew up in suburban Los Angeles. As a kid, he liked to turn over rocks to see what critters might be hiding underneath. Today as a world-famous scientist, Novacek is still unlocking secrets hidden beneath rocks—and within them.

Novacek is a paleontologist—a fossil expert. He studies the fossils of dinosaurs and early mammals and the rocks in which the fossils form. Then he can figure out when the animals lived, how they lived, and how they changed through time. Novacek does more than study fossils—he finds them and digs them up. His fossil-hunting expeditions take him all over the world. The expeditions are thrilling, but they can be dangerous too. Besides the bites and stings of animals, Novacek puts up with searing heat and the injuries that come from hiking over rugged landscape.

For Michael Novacek the risks are well worth it. He has found thousands of fossils. In fact, in Mongolia, north of China, he discovered the world's richest site of fossils from the Cretaceous period (65 to 140 million years ago). Novacek's career has been one big adventure, and there's no end in sight.

Lab zone Take-Home Activity

Michael Novacek is a curator of paleontology at the American Museum of Natural History in New York City. Visit the museum online, either at home or at the library. Explore the museum's exhibits. Then make a poster that highlights one or more exhibits.

264

Chapter 10
Reshaping Earth's Surface

You Will Discover

- how Earth's surface is changed by mechanical weathering and chemical weathering.
- how Earth's surface has changed throughout Earth's history.
- how river systems form and change.
- how waves and wind erosion change coastlines.

What processes change Earth's landforms?

erosion

weathering

chemical weathering

mechanical weathering

Chapter 10 Vocabulary

sediment

deposition

Explore How can you make a topographic map?

The probes *must* stand straight.

Materials

safety goggles

modeling clay

ruler

plastic Petri dish bottom

2 probes

dental floss

posterboard
(or cardboard)

What to Do

1 Use clay to make a **model** of a cone-shaped mountain 8 cm tall and place it in a Petri dish.

2 Push two probes straight down into the mountain.

3 Remove the probes. Use dental floss to slice the bottom from your mountain. Use the dish as a guide.

4 Place the slice on posterboard and trace around it. Mark the location of the holes by pushing a pin through each hole into the posterboard.

Mark the locations of the holes with a pen.

Make sure to line up the holes before you trace around each slice.

5 Repeat steps 3 and 4 until the entire mountain has been sliced.

Explain Your Results

1. What is the difference in height between one slice and the next in your **model** of a mountain? Explain.

2. **Infer** What does the space between each line on your map represent?

Process Skills

You can **infer** the steepness of an area by the spacing of lines on a topographic map.

How to Read Science

Draw Conclusions

A good reader puts together facts he or she reads and then infers a new idea, or a **conclusion.** Sometimes a reader may have more than one conclusion. Some facts are highlighted in the paragraph below.

- Try to make a logical conclusion from the facts you read.

- Use your own knowledge and experience to help you draw conclusions.

- Check to make sure that your conclusions are supported by the facts.

Science Article

Topographic Maps

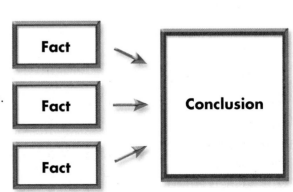

If you want to find out what kinds of landforms are in a particular area, use a map. You can find some landforms, such as a mountain, on a road map. But a road map might show where a mountain is located only with an *X*. A topographic map also shows where the mountain is. In addition, it shows the mountain's shape and height. If you planned to go hiking, which kind of map would you use to find the quickest way through unfamiliar land?

Apply It!

Make a graphic organizer similar to this one. List the facts from the science article. Then write a **conclusion.**

```
┌────────┐
│  Fact  │ ──→
└────────┘        ┌──────────────┐
┌────────┐        │              │
│  Fact  │ ──→    │  Conclusion  │
└────────┘        │              │
┌────────┐        └──────────────┘
│  Fact  │ ──→
└────────┘
```

You Are There!

Shhhh! Listen. There is little sound anywhere. An occasional insect buzzes by your ears. In the distance, you can hear a bird singing. Now and then you hear a splash—a fish leaps into the air from the lake waters. The quiet peacefulness is amazing. But things weren't always this quiet here. Both the lake and the mountains came about through a violent start. But since they formed, quieter, slower processes have been changing their features. What are those processes?

AudioText

How does Earth's surface change?

Badlands National Park

Earth's surface is made up of many different features called landforms. As Earth's surface changes constantly, these landforms are shaped both suddenly and slowly.

Earth's Features

Do you see the river here in Badlands National Park? No? That's because it's far below the tops of the canyons. These canyons began with the flow of water over flat land. The water carved the landscape over a very long period. Over the years, the moving water dug deeper and deeper into Earth's surface to form the deep canyons we see today.

Even frozen waters can carve into Earth's surface. Many North American lakes, including the Great Lakes between the United States and Canada, were carved out by glaciers on the move. Glaciers are huge masses of slowly moving ice. As glaciers moved, they carried along huge amounts of rock and soil that dug out the lakes' bottoms.

Other landforms on Earth have also been shaped by both gradual and dramatic events. Rivers shift as they carry and deposit **sediments,** solid particles that are moved from one place to another. Although they are flat, plateaus share with mountains their high elevation compared to the land around them. Plains are also flat but support grasslands. The Great Plains of North America is actually a huge, high plateau.

1. **✓Checkpoint** Describe three ways that landforms were created on Earth's surface.
2. **Social Studies** in Science Find out what major landforms can be found in your state. Draw a map that shows the location of each. If possible, include a picture of each.

Weathering and Erosion

If you could go back and visit a particular place in your neighborhood 10 years ago, you might notice some changes. Few of those changes would be to its landforms. But if you could go back thousands of years, you'd probably be surprised how different the landforms were.

Many changes on Earth's surface can be seen only over thousands of years or more. These changes often are caused by the weathering and erosion of Earth's surface.

Weathering is the process of breaking down rock into smaller pieces. Some weathering takes place when forces such as water and ice break down rock. This process is called **mechanical weathering.** During mechanical weathering, the minerals that make up the rock do not change.

Most rocks have small cracks in their surfaces. These cracks may be smaller than the width of a hair, but it is in these cracks that mechanical weathering begins. Water can seep into these cracks and freeze. The freezing water expands and pushes against the sides of the crack, making it larger. When the ice melts, water moves back into the cracks again. The rock freezes and thaws over and over again, making the cracks larger each time.

Sometimes soil forms in the cracks of the rock. Plants begin to grow, and their roots push the crack open even farther. Some types of plants can produce chemicals that eat into rocks to cause cracks and holes.

During **chemical weathering,** the actual minerals that make up rock change. The change can be caused when the minerals react with other substances in the environment, such as water or oxygen, to change the mineral content of rocks.

Weathering and erosion shaped this rock.

1930
Little rain falls in the southern plains, but crops flourish.

1934
Fewer dust storms, but they spread as far as New York. About 35 million acres of farmland have been destroyed.

1935
Many cattle are destroyed because crops cannot be grown to feed them. About 850,000,000 tons of topsoil blow from the southern plains. The Soil Conservation Service is established to develop conservation programs.

Dust Bowl

1931
Severe drought hits the midwest and southern plains. Dust begins to blow.

1932
Fourteen dust storms hit the area.

1933
Thirty-eight dust storms occur.

1936
The number of dust storms increases.

1938
Conservation methods, including replowing farmland into furrows and planting trees, result in 65 percent less soil blowing.

1939
Rains arrive, bringing an end to the drought.

What happens to the pieces of rock when weathering breaks them apart? **Erosion** is the process by which soil and sediments are transferred from one location to another—usually by wind, water, ice, and gravity. Erosion can carry eroded materials for hundreds of kilometers.

Weathering and erosion continuously change Earth's surface. Over time, these processes can flatten mountains or dig deep canyons in layers of rock.

Soil Erosion

Erosion can have more immediate effects too. When areas of soil are not covered by plants, the soil can be eroded easily. The roots of plants help prevent soil erosion. That's one reason farmers plant cover crops—crops planted between harvests to reduce erosion. The cover crops also add nutrients to the soil.

When soil erodes, a chain of destructive events might occur. One example is what happened in the southern plains of the United States in the 1930s. Years of drought and poor farming practices left many areas of soil bare. The area became known as the Dust Bowl because of the severe dust storms that blew for eight years. The blown dust was so heavy that children wore dust masks to school. In some places the dust was so thick that people couldn't see even during the day. Dust piled up like snow drifts.

The drought affected not only the land. People had health problems. Some died. Dust damaged cars and farm equipment. Farmers lost their land. Millions of people were left without jobs. Along with the bad came the good. Farmers learned better farming methods and an era of soil conservation began. People learned to take care of the land.

✓ Lesson Checkpoint

1. Water can seep into rocks and dissolve minerals. The dissolved minerals can be washed away. What type of weathering is this? Explain your answer.
2. The Mississippi River carries sediments from Minnesota to the Gulf of Mexico. What is the name of this process?
3. **Draw Conclusions** Over the next 100 years, are Earth's landscapes likely to remain the same? Why or why not? How about over the next 10 years?

How does water affect Earth's features?

Through erosion, water changes the shape and design of Earth's surface. As it flows downhill in complicated, ever-changing systems of streams and rivers, water carries and deposits many tiny pieces of rock and soil.

Deposition

Did you ever get hit by a huge splash of water? If you did, you know that water can hit with quite a force. All moving water has energy, and water running downhill is the main process that shapes Earth's surface. During mechanical weathering, the high energy of running water can break down rock and soil into bits of sediments. Water can also chemically weather rock when it dissolves minerals and other materials in the rock. This process changes the mineral make-up of rock.

The sediments that form during weathering are eroded and deposited at another location. This process of adding sediments to a new place after being carried from another is called **deposition.** In the process of deposition, the shape and direction of a river's flow changes. You can see some effects of erosion and deposition in the picture.

Minerals in Lakes and Oceans

As rivers flow to the ocean, they carry along sediments and dissolved minerals. Ocean plants and animals use some of these dissolved minerals to carry on life processes. Other dissolved minerals settle out of the water and form mineral deposits in lakes, along the coast, and on the ocean floor.

One mineral carried by water is salt. Rivers carry an estimated four billion tons of dissolved salts to the oceans each year. As ocean water evaporates, it leaves behind dissolved salts and other minerals. As a result of this process over thousands of years, the amount of salt in the ocean has increased.

Flowing water picks up sediment as it travels across land.

Falling water can cause mechanical and chemical weathering.

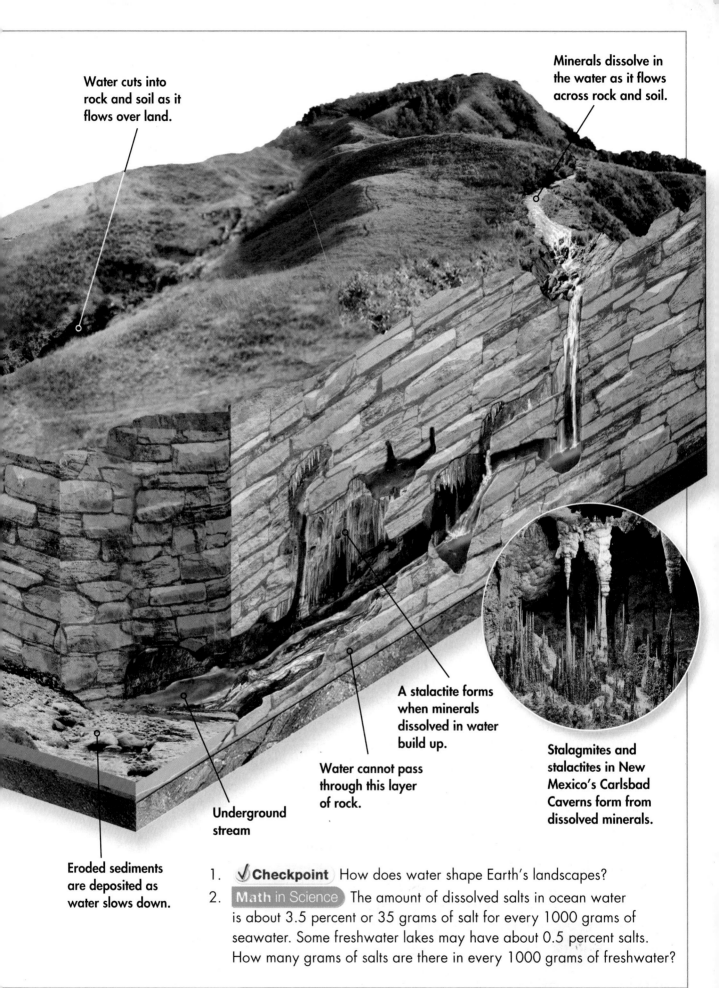

Water cuts into rock and soil as it flows over land.

Minerals dissolve in the water as it flows across rock and soil.

A stalactite forms when minerals dissolved in water build up.

Water cannot pass through this layer of rock.

Underground stream

Stalagmites and stalactites in New Mexico's Carlsbad Caverns form from dissolved minerals.

Eroded sediments are deposited as water slows down.

1. ✔ **Checkpoint** How does water shape Earth's landscapes?

2. **Math** in Science The amount of dissolved salts in ocean water is about 3.5 percent or 35 grams of salt for every 1000 grams of seawater. Some freshwater lakes may have about 0.5 percent salts. How many grams of salts are there in every 1000 grams of freshwater?

275

River Systems

You might picture a river as a flat, quiet body of water, but it can change quite a lot over time. Rivers and streams are dynamic systems, which means they are always changing.

A stream begins on land that is higher than sea level. Its water flows because gravity pulls the water downward to a lower area. As a stream flows, other streams may join it, until a river forms. The flowing river water wears down soil and rock and carries the sediments away.

The sediments a river carries can be deposited in different places. That's because as water slows down, it has less energy and can carry less sediment. Heavier sediments are deposited first. Finer, lighter ones can be carried for hundreds of kilometers. Waters often slow down at the low areas at the mouth of the river. There fine sediments are deposited in areas called river deltas.

This fan-shaped deposit of sediments in Death Valley, California, marks the end of the road for sediment carried from far upriver.

Bends in rivers can become more dramatic as sediments are deposited. Sometimes deposition can cut the bends off from the rest of the river, forming lakes.

Floodplains

When rivers and streams flood their banks, their water often slows down and sediments are deposited. Flooding can move huge amounts of sediments to places that would otherwise never receive them. A floodplain is that part of the landscape that is likely to receive the overflow water and sediment from a flooded river.

In some places farmers depend on flooding. That's because the sediments add to the soil important nutrients for growing crops. Often, however, floods are very destructive. Those living in the floodplain can lose homes, villages, or even their lives.

The Nile has flooded local homes here in the Sudan.

The Mississippi River

Fan-shaped deposits can be especially obvious where mountains drop rapidly to the water below that receives the river's sediments.

Beginning as a stream flowing out of Lake Itasca, Minnesota, the Mississippi River becomes one of the largest river systems in the world. Water from 31 states drains into the Mississippi before it reaches the Gulf of Mexico. The land drained by a river is called its drainage basin. How many of these facts about the Mississippi River did you know?

- The river's length is 3,705 kilometers.

- The area of its drainage basin is 3.2 million square kilometers.

- Each second 600,000 cubic feet of its water empties into the Gulf of Mexico.

- The river provides habitats for 241 fish species, 38 species of mussels, 45 amphibian species, and 50 species of mammals. It also serves 40 percent of the nation's migratory birds.

✓ Lesson Checkpoint

1. What is the source of much of the salt in ocean water?
2. Why do sediments settle out of flowing water as it slows down?
3. **Writing in Science** **Narrative** Describe a journey from the point of view of one grain of sand. Start your trip as the sand grain is first worn away from a mountaintop rock. Describe events as the grain is carried a long distance and deposited in a river delta.

How do waves affect coastal landforms?

The well-known surfing waves in Hawaii define the adjective *tubular*. As the very powerful waves begin to break, they fold over and stretch along the length of the waves, forming a tube in which surfers can ride along with the wave.

Wind Waves
The circular movement of water gets smaller as you go deeper into the water. Wave energy is strongest at the water's surface.

High-energy ocean waves cause erosion along coasts. Waves wear down coastal landforms and build up new ones. Because of waves and wind, coastal landforms are always changing.

Wave Energy

Can you imagine being hit by the huge wave in the picture? Like any wave, this one carries energy. In fact, ocean waves carry and pass along a great deal of energy.

If you have ever watched ocean waves, you probably thought that the water moves forward with the waves. But only energy moves. The water stays in the same spot, rising and falling in a circular motion. As a wave approaches, the water moves slightly forward and then downward and back in a circular loop. Each time a wave passes, the water ends up just about where it started.

As waves move toward shore, the shallower ocean bottom interferes with the waves' movements. The ocean floor can cause the bottom of waves to slow down. The tops of the waves continue to move quickly, so the tops tumble forward. Eventually the waves tumble toward shore to form a breaker.

Causes of Waves

The familiar waves we spot at the beach are often caused by wind. These waves form in the open ocean. As winds touch ocean water, energy transfers from the wind to the water, forming waves. The size of waves depends on the speed of the wind, how long it blows, and on how much of the sea it blows over.

Waves are also formed through tectonic activity. Volcanic eruptions, earthquakes, and landslides take place underwater or along coasts. These events can form tsunamis, waves that travel at incredible speeds and reach great heights before they crash into the shore.

Tsunamis can cause tremendous damage and loss of life. On December 26, 2004, a powerful earthquake erupted in the Indian Ocean near Sumatra, Indonesia. It caused deadly tsunamis to crash the shore of several countries. More than 100,000 people were killed.

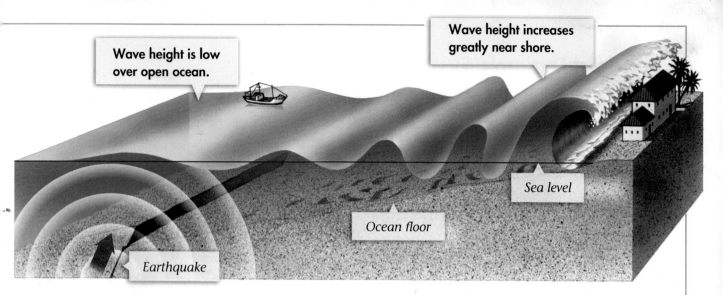

Wave height is low over open ocean.

Wave height increases greatly near shore.

Sea level

Ocean floor

Earthquake

Tsunami
Compare the tsunami with wind waves on page 278.

Wave Characteristics

Scientists use certain characteristics to describe all waves, including water waves. The highest part of a wave is the crest. The lowest part is the trough. The heavy dotted line shows the water's position before a wave passes through it. If you measure from that line to the crest or the trough, you know a wave's amplitude.

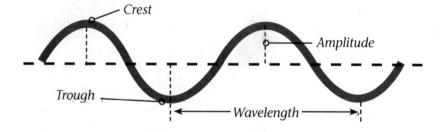

Crest

Amplitude

Trough

Wavelength

On a calm day, the amplitude of ocean waves is small. But when strong winds blow, the waves pick up energy, and the amplitude greatly increases.

Wavelength is the distance from one crest to the next or from one trough to the next. The wavelength of small ripples of water may only be a few millimeters. Those of huge waves may be several meters.

1. ✔**Checkpoint** Identify and define four wave characteristics.
2. ☉ **Draw Conclusions** Why do you think tsunamis are so destructive?

Beaches: Dynamic Systems

With all the energy carried by waves, it's not so surprising that they can dramatically change an ocean beach. The great amounts of energy in large waves can cause cracks in even huge rocks. Over time, the cracks can become larger, until finally pieces of rock break off.

Waves also carry sediments, such as stones and sand, that can wear down coastal landforms. When these sediments hit coastal features, they act like sandpaper to wear away rock.

Waves also build up beaches by moving sand along the shore. The way the sand moves depends on the angle at which waves strike the shore. When waves move at an angle toward the shoreline, they push water along the shoreline. The movement of water, called a longshore current, can move materials from the shoreline to an area in the water away from the shore. One landform created this way is a sandbar, which you can see in the picture below. Sandbars are ridges of sand, shells, and stones. The tops of the sandbars can be above or below water.

The steep, rocky towers of Australia's "Twelve Apostles" show the work of the ocean's energy over a very long period.

This sandbar formed when waves carried sand.

Lagoons are quiet places where sand, rock, or islands separate the water body from the open ocean. Water moves between lagoon and ocean through one or a few narrow passes. Waves and currents build the barriers that form a lagoon.

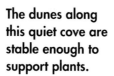

The dunes along this quiet cove are stable enough to support plants.

Wind, too, can change landforms along a coast. On rocky shores, wind can shape cliffs and large rocks into amazing shapes. Along quieter, sandy coastlines, wind can blow loose sand into piles, called dunes, along the edge of a beach. Beach dunes are usually small but can be very large.

Coastal landforms are constantly changing as water and wind act on them. Not all beaches are the same. The color and texture of any beach are determined by the sources of its sand and rock. White sand comes from a very different kind of rock than does the black sand of Hawaii's famous volcanic rock beaches. Even major structures that make up a beach, such as rocky cliffs or flat patches of sand, are very different from one beach to another.

✓ Lesson Checkpoint

1. What are two examples of mechanical weathering along an ocean beach?
2. What agent of erosion builds sand dunes?
3. **Draw Conclusions** Why is a beach more likely to change rapidly if it is placed along a river mouth where there are many winter storms than if it is found along a quiet stretch where there are no rivers and few storms?

Investigate How can you grow a stalactite?

Water can carry dissolved minerals from place to place. In some caves when mineral-rich water drips from the ceiling, a small amount of minerals can be left behind. Over a long time, icicle-shaped deposits called stalactites can be formed.

Materials

2 large cups

Epsom salt

tub and very warm water

spoon, tape,
2 large paper clips

small pan and cloth strip

Process Skills

Making and using a model can help you understand how stalactites form.

What to Do

1 Add enough very warm water to fill each cup $\frac{3}{4}$ full.

2 Add 18 level spoonfuls of Epsom salt to each cup. Stir well.

3 Put the cups in the corners of the tub as shown. Tape each cup to the sides of the tub. Place your **model** where it will be out of the way.

4 Attach the paper clips to the ends of the cloth. Hang the cloth between the two containers. Place the pan under the cloth.

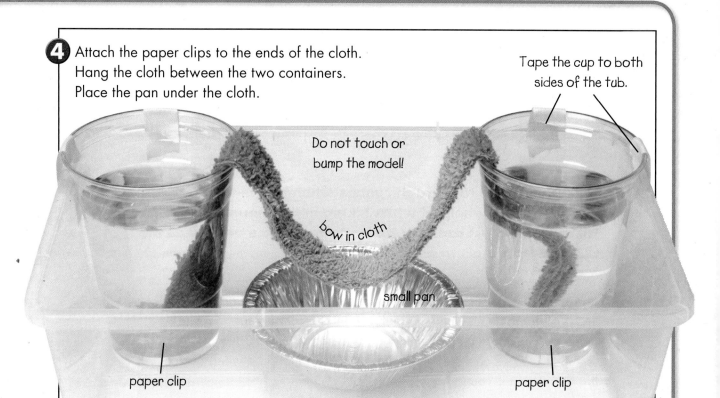

Tape the cup to both sides of the tub.

Do not touch or bump the model!

bow in cloth

small pan

paper clip

paper clip

tub

5 Record your **observations** of the cloth strip every day for 8 days.

Stalactite Formation

Day	Length (mm)	Description (shape, color)
1		
2		
3		
4		
5		

Explain Your Results

1. How does the Day 8 length of your stalactite compare with those of others in your class?

2. What part of your **model** represents mineral-rich water dripping in a cave? Explain.

Go Further

What other materials could you use to make stalactites? Make and carry out a plan to find out.

Math in Science

Topographic Maps

Hikers often use topographic maps when planning hikes. This is especially helpful when hiking in the mountains. Hikers there must consider the vertical distance as well as the distance from start to finish.

A topographic map shows the elevation of the land (how high it is above sea level) using contour lines. Every point along a contour line is at the same elevation. The elevation of each contour line is marked somewhere on the line. The difference in elevation from one line to the next is called the contour interval. The land between contour lines slopes up if you move toward another line with a higher elevation or down if you move toward a line of lower elevation.

Shown here is a drawing and a topographic map of the same mountain. The lowest contour line on this map is at an elevation of 540 meters. Locate it on the map. Every fifth contour line is drawn darker to make it easier to read the map. Point A on the map is near, but still below, the summit of the mountain. Points B, C, and D are starting points for three different hiking trails.

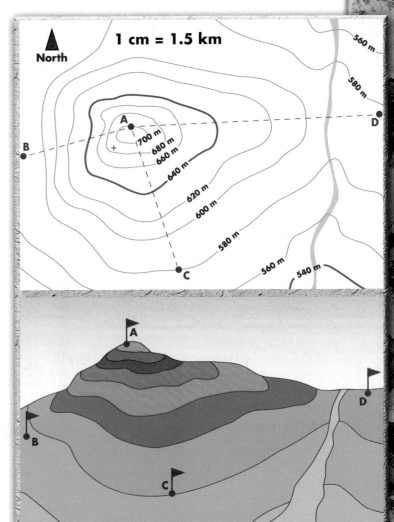

1 cm = 1.5 km

North

560 m
580 m
700 m
680 m
660 m
640 m
620 m
600 m
580 m
560 m
540 m

A
B
C
D

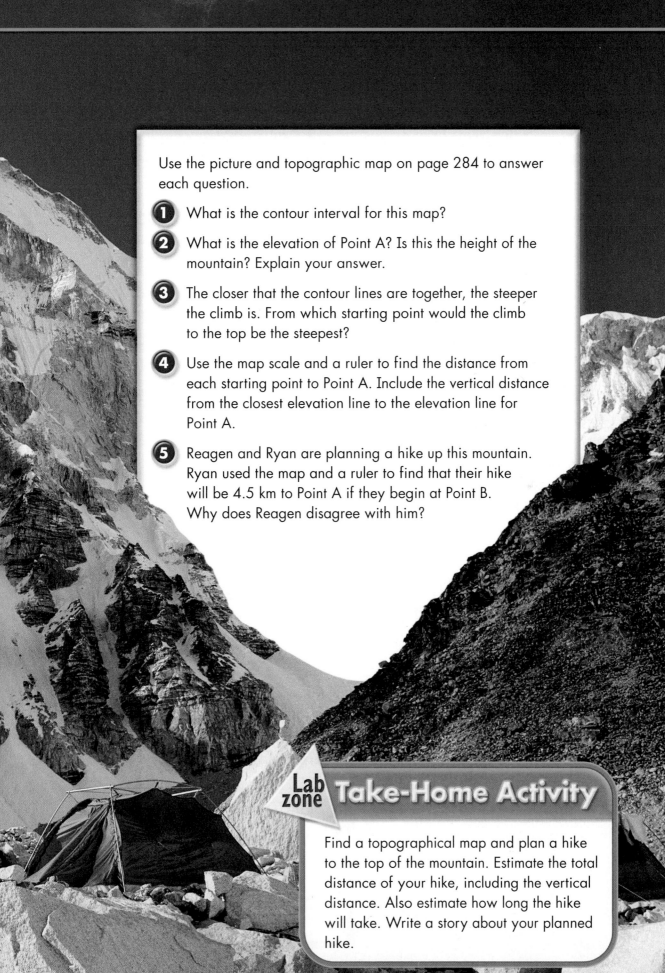

Use the picture and topographic map on page 284 to answer each question.

1. What is the contour interval for this map?

2. What is the elevation of Point A? Is this the height of the mountain? Explain your answer.

3. The closer that the contour lines are together, the steeper the climb is. From which starting point would the climb to the top be the steepest?

4. Use the map scale and a ruler to find the distance from each starting point to Point A. Include the vertical distance from the closest elevation line to the elevation line for Point A.

5. Reagen and Ryan are planning a hike up this mountain. Ryan used the map and a ruler to find that their hike will be 4.5 km to Point A if they begin at Point B. Why does Reagen disagree with him?

Lab zone Take-Home Activity

Find a topographical map and plan a hike to the top of the mountain. Estimate the total distance of your hike, including the vertical distance. Also estimate how long the hike will take. Write a story about your planned hike.

Use Vocabulary

chemical weathering (p. 272)	mechanical weathering (p. 272)
deposition (p. 274)	sediment (p. 271)
erosion (p. 273)	weathering (p. 272)

Choose the term from the list above that best matches each phrase.

1. Adding sediments to a new place after being carried from another

2. Movement of materials from Earth's surface through the action of wind, water, and ice

3. Rock is broken down but the minerals that make up the rock do not change

4. Process that changes the mineral make-up of rock

5. Solid particles that are moved from one place to another

6. The process of breaking down rock into smaller pieces

Explain Concepts

7. Describe how water running downhill is the main process that shapes Earth's landscapes.

8. Explain how salts collect in the ocean.

9. How are the processes of weathering, erosion, and deposition related?

10. How do erosion and deposition affect beaches?

11. Describe two examples of mechanical weathering.

12. What are two sources of energy for water waves? Explain.

Process Skills

13. **Interpreting Data** The height of ocean waves is determined by the speed of the wind, the distance across the water the wind travels, and the amount of time that the wind blows. According to the graph, what are the wave heights reached at wind speeds of 5 meters/second, 15 meters/second, and 25 meters/second? Between which wind speeds do the wave heights seem to be increasing most rapidly?

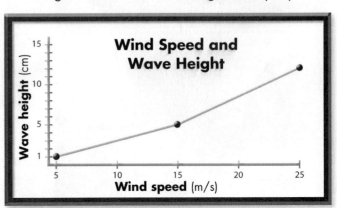

Wind Speed and Wave Height

Wave height (cm)

Wind speed (m/s)

14. Model Draw a model that explains the movement of water in an ocean wave.

 ## Draw Conclusions

15. Read the following passage, and then fill in a graphic organizer similar to the one below. List three facts from the passage, and then make a conclusion about changes that take place on Earth's surface.

> The water in rivers slowly dissolves rock and carries away sediment from the land. Wind and waves constantly change coastal areas. Earthquakes, floods, volcanoes, and other sudden events can dramatically change the landscape.

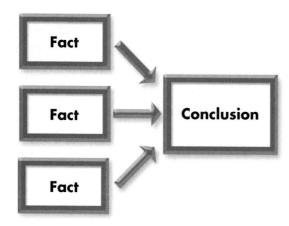

 ## Test Prep

Choose the letter that best completes the statement or answers the question.

16. Broken-down rock and soil are moved from place to place on the Earth's surface through
 Ⓐ tectonic activity.
 Ⓑ chemical weathering.
 Ⓒ wave action.
 Ⓓ erosion and deposition.

17. Water flows in a river because of
 Ⓕ erosion.
 Ⓖ gravity.
 Ⓗ deposition.
 Ⓘ weathering.

18. What is the most important reason that rivers and streams cause erosion?
 Ⓐ Their moving water has energy.
 Ⓑ They flood their banks.
 Ⓒ They deposit sediments in deltas.
 Ⓓ They create deltas.

19. Explain why the answer you chose for Question 18 is the best. For each of the answers that you did not choose, give a reason why it is not the best choice.

20. Writing in Science **Expository** Summarize the many processes and events that change Earth's surface. Divide them into two groups, those that cause sudden, dramatic change, and those that cause slow and steady change over time.

Web Editor

How would you like to spend each day learning from NASA scientists what they have discovered about the changes in Earth's surface? You would meet with scientists to hear about exciting things they have found. You would also see fantastic images from all over the world taken by satellites in space.

As a writer or editor for a Web site like NASA's, you might help everyone understand what scientists are discovering every day. Your stories might be about events on the Earth's surface that can only be seen in their entirety from space. You might select the best satellite image to include on the Web page and explain the image with a caption.

Editing for a scientific Web site is just one of the many areas in which Web editors are needed. You could also be a Web site editor in the areas of history, technology, music, or sports, to name just a few.

Rebecca Lindsey wrote an article for NASA's Earth Observatory Web site about how a landslide blocked a river in Tibet and formed a new lake.

Lab zone Take-Home Activity

Research an image on NASA's Earth Observatory Web site at http://earthobservatory.nasa.gov. Write a short article that explains what the image shows.

Chapter 11
Earth's Resources

You Will Discover

- what renewable and nonrenewable resources are.
- how land, air, and water provide resources.
- how resources are connected.
- what some energy resources are.
- how fossil fuels form.
- how the harmful effects of using fossil fuels can be reduced.

online
Student Edition
pearsonsuccessnet.com

How can we use Earth's resources wisely?

natural gas

fossil fuel

nonrenewable resource

geothermal energy

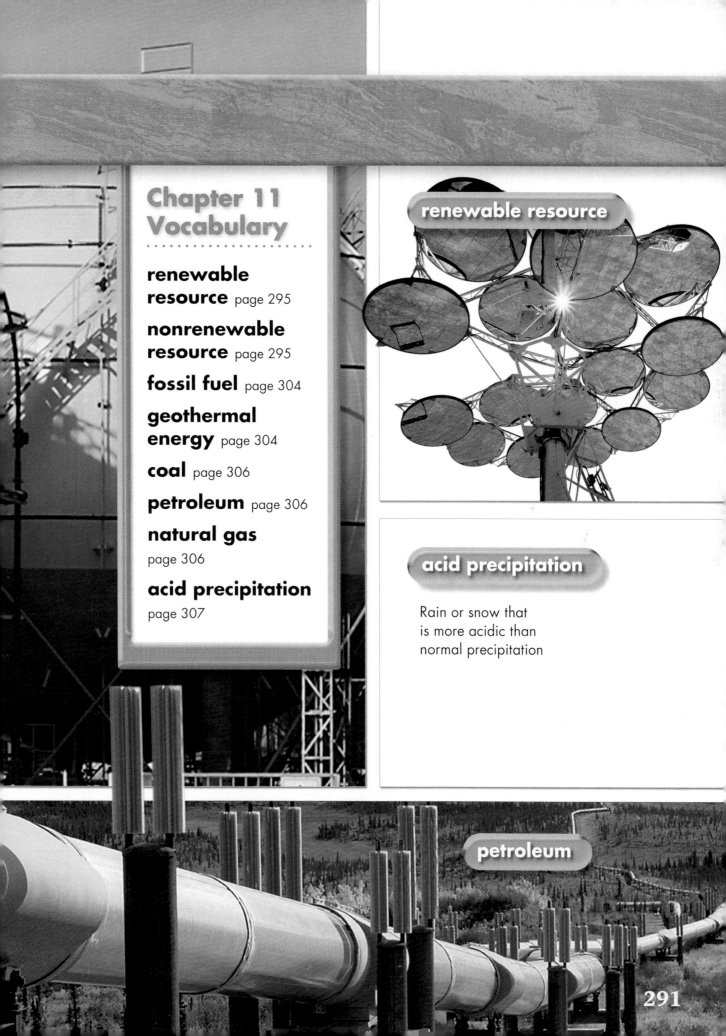

Chapter 11 Vocabulary

renewable resource

acid precipitation

Rain or snow that is more acidic than normal precipitation

petroleum

Explore What resources were used to make things in your classroom?

Materials

classroom objects

What to Do

1 Look around the classroom. Find objects made from the resource categories. Use the chart to **classify** them.

2 Use a chart to help record and **communicate** your findings.

3 Repeat steps 1 and 2 until the chart is complete.

Resource Category Chart

Resource Category	Object
Renewable	
water	
tree or other plant	
animal	
Nonrenewable	
rock or mineral	
fossil fuel	

Explain Your Results

1. What objects made from nonrenewable resources can be replaced with objects made from renewable resources?

2. **Communicate** Write a main idea statement that tells what you learned in this activity. Give details to support your statement.

Process Skills

When you share information about your observations and data, you **communicate**.

How to Read Science

Main Idea and Details

One strategy you can use to help you understand the information a writer wants to **communicate** is to identify the **main idea** of a passage. The main idea is the most important idea in a reading selection. **Details** make the main idea clearer.

- Identify the main idea of the paragraph. Often the main idea is stated in the paragraph's topic sentence. The topic sentence is marked in the paragraph below.

- Find details that support or expand upon the main idea.

Science Article

Water as a Resource

Water is a valuable resource that is used by humans in many different ways. We use it for cooking, cleaning, and bathing. Farmers use it to irrigate crops and for livestock. Large ships carry goods between countries over oceans worldwide. People use boats to travel from one location to another. Without water resources, we would not be able to boat, swim, or fish.

Apply It!

Make a graphic organizer like this one. Identify the **main idea** in the paragraph and list the **details** that support it.

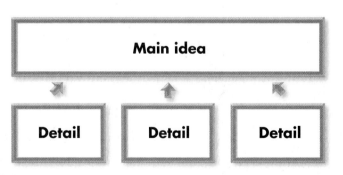

Main idea

| Detail | Detail | Detail |

You Are There!

A cool breeze from the ocean brushes your skin, and you can smell the salt in the air. The gentle slapping you hear is the lapping of waves against the dock. Seabirds call to each other as they glide by you. The roaring of boat motors becomes louder as you walk down the dock to look at today's lobster catch. Which of these pleasures would you miss if this water resource disappeared?

What are Earth's natural resources?

All living things share resources that can be renewable or nonrenewable. The way in which we use one resource can affect other resources.

Renewable and Nonrenewable Resources

How often do you think about the air, water, and land around you? Try to imagine what life would be like without a seemingly endless supply of these resources. Air, water, and land are just a few of the many resources on Earth.

Some resources, called **renewable resources,** can be replaced through natural processes almost as fast as they can be used. Sunlight and wind are examples of renewable resources. Trees and cotton are also renewable resources. They can be replanted once they are used. If they are used wisely, renewable resources can last indefinitely.

Nonrenewable resources cannot be replaced as fast as they are used. Some nonrenewable resources, such as minerals and fossil fuels, take millions of years to form.

When using resources, consider the benefits and costs. For example, cutting trees to make lumber for homes may seem like a benefit. But the cost might be that certain organisms lose their habitats. Understanding how resource use affects Earth can help you make informed decisions.

1. ✅ **Checkpoint** How are renewable and nonrenewable resources alike and different?
2. 🎯 **Main Idea and Details** Write a main idea statement about the use of Earth's resources. Then list at least three details to support your main idea.

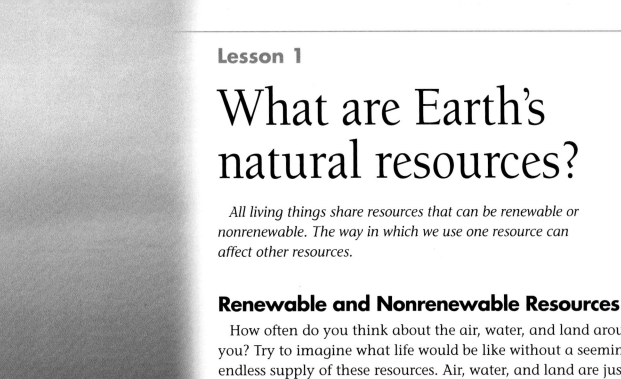

Air Resources

One reason that life on Earth is possible is because of the gases of its atmosphere. Nitrogen, oxygen, and carbon dioxide are gases that are essential to life. These gases are renewable resources because they cycle in the environment. But the air can become polluted.

Air pollution results when certain substances are put into the atmosphere. Many of these substances are produced when fuels such as coal, oil, and natural gas are burned. Air pollution can affect all living organisms, including humans. When air is polluted, some people have trouble breathing.

Each day the Environmental Protection Agency (EPA) lets people know how clean their air is. The EPA rates the air with an air quality index (AQI) color, which you can see below. The colors go from green to maroon. You can find AQI information in your local newspaper or on the EPA Web site.

Pollutant: Ozone

Today's Forecast: 130

Quality: Unhealthy for Sensitive Groups

Children and people with asthma are the groups most at risk.

Land Resources

The quartz in this rock can be used to make glass, cement, sandpaper, and electronic equipment.

If you think about all the ways we depend on land, you will realize how important it is. Land resources include farmlands, grazing lands, soil, minerals, forests, and wildlife. People build houses and other structures on land.

Soil covers much of Earth's land, and people use it to grow crops and other plants. Without soil, you wouldn't have much of the food you eat. Soil may take hundreds of years to form, and it can be easily eroded by wind and water. Many farmers take steps, such as rotating crops and limiting areas of bare soil, to reduce soil erosion.

Land also provides us with the many minerals we use every day. The automobile, bus, or bike you ride is made with the mineral iron. Iron also is used to build many buildings and machines. Limestone, a rock containing the mineral calcite, is used to make cement, which is used to make buildings, bridges, and sidewalks. Minerals take thousands of years to form, so they are nonrenewable resources.

Forests

Did you use paper today? Did you sit on furniture made of wood? Have you used anything made of rubber lately? If you did, you probably used a product that came from a forest. Many materials we use every day come from forests. Some nuts, fruits, and even medicines come from rain forests. Scientists are researching forest plants for other medicines that may be able to treat diseases.

Forests also provide a habitat for many species. When forests are cut down, these species may not be able to adapt to a new environment. Some species become extinct as large tracts of forests are cut down.

Forests play an important role in controlling carbon dioxide in Earth's atmosphere. Too much carbon dioxide in the atmosphere can trap heat, causing temperatures to get warmer. The result can be harmful to Earth's organisms that cannot adjust to the higher temperatures. Trees take in carbon dioxide and release oxygen during photosynthesis. When large portions of forests are cut down and burned, more carbon dioxide remains in the atmosphere.

Many of the forests in the United States are public lands. But others are owned privately—often by lumber and paper companies that cut trees to make their products. These companies provide valuable products that we use every day, and they employ many people. The United States Forest Service works with these companies to conserve forest resources by encouraging logging methods that maintain forests as renewable resources. Part of the process is figuring out how often and where to cut and plant trees to keep a constant supply.

What products do you use that come from forests?

Apples are a food crop that can be eaten raw or cooked. What are some food products made from apples?

1. ✓ **Checkpoint** Do you think soil is a renewable or nonrenewable resource? Explain why you think so.

2. ⊚ **Main Idea and Details** Why are forests an important resource? Use a graphic organizer to answer the question.

Water Resources

How many different ways have you used water today? Could you have done the same things without water? Some of the ways we use water are obvious—bathing, cleaning, drinking, cooking, growing crops, or swimming. Many industries use water too. But many water uses aren't as easy to see. The cells of all living things need water for life processes. Without water, the cells would die. For this reason, all living things need a source of water.

Water is considered a renewable resource because it is recycled in the water cycle. But if water becomes polluted, it cannot be used safely. As water flows across land, it can pick up pollution, including fertilizers and pesticides. Chemicals from industry are another source of water pollution.

Some industries remove water from lakes and rivers. They use it to cool equipment that becomes hot. When the water is returned to the lake or river, its temperature is higher than it was originally. Even a small increase in temperature can lead to changes in an ecosystem and affect organisms.

About 75 percent of Earth's surface is covered by water. So you might wonder why we should worry about some of it being polluted. Most of Earth's water is in the ocean's salt water. Many organisms—including humans—cannot use salt water. Fresh water makes up only about three percent of Earth's water, and much of that fresh water is frozen, such as in glaciers. Frozen water is not available for use. Because freshwater organisms can use so little of Earth's water, preventing pollution is important.

Although most places in the United States have enough water, some places have water shortages. The problem can result when populations grow. They need more water than the area can supply. People living in some areas must get fresh water from faraway sources or by removing salt from ocean water.

Many food products, including fish, come from water. What other food products do fresh and salt water produce?

How has the use of water for public supply changed from 1960 to the present?

- Public supply
- Rural domestic and livestock
- Irrigation
- Thermoelectric power
- Other industrial use

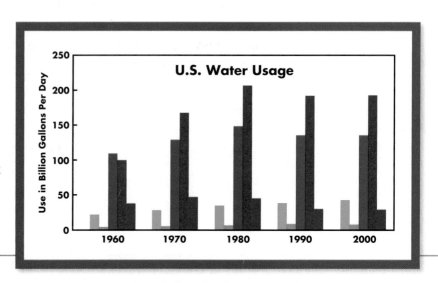

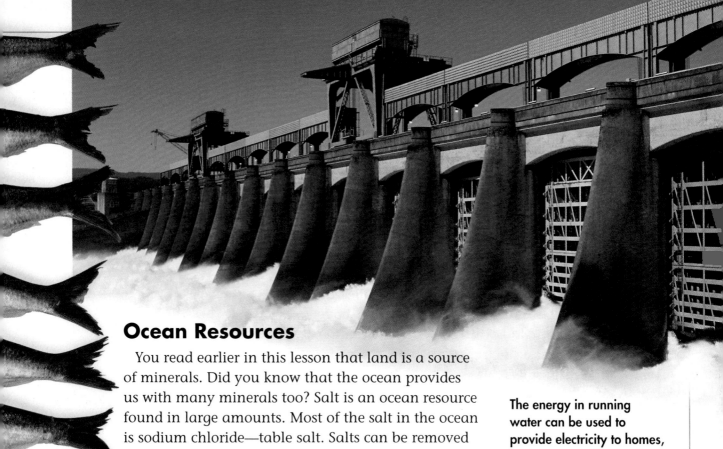

Ocean Resources

You read earlier in this lesson that land is a source of minerals. Did you know that the ocean provides us with many minerals too? Salt is an ocean resource found in large amounts. Most of the salt in the ocean is sodium chloride—table salt. Salts can be removed from ocean water when the water evaporates.

Other minerals, such as tin, magnesium, iron, and copper, can be found in large amounts on the ocean floor. Many of these minerals form around a small object such as a shark's tooth. These lumps of minerals are called nodules.

Minerals aren't the only resources on the ocean floor. Deposits of oil and natural gas exist beneath the ocean floor. Wells can be drilled deep into the ocean bottom to remove these products.

Another source of energy can be found in Earth's oceans. Can you guess what it is? Moving ocean water has a lot of energy. Today we can capture the energy of the ocean tides and use it to generate electricity. Tidal energy is inexpensive and does not pollute the environment—and it is a renewable resource. Unfortunately, only a few places in the world have the right kind of coastline to produce tidal energy.

The energy in running water can be used to provide electricity to homes, businesses, and industries.

These tiny organisms are only one of the many species that form plankton. Plankton are important in both ocean and freshwater food chains. Because many plankton species can carry on photosynthesis, they form the base of some food chains.

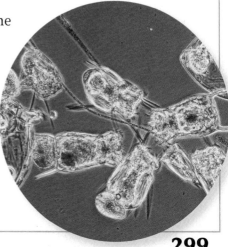

1. ✓**Checkpoint** Why is water important to all living organisms?

2. **Math** in Science Approximately how many more gallons of water were used per day for irrigation than for other industries in 1990?

Connections Among Resources

Although Earth has a plentiful supply of many resources, the supply can be affected by human activities. Air, land, and water can become polluted. Habitats can be changed or destroyed. Supplies can be used up more quickly than they can be replaced.

How much of Earth has been affected by human activities? In 1865, author and naturalist George Marsh asked a similar question. Since then, many other scientists have been trying to answer that question.

Recently a group of scientists got together to find an answer. The result is the map on this page, called the Human Footprint. It shows how much humans have impacted—or affected—Earth's ecosystems. Human impact is rated on a scale from 0 to 100. A score of 0 shows the least impact.

By studying the data, scientists found that 83 percent of Earth's total land has been influenced by human activity. They also discovered that 98 percent of the land where it is possible to grow rice, wheat, and maize—the world's three main crops—is directly affected by human activities. Some of the effects are harmless, but others are not. Scientists say that one reason they wanted to do the study is so that people will understand that they affect the environment. They want people to know that they can make choices that will enable them to lessen the harmful effects and increase the helpful effects.

Human Footprint Map

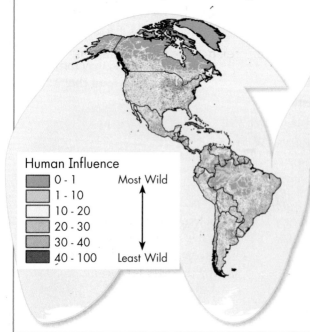

Human Influence

■ 0 - 1	Most Wild
■ 1 - 10	
□ 10 - 20	
■ 20 - 30	
■ 30 - 40	
■ 40 - 100	Least Wild

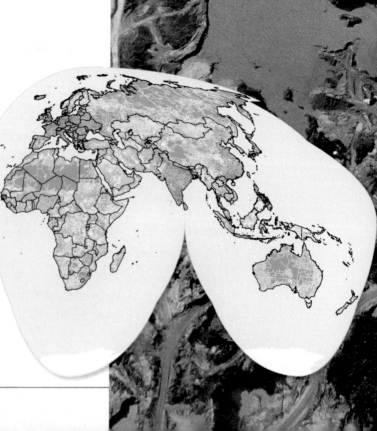

Reducing the Impact

Were you surprised to learn how much of Earth has been affected by humans? What can you and others do to reduce the harm done to Earth and its resources?

Knowing how all Earth's parts—its land, water, air, and living organisms—are interconnected can help people make good choices about their activities. For example, look at the photo to the left to see the chain of causes and effects that begin with clearing large areas of forest. The pollution that results affects all organisms that depend on water from the rivers. The resulting erosion can wash away valuable soil, which can make growing trees and other plants in those areas difficult or impossible. Any organisms that depended on the soil will have to move to new habitats or die. What would happen to organisms that depended on the soil organisms? Can you see how one act—cutting trees—can have many effects?

Recall that some resources are nonrenewable, including minerals, coal, oil, and natural gas. If humans don't manage these resources wisely, they will run out. Part of managing a resource includes conservation. To conserve resources, use them only when necessary.

One way you can practice conservation is to use the three Rs: Reduce, Recycle, Reuse. The chart gives you some ideas about how to use the three Rs. What other ways can you think of?

✓ Lesson Checkpoint

1. Why is conserving resources important?
2. Explain how the use of one resource may affect other resources.
3. **Writing in Science** **Expository** Write a newspaper article about a series of events that result from carelessly using or polluting a resource. Your article can be real or one that you make up. For example, you might report about what happens downstream when a factory releases harmful chemicals in a river.

When large areas of forests are cleared for timber, topsoil is easily eroded and washed into nearby streams and rivers.

Where do we get energy?

Every day humans use energy from a variety of sources. These sources include fossil fuels, wind, water, solar energy, nuclear energy, and geothermal energy.

Energy Needs

The picture on this page shows what Earth looks like at night. Hundreds of satellite images were put together to make the picture. You can see that human-made light shows up all across the planet. Can you see the areas that have the most light?

As you can guess from the picture, one of the largest uses of energy on Earth is to produce light. But energy is needed for many other uses. Each time you ride in a car, bus, or train, you are taking part in an activity that uses energy. When you use a computer, watch TV, or listen to a CD, you are using energy. Cooking, heating and cooling your home, and doing laundry require energy.

Businesses use energy to power computers, phones, fax machines, copy machines, and cash registers. Energy powers industrial machines that make products. Theaters use energy to show movies, and restaurants use it to cook food and to keep the food from spoiling. Ships, trucks, and trains need energy to transport goods around the world.

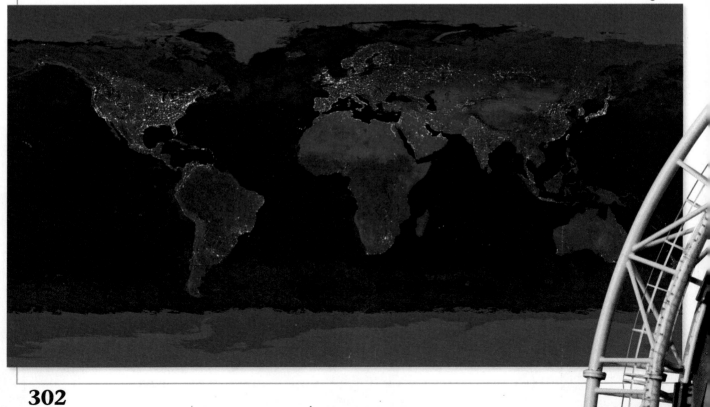

Earth at night

Energy Needs Over Time

The need for energy resources in most areas of the world has changed over time. Early societies used some energy resources, such as wood, for light, heat, and cooking. Even early farming societies used energy, but compared to today's energy use, they didn't use much. They depended on animals to pull plows and other farm equipment.

In the late 1700s, people in the United States began to use industry to meet their needs. Tasks that in the past were done by people and animals were now done by machines. Factories began producing clothing, furniture, building equipment, farm machines, and later automobiles. Making these products required a source of energy, often electricity.

As the country's population grew, the demand for products also increased. New factories opened, and the need for energy increased. The demand for more energy continues today. Look at the graph to see how we use energy.

Much of the increase in the use of energy results from the use of more electricity. Except for lightning, electricity is not a resource found in nature. Where does the energy come from? You'll find out on the next few pages.

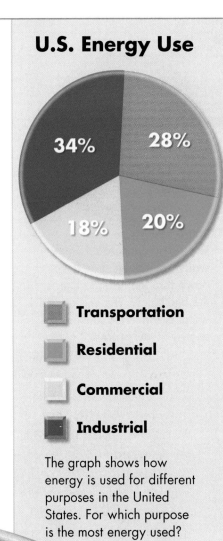

U.S. Energy Use

34% 28% 18% 20%

- **Transportation**
- **Residential**
- **Commercial**
- **Industrial**

The graph shows how energy is used for different purposes in the United States. For which purpose is the most energy used?

This roller coaster uses electrical energy to take people on an exciting ride.

1. ✓**Checkpoint** List ways that you use energy resources every day. Identify those sources you could not do without.

2. **Writing in Science** **Expository** Write a few paragraphs that tell how energy needs have changed over time. Predict how they will change in the future. Give reasons for your prediction.

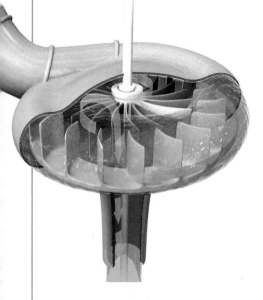

Electricity is generated when water behind this dam flows down through turbines like the one below. The energy of water is converted to electrical energy in this process.

Sources of Energy

The world is full of energy sources. You probably are familiar with some, such as oil, natural gas, and coal. These energy resources are called **fossil fuels**—energy sources made from the remains of living organisms. You'll learn more about fossil fuels later in this chapter. Other energy sources may not be as familiar as fossil fuels even though they are all around you.

Energy from Moving Water

Moving water can be used as an energy source. You read about tidal power earlier in this chapter. The water of moving rivers can also be used to produce electricity.

Hydroelectric power, also called hydropower, is produced when dams are built across waterways. Water flows against the blades of a turbine, causing the blades to turn. The energy of the turning blades is converted to electrical energy inside a generator. Advantages of hydropower are that it doesn't release pollution, and it is renewable. A disadvantage of hydropower is that wildlife habitats can be destroyed when a river is dammed and the land behind the dam floods. In 2002, about three percent of energy in the United States was generated by hydropower.

Energy from Atoms and Earth's Heat

Nuclear energy comes from the heat produced when atoms split apart. Nuclear energy is a nonrenewable resource. In 2002, about eight percent of the total energy used in the United States came from nuclear energy. Nuclear energy doesn't pollute the air. But waste materials from nuclear power plants can be harmful to many organisms, including humans. The wastes must be disposed of very carefully.

If you could go deep into Earth's interior, you would find that it is very hot. The energy of the heat inside Earth is called **geothermal energy.** In some places, geothermal energy heats water below Earth's surface. When scientists drill into certain parts of Earth's crust, the hot water is released in the form of steam. The steam can turn turbines. Inside geothermal power plants, the turbines run generators that make electricity. Geothermal energy, a renewable resource, is more available in some areas of the world than others.

Geothermal energy may cause some pollution when carbon dioxide and hydrogen sulfide gases are released into the atmosphere.

SciLinks Take It to the Net
pearsonsuccessnet.com · keyword: fossil fuel
code: g6p304

Energy from Sunlight and Wind

Energy that comes from the Sun is solar energy. It can be used directly to heat homes and buildings. Solar energy can be converted to electricity without using turbines. Solar energy is renewable and does not produce pollution. However, with today's technology, solar energy can't be used efficiently everywhere. In 2002, less than one percent of energy in the United States was supplied by solar energy.

Wind energy is used to turn the blades of large wind turbines, which generate electricity. Wind energy is a renewable resource that does not produce pollution. The use of wind as a source of energy may not be efficient in some areas where wind may not be steady or constant. Many states use wind energy as a source of electricity.

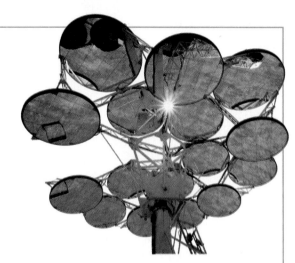

Water circulated through pipes in these solar collectors is heated by the Sun's energy. The heated water is pumped through radiators to provide heat and hot water to homes and other buildings.

An area where there are a large number of wind turbines is called a wind farm.

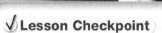

Clouds of water droplets are rising from the cooling towers of this nuclear power plant.

Lesson Checkpoint

1. Which sources of energy are nonrenewable, and which are renewable?

2. Make a three-column table. In the first column list the energy sources discussed in this lesson. In the second column, list advantages of each source. In the third column, list the disadvantages.

3. **Main Idea and Details** Give details to expand on this main idea: Moving water can be used as an energy source.

Coal can be mined from below Earth's surface.

Oil from remote areas of the world, such as Alaska, is transported through a pipeline to areas where it is processed.

After natural gas is removed from underground, it is stored in large tanks.

How are fossil fuels formed and used?

Fossil fuels are nonrenewable energy resources. They take millions of years to form and exist in a limited amount. The burning of fossil fuels can result in air and water pollution.

Types of Fossil Fuels

When you ride in a car or cook on a gas stove, you are indirectly using energy from the Sun. How can that be? Fossil fuels form from organisms that lived long ago. Those organisms were either plants that captured the energy of sunlight, or they were organisms that got energy by eating plants or organisms that ate plants. When the organisms died, some of the energy stored in their bodies was changed into the energy of the fossil fuels. Today when we burn fossil fuels, we are releasing that stored energy—energy that plants captured from the Sun millions of years ago!

Coal is a solid fossil fuel. Until 1960, it was the world's primary energy source. At one time, it was the most common fuel used in the United States. It was burned to heat homes and to power trains. Today most coal is burned in power plants to produce electricity.

Petroleum, also called crude oil or oil, is a liquid fossil fuel. It has been used for more than 5,000 years. The ancient Egyptians used it as a medicine for wounds and as a fuel in lamps. Today we use petroleum products such as gasoline, jet fuel, home-heating oil, and kerosene.

Natural gas is a fossil fuel that is a mixture of gases. More than 2,000 years ago, the Chinese used bamboo poles to pipe natural gas from shallow wells. They burned the gas to heat large pans of seawater. As the water evaporated, the dissolved salt in the water remained.

Today natural gas is used to heat homes and produce electricity. The stove or clothes dryer in your home may use natural gas.

Oil and natural gas can both be found beneath the ocean floor. Large drills are lowered from ocean platforms to explore for oil and gas.

Using Fossil Fuels

Most of the energy used in the United States comes from fossil fuels. Although the United States has large amounts of coal, it is a nonrenewable resource. The supply of coal—and all fossil fuels—can run out. That's one reason scientists are trying to find alternate sources of energy. In addition, getting, processing, and using fossil fuels can cause problems.

When fossil fuels burn, gases are produced. Some of these gases—called greenhouse gases—trap heat in the air. The result is called the greenhouse effect. Some scientists are concerned because as more greenhouse gases are produced, more heat is trapped. The extra heat might cause Earth to become warmer. Organisms that cannot adjust to the warmer temperatures would die. Land could become too dry to grow crops.

Other gases released when fossil fuels burn can combine with water vapor in the air. The result can be **acid precipitation**—rain or snow that is more acidic than normal precipitation. Acid precipitation can harm living organisms, buildings, and statues. For example, many organisms that lived in some North American lakes have died because of acid precipitation.

Burning fossil fuels also leads to smog, a brownish-yellowish haze that settles over some areas on sunny days. Smog can be harmful to living organisms and can cause respiratory problems in humans.

Reducing Fossil Fuel Problems

What can you do to reduce the harmful effects of fossil fuel use? The obvious answer is to use less fossil fuel. But how? Carpool, ride a bike, use public transportation, walk—these are a few things you can do. Also, turn off lights and appliances when you aren't using them. As an adult you may have to make decisions about energy sources. Being informed will help you make better decisions. Prepare yourself by learning about other forms of energy, such as solar, wind, or water.

1. ✓**Checkpoint** What are some ways to reduce the use of fossil fuels?
2. 🎯 **Main Idea and Details** Write a main idea statement about the problems of using fossil fuels. Support your statement with at least three details.

How Coal Forms

Coal, petroleum, and natural gas formed from the buried remains of organisms that lived millions of years ago. But each formed in a slightly different way and from different kinds of organisms. The processes are summarized in the diagrams.

Coal formed from swamp plants. When the plants died, they were buried in the water and mud of the swamps. There the dead plants formed a layer of dead material, called peat. Over time more dead plants, mud, sand, and other sediments were deposited over the peat layer. Pressure from the layers of sediment above and heat within Earth changed the peat into lignite, a soft form of coal.

Notice in the diagram that more pressure and heat changes coal to a different form at each stage. Each type of coal has more carbon than the coal formed at the stage before it. The higher the percent of carbon, the cleaner the coal will burn. Anthracite, the hardest form of coal, is the cleanest burning. In the United States, 97 percent of anthracite is found in Pennsylvania.

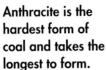

Anthracite is the hardest form of coal and takes the longest to form.

1 Dead swamp plants sink to the bottom of the swamp water and form peat.

2 Heat and pressure from sediment layers above the peat slowly change it to lignite. Lignite is a brownish-black coal with a lot of water.

3 More heat and pressure change lignite to bituminous coal, the most common form of coal used in the United States.

4 Anthracite is the last stage of coal formation. It is the hardest form of coal.

1 Ocean organisms die, sink, and become buried by layers of sediment.

2 Pressure and heat act on the decaying material to form oil and natural gas.

3 Oil and natural gas move up towards Earth's surface.

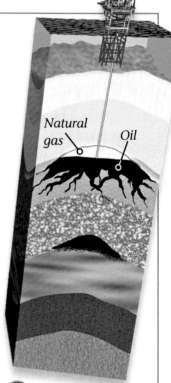

Natural gas

Oil

4 Oil and natural gas become trapped when they cannot pass through the rocks.

Oil and natural gas are drilled for by offshore oil rigs.

Oil and Natural Gas

Oil and natural gas formed in processes similar to those that produced coal. But they formed from the remains of tiny organisms that lived in ocean water. Since natural gas is lighter than oil, it is often found on top of oil. The areas of trapped oil and natural gas can be drilled into and the deposits recovered for energy use.

1. **✓Checkpoint** How does lignite differ from anthracite?

2. **Social Studies** in Science Use the Internet or an electronic encyclopedia to find out where large deposits of natural gas and petroleum can be found. Draw a world map that shows the location of those deposits.

309

Processing and Delivering Petroleum

When petroleum is removed from the ground, it is a mixture of many different kinds of products. These products can be separated at an oil refinery. There, the crude oil is heated. As the temperature of the oil rises, different parts of the oil can be removed at different temperatures. These substances are then processed to make them pure, removing materials such as water, salts, or oxygen. The finished products are often stored at the refinery until they are shipped to gas stations, airports, or factories. You can see how this process works in the diagram.

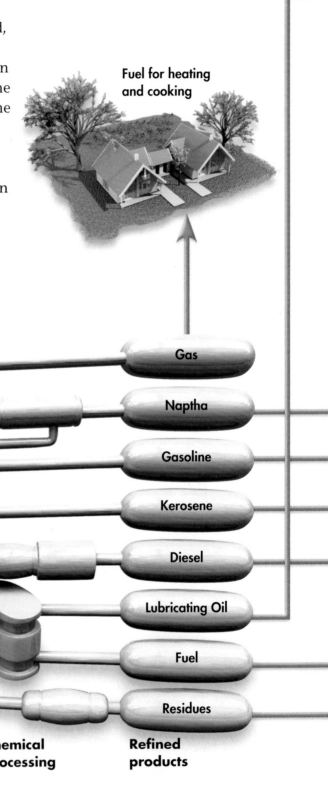

Fuel for heating and cooking

Crude oil

Gas

Naptha

Gasoline

Kerosene

Diesel

Lubricating Oil

Fuel

Residues

Boiler
(Oil boils to form gases.)

Separating column
(Gases rise, cool, condense, and separate.)

Chemical processing

Refined products

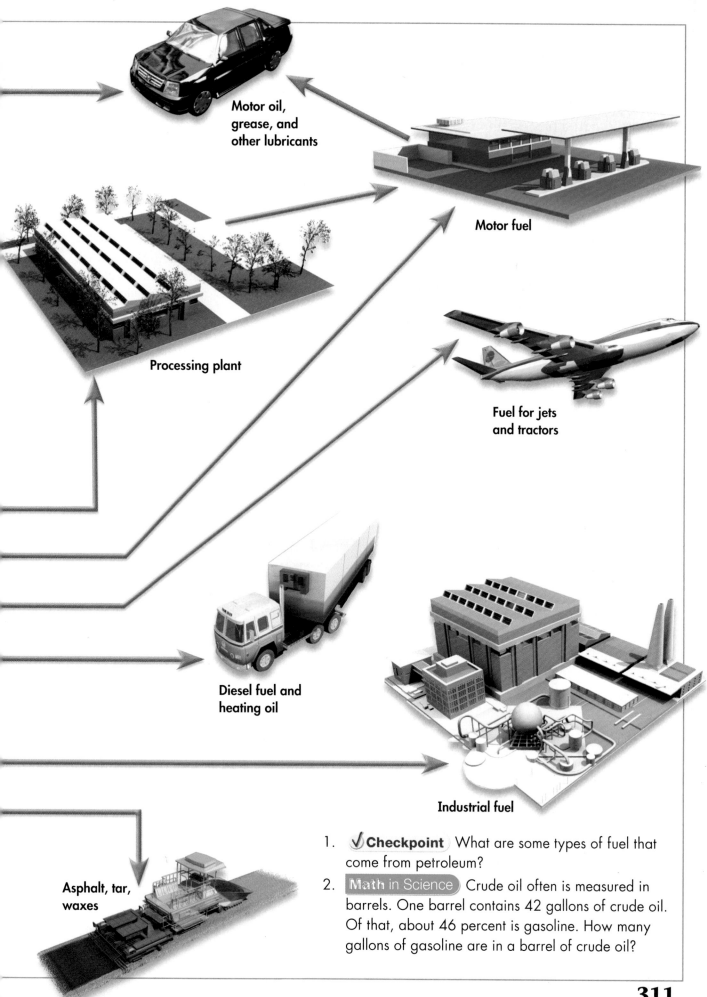

Motor oil, grease, and other lubricants

Motor fuel

Processing plant

Fuel for jets and tractors

Diesel fuel and heating oil

Industrial fuel

Asphalt, tar, waxes

1. ✔ **Checkpoint** What are some types of fuel that come from petroleum?

2. **Math in Science** Crude oil often is measured in barrels. One barrel contains 42 gallons of crude oil. Of that, about 46 percent is gasoline. How many gallons of gasoline are in a barrel of crude oil?

Coal Mining and Reclamation

Because coal is a solid, it is removed from the ground in a process that is different than the one used to remove natural gas and petroleum. Coal that is buried deep below Earth's surface is removed by digging underground tunnels. The coal is removed and brought to the surface, leaving behind huge caves.

Coal that is within 30 meters of Earth's surface is usually removed by a process called strip mining. During strip mining, soil and rock are removed from Earth's surface to expose the coal.

Both methods of mining coal can have harmful effects on the environment and its organisms. When land is stripped of soil, plants cannot grow and animals lose shelter. Soil can erode and the land can become unusable. Deep coal mining can pollute water. The large caves produced by mining can cause the ground above to collapse.

Land that is mined can be reclaimed, or put to productive use. Both federal and state laws require reclamation of land disturbed by strip mining and deep mining. The pictures show how strip-mined land can be managed and reclaimed.

✓ Lesson Checkpoint

1. How are coal, natural gas, and petroleum deposits removed for human use?
2. What are three problems caused by using fossil fuels?
3. **Writing in Science** **Persuasive** Write a letter to your state senator urging him or her to pass laws to help reduce the use of fossil fuels. Support your viewpoint with reasons why burning fossil fuels is harmful.

During Mining

A Water Management
Water is important to both the public and the mining process. To protect water quality, mine operators monitor water quality at all stages of the mining process. They develop methods to allow water to flow naturally and without pollution through mining areas.

B Water Treatment
Miners establish water treatment facilities at the mining site, such as settling ponds, to allow sediments and other solids to settle out of mining water before it is reintroduced to streams.

C Waste Storage
The correct handling of wastes produced during the mining process can make the reclamation process easier. The upper topsoil layer at the site can be saved for use after the mining operations are completed. Some wastes can safely be buried underground.

D Chemical Recovery
Chemicals that are used to remove minerals from rock can be collected and disposed of properly.

E Protecting Air Quality
State and federal laws and regulations have established strict guidelines for maintaining air quality at mining sites. Methods for maintaining air quality include using scrubbers and other devices to trap air pollutants and then recycling the pollutants.

F Ecosystem Protection
Care must be taken during the mining process and reclamation to ensure that wildlife populations are not permanently affected. Issues to be considered include ecosystem relationships and protections of wetlands and other habitats.

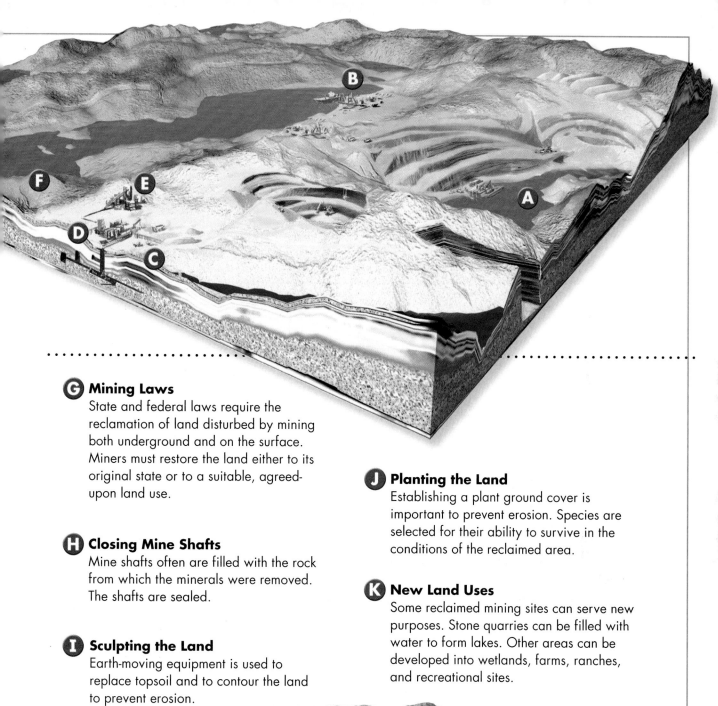

G Mining Laws
State and federal laws require the reclamation of land disturbed by mining both underground and on the surface. Miners must restore the land either to its original state or to a suitable, agreed-upon land use.

H Closing Mine Shafts
Mine shafts often are filled with the rock from which the minerals were removed. The shafts are sealed.

I Sculpting the Land
Earth-moving equipment is used to replace topsoil and to contour the land to prevent erosion.

J Planting the Land
Establishing a plant ground cover is important to prevent erosion. Species are selected for their ability to survive in the conditions of the reclaimed area.

K New Land Uses
Some reclaimed mining sites can serve new purposes. Stone quarries can be filled with water to form lakes. Other areas can be developed into wetlands, farms, ranches, and recreational sites.

Reclaimed Land

Investigate What happens at a water treatment plant?

Materials

4 cups and spoon

polluted water and measuring cup

alum, sand, gravel

clock

cotton and bottle with bottom cut off

ruler and tape

Process Skills

Making a model of the water treatment process can help you understand how water can be purified for drinking.

What to Do

1 Label the cups A, B, C, D.

2 Gently shake the polluted water to mix it. Pour about 150 mL into cups A, B, C.

3 **Observe** how the water in cup A looks. Record your observations.

Water Treatment

Container	Appearance
Cup A	
Cup B • after 5 minutes	
• after 10 minutes	
• after 15 minutes	
• after 20 minutes	
Cup D	

4 Add 2 spoonfuls of alum to cup B and stir for 1 minute.

5 Observe the water in cup B every 5 minutes for 20 minutes. Record your observations. This is a **model** of the way chemicals are used in the water treatment process.

6 Make a water filter using the bottle with the bottom cut off. Place the filter above cup D.

7 Gently pour the water from cup C into the filter. Try not to pour any of the mud at the bottom of cup C into the filter. Try not to disturb the filter's sand layer.

8 Wait until all the water has moved through the filter into the cup. Observe the water in cup D and record your observations.

sand, 5 cm height

gravel, 5 cm height

cotton

This is a model of the way filters are used in the water treatment process.

Be careful!

Do not drink the water.

Explain Your Results

1. In your **model** of the water treatment process, what was represented by the water in cup A? cup B?

2. What part of the water treatment process is not shown in this model?

Go Further

How would changing the amount of sand, pea gravel, and cotton affect the quality of the filtered water? Develop a plan to answer this or any other questions you may have.

315

Hybrid Cars

While a car is being driven, only about 15% of the energy stored in the gasoline is used to move the car and to run accessories, such as an air conditioner. The rest of the energy is lost to the environment. Scientists are constantly working to reduce the amount of wasted energy. Hybrid cars are now being produced that are more fuel-efficient than conventional vehicles.

A hybrid car has a gasoline engine like those found in most cars, but also has an electric motor to assist or replace the work of the gas engine. The electric motor operates during low speed driving and when extra power is needed for acceleration or increased elevation. When the hybrid is slowing down or coming to a stop, the motor changes normally wasted energy into electric energy. This energy is stored in batteries for later use.

The double bar graph on the next page compares the fuel economy of four vehicles. The data came from a manufacturer of hybrid cars, and it compares fuel economy only.

When analyzing data, it is important to know the source so that you can identify any possible bias in the data or in the conclusions presented.

1 Internal Combustion Engine

2 Transmission

3 Electric Motor

4 Intelligent Power Electronics

5 Conventional Fuel Tank

6 Advanced Batteries

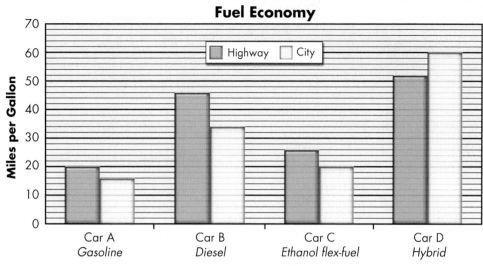

Fuel Economy

Miles per Gallon (y-axis): 0, 10, 20, 30, 40, 50, 60, 70

Legend: ■ Highway □ City

Car A — Gasoline
Car B — Diesel
Car C — Ethanol flex-fuel
Car D — Hybrid

Vehicle and Type

Use the graph above to answer each question.

① Notice that the fuel economy of the hybrid is higher than the others. In what other way is it different from the data for the other three vehicles?

② Find the average fuel economy for each of the four cars.

③ A driver expects to pay $750.00 to purchase a year's worth of fuel for the hybrid. If fuel costs $2.80 per gallon, how many miles of driving are expected? (Hint: Use the average fuel economy you found for the hybrid in Question 2.)

④ The manufacturer says it is clear that a hybrid is the cheapest car to own and it will solve our energy problem. Why is the information presented not enough to support these conclusions? What other information would you want?

Lab zone Take-Home Activity

Use a library or the Internet to do additional research on fuel-efficient vehicles. What other alternatives are there? What are the pros and cons of each type? Does the information reflect any bias by the source of the information? Write your conclusions and present them to the class.

Chapter 11 Review and Test Prep

Use Vocabulary

acid precipitation (p. 307)	**nonrenewable resource** (p. 295)
coal (p. 306)	
fossil fuel (p. 304)	**petroleum** (p. 306)
geothermal energy (p. 304)	**renewable resource** (p. 295)
natural gas (p. 306)	

Use the term from above that best completes each sentence.

1. A liquid fossil fuel that formed from ocean water organisms is _____.

2. Rain or snow that has a large amount of acid is _____.

3. A solid fossil fuel that formed from swamp plants is _____.

4. A renewable resource that is generated from the heat in Earth's interior is_____.

5. A resource that can be replaced as fast as it is used is a _____.

6. An energy source made from once-living organisms is a _____.

7. A fossil fuel found in the form of a gas is _____.

8. A resource that cannot be replaced as fast as it is used is a _____.

Explain Concepts

9. Explain why air is an important resource.

10. Minerals and fossil fuels are both resources. How are they alike and different?

11. How are fossil fuels and acid precipitation related?

12. **Interpret Data** The table shows the amounts of two greenhouse gases released into the air in the United States for three different years. How would you describe the change in the amount of carbon dioxide released from 1990 to 2000? How does this compare to the amount of methane released?

Released Greenhouse Gases
(million metric tons)

Gas	1990	1995	2000
Carbon dioxide	4,900	5,200	5,800
Methane	31.7	31.1	28.2

13. Classify A biomass fuel is a fuel formed from the products of living organisms. Wood is a biomass fuel. Would you consider biomass fuels renewable or nonrenewable? Why?

14. Predict A company is built along a river that has large populations of fish and other organisms. The company plans to draw water from the river to cool its machinery that heats up as it cuts large pieces of metal. The company will release the heated water back into the stream. What is likely to happen to some of the organisms living in the river? Explain your answer.

Main Idea and Details

15. Make a graphic organizer like the one shown below. Fill in some details for each main idea.

Main Idea	Details
A variety of land resources exist on Earth.	
Water resources are essential for life.	
Plants and animals use air resources.	

Test Prep

Choose the letter that best completes the statement or answers the question.

16. Which is a nonrenewable resource?
   Ⓐ solar energy   Ⓒ wind
   Ⓑ hydropower   Ⓓ nuclear energy

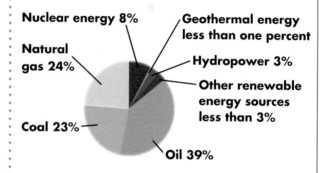

Nuclear energy 8%

Geothermal energy less than one percent

Natural gas 24%

Hydropower 3%

Other renewable energy sources less than 3%

Coal 23%

Oil 39%

17. According to the above graph, what percent of energy came from renewable energy sources?
   Ⓕ 24 percent   Ⓗ 8 percent
   Ⓖ 23 percent   Ⓘ 6 percent

18. Strip mining coal can affect all of the following resources EXCEPT
   Ⓐ water.   Ⓒ the Sun.
   Ⓑ land.   Ⓓ wildlife.

19. Explain why the answer you chose for Question 18 is best. For each of the answers you did not choose, give a reason why it is not the best choice.

20. Writing in Science **Persuasive** Using alternate sources of energy sometimes costs more than using fossil fuels. Would you support laws that require the use of alternate sources? Write a letter to persuade others to agree with your opinion.

GEOCHEMIST

Suppose that an abandoned mine is located near your community. People want to know if rainwater is becoming contaminated with metals as it trickles through the mine on its way to the groundwater. Who can answer this question? A geochemist can.

A geochemist studies the chemicals that make up Earth materials such as rocks, minerals, water, and oil. Many geochemists work on environmental issues. For example, a geochemist might analyze samples of water and rock from a mine. This person could tell if the water is being contaminated and what kinds of rocks are causing the contamination. The geochemist can then help people take steps to clean up the area.

Many other geochemists specialize in finding resources such as oil or minerals. They use their knowledge to help companies obtain these materials with as little environmental damage as possible.

No matter what the specialty, geochemists must be good observers and problem solvers. Some of their work takes place in a lab, but much is also done outside where they have to be on site to collect samples. In fact, a career in geochemistry is a terrific way to combine science with the great outdoors.

W322

Lab zone Take-Home Activity

Make a map that shows how rock piles from an abandoned mine might be contaminating a river that flows through a community. Place *X*s where you think a geochemist would want to take samples of water, rock, and soil.

You Will Discover

- characteristics of Earth's atmosphere.
- how winds form.
- how water vapor causes humidity and clouds.
- different ways precipitation forms.
- the role of air masses in weather.
- how to be safe in severe weather.
- what factors can affect climate.

Chapter 12

Climate and Weather

online
Student Edition
pearsonsuccessnet.com

Web Games
Take It to the Net
pearsonsuccessnet.com

What causes Earth's weather and climate?

atmosphere

climate

weather

meteorologist

A scientist who studies weather

air pressure

humidity

relative humidity

front

air mass

Explore How can you show the presence of air if you cannot see it?

Materials

plastic bottle and water

modeling clay

funnel

pencil

What to Do

1 Use clay to seal the funnel in the bottle.

2 Slowly pour the water into the funnel. **Observe** what happens.

3 Use the pencil to make a hole in the clay surrounding the bottle. Observe what happens.

Careful **observations** can help you **infer** the existence of something that cannot be seen directly.

Explain Your Results

1. Compare your **observations** in step 2 and in step 3. What causes the difference?

2. **Infer** Use your observation in step 3 to explain your observation in step 2.

How to Read Science

Cause and Effect

When you read science, understanding what happens and why it happens is important. The reason something happens is the **cause.** The result is the **effect.** Identifying causes and their related effects when you read can help you understand difficult ideas. Sometimes cause-and-effect relationships are stated directly. Other times you will have to **infer** the information. The causes and effects are marked in the newspaper article below.

- Look for words that signal a cause-and-effect relationship: *because, so, caused, as a result, since,* and *thus.*

- A cause may have more than one effect. An effect can have more than one cause.

Newspaper Article

Wind Topples Trees

Visitors to Newgate Park will notice it looks a little different. High winds hit the park on Tuesday. As a result, several of the trees there blew over. Scientists explained that the winds were caused when cold air suddenly moved into the area. Local nature groups are concerned. The trees that blew over were home to some endangered birds, so those birds now have no home.

Apply It!

Make a graphic organizer like this one. Fill in the graphic organizer to show what **caused** Newgate Park described in the article to look different. Be sure to include the **effects.**

325

You Are There!

You can hear the gentle waves of the ocean as they break against the rocks. The last of the Sun's warmth keeps the rocks hot as the Sun slowly slips towards the horizon. As the Sun sets through the clouds, light is filtered by particles in the atmosphere. Will tomorrow be as beautiful? Or do the clouds mean that a storm is on its way?

AudioText

What is Earth's atmosphere?

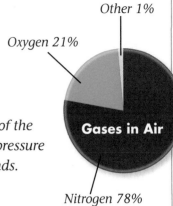

Other 1%

Oxygen 21%

Gases in Air

Nitrogen 78%

Earth's atmosphere is made up of gases. Each layer of the atmosphere has its own characteristics, including air pressure and temperature. Differences in air pressure cause winds.

Gases in Air

Usually you can't see it, smell it, or even hear it, but Earth's air surrounds you all the time. The blanket of air that surrounds a planet, including Earth, is called its **atmosphere.** Earth's atmosphere is made up mostly of nitrogen and oxygen gases. Very small amounts of about ten other gases also are part of it. Gravity keeps these gases from escaping into space. Compared to Earth's total size, its atmosphere is a very thin layer.

Where did the gases in Earth's atmosphere come from? Would it surprise you to learn that many of them were once part of the molten rock within Earth? As molten rock cooled, gases such as nitrogen, water vapor, and carbon dioxide were released. Some of the gases were trapped within Earth. Many escaped as volcanoes erupted, a process that has been going on for more than four billion years.

Earth's atmosphere didn't always have the oxygen it has today. As plants spread across the planet, they took in carbon dioxide from the atmosphere and released oxygen during the process of photosynthesis. Over millions of years, the amount of oxygen in Earth's atmosphere reached its present level.

Today the amounts of nitrogen, oxygen, and some other gases remain about the same from one place on Earth to another. But the amount of water vapor in the atmosphere can change. In some areas of the world, such as polar regions, the amount of water vapor in the air might be almost zero. In other areas, such as tropical regions, as much as four percent of the air may be made up of water vapor.

1. **✓Checkpoint** How do the gases in Earth's air differ from place to place?
2. **Cause and Effect** What change caused oxygen to build up in Earth's atmosphere?

Air Pressure and Altitude

When air was pumped out of the metal can above, the outside air pressure became greater than the inside air pressure. The force of air pushing in caused the can to collapse.

If you have ever driven up or down a mountain, flown in a plane, or ridden a fast-moving elevator in a tall building, you may have felt the effects of a change in air pressure. Your ears may have "popped" as you rose. They may have felt full and possibly ached when you descended. This happens because air pressure changes with altitude.

When you descend, the pressure on your ears is increasing. The "popping" that you feel in your ears happens as the pressure inside your ears becomes equal to the pressure outside your ears.

Airplane cabins are pressurized to help passengers stay comfortable at the high altitudes at which most planes fly. The air pressure at the part of the atmosphere where many planes fly is less than half of that at Earth's surface.

A barometer is the instrument used to measure air pressure.

Air Pressure and Temperature

When you look at the air, you probably don't think much is going on. But the gases in air are made of particles that are constantly moving. They bump into and off other matter. **Air pressure** is the measure of force per unit area with which air particles push on matter. For example, when you blow up a balloon, the air particles that you blow into the balloon push on the side of the balloon to make it get larger. In other words, the balloon gets larger because of air pressure.

Air in the atmosphere pushes on matter too. Air pushes on all sides of an object, not just down. Right now air is pushing on all parts of your body. Can you feel it? Probably not. The reason is that air pushes equally from all sides. That means that the air inside your body pushes out with the same force that air on the outside pushes in.

The force with which air pushes on matter is related to the temperature of the air. The particles in cool air are closer together than those in warm air—they are packed together more tightly. The result is that cool air has greater air pressure. The amount of water vapor in the air also affects air pressure. Moist air has less pressure than dry air.

Air pressure is greatest at Earth's surface. That's because more air particles are above to push down. As you rise higher above Earth, air pressure decreases.

Layers of the Atmosphere

Earth's atmosphere isn't the same from top to bottom. It is made of layers, and each layer has its own characteristics. Read about the characteristics of each layer on the next page.

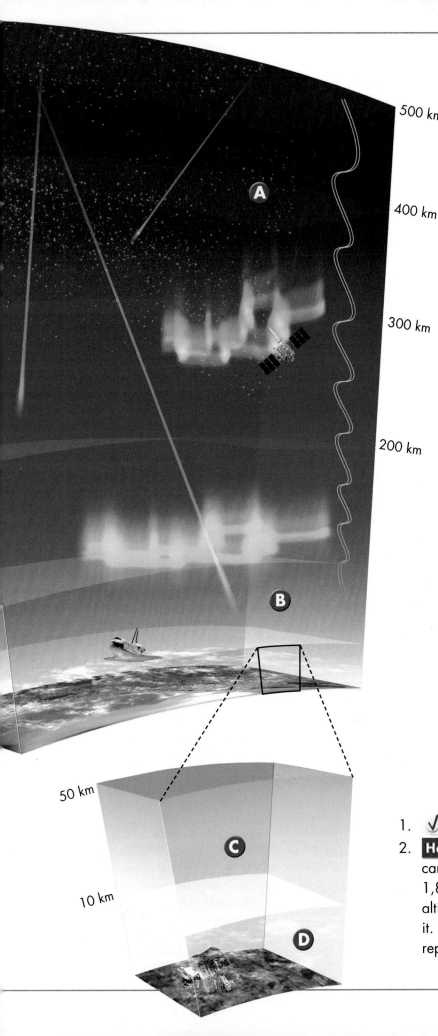

A Thermosphere
The air particles in the thermosphere are far apart. Sometimes, particles of gas in this layer are disturbed by electrical energy from the Sun. When this happens, glows, or auroras, occur that can be seen in the night sky at high latitudes.

B Mesosphere
The mesosphere is the coldest layer. Temperatures get cooler as you move higher in this layer.

C Stratosphere
Temperature increases with altitude in the stratosphere. This layer contains most of the atmosphere's ozone. Ozone is a gas that absorbs harmful ultraviolet rays from the Sun, preventing them from reaching Earth's surface.

D Troposphere
The troposphere is the layer in which you live. More than 75 percent of all the air in the atmosphere is in this layer. All weather takes place here. Temperatures are warmest near Earth's surface. As altitude increases, air temperature and pressure decrease.

1. ✓Checkpoint What is air pressure?
2. Health in Science Altitude sickness can affect people at altitudes above 1,800 meters. Find out what causes altitude sickness and how to prevent it. Summarize your findings in a short report.

Causes of Winds

You step out the door and a gust of wind almost blows you over! It's hard to believe that particles of air can hit you with such force. Where do the forces of wind come from?

Wind is moving air, caused by differences in air pressure. In general, air moves from areas of high pressure to areas of low pressure. Think about a balloon. When you let air out of a balloon, air rushes from inside the balloon where pressure is higher to where pressure is lower outside the balloon. You can feel wind.

Global Winds

Differences in air pressure are caused partly by differences in air temperature. When air is heated, its particles move faster and farther apart. The air becomes less dense. The lighter, warmer air moves upward, as cooler, denser air falls. This transfer of heat by the movement of air particles is called convection. Winds blow across Earth as warm air from regions near the equator rise and cold air from polar regions falls.

Winds do not just move in one big circle between the equator and the poles. As warm air rises over the equator, it begins to cool. At about 30° north and south of the equator, the air cools enough—and the pressure becomes high enough—to cause the air to sink back towards Earth's surface. The sinking air produces winds that blow near Earth's surface back toward the equator. These winds are called the trade winds and blow from east to west. You can see other global winds in the diagram.

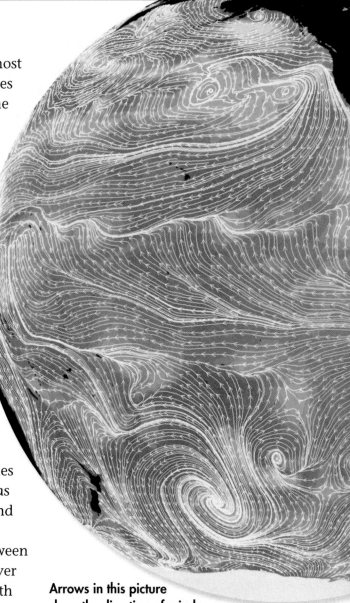

Arrows in this picture show the direction of winds over the Pacific Ocean on a particular day. Light winds are blue. Orange areas are strong winds.

The westerlies are winds that blow close to Earth's surface from west to east between 30° and 60° latitude. In the polar regions, between 60° and 90° latitude, winds near Earth's surface generally move from east to west and are called easterlies.

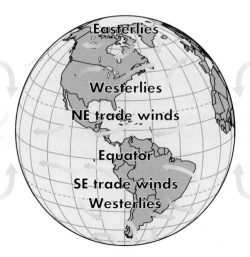

Easterlies
Westerlies
NE trade winds
Equator
SE trade winds
Westerlies

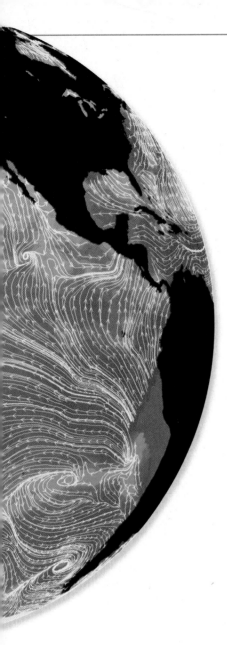

Local Winds

The rising and sinking of air also can create local winds. If you live near a large body of water, such as a lake or the ocean, you've probably experienced an example of this. The temperature of water doesn't change as quickly as the temperature of land. During the day while the sun is shining, the temperature of the land increases. The air above the land also gets warmer and rises. This air is replaced by cool air that blows in from over the water. The result is that winds move from the water toward land.

At night when land has cooled down, the flow of air is reversed. The temperature of the water is warmer than that of the land. Air over the water is warmed and rises. This air is replaced by cooler air that blows out from over the land. This pattern of airflow helps keep the air temperatures of land near bodies of water warmer and more even than temperatures inland.

Winds and Local Weather

When the air rises and cools near the equator, water vapor in the air condenses. The result is that areas near the equator have rains almost every day. At 30° north or south latitude, the air coming back down to Earth's surface is very dry. Some of the world's deserts, such as the Sahara Desert, are located in these regions.

Local weather is affected by another type of wind—the jet stream. A jet stream is a narrow belt of high-speed wind that blows in the upper troposphere and lower stratosphere. Jet streams always move from west to east in direction. In North America the jet stream affects day-to-day weather and seasons. In the winter, this jet stream can bring cold arctic air to states as far south as Kentucky. In the summer, the jet stream brings hot air north into Canada.

Winds are created by differences in air pressure. The greater the difference in pressure between two air masses, the stronger the wind will be.

✓ Lesson Checkpoint

1. How would air pressure change as you drove up and then down a mountain road?
2. What are the layers of Earth's atmosphere? How do they differ?
3. Writing in Science **Narrative** Write an account of winds forming from the viewpoint of a particle of air. Be sure to describe temperatures and movement.

331

How do clouds and precipitation form?

Water enters the atmosphere as part of the water cycle. Clouds form when air containing water vapor rises and cools. Precipitation may fall from clouds as rain, sleet, snow, or hail.

Humidity

Are you one of those people whose hair suddenly gets curly when you step outside on hot, muggy days? Or perhaps your straight hair just gets flat. The change in your hair may be due to humidity. **Humidity** is the amount of water vapor in the air.

Water enters the atmosphere as part of the water cycle. The amount of water vapor in air depends on the air temperature. Warm air has more water than cool air. As air gets cooler, water vapor condenses—changes from a gas to a liquid—to form dew, fog, or clouds.

Regardless of the temperature, there is a limit to the amount of water air can contain. **Relative humidity** is the amount of water vapor the air *actually* contains compared with the amount it *could* contain at that temperature. For example, if the relative humidity is 50 percent, the air has half of the amount of water it can contain at that temperature. On hot, humid days, the relative humidity can be almost 100 percent. At 100 percent relative humidity, air cannot contain any more water vapor.

Clouds

Clouds form when air rises and cools. Cooler air contains less water vapor, so the water in the rising air condenses to form tiny droplets. The droplets form around tiny particles in the air, such as dust, smoke, and salt. Clouds are a collection of millions of these tiny water droplets. Sometimes the temperature in the clouds is so cold that the water droplets freeze to form ice crystals. A cloud grows in size as more water droplets or ice crystals form.

Clouds are classified according to their shape and their height above Earth's surface. The three main forms of clouds are cirrus, cumulus, and stratus. All others are a modified form or a combination of these forms.

1. Cirrus clouds are thin and look feathery. Because they form high in the atmosphere where temperatures are below 0°C, cirrus clouds are made of ice crystals. These clouds do not usually result in precipitation.

2. Fluffy cirrocumulus clouds form high in the atmosphere. These clouds are made of ice crystals and do not usually result in precipitation.

3. Dark, heavy cumulonimbus clouds can reach high into the atmosphere. Cumulonimbus clouds are also called thunderheads because they usually result in a short, heavy rainfall or a thunderstorm.

4. Cumulus clouds usually form within two kilometers of Earth's surface. They are puffy clouds that stack up on top of one another. They usually form late in the day, when air warmed by land is rising into the atmosphere.

5. Stratus clouds form between two and six kilometers above Earth's surface. They are flat, white clouds that will produce mist or a steady drizzle.

1. √Checkpoint What is the relationship between humidity and relative humidity?

2. Writing in Science **Descriptive** Write a type of poem called a cinquain that describes one type of cloud shown on this page. Write the cinquain this way: The first line is a noun. The second is two adjectives. The third line is three verbs ending in -ing. The fourth is two words, and the fifth line is one word.

333

How Precipitation Forms

Rain, sleet, snow, and hail—chances are the area where you live gets at least one of these forms of precipitation. Precipitation is all the forms of moisture that fall from the atmosphere to Earth's surface. A cloud must have a lot of moisture before it can produce precipitation.

The water droplets and ice crystals in clouds can be very small, but they can get larger as more water clings to them. Precipitation forms when the drops or crystals become large enough to fall. The precipitation can be made of large water droplets, ice crystals, or both. Follow along in the diagram as you read how some types of precipitation form.

Rain and Snow

Some rain forms when water droplets fall from clouds through temperatures that are above freezing—0°C. However, most rain forms from ice crystals. That happens when the temperature directly beneath the clouds is above freezing. As the ice falls from the cloud, it melts to form rain.

If the temperature below the cloud is below freezing, the falling ice crystals continue to combine to form snowflakes. The crystals that make up snow can be feathery six-sided snowflakes or flat hexagons. The temperature and amount of moisture in a cloud determines the shape of the snowflakes. If the air where the snow falls is very cold, the snowflakes will be in the form of dry snow. Warmer ground temperatures produce a wet snow.

Sleet and Hail

Sleet forms when rain falls through a layer of freezing air that is large enough to freeze the rain. As water drops pass through the colder air, they freeze and reach the ground as small particles of ice that are the size of a raindrop.

Glaze, also called freezing rain, occurs when raindrops pass through cold air that is not cold enough to freeze the drops. The raindrops freeze when they hit a freezing surface.

Hail is precipitation that occurs in the form of hard, round particles of ice. This type of precipitation usually forms in warmer summer months. Hail forms inside cumulonimbus clouds when winds toss the ice crystals up and down. As the crystals move up and down, droplets of water attach to them and freeze. The hailstone continues to grow this way until it becomes too heavy to remain in the clouds. It then falls to the ground. Some hailstones can become as large as baseballs.

Drizzle

Warm

How Precipitation Forms

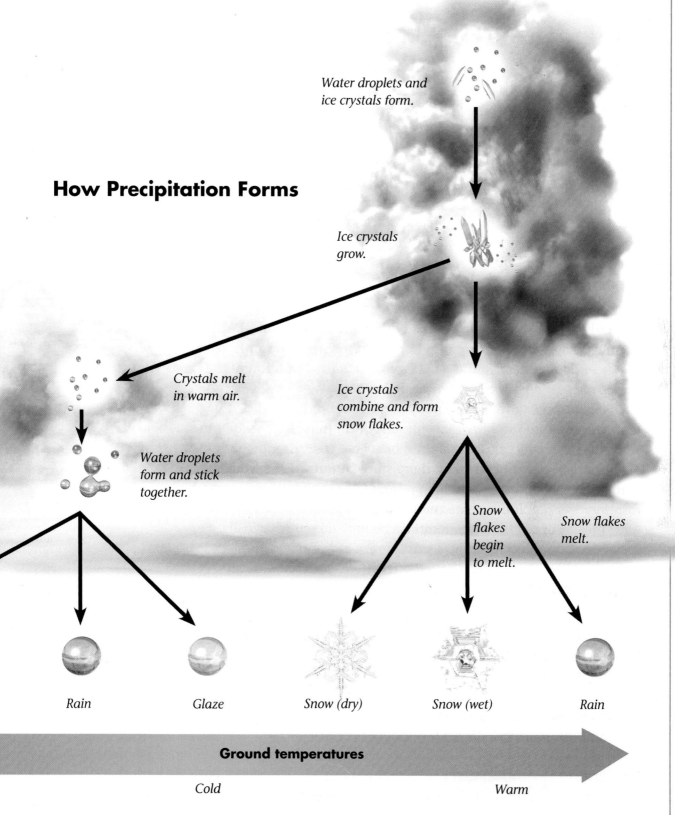

Water droplets and ice crystals form.

Ice crystals grow.

Crystals melt in warm air.

Ice crystals combine and form snow flakes.

Water droplets form and stick together.

Snow flakes begin to melt.

Snow flakes melt.

Rain

Glaze

Snow (dry)

Snow (wet)

Rain

Ground temperatures

Cold

Warm

✓ **Lesson Checkpoint**

1. When clouds form, why don't the water droplets in them fall to the ground immediately?

2. What determines whether precipitation falls as rain or snow?

3. 🎯 **Cause and Effect** What causes hail to form?

Lesson 3

What causes weather and climate?

Weather is the day-to-day condition of the atmosphere. It includes air temperature, humidity, wind speed, and precipitation. Meteorologists make weather forecasts by gathering weather data. Climate is the pattern of weather that occurs in an area over a long period.

Air Masses and Fronts

You may have seen a weather map like the ones on these pages. Probably the most noticeable parts of the weather map are the symbols showing air masses and fronts. Air masses and fronts produce the weather around you. **Weather** is the condition of the atmosphere at a particular time and place.

An **air mass** is a very large body of air that has a similar temperature and humidity throughout. An air mass forms when the same air stays over an area for days or even a week or more. The air mass gets its temperature and moisture characteristics from the area of Earth's surface over which it forms. For example, an air mass forming over a polar region would be cold.

Air masses of different temperatures usually do not mix easily. Instead, a boundary forms between them. The boundary that forms between air masses is called a **front.** Weather at a front often is cloudy or stormy. **Meteorologists**—scientists who study the weather—track the movements of air masses to predict weather conditions. Study the diagram below to see what happens when fronts meet.

Cold Front

A mass of cold air runs into a mass of warm air, forcing the warm air above the cold air. As the warm air rises, it cools and condenses. Clouds form, and heavy rain or snow may follow. Cold fronts move more quickly than warm fronts.

Stationary Front

A warm air mass and a cold air mass meet but neither one moves toward the other. As the name implies, a stationary front does not move quickly. It can stay over an area for several days. The weather produced is similar to a warm front.

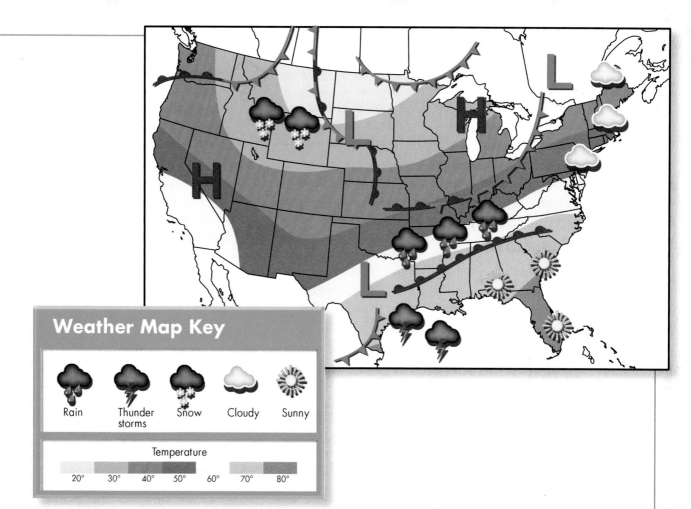

Weather Map Key

| Rain | Thunder storms | Snow | Cloudy | Sunny |

Temperature
20° 30° 40° 50° 60° 70° 80°

Cold Front

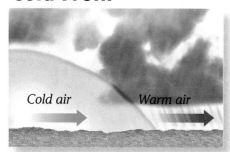

Cold air   Warm air

Warm Front

Warm air   Cold air

Warm Front

A mass of warm air runs into a mass of cooler air. The warm air is forced above the cooler air. As the warm air rises, it cools and condenses, forming clouds. Periods of steady rain or drizzle result.

1. ✅ **Checkpoint** How are air masses and fronts related?
2. **Writing in Science** Write a paragraph that explains how Earth's surface affects the characteristics of an air mass. Use the terms *temperature, humidity,* and *moisture.*

Severe Weather

You are outside and suddenly you hear thunder. What should you do? Your friend says that thunder can't hurt you, but you know that the lightning that goes with it can. Knowing what to do when severe weather happens is important. Read about each type of severe weather. Then study the information in the chart on the next page so that you know what to do when severe weather comes your way.

Thunderstorms

A thunderstorm is a small, intense storm that produces strong winds, heavy rain, lightning, and thunder. Thunderstorms occur all the time on Earth. Right now, about 1,800 of them are happening around the world. They tend to happen more in spring and summer months, but they can pop up any time of the year.

Every thunderstorm has lightning, so all thunderstorms are dangerous. Every year lightning kills more people than tornadoes do. And the storm's heavy rain can cause flash flooding, which also is very dangerous.

Tornadoes

A tornado is a violent, funnel-shaped column of air that extends from a thunderstorm to the ground. The winds of a tornado can reach 512 kilometers an hour. They form very quickly from thunderstorms, so they are difficult to predict. The path of a tornado also can change quickly. That makes predicting their path difficult too.

Tornadoes can happen in any part of the United States, but they are most common in the plains area between the Rocky Mountains and the Appalachians. Tornadoes are always dangerous.

Hurricanes

A hurricane is a large spiraling storm that forms over warm ocean waters—the southern Atlantic Ocean, Caribbean Sea, Gulf of Mexico, and eastern Pacific Ocean. The winds of a hurricane blow at least 119 kilometers per hour. These strong winds can cause a lot of damage when they hit land.

Hurricanes begin as thunderstorms in areas of low pressure over warm ocean water. Winds blow into the low-pressure area. Because Earth rotates, these winds spiral around the area. Moisture is added to the warm air of the hurricane by evaporation of ocean water. As the warm air rises, the water condenses. The process releases a lot of energy. Large amounts of warm, moist air keep a hurricane moving. When it moves across colder waters or drier land, the hurricane loses its source of energy and dies.

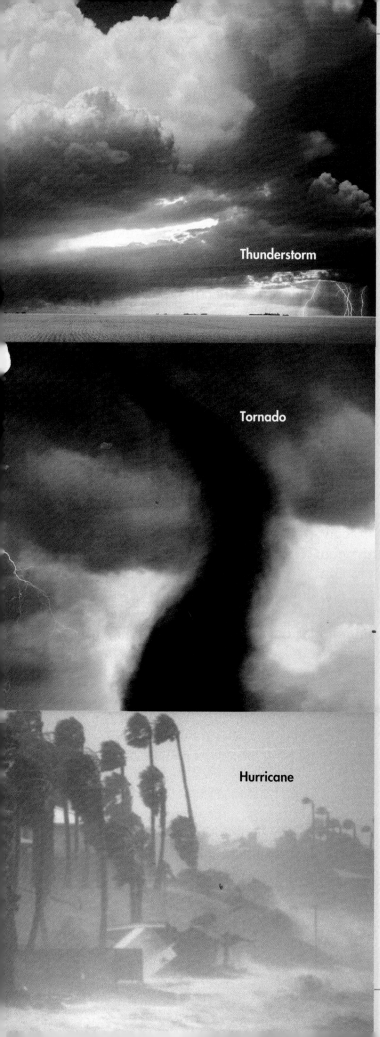

Thunderstorm

Tornado

Hurricane

Severe Weather Safety

Thunderstorms

- Find shelter in a building or car. Keep car windows closed.
- In the woods: Take shelter under the shorter trees. If boating or swimming, go to land and find shelter.
- Outside in an open space: Squat low to the ground. Place your hands on your knees with your head between them. Make yourself as small as possible.

Tornadoes

- Take shelter underground in a basement or storm shelter.
- No basement or shelter: Go to an inside room, hallway, or closet on the first floor away from windows.
- Outside: Lie flat in a ditch. Lie facedown and cover your head with your hands.

Hurricanes

- Prepare a disaster plan and a disaster supply kit ahead of time.
- Evacuate if told to do so. If you don't need to evacuate, stay indoors.
- Avoid using the phone except for emergencies.

1. ✔**Checkpoint** What should you do if you are outdoors when each of these types of storm hits: thunderstorm, hurricane, tornado?

2. **Math in Science** Light travels at 299,792 kilometers per second, so when lightning flashes, you see it immediately. Sound travels much more slowly—about 1.7 kilometers in five seconds. If you see lightning and then hear thunder about 15 seconds later, how far away was the lightning?

339

Predicting Weather

On your way to the ballpark, you look at the bright Sun in the sky. Good day for a game. By the time you get to the park, dark clouds have filled the sky. Weather can change quickly, and storms can catch you unprepared. A weather forecast can help you prepare for weather. You can find weather forecasts on television, the newspaper, the radio, and the Internet. In the event of severe weather, these sources also give warnings and instructions.

Weather forecasting begins with looking at weather conditions all over the world. Meteorologists gather information about the factors that make up the weather—precipitation, temperature, wind speed, humidity, and air pressure. Then they use computers to analyze the information and make predictions. In the United States, the National Weather Service operates the computers. Forecasters all over the world use this information to predict the weather both nationally and locally.

Gathering Data

What tools do meteorologists use to gather weather information? You probably are familiar with some forecasting tools. Thermometers measure temperatures. Barometers measure air pressure, and anemometers measure wind speed. Simple rain gauges measure any precipitation that falls.

Today meteorologists have more advanced methods for gathering weather data. The Automated Surface Observing System (ASOS) program is run by the National Weather Service, the Federal Aviation Administration, and the Department of Defense. The system is a group of sensors that measures, collects, and broadcasts weather data. ASOS provides up-to-date information 24 hours a day, every day of the year.

Knowing what is happening on Earth's surface isn't enough to make good weather forecasts. Meteorologists also gather information from above Earth. Twice a day at almost 900 stations around the world, scientists release weather balloons. The balloons gather information about Earth's weather from the troposphere.

Another important tool, Doppler radar, uses radio waves to measure wind speed and precipitation. It also gives scientists information about the direction in which a storm is moving. By watching the movement of a storm and the winds within it, scientists are better able to predict severe weather. Being able to make accurate weather predictions can save lives.

Scientists can collect data about global climate changes and weather from this weather station high atop Mount Washington in New Hampshire.

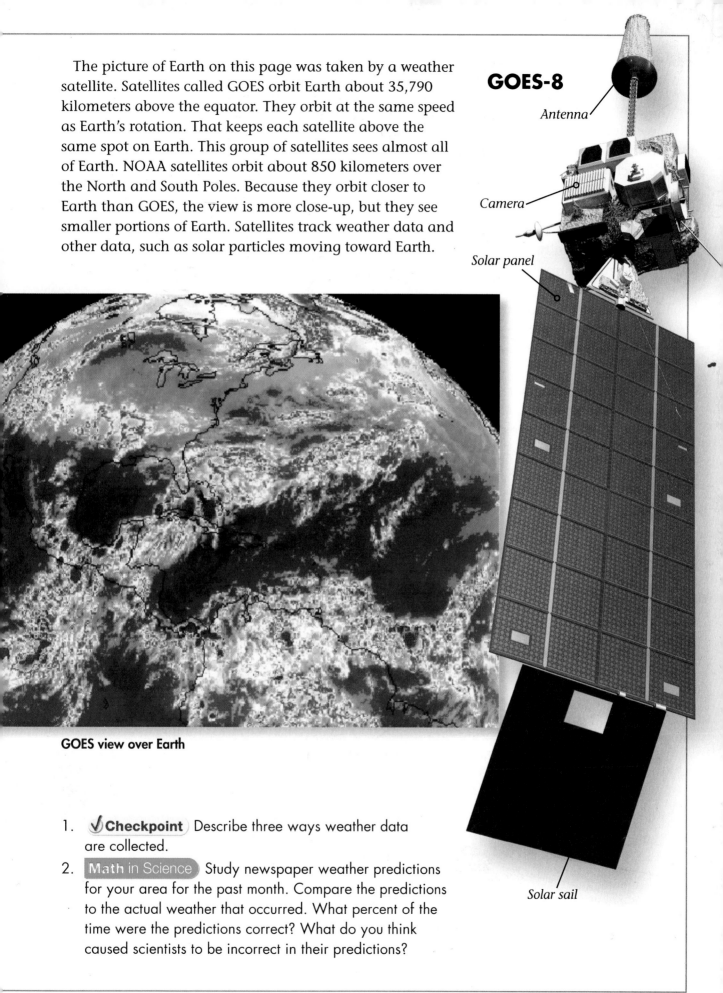

The picture of Earth on this page was taken by a weather satellite. Satellites called GOES orbit Earth about 35,790 kilometers above the equator. They orbit at the same speed as Earth's rotation. That keeps each satellite above the same spot on Earth. This group of satellites sees almost all of Earth. NOAA satellites orbit about 850 kilometers over the North and South Poles. Because they orbit closer to Earth than GOES, the view is more close-up, but they see smaller portions of Earth. Satellites track weather data and other data, such as solar particles moving toward Earth.

GOES-8

Antenna

Camera

Solar panel

Solar sail

GOES view over Earth

1. ✓ **Checkpoint** Describe three ways weather data are collected.
2. **Math in Science** Study newspaper weather predictions for your area for the past month. Compare the predictions to the actual weather that occurred. What percent of the time were the predictions correct? What do you think caused scientists to be incorrect in their predictions?

Climate

As you now know, weather is the condition of the atmosphere at a particular time. Weather in an area can change constantly. **Climate,** however, is the pattern of weather that occurs in an area over a long period— usually at least 30 years. The climate of an area is usually described in terms of its average temperatures and average precipitation.

You probably know that climate differs from one area of Earth to another. Do you know what causes the differences? Many factors can affect climate. For example, because Earth is round, different parts receive different amounts of sunlight. Those areas that receive less sunlight will have colder climates.

Large bodies of water also affect climate. Water warms and cools more slowly than does land. As a result, temperatures near oceans and lakes are milder than those further inland. The warm and cold currents in large bodies of water also affect climate.

Pollution is another factor that affects climate. Pollutants such as carbon dioxide, which is produced when fossil fuels burn, can contribute to a worldwide increase in temperature, called global warming. The amount of carbon dioxide in the atmosphere has increased over the last 150 years. Some scientists think that this increase has led to global warming. Rising global temperature can cause sea levels to rise and can affect forests, crops, and water supplies. It could also have an effect on ecosystems and human health.

People can control some factors that affect climate, such as the amount of carbon dioxide in the atmosphere. The photos on these pages show other factors that affect climate. How many of these can people control?

The angle at which sunlight hits a particular area on Earth is one factor that determines the area's climate.

✓ Lesson Checkpoint

1. What is the difference between weather and climate?
2. Explain how warm fronts and cold fronts affect weather.
3. ⊙ **Cause and Effect** How do large bodies of water affect climate?

Some Factors That Affect Climate

Volcanic eruptions release large amounts of ash and smoke into the atmosphere. These materials can block sunlight, causing Earth to cool.

The Gulf Stream, a warm-water current that flows northward through the Atlantic Ocean, brings warmth from the equator toward the North Pole. Air warmed by this current helps keep the climates of England and Ireland in Northern Europe mild in winter.

Earth's polar regions receive less solar radiation, and ice reflects much of it. This keeps these areas cold. Arctic regions have an average winter temperature of about −30°C.

As air rises over mountains, it cools, and water vapor condenses. The areas of the western slopes of mountains receive a lot of rainfall. The eastern slopes are generally dry.

Water from oceans and other bodies of water evaporates and helps make the climate more humid. As moist air moves over land, it can cause precipitation.

When forests burn, carbon dioxide is released into the atmosphere. Also when forests burn or are cut, fewer trees remain to absorb carbon dioxide. Increasing levels of carbon dioxide in the atmosphere may be causing global warming.

Low clouds, such as stratocumulus clouds, reflect sunlight, which makes Earth cooler. However, high clouds, such as cirrus clouds, help keep Earth warm by trapping heat from solar radiation in the atmosphere.

Investigate How can you make a model of a tornado?

A tornado is a violent windstorm characterized by whirling winds within a funnel-shaped cloud. A tornado's movements are difficult to see in air but can be imitated—and seen—in water.

Materials

2 plastic bottles and colored water

funnel

washer

duct tape

paper towels

Process Skills

Making and using a model of a tornado can help you form a mental picture of the winds in a tornado.

What to Do

1. Pour colored water into a plastic bottle to fill it $\frac{3}{4}$ full. Dry the opening and place the washer over it.

2. Place the second bottle upside down with its opening over the washer. Tape bottles together.

3. Carefully turn the bottles so the empty bottle is the bottom bottle. **Observe** what happens.

4 Gently twist or turn the bottles clockwise. Observe what happens.

Bottle Tornado

	Motion	Observations
Trial 1	gentle twist	
Trial 2	gentle twist	
Trial 3	quick twist	
Trial 4	quick twist	

5 Repeat steps 1–4, twisting the bottles quickly. Observe your **model**.

Explain Your Results

1. What happens in your **model** if the bottles are left to stand, without twisting? Explain.

2. How did twisting the bottle make the difference between forming and not forming a "tornado"?

Go Further

How else could you make a model of a tornado? Write a plan others could follow.

Math in Science

WEATHER UNDER PRESSURE

To better understand air pressure, you might think of a very tall blanket of air. This blanket of air is always pushing on you from all directions.

How hard the air pushes on you depends partly on how thick the blanket is. On a high mountain, air pressure is lower because the blanket is thinner, so there is less air pushing down from above. How hard the air pushes on you also depends on how closely packed the air particles are. The tighter the air particles are packed together, the heavier the air is and the greater the air pressure. When air gets warmer, air particles spread out, reducing air pressure.

Changes in air pressure can give us clues as to what is happening with the weather. The following weather data is for an area into which a warm front is moving. In weather reports, air pressure is usually reported in "inches of mercury," due to the longtime use of the mercury barometer. Some reports use units called "millibars." One inch of mercury equals about 33.87 millibars.

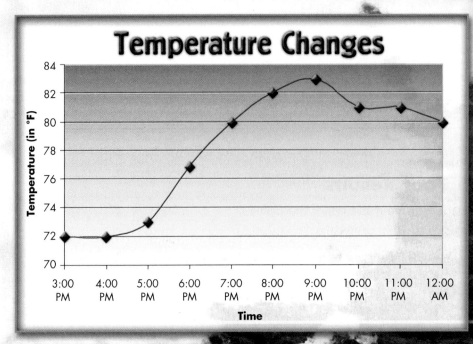

Temperature Changes

e Tools Take It to the Net
pearsonsuccessnet.com

Time	Air Pressure (inches of mercury)	Sky Conditions
3:00 PM	30.86	partly cloudy
4:00 PM	30.77	partly cloudy
5:00 PM	30.71	cloudy
6:00 PM	30.42	cloudy
7:00 PM	29.83	cloudy
8:00 PM	29.71	light showers
9:00 PM	29.59	heavy showers
10:00 PM	29.51	light showers
11:00 PM	29.47	light showers
12:00 AM	29.46	cloudy

Use the graph on page 346 and the chart above to answer the questions.

1. Find the highest and lowest air pressure readings on the chart. Express each of these in millibars. Round your answers to the nearest whole number.

2. What is the highest temperature reading on the graph? At what time of day did this occur? Why is this an unusual time of day for a high temperature reading? Can you explain it?

3. Describe the trend in air pressure through the day.

4. Use the data given to make an argument to support this statement: A drop in air pressure is a warning that a storm might occur.

5. What change in air pressure might you expect as a cold front moves into the area?

Lab zone Take-Home Activity

Collect your own air pressure data at several times during the day or over several days. Hourly readings may be obtained on the Internet or television, or from a barometer. Look for a trend in your data and make your own weather prediction based on the trend. Was your prediction correct?

Use Vocabulary

air mass (p. 336)   front (p. 336)

air pressure
(p. 328)

atmosphere
(p. 327)

climate (p. 342)

humidity (p. 332)

meteorologist
(p. 336)

relative humidity
(p. 332)

weather (p. 336)

Use the vocabulary term from the list above that best matches each description.

1. The amount of water vapor in the air

2. The boundary that forms between air masses

3. A scientist who studies weather

4. A large body of air that has a similar temperature and humidity throughout

5. The condition of the atmosphere at a particular time and place

6. The blanket of air surrounding a planet

7. The amount of water vapor the air contains compared with the maximum it can hold at that temperature

8. The pattern of weather in an area over a long period

9. The measure of force with which air particles push on matter

Explain Concepts

10. Explain why air pressure decreases as you go higher in the atmosphere.

11. Explain how each of the following can affect climate: mountains, oceans, pollution, and forest fires.

12. The diagram shows a front. Identify the type of front and then explain what is happening.

Process Skills

13. Model Draw a diagram to show how a cloud forms.

14. Infer A thunderstorm warning has been announced by the local weather forecaster. What should you do?

Cause and Effect

15. Make a graphic organizer like the one shown below. Identify the causes that result in global wind movement.

| Causes | → | Effect |

Test Prep

Choose the letter that best completes the statement or answers the question.

16. Which of the following would meteorologists use to measure the speed and direction of a storm?
Ⓐ barometer
Ⓑ thermometer
Ⓒ humidity
Ⓓ Doppler radar

17. In which layer of the atmosphere does most weather take place?
Ⓕ thermosphere
Ⓖ mesosphere
Ⓗ stratosphere
Ⓘ troposphere

18. What results from differences in air pressure?
Ⓐ rain
Ⓑ wind
Ⓒ humidity
Ⓓ evaporation

19. Explain why the answer you chose for Question 16 is best. For each of the answers you did not choose, give a reason why it is not the best choice.

20. Writing in Science **Descriptive** Write a paragraph describing a thunderstorm as it passes over your home. Include details about the clouds, the winds, the precipitation, and the air temperature.

El Niño and the "BIG BELCH"

Like living animals such as cows and sheep, the Earth sometimes "burps." During El Niño years in particular, the planet suddenly releases large amounts of gas, just as you might after drinking a carbonated beverage.

Every three to seven years, the temperature of the Pacific Ocean along the equator warms up a great deal. The phenomenon was given the name El Niño, or "The Child," by people in Peru. El Niño changes "normal" weather patterns around the world.

The reason scientists sometimes call the changes "a big belch" is because two greenhouse gases in the atmosphere, methane and carbon dioxide, increase significantly during El Niño years. So much gas is released that some scientists compare it to Earth having a planet-sized case of heartburn.

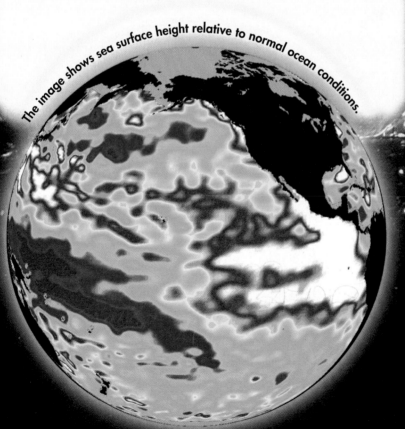

The image shows sea surface height relative to normal ocean conditions.

Many greenhouse gases result from people burning fossil fuels. That factor doesn't change during El Niño years, so why do methane and carbon dioxide increase so much? Scientists thought that the increase was due to a change in the life cycle of plants during El Niño years. But now NASA scientists think wildfires may get the "big belch" started. In El Niño years, large areas in the tropics become very dry, and fires can result. During the 1997–1998 El Niño, huge fires burned in Mexico and Southeast Asia, for example.

At the same time that burning plants are releasing huge amounts of carbon dioxide into the atmosphere, fewer plants are growing in the dry tropics. Plants take in carbon dioxide from the air. With less plant growth, less carbon dioxide is taken in by plants. Just a small change in the amount absorbed by plants is enough to give Earth heartburn.

Lab zone Take-Home Activity

Research the effect of greenhouse gases on Earth. Find out ways to reduce the amount of these gases in the atmosphere. Use the information to make a pamphlet that informs the public about ways to reduce greenhouse gases.

EDWARD R. COOK

Edward Cook is sometimes known as Dr. Dendro. Dendro comes from a Greek word meaning "tree." Is Cook a tree doctor? Not quite. But trees are a very important part of his work.

Cook is a paleoclimatologist. That's a person who studies climates of the past. How can someone tell what climates were like hundreds or even thousands of years ago? Cook uses tree rings.

Tree rings form a pattern of circles that you can see on a tree stump or at the end of a log. Each year a tree grows a layer of wood under the bark. This layer becomes another ring. By counting the rings, you can tell how many years the tree lived. But that's not all. If the temperatures and amounts of precipitation are good for tree growth, the tree ring will be wide. Narrow rings usually means temperatures were too cold or there was too little rainfall for good tree growth that year.

Scientists use a borer to take pencil-thin cores of wood from trees. The trees are unharmed. By examining the ring marks in the cores, Cook can tell, for example, that Texas had a drought from 1703 to 1709. That's more than just an interesting bit of information. Cook knows that by studying weather patterns of the past, scientists can better predict weather patterns of the future.

Lab zone Take-Home Activity

Find a tree stump, a log, or a thick branch that has been cut from a tree. Count the rings to see how old the tree or branch is. Are some rings wider than others? What does this tell you about the weather in those years?

Unit B Test Talk

Choose the Right Answer

Multiple choice test questions have several possible answers. To choose the right answers, first read the passage and then think about the main idea.

> **Acid precipitation** is any form of precipitation, such as rain, sleet, or hail, that is acidic. The **pH** of a substance tells its level of acidity. Substances are rated from 1 to 14 on the pH scale. Any substance with a pH below 7 is acidic. The lower the number, the more acidic the substance. Acid precipitation may have a pH lower than 5.6.
>
> Automobiles, electric power plants, and certain industries may use fossil fuels, such as coal and oil. When fossil fuels burn, they release chemicals that can combine with water vapor in the air to form acid precipitation. When it falls, acid precipitation can harm or kill living organisms. It also can damage buildings, statues, and other structures.
>
> Acidic substances that fall to Earth's surface are called **acid deposition.** Acidic substances may fall in wet form as acid precipitation. They may also fall in dry form. Solid particles may fall directly onto the ground, plants, or buildings and form acidic substances.

Read each question carefully, and then read every answer choice. To choose the right answer, first eliminate answers that you know are incorrect.

Use What You Know

1. Which of these pH values is least acidic?
   Ⓐ 2
   Ⓑ 4
   Ⓒ 7
   Ⓓ 9

2. An acidic substance that falls to Earth either wet or dry is acidic
   Ⓕ deposition.
   Ⓖ fossil fuel.
   Ⓗ precipitation.
   Ⓘ water vapor.

3. Acid precipitation forms when chemicals from burning fossil fuels combine with
   Ⓐ carbon dioxide.
   Ⓑ nitrogen.
   Ⓒ sulfur.
   Ⓓ water vapor.

4. Which is a likely pH for acid rain?
   Ⓕ 5.2
   Ⓖ 6.1
   Ⓗ 8.3
   Ⓘ 12.2

353

Unit B Wrap-Up

Chapter 8

How does the theory of plate tectonics explain Earth's landforms?
- Earth's lithosphere is composed of plates.
- The plates are constantly moving—toward each other, away from each other, or past each other.

Chapter 9

How do rocks and minerals form soils?
- Rocks are made of minerals.
- Rocks break down during weathering and then mix with organic materials to form soil.

Chapter 10

What processes change Earth's landforms?
- Weathering breaks down rock into smaller pieces, which can be carried to other locations by erosion.
- During deposition, sediments carried by wind or water are deposited in new locations.

Chapter 11

How can we use Earth's resources wisely?
- Earth's land, water, and air resources can be renewable or nonrenewable.
- Recognizing how Earth's resources are interconnected and using resources wisely are ways to make good choices about resources.

Chapter 12

What causes Earth's weather and climate?
- When air masses with different temperatures and humidity meet, precipitation may result.
- Many factors, including location on the Earth, nearby bodies of water or mountains, and human activities, can affect an area's weather and climate.

Performance Assessment

Model Earth's Interior

What are the layers of Earth's interior? Use modeling clay to make a model of Earth. Make the model a half sphere to show the inside layers. A different color of clay can represent each layer. Consider the relative thicknesses of each layer when determining the thickness of each layer of clay. After you have finished, tape paper to toothpicks to make small flags. Write the name of each of Earth's layers on a flag, and insert the flags into your clay model.

Read More About Earth Science

Look for books like these in the library.

Lab zone Full Inquiry

Experiment How fast does water flow through soils?

Water will flow through some soils more quickly than others.

Materials

spoon, timer (or clock with a second hand)

paper plate, paper towels, tape

clay soil, loam soil, sand, gravel

water, graduated cylinder, measuring cup

2 cups, 4 foam cups with bottoms cut out, 4 coffee filters

Process Skills

You **control variables** when you change only one thing in an **experiment**.

Ask a question.

How does the type of soil—and particle size—affect how fast water moves through it?

State your hypothesis.

Look at the four types of soil. Note the particle size of each. If you pour water on clay soil, loam soil, sand, and gravel, which material will the water move through fastest? Write your hypothesis.

Particle Size Chart

Type of Soil	Particle Size
Clay soil	less than 0.002 mm
Loam soil	0.002 – 2 mm
Sand	0.05 – 2 mm
Gravel	greater than 2 mm

Identify and control variables.

You will pour 50 mL of water on each type of soil. You will **observe** how much water moves through each type of soil in 5 minutes. Everything else in your **experiment** must remain the same.

Test your hypothesis.

1️⃣ Before beginning your experiment, first put a spoonful of each soil sample on a paper plate. **Observe** the color and texture of each soil. Record your observations in a data table.

graduated cylinder
with 50 mL of water

2️⃣ Use the foam cups that have had their bottoms cut out. Cover the bottom end of each with a coffee filter. Tape the coffee filter to the cup.

foam cup with
bottom cut out

100 mL of soil

coffee
filter
taped to
foam cup

3️⃣ Use a measuring cup to put 100 mL of clay soil in one of the foam cups.

4️⃣ Put the foam cup in a plastic cup. Use a graduated cylinder to **measure** and pour 50 mL of water into the foam cup.

plastic cup

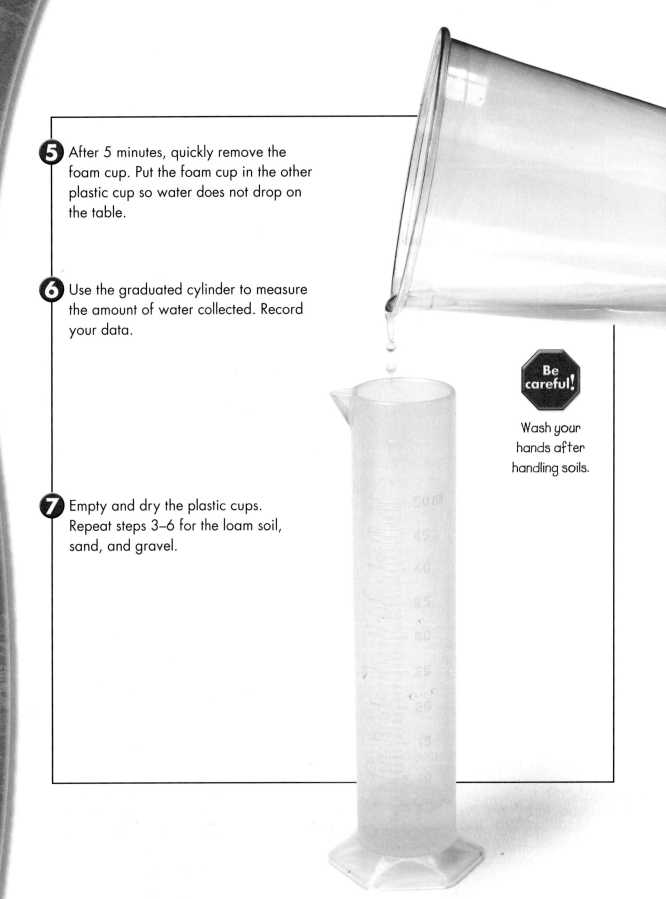

5 After 5 minutes, quickly remove the foam cup. Put the foam cup in the other plastic cup so water does not drop on the table.

6 Use the graduated cylinder to measure the amount of water collected. Record your data.

Be careful!

Wash your hands after handling soils.

7 Empty and dry the plastic cups. Repeat steps 3–6 for the loam soil, sand, and gravel.

Collect and record your data.

Soil Type	Texture and Color of Soil	Amount of Water Collected (mL)
Clay soil		
Loam soil		
Sand		
Gravel		

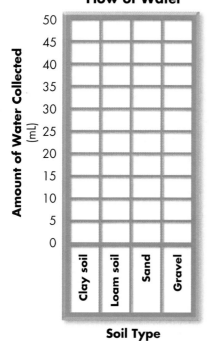

Soil Type and Flow of Water

Amount of Water Collected (mL)

50
45
40
35
30
25
20
15
10
5
0

Clay soil Loam soil Sand Gravel

Soil Type

Interpret your data.
Use your data to make a bar graph. The graph should show how much water moved through the soil in 5 minutes. Look closely at your graphs. Describe how the type of soil—and the particle size—affected how fast the water moved through it.

State your conclusion.
Explain how the type of soil affected how quickly water moved through the soil. Compare your hypothesis with your results. **Communicate** your conclusion.

Go Further
Would the water move at the same rate if the soil types were already wet at the beginning of the experiment? Design and carry out a plan to investigate this or other questions you may have.

Science Fair Projects

Fault Formation

A fault is a break in Earth's crust that usually forms as a result of the movement of tectonic plates.

Idea: Design and build a model showing different ways that faults form. Investigate the types of places on Earth where faults are most likely to form.

River Migration

Rivers constantly change their shapes and location due to soil erosion, drought, and other factors.

Idea: Create a model river. Experiment to find how factors such as soil composition, vegetation, and slope of the land affect the rate at which a river changes its shape.

Desalination of Ocean Water

Can ocean water be used as a source of fresh water? Desalination is the process of removing salt from ocean water.

Idea: Demonstrate ways of removing salt from ocean water. Research places where this process is used. Explore the conditions for which desalination is useful.

Using Scientific Methods

1. Ask a question.
2. State a hypothesis.
3. Identify and control variables.
4. Test your hypothesis.
5. Collect and record your data.
6. Interpret your data.
7. State your conclusions.
8. Go further.

EC CRU 10 9 8 7 6 5 4 3 2

Unit C

Physical Science

Chapter 13

Matter

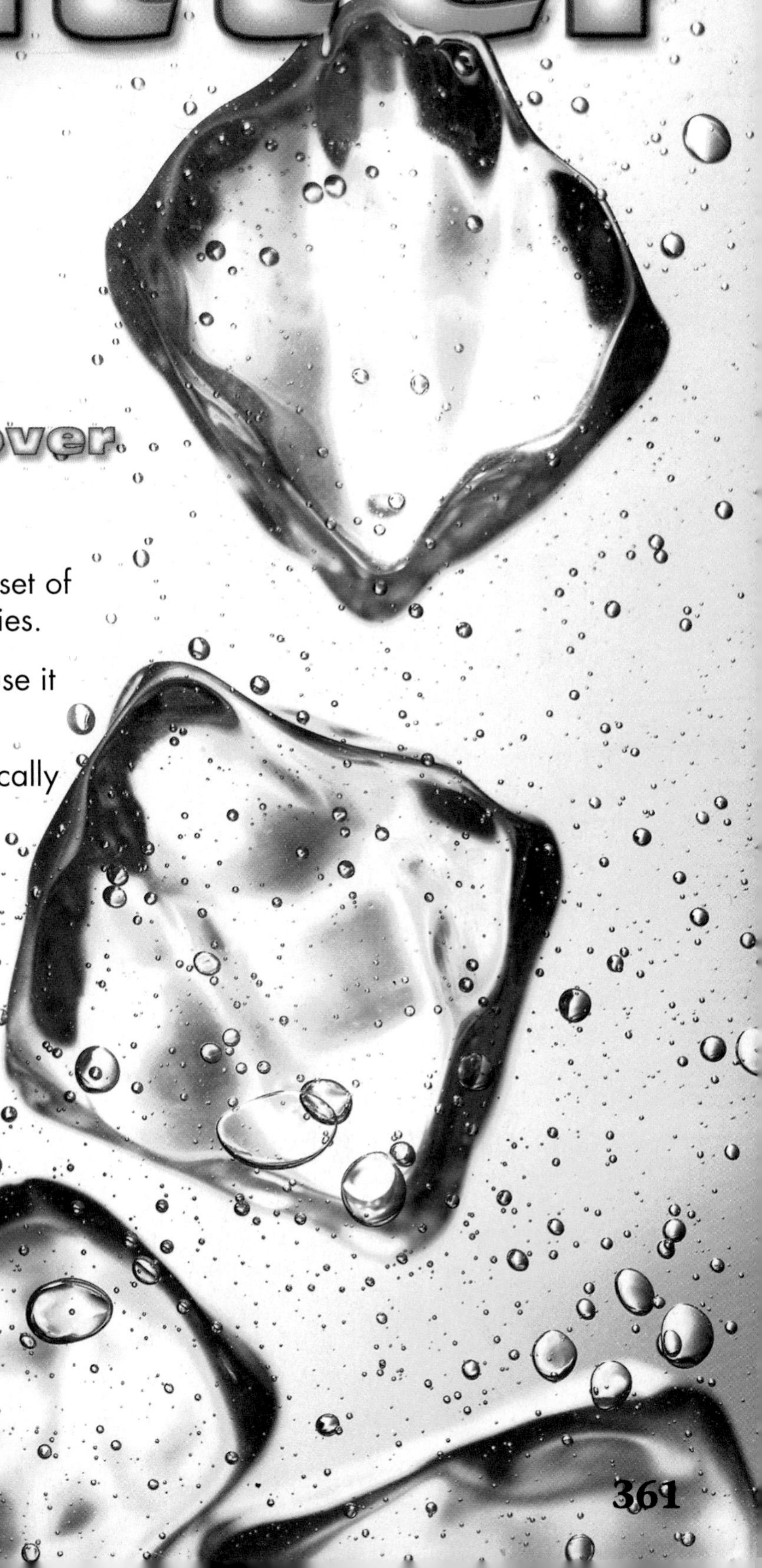

You Will Discover

- what chemical and physical properties are.

- that a substance has a unique set of chemical and physical properties.

- how to calculate density and use it to identify a substance.

- how matter can change chemically and physically.

online
Student Edition
pearsonsuccessnet.com

361

How can the properties of matter change?

physical property

physical change

chemical change

chemical property

Chapter 13 Vocabulary

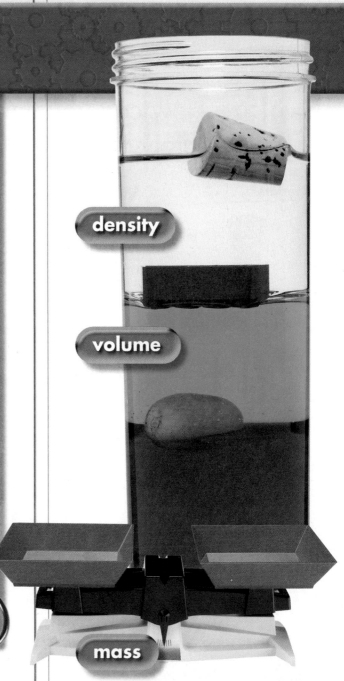

density

volume

mass

condensation

weight

Explore How can you find the volume of an irregular solid?

Materials

graduated cylinder and water

8 gram cubes

modeling clay

What to Do

1 Pour 25 mL of water into the graduated cylinder.

2 Drop 8 gram cubes into the graduated cylinder. Notice that the volume increases. **Measure** and record the new volume. Remember: each cube has a volume of 1 cm³.

3 Remove the cubes and the water. Repeat steps 1 and 2, but put the clay in the water. Record the new volume.

Process Skills

By **measuring** in **sequence** the changes in the volume in the graduated cylinder, you can find the volume of an irregular solid.

Explain Your Results

1. What is the volume of a gram cube in milliliters? Compare the sizes of a milliliter and a cubic centimeter. What is the volume of the clay in milliliters and in cubic centimeters?

2. Change the shape of the clay. **Measure** its volume. Did the volume change?

How to Read Science

Reading Skills

Sequence

Understanding science concepts sometimes means understanding the order in which events happen. This step-by-step order of events is called **sequence.**

- Look for clue words, such as *first, next, then, after, last,* and *finally,* that signal sequence.

Some clue words are marked for you in the activity procedure below.

Activity Procedure

Finding a Marble's Volume

First, gather these materials: a marble, a graduated cylinder, and some water. Next, put about 50 mL of water into the graduated cylinder. Record the exact amount of water. After you place the marble in the water, find and record the new volume of water. Finally, subtract the original volume of water from the new volume to find the volume of the marble.

Apply It!

Make a graphic organizer like this one. Fill in the steps to show the **sequence** of events for **measuring** and finding volume in the activity procedure.

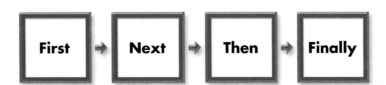

| First | → | Next | → | Then | → | Finally |

You Are There!

This Japanese macaque is soaking in a hot spring fed by a volcano. You can almost see the steam rising and feel the sting of ice on your face. Imagine the shock of heat as the water hits your cold toes! The macaque, the water, the ice, and even the rock and air have something in common. Do you know what it is?

AudioText

Lesson 1

What is matter?

All matter has volume, mass, density, boiling point, freezing point, and other properties. These properties can be described as physical properties or chemical properties. Matter can change chemically and physically.

Measuring Matter

You probably know that the macaque, the rocks, and the water in the picture are matter. But did you know that the air surrounding the macaque also is matter? Matter is anything that has mass and takes up space. Everything you see is matter, whether it is tiny or huge, hard or soft, or even wet or dry. Some matter, such as the air, you can't even see.

Mass is a property of matter that can be measured. An object's **mass** is the amount of matter that makes up that object. Mass is measured in grams. The mass of an object does not depend on the object's shape. A piece of paper has the same mass whether it lies flat, is folded in half, or is shaped into a fancy paper boat.

Volume is another property of matter that you can measure. **Volume** is the amount of space that something takes up. The volume of a liquid is measured in milliliters (mL). A solid's volume is measured in cubic centimeters (cm^3). You can find the volume of some kinds of solids by multiplying the length by the width by the height. For example, a block of iron that measures 2 centimeters by 2 centimeters by 4 centimeters has a volume of 16 cubic centimeters, or 16 cm^3.

1. ✔**Checkpoint** What are you measuring when you measure an object's mass?
2. **Math** in Science What is the volume of a block of wood that measures 1 cm by 4 cm by 2 cm?

Mass and Weight

People often confuse mass and weight, but they are different properties of matter. Mass is a measure of the amount of matter in an object. The mass of an object stays the same no matter where the object is in the universe. You can find the mass of an object by using a balance.

Balance

Weight is a measure of the pull of gravity on an object. Weight can change if the object moves to a place with a different force of gravity. Your mass would be the same on Earth as it is on the Moon. But your weight on Earth is six times greater than it would be on the Moon! Weight is measured with a spring scale in units called newtons. A newton is equal to about a quarter of a pound—a unit of weight you are more likely familiar with.

Spring scale

Density

Did anyone ever ask you this riddle: Which weighs more—a pound of feathers or a pound of lead? Do you know the answer? Both the feathers and the lead weigh the same—one pound. But one pound of feathers would be a lot larger than one pound of lead. How can that be? The reason is that the matter that makes up lead is more tightly packed than the matter that makes up feathers. The lead has a greater density. **Density** is a measure of the amount of matter in a given space. Another way to say this is that density is mass per unit volume.

Think of density this way. Suppose you have a cube of lead that measures one centimeter on each side. Its volume would be one cubic centimeter. Its mass would be 11.35 grams. The same size cube of cork would have the same volume—1 cubic centimeter. But its mass would be smaller—0.24 grams. The particles that make up matter are more tightly packed in the lead than in the cork. The lead cube would be heavier.

Finding the density of a substance is easy if you know its mass and volume. Use this formula:

$$\text{density} = \frac{\text{mass}}{\text{volume}} \text{ or } \frac{m}{v}$$

For example, suppose you have an object with a mass of 30 grams and its volume is 15 cubic centimeters. What is its density?

$$\text{density} = \frac{m}{v} = \frac{30g}{15cm^3} = \frac{2g}{cm^3}$$

One cubic centimeter of this substance has a mass of 2 grams.

Can you tell what's happening in this tube? The substances—both liquids and solids—have different densities. A substance that is less dense will float on a substance that is more dense. The densest liquid is on the bottom, and the least dense floats at the top.

Using Density to Identify Substances

By now you might be wondering how knowing the density of a substance is useful. You can use density to identify an unknown substance. Every substance has a particular density. For example, if you have a small cube of lead or a large lead pipe, the density of the lead is the same—11.35 grams per cubic centimeter. Also the density of a particular substance usually differs from that of any other substance.

Suppose you have an unknown piece of metal and want to find out what it is. First, measure its mass and volume, and then use the mass and volume to calculate the density. Once you know the density, you can use a table like the one on this page to identify the metal. If you find that the density of your unknown metal is 10.50 grams per cubic centimeter, what metal do you have?

Oil is less dense than water, so it floats on the water. That's why oil that is spilled in an accident is likely to wash up onto the beach.

✓ Checkpoint

1. If you dropped a cork in a container of water, would it sink or float. How do you know?

2. Math in Science A block of a substance is 2 cm wide, 1 cm high, and 5 cm long. It has a mass of 6.8 grams. What is its density? Use the table to identify the substance.

Densities of Common Materials

Material	Density (g/cm³)
Gold	19.32
Lead	11.35
Silver	10.50
Copper	8.96
Rubber	1.10
Water	1.00
Cork	0.24
Wood	
White oak	0.68
Balsa	0.16

Physical Properties of Matter

Density is just one of the properties that can be used to describe matter. You learned that the density of copper is 8.96 grams per cubic centimeter. Look at the copper in the picture below. What other properties describe copper?

Did you describe copper as shiny and solid? Those are some of copper's physical properties. **Physical properties** of matter are those that can be seen or measured without changing the substance into something else.

The pieces of copper in the picture show two other physical properties. The copper is malleable, which means it can be spread or shaped by being pounded with a hammer or by being forced through rollers. Copper can also be made into wire, which means that it is ductile.

You might recognize copper as the material that makes up electrical wires. That's due to another physical property—its ability to conduct heat or electricity. Wood does not conduct heat or electricity well, which is why cooking spoons are often made of wood.

Other physical properties of matter include whether a substance can be dissolved in other substances, whether it is magnetic, and the temperatures at which the substance freezes and boils. A substance's physical properties are the same no matter how much of the substance there is.

The temperature at which a liquid boils is a physical property.

All pure water freezes and melts at 0°C. The temperatures at which substances freeze and melt are physical properties.

Copper

370

Many substances are changed when they mix with acids. The specific way a substance changes when mixed with another substance is a chemical property. You can tell that the zinc nail is changing into another substance in the acid by the bubbles it releases. But the gold in the bracelet doesn't change.

Chemical Properties of Matter

Another way to describe matter is to describe its chemical properties. A substance's **chemical properties** tell how the substance forms new substances when it reacts with something else. The wood in the fireplace is burning. As the wood burns, it will change into new substances—ash and gases. A substance's ability to burn is called flammability. Wood is flammable, but iron is not.

We know that wood is flammable, as it is the choice fuel for our fireplaces and bonfires.

Some Common Properties		
Substance	**Physical Property**	**Chemical Property**
Wood	Does not conduct electricity	Flammable
Iron	Malleable	Combines with oxygen to form rust
Water	Colorless and odorless	Does not burn
Copper	Conducts electricity	Combines with oxygen to form the mineral cuprite

✔Lesson Checkpoint

1. How do physical properties and chemical properties differ?
2. 🎯 **Sequence** Use sequence words—*first, next, after,* and *finally*—to explain how to find the density of a substance.
3. Writing in Science **Description** Choose an object and write a description of its physical properties.

Lesson 2

How can matter change?

Matter can be in any of four states—solid, liquid, gas, or plasma. Matter can change from one state to another. When these changes take place, the energy of the particles making up a substance changes.

States of Matter

Look closely at your desk. Is it moving? You probably answered that it is not. But there is a buzz of activity in the matter that makes up your desk.

All matter is made up of tiny, moving particles. These particles are too tiny to be seen without a very powerful microscope. The particles constantly move and bump into each other. The speed of the particles and how strongly they are attracted to one another determine whether the matter is a solid, liquid, gas, or plasma. These four forms of matter are called the states of matter. Study the diagrams to the right as you read about solids, liquids, and gases.

Solids

You can tell the differences among the states of matter by looking at their shape and volume. A solid has a definite shape and volume. Its particles are very close together, and they don't move very fast. A strong attraction for each other holds the particles together. You can move a solid from place to place, but it will still have the same shape and volume. Your chair, the floor, and the hair on your head are examples of solids.

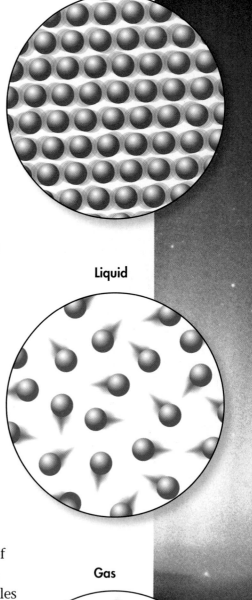

Solid

Liquid

Gas

The beautiful aurora borealis, known as the northern lights, is an example of a plasma. Auroras are formed when high-energy charged particles from the Sun interact with gases in the high atmosphere.

Liquids

A liquid has a definite volume but no definite shape. The particles that make up a liquid move fast enough to break through some of the attraction between them. This allows the particles to slide past each other. The result is that a liquid takes the shape of the container that holds it. You can pour a small container of juice into a cup. The shape of the juice will change, but its volume stays the same.

Gases

A gas has no particular shape or volume. Its particles move fast enough to break away from one another, and they move in many different directions. A gas will spread out to take the shape of the container it is in. You can't see the air that you breathe, but it is made up of gases that fill up and take the shape of the room that you are in, or the car, elevator, or plane in which you ride. But gases fill tiny spaces as well: small jars, balloons, or beach balls.

Plasma

Plasma is the state of matter that does not have definite shape or volume. Does that sound like a gas? Plasmas have some properties of gases and some that are different from those of gases. The particles that make up plasmas have electric charges, so plasmas can conduct electricity. Plasmas are found in lightning, fire, welding arcs, and fluorescent and neon light tubes. Plasmas are not common on Earth. But scientists believe that 99 percent of the known matter in the universe, including the Sun, is made of plasma.

√ Checkpoint
1. How do particles differ in the four states of matter?
2. **Technology** in Science A plasma TV uses plasma to produce pictures on its screen. Find out how plasmas are used to produce the pictures. Report your finding to the class.

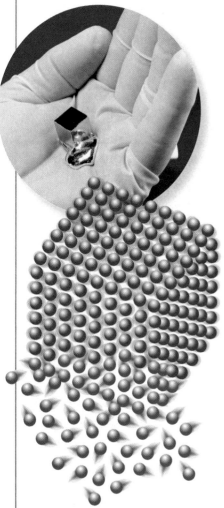

Gallium is a metal with a melting point so close to normal human body temperature that it would melt in your hand!

Solids melt as their particles gain energy.

Changes of State

If you look around you, you will see that some things are solids, some liquids, and others gases. We are used to seeing oxygen as a gas, iron as a solid, and mercury as a liquid. Why do different substances at the same temperature exist in different states?

Recall that the particles that make up matter have a force of attraction between them. The attractions between particles of some kinds of matter are stronger than those of others. For example, the attraction between the particles that make up iron is stronger than the force of attraction between the particles of oxygen gas in the air. That's why iron is a solid and oxygen is a gas at normal temperatures and pressures.

Temperature can affect the force of attraction between particles. If you heat a substance, its particles will gain energy and move faster. If you add enough heat, the particles will gain enough energy so that they can break some of the force of attraction between them. The solid becomes a liquid. Heat the substance even more and the particles will break completely free of the forces of attraction. The liquid has become a gas.

Melting and Freezing

Now think about the solid iron and what might happen to it if it were heated to very high temperatures. Eventually the iron would turn to a liquid, which we call molten iron. The process by which a solid becomes a liquid is called melting. A substance becomes a liquid when it is heated to its melting point. The melting point of lead is 327.5ºC—much higher than the melting point of water at 0ºC.

Melting happens when a solid gains heat. What do you think happens if a liquid loses heat? When that happens, its particles slow down and form a solid. This process is called freezing. The temperature at which a substance freezes is its freezing point. A substance freezes and melts at the same temperature. Each substance has a particular melting and freezing point.

A substance will melt more slowly in an insulated container than it will in an open one. The reason is that the insulation slows down the movement of heat into the melting substance.

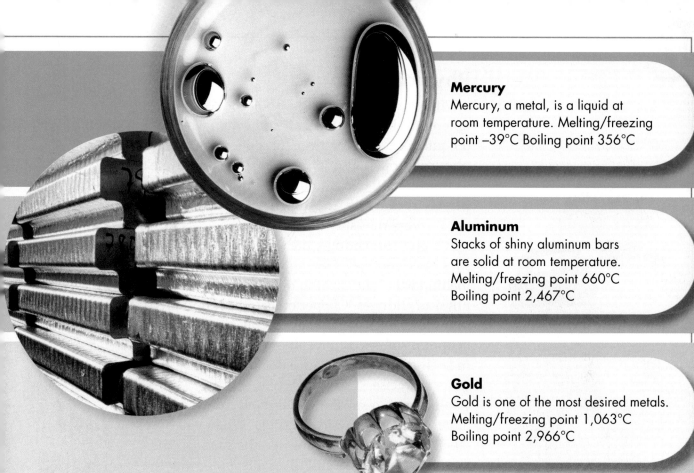

Mercury

Mercury, a metal, is a liquid at room temperature. Melting/freezing point –39°C Boiling point 356°C

Aluminum

Stacks of shiny aluminum bars are solid at room temperature. Melting/freezing point 660°C Boiling point 2,467°C

Gold

Gold is one of the most desired metals. Melting/freezing point 1,063°C Boiling point 2,966°C

The outside of this can is chilled to the point that the water vapor around it turns from a gas to drops of water.

Boiling

When you boil a pan of water, you might notice that the air around the pan gets more humid. That's because as water is heated, its particles speed up. Eventually, at its boiling point, the water gains enough heat to change to a gas—water vapor. The particles that make up the water have broken free from each other.

If the water particles in the air cool, they lose energy. The particles slow down and move closer together. When they get close enough, their attraction for each other causes them to form a liquid. This change of state from a gas to a liquid is called **condensation.**

Like adding or removing heat, changing the air pressure around a substance can change the substance's energy and cause it to boil or melt. You might think water would never freeze at room temperature, but it would at air pressures 10,000 times higher than normal! And at very low air pressures, water might change from a liquid to a gas without being heated.

✔Checkpoint

1. How is temperature related to the states of matter?
2. 🔄 **Sequence** You are given three cups of liquids that look identical. Use sequence words—*first, next, after,* and *finally*—to explain how you might tell whether the liquids are the same or different.

375

Physical Changes

When a substance melts or boils, it doesn't change into a different substance. Water is still water, whether it is a solid, a liquid, or a gas. Melting, freezing, and boiling points are physical properties of a substance. A change of state, such as from a solid to a liquid, is a physical change. During a **physical change,** the appearance of a substance changes but its properties stay the same.

In a physical change, the size, shape, or state of the substance changes. Sawing wood, shredding paper, melting wax, and grating a potato are examples of physical changes. Copper ore can be hammered into sheets, and gemstones can be carved into beautiful shapes as a result of physical changes. In each case, the substance does not change into something else.

Sometimes, a substance can look completely different after a physical change. When you dissolve sugar crystals in water, the sugar seems to disappear. But it's still there. Just boil away the water, and you'll find sugar crystals again.

Think about what's happening to this potato. It has been peeled and shredded, but anyone can tell that potatoes are in the pan. Grating causes physical changes, but the potato is the same substance it was at the beginning of the dinner preparations. Cooking causes chemical changes.

Chemical Changes

The wax of the candles to the right is melting, which is a physical change. But what about the burning wick? What kind of change is taking place there? When you burn a candle, the substance that makes up the candlewick undergoes a chemical change. During a **chemical change,** one or more substances change into completely new substances with different properties.

The burning candlewick and the oxygen gas in the air undergo a chemical change during burning. The process produces three new substances—ash, carbon dioxide gas, and water vapor. None of the new substances has the same properties as the candlewick or the oxygen gas.

Chemical changes often give clues that they are happening. Heat, light, sound, permanent color change, and fizzing often are caused by a chemical change. What clues can you find in the pictures on the next page?

Substances Switch Places

Sometimes the particles that make up different substances can switch places to make new substances. In this chemical change, two clear substances were mixed together. The result was that one of the new substances that formed is the yellow substance you see. The other new substance dissolves in the water so you can't see it.

Substances Combine

In this type of chemical change, the particles of two substances combine to make a new substance. The metal of the ship combined with oxygen in the atmosphere to form rust.

Substance Breaks Apart

Hydrogen peroxide is made up of hydrogen and oxygen particles. Light can cause a chemical change to take place in which the hydrogen peroxide breaks down into hydrogen gas and oxygen gas.

✔ Lesson Checkpoint

1. What happens to the particles that make up water as the water is heated?

2. When water and concrete mix are combined, the material becomes warm and a hard solid forms. Is this a physical change or a chemical change? Explain your reasoning.

3. (Art in Science) Draw pictures to show how the particles in the three states of matter differ.

Investigate How does temperature affect particle motion?

Everything we see is made up of small particles. Those particles are always moving. The greater the temperature, the faster the particles move.

Materials

3 cups

masking tape and measuring cup

room-temperature water, cold water, very warm water

red food coloring and red colored pencil

clock with a second hand

Process Skills

Data you collect can help you make an **inference** about the relationship between temperature and particle motion.

What to Do

1 Label the 3 cups A, B, and C.

2 Add 150 mL room-temperature water to cup A. Let the water stand for 1 minute.

3 After the water is still, gently add 3 drops of food coloring. Place the drops on top of the water and in the center of the cup. Do not mix or stir.

4 **Observe** the cup at 15 seconds, 30 seconds, 1 minute, and 3 minutes after adding the food coloring.

5 Draw pictures to show how the coloring moves through the cup.

6 Add cold water to cup B. Repeat steps 3–5.

7 Add very warm water to cup C. Repeat steps 3–5.

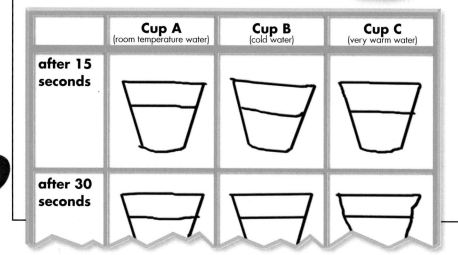

Color Movement

	Cup A (room temperature water)	Cup B (cold water)	Cup C (very warm water)
after 15 seconds			
after 30 seconds			

Explain Your Results

1. Was there a difference in the movement of the coloring through the very warm water compared to movement through the cold water? Describe what you observed.

2. **Infer** What might have caused the food coloring to move? What might have caused the coloring to move more quickly?

Go Further

How might adding salt to the water affect the rate of particle distribution? Make a plan to answer this or any other questions you may have.

GRAPHING CHANGES

Scientists often show data for more than one substance on the same graph. A double or triple line graph is helpful for comparing data for two or three substances.

Three solid substances of the same mass were heated at a constant rate. The triple line graph below shows the changes in temperature of each substance. Notice the similar patterns of alternating climbs and plateaus for each line. A plateau represents a period when thermal energy was being added to the substance but there was no change in its temperature. During this time, all the energy being added is used in changing the state of the substance. The first plateau appears when a substance is at its melting point, changing from a solid to a liquid. The second plateau appears when a substance is at its boiling point, changing from a liquid to a gas.

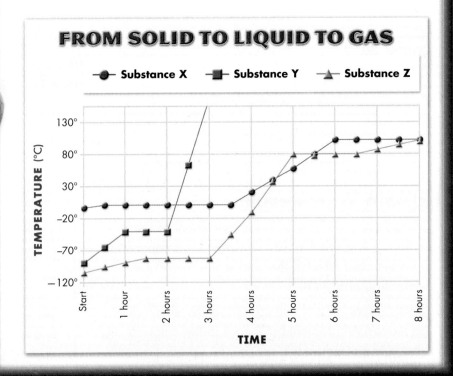

FROM SOLID TO LIQUID TO GAS

● Substance X   ■ Substance Y   ▲ Substance Z

Answer each question. Use the graph on page 380.

1. What is the boiling point of substance Z?

2. Do you think any of these substances could be water? Explain.

3. Substance Y is the densest and substance Z is the least dense. What trend do you see with these substances relating density and boiling point?

4. After 8 hours, substances X and Z are at the same temperature. How would you predict which substance would be hotter after one more hour?

5. Which substance changed from a solid to a liquid the fastest? How could you tell?

Lab zone Take-Home Activity

Caution: *Work with an adult to do this activity.* Add ice to a pan of cold water to make it as cold as you can. Then heat the pan of cold water on the stove. Using a cooking thermometer, measure and record the water's temperature every 30 or 60 seconds. Be sure the thermometer does not touch the pan. Plot your data on a graph. Does your graph follow a pattern similar to those on this page? Can you explain any differences?

Chapter 13 Review and Test Prep

Use Vocabulary

chemical change (p. 376)   mass (p. 367)
chemical property (p. 371)   physical change (p. 376)
condensation (p. 375)   physical property (p. 370)
density (p. 368)   volume (p. 367)
weight (p. 368)

Use the vocabulary term from the list above that best completes each sentence.

1. During a _____, a substance mixes with another substance and changes into completely new substances with different properties.

2. The measure of the mass per unit volume of a substance is its _____.

3. A _____ tells how a substance forms new substances when it mixes with something else.

4. The change of state from a gas to a liquid is called _____.

5. An object's _____ is the amount of space that it takes up.

6. A _____ can be seen or measured without changing the substance into something else.

7. An object's _____ is the amount of matter that makes up that object.

8. During a_____, the appearance of a substance changes but its properties stay the same.

9. The measure of the pull of gravity on an object is its _____.

Explain Concepts

10. How does plasma differ from gases?

11. For each change below, decide if it is a physical change or a chemical change. Then tell how you know.
    - chopping wood
    - chocolate melting
    - a candle burning
    - a nail rusting

12. Using the information in the chart below, calculate the densities for liquids A, B, C, and D. Based on what you already know, which liquid is probably water? If all the liquids were poured into a column (hydrometer) and allowed to separate, what would be their order, from top to bottom?

Liquid	Mass	Volume
A	12.2 g	11.1 mL
B	21.3 g	22.5 mL
C	19.1 g	19.1 mL
D	15.5 g	31.8 mL

13. Classify Study the picture of the zinc nail and gold bracelet in vinegar on page 371. Make a list of properties for zinc and for gold. Then classify each property as chemical or physical.

 **Sequence**

14. Describe in sequence what would happen to the particles in an ice cube from the time the cube is heated until the particles form water vapor. Use a graphic organizer like this one.

First → **Next** → **Last**

 Test Prep

Choose the letter that best completes the statement or answers the question.

15. When it goes through a chemical change, a substance changes
   Ⓐ in shape or size.
   Ⓑ into another substance.
   Ⓒ in color.
   Ⓓ into another state of matter.

16. All of the following are physical properties of a substance EXCEPT
   Ⓕ its form at a given temperature.
   Ⓖ its density.
   Ⓗ its boiling point.
   Ⓘ its flammability.

17. Chemical properties describe how a substance changes when it
   Ⓐ reacts with another substance.
   Ⓑ changes into a different state of matter.
   Ⓒ adds or loses mass.
   Ⓓ gains or loses energy.

18. Even if you change the mass of a substance, the substance will always have the same
   Ⓕ weight.
   Ⓖ volume.
   Ⓗ pull from gravity.
   Ⓘ density.

19. Explain why the answer you chose for Question 15 is the best. For each of the answers that you did not choose, give a reason why it is not the best choice.

20. Writing in Science **Expository**
You have an unknown solid that you would like to identify. Explain how you would use the solid's chemical and physical properties to identify it. Use the terms *mass, weight, density, boiling point,* and *freezing point.*

Antoine Lavoisier

In 1782, America was nearing the end of the Revolutionary War. At the same time, another important event was taking place in a laboratory in Paris, France.

The French chemist Antoine Lavoisier was making one of the most important discoveries in science. His experiments showed that the mass of materials before a chemical change was the same as the mass of the materials after the chemical change. These experiments led Lavoisier to conclude that matter cannot be created or destroyed. It can only change from one form to another.

Lavoisier made many other discoveries. For example, he showed that air is a mixture of gases. He proved that one of these gases, oxygen, is needed to make fire. He also showed that oxygen is needed for breathing and to make metals rust.

Lavoisier could have done much more, but his life ended tragically. After the French Revolution, Lavoisier was arrested and executed because he was part of a company that collected taxes for the government.

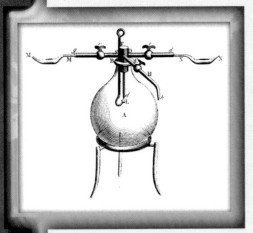

Lavoisier's hydrogen burner (1784) burned hydrogen in air to produce water, which he took as proof that water was a compound of hydrogen.

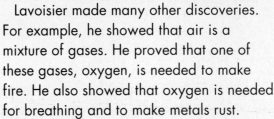

Lab zone Take-Home Activity

Lavoisier made important discoveries because he did careful experiments and followed the methods of science. Make a flowchart that shows the methods of science and how they connect to one another.

You Will Discover

- what all matter is made of.
- how matter can be classified as one of three types—element, compound, or mixture.
- what acids and bases are.

online
Student Edition
pearsonsuccessnet.com

Chapter 14

Building Blocks of Matter

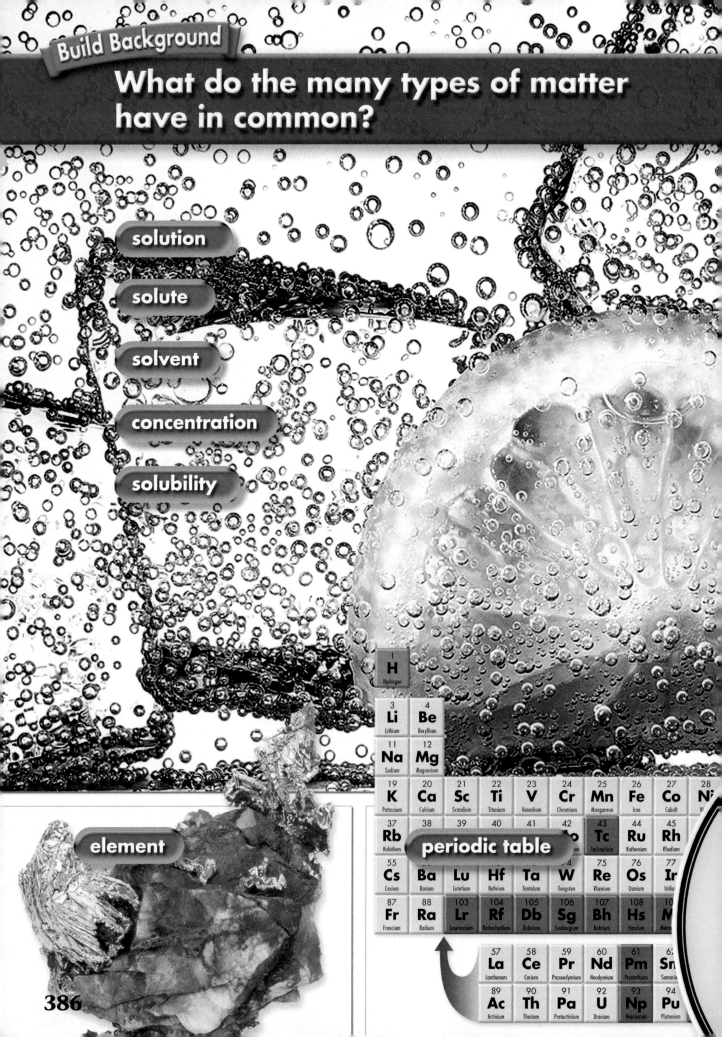

What do the many types of matter have in common?

solution

solute

solvent

concentration

solubility

element

periodic table

1 **H** Hydrogen									
3 **Li** Lithium	4 **Be** Beryllium								
11 **Na** Sodium	12 **Mg** Magnesium								
19 **K** Potassium	20 **Ca** Calcium	21 **Sc** Scandium	22 **Ti** Titanium	23 **V** Vanadium	24 **Cr** Chromium	25 **Mn** Manganese	26 **Fe** Iron	27 **Co** Cobalt	28 **N**
37 **Rb** Rubidium	38	39	40	41	42	43 **Tc** Technetium	44 **Ru** Ruthenium	45 **Rh** Rhodium	
55 **Cs** Cesium	56 **Ba** Barium	**Lu** Lutetium	**Hf** Hafnium	**Ta** Tantalum	**W** Tungsten	75 **Re** Rhenium	76 **Os** Osmium	77 **Ir** Iridium	
87 **Fr** Francium	88 **Ra** Radium	103 **Lr** Lawrencium	104 **Rf** Rutherfordium	105 **Db** Dubnium	106 **Sg** Seaborgium	107 **Bh** Bohrium	108 **Hs** Hassium	10 **M**	

57 **La** Lanthanum	58 **Ce** Cerium	59 **Pr** Praseodymium	60 **Nd** Neodymium	61 **Pm** Promethium	62 **Sn** Samaria
89 **Ac** Actinium	90 **Th** Thorium	91 **Pa** Protactinium	92 **U** Uranium	93 **Np** Neptunium	94 **Pu** Plutonium

mixture

compound

Explore How can you describe an object you cannot see?

Materials

clay with mystery object

toothpick

What to Do

1 Make up a list of questions about what is inside the ball.

Poke the clay ball with the toothpick.

2 Use a toothpick to learn about the object. Record your observations.

3 Use your results to draw a picture of what is inside the ball.

Description of Object	Drawing

4 Remove the clay. Compare the object inside with your drawing.

Explain Your Results

1. What did you **infer** about the object? What evidence supports your inference?

2. What other tests might have helped you learn about the object?

Process Skills

Comparing and contrasting the results of tests can help you **infer** what is inside a lump of clay.

Compare and Contrast

Sometimes it is useful to **compare** and **contrast** characteristics of items to fully understand them. Use the following tips to find comparisons and contrasts when reading science articles.

- When comparing two items, tell how they are alike. When contrasting two items, tell how they are different.

- You can use the information you read to **infer** how things are alike and different.

Science Article

Matter and Atoms

Like all matter, boron and nitrogen are made of atoms. These atoms are so small that they can only be seen with very powerful microscopes. Their atoms have protons, neutrons, and electrons, but the number of these parts differs. Boron atoms contain five protons, and nitrogen atoms contain seven protons. That's why they are different substances with different properties.

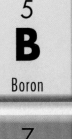

Apply It!

Make a graphic organizer like this one. List the facts from the science article to **compare** and **contrast** boron and nitrogen.

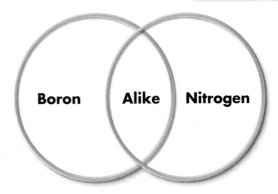

You Are There!

Wow, what a ride! You are riding a tiny atom that's going in a huge circle. Racecar drivers think driving on their track is fun. This ride is awesome! Oh no, you are about to collide with another atom. You can't avoid the collision. Crash! You're now stuck to the other atom. Fantastic! You just created a new substance.

AudioText

Lesson 1

How did we learn about atoms?

Carbon atom

Proton

Neutron

Electron

All matter is composed of tiny particles. Pure substances such as aluminum and carbon are made of similar particles called atoms.

Structure of the Atom

Charcoal and aluminum foil do not appear to have anything in common. However, these materials are made up of tiny particles called atoms. An atom is the smallest whole piece of matter. If you were able to see the structure of aluminum or carbon, you would find that it was made from tiny atoms joined together.

Aluminum atom

Atoms are difficult to study because they are so small, so scientists use models to help picture them. The model of the atom has changed over time as scientists gathered information. Today scientists use the electron cloud model to represent an atom. In the electron cloud model, an atom has two distinct regions—the nucleus and the electron cloud. The nucleus is located in the center of the atom. It is composed of protons and neutrons. A proton is a particle that has a positive charge. A neutron is a particle that has no charge.

The nucleus of an atom is surrounded by the electron cloud. This part of the atom contains electrons and a great deal of empty space. An electron is a particle that has a negative charge. Scientists also have found even smaller particles that compose protons and neutrons. Many details about these particles are still being worked out by scientists.

1. **✓Checkpoint** Describe the electron cloud model of an atom.
2. **⊙ Compare and Contrast** Tell how protons, neutrons, and electrons are alike and different.

391

History of the Atom

Throughout history, people have thought that all matter is made of combinations of a few basic parts. For example, the ancient Greeks thought that all matter was made from four elements—earth, fire, air, and water. Today scientists know that all matter is made of atoms and that atoms are made of smaller particles—protons, neutrons, and electrons. But it took over 2000 years for today's model of the atom to develop. The Greek philosopher Leucippus is usually given credit for thinking of the idea that matter is made of smaller particles. His student, Democritus, further developed the idea and gave the particles the name *atomos,* meaning "indivisible." Atoms, according to Democritus, were all hard solids that could not be destroyed. He thought that all atoms were made of the same material in different sizes and shapes.

Another Greek philosopher, Aristotle, disagreed with Democritus. Aristotle believed that matter could be divided and subdivided indefinitely. Aristotle had many followers, and his ideas about the atom were believed by many until the 17th century.

The Greek ideas about atoms were not based on scientific observation, measurement, or experimentation. The Greeks used mathematics and reasoning to form their ideas. But in 1803, the British scientist John Dalton used scientific experimentation to prove that atoms exist. Dalton's atomic theory stated that all matter is made of atoms that cannot be created, divided, or destroyed.

As you can see in the time line on the next page, since Dalton's time, the model of the atom has undergone many changes. As technology has changed throughout the years, more and more information has been discovered. Today the electron cloud model is widely accepted as being a good working model of the atom. But it too may change as scientists learn new information.

Aristotle was a student of Plato, another Greek philosopher.

✓ Lesson Checkpoint

1. What might happen to cause scientists to change the model of the atom?

2. How does the way scientists today develop ideas differ from the way the Greek philosophers developed ideas?

3. **Compare and Contrast** Use a graphic organizer to show how Thomson's model of the atom is like and different from Dalton's model.

A Changing Atomic Model

5th century B.C. Democritus, a Greek philosopher, proposed that all matter was made of indivisible particles called atoms. Aristotle disagreed, and his views were considered correct until John Dalton found proof that atoms exist.

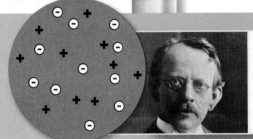

1803 John Dalton proposed that atoms were small solid spheres. His model of the atom resembled a billiard ball.

1897 Joseph John Thomson proposed that atoms were positively charged spheres with negatively charged particles embedded into them. This model is often called the plum pudding model. Thomson is credited with discovering the electron.

1911 Ernest Rutherford found that most of the mass of the atom was located in the center of the atom. He called the center a nucleus. His model resembled the solar system. In his model, negatively charged electrons orbit a dense positively charged nucleus.

1913 Niels Bohr proposed that electrons traveled in fixed orbits called shells. Electrons cannot move from one shell to another without gaining or losing energy.

1920s Erwin Schrödinger and Werner Heisenberg proposed the electron cloud model for the atom.

Gold is a metal that is often used in jewelry.

Silver and copper are metals that are used in jewelry and electrical wiring.

Elements in the Human Body

All living and nonliving things are composed of elements, including your body. This circle graph shows most of the elements that make up the human body. Notice that your body contains over 60 percent oxygen by mass. Oxygen is found in water, proteins, sugars, and fats in the human body.

- Oxygen 65%
- Carbon 18%
- Hydrogen 10%
- Nitrogen 3%
- Calcium 1.5%
- Phosphorus 1.0%
- Other 1.5%

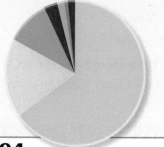

How are elements grouped?

Scientists classify matter that has similar characteristics. Matter can be classified as elements, compounds, or mixtures. Some compounds also can be classified as acids or bases.

Elements

It's amazing to think that all the matter around you is made of tiny atoms. Most things are made of more than one kind of atom. For example, water is made of oxygen atoms and hydrogen atoms. But some kinds of matter, called **elements,** are each made up of only one type of atom. An element cannot be separated into simpler substances by physical or chemical means. Elements that you might be familiar with are carbon, aluminum, gold, silver, and copper. Because each element is made of only one kind of atom, elements are called pure substances. Each pure substance is made of only one kind of particle—in this case, atoms.

Less than 100 different elements occur naturally on Earth. All matter found in nature on Earth and everything that we have found in space is made of these elements. You might wonder how less than 100 different elements can make the seemingly endless variety of matter. It's somewhat like the alphabet. The 26 letters of our alphabet can make all the words in the largest dictionary. In a similar way, elements combine in different ways to form everything that is matter.

Elements and Their Atoms

The atoms of each element are different from the atoms of all other elements. And all the atoms of an element are the same. Each element can be identified by the number of protons in the nucleus of its atom. All matter with 79 protons in the nucleus of its atom is gold. All matter with six protons in its nucleus is carbon, and so on.

Atoms of elements have no electrical charge because they have the same number of protons and electrons. An element with six protons in its nucleus must also have six electrons in the electron cloud. With six positive charges and six negative charges, the overall charge of the atom is zero.

Symbols for Elements

Scientists have developed a shorthand method for writing the names of elements. Each element has a unique chemical symbol. Chemical symbols are a single letter, or two- or three-letter combinations. Usually, the chemical symbol is the first letter in the name. If that symbol is used by another element, another letter from the name is added. Some elements that were discovered in ancient times were given Greek or Latin names. Some of these elements have symbols from their old name. For example, the symbol for gold is Au for the Latin name *aurum*. Newly discovered elements are given temporary three-letter names based on the Latin name for the number of protons found in the nucleus. You can see the symbols for all the elements on pages 396–397.

Mercury is the only metal that is liquid at room temperature.

Classifying Elements

Each element has a unique number of protons and electrons. This unique set of protons and electrons gives each element a unique set of properties. Scientists use these properties to place each element into one of three groups— metals, nonmetals, and metalloids.

Metals are elements that are usually hard, are good conductors of heat and electricity, and are capable of being drawn into wires and hammered into sheets. Nonmetals are elements that are usually brittle, are poor conductors of heat and electricity, and cannot be hammered into sheets or made into wires. Metalloids are elements that have some properties of both metals and nonmetals.

The element neon is used in colorful signs.

Silicon is an element that is used to make computer parts.

1. ✔ **Checkpoint** Atoms often are referred to as the building blocks of matter. Why do you think atoms were given this title?
2. What are the most common elements in the human body?
3. **Health in Science** Calcium, potassium, and sodium are elements that are required by the body for good health. Find out how each of these elements is used by the body.

The Periodic Table

Suppose you go to the bookstore to buy a particular book. When you get there, the books are not organized in any way. Mysteries, autobiographies, and poetry books are all mixed together with other kinds of books. How easily would you be able to find the book you are looking for? Scientists had a similar problem before they came up with a way to organize the elements. Today all of the known elements are organized in the **periodic table.**

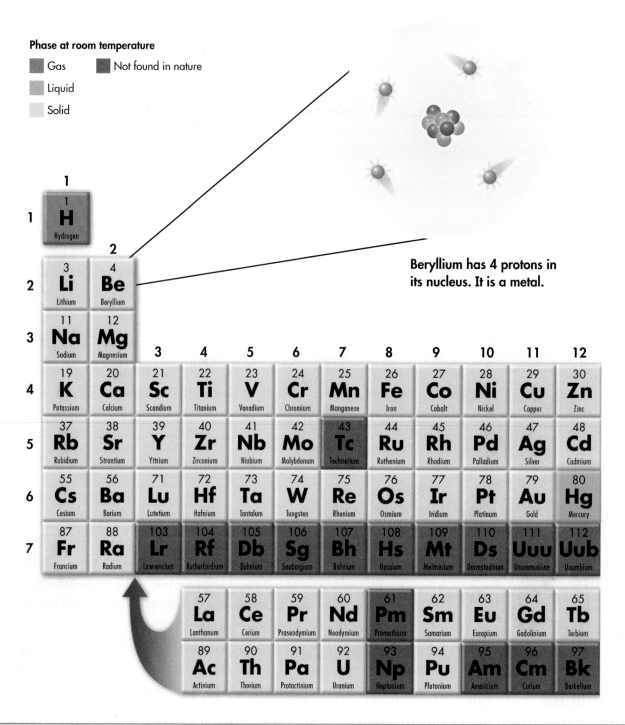

Phase at room temperature

- Gas
- Liquid
- Solid
- Not found in nature

Beryllium has 4 protons in its nucleus. It is a metal.

The periodic table lists the elements in order of increasing atomic number from left to right. The atomic number of an element is the number of protons in the nucleus of its atom. Elements on the left side of the table are metals. Elements on the right side of the table are nonmetals. Metalloids are along each side of the zig-zag line between the metals and nonmetals on the table. Although aluminum is along the zig-zag line, it is not a metalloid. It is a metal. Aluminum is an exception to the rule that all elements touching the zig-zag line are metalloids.

At the bottom of the periodic table are two series of elements called the Lanthanide series and the Actinide series. Look at the atomic number of the first member in the Lanthanide series. Lanthanum, atomic number 57, should follow Barium, atomic number 56 in the table above. The first element in the Actinide series should follow the element radium. These elements are pulled to the bottom of the periodic table for convenience. If these elements were placed in the table above, the table would be extremely wide. These elements are pulled to the bottom of the table so that the periodic table will fit nicely on a page.

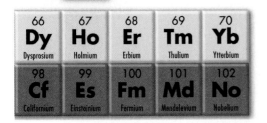

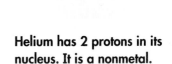

Helium has 2 protons in its nucleus. It is a nonmetal.

1. ✓ **Checkpoint** How many protons do the elements beryllium and helium each have?

2. Use the information in the table to draw a model that shows the number of electrons and protons in a lithium atom.

3. **Technology in Science** Scientists have made some elements in the laboratory. Find out which elements scientists made.

Information on the Periodic Table

If you want to find information about a word, you go to a dictionary. If you want information about an element, go to the periodic table. The periodic table contains a great deal of information about the elements. The word *periodic* means "a regular, repeated pattern."

Each individual block in the periodic table contains information about a particular element. Look at the block for chromium to find out what information you can get about each element on the periodic table on pages 396–397. Other periodic tables may give more or less information about each element.

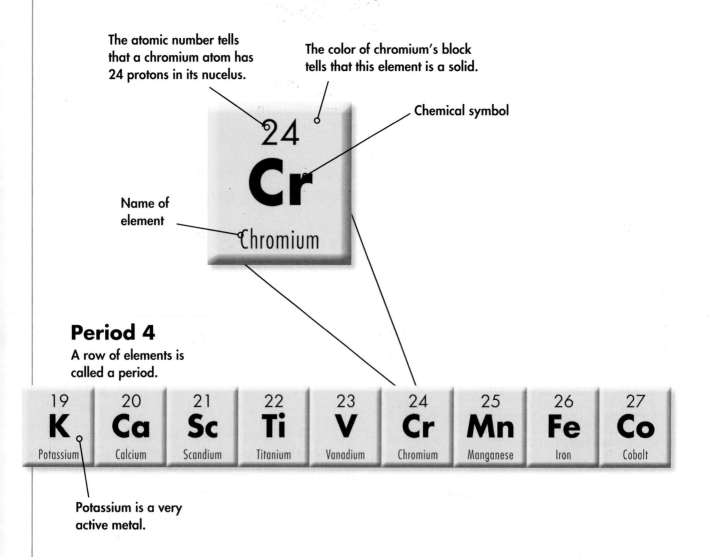

The atomic number tells that a chromium atom has 24 protons in its nucelus.

The color of chromium's block tells that this element is a solid.

Chemical symbol

Name of element

24
Cr
Chromium

Period 4
A row of elements is called a period.

19	20	21	22	23	24	25	26	27
K	**Ca**	**Sc**	**Ti**	**V**	**Cr**	**Mn**	**Fe**	**Co**
Potassium	Calcium	Scandium	Titanium	Vanadium	Chromium	Manganese	Iron	Cobalt

Potassium is a very active metal.

Columns and Rows

The location of an element on the table also gives information about the element's properties. As you move across a row or down a column, the elements' properties change in a predictable way.

The periodic table has 18 columns. These columns are called groups or families. Like members of a family, elements in a family resemble each other. They react with other substances in similar ways. Groups are numbered from 1 to 18.

The elements in Group 1 are all metals that react strongly with water. Hydrogen is an exception. Its atomic structure is similar to other elements in Group 1, but it does not have similar chemical properties. The elements in Group 18 barely react at all with other elements. They are called inactive elements.

The periodic table's seven rows are called periods. Unlike the elements in a group, the elements in a period have very different properties. For example, the elements in Period 4 change from very active metals to less active metals to metalloids and then to nonmetals. The first element in a period always reacts violently. The last one is always inactive.

√ **Lesson Checkpoint**

1. In which groups and periods are nitrogen, xenon, and cesium found?

2. Is bromine a metal or nonmetal? Is it a solid, liquid, or gas at room temperature? What is its chemical symbol?

3. ⊙ **Compare and Contrast** Find the elements oxygen and calcium on the periodic table. Tell how they are alike and different.

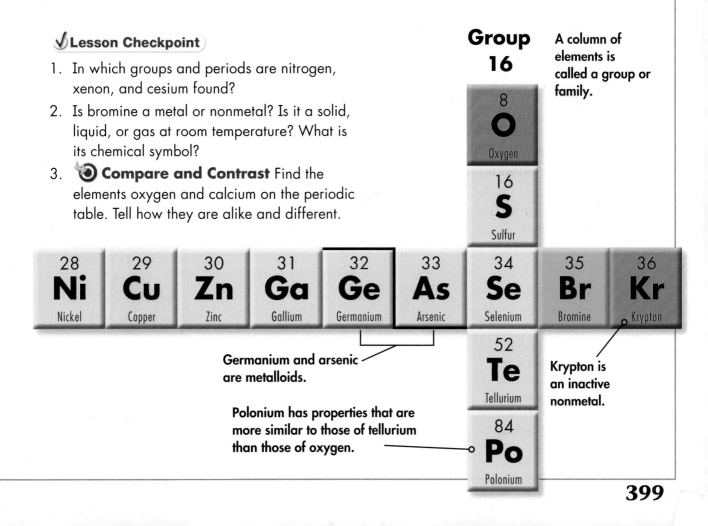

Group 16

A column of elements is called a group or family.

| 8 O Oxygen |
| 16 S Sulfur |

| 28 Ni Nickel | 29 Cu Copper | 30 Zn Zinc | 31 Ga Gallium | 32 Ge Germanium | 33 As Arsenic | 34 Se Selenium | 35 Br Bromine | 36 Kr Krypton |

| 52 Te Tellurium |
| 84 Po Polonium |

Germanium and arsenic are metalloids.

Krypton is an inactive nonmetal.

Polonium has properties that are more similar to those of tellurium than those of oxygen.

399

Lesson 3

What are compounds and mixtures?

Elements combine in exact ratios to form compounds. Compounds have properties that differ from the properties of the elements that make them. The substances that form mixtures do not combine in exact ratios. Substances in a mixture retain their own properties.

Atoms Together

The table salt in the picture is different from the elements you read about in Lesson 2. Table salt is made of more than one element. Most atoms found in nature are not found as elements but are found in compounds. A **compound** is a substance composed of two or more elements that are chemically combined to form a new substance with different properties. Table salt is a compound.

Many components of your body are made of compounds. For example, water is a compound, and it makes up about 60 percent of your body. Other compounds, called proteins, make up much of your skin, bones, tendons, and ligaments. Compounds also make up the membranes surrounding the cells in your body and the DNA that determines the traits you inherit.

Each element will react in a different way when it combines with different substances. When sodium combines with chlorine, it forms sodium chloride. But when it combines with water, it reacts violently to form hydrogen gas and sodium hydroxide.

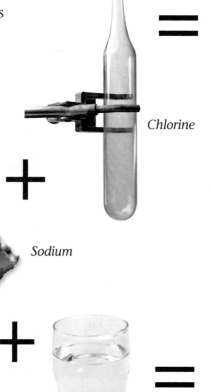

Chlorine

Sodium

Water

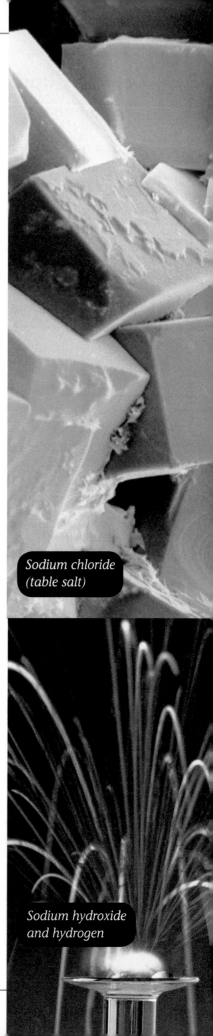

Sodium chloride (table salt)

Sodium hydroxide and hydrogen

400

Each particle of a compound is made of exactly the same ratio of elements. For example, every particle of table salt contains one atom of sodium combined with one atom of chlorine. Each particle of water is made of two atoms of hydrogen and one atom of oxygen.

The properties of a compound differ from the properties of the elements that form it. Sodium, chlorine, and the sodium chloride they form have very different properties. You might be surprised to learn that the element chlorine is a greenish yellow, poisonous gas. When sodium, a silvery, white metal, combines with chlorine, sodium chloride forms. You eat sodium chloride every day—it's table salt! Table salt has properties that are different from those of sodium and chlorine.

Chemical Formulas

Scientists not only use symbols for elements, they also use symbols for compounds. Every compound has its own chemical formula. A chemical formula consists of two parts—symbols for the elements and subscripts. A chemical formula contains a chemical symbol for every element that is present in a particle of the compound. The subscript tells how many atoms of each element are present. For example, the chemical formula for water is H_2O. The formula tells you that water contains the elements hydrogen and oxygen. The subscript tells you two atoms of hydrogen and one atom of oxygen combine to make water. The subscript for an element follows the element's chemical symbol. The subscript 1 is never written in a chemical formula. If there is no subscript written, then you know that there is only one atom present.

Elements and Compounds in Products

Foods, household chemicals, and over-the-counter medicines have labels on their packaging that identify the elements and compounds in the product. Federal laws tell manufacturers what information is required on each type of product. The labels on over-the-counter medications must give the active and inactive ingredients found in the product. Labels on household chemicals tell the ingredients in the product.

Labels on food packaging list the nutrients that are contained in that food. The elements sodium and potassium are found in these dried apricots. The other nutrients listed are compounds. The compounds listed on this label are compounds found in most living things. Many living things contain fats, carbohydrates, proteins, and water in their cells.

1. ✔**Checkpoint** The chemical formula for glucose, a type of sugar, is $C_6H_{12}O_6$. Is glucose an element or a compound? How do you know?

2. How many atoms of hydrogen are in a particle of glucose?

3. 🔵 **Compare and Contrast** How do the elements sodium and chlorine differ from the table salt they form? How are they alike?

401

The components of this soup are not chemically combined.

Mixtures

Elements and compounds are two ways matter can be classified. You know that elements contain one type of atom. Compounds are made of two or more atoms combined in fixed ratios. Matter that cannot be classified as an element or a compound is usually a mixture. A **mixture** is a combination of substances in which the atoms of the substances are not chemically combined. Mixtures can be a combination of elements, compounds, or both. Look at the picture on the next page to see how elements and compounds make up sand—a mixture.

Substances in a mixture retain their own properties. For example, the vegetable soup in the picture contains chicken, noodles, celery, carrots, and other vegetables. The vegetables are separate and can be easily identified. The components of a mixture do not have a definite ratio. One bowl of soup may have more carrots than another bowl.

Separating Mixtures

Mixtures also can be easily separated. If you don't like the carrots in the soup, you could easily pick them out. Some mixtures are more difficult to separate because the components are very small. How do you separate a mixture with smaller components, such as salt, iron filings, and sand?

Mixtures can be separated using the physical properties of the substances that it contains. For example, the iron filings in the salt-iron-sand mixture are magnetic. You can separate them from the mixture using a magnet. What remains is a mixture of salt and sand. If you add water to the salt-sand mixture, the salt will dissolve. Then pour the water-salt-sand mixture through a filter paper. The sand will collect on the filter paper. The remaining water-salt mixture can be separated by evaporating the water. Solid salt particles will remain.

A filter can be used to separate components of a mixture. Here the larger particles cannot move through the filter but the smaller water particles can.

The coffee in this pot is a mixture. The coffee can be separated from the water by evaporation.

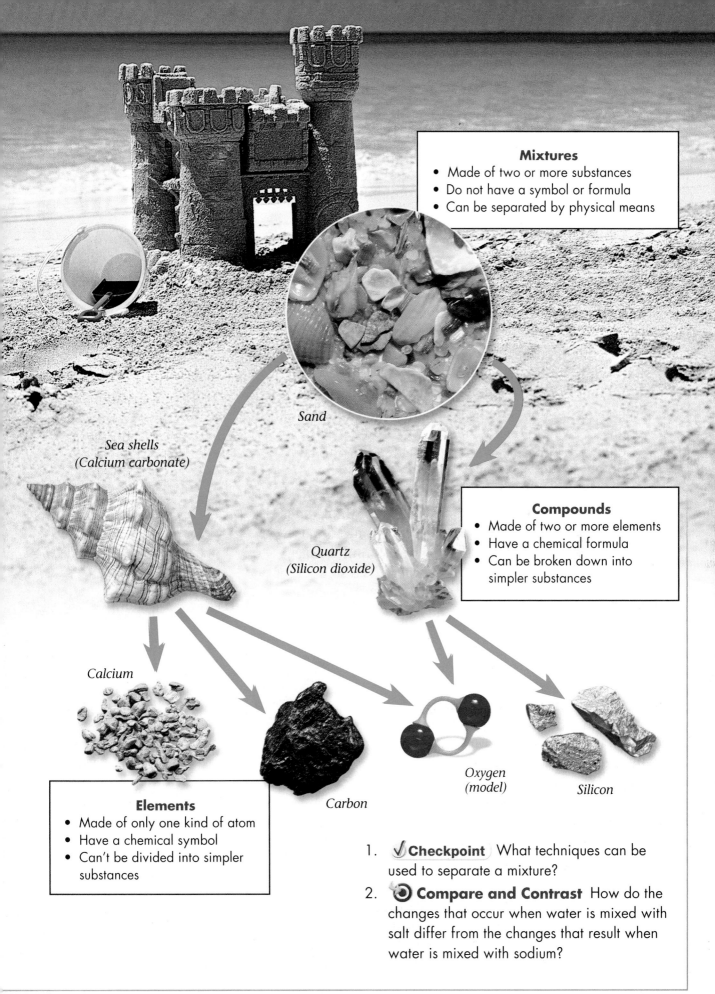

Mixtures
- Made of two or more substances
- Do not have a symbol or formula
- Can be separated by physical means

Sand

*Sea shells
(Calcium carbonate)*

*Quartz
(Silicon dioxide)*

Compounds
- Made of two or more elements
- Have a chemical formula
- Can be broken down into simpler substances

Calcium

Carbon

*Oxygen
(model)*

Silicon

Elements
- Made of only one kind of atom
- Have a chemical symbol
- Can't be divided into simpler substances

1. ✅ **Checkpoint** What techniques can be used to separate a mixture?

2. 🔎 **Compare and Contrast** How do the changes that occur when water is mixed with salt differ from the changes that result when water is mixed with sodium?

403

Solutions

Seeing the individual substances in the soup pictured on page 402 is easy. But some mixtures appear the same throughout. These mixtures are solutions. A **solution** forms when one substance dissolves in another. Salt water is a solution you probably are familiar with.

A solution has two components—the solute and the solvent. The **solute** is the substance that is dissolved. The **solvent** is the substance in which the solute is dissolved. When you dissolve salt in water, the salt is the solute. Water is the solvent.

When a substance dissolves, it breaks down into very small particles. The solute particles mix evenly with the solvent particles. That's why a solution appears to be a single substance. The particles in a solution are so small that they can't even be seen with a microscope. These particles remain evenly mixed and do not settle to the bottom of a container over time.

You might think that all solutions are made with water. Many solutions are made with solvents other than water. Solutions can be combinations of solids, liquids, or gases. Metals form solid solutions. For example, stainless steel, which is used in knives, forks, and spoons, is a solution of solids—chromium, nickel, and iron. Vinegar is a solution of the liquids water and acetic acid.

Chromatography

Differences in solubility can be used to identify substances in a mixture. This paper shows the separation of color pigments that are found in the rose petals. As the liquid moves up the paper strip, particles of pigments dissolve in the liquid. The result is bands of different substances, in this case pigments. Many police departments use this procedure, called chromatography, to separate and identify all kinds of substances.

Yellow gold used in jewelry is a solution of gold and copper.

This whipped cream is a liquid-gas solution of butter fat and air.

Carbon dioxide gas and water form a solution when under pressure. When the bottle or can of soda is opened, the gas is no longer under pressure and it is no longer soluble. The carbon dioxide gas rises to the top of the glass and escapes into the atmosphere.

Concentration

All solutions do not contain the same amounts of solute and solvent. The measure of the amount of solute dissolved in a solvent is **concentration.** Solutions can be described as concentrated or dilute. White vinegar found in most kitchens is a dilute solution of acetic acid and water. More concentrated solutions of acetic acid are found in laboratories and in manufacturing facilities that make pickled vegetables, such as dill pickles.

If you have ever tried to sweeten iced tea, you know that it's difficult to dissolve sugar after ice has been added to the glass. This is an example of a property known as solubility. **Solubility** is the maximum amount of solute that can be dissolved in a solvent at a particular temperature. Solubility usually is expressed in grams of solute per milliliter of solvent.

The speed at which a substance dissolves is improved by mixing or stirring the solution. Increasing the temperature of the solvent and crushing the solute into smaller pieces also makes substances dissolve faster.

You may have noticed that sometimes sugar falls to the bottom of a glass of iced tea. No amount of stirring will make the sugar dissolve. All solutions reach a point in which no more solute can be dissolved in the solvent. This point is known as saturation. Once a solution reaches this point, additional solute will settle at the bottom of the container. The solution has reached its saturation point.

1. ✓**Checkpoint** Give an example of a solution and identify the two components.
2. 🔾 **Compare and Contrast** What are the similarities and differences in solutions and compounds?

Acids
- Taste sour (NEVER taste a substance to test for the presence of acids.)
- React strongly with some metals to form new compounds
- Change blue litmus paper to red

Bases
- Taste bitter (NEVER taste a substance to test for the presence of bases.)
- Feel slippery
- Change red litmus paper to blue

Acids and Bases

When you think of acid, you may think of a liquid that burns holes in anything it touches. You may be surprised to learn that many of the foods you eat contain acids—sour candies, pickles, milk, and citrus fruits are just a few. These substances contain weak acids. Your body cells also contain weak acids that help keep the body healthy and alive.

Some acids are strong. They can burn your skin and are poisonous. Touching an acid to identify it is dangerous. Instead, you can use an indicator. An indicator is a compound that changes color in the presence of an acid. For example, acids cause one kind of indicator, blue litmus paper, to change to red.

Many products you use contain bases. Shampoo, oven cleaners, and drain cleaners contain bases. Strong bases react strongly with some substances. In fact, strong bases will burn your skin just as strong acids will burn. And they are poisonous. Bases turn red litmus paper blue.

More acidic

0   1   2   3   4   5   6

Stomach lining

Hydrochloric acid

Carbonated beverage

Potato

Rainwater

Milk

The pH scale

To measure the strength of acids and bases, scientists use a pH scale, similar to the one below. This scale ranges from 0 to 14. Substances with a pH between 0 and 7 are acids. Acids decrease in strength as the number increases. The pH of bases ranges from 7 to 14. The strength of bases increases as the pH number increases. A pH of exactly 7 is neutral.

✓ **Lesson Checkpoint**

1. Explain what you can tell about a compound with the formula $C_6H_{12}O_6$.
2. What is a saturated solution? Use the terms *solute, solvent,* and *dissolve* in your answer.
3. Writing in Science **Persuasive** Write a news article for younger students explaining what acids and bases are and why being careful around them is important.

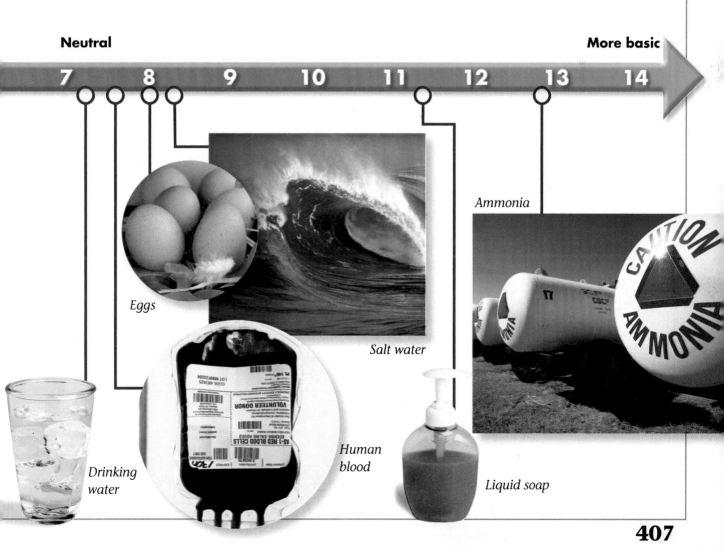

Neutral

More basic

7   8   9   10   11   12   13   14

Eggs

Salt water

Ammonia

Drinking water

Human blood

Liquid soap

Investigate How can you measure pH?

Materials

6 small cups   masking tape

6 pH strips

vinegar
blue dish detergent
carbonated beverage
lemon juice
baking soda solution
antacid solution

Process Skills

An **operational definition** is a definition that involves a **measurement** or careful **observation.** It is made in measurable or observable terms.

What to Do

1 Label each small cup.

 Be careful! Wear your safety goggles.

Do NOT mix up the spoons

2 Put 2 spoonfuls of each liquid in the correct cup.

3 **Measure** the pH of blue dish detergent. Very briefly, touch a pH strip to the blue dish detergent. Carefully **observe** the color of the pH strip.

4 Match the color of the pH strip to the pH Key. Record the pH in column 2 of the chart.

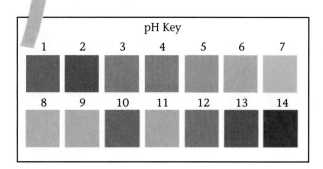

pH Key

5 Repeat step 3 for each liquid.

6 Scientists sometimes use a special kind of definition called an **operational definition.** Here is an example.

> A base is a substance, that when tested,
> has a pH reading greater than 7.

An operational definition tells a way to test if something meets the definition. Use the operational definition of a base to complete column 3 in the chart.

Column 1	Column 2	Column 3	Column 4
Liquid	**pH**	**Is it a base?**	**Is it an acid?**
Vinegar			
Blue dish detergent			
Carbonated beverage			
Lemon juice			
Baking soda solution			
Antacid solution			

Explain Your Results

1. First, **make** an **operational definition** of an acid. Use the operational definition of a base as your guide. Then, complete column 4.

2. Based on your **observations,** list the liquids in order from strongest acid to strongest base.

Go Further

What are the pH values of some common beverages? Make and carry out a plan to find out.

Math in Science

BALANCING EQUATIONS

Just like a mathematical equation is a short way to show a mathematical relationship, a chemical equation is a short way to describe a chemical reaction. A mathematical equation uses numbers, variables, and operation symbols. A chemical equation uses symbols for elements, formulas for compounds, and the plus sign. Instead of the equal sign, a chemical equation uses an arrow.

When you work with a mathematical equation, you must keep it balanced. Also to accurately show a chemical reaction, a chemical equation must be balanced. The number of atoms of any element must be the same on both sides of the arrow.

The chemical equation for hydrogen reacting with oxygen to form water is shown below. This equation is not yet balanced.

$$H_2 + O_2 \longrightarrow H_2O$$

The subscripts show that the left side of the equation has 2 atoms of hydrogen and 2 atoms of oxygen. The right side has 2 atoms of hydrogen, but only 1 atom of oxygen.

To balance the equation, 2 atoms of oxygen are needed on the right side, so the number 2 can be written in front of H_2O. This results in doubling everything in the formula H_2O.

$$H_2 + O_2 \longrightarrow 2H_2O$$
$$2H_2 + O_2 \longrightarrow 2H_2O$$

Now there are 2 atoms of oxygen on each side, but the hydrogen atoms are unbalanced. There are 2 on the left, but 4 on the right. Try doubling the number on the left.

The equation is now balanced. There are 4 hydrogen atoms on each side and 2 oxygen atoms on each side.

Any number written in front of a formula multiplies the number of atoms of each element. For example, $4H_3PO_4$ has 12 hydrogen atoms, 4 phosphorus atoms, and 16 oxygen atoms.

For each formula, find the number of each kind of atom.

1 $2MgO$

2 $4Fe_2O_3$

3 $2H_2SO_4$

Balance each equation.

4 $Mg + O_2 \longrightarrow MgO$

5 $C + Cl_2 \longrightarrow CCl_4$

6 $Al + O_2 \longrightarrow Al_2O_3$

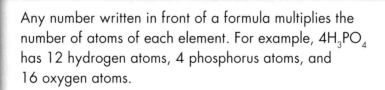

Lab zone Take-Home Activity

Gather about 25 coins including pennies, nickels, dimes, and quarters. Sort the coins into four piles by denomination. For each pile, count the coins and find the value. Also find the total value. Record the data. Mix up the coins and make four random piles. Count and find the value in each pile and the total. Compare the data with the first count. Which numbers have changed? Which have not? Write a paragraph comparing this activity with balancing the number of atoms in a chemical equation.

Use Vocabulary

compound (p. 400)	**periodic table** (p. 396)
concentration (p. 405)	**solubility** (p. 405)
	solute (p. 404)
element (p. 394)	**solution** (p. 404)
mixture (p. 402)	**solvent** (p. 404)

Replace the underlined terms with the correct vocabulary terms from the list above.

1. A <u>mixture</u> is a substance composed of two or more elements that are chemically combined.

2. The two parts of a solution are <u>elements</u> and <u>compounds</u>.

3. All of the known elements are organized in the <u>solubility table</u>.

4. Gold, silver, and copper are examples of a <u>compound</u>.

5. A tossed salad is an example of a <u>compound</u>.

6. The measure of the amount of solute dissolved in a solvent is <u>solubility</u>.

7. The maximum amount of solute that can be dissolved in a solute at a particular temperature is <u>concentration</u>.

8. A <u>compound</u> is a mixture that appears to be a single substance.

Explain Concepts

9. Describe the differences between an element, a compound, and a mixture.

10. You have an unknown element that needs to be identified. The element sample has been hammered into a sheet. It is a good conductor of heat. What can you tell about this element? Explain your answer.

11. The graph shows the solubility of glucose, a type of sugar, at different temperatures. How much more sugar could be added to 100 mL of water if its temperature was raised from 50°C to 70°C? What would happen if the 70°C water was cooled to 30°C?

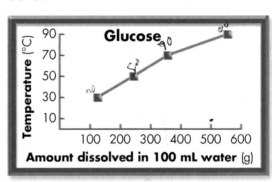

12. Model Make a model of a lithium atom showing the correct number and electrical charge of the protons, neutrons, and electrons. Use four neutrons in your model.

13. Classify Use the periodic table on pages 396–397 to answer these questions about each element below. What is its group and period numbers? Is the element a metal, nonmetal, or metalloid? Is it a solid, liquid, or gas?
- lithium
- tungsten
- arsenic
- krypton

14. Infer whether each of the following substances are soluble or insoluble in water.
- sand
- sugar
- salt
- vinegar

Compare and Contrast

15. Make a graphic organizer like the one shown below to compare and contrast acids and bases.

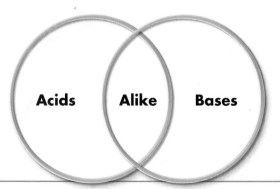

Acids   Alike   Bases

 Test Prep

Choose the letter that best completes the statement or answers the question.

16. Which substance is a compound?
- Ⓐ carbon
- Ⓑ chlorine
- Ⓒ sodium chloride
- Ⓓ sodium

17. Where are the nonmetals located on the periodic table?
- Ⓕ left side
- Ⓖ right side
- Ⓗ along the zig-zag line
- Ⓘ at the bottom

18. A property of bases is that
- Ⓐ it feels slippery and has a bitter taste.
- Ⓑ it reacts strongly with some metals to form new compounds.
- Ⓒ it tastes sour.
- Ⓓ it turns blue litmus paper red.

19. Explain why the answer you chose for Question 16 is best. For each of the answers you did not choose, give a reason why it is not the best choice.

20. Writing in Science **Expository**
Suppose you are writing an article for a local newspaper about solutions. Write a paragraph that could be used in the article describing a solution.

The DIME Challenge

What do you think it would be like to conduct an experiment in a NASA test facility, just like NASA scientists do? In April every year, four teams of high school students get to find out.

Each year, NASA invites teams of high school students to design and build a science experiment using microgravity—the near weightlessness that astronauts experience in outer space. The competition is called DIME, which stands for Dropping in a Microgravity Environment.

Each team designs an experiment that will use a NASA "microgravity drop tower" at the Glenn Research Center in Cleveland, Ohio. A drop tower is a facility that creates a microgravity environment. The only way microgravity can be achieved on Earth is to put an object in free fall. In other words, you drop it from a high place.

Student-designed apparatus

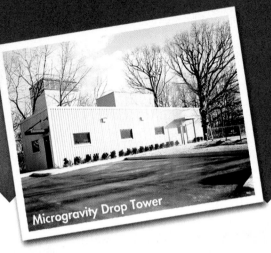
Microgravity Drop Tower

The Glenn drop tower is eight stories tall. When an object drops that distance, it experiences microgravity for just 2.2 seconds. Each experiment must be designed to find results in that short time. Most of the experiments that teams have conducted have involved burning, because flames can spread quickly.

Teams that enter the competition consist of four high school students and an adult advisor. Although teams enter from all across the United States and Puerto Rico, only four experiments are chosen. NASA then pays to bring the four teams to Cleveland to conduct their experiments.

For the winning teams, conducting the experiment is a dream come true. They use the same facility and measuring tools, such as high-speed video cameras, that NASA and university scientists use.

Lab zone Take-Home Activity

Think of an experiment that you would like to conduct at the Glenn Research Center's drop tower. Outline the experiment and the question you would hope the experiment could answer. DIME rules do not allow the use of a living organism in the experiment. Otherwise, let your imagination be your guide!

Chemical Technician

You can learn about science in many ways. You can read about it, talk about it, and think about it. You can also investigate it with activities and experiments. If this is your favorite way to learn science, you might like to be a chemical technician.

Chemical technicians work with chemists. For example, a chemist might identify a problem and an experiment to solve it. The chemical technician would help design, set up, and run the experiment. The technician works closely with the chemist to make observations, record data, and help develop conclusions.

Some chemical technicians do basic research in universities and private or government laboratories. Other technicians work for companies to help invent or improve products. They might work on the product itself or the packaging of the product.

Computers are part of many experiments that chemical technicians run. So strong computer skills are a must for this career. It's important to take lots of science and math courses too. Most technicians have at least a two-year college degree. Some of the skills are learned or sharpened during on-the-job training.

Lab zone Take-Home Activity

Look for a product that you think a chemical technician might have helped develop. (Hint: It could be just about anything.) Write a paragraph explaining how you think the technician was involved.

Chapter 15

Forces and Motion

You Will Discover

- how forces affect the motion of objects.
- how friction affects motion.
- how gravity affects objects.
- how to describe motion.
- what the laws of motion are.

online
Student Edition
pearsonsuccessnet.com

How are forces and motion related?

force

friction

speed

velocity

418

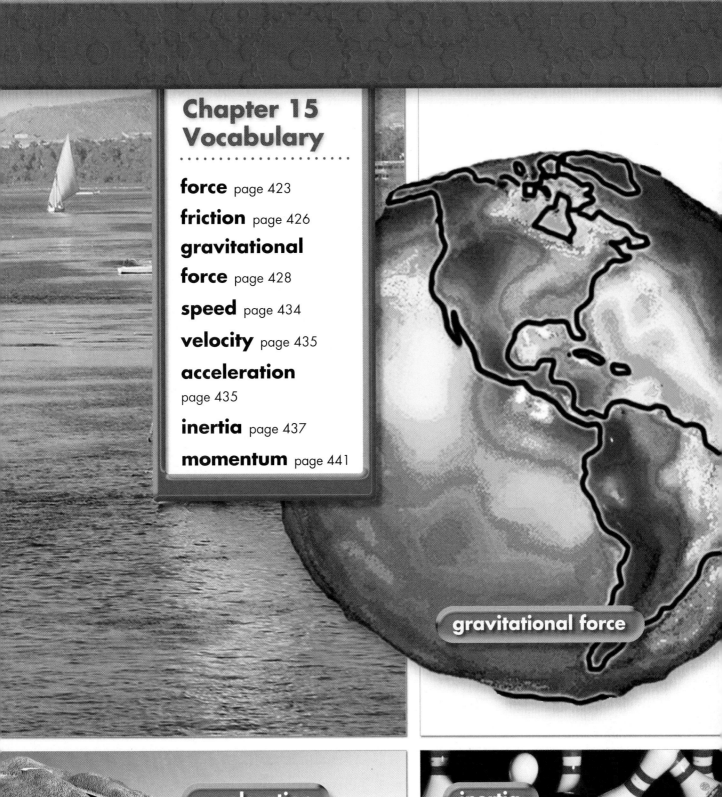

Chapter 15 Vocabulary

gravitational force

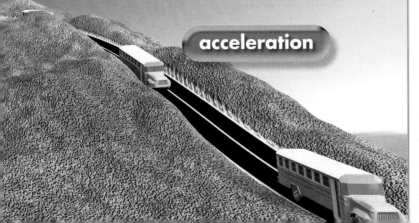

acceleration

inertia

momentum

Explore How can you weigh an object with a spring?

Tape the string to the wall.

Tape the paper strip to the wall.

Materials

spring

2 pieces of string

tape

paper strip

paper cup

10 washers

meterstick

What to Do

1 Tie a string to one end of the spring. Tape the string to the wall.

2 Tape a paper strip to the side of the wall.

3 Tape a string to a cup to make a handle. Place the cup on the free end of the spring. On the paper strip mark the height of the bottom of the cup.

4 Put 2 washers in the cup. Mark the new height of the bottom of the cup.

5 Use the meterstick to find the distance the spring stretched.

6 Repeat steps 4–5 using 4, 6, 8, and 10 washers.

0 washers

Mark the height of the bottom of the cup.

Process Skills

You can use data you collect to help **predict** further results.

Explain Your Results

1. How is weight related to the amount of stretch in the spring?

2. How can you use your data to **predict** how far 14 washers will stretch the spring?

How to Read Science

TARGET SKILL Predict

When you **predict** an outcome, you guess what will happen next. You base your prediction on facts and what you know about the pattern of events that have happened before. To make a prediction, follow these strategies.

• List events or actions in order. Think about how they might be connected.

• Relate the events or actions to past experience.

• Make a reasonable guess about what will happen.

Science Article

Using a Spring Scale

A spring scale can be used to measure force. When a force is applied to a spring scale, the force pulls on a spring attached to a scale. The scale shows the strength of the force. A large force will cause the spring to stretch more than a small force. You attach an empty cup to the spring scale. What will happen to the spring if you fill the cup with sand?

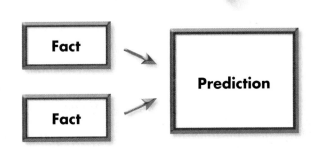

Apply It!

Make a graphic organizer like this one. List the facts from the article. Use the facts to write a **prediction** about what will happen to the spring.

Fact	→	
Fact	→	**Prediction**

Standing in front of the Leaning Tower of Pisa, you think you must be imagining. Why doesn't the tower fall? As the tower was built, the soft ground shifted. The weight of the tower pulled it over. Over time, workers have found ways to support the tower. Forces made the tower lean, but forces also keep the tower from falling. What are these forces?

AudioText

Lesson 1

What happens when forces act on objects?

Some forces act only if objects touch. Others can act at a distance. More than one force usually acts on an object. Friction resists the motion of two surfaces past each other.

Forces

How can this elephant balance on a ball? Like the Leaning Tower of Pisa, the elephant stays upright because of the forces acting on it. A **force** is a push or pull. A force has both size and direction.

Some forces act only if objects touch. For example, when you use your hands to push a heavy box, your hands and the box touch. The elephant touches the ball while pushing down on it. The ball touches the elephant as it pushes upward.

Other forces act even if objects do not touch. Earth's gravity pulls on you when you jump up. Objects with an electrical charge attract or repel each other from a distance. If two magnets are close, you can feel them pushing or pulling on each other without touching.

The elephant applies a force against the ball.

Measuring Forces

Forces are measured in units called newtons (N). One newton is the force needed to change the speed of a one-kilogram object by one meter per second each second. You need a force of about one newton to lift a small apple. Force can be measured using a spring scale. You attach an object to one end of the scale and hold up the other end. A spring inside stretches to show the force needed to support the object.

1. ✓ **Checkpoint** What two things should you describe about a force that acts on an object?
2. **Writing in Science** **Descriptive** Tell about a situation in which a force acts when objects touch. Describe another situation in which a force acts at a distance.

The downward force of a water strider on the water is balanced by the upward force of the water on the water strider.

Forces on Objects

A high-flying kite soars through the air, swerving up and around. What forces are acting on the kite? The weight of the kite pulls it down, and the force of the wind pushes it up. You guide the kite by applying force to the string. Like the kite, most objects have more than one force acting on them.

The combination of all of the forces acting on an object determines the effect of the forces. Some forces act in the same direction. Others act in different directions.

You might compare the forces acting on an object to a tug-of-war with a rope. Some people pull the rope one way, and others pull the opposite way. If the forces pulling one way are stronger than the forces pulling in the opposite direction, the rope moves in the direction of the stronger force. The forces are unbalanced. Unbalanced forces can cause an object at rest to move. They can also change the speed or direction of a moving object. Balanced forces cause no change in motion, even if an object is moving. If the forces of the two sides are the same, the motion of the rope doesn't change.

The force of the wind against the sail causes a sailboat to move through water. By rotating the sail, the sailboat's direction of motion can be changed.

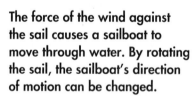

To find the overall effect of forces acting on an object, you add the forces together. The resulting force is called the net force. It works like this: If a 5 N force pulls an object to the right, and a 3 N force pulls to the left, the overall effect is the same as a 2 N force pulling to the right. The net force is 2 N to the right.

The net force on an object, however, doesn't always determine the direction that an object moves. It determines the *change* in an object's motion. Suppose a bicycle rider is moving quickly along a flat sidewalk and lightly applies the brakes. The bike continues along the sidewalk, but the force of the brakes acts in the opposite direction. The bike moves more slowly. A stronger force could stop the bicycle.

The arrows show the directions of forces that allow the strong wire cables to support the weight of the road and the automobiles that cross it.

1. ✓ **Checkpoint** How do balanced forces affect the motion of an object?

2. 🎯 **Predict** Draw and label arrows showing forces acting on a ball that is rolling to the right. A 15 N force pushes to the right. A 9 N force pushes to the left. What is the net force on the ball? How will the net force affect the motion of the ball?

Balanced forces are needed for a safe suspension bridge.

Friction

. Why does a soccer ball slow down when you roll it across the ground? Friction is the reason. **Friction** is the force that resists the movement of one surface past another. The rough surface of the ground stops the soccer ball by pushing against it. Friction is a force opposite of the direction of the ball's motion.

The table describes three types of friction. Rolling friction and sliding friction act on objects that are moving. Rolling friction resists the motion of a skateboard's wheels. Pushing a heavy box across the floor is hard because of sliding friction. The box is easier to push, however, after it starts to move. When you first push on the box, static friction resists its movement. Static friction is usually stronger than sliding friction.

Type of Friction	Description
Rolling	Resists the motion of a rolling object
Sliding	Resists the motion of a sliding object
Static	Resists the motion of an object just as it begins to move

The floor of a bowling lane must be polished to reduce rolling friction between the wood and the ball.

Friction depends on the type of surfaces rubbing against each other and how strongly they are pushed together. Friction is mainly caused by rough surfaces. Even surfaces that seem to be smooth are rough if you look at them with a microscope. Tiny bumps and holes on the surfaces catch on each other, slowing the movement of the surfaces.

Friction usually is greater for rougher surfaces. If both surfaces are very smooth and flat, however, the attraction of their particles increases their friction. A soft or rubbery surface also has more friction because it easily bends. Movement also may be slowed when the particles of the two surfaces attract. The surfaces then stick to each other.

Heat produced by friction can wear out these engine parts and reduce efficiency.

Oil and grease are used on engine parts to decrease friction by reducing contact between rough surfaces.

Oil

Grease

Helpful and Harmful Friction

Friction is useful for many things you do every day. Without friction, walking across a room would be like walking on ice. You depend on friction between your feet and the floor to keep you from slipping. If you ride on a scooter, friction between the wheels and the ground keep you from spinning your wheels. Friction also prevents your feet from slipping off the scooter. When the driver of a car applies the brakes, friction of the brake pads against the brake drum slows the car.

Friction can also be harmful. When objects rub together, heat is produced. If you rub your hands together quickly, your hands begin to feel warm. Energy from your hands changes to thermal energy because of the friction of your hands. Heat produced by friction makes engines run less efficiently. Friction between wind and soil can cause erosion. Friction also wears away the rubber on car tires and forms holes in the soles of shoes.

✓ Lesson Checkpoint

1. Give an example of static friction on an object.
2. Name a way not mentioned in the text that friction is helpful.
3. **Writing in Science** **Expository** Explain how the usefulness of machine parts depends on the materials they are made from and how well they fit together.

The metal surface of a car's engine may feel smooth, but this photo, taken with an electron microscope, shows the many bumps and cuts in the surface that can increase friction.

Lesson 2

How does gravity affect objects?

All objects exert a gravitational pull on all other objects. Gravitational force affects objects on Earth as well as stars, planets, and all other objects in the universe.

Gravitational Force

Toss a ball into the air and you know it will fall down. Earth's gravity pulls all objects on Earth toward Earth's center. But the pull of Earth's gravity isn't the only gravitational force. **Gravitational force** is the force of attraction between any object and every other object in the universe. Gravitational force holds water in the oceans and holds the air near Earth. It affects the way plants grow and the way your bones develop. Life on Earth depends on gravity in many ways.

In the 17th century, Isaac Newton, an English scientist, was the first to explain many details about gravity. He realized that gravity depends on the masses of the two objects that exert gravitational forces on each other. The greater the mass of an object, the stronger its gravitational force. The book you are reading pulls on you with a gravitational attraction, and you pull on the book. You don't feel the gravitational pull of the book because both you and the book have low mass. But you feel Earth's gravity because Earth has such a large mass. Astronauts on the Moon experience a lower gravitational force because the Moon has less mass than Earth.

On Earth an apple experiences a gravitational force of about 1 N.

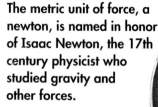

The metric unit of force, a newton, is named in honor of Isaac Newton, the 17th century physicist who studied gravity and other forces.

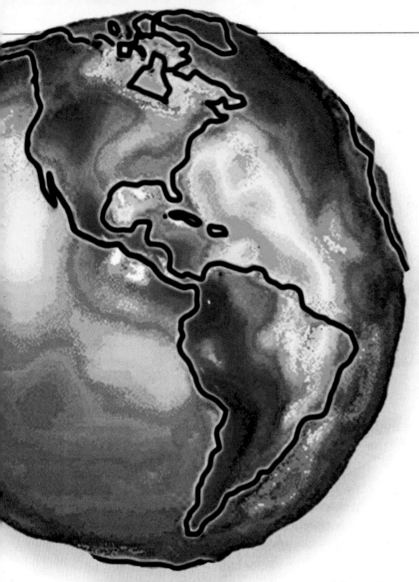

Gravitational force is not the same at all places on Earth. This gravitational map shows how Earth's gravity varies slightly. Red areas show where the Earth's gravity is highest. Dark blue areas show where gravity is lowest.

The Moon's gravity is about one-sixth the gravity on Earth. An apple's mass experiences a gravitational force of less than 0.2 N.

Newton also realized that gravitational force depends on the distance between two objects. If the distance between objects increases, the gravitational pull between them decreases. Earth's gravitational pull on you is slightly less when you are in an airplane than when you are standing on Earth's surface.

You can measure Earth's gravitational pull on your body—just weigh yourself. An object's mass—the amount of matter that makes up the object—is the same everywhere in the universe. Weight depends on your location. You weigh more on Earth than on the Moon. Like all forces, weight can be measured in newtons.

1. ✓Checkpoint Why don't you notice the gravitational pull of your school desk?

2. Health in Science Explain why your weight would change if you went to the Moon but your mass would not.

429

Gravity and the Universe

Newton's theory of gravity showed that the force that causes a baseball to fall to Earth also moves the planets and stars. The Moon revolves around Earth because of the gravitational pull between the Moon and Earth. Earth and all the planets of the solar system stay in orbit around the Sun because of the gravitational pull between the Sun and the planets. Without the pull of gravity, the Moon and all the planets would shoot straight into outer space.

The masses of Earth and the other planets in our solar system are much less than the mass of the Sun. The pull of the planets therefore has little effect on the Sun's motion. In other solar systems, some planets have masses much closer to the masses of their stars. In those cases, the gravity of a planet can cause a star to wobble. Astronomers use this wobble as a way to locate faraway planets.

If gravity is larger for objects with more mass, why don't you feel the gravitational pull of the Sun? Remember that gravitational force depends on distance as well as mass. The Sun's mass is about 330,000 times greater than Earth's mass. Your distance from the Sun's center, however, is about 23,000 times greater than the distance to Earth's center. The strength of the Sun's gravitational pull quickly decreases with distance. If you were an equal distance from the Sun and from Earth, the Sun's pull on you would be much stronger. Because you are so far away from the Sun, you only experience Earth's gravity.

Gravity is different on every planet and moon. Mars, for example, has a mass that is about one-tenth the mass of Earth. You might expect, then, that gravity on Mars would be one-tenth as strong as Earth's gravity. In fact, the gravity on Mars is about one-half the gravity on Earth. The difference is due to the planet's size. The radius of Mars is about one-half the radius of Earth. In other words, the distance from the surface of Mars to its center is about half that of Earth. The gravitational pull of a planet depends on the distance to its center.

1 The gravitational force of the Moon lowers the tide and exposes the land between the island of Mont Saint Michel and the coast of France.

2 High tides cause the island of Mont Saint Michel to be surrounded with water.

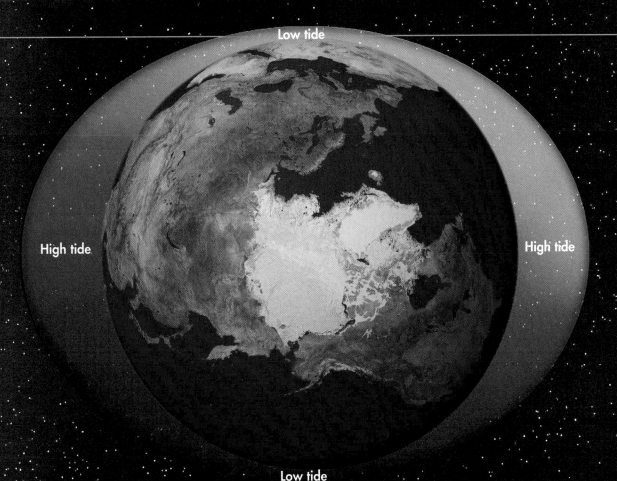

Low tide

High tide

High tide

Low tide

Tides

A tide is a rise or fall in water level near the ocean's shore. Most coastal areas around the world have two high tides and two low tides each day. The illustration shows how this happens.

The gravitational force of the Moon pulls on everything on Earth, including its water. But the pull is more noticeable in liquids than in solids. That's because the particles that make up liquids can move more easily than the particles in a solid. This difference causes ocean water to be pulled slightly away from Earth. Earth is pulled slightly away from the water on the side opposite the Moon. As Earth spins on its axis, the part of Earth facing the Moon experiences a high tide. The opposite side of Earth also has a high tide. The other parts of Earth experience a low tide. The Sun also pulls on Earth's water, but because of the distance, the effect is much smaller.

✓ Lesson Checkpoint

1. Why do most coastal areas have two high tides each day?
2. How would you expect Earth's gravitational pull on you high in the Rocky Mountains to be different from the pull at a seashore?
3. Writing in Science **Expository** Write a paragraph explaining why the Moon has a greater effect on Earth's tides than the Sun does.

Lesson 3

How can you describe motion?

A description of motion depends on the frame of reference from which the motion is viewed. Speed, velocity, and acceleration are used to describe motion.

Observing Motion

Riding on a roller coaster like the one to the right can make you feel as if you are flying. You rise high into the air, then down again, over and over. What do you see as the roller coaster moves around? At the highest point, you glance down and see other rides, games, and people that look very small. As you loop downward, objects on the ground seem to move toward you. Then, as you rise, objects on the ground seem to move away. Are the objects on the ground actually moving?

In order to determine an object's motion, you must view it in relation to another object that appears to stay in place. In other words, the way you describe motion depends on your frame of reference. A frame of reference is the object an observer uses to detect motion.

When riding on a roller coaster, the seat in which you ride may be your frame of reference. In that case, you aren't moving relative to the seat. If you use the ground as your frame of reference, however, the ground seems perfectly still. The chair in which you are riding appears to move up, around, and down.

How would you describe your motion right now? Motion is usually described using Earth as a frame of reference. If you are sitting still, you are not in motion relative to Earth. Relative to the Sun, however, Earth is whirling through space. Earth is also spinning on its axis. You are not aware of these motions because objects around you are also motionless in this frame of reference.

Kinds of Motion

How would you describe the motion of one of the seats on the Ferris wheel? Its path is called circular motion. Circular motion takes place around a central point. The central point for the seat's motion is the axle of the ride. When a roller coaster travels in its loops, it too is using circular motion. Other examples of circular motion include the orbits of planets around the Sun and the wheel of a bicycle as it turns to move the bike.

Although the wheel of the bicycle moves in a circular pattern, the bike itself travels in a straight line. Straight-line motion can be seen as you watch a parade move down a street or when someone makes a "bee line" for the door.

Circular motion and straight-line motion may be easy to observe. Vibrational motion can be more difficult to see. A vibration is a rapid back-and-forth movement. The strings on a cello vibrate to make sounds, as do your vocal cords.

A person observing this Ferris wheel from the ground probably would say the seats are moving. How does using the red supports that hold up the wheel as a frame of reference show motion?

If you were riding in the blue seat at the top left and using the seat as your frame of reference, the ground would appear to first move farther away and then move closer.

1. ✓ **Checkpoint** Describe the motion of a bus from the point of reference of a person riding on the bus.

2. **Writing in Science** **Narrative** Write a short paragraph describing the motion of a boy on a skateboard zooming past a cat. Write from the frame of reference of the boy. Then write another paragraph from the frame of reference of the cat.

433

Calculating Speed

The bus below is winding its way along the hilly road. How can you figure out its speed? **Speed** is a measure of how fast an object is moving.

You can find speed by dividing the distance traveled by the time needed to move that distance. Speed is often measured in kilometers per hour. If the bus travels between two points that are 9 kilometers apart in 10 minutes, you can find its speed using this equation:

$$\text{average speed} = \frac{\text{distance}}{\text{time}} = \frac{9 \text{ km}}{10 \text{ min}} \times \frac{60 \text{ min}}{1 \text{ h}} = 54 \text{ km/h}$$

This speed for the entire trip—54 km/h—is the average speed of the trip. But the bus probably didn't travel at the same speed during the entire trip. An object's speed at any moment is instantaneous speed. The speedometer of a car tells the instantaneous speed that the car is traveling.

Velocity

How does the bus's motion change if it makes the trip in the opposite direction? The distance traveled is the same. It may also have the same travel time. So the bus's average speed would remain the same. The direction of motion, however, is different. Its velocity also changes.

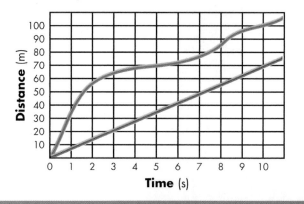

From a distance/time graph, you can infer whether a moving abject's instantaneous speed is changing. A straight line indicates constant speed.

Velocity is the speed of an object in a particular direction. On the bus's first trip, its velocity would be 54 km/h east. On the return trip, its velocity would be 54 km/h west. A change in either speed or direction causes a change in velocity.

The velocity of an object moving along a curved path constantly changes even if the speed of the object is constant. The velocity changes because the direction of the object is always changing.

Acceleration

The motion of moving objects usually isn't constant. The instantaneous speed and direction of motion may change. **Acceleration** is the rate at which velocity changes. The bus in the picture accelerates when it speeds up.

Acceleration isn't just going faster. Acceleration also happens when an object slows down or changes direction. Each time the bus moves slower or travels around a curve, it is accelerating.

The velocity of an object can only change if a force acts on the object. Acceleration is therefore the result of unbalanced forces acting on the object.

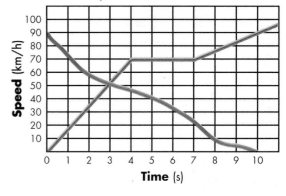

A speed/time graph shows the speed of an object at any time. You can infer whether the object is accelerating. A straight line indicates constant acceleration. A curved line indicates changing acceleration. A horizontal line indicates constant speed.

✓ Lesson Checkpoint

1. What is the difference between instantaneous speed and average speed?

2. A car traveling along a curved road at 80 km per hour slows down to 65 km per hour. Is the car accelerating? Explain your answer.

3. **Math in Science** According to the graph on page 434, for the first 5 seconds, what is the average speed of the moving object represented by the blue line?

435

Lesson 4

What are the laws of motion?

A force is needed to change an object's motion. An object accelerates in response to an unbalanced force. A force on an object causes an equal but opposite reaction force.

Studying Motion

For hundreds of years, scientists tried different experiments to try to explain motion. One of those scientists was Galileo Galilei, who in the 1600s studied falling objects and the idea of gravity. At the time, people thought that objects slowed down and stopped by themselves. They did not yet understand friction.

It wasn't until 1686 that Isaac Newton published his book *Principia.* In it he related forces to the motion of objects. Newton's book put the ideas of many scientists together in a way that people could understand them.

Galileo Galilei

First Law of Motion

Newton's first law of motion describes the motion of an object that has equal forces acting on it.

Newton's First Law of Motion

An object at rest remains at rest, and an object in motion remains in motion at constant speed and in a straight line, unless acted on by an unbalanced force.

The first part of this law is not surprising. You know that if you place your book on a desk, the book will not move unless you pick it up or another force acts on it. If you place a soccer ball on a field, you have to kick the ball to move it.

This crash-test dummy shows the effect of inertia. If a car stops suddenly, the forward motion of people in the car continues. The force that stopped the car does not stop the people. The force of a seat belt or air bag stops a person's forward motion.

The second part of the law may surprise you—an object stays in motion. Motion in your everyday life doesn't seem to obey Newton's first law. If you kick a soccer ball, it moves for a while and then gradually slows down and stops. To keep your bicycle moving, you have to continually push on the pedals.

Why do the objects slow down? Friction is one explanation. Objects in motion can be stopped by friction. When bicycle wheels touch the ground, the ground exerts a frictional force. Air friction also slows the motion as air particles push against the bicycle. Other forces, such as gravity, may also slow an object's movement.

Inertia

Newton's first law of motion is sometimes called the law of inertia. **Inertia** is the tendency of an object to remain at rest or in constant motion unless a force acts on it. Because ice has little friction, inertia allows an ice skater to glide long distances. A rock sitting on the ground stays still because of inertia.

Suppose you had two jars of the same size. One is filled with feathers and the other is filled with pennies. Which jar would be harder to move? If you said the pennies, you are right. But why? Both are the same size. The jar of pennies is more difficult to move because it has more mass. The amount of inertia an object has depends on its mass. The greater the mass of an object, the greater its inertia.

1. ✓Checkpoint What does Newton's first law say about a moving object if the forces on the object are balanced?
2. Writing in Science **Expository** Write a paragraph explaining the forces on a baseball flying through the air. Use Newton's first law of motion to explain the ball's motion.

Second Law of Motion

Newton's first law of motion states that unbalanced forces cause a change in motion, but how does the motion change? According to Newton's second law of motion, a force causes an object to accelerate.

Newton's Second Law of Motion

The acceleration of an object depends on the mass of the object and the size of the net force applied.

First, consider how mass affects motion. Look at the two dogs in the wagons. The large dog has greater mass than the smaller dog. You have to exert only a small force to pull the wagon with the small dog. But the same force applied to the wagon with the large dog will not accelerate the wagon as much. In other words, if you apply the same force, the greater the mass, the smaller the acceleration.

Now suppose you give the wagon with the small dog a push. The wagon will travel at a certain speed. If you give the same wagon a harder push, it will move faster. Stated another way, an object's acceleration will increase as the net force increases. Likewise, the acceleration will decrease as the net force decreases.

What effect would pulling on these two wagons with equal force have on the wagons?

Using an Equation

The second law of motion can be written as an equation.

acceleration = force ÷ mass

In the equation, force refers to the net force applied to the object. Mass refers to the object's mass, and acceleration to the object's acceleration. The equation shows that both force and mass affect acceleration.

Not all forces cause a change in motion. Only unbalanced forces cause an object to accelerate. If you and a friend push on opposite sides of a box with the same force, the box will not move. However, if you push with a greater force than your friend does, the box will begin to accelerate. It will continue to accelerate as long as the forces on the box are not balanced.

The direction of an object's acceleration depends on the direction of the forces on the object. Place a coin on a desk and give it a small push. The coin accelerates in the direction of the force. If you push on it from two directions, it accelerates in the direction of the unbalanced force.

The force of the snowplow causes the ice and snow to accelerate. If the force of friction equals the force of the snowplow, the ice and snow will not accelerate.

1. ✓**Checkpoint** Newton's second law shows the relationship among which three quantities?
2. ⟳ **Predict** Suppose you are riding on a bicycle. You stop to place a heavy object on the back of the bike. How will the increased mass affect the bike's acceleration if you pedal with the same force? Explain your reasoning.

Third Law of Motion

Why does a rubber ball bounce if you toss it on the ground? The force of your hand is downward, but the ball bounces upward. Newton's third law of motion explains the motion of the ball.

Newton's Third Law of Motion

When a force is applied to an object, the object exerts an equal force in the opposite direction.

A falling ball exerts a downward force on the ground, and the ground exerts an equal but upward force on the ball. The push of the ground causes the ball to bounce upward.

Newton's third law of motion is sometimes called the law of action and reaction. For every action, there is an equal and opposite reaction. When you pull on a doorknob to open a door, you feel a force working against you. Your pull on the doorknob is the action force, and the doorknob's pull in the opposite direction is the reaction force. When a cat jumps into the air, it bends its legs and pushes its feet very hard against the ground. The ground exerts an equal force, pushing the cat into the air. The cat's push against the ground is the action force. The ground's opposite but equal push is the reaction force.

Newton's third law of motion explains the result when two objects collide, or hit against each other. Think about a basketball rolling along the ground. It strikes a bowling ball that is sitting still. During the collision, the two balls exert equal and opposite forces on each other. The mass of the bowling ball is much greater than the mass of the basketball. The basketball experiences greater acceleration and it changes direction. It rolls away from the bowling ball. The bowling ball moves forward with less acceleration.

Why does this leopard move upward when it pushes downward on the rock?

440

What action-reaction forces cause this rowing boat to move forward?

These oryx are applying equal but opposite force.

Momentum

The difference in the reactions of the basketball and the bowling ball is explained by momentum. **Momentum** can be used to find the force needed to stop a moving object. An object's momentum depends on its mass and velocity. The more momentum an object has, the harder it is to stop the object or change its direction.

When a moving object hits another object, some or all of the momentum of the first object is transferred to the other object. The total momentum before the collision equals the total momentum afterwards. This is known as the law of conservation of momentum.

The momentum of the basketball before it hits the bowling ball must equal the momentum of the basketball and bowling ball after the collision. The bowling ball starts moving because it gets some momentum from the basketball.

✓ Lesson Checkpoint

1. A bowling ball rolls down a lane and strikes a bowling pin. Which is greater, the force of the ball on the pin or the force of the pin on the ball? Explain.

2. Which has greater momentum, a car sitting still or a pebble rolling down a hill? Explain.

3. **Predict** An adult and a child are ice skating. The child pushes away from the adult. The child moves backward. What will happen to the adult?

441

Investigate How can an object stay the same but weigh less?

The weight of an object is the result of the force of gravity acting on that object and pulling downward, toward Earth. You can use water to make the object weigh less.

Materials

4 pieces of string

8 washers

metric ruler

tape

2 plastic cups and water

spring scale

What to Do

Part A

1 Tie 2 washers to a ruler. Hang the ruler and washers from a table. Balance the ruler by sliding the washers back and forth until the ruler is parallel to the floor.

2 Place 1 cup under each washer.

3 Fill one cup with water, leave the second cup empty. **Observe** what happens.

4 Remove the ruler and washers from the table.

Part B

5 Hang a spring scale holding 2 washers from the table. Record the weight of the washers.

6 **Predict** Will the spring scale show that 2 washers suspended in water weigh more than, about the same as, or less than 2 washers suspended in air?

7 Test your prediction. Record your results.

8 Repeat steps 4–6 with 4, 6, and 8 washers. Record your results.

Number of Washers	2	4
Weight in air = Gravitational force (direction of force (*up* or *down*) _____)		
Weight in water (direction of force (*up* or *down*) _____)		
Buoyant force = weight in air − weight in water (direction of force (*up* or *down*) _____)		

Explain Your Results

1. What direction is the buoyant force? Explain.

2. What information did you use to make your prediction in step 6?

3. **Communicate** Use the direction of the forces acting on the washer to explain the statement "buoyant force = weight in air − weight in water."

Go Further

How will your results change if you repeat the activity with objects that are the same weight but have different volumes? Make a plan to answer this and other questions you may have.

Math in Science

PROPORTIONS AND SPRINGS

Pogo sticks were first patented in 1919 and were very popular in the 1920s. There were theater shows on pogo sticks and contests for the most jumps. Some people are still enjoying pogo sticks today.

A spring is the main part in a pogo stick. The distance a spring stretches or is squeezed is directly proportional to the force put on it. This means that if the force pulling or pushing on a spring doubles, the spring will stretch (or be squeezed) twice as much, three times the force will triple the stretch or squeeze, and so on.

When you jump on a pogo stick and the tip comes down to touch the ground, the spring compresses—gets squeezed. The spring reaches its maximum compression quickly. The maximum compression is proportional to the total force pushing on the spring. The forces that compress the spring include your weight, the weight of the pogo stick pushing down on the spring, and the force of the ground pushing up on the spring.

If a total force of 400 N on a pogo stick compresses the spring 20 cm, how much would the same spring compress with a total force of 200 N? The answer can be found by solving this proportion.

$$\frac{400}{20} = \frac{200}{c}$$

$$400c = 4000$$

$$c = 10$$

The spring will compress 10 cm.

Use the information on page 444 to answer each question.

1. If a total force of 400 N on a pogo stick compresses the spring 20 cm, how much total force is needed to compress the same spring 32 cm?

2. On another pogo stick, the spring compresses 15 cm with a total force of 230 N. How much would this spring compress with a total force of 300 N? Round your answer to the nearest tenth of a centimeter.

3. After its maximum compression, the spring on a pogo stick will begin to expand. It will keep expanding to a length greater than its original length before the jump. If a 40 cm spring expands to a length of 44 cm, what is the percent increase in length?

Lab zone **Take-Home Activity**

This activity will help you decide if the proportionality rule for springs is also true for rubber bands. Hook a bent paper clip through a plastic bag to make a basket. Hang the other end of the clip on a rubber band. Put two pennies in the bag as weights and measure the stretch of the rubber band. Then do the same with four pennies in the bag, and then eight pennies. Did the amount of stretch double when the weight doubled? Explain.

Use Vocabulary

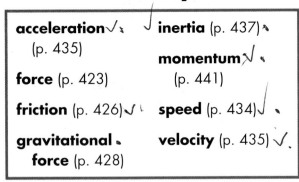

acceleration (p. 435)	**inertia** (p. 437)
force (p. 423)	**momentum** (p. 441)
friction (p. 426)	**speed** (p. 434)
gravitational force (p. 428)	**velocity** (p. 435)

Use the vocabulary term from the list above that best completes each sentence.

1. The mass and acceleration of an object determines its _____.

2. A force that opposes the motion of a ball rolling across the ground is _____.

3. Your weight is the _____ that pulls you toward Earth.

4. The speed and direction of an object is its _____.

5. The product of mass and velocity is _____.

6. An object remains at rest unless a force acts on it because of its _____.

7. A measure of how fast an object moves is _____.

8. Unbalanced forces on an object cause _____.

Explain Concepts

9. After reading Newton's first law of motion, a student claims that an object moving at a constant speed in a straight line has no forces acting on it. Is the student correct? Explain your answer.

10. Identify the effect of each of the actions below. Use Newton's laws to explain the results.
    A. You pushed against a wall.
    B. An unbalanced force acts on an object.
    C. An empty grocery cart runs into a parked car.

11. The length of the force arrows in the picture below shows the relative strength of the forces acting on the box. If the box were sitting still on a table, what would be the result of all the forces acting on the box?

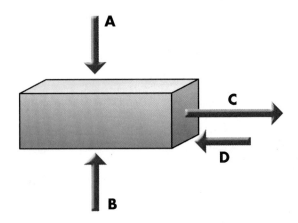

12. **Communicate** Prepare and give a presentation to the class about how friction is important in football, gymnastics, or some other sport.

13. **Make a Hypothesis** Make a ramp by supporting one end of a long board with a book. Attach a rubber band to a toy car and pull the rubber band to move the car up the ramp. Note how far the rubber band stretches as you pull on the car. How far do you think the rubber band will stretch if you cover the board with sandpaper? Test your prediction and explain the results.

Predict

14. An object weighs 100 N. Predict how the object's weight would change if it were placed on Mars. Use a graphic organizer like the one below.

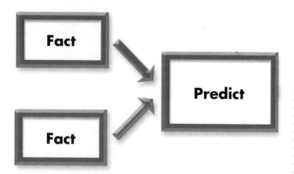

Test Prep

Choose the letter that best completes the statement or answers the question.

15. Which type of friction acts on a box that is moving down a ramp?
   Ⓐ gliding
   Ⓑ rolling
   Ⓒ sliding
   Ⓓ static

16. Which is a force that keeps planets in orbit?
   Ⓕ friction
   Ⓖ inertia
   Ⓗ gravity
   Ⓘ speed

17. Which can be used to figure out the force needed to stop a moving object?
   Ⓐ acceleration
   Ⓑ friction
   Ⓒ momentum
   Ⓓ speed

18. Which is the unit of force?
   Ⓕ m/s
   Ⓖ kilogram
   Ⓗ newton
   Ⓘ km/h

19. Explain why the answer you chose for Question 17 is best. For each of the answers you did not choose, give a reason why it is not the best choice.

20. Writing in Science **Persuasive** Write a paragraph in support of having airbags in cars. Use Newton's second law of motion to support your argument.

Albert Einstein

When Albert Einstein was 5 years old, his father showed him a magnetic compass. Young Albert was fascinated with it. No matter how he turned the compass, the needle would point in the same direction. He wondered what kept the needle pointing north. Einstein's curiosity and constant wondering would make him one of the greatest scientists the world has ever known.

Einstein was a genius. Like many geniuses, Einstein thought about things in different ways. He was able to come up with ideas that no one had ever thought about before—and show them to be correct.

One of these ideas was that matter and energy are interchangeable. In other words, matter can be changed into energy, and energy can be changed into matter. His famous equation, $E = mc^2$, shows that a tiny amount of mass can be changed into a huge amount of energy. This idea led to the use of nuclear power.

Einstein used math to explain and prove his ideas. For example, he developed a theory that predicts no matter can go as fast as the speed of light. Experiments in modern laboratories have shown Einstein to be correct.

Lab zone Take-Home Activity

Einstein lived a quiet yet interesting life. Find out more about him. Then on poster board, create a time line of the major events in his life.

Chapter 16
Machines

online
Student Edition
pearsonsuccessnet.com

You Will Discover

- how machines make work easier.
- what some simple machines are.
- how simple machines can be put together to make compound machines.

How do machines make work easier?

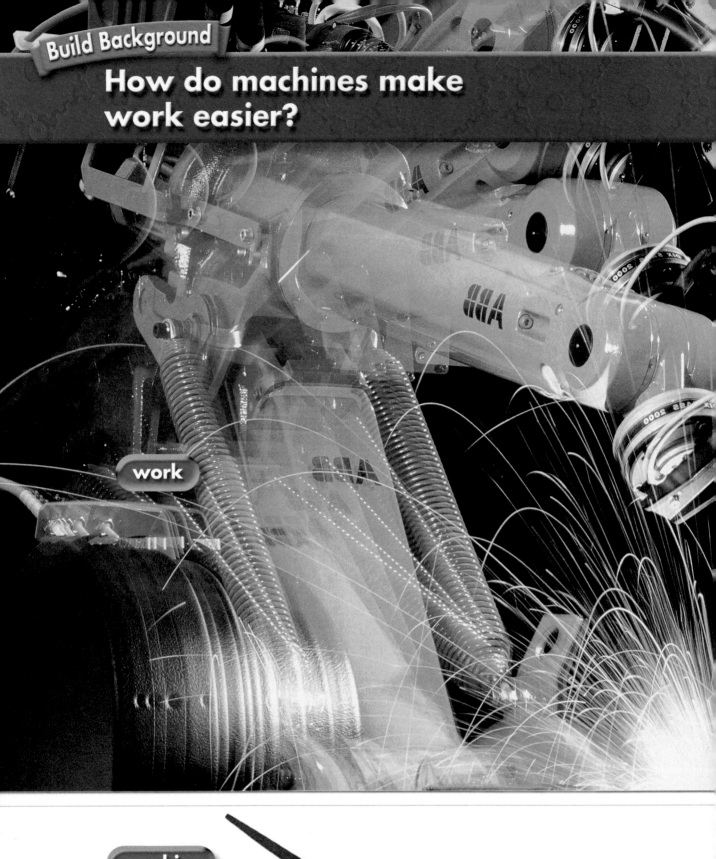

work

machine

simple machine

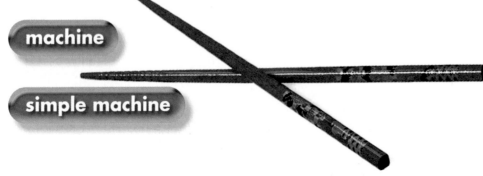

Chapter 16 Vocabulary

effort force

load

fulcrum

compound machine

451

Explore How can you balance different weights?

Materials

modeling clay

soup can

10 washers

meterstick

tape

What to Do

1 Put a piece of clay on each side of the can to hold it in place.

force A

Tape additional washers on top of these washers.

2 Tape 2 washers to each end of a meterstick. Balance the meterstick and weights on the can.

3 Record your **observations**.

clay

fulcrum

4 Double force A by taping 2 more washers to the A end of the meter stick. Balance the meterstick without changing force B.

clay

5 Record your results.

6 Double force A again. **Predict** where the fulcrum must be to balance the meterstick.

Do not add washers to this end.

7 Test your prediction.

force B

Process Skills

To help **predict** how to balance a system that is not balanced, first **observe** the cause-and-effect relationships in a balanced system.

Explain Your Results

1. When you increased force A, how did you change the distance from the fulcrum to force A to balance the meterstick?

2. **Predict** If you increase the force at one end, which direction must you move the fulcrum to balance the meterstick?

Cause and Effect

When you talk about **cause** and **effect,** you tell what happens (effect) and why (cause). Often the effect of one event will become the cause of another event. Some causes and effects are marked in the lab report. Can you find others?

Lab Report

Using a Lever

I piled several large books on the table. First, I tried to lift the pile by placing my finger underneath and lifting. I could not lift the books. Next, I placed a ruler under the books. I put an eraser under the ruler near its center. I pushed down on one end of the ruler.

Apply It!

Use a graphic organizer like this one to **predict** the **effect** on the book when the person pushes down on the ruler.

Cause	→	Effect

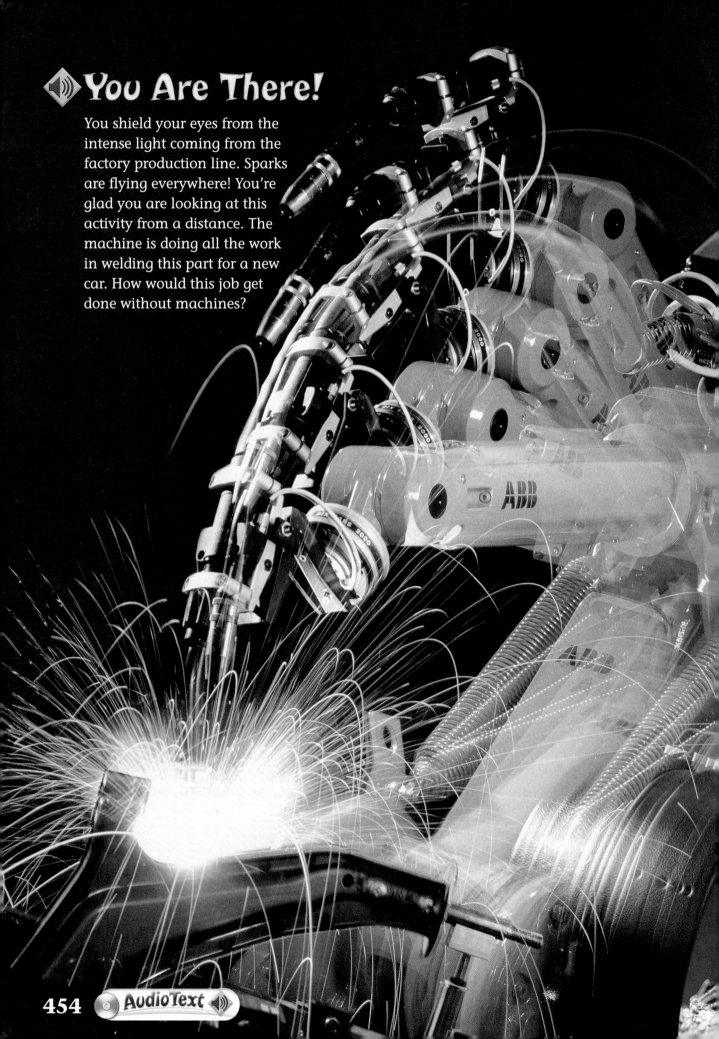

◀)) You Are There!

You shield your eyes from the intense light coming from the factory production line. Sparks are flying everywhere! You're glad you are looking at this activity from a distance. The machine is doing all the work in welding this part for a new car. How would this job get done without machines?

AudioText ◀))

How do machines help people work?

In science, work *means "using force to move an object a certain distance." A machine is any device that helps people do work.*

Measuring Work

What do you think of when you use the word *work?* Do you think of cleaning your room or doing your homework? Do you think of jobs that adults in your family do to make a living? In our everyday lives, all these examples seem to fit the definition of *work.*

In science, however, **work** means using force—pushing or pulling—in order to move an object a certain distance. No matter how much force you use, if something doesn't move, you haven't done work.

Suppose you want to move a piano from one room to another. A team of movers could push the piano on its rollers across the floor. When they rolled the piano in its new position, they could truly say, "We've done some work!" If you tried to move the piano by yourself, though, you probably wouldn't be able to budge it. You might struggle, strain, and sweat a lot, but you couldn't say, "I did work," if the piano didn't move.

To find how much work is done, use this formula:

$$\text{work} = \text{force} \times \text{distance}.$$

Work is measured in a unit called the joule. The abbreviation for joule is J.

$$1 \text{ joule (J)} = 1 \text{ newton (N)} \times 1 \text{ meter (m)}$$

For example, suppose you push on a box with a force of 200 newtons. The box moves 1 meter. The work done is 200 N × 1 m, or 200 J.

1. ✓**Checkpoint** Use the work formula to explain the scientific definition of *work.*

2. **Math** in Science Suppose you want to find the work done, and the distance is given in centimeters. What will you need to do to the distance value in order to use it correctly in the formula?

How are these leafcutter ants doing work?

Work and Machines

Do you know what a machine is? Perhaps you imagine a large, noisy object with many moving parts. Not all machines are complicated, and many don't have moving parts. In science a **machine** is any device that helps people do work. A machine can be quite simple.

You probably don't think of nail clippers or chopsticks as machines, but they are **simple machines.** A simple machine is a tool made up of one or two parts. Think about the way you use chopsticks. You hold them in the middle and squeeze the ends together to grasp bits of food. You then move the food to your mouth. Because you are using force to move something, you are doing work—with help from the chopsticks.

The kind of machine that most people think of when they think of a machine is a compound machine. A compound machine helps people do work too, but it has many parts. A **compound machine** contains one or more simple machines among its parts. You probably can think of many compound machines. Some, such as cars, trucks, and airplanes, have thousands of parts.

These nail clippers are a machine that can do work.

Chopsticks help you do work.

How Machines Help

There is nothing magic about what a machine can do for you. Every machine makes some kind of tradeoff that helps you in some way. Recall that work is equal to force times distance. Some machines decrease the force required to do a task. A car jack is an example. If you tried to lift a car without a machine, you wouldn't be able to supply enough force. But when you use a car jack, the task becomes much easier. The jack decreases the required force by increasing the distance over which the force is applied.

Think about twisting a screw-top lid on a jar. A person might be able to force the lid onto the jar top by slamming down hard with a fist. However, screwing on the top is a lot easier. When you screw on the lid, you apply the force over more distance as you turn and turn the lid, but you don't have to use as much force.

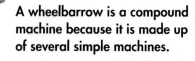

A wheelbarrow is a compound machine because it is made up of several simple machines.

456

Machines and Friction

In order for a machine to do its job, work must go into it. If you supply a force—a push or a pull—on a machine, you are doing work. Sometimes the work that goes into a machine comes from another energy source, such as a battery.

You might think that the amount of work that a machine does is equal to the amount of work put into it. But the amount of work done by a machine is less than the amount put into it. Why? The answer is friction.

You've probably noticed that often when you use a machine, it gives off heat. The heat is produced as a result of the friction between the moving parts of the machine. In general, the more moving parts a machine has, the more work is lost to friction.

People who design machines try to make machines more efficient by reducing the friction between the machine's parts. One way to do this is by using lubricants. Lubricants include substances such as oil, wax, and grease.

Another way to reduce friction is to use wheels, rollers, or balls. The ball bearings placed in the wheels of inline skates reduce friction. Using a lubricant would reduce friction even more.

✓ Lesson Checkpoint

1. How do machines make doing work easier?
2. 🌀 **Cause and Effect** How does friction affect the work of a machine?
3. Math in Science Suppose you need to move a board that is nailed to the floor. You pry down with a crow bar with a force of 300 newtons. You move the piece of wood 0.5 meters. How much work did you do?

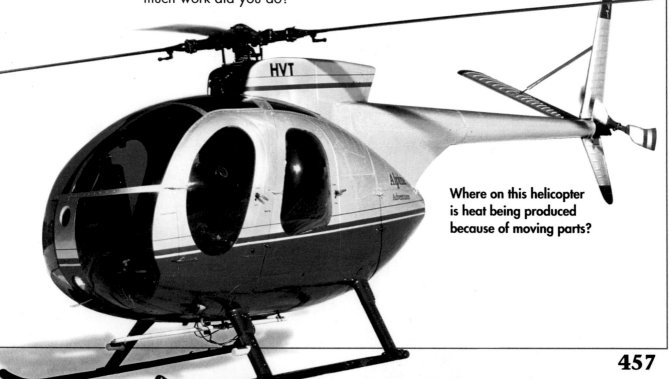

Where on this helicopter is heat being produced because of moving parts?

457

Lesson 2

What are types of simple machines?

There are six basic types of simple machines.
Each machine works in a unique way to help you do work.

Types of Simple Machines

If you study the parts of any compound machine, you will find that it is made from two or more simple machines. The six types of simple machines are the lever, inclined plane, wedge, screw, wheel and axle, and pulley.

Lever

The objects pictured on these two pages have something in common that helps make work easier. Do you know what it is? They all contain a simple machine called a lever. A lever is made of one or more bars resting on a support. The support is called the **fulcrum.**

The crowbar in the picture is a lever. The curved part at the bottom of the crowbar is the fulcrum. The cinder block, which is also called the **load,** is on one end of the bar. It applies a force on the crowbar. A force is applied to the opposite end, which lifts the load. This applied force is also called the **effort force.** When a person pushes on the crowbar to move something, the force created by the person pushing (the effort force) will be less than the force applied to the load, but the effort force moves the handle a greater distance than the load moves.

The fulcrum of a lever doesn't have to be right in the middle. The order of fulcrum, load, and effort force can be different, depending on the type of lever. If the fulcrum is closer to the load, less force will be required to move the load, but the load will not be lifted as high. If the fulcrum is closer to the effort force, more force will be required, but the load will be lifted higher. In both examples, the trade off is between force and distance.

Key	
E	Effort force
F	Fulcrum
L	Load

Types of Levers

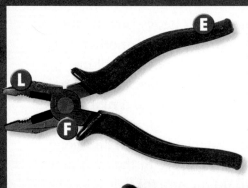

First-Class Lever

Can you find the fulcrum in this pair of pliers? It's in the middle, between the effort force and the load. The effort force is the force you apply when you squeeze the handles. The load is the item you will grab with the "nose" end of the pliers. A first-class lever, such as pliers, has the effort force at one end, the load at the other end, and the fulcrum between them.

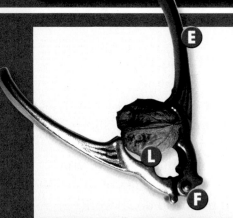

Second-Class Lever

A second-class lever, such as a nutcracker, has the effort force at one end, the fulcrum at the other end, and the load in the middle. The fulcrum of the nutcracker is at the closed end, where the two bars connect. The effort force is the force you apply when you squeeze the handles. The load is the nut you want to crack.

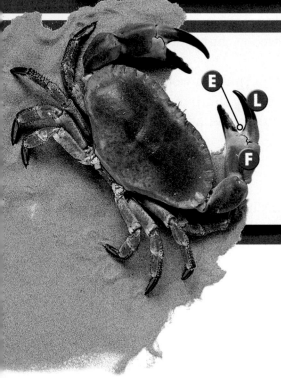

Third-Class Lever

You probably don't think of crab claws as levers. Can you find the fulcrum? It is the joint that connects the two halves of the claw with the crab arm. The effort force is the force the crab applies with muscles in the middle of its claw. The load is the tasty morsel the crab pinches and grabs with the sharp ends of its claw. A third-class lever, such as the crab claw, has the fulcrum at one end, the load at the other, and effort force in the middle.

1. ✓**Checkpoint** How do first-class, second-class, and third-class levers differ?

2. **Health in Science** Your elbows and knees are types of fulcrums. Sometimes, these parts of the body must handle strong forces applied in activities such as sports. Find out how you can protect knees and elbows when doing sports activities such as playing ball or riding a bike. Use the Internet or your library. Make a list of helpful hints.

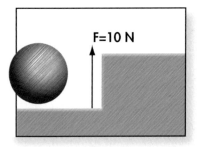

F=10 N

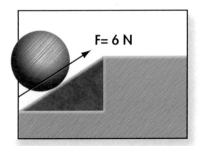

F= 6 N

Inclined Plane

Would you rather carry a heavy box up a flight of stairs or use a ramp? A ramp is another type of simple machine called the inclined plane. An inclined plane is a slanted surface. A ramp makes moving a load from a low place to a higher place easier.

The inclined plane offers a trade off between distance and force. You can see in the diagrams that moving a load up a ramp takes less force than lifting it straight up. But the load travels farther up the ramp. In both cases, you do the same amount of work.

The Wedge

Not all inclined planes are as simple as a ramp. The left picture on the bottom of the page shows the part of a ship called the prow. The prow is a wedge. A wedge is a simple machine made of one or two inclined planes. The slanted edges of the inclined planes come to a point. To do its work, the wedge must be moving. A force directed at the flat end of the wedge drives the point forward. The inclined planes of the wedge change the direction of the force.

A wedge can be used for splitting wood or for digging in the ground. Many sharp tools are made of inclined planes—saws, knives, needles, and axes.

The Screw

The bottom part of this light bulb is a modified inclined plane. Thinking of a screw as an inclined plane may seem strange. But a screw is an inclined plane that is wrapped in a spiral. The ridges on a screw are called threads. If you could unwind the threads of a screw, you would see they form an inclined plane. A screw decreases force and increases distance. Screws often are used as fasteners.

This winding road on a mountainside is an inclined plane. Cars must travel quite a distance to get to the mountaintop, but they can go there more easily than driving straight up.

The ship's prow is a wedge. It helps the ship move more easily through the water.

Which part of the wheel and axle moves the greater distance?

Wheel and Axle

Did you ever ride on a Ferris wheel similar to the one in the picture? If you did, you were riding on a simple machine called a wheel and axle. A wheel and axle is made of a wheel with a rod joined at the wheel's center. You can see in the picture how much larger the diameter of the wheel is than that of the axle. The wheel turns through a much greater distance than the axle. But the smaller turn of the axle is much more powerful.

A wheel and axle can increase a force or increase the distance through which a force acts. Think about a water faucet in the shape of a wheel that you turn with your hand. The force you put into turning the faucet changes into a larger force in the tiny axle, which opens up the water valve. Can you imagine what it would be like to turn on the faucet if it consisted of just the axle without the wheel?

1. ✔**Checkpoint** Explain how a wedge and a screw are related to the inclined plane.
2. 🔄 **Cause and Effect** You want to move a heavy box up the four front steps of your home. You decide to use a ramp. How will using the ramp affect the distance the box must be moved?

461

Pulley

A pulley is a grooved wheel with a rope or chain around it. A load is attached to one end of the rope and the effort force is applied to the other end. There are two types of pulleys: fixed pulleys and movable pulleys. A fixed pulley stays in one position as the wheel spins. It lets you pull down on one end to lift up the load on the other end. It changes the direction of the force, but it doesn't reduce the effort force you must use. A downward pull on the rope causes the load to move upward.

Unlike a fixed pulley, a movable pulley is attached to the object being moved. As a force is applied to the load, the pulley moves along with the load. Movable pulleys decrease the force you must apply, but the force you use is applied over a greater distance. You must make both sides of the rope move in order to move the load.

Fixed pulley   *Moveable pulley*

Escalators are machines that use pulleys.

Several pulleys can be used with the same rope in a system called a block and tackle. Each pulley added to the compound system reduces the amount of effort required to lift the load. A block and tackle with a lot of pulleys could help lift a very heavy load, such as a piano.

Block and tackle

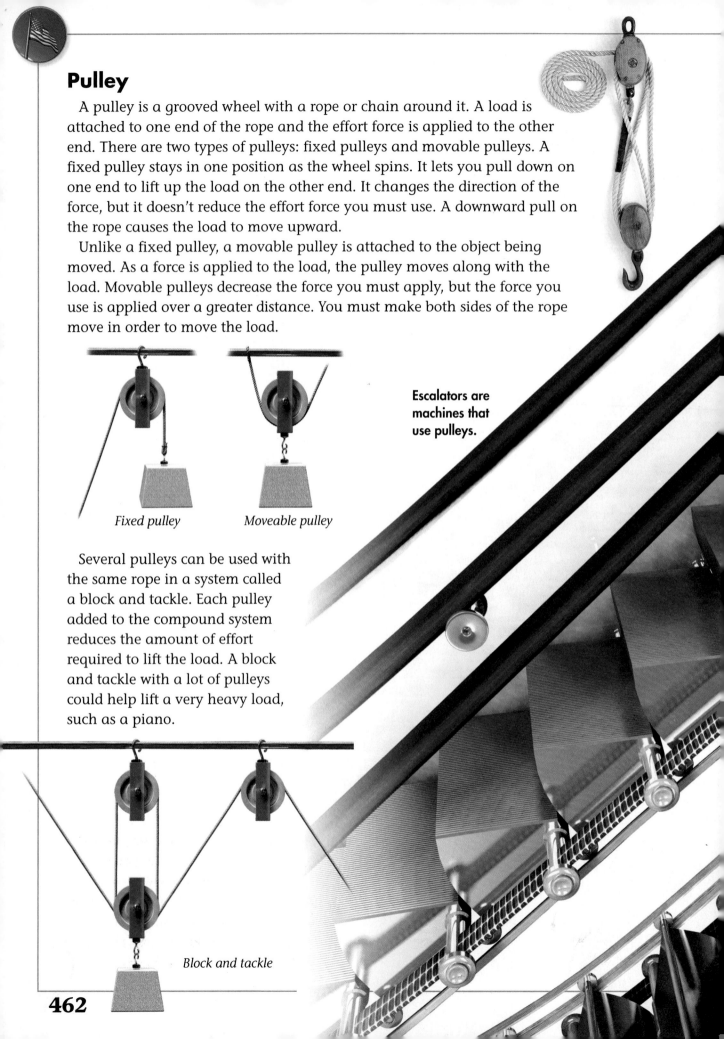

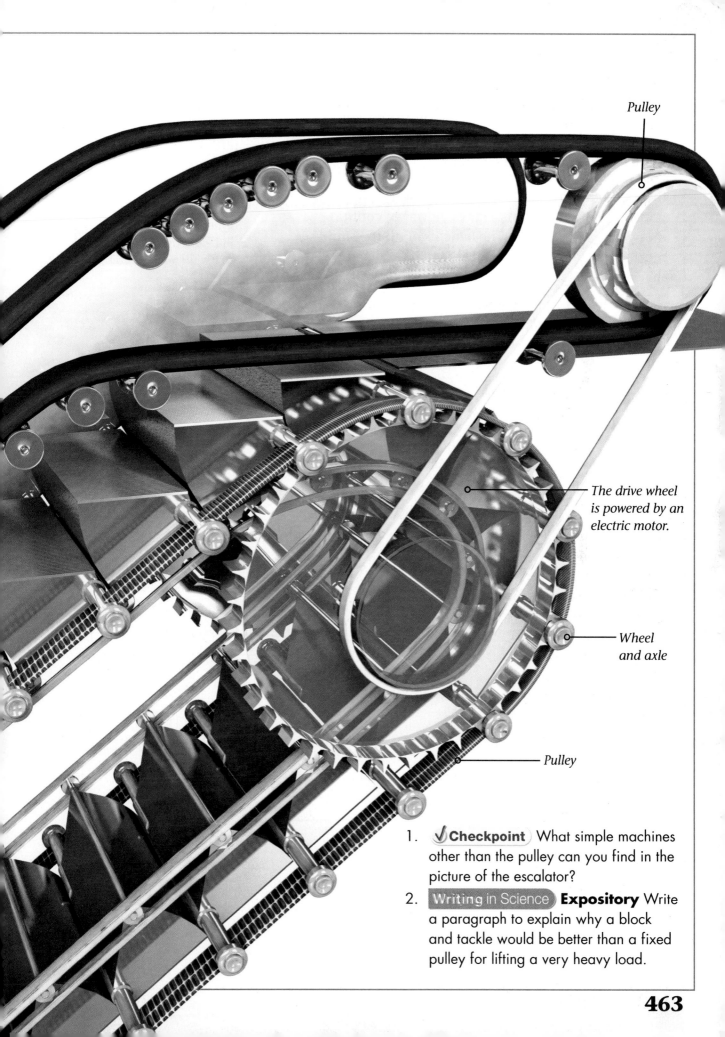

Pulley

The drive wheel is powered by an electric motor.

Wheel and axle

Pulley

1. ✓**Checkpoint** What simple machines other than the pulley can you find in the picture of the escalator?

2. **Writing in Science** **Expository** Write a paragraph to explain why a block and tackle would be better than a fixed pulley for lifting a very heavy load.

463

Compound Machines

Almost all the machines you see and use are compound machines—the automobile or bus you ride in, the elevator that carries you from one floor to the next, even the stapler you use to fasten together your papers. Many compound machines, such as this sailboat, have hundreds or even thousands of parts. Even the largest machines, however, contain many simple machines. The benefits of all the simple machines add up to the greater benefit provided by the compound machine.

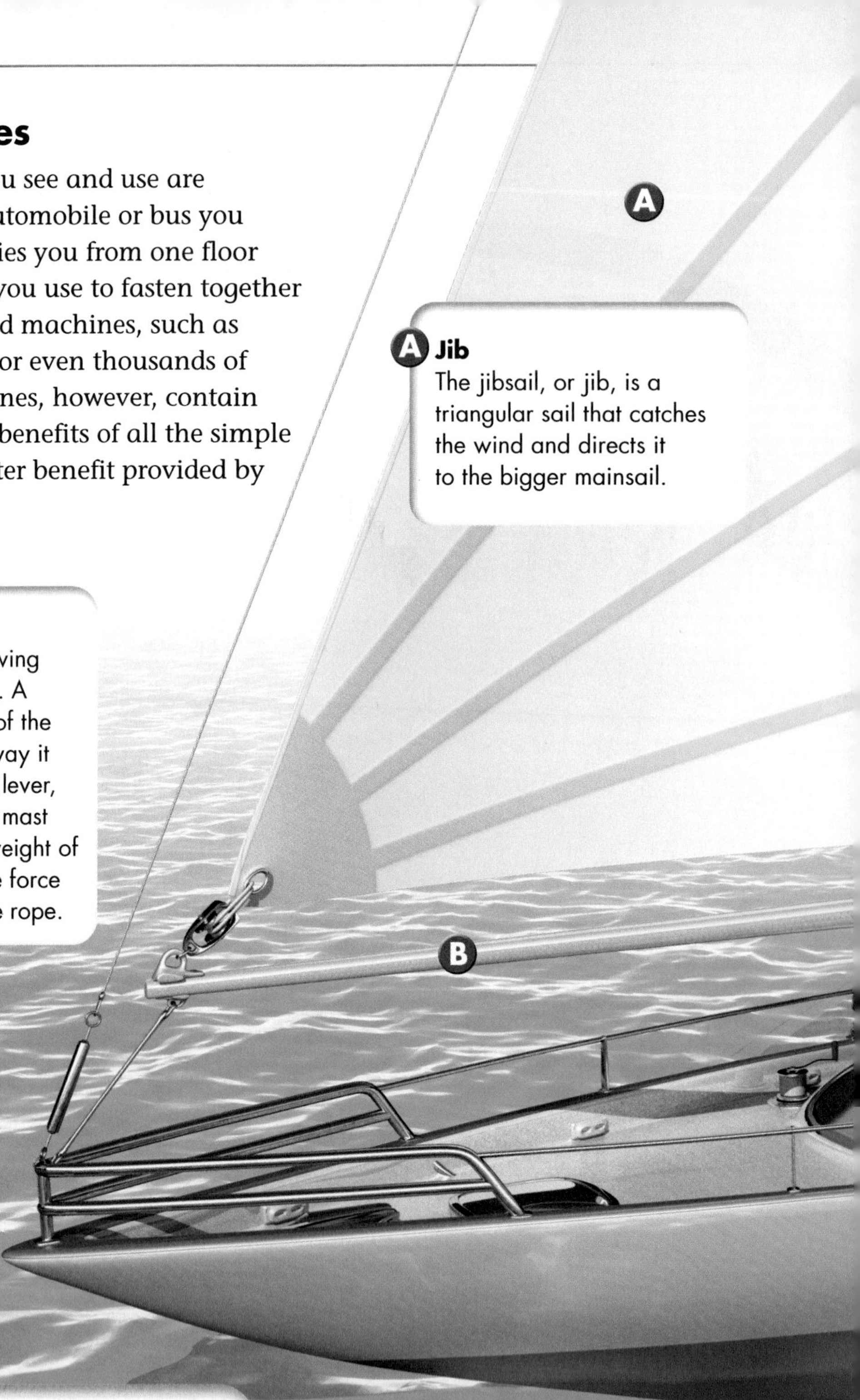

A Jib

The jibsail, or jib, is a triangular sail that catches the wind and directs it to the bigger mainsail.

B Boom

The boom's end can swing freely around the mast. A rope along the length of the boom controls which way it swings. The boom is a lever, with the fulcrum at the mast joint. The load is the weight of the sail above, and the force is applied by the guide rope.

✓ Lesson Checkpoint

1. Explain how the following are related: fulcrum, load, effort force.
2. How is a screw like an inclined plane?
3. **Art in Science** Design a compound machine to perform a particular task. Draw your design and label the simple machines that make up your compound machine. Use labels or write a paragraph to explain how your machine works.

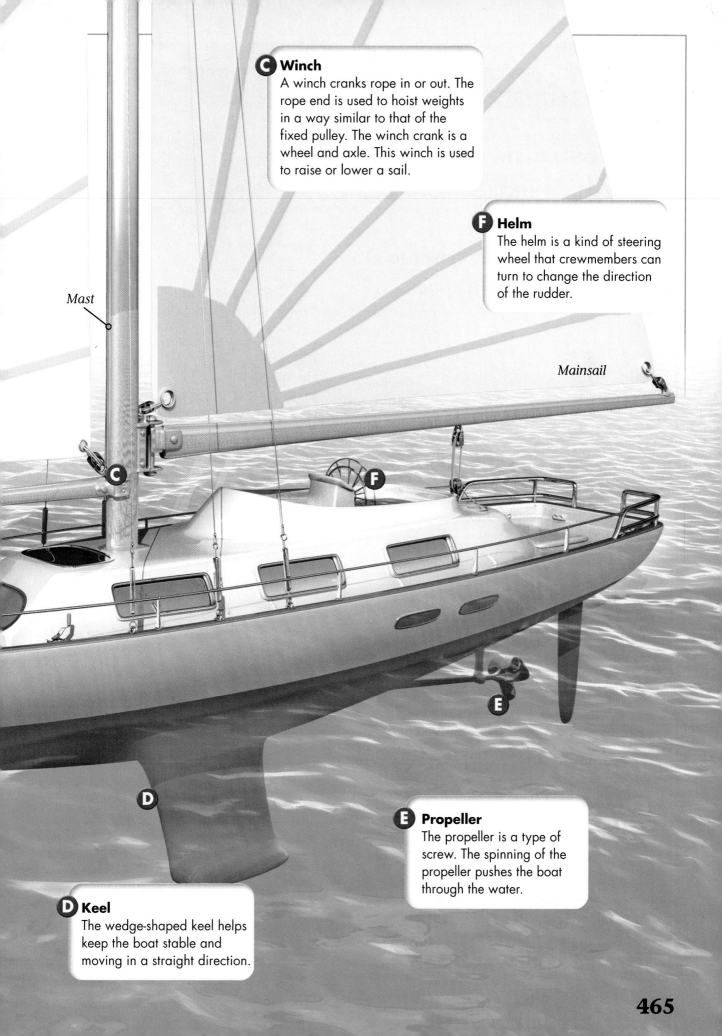

C **Winch**
A winch cranks rope in or out. The rope end is used to hoist weights in a way similar to that of the fixed pulley. The winch crank is a wheel and axle. This winch is used to raise or lower a sail.

F **Helm**
The helm is a kind of steering wheel that crewmembers can turn to change the direction of the rudder.

Mast

Mainsail

E **Propeller**
The propeller is a type of screw. The spinning of the propeller pushes the boat through the water.

D **Keel**
The wedge-shaped keel helps keep the boat stable and moving in a straight direction.

465

Investigate How can a wheel and axle make work easier?

Materials

paper cups

masking tape

string

spool with pencil

washers

meterstick

Process Skills

You can **observe** a model to learn how a wheel and axle help you do work.

What to Do

1 Label the cups A and B. On each, tape a short string to make a handle. Tie a long string onto each handle.

short pieces of string

Onto each "handle" tie a long string.

2 Use tape and the 2 remaining pieces of string to hang the pencil from a table.

3 Tape the long string from cup A onto the spool. Turn the pencil to lift cup A to the top. Have a partner hold it there.

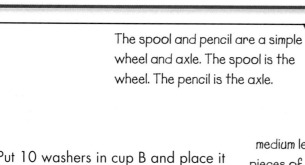

The spool and pencil are a simple wheel and axle. The spool is the wheel. The pencil is the axle.

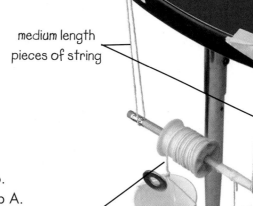

medium length pieces of string

long pieces of string

4 Put 10 washers in cup B and place it under the pencil. Tape the long string from cup B onto the pencil. The string should be taut.

5 Ask the partner holding cup A to let go. **Measure** and record the height of cup A.

6 Gently add washers one at a time to cup A until it moves to the floor. **Observe** what happens to cup B. Measure and record the height of cup B.

	Cup A	Cup B
Height at start (cm)	____ cm	0 cm
Height at end (cm)	0 cm	____ cm
Distance moved (cm)	____ cm down	____ cm up
Number of washers at start	0 washers	10 washers
Number of washers at end	____ washers	10 washers

Explain Your Results

1. Using a wheel and axle, only ____ washers in cup A were needed to lift 10 washers in cup B. However, cup A had to move down ____ cm to lift cup B up only ____ cm.

2. Based on your **observations**, how could the wheel and axle help you do work? Explain.

Go Further

What would happen if the axle and wheel were the same circumference? Make a plan to answer this and any other questions you may have.

467

Math in Science

Mathematics and MACHINES

We are surrounded by machines that make our lives easier. Scissors, doorknobs, and stairs are all examples of simple machines that we use regularly. Some of the same tasks could be accomplished with a variety of machines.

Suppose you need to load a heavy box (1,200 N) onto the back of a truck. You have several options for loading the box. First, you could lift it 1.5 m into the back of the truck. How much work would this take?

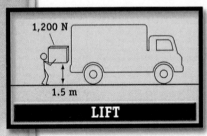
LIFT

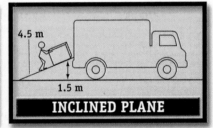
INCLINED PLANE

SIMPLE PULLEY

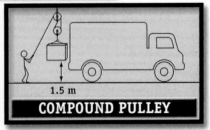
COMPOUND PULLEY

Remember: Work (in joules) = force (in Newtons) x distance (in meters).

$W = 1{,}200 \text{ N} \times 1.5 \text{ m}$
$W = 1{,}800 \text{ N} \times \text{m}$
$W = 1{,}800 \text{ J}$

In this case, the force is the weight of the box, in Newtons. The distance is the height of the truck bed from the ground.

The total work to lift the box would be 1,800 J.

eTools Take It to the Net
pearsonsuccessnet.com

You could also use a machine to load the box. You can choose a ramp (inclined plane), a simple pulley, or a compound pulley. These options are pictured for you on page 468. Friction works against all machines, so the actual force required is greater than what would be expected, but they can still make the job easier.

Answer each question. Use the pictures on page 468.

1. If the force required to load the box using the ramp is 440 N and the ramp is 4.5 m long, what is the amount of work done?

2. The work done to load the box using the simple pulley is 1,845 J. Compute the force needed. Considering your answer, how does a simple pulley help?

3. If you use the compound pulley, you will need to pull twice the distance but with less force. The force you need is equal to one half the weight of the box plus 25 N. What is the force needed?

4. If you are only able to exert a force of 550 N, which machine should you use? Which machine requires the most work to use?

5. Predict how the force needed would change if you used a ramp that is twice as long as the one pictured. Explain your answer.

Lab zone Take-Home Activity

Using a board or other long, flat surface, set up an inclined plane. Find a way to attach a rubber band to various objects that can be pulled up the inclined plane. As you pull an object up, try to maintain a constant speed. Measure the length of the rubber band as you are pulling. Experiment with objects of different weights and materials and change the angle of the incline. Record your results and use them to explain the advantages and disadvantages of using an inclined plane.

Use Vocabulary

compound machine (p. 456)	**load** (p. 458)
effort force (p. 458)	**machine** (p. 456)
fulcrum (p. 458)	**simple machine** (p. 456)
	work (p. 455)

Choose a term from the box that best matches each clue.

_____ **1.** Any device that helps people do work

_____ **2.** Has one or just a few parts

_____ **3.** The support on a lever

_____ **4.** The force applied to a lever by a person or another machine

_____ **5.** Has many parts; contains one or more simple machines

_____ **6.** The force of an object on a lever

_____ **7.** Using a force to move something

Explain Concepts

8. Explain how the scientific definition of *work* differs from the everyday meaning of *work*, as in "chores."

9. What are the six kinds of simple machines? Give an example of each.

10. Explain why the amount of work that a machine does is less than the amount put into the machine.

11. What are two ways to reduce the friction produced when parts of a machine move? Give examples.

Process Skills

12. Collect Data The pictures show how four different ramps were used to move a heavy box. Use the information to draw a force-distance graph. Then calculate the amount of work done with each ramp.

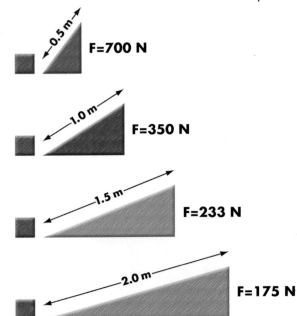

0.5 m F=700 N

1.0 m F=350 N

1.5 m F=233 N

2.0 m F=175 N

13. Classify Draw the three types of levers. Identify the fulcrum, effort force and load in each.

 **Cause and Effect**

14. Lifting a load of 200 N with a single movable pulley requires 100 N of force. What would be the effect on the amount of effort force required to move the load if a block and tackle were used? Explain your answer.

 Test Prep

Choose the letter that best answers the question.

15. How much work is done when a 5 N force moves a load 2 m?

Ⓐ 1 J
Ⓑ 2.5 J
Ⓒ 5 J
Ⓓ 10 J

16. Suppose you twist the lid of a pickle jar to tighten it. What simple machine are you using?

Ⓕ pulley
Ⓖ lever
Ⓗ screw
Ⓘ wheel and axle

17. A block and tackle is made from

Ⓐ a series of pulleys.
Ⓑ a wheel and axle.
Ⓒ two inclined planes.
Ⓓ two screws.

18. Which item is NOT a compound machine?

Ⓕ pliers
Ⓖ manual can opener
Ⓗ electric can opener
Ⓘ bicycle

19. Explain why the answer you chose for Question 15 is best. For each of the answers you did not choose, give a reason why it is not the best choice.

20. **Writing in Science** **Expository**
Write directions for using a pulley to lift a very heavy load. Include a description of the kind of pulley to use.

MACHINIST

Did you ever look at a car engine? It's an amazing machine. Hundreds of metal parts work together to make the car move. The parts work together because they are the exact shape and size they are supposed to be.

Machinists use machines to make precise metal parts. These parts are then put together to make many of the products that we use every day.

Machinists plan their work carefully. First, they study blueprints or written instructions for the part they will be making. Next, they decide what materials and tools to use. They plan out how they will shape the material each step of the way. Then they begin to cut, drill, shave, and shape the material to make the exact part needed.

A lot of the machines that make metal parts contain computers. So machinists often need some computer skills. Most machinists learn their skills in a technical school or two-year college after high school. Some become apprentices and learn through on-the-job training while attending classes.

Lab zone Take-Home Activity

Look at a machine that has metal parts. It might be a bicycle, a kitchen gadget, or a tool such as a wrench. Observe how the parts fit together. Then imagine that one of the parts was a different size or shape. How would that affect the working of the machine?

Chapter 17

Changing Energy Forms

You Will Discover

- what different kinds of energy are.
- what electric current and electric circuits are.
- how series and parallel circuits differ.
- how magnetic domains cause magnetic fields.
- how electricity and magnetism are related.

online
Student Edition
pearsonsuccessnet.com

How can energy change from one form to another?

energy

electric current

electric circuit

474

Chapter 17 Vocabulary

magnetic domain

kinetic energy

The energy of a moving object

potential energy

The energy due to the position of an object

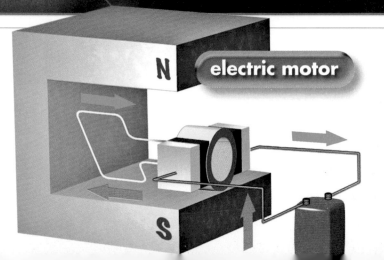

electric motor

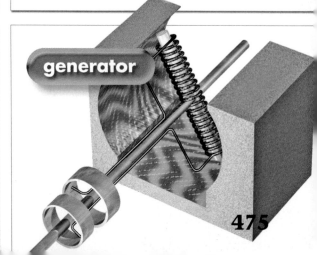

generator

Explore How can marbles pass along energy?

Materials

8 marbles

ruler with groove

What to Do

1 Place the ruler on a flat, level surface.

2 Place 5 marbles in the groove of the ruler. Marbles should be in the center of the ruler and touch one another.

3 Place another marble in the groove and about 3 cm from the group of marbles.

4 **Predict** what will happen when you push the single marble so that it suddenly hits the marble group?

5 Test your prediction. **Observe** what happens. Compare your prediction with your observation.

6 Repeat steps 4 and 5 for two and then three marbles.

Process Skills

Observing the sequence of actions when marbles are in motion, can help you understand how marbles transfer, or pass along, energy.

Explain Your Results

1. Describe the pattern you **observed.**

2. What did you observe about the energy of the marble you pushed when it hit the standing marbles?

Sequence

When you read a description of a natural process or a scientific experiment, you may notice that the details are presented in a step-by-step order. The **sequence** may be in time order or in logical order. Understanding the sequence of events from beginning to end will help you figure out many science processes. **Observing** and noting the sequence of events that happen during a science activity will help you understand your results.

- Look for the starting event or process.

- Decide what step or outcome logically follows each event or process.

Science Article

Making a Magnetic Compass

Making a magnetic compass is easy. Fill a bowl about half full of water. Any size bowl will do, but a smaller one is better. Then rub a needle with a bar magnet several times. Be sure to rub in the same direction and with the same end of the magnet each time. Place the needle through a small cube of sponge. Put the sponge in the water. The needle will point in a north/south direction.

Apply It!

Make a graphic organizer like this one. Show the **sequence** of steps for making a magnetic compass.

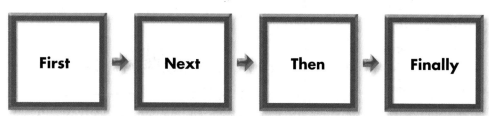

First → Next → Then → Finally

You Are There!

You watch through a protective window as the high-powered laser light is turned on. Blinding sparks of hot metal shoot out in all directions. Energy from the invisible light beam changes to heat energy that melts a smooth cut in the metal. It's a good thing you're watching through a protective window. This laser delivers a lot of energy to a small area. Even the reflection of the beam would damage your eyes or skin in less than a second.

AudioText

Lesson 1

How can energy change?

Energy exists in many different forms. Energy can change from one form to another, but it is never lost completely.

Energy and Work

Think of all the ways you change things. You change an apple by cutting it in half. You flip a switch to light up a room. Pushing a book changes its location. Every change involves energy, and energy is related to work. That's why energy and work use the same unit, the joule. When you do work, you change an object by transferring energy to it. **Energy** is the ability to cause change or to do work. Energy is a property of all matter.

Forms of Energy

Mechanical energy is the energy an object has because of its movement or position. **Kinetic energy** is the mechanical energy of a moving object. A ball rolling across the floor has kinetic energy as long as it keeps moving. **Potential energy** is mechanical energy due to position. Any object above the ground, such as your book sitting on your desk, has potential energy.

Energy has many other forms. Chemical energy is stored in the bonds between atoms. You get chemical energy from the food you eat. A car's engine uses chemical energy stored in gasoline. The nucleus of an atom stores nuclear energy. This energy can be released when atoms break apart. Reactions like this take place in nuclear power plants.

Another kind of energy, thermal energy, moves from one object to another as heat. Electrical energy is energy that results from the movement of electrons. Televisions and lights rely on electrical energy.

1. ✔**Checkpoint** Describe the two types of mechanical energy. Give an example for each.

2. **Writing** in Science **Narrative** Write about how you used chemical, thermal, and electrical energy during the past day.

Energy Changes

Almost everything that happens around you involves the change of energy from one form to another. Think about the different forms of energy involved in drinking a glass of orange juice. The energy changes begin with the Sun. The Sun's nuclear energy changes to radiant energy that travels through space to Earth. The leaves of an orange tree take in this radiant energy. During photosynthesis, the leaves change the radiant energy to chemical energy stored in the plant's cells. When you drink orange juice, you take in this stored chemical energy. Your body changes some of the chemical energy to thermal energy to keep you warm. Some thermal energy is lost to the air as heat. You change chemical energy to kinetic energy as you move around.

All forms of energy can be used to create forces to do work. Think about the kinetic energy of moving wind and water. It can create forces strong enough to blow down trees or move rocks. Geothermal energy in hot underground springs can force geysers to spurt water high into the air. At the seashore, the energy of tides and waves results in forces that wear away sand and rocks.

Each kind of energy can be changed into thermal energy. Rub your hands together. What happens? Do your hands get warmer? That's because of energy changes that result from friction. Friction causes the mechanical energy of your moving hands to change to thermal energy.

Thermal energy also results when something burns. For example, chemical energy is stored in wood. When wood is burned, some of the chemical energy changes to thermal energy. The thermal energy may move as heat that warms the nearby air. Some of the chemical energy changes to radiant energy that warms you if you stand near the burning wood.

A geyser can release a lot of stored energy.

What kinds of energy are stored in each of these objects?

Conservation of Mass and Energy

In all of these energy changes, energy is never lost completely. It only changes form. Think about this example. If you drop a rubber ball onto a hard floor, the ball bounces a few times and then stops. Each bounce is lower than the one before it because the ball loses some energy as heat and sound. The energy lost from the ball is gained by the floor and the air.

Until the 1900s scientists had never found a process in which energy was lost. This fact had been observed so often that scientists called it the law of conservation of energy. Scientists also had stated a similar law about matter, called the law of conservation of mass. First discovered by Antoine Lavoisier in 1784, it stated that matter could not be created or destroyed.

Then scientists discovered that energy and matter can be changed into each other under extraordinary conditions. For example, nuclear energy results when matter changes to energy. Because of this new evidence, scientists developed a new law that states that the total amount of matter and energy does not change.

Both this firefly and the light wands convert chemical energy into light energy.

✓ Lesson Checkpoint

1. Where do plants get the chemical energy they need to grow?
2. Explain why the work needed to operate a machine must always be more than the work done by a machine. Hint: Think about friction.
3. **Writing in Science** **Descriptive** Write a paragraph describing the energy changes involved in tossing a ball into the air.

481

How are electricity and magnetism related?

Electric charges travel as an electric current in a circuit. Magnets are surrounded by a magnetic field. Moving electric charges produce a magnetic field. A changing magnetic field produces an electric current.

Water turns giant blades called turbines at a power plant, changing mechanical energy to electrical energy.

Electric Current

What would your life be like if you had no electrical energy? Lamps, computers, stoves, flashlights, cars, and all other things that use electrical energy would be useless. What would schools, dentist offices, and stores be like? Hardly a minute goes by each day without electrical energy affecting your life.

Recall that atoms have a central nucleus surrounded by a cloud of electrons. The nucleus has protons with positive charges and neutrons with no charge. The electrons have negative charges and are held around the nucleus. In most atoms, the number of positive and negative charges are equal. For that reason, atoms usually have no charge.

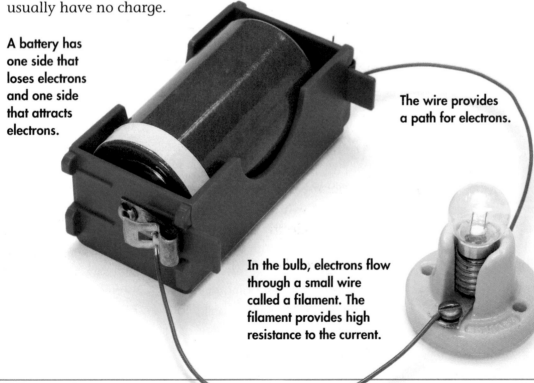

A battery has one side that loses electrons and one side that attracts electrons.

The wire provides a path for electrons.

In the bulb, electrons flow through a small wire called a filament. The filament provides high resistance to the current.

In some materials, such as copper, electrons are not tightly held by the atoms. These electrons can move from atom to atom. This flow of electrons causes an electric charge to move along atoms. For example, when you turn on a light, electrons start flowing through the wire in the lamp. All electrons have negative charges, so they repel, or push away from, each other. When the electrons from one atom flow to the next atom, the repelling effect pushes the electrons in the second atom along to the next atom. This process continues as electric current. An **electric current** is a flow of electric charge in a material.

A material that allows electrons to flow easily through its atoms is a good electrical conductor. Copper is a good conductor. This property makes copper a good choice for electrical wires. In other materials, called insulators, electrons do not move easily. Current does not flow easily in an insulator. Rubber is a good insulator.

Electric Circuit

Electric current can flow only when it can travel in a complete path back to its starting position. An **electric circuit** is a closed path along which current can flow. A simple circuit must have a source of electrical energy, such as a battery. A circuit also needs a wire or other material through which the current can flow. Many electric circuits also have a switch. When the switch is open, a break in the circuit prevents the flow of current. A device such as a light bulb that can change the electrical energy to a useful form of energy is also part of a simple circuit.

The wire inside a light bulb resists, or slows, the flow of electrons. This resistance causes electrical energy to change to thermal and radiant energy. The result is the light you see when electricity travels through a light bulb.

The energy source in a circuit provides the push that moves electrons through an electric circuit. Volts measure how strongly the electrons are pushed. Electric stoves and a few other home devices use 220-volt electric current. Toasters and most everything else in your home use 110-volt current. Using the wrong amount of volts can damage an electric device.

1. **✓Checkpoint** What advantage do parallel circuits have over series circuits?

2. **⟳ Sequence** Look at the series circuit on this page. Describe the movement of current as it leaves the negative side of the battery until it reaches the positive side.

Series Circuit
A series circuit has only one path along which current can flow. Current flows from the negative side of the battery, through each of the light bulbs, and back to the positive side of the battery. If you remove a bulb, the circuit is broken and the other bulb will go out.

Parallel Circuit
A parallel circuit has more than one path along which current can flow. Homes and businesses use this type of wiring. If one bulb is taken out, the other bulb still glows. The current still has a path along which to flow.

Magnetic Fields

Have you ever played with magnets? If you did, you probably know that each magnet has a north pole and a south pole. As you can see in the picture below, if you bring opposite poles of two magnets together, the magnets will attract, or pull toward, each other. If you bring similar poles together, the magnets will repel, or push away from, each other. The space around a magnet in which the magnet can exert a force on other magnets is called the magnetic field. The field is strongest at the poles. Magnets attract or repel because of their magnetic fields.

Not all materials can be magnetic. The movement of electrons about the nucleus of an atom causes each atom to be slightly magnetic. For most materials, the magnetic fields face in every direction and cancel each other out. But in some materials, such as iron, cobalt, and nickel, the magnetism of the atoms is stronger. The atoms line up in groups called domains. A **magnetic domain** is a large number of atoms with their magnetic fields pointing in the same direction.

Each magnetic domain is like a small magnet, with a north and south pole. If the domains are pointing in different directions, the material is not a magnet. Some materials can be made into magnets. If they are placed in a magnetic field, their domains will line up with the field. The materials will then be magnets.

What do you think would happen to a magnet if you broke it in half? Would you have a north-pole magnet and a south-pole magnet? If you break a magnet in half, you don't end up with a north-pole magnet and a south-pole magnet. The magnetic domains still point in the same direction as the original magnet. You end up with two smaller magnets, each having a north and a south pole.

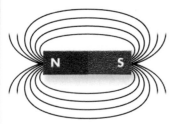

Magnetic field

This iron is not magnetized. The magnetic domains of its atoms point in different directions.

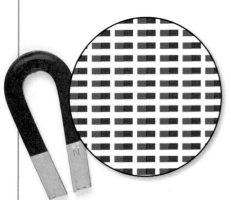

Most magnetic domains in a magnet point in the same direction.

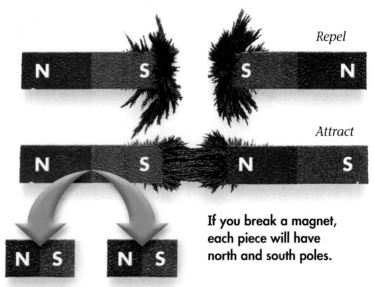

Repel

Attract

If you break a magnet, each piece will have north and south poles.

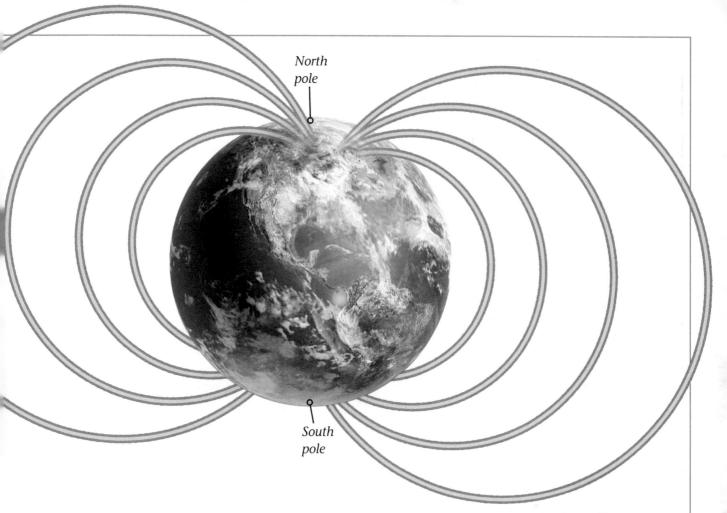
North
pole

South
pole

Earth acts like a
giant magnet.

Earth as a Magnet

All compass needles align in a north/south direction.
Did you ever wonder why? In 1600, an English physician,
William Gilbert, suggested that the reason is because Earth
acts like a giant magnet.

Imagine a giant bar magnet running through Earth. Earth
is surrounded by a magnetic field, similar to the field around
a bar magnet. The poles of the imaginary magnet are located
near, but not exactly at, Earth's geographic poles. You can
imagine lines of magnetic force that start inside Earth and
push out from the South Pole. The force lines circle around to
the North Pole. A compass points to Earth's magnetic north
and south.

The magnetic tip on a
compass aligns with
Earth's magnetic field.

1.   ✓ **Checkpoint** Why can't a magnet have just a north pole?
2.   **Writing** in Science **Narrative** Write a short story about
     a person with a "magnetic personality." Relate your story to
     things you know about magnetism.

485

Electromagnets

People have known about magnetism for more than a thousand years. But in 1820, a teacher made an amazing discovery. One night, the Danish physicist Hans Christian Oersted was showing his students an electric current in a wire. He had a magnetic compass nearby. He noticed that each time the current was turned on, the needle in the compass moved. Oersted already knew that a compass moves if it is in a magnetic field. He had just found out that moving electrical charges create a magnetic field.

The relationship that Oersted discovered is known as electromagnetism. All electric charges are surrounded by an electric field. If the charges are moving, they are also surrounded by a magnetic field. This property is useful for making strong magnets called electromagnets.

How does electromagnetism work? The magnetic field around a wire that is carrying current circles around the wire. If the wire is shaped into a coil, the overall magnetic field is like the field around a bar magnet. You can make the magnetic field stronger by adding more coils or by putting an iron core into the coil of wire. As current flows through the wire, it magnetizes the iron. This adds to the magnetic field.

Using Electromagnets

Electromagnets are very useful because the current in the wire can be controlled. It can be turned on or off. Electromagnets only attract magnetic objects when the current is turned on. This property is used when large electromagnets in cranes move heavy loads of metal. Turn on the current, and the magnet picks up the metal. Turn off the current, and the magnet releases it.

You probably use electromagnets very often. Televisions, CD players, and radios use electromagnets to change electrical energy to mechanical energy. The mechanical energy is used to make sounds by causing the speaker to vibrate. Fans, hair dryers, computers, and anything else with an electric motor use electromagnets.

When electricity flows through this wire a magnetic field forms around the wire.

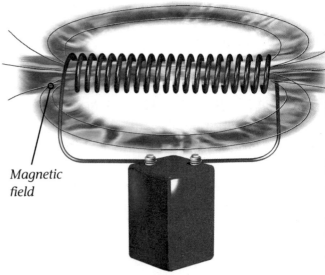

Magnetic field

Oersted accidentally discovered the relationship between moving electric charge and magnetism while using a setup like this.

Electric Motor

An **electric motor** is a device that changes electrical energy to kinetic energy. One common kind of small motor is composed of a permanent magnet, an electromagnet, and a device that changes the direction of the electric current flowing through the electromagnet.

When current passes through the electromagnet, each pole is attracted to the opposite pole of the fixed magnet. This causes the electromagnet to turn. Just as the unlike poles line up, the direction of current in the electromagnet reverses, and the poles of the electromagnet reverse. Because two like poles are now near each other, they repel each other. This causes the electromagnet to keep turning. The current in the electromagnet constantly changes direction after each turn.

An Electric Motor

Permanent magnet

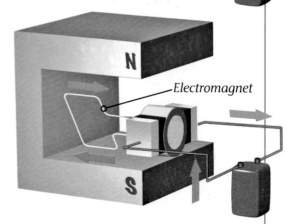

Electromagnet

1. **✓ Checkpoint** Draw an electric motor. Use labels to explain how electricity and magnetism work together in the motor.

2. **⊙ Sequence** Make a numbered list, in your own words, of steps in which an electric motor changes electrical energy to kinetic energy.

Changing Magnetism into Electricity

Oersted had shown that moving electric charges produce a magnetic field. The natural question, then, was whether a magnetic field could also produce an electric current in a wire. In 1831, the English scientist Michael Faraday showed that the answer is "yes."

Electromagnetic induction is the process in which a changing magnetic field produces an electric current. If you move a bar magnet through the center of a wire coil, the wire experiences a changing magnetic field. This produces a current in the wire. Moving the magnet faster produces a stronger current. You can also produce a current by moving the wire and keeping the magnet still. Electromagnetic induction is used to produce almost all of the electrical energy for homes, schools, and work. Study the concert picture to see how electrical energy can be changed to other useful forms of energy.

Generators

A **generator** is a device that changes mechanical energy into electrical energy. The two main parts of a small generator are a permanent magnet and a coil of wire. A source of mechanical energy causes the coil to spin in the field of the magnet. As the coil spins, an electric current is produced, and the direction of the current changes. A current that regularly changes direction is called an alternating current.

Sometimes a turbine is used to turn the coils in generators. A turbine is a wheel attached to a rod that attaches to the coil. Water, steam, and other sources of energy are used to make the turbine move. Study the picture to see how a generator can produce electricity to run a concert.

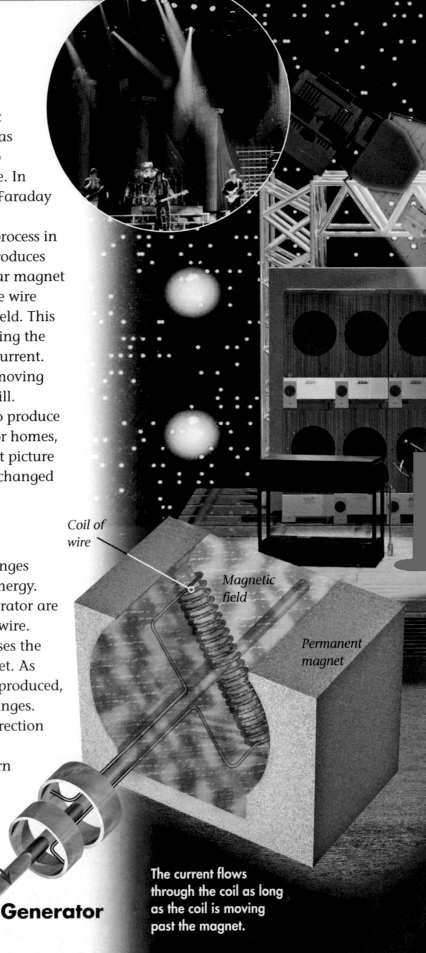

Coil of wire

Magnetic field

Permanent magnet

Generator

The current flows through the coil as long as the coil is moving past the magnet.

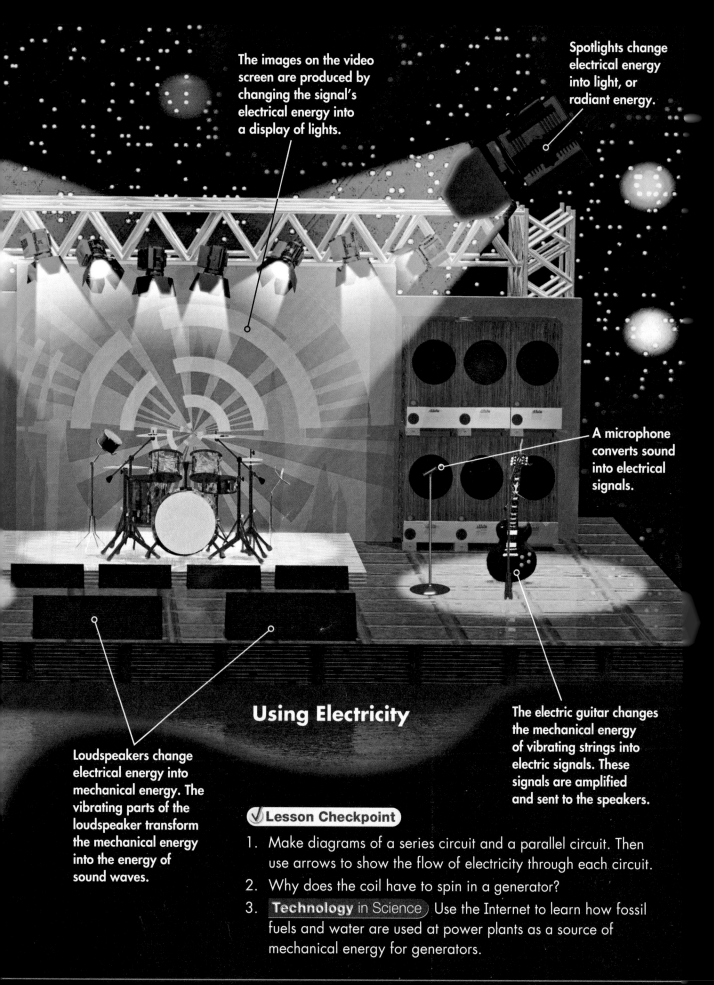

The images on the video screen are produced by changing the signal's electrical energy into a display of lights.

Spotlights change electrical energy into light, or radiant energy.

A microphone converts sound into electrical signals.

Using Electricity

The electric guitar changes the mechanical energy of vibrating strings into electric signals. These signals are amplified and sent to the speakers.

Loudspeakers change electrical energy into mechanical energy. The vibrating parts of the loudspeaker transform the mechanical energy into the energy of sound waves.

☑ **Lesson Checkpoint**

1. Make diagrams of a series circuit and a parallel circuit. Then use arrows to show the flow of electricity through each circuit.
2. Why does the coil have to spin in a generator?
3. **Technology** in Science Use the Internet to learn how fossil fuels and water are used at power plants as a source of mechanical energy for generators.

489

Investigate How does a circuit board work?

The smallest circuits used in computers are placed on silicon chips. These circuits then are placed on printed circuit boards—plastic boards carrying a maze of tiny flat wires.

Materials

safety goggles, sissors

index card, cardboard, glue

hole punch and 12 fasteners

battery and battery holder

flashlight bulb and holder

wire

Process Skills

You can infer how a circuit board works by **observing** a **model** of an electronic quiz board.

What to Do

1 Fold an index card as shown. Cut along the fold lines. You will need 12 squares.

2 Choose a topic for your model of an electonic quiz board. Write a question on each of 6 squares. On the other 6 squares, write the answers.

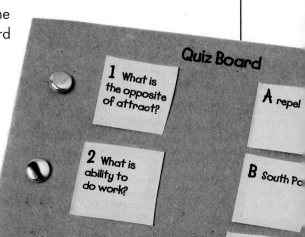

3 Glue the questions on the left side of the cardboard and the answers on the right side. Remember to mix up the order of the answers.

Wear safety goggles.

4 Punch a hole next to each question and answer. Put a fastener through each hole.

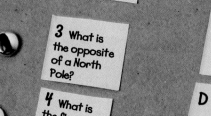

Quiz Board

1 What is the opposite of attract?

A repel

2 What is ability to do work?

B South Po

3 What is the opposite of a North Pole?

C electric current

4 What is the flow of electric charges?

D energy

5 On the back of the cardboard, use a piece of wire to connect the fastener for each question with the fastener for the correct answer.

6 Connect the battery, bulb, and wires as shown in the picture at the right.

7 Touch one testing wire to the fastener next to a question. Touch the other testing wire to the fastener next to the correct answer. **Observe** what happens.

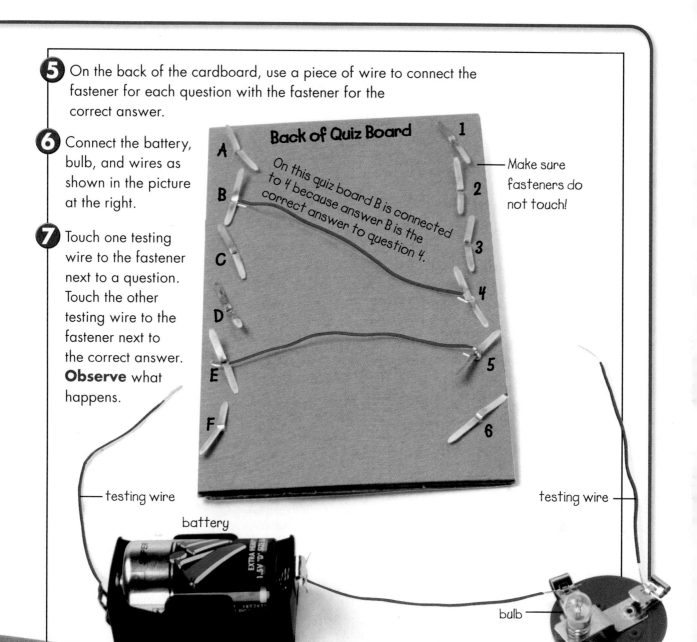

Back of Quiz Board

On this quiz board B is connected to 4 because answer B is the correct answer to question 4.

Make sure fasteners do not touch!

testing wire

battery

testing wire

bulb

Explain Your Results

1. What did you **observe** when you touched the testing wires on your **model** to two items that matched? What can you **infer** from your observation?

2. Suppose the test wires touched two matching items but the bulb did not light. What could be wrong?

Go Further

How can you wire your quiz board with a switch? Make a plan to answer this and any other questions you may have.

Solving Energy Problems

Fossil fuels are limited, but there are many other sources of energy. Energy sources that can be replaced are called renewable resources. Wind, solar, and tidal energy are examples of renewable energy sources. If you have ever been hit by a large ocean wave, you know that it has energy—the ability to do work. The challenge for scientists and engineers is to change these renewable sources of energy into other, useable forms.

Hydroelectric generators change the renewable potential energy of water into electricity. The hydroelectric complex at the Itaipu Dam, between Paraguay and Brazil, is considered one of the marvels of the modern world. The amount of energy produced by Itaipu each year for Brazil and Paraguay is about the same as California's total energy requirement. Each year, use of this dam avoids more than 61 million metric tons of carbon dioxide emissions by not using fossil fuels. The table below contains some other facts about this amazing energy converter.

In the table you will see some units that might be unfamiliar. The letter P is the symbol for the metric prefix *peta*, which means "quadrillion," or "10^{15}." So, PJ stands for "petajoule" or "1 quadrillion joules." The letter G is the symbol for the metric prefix *giga*, which means "billion," or "10^9." Remember Wh means "watt-hour." So, GWh stands for "1 billion watt-hours."

Itaipu Hydroelectric Power Plant

Height of the dam	196 m
Area of lake	1,350 sq. km
Elevation of lake surface	222 m above sea level
Elevation of water intake	187 m above sea level
Potential energy of lake	94.8 PJ
Potential energy actually used	54.9 PJ
Energy produced yearly	75,000 GWh
Cost to build	$20 billion U.S. dollars

Use the information on page 492 to answer each question.

1. How far below the lake's surface is the water intake?

2. What percent of the lake's potential energy is actually used? Round your answer to the nearest tenth of a percent.

3. Itaipu Dam is about the same height as a building of how many stories? One story is about 3 meters high.

4. If the value of electrical energy is $100,000 for 1 GWh, what is the value of the energy produced by the plant each year? About how many years would it take for the energy plant to produce $20 billion worth of electricity? In your opinion, was it a good idea to build the Itaipu power plant? Explain.

Lab zone Take-Home Activity

Make a list of as many things as you can from around your home, school and community that use energy. You can include both living and nonliving things. Then try to create three different systems for classifying all the items on your list. For example, classify them as living or nonliving or by what type of energy they use.

Chapter 17 Review and Test Prep

Use Vocabulary

electric circuit (p. 483)	**generator** (p. 488)
electric current (p. 483)	**kinetic energy** (p. 479)
electric motor (p. 487)	**magnetic domain** (p. 484)
energy (p. 479)	**potential energy** (p. 479)

Use the vocabulary term from the list above that best completes each sentence.

1. A large number of atoms with their magnetic fields pointing in the same direction is a(n) _____.

2. The ability to cause change or to do work is _____.

3. A(n) _____ is a device that changes electrical energy to mechanical energy.

4. A changing magnetic field produces a(n) _____ in a wire.

5. Electric charge can only move through a(n) _____ if it is closed.

6. A(n) _____ changes mechanical energy into electrical energy.

7. The mechanical energy of a moving object is _____.

8. The mechanical energy due to position is _____.

Explain Concepts

9. Explain the energy changes that occur when you use an electric fan.

10. Why does the wire in an electric motor have to be coiled?

11. Suppose you have two bar magnets. Magnet A has its north and south poles marked. Magnet B does not have its poles marked. How can you identify the poles on Magnet B?

12. The diagram shows an electrical circuit. The piece of foil acts like a switch. Would electric current travel through this circuit? Explain your answer.

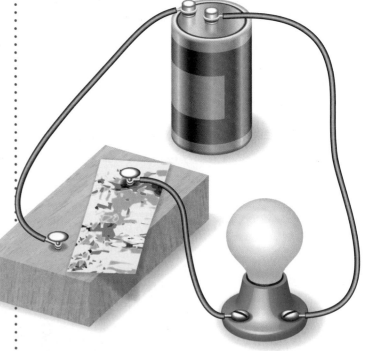

Process Skills

13. Model Draw a diagram of a series circuit with two bulbs. Use labels to show the energy transfer that takes place.

14. Predict whether a generator would work if the permanent magnet rotated rather than the coil of wire.

Sequence

15. Make a copy of the graphic organizer shown below. Fill in the blanks to show energy conversions that may be involved if you eat an apple and then use the energy for running. Start with the Sun's energy hitting a leaf of the apple tree.

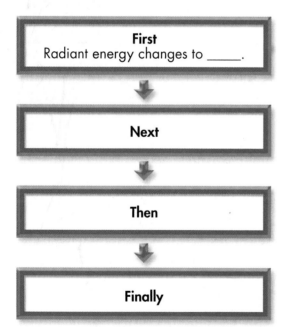

First
Radiant energy changes to _____.

↓

Next

↓

Then

↓

Finally

 Test Prep

Choose the letter that best completes the statement or answers the question.

16. Which is the energy stored in the bonds between atoms?
Ⓐ chemical energy
Ⓑ electrical energy
Ⓒ nuclear energy
Ⓓ thermal energy

17. What term refers to the push that moves electrons through a circuit?
Ⓕ charge
Ⓖ current
Ⓗ resistance
Ⓘ voltage

18. What effect does increasing the number of coils have on an electromagnet?
Ⓐ Magnetic field increases.
Ⓑ Energy is destroyed.
Ⓒ Magnetic field decreases.
Ⓓ Energy is created.

19. Explain why the answer you chose for Question 18 is best. For each of the answers you did not choose, give a reason why it is not the best choice.

20. Writing in Science **Expository** Compare and contrast an electric motor and a generator. Discuss their designs, uses, and energy conversions.

Computer Engineer

A licensed pilot, Debbie Martínez works for NASA as a computer engineer. She helps design software and instruments that NASA uses for research. Pilots use simulators to test the results of the research. NASA's flight simulation research makes flying safer for everyone.

How do you think pilots are trained to fly new aircraft? They don't simply fly the aircraft. That would be too dangerous. Instead, pilots train in flight simulators. Simulators are life-size models of aircraft that move like the real thing, but stay on the ground. Simulators mimic what it is like to actually fly a plane, helicopter, or even a spacecraft.

Many different people work together to build these simulators, including computer and electronics engineers. They work with researchers to design and develop electrical and electronic equipment and processes. They might work on radar, computers, and video equipment. As an engineer, you would work on a project from the time the product is first discussed and researched until it is manufactured.

If you like to work on a team, are creative, are good with details, and can express yourself well, you might consider a career as an electronics or computer engineer. You will have to get a college degree. But your education will not end then. Engineers must keep up with new information and technology in their field.

Lab zone Take-Home Activity

Engineers helped develop the simulator for training pilots. What process would you like to develop a training simulator for? What are some of the factors you would have to consider as you develop the simulator?

You Will Discover

- how thermal energy is transferred between objects by conduction, convection, and radiation.
- how waves carry energy.
- what the characteristics of light are.

online
Student Edition
pearsonsuccessnet.com

Discovery Channel School
Student DVD
DISCOVERY CHANNEL SCHOOL

Chapter 18
Thermal and Light
ENERGY

How are thermal energy and light energy transferred?

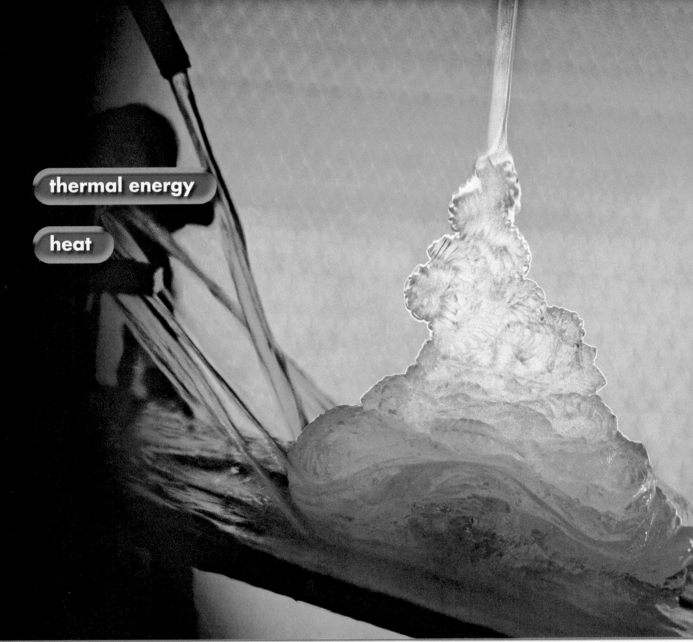

thermal energy

heat

conduction

Heat transfer between two objects that touch

conductor

A material that easily transfers heat

convection

498

Chapter 18 Vocabulary

insulator

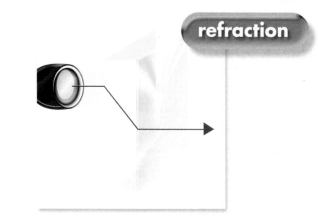

refraction

radiation

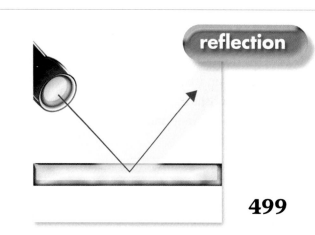

reflection

499

Explore What can you observe about heat and sunlight?

Materials

safety goggles

plastic bottle

balloon and string

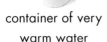

container of very warm water

3 paper towels

What to Do

1 Stretch the balloon over the neck of the bottle. Tie a string around the bottle and balloon to make certain no air can get in or out of the bottle.

2 Place the bottle in a container of very warm water until the bottle becomes warm. **Observe** the balloon. Record any changes you see.

Hold the bottle upright in the water.

Be careful!

Wear your safety goggles.

3 Remove the bottle from the water. Dry the bottle. Allow it to cool to room temperature.

4 Place the bottle in bright sunlight. Observe and record any changes.

Process Skills

If you compare and contrast what happens to a balloon under different conditions you can **infer** the relationship between heat and sunlight.

Explain Your Results

1. Compare and contrast the effect that warm water and bright sunlight had on the bottle with the balloon.

2. Think about your answer. What might you **infer** about the relationship between heat and sunlight?

How to Read Science

Compare and Contrast

Understanding new ideas that you read about in science can sometimes be difficult. A good way to make learning easier is to **compare** and **contrast.** Compare means to tell how things are alike. Contrast means to tell how things are different. Thinking about how things are alike and different will help you understand science information.

Observe the illustration below, which shows two ways you can make waves with a rope. Use the pictures to **infer** how the waves are alike and how they are different.

Waves

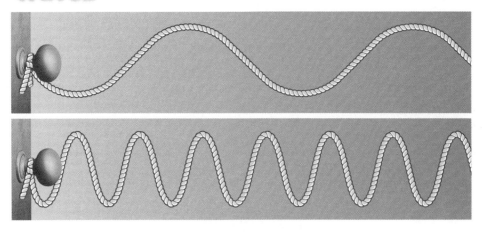

Apply It!

Copy this graphic organizer. Use it to **compare** and **contrast** the two types of waves made with a rope.

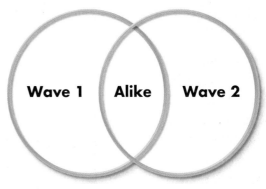

Wave 1   Alike   Wave 2

🔊 You Are There!

You stare in wonder as the glassblower gathers the glowing, liquid glass onto a rod. Even at a safe distance, the heat from the roaring furnace warms your face and reminds you that liquid glass is unbelievably hot. The glassblower turns the rod over and over to shape the glass. The glass flows first one way, and then the other. But slowly, as the glass cools, it flows less. Gradually, the cooling glass becomes a solid.

AudioText 🔊

How is thermal energy transferred?

Thermal energy is the total kinetic and potential energy of the particles in a substance. Heat is thermal energy that moves from one substance to another. Heat can move by conduction, convection, and radiation.

Thermal Energy

When you look at the molten glass, it is easy to see that its particles are moving. The molten glass flows. But a solid object, such as a glass pitcher, seems to be perfectly still. Are you surprised to find out that it's not?

All matter is made of particles that are always moving. The particles have kinetic energy, or energy due to motion. The particles in a substance always pull on each other. This means the particles have potential energy, or energy due to position. Particles in a gas can move freely. They do not pull strongly on each other. Particles in a liquid can only flow around each other. They pull more strongly on each other than gas particles do. The particles in a solid pull strongly on each other. They vibrate, but they cannot move from their fixed position.

The total kinetic and potential energy of the particles in a substance is **thermal energy.** The amount of thermal energy depends on the amount of the substance. If you have a cup of water and you pour half of it out, the part that is left has half the number of particles. It therefore has half the thermal energy that the full cup of water had.

Thermal energy determines how warm a substance feels. A warm cup of water has more thermal energy than a cool cup of water. The warm and cool water have about the same number of particles, but the particles in the warm water are moving faster. They have more kinetic energy. Therefore, they have more thermal energy and feel warmer.

1. ✓**Checkpoint** What is the difference between kinetic energy and potential energy?
2. **Writing in Science** **Expository** You place a cup of water in a freezer and it changes to ice. Explain what happens to the thermal energy of the water.

Heat

You've probably measured your kinetic energy many times, but you may not have known it. Temperature is a measure of the average kinetic energy of an object's particles. When you take your temperature with a thermometer, your body heat increases the kinetic energy of particles of a liquid in the thermometer. The thermometer then shows the average kinetic energy of particles in your body.

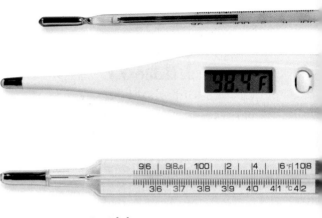

Temperature is not the same as thermal energy. Temperature depends only on the average kinetic energy. Thermal energy is the sum of kinetic and potential energy. Unlike thermal energy, temperature does not depend on the amount of a substance. If you split an object in half, each part has half as many particles. But the temperature does not change. The average kinetic energy is the same.

Liquid thermometers measure temperature change when increased kinetic energy causes a liquid to expand. Digital thermometers measure temperature change when increased kinetic energy causes a metal to expand.

Thermal energy that can move from one substance to another is called **heat.** Heat always moves from a warmer substance to a cooler one. An increase in temperature means that heat moves into a substance. When heat moves into a substance, the average kinetic energy of the particles rises. The extra kinetic energy increases the particles' vibrations. Particles vibrate faster when a substance is heated.

The movement of heat from one substance to another can occur between objects that touch and objects that don't touch. The three types of heat transfer are conduction, convection, and radiation.

The lynx warms the snow as heat moves from particles in its body to particles in the snow.

Conduction

Heat transfer between two objects that touch is called **conduction.** Think about what happens if you place ice cubes in a glass of warm lemonade. Do the ice cubes cool the lemonade, or does the lemonade warm the ice cubes?

The temperature of the ice cubes is lower than the temperature of the lemonade. The particles that make up the lemonade are vibrating faster than the particles of the ice. When the ice touches the lemonade, the particles in the lemonade bump against the ice particles. This causes the ice particles to move faster and faster. Heat flows from the warmer lemonade to the cooler ice. The lemonade particles slow down. Conduction of heat has warmed the ice and cooled the lemonade.

When heat moves by conduction, the particles in the substances do not change their location. Energy is passed from particle to particle as the particles vibrate and bump against other particles. This movement of energy may occur between a warmer substance and a cooler one. It may also occur between the warm part of an object and a cooler part of the same object.

1. ✓**Checkpoint** Why doesn't the temperature of an object change if you break the object in half?

2. **Technology** in Science Heat naturally moves from warm to cool objects, but refrigerators reverse this movement. Research and write a paragraph that explains this process.

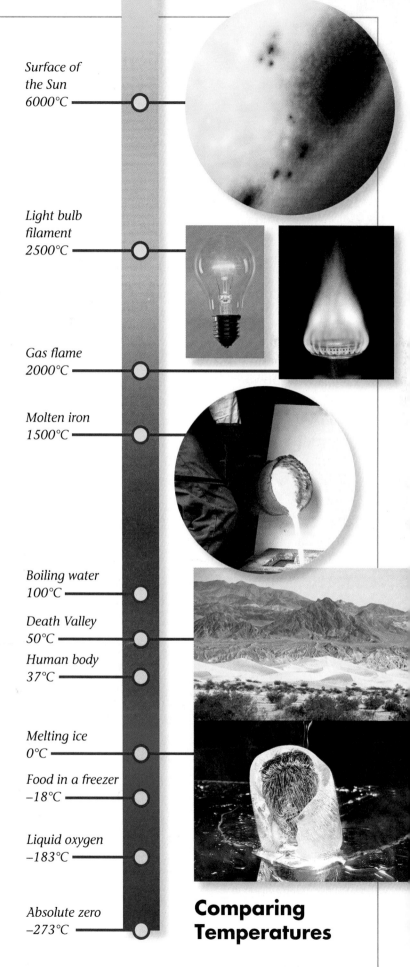

Surface of the Sun
6000°C

Light bulb filament
2500°C

Gas flame
2000°C

Molten iron
1500°C

Boiling water
100°C

Death Valley
50°C

Human body
37°C

Melting ice
0°C

Food in a freezer
−18°C

Liquid oxygen
−183°C

Absolute zero
−273°C

Comparing Temperatures

505

Convection

A hang glider soars through the air, swooping up and circling again and again. The wings of the glider provide balance, but how is the glider able to move upward? Hang gliders depend on the movement of thermal energy in the air.

Heat moves from the warm ground to the air just above it by conduction. As with solids, the kinetic and potential energy of particles in a fluid—a liquid or gas—increases if the fluid touches a warmer object. Energy from the warmer object moves into the fluid. As the fluid becomes warmer, its particles move faster. The density of a fluid decreases as the fast-moving particles spread apart.

A fluid with a higher density sinks below a fluid with a lower density. This causes the lower-density fluid to rise. When this happens, the rising fluid carries thermal energy along with it. **Convection** is the transfer of thermal energy by the movement of the particles of a liquid or a gas. This movement results in a stream of fluid called a convection current. Hang gliders can fly great distances as they are continually pushed upward by convection currents along the way.

Convection currents in the air cause winds to form. As warm air rises, cooler air rushes in to fill its place near the ground. The rising warm air becomes cooler and begins to fall. The cooler air near the ground becomes warmer and begins to rise.

A pot of boiling water is another example of convection. If you place a pot of water on a stove, the temperature of the pot rises by conduction. Heat moves from the stove to the pot. The pot then warms the water that touches it by conduction as heat moves from the pot to the water. The warm water is less dense than the cooler water above it. The cool water then sinks, causing the warm water to rise. The rising and falling of warmer and cooler water increases the temperature of the entire pot of water.

Hang gliders can stay in the air longer because of convection. They are pushed upward as they fly through rising currents of warm air called thermals.

Radiation

For the chameleon, a good way to spend a sunny afternoon is sitting on a rock. Like all reptiles, chameleons warm their bodies with energy from the Sun. This energy must travel from the Sun to Earth through space that has almost no matter. **Radiation** is the transfer of thermal energy as waves. It can involve energy transfer through matter or across empty space.

Energy from these lamps moves by radiation to keep the food warm.

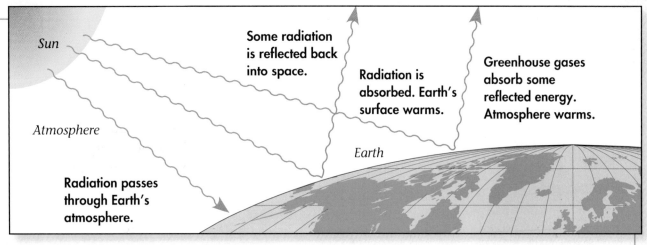

Sun

Atmosphere

Some radiation
is reflected back
into space.

Radiation is
absorbed. Earth's
surface warms.

Greenhouse gases
absorb some
reflected energy.
Atmosphere warms.

Earth

Radiation passes
through Earth's
atmosphere.

When solar radiation reaches Earth's atmosphere, some of the energy is reflected back toward space. The rest of the radiation reaches Earth. Like the atmosphere, Earth's surface reflects some radiation and absorbs the rest. The absorbed radiation heats Earth's surface, which releases some of this heat back into the atmosphere. There gases, such as carbon dioxide and water vapor, absorb the energy and become warmer. These gases surround Earth and act like a blanket to hold heat. This process by which the atmosphere holds heat is called the greenhouse effect.

The greenhouse effect is a natural process. Without it, Earth would be a cold, lifeless planet. But some scientists are concerned that the increase in some atmospheric gases, such as carbon dioxide, will cause the atmosphere to become too warm. Increased temperatures can have a harmful effect on Earth's ecosystems.

Energy from the Sun warms a chameleon by radiation. The chameleon is also warmed by conduction. Heat moves from the rock into the chameleon's body.

1. ✓**Checkpoint** Why is radiation the only type of heat transfer by which the Sun's energy can move to Earth?

2. **Art** in Science Draw an illustration that explains convection currents.

Insulation

Brrr! It's a cold winter day, and you're getting ready for school. You put on a thick coat, scarf, and gloves to keep warm. Now that you've learned about different types of heat transfer, can you explain how a coat, scarf, and gloves keep you warm?

Winter clothes keep you warm because they insulate you against the cold. An **insulator** is a material that does not easily transfer heat. Other materials, such as metals, are **conductors.** They transfer heat easily.

What causes a material to be either an insulator or a conductor? Recall what happens when heat moves from a warmer object to a cooler one. Particles in the warmer object move faster. If the warmer object touches the cooler object, particles in the warmer object bump against particles in the cooler object. Particles in the cooler object then move faster and faster. Their kinetic energy rises. The temperature of the cooler object rises by conduction.

This scarf is made of a material that contains air pockets. A scarf keeps you warm because thermal energy doesn't easily move through air.

A shiny surface on the thermos slows heat transfer by radiation.

A pocket of insulating air inside a thermos slows the conduction of heat.

Some materials are good conductors because their atoms can easily vibrate to transfer heat. Metals, such as copper and silver, are good conductors because of the movement of electrons. Some electrons are not tightly held to the atoms of the metals. These electrons can move easily. They carry energy from place to place. You may have realized that metals are good conductors when you've stirred hot soup with a spoon. After a short while, you can feel the heat in the spoon.

Liquids and gases are usually better insulators than solids because their particles are farther apart. Empty space is also a good insulator. Heat cannot move through empty space by conduction or convection.

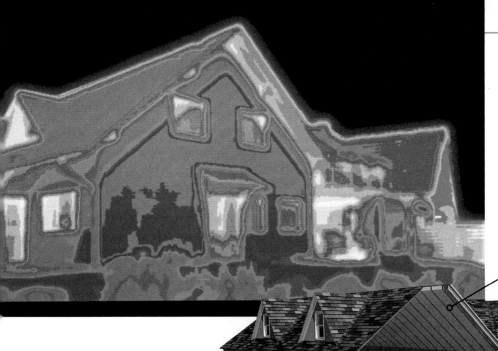

This photograph was taken with a thermal camera that detects heat loss in buildings. Yellow areas show where the house has little insulation and heat can easily escape. Blue areas show where the house is well insulated with little heat loss.

The roof and attic are lined with fiberglass insulation.

Windows have a double layer of panes. The air between the panes is a good insulator.

Floors are covered with carpet.

Air-filled insulation such as foam is packed into hollow walls.

Using Insulators

Understanding insulators is important in choosing clothes for cold weather. Layers of materials will keep you warmest. They contain pockets of air. Because air is a good insulator, heat cannot easily escape from your body.

Insulating materials are also important in home building. If you've ever seen a house being built, you may have seen thick layers of insulating material placed in the walls and attic. Air pockets within the layers slow the movement of heat out of a home on cold days. They also slow the movement of heat into a home on hot summer days. Some houses have windows with double layers of glass. The pocket of air between the layers is insulation against the movement of heat through the window.

Insulation is one way that animals protect themselves from the cold in winter. Some animals have thick layers of insulating fat. Animals may also have fur or hair that traps heat close to their bodies.

Fluffy down feathers have pockets of air that trap heat near a goose's body. People sometimes use these insulating feathers for winter coats and blankets.

✓ Lesson Checkpoint

1. How does a liquid thermometer show that you have a fever?
2. Why are you warmer if you wear layers of clothing on a cold day?
3. 🔄 **Compare and Contrast** Explain how conduction, convection, and radiation are alike and how they are different.

Lesson 2

How do waves carry energy?

Waves, such as sound and light, carry energy. When light strikes matter, it may be absorbed, transmitted, or reflected. Light may change direction when it moves from one material to another.

Water waves carry energy.

Types of Waves

Have you ever dropped a rock into a pool of water? Waves spread out in all directions from the point where the rock enters the water. The rock causes molecules in the water to move back and forth as a vibration. A wave carries energy away from a vibration.

The illustrations below show the two main types of waves. Notice their differences. When waves move through matter, the matter does not move along with the wave. When transverse waves move through matter, they cause the matter to move in a direction different than the wave moves. If the wave is moving to the right, molecules in the matter move up and down. If a compressional wave is moving through matter, the matter moves back and forth in the same direction as the wave. The particles in the matter move forward and then backward, over and over again.

An important type of compressional waves is sound. As with all waves, sounds are caused by vibrations. Think about what happens if you strike your pencil against a desk. The force of your pencil causes molecules in the desk and air next to it to vibrate. These vibrations cause nearby air particles to vibrate, and they cause other molecules to vibrate. The vibrations move outward through the air in all directions. You hear sound when the vibrations reach your ear. You can also hear the pencil striking the desk if you place your ear against the desk. Sound waves can travel through matter, but they cannot travel through empty space.

Transverse wave

Compressional wave

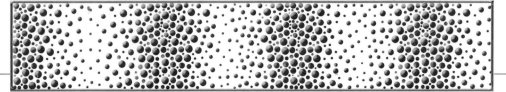

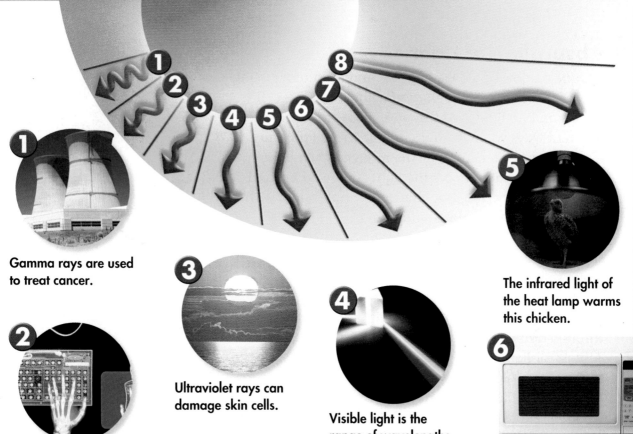

1 Gamma rays are used to treat cancer.

2 X rays pass through soft body tissue but not through bones.

3 Ultraviolet rays can damage skin cells.

4 Visible light is the range of wavelengths that humans can see.

5 The infrared light of the heat lamp warms this chicken.

6 Microwaves are used for satellite signals and for cooking food.

7 Television signals are short-wavelength radio waves.

8 Radio waves carry signals that represent sound.

Electromagnetic Spectrum

You just read about sound waves that travel through matter. Like sound, light travels as a wave, but unlike sound, light can travel through empty space. Light travels as transverse waves.

Visible light is only one of the many kinds of waves that travel to Earth from the Sun. If you arranged all the kinds of waves from the shortest wavelength to the longest wavelength, you would get a pattern similar to the one shown in the diagram above. The pattern is called the electromagnetic spectrum.

Notice that the wavelength becomes longer as you move from left to right across the spectrum, but the frequency becomes shorter. Like all waves, those of the electromagnetic spectrum carry energy. Waves with a shorter wavelength have more energy than those with a longer wavelength.

1. ✓**Checkpoint** What type of wave carries more energy—radio waves or visible light?
2. 🔁 **Compare and Contrast** Tell how transverse waves and compressional waves are alike and different.

Absorption of Light

Shine a light on a piece of glass, and most of the light travels through it. Shine the same light on a piece of metal, and no light goes through. Light can behave in different ways when it strikes matter. Some light may be absorbed, or taken in, by the matter. When light enters a material, some of the light energy is changed into heat energy. You may have noticed this on a warm summer day. Dark-colored materials absorb more sunlight than light-colored materials. Wearing a black shirt, for example, makes you warmer than wearing a white shirt.

Light may also pass through a material without being absorbed. The amount of light that passes through a material depends on the type of material. Almost all light passes through transparent materials, such as clear glass and water. Translucent materials only allow some of the light that strikes them to pass through. Waxed paper is a translucent material. Opaque materials don't allow any light that strikes them to pass through. Wood, rocks, and metals are examples of opaque materials.

All electromagnetic waves travel through empty space at the speed of light—300,000 kilometers per second. Light travels through matter at speeds less than this. But light doesn't pass through all materials at the same speed. The particles that make up matter cause light to slow down. The speed that light passes through a material depends on the type of material. Unlike sound waves, light usually travels slowest through solids because they have the highest density. Light travels faster through liquids, and even faster through gases.

Refraction and Reflection

Light changes speed when it moves from one material to another. If a beam of light strikes the border of two materials at an angle, the change in the speed of the light changes its direction. **Refraction** is the change in direction of light when it moves from one material to another. You can see refraction by placing a spoon in a glass of water and looking at it from the side. The spoon seems to be bent. This happens because light changes direction when it moves from the water to the air.

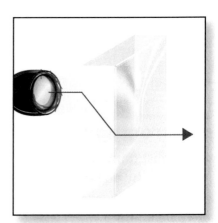

Absorption

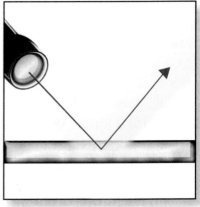

Refraction

Reflection

Refraction distorts this photo taken under water.

Light that isn't absorbed and doesn't pass through a material is reflected. **Reflection** is the bouncing of light rays off the surface of a material. If the surface is smooth, you may be able to see your reflection in the material. When light strikes a mirror, for example, the light reflects back so that you can see yourself.

Think about places where you can see your reflection. Why can't you see your reflection when you look at a wall or a book? These surfaces may seem smooth. Using a magnifying glass, however, you can see many bumps and holes. Light that strikes these surfaces bounces off in many directions. A surface must be smooth enough for light to bounce back to your eyes in order for you to see a clear reflection.

✔️ Lesson Checkpoint

1. Why can't sound travel through empty space?
2. Why will you likely be cooler if you wear a light-colored shirt instead of a dark-colored shirt on a warm day?
3. 🎯 **Compare and Contrast** Write a paragraph explaining ways light and radio waves are alike and ways they are different.

Seeing Color

The wavelengths of light that an object absorbs and reflects determine its color.

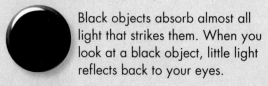 Black objects absorb almost all light that strikes them. When you look at a black object, little light reflects back to your eyes.

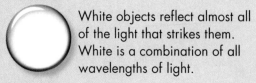 White objects reflect almost all of the light that strikes them. White is a combination of all wavelengths of light.

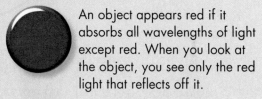 An object appears red if it absorbs all wavelengths of light except red. When you look at the object, you see only the red light that reflects off it.

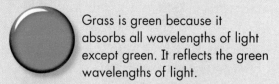 Grass is green because it absorbs all wavelengths of light except green. It reflects the green wavelengths of light.

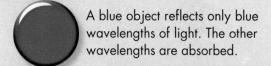 A blue object reflects only blue wavelengths of light. The other wavelengths are absorbed.

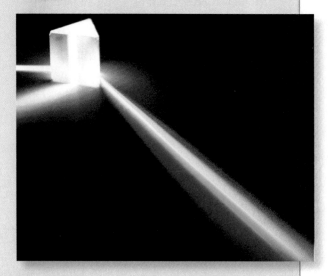
White light contains all wavelengths of visible light. The colors of light bend different amounts when they pass through a prism. This same effect allows you to see different colors in a rainbow.

513

Investigate How does heat move?

Materials

paper cup with lid

thermometers and clay

foam cup

very warm water and cold water

clock
(with a second hand)

metric ruler

What to Do

1 Push a thermometer through the lid of a paper cup about 5 cm. Use clay to hold the thermometer to the lid.

2 Fill a paper cup with very warm water. Cover the cup with the lid from step 1.

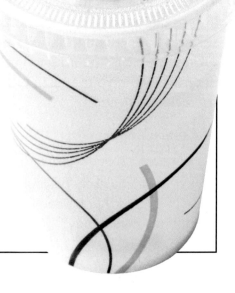

3 Measure the temperature of the very warm water. Use a chart to **collect** your **data**.

Process Skills

Collecting and **interpreting data** in this **investigation** can help you understand the movement of heat.

4 Fill the foam cup $\frac{1}{4}$ full with cold water. Take the temperature of the cold water.

5 Place the cup with very warm water inside the cup with cold water.

6 Record the temperature reading of each thermometer every minute. Stop when temperatures are nearly the same.

Time (minutes)	Temperature (°C)	
	Warm Water	Cold Water
0 (start)		
1		
2		
3		

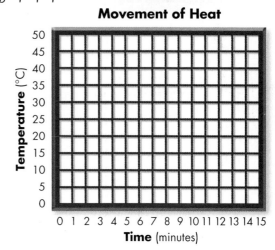

Your teacher may wish you to use graph paper.

Movement of Heat

7 Plot both sets of data from your **investigation** on the same graph. Use a dotted line for the warm water and solid line for the cold water.

Explain Your Results

1. **Interpret Data** What does your data table show? What does your graph show?

2. Does heat move from a warmer object to a cooler one or from a cooler object to a warmer one? Use the results of your **investigation** to support your answer.

Go Further

What would happen if you put the cold water in the paper cup and the very warm water in the foam cup? Make a plan to find out.

Solving Combustion Problems

Combustion is a chemical reaction in which a substance combines with oxygen and releases energy. A common example of combustion is a candle burning. A flame occurs when gases combust quickly, releasing heat and bright light.

In a candle, evaporated wax combines with oxygen in the air to produce heat and light. If you look at a candle flame closely, you will see different colors. The color is an indication of how complete the combustion is and also how hot the flame is. The bottom of the flame is blue, and the outer edge is white. These colors show that more complete combustion is taking place and the flame is hotter. The inside of the flame is more yellowish orange, which means less complete combustion is taking place and the flame is not as hot.

Candle Flame Temperature

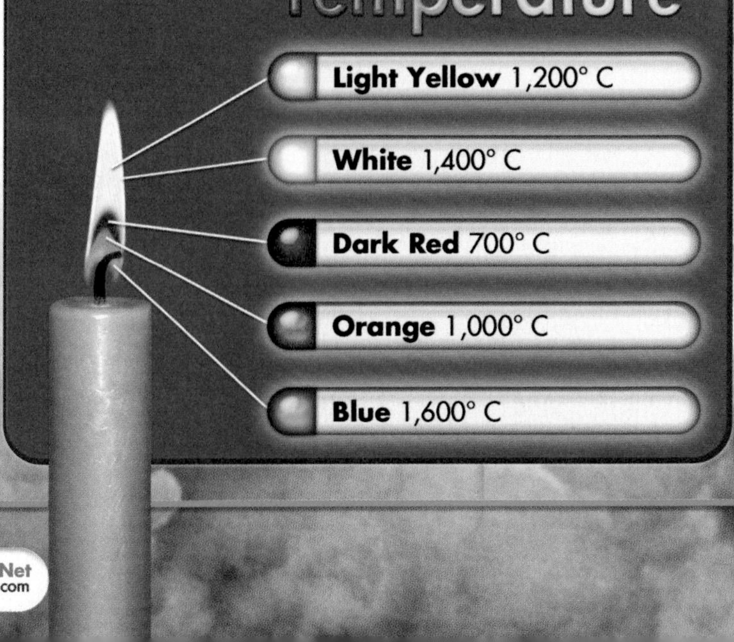
Light Yellow 1,200° C
White 1,400° C
Dark Red 700° C
Orange 1,000° C
Blue 1,600° C

e Tools Take It to the Net pearsonsuccessnet.com

Answer each question. Use the chart on page 516.

1. The surface temperature of a star is much hotter than a candle flame, but it is estimated by color, using the same rules. Use what you've learned to write the names of the following five stars in order from hottest surface temperature to coolest.

   Aldebaran: orange
   Betelgeuse: red
   Polaris: yellow
   Rigel: bluish white
   Sirius B: white

2. A candle is burning at the rate of 1.5 cm per hour. The candle is now 2.25 cm tall. If it was originally 12 cm tall, how long has it been burning?

3. While the space shuttle is launching, combustion in the engines burns fuel at the amazing rate of about 76,000 L (the volume of a swimming pool) every 10 seconds. If the engines fire at full throttle for 8 minutes, how much fuel will be used?

4. Only about 8% of the electrical energy of a standard light bulb is converted to light. The rest of the energy is lost as heat. If a 100-watt light bulb uses $42 worth of electrical energy in a year, what is the cost of the wasted heat?

Lab zone Take-Home Activity

Use crayons or markers to make a spectrum of red, orange, yellow, white, and blue. Label the spectrum with *Coolest* on the left and *Hottest* on the right. Arrange the colors in that order.

Chapter 18 Review and Test Prep

Use Vocabulary

conduction (p. 505)	**radiation** (p. 506)
conductor (p. 508)	**reflection** (p. 513)
convection (p. 506)	**refraction** (p. 512)
heat (p. 504)	**thermal energy** (p. 503)
insulator (p. 508)	

Determine whether each statement is true or false. Write *true* if it is true. If it is false, replace the underlined term with another vocabulary term to make the statement true.

1. The movement of thermal energy by rising currents is <u>conduction</u>.

2. The total kinetic and potential energy of the particles in a substance is <u>thermal energy</u>.

3. A <u>conductor</u> does not transfer heat easily.

4. Thermal energy that moves from one substance to another is <u>heat</u>.

5. Heat transfer between two objects that touch is <u>convection</u>.

6. <u>Connection</u> is the change in direction of light when it moves from one material to another.

7. If you stand near a hot fire, you feel the warmth because of <u>radiation</u>.

8. <u>Reflection</u> is the bouncing of light rays off the surface of the material.

9. An <u>insulator</u> transfers heat easily.

Explain Concepts

10. Suppose you have a large container of warm water. You pour half the water into a second container. Tell whether the amount of thermal energy and the temperature in the first container would be affected after half the water is poured into the second container.

11. Why do some objects appear black? Why do other objects appear white?

12. Identify and describe the ways that heat is being transferred in the picture below.

Process Skills

13. Predict Would you expect a light wave to change speed as it moves from the air into a glass window? Would you expect it to change direction? Explain your answers.

14. Experiment Which is a better heat insulator—cotton or nylon? Design an experiment to answer this question. Write a paragraph that describes your experiment.

Compare and Contrast

15. Make a graphic organizer like the one shown below. Show how thermal energy and temperature are alike and how they are different.

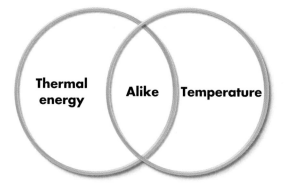

Thermal energy   **Alike**   **Temperature**

Test Prep

Choose the letter that best completes the statement or answers the question.

16. Which electromagnetic waves have higher frequencies than ultraviolet waves?
   Ⓐ infrared waves
   Ⓑ microwaves
   Ⓒ radio waves
   Ⓓ X rays

17. If a compressional wave moves through matter from left to right, the matter
   Ⓕ moves from left to right.
   Ⓖ moves up and down.
   Ⓗ moves back and forth.
   Ⓘ does not move.

18. When heat moves by conduction from one end of a metal spoon to the other,
   Ⓐ the temperature of the spoon decreases.
   Ⓑ the thermal energy of the spoon increases.
   Ⓒ particles move from one end of the spoon to the other.
   Ⓓ vibrations are passed among particles of the spoon.

19. Explain why the answer you chose for Question 18 is best. For each of the answers you did not choose, give a reason why it is not the best choice.

20. Writing in Science **Descriptive** Write a paragraph that describes how insulators prevent the movement of heat.

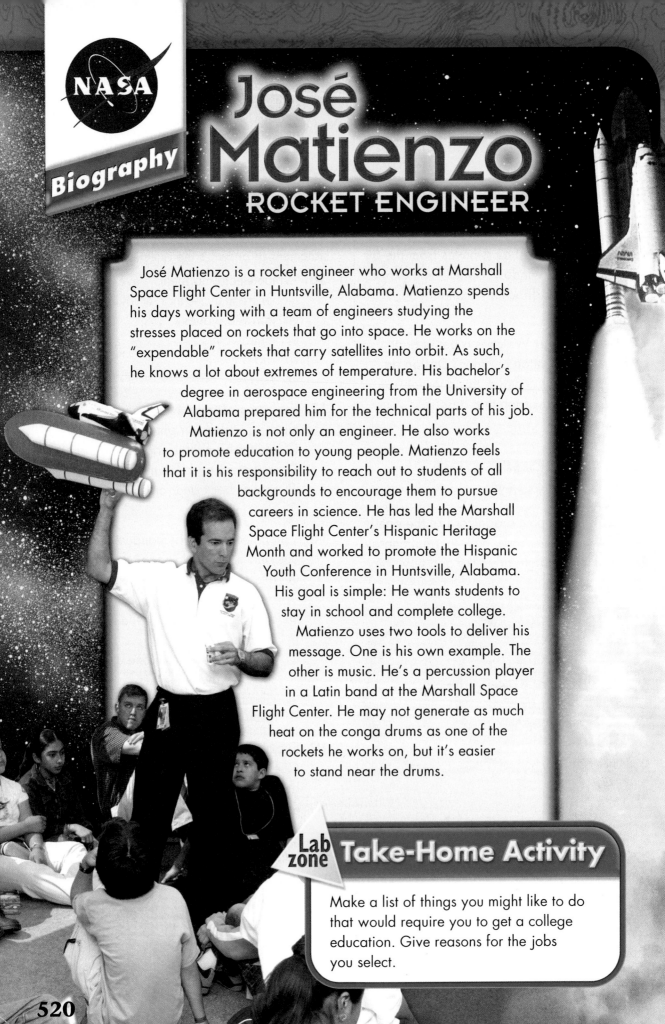

José Matienzo
ROCKET ENGINEER

José Matienzo is a rocket engineer who works at Marshall Space Flight Center in Huntsville, Alabama. Matienzo spends his days working with a team of engineers studying the stresses placed on rockets that go into space. He works on the "expendable" rockets that carry satellites into orbit. As such, he knows a lot about extremes of temperature. His bachelor's degree in aerospace engineering from the University of Alabama prepared him for the technical parts of his job. Matienzo is not only an engineer. He also works to promote education to young people. Matienzo feels that it is his responsibility to reach out to students of all backgrounds to encourage them to pursue careers in science. He has led the Marshall Space Flight Center's Hispanic Heritage Month and worked to promote the Hispanic Youth Conference in Huntsville, Alabama. His goal is simple: He wants students to stay in school and complete college.

Matienzo uses two tools to deliver his message. One is his own example. The other is music. He's a percussion player in a Latin band at the Marshall Space Flight Center. He may not generate as much heat on the conga drums as one of the rockets he works on, but it's easier to stand near the drums.

Lab zone Take-Home Activity

Make a list of things you might like to do that would require you to get a college education. Give reasons for the jobs you select.

520

Unit C Test Talk

Use Information from Text and Graphics

When taking a test with text and graphics, read the text first. Then study the graphics to see how they relate to the information you just read. Use information from the text and graphics to answer the text question.

Forces—pushes or pulls—act on all objects on Earth. Newton's laws explain how these forces act. Newton's first law says that when an object is moving, a force is required to change the objects speed or its direction. An object at rest remains at rest unless acted upon by a force.

Newton's second law states that an object's acceleration depends on the mass of the object and the amount of force applied. The larger the mass, the more force is needed to move the object.

Newton's third law of motion states that when a force acts on an object, the object exerts an equal and opposite force in the opposite direction. For example, two forces are acting on the dog in the picture—gravity and the wagon. Gravity applies a downward force to the dog, and the wagon applies an upward force.

To answer the questions, read the text and then look at the graphic. Graphics are pictures or diagrams. Study the graphic to see how it helps explain the text.

Use What You Know

1. Newton's first law states that a ball sitting on the ground will not move unless
   (A) unbalanced forces act on it.
   (B) no forces act on it.
   (C) a single force acts on it.
   (D) balanced forces act on it.

2. An object's acceleration depends on the mass of the object and the
   (F) object's speed.
   (G) shape of the object.
   (H) amount of force applied.
   (I) distance the object travels.

3. Newton's third law of motion describes the
   (A) acceleration of a single object.
   (B) interaction of two objects.
   (C) motion of an object at constant speed.
   (D) electrical and magnetic force.

4. The force of Earth's gravity on an object pulls in which direction?
   (F) upward
   (G) downward
   (H) to the left
   (I) to the right

521

Unit C Wrap-Up

Chapter 13

How can the properties of matter change?

- During a physical change, the appearance of a substance changes but its chemical properties stay the same.
- During a chemical change, one or more substances change into new substances with different properties.

Chapter 14

What do the many types of matter have in common?

- All matter is made of atoms.
- Slightly more than 100 different elements combine to form all the matter on Earth.

Chapter 15

How are motion and forces related?

- Forces can change the direction and speed of moving objects.
- The relationship of forces and motion is stated in Newton's three laws of motion.

Chapter 16

How do machines make work easier?

- Machines change the force required to do a task, or they change the direction or the distance over which the force is applied.
- All machines are made from one or more simple machines.

Chapter 17

How can energy change from one form to another?

- Energy can exist in many forms including mechanical, chemical, nuclear, thermal, and electrical.
- All forms of energy can be used to produce a force to do work.

Chapter 18

How are thermal energy and light energy transferred?

- Thermal energy can be transferred by convection, conduction, and radiation.
- Light energy is transferred as waves.

Performance Assessment

Relating Force and Distance

Build a ramp with a board and a book. Measure the height of the ramp. Tie a string around a book. Attach the string to a spring scale. Use the spring scale to pull the book up the ramp. Record the reading on the spring scale. Add another book and repeat the procedure. Continue by adding three more books, one at a time. Use the data you collect to make a force/distance graph.

Read More About Physical Science

Look for books like these in the library.

Full Inquiry

Experiment How can you slow the rate at which ice melts?

Materials

ice cubes and
3 plastic cups

masking tape

newspaper
and wool cloth

clock and balance

Process Skills

When you plan an **experiment** and determine what you will change and what you must not change, you are **identifying and controlling variables.**

Ask a question.
How can you slow the rate at which ice melts?

State a hypothesis.
If a cup containing an ice cube is wrapped in newspaper and another cup containing an ice cube is wrapped in wool cloth, which ice cube will take longer to melt? Write your **hypothesis**.

Identify and control variables.
The **variable** you will change is the insulating material—newspaper or wool cloth.

> The variable *you change* is the independent variable.

Use enough layers of newspaper so that the thickness of the newspaper wrapping and the wool cloth are the same. The size of the newspaper wrapping and the wool cloth must be the same too. Be sure the mass and shape of the ice cubes are also the same.

> Controlled variables are things *you need* to keep the same if you want a fair test.

The variable you will measure in this **experiment** is the length of time it takes for the ice cubes to melt completely.

> The variable *you measure* is the dependent variable.

For comparison, test an unwrapped cup containing an ice cube.

Test your hypothesis.

1 Write the directions explaining how you will wrap the cups with the newspaper and the wool cloth. Label the cups A, B, and C. Put an ice cube in each cup.

2 Place cups A and B on a balance to be sure the ice cubes have the same mass. Then check cups B and C.

If necessary, change the ice cubes to find ones that balance.

3 Wrap cup A with newspaper. Wrap cup B with wool cloth. Leave cup C unwrapped.

Use tape to hold the insulating material closed.

4 Observe the cups. Record the amount of time needed for each ice cube to melt completely.

Every 10 minutes carefully pull back the insulating materials a little to check if the ice cubes are completely melted.

Collect and record your data.

Insulating Material	Melting Time (minutes)
newspaper (Cup A)	
wool cloth (Cup B)	
none (control) (Cup C)	

Compare your data with the data other groups obtained. Discuss your results.

Interpret your data.
Use your data to make a bar graph showing your results. Look closely at your graphs. Compare the effectiveness of the insulating materials.

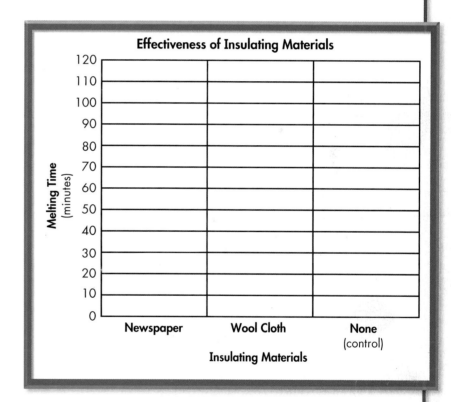

Effectiveness of Insulating Materials

Melting Time (minutes)

120 110 100 90 80 70 60 50 40 30 20 10 0

Newspaper   Wool Cloth   None (control)

Insulating Materials

State your conclusion.
Explain the results of your test. Compare your hypothesis with your results.
Communicate your conclusion.

Go Further

Can you think of other ways you might be able to slow the rate at which ice melts? Design and carry out a plan to investigate this or other questions you may have.

Science Fair Projects

Super Conductors

Some materials conduct electricity.

Idea: Make an electric circuit with a battery, a wire, and a flashlight bulb. Connect the wires to various objects, such as scissors, a plastic spoon and a metal spoon. Observe whether the bulb shines.

Food Detectives

Many foods are acidic.

Idea: Use common foods and pH paper to find out which foods you eat are acidic.

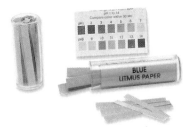

Cooling Rates

The size of a water sample affects its cooling rate.

Idea: Use water, several sizes of plastic cups, and thermometers to show how the amount of water in a cup affects the cooling rate.

Using Scientific Methods

1. Ask a question.
2. State a hypothesis.
3. Identify and control variables.
4. Test your hypothesis.
5. Collect and record your data.
6. Interpret your data.
7. State your conclusions.
8. Go further.

Unit D
Space and Technology

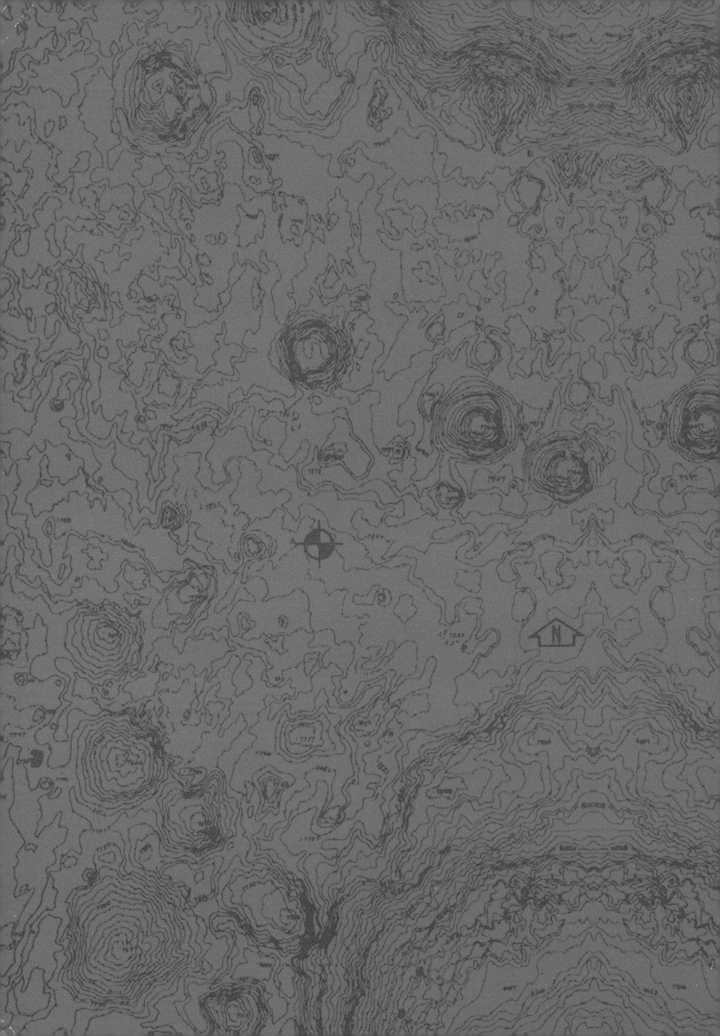

You Will Discover

- what Earth's Sun and Moon are like.
- what causes the phases of the Moon.
- how Earth-Moon-Sun relationships relate to days, years, and seasons.
- what causes solar and lunar eclipses.

Chapter 19

Earth, Sun, and Moon

online
Student Edition
pearsonsuccessnet.com

Build Background

What are the effects of the movements of Earth and the Moon?

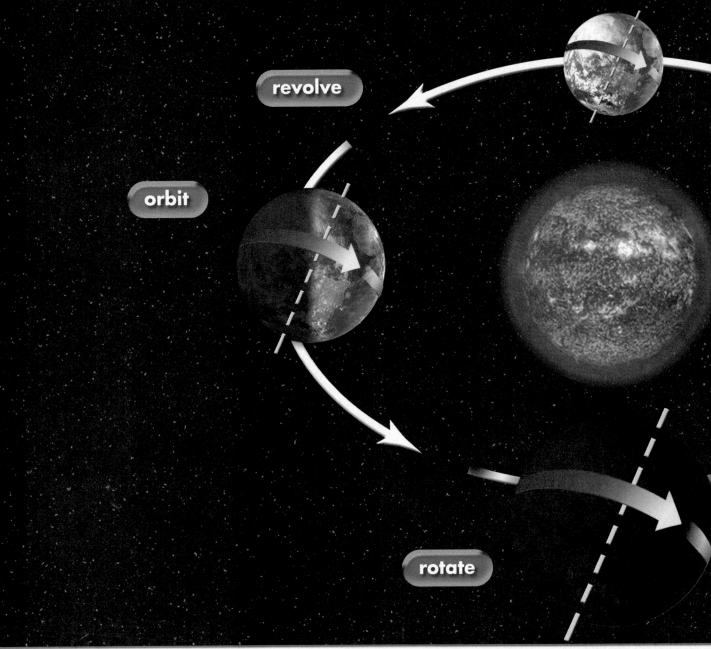

revolve

orbit

rotate

lunar eclipse

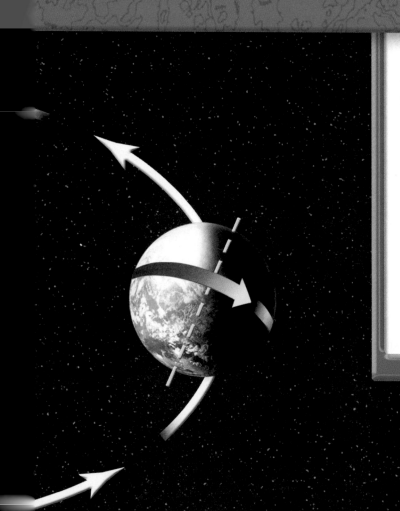

solar eclipse

Explore How can you make a sundial?

A sundial can show one effect of Earth's movement.

Materials

posterboard

drawing compass and modeling clay

ruler and unsharpened pencil

directional compass and clock

marker

What to Do

1 Draw a 9 inch circle on the posterboard. Mark the center of the circle and draw a line through it. Write *noon* at one end of the line.

2 Place a small mound of clay at the center of the circle. Press the eraser end of a pencil into the clay so the pencil stands upright.

3 Take your sundial and a directional compass outside on a sunny day. Place the sundial so that "noon" on your sundial points north.

noon

N

At noon, the pencil's shadow falls along a line pointing north

4 **Observe** the pencil's shadow moving around the sundial. At each hour, mark the position of the shadow. Mark as many hours as you can.

Explain Your Results

Infer How could you change your sundial to tell Daylight Saving Time?
(Hint: 1 P.M. Standard Time = 2 P.M. Daylight Saving Time)

Process Skills

You can make an **inference** based on your experience and **observations**.

How to Read Science

 TARGET SKILL

Main Idea and Details

The **main idea** tells what a paragraph is about. Knowing how to quickly find the main idea of a paragraph can help you understand and remember what you read.

- Sometimes the main idea is not stated. You must **infer** it.

- Look for **details** that give clues to the main idea. Then put together the facts to figure out the main idea.

Science Article

Seeing the Moon

When you look at the Moon at night, it's hard to believe that it doesn't give off its own light. What you see is sunlight bouncing off the Moon. When the Moon is between Earth and the Sun, the back part of the Moon is lit. We can't see that part from Earth. At that time, the part of the Moon facing Earth is dark, so you can't see the Moon when you look at the sky.

Apply It!

Make a graphic organizer like this one. Record **details** from the paragraph. Then write a **main idea** sentence.

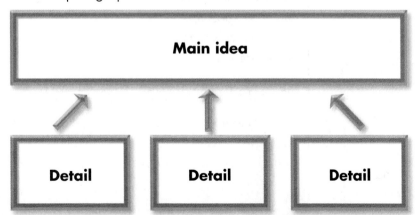

Main idea

Detail   Detail   Detail

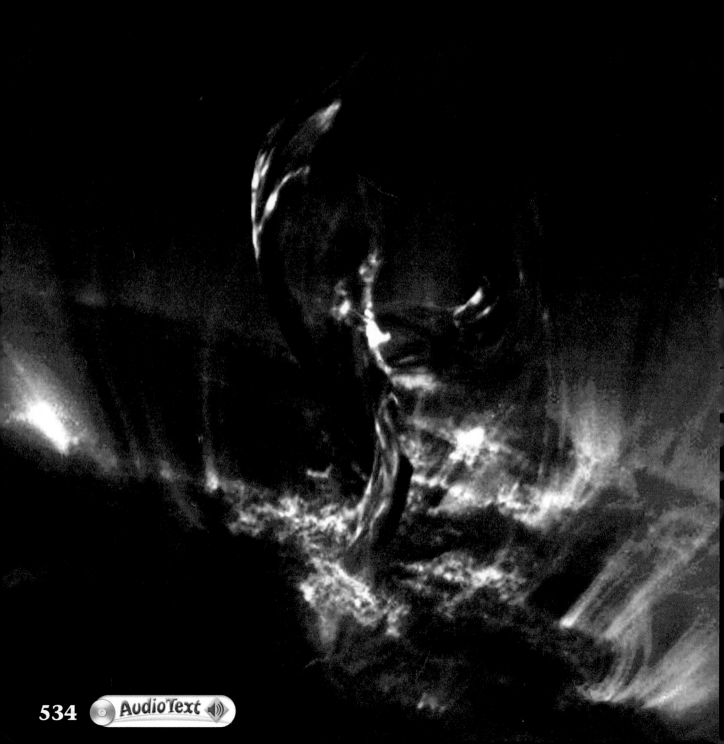

You Are There!

A trip to the Sun wouldn't be much fun! Even the coolest regions are thousands of degrees hotter than Earth. But if you could somehow withstand the intense heat, you would see a swirl of glowing gases. Nearby you might see a tremendous ring of gases thousands of miles high. Huge flares of unimaginably hot gases would suddenly burst out into space above you. What are these huge flares?

AudioText

Lesson 1

What are the characteristics of Earth's Sun and Moon?

The Sun provides Earth with the heat and light needed to sustain life. The Moon revolves around Earth. The Moon's phases are caused by its position relative to Earth and the Sun.

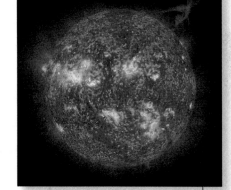

Solar prominence

Our Sun

Our Sun is a star, just like all the stars you see in the night sky. The Sun appears larger only because it is much closer to Earth. The Sun looks like a ball of fire, but it isn't burning at all. The Sun is made of hot gases called plasma. The plasma is so hot that it glows, like the glow of the wire in a light bulb.

The inner part of the Sun is a dense core with a temperature around 15,000,000°C. Reactions among particles in the core release energy, part of which provides light and heat for Earth. Life couldn't exist on Earth without energy from the Sun. Plants use the light energy to produce food for themselves and for other organisms that eat plants. Without the Sun's energy, Earth would be a cold, lifeless rock.

The Sun has no solid surface. Outside the core are swirling layers of plasma. Huge loops of gases, called prominences, extend thousands of kilometers out from the Sun. Some prominences are held in place for weeks. Others explode into space. Intense, temporary releases of energy from the Sun's surface are called solar flares. Energy from these flares sometimes reaches Earth. This energy can cause beautiful light displays called auroras, usually seen near Earth's poles.

1. ✓**Checkpoint** What causes the light that the Sun produces?
2. ◎ **Main Idea and Details** Write a main idea statement about the Sun from the paragraphs above. Give details to support your main idea.

535

Earth's Moon

Looking at the Moon on a clear night, you might think that it shines like the Sun. But the Moon has no light of its own. The light you see is the sunlight that reflects off the Moon's surface. Unlike the Sun with its swirling hot plasma, the Moon is like a giant rock in space. The Moon has almost no atmosphere.

The Moon **rotates,** or spins, on its axis while it revolves around Earth. **Revolve** means to "move on a path around an object." Features of the Moon are easy to spot because its same side always faces Earth. Why do we only see one side? The time for one rotation and one revolution of the Moon are the same as Earth days. Each time the Moon revolves around Earth, it also rotates one time.

Phases of the Moon

If you look at the Moon each night for a month, you'll notice that it seems to change shape. Of course, the Moon doesn't really change shape. The phases of the Moon are the different shapes that the Moon seems to have. The shapes change because the size of the lighted part that we can see from Earth changes. Only the half of the Moon that faces the Sun at any time is lighted. The phases you see depend on the positions of the Moon, Earth, and the Sun.

A new moon is the dark phase of the Moon. During a new moon, the side of the Moon facing Earth is not lighted. On nights just after a new moon, the Moon begins to wax. *Waxing* means "gradually growing larger." The Moon is waxing when more of its lighted part can be seen each night. A full moon is the completely lighted phase of the Moon. On nights after a full moon, the Moon begins to wane. *Waning* means "gradually becoming smaller." The Moon is waning when less of its lighted part can be seen each night. The Moon continues to wane until you once again see a new moon, and the cycle continues. A complete cycle of Moon phases occurs about every 29.5 days.

Waxing Crescent

As the Moon begins to wax, a crescent of light begins to show on the side.

First Quarter

As the Moon continues to wax, you can see half of its lighted side.

Astronauts on this *Apollo 16* mission to the Moon in 1972 collected samples, performed experiments, and took photographs.

Waxing Gibbous

The Moon continues to wax. The shape of the Moon we see is now called gibbous.

Full Moon

About two weeks after a new moon, the Moon appears fully lighted. It has completed half its path around Earth.

Waning Gibbous

The Moon begins to wane. The gibbous shape is now on the left side of the Moon.

Third Quarter

The Moon has now traveled about three quarters of its path around Earth. The lighted half you see is now on the side opposite that of the First Quarter.

Waning Crescent

The Moon is now waning. Each night, the lighted portion grows smaller until only a thin crescent of light is visible.

Astronaut Buzz Aldrin took this photo of his boot print in the Moon's soil during the *Apollo 11* mission.

The *Apollo 11* astronauts brought rocks from the Moon back to Earth. Scientists studied microscopic views of the rocks to learn about their properties.

Learning About the Moon

Although the Moon has been known to humans since prehistoric times, the first visit to the Moon by a spacecraft didn't happen until 1957. That year the unmanned Soviet spacecraft *Luna 2* landed on the surface of the Moon. Ten years later, *Apollo 11* astronauts Edwin "Buzz" Aldrin and Neil Armstrong were the first humans to land on the Moon. Their landing was followed by five more Moon landings, the last in 1972.

Scientists study information they collected on those journeys to learn about the Moon, Earth, and the entire solar system. Because the Moon has almost no atmosphere, its surface remains undisturbed. Scientists can study the craters and other features of the Moon's surface to help determine the age of the Moon and of Earth.

✓ Lesson Checkpoint

1. Explain why the same side of the Moon always faces Earth. Use the terms *rotate* and *revolve*.

2. **Technology** in Science Space exploration began on October 4, 1957, when the Soviet Union launched *Sputnik 1*. Find out what other spacecraft were launched between that date and the last mission to the Moon in 1972. Draw a time line of those events.

537

Lesson 2

What are the effects of the movements of Earth and the Moon?

Days, years, and seasons are caused by Earth's rotation, revolution, and tilt on its axis. The changing positions of the Sun, Moon, and Earth can cause solar and lunar eclipses.

In the evening, the Sun appears to sink below the western horizon.

At midnight, the side of Earth opposite to you experiences the noon Sun.

Earth on its Axis

Think about a time thousands of years ago, before telescopes had been invented and before astronauts had ever traveled into space. What did people think of Earth and its Sun? If you look at the daytime sky, the Sun rises in the east and sets in the west. People naturally thought the Sun was moving around Earth.

We now know that the Sun is the center of our solar system and that Earth and other planets revolve around the Sun. Earth also rotates on its axis, an imaginary line between its poles. A day is the total time for a planet to make one complete rotation. The Sun seems to revolve around Earth because of Earth's rotation.

If you wake up early in the morning, you might see the Sun just beginning to rise above the eastern horizon. The Sun always seems to rise in the east because Earth spins from west to east. Because you spin along with Earth, the Sun is first visible in the east. You experience daytime as long as the Sun is visible from your location on Earth. Daytime ends when Earth has turned enough that the Sun seems to set in the west. Nighttime is when the Sun is no longer visible to you.

To understand Earth's rotation, picture Earth spinning on a pole. The speed of Earth's rotation at the equator is about 1,670 km/h.

Heat from the Sun is most intense around noon when the Sun is at its highest point.

As the Sun rises in the eastern sky, sunlight begins to warm Earth.

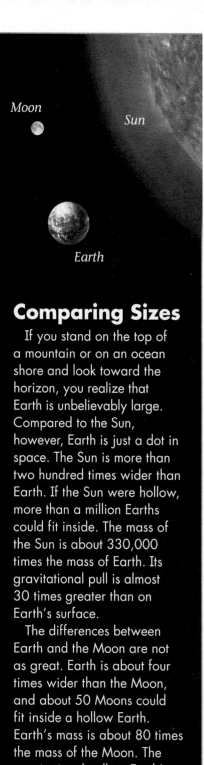

Moon

Sun

Earth

Comparing Sizes

If you stand on the top of a mountain or on an ocean shore and look toward the horizon, you realize that Earth is unbelievably large. Compared to the Sun, however, Earth is just a dot in space. The Sun is more than two hundred times wider than Earth. If the Sun were hollow, more than a million Earths could fit inside. The mass of the Sun is about 330,000 times the mass of Earth. Its gravitational pull is almost 30 times greater than on Earth's surface.

The differences between Earth and the Moon are not as great. Earth is about four times wider than the Moon, and about 50 Moons could fit inside a hollow Earth. Earth's mass is about 80 times the mass of the Moon. The gravitational pull on Earth's surface is about six times stronger than on the Moon's surface. That's why an object that weighs 60 newtons on Earth would only weigh 10 newtons on the Moon.

When you wake up on a winter morning, it may still be dark outside. If you wake up at the same time in summer, it may have been light outside for hours. The number of hours of daylight changes throughout the year. Notice on the globe how Earth is tilted on its axis. One half of Earth is usually tilted slightly toward the Sun. That side has more daylight hours and fewer nighttime hours. The other half of Earth has fewer daylight hours and more nighttime hours.

The tilt of Earth's axis has an even greater effect at the poles. When the northern part of Earth is tilted toward the Sun, the Sun never fully sets at the North Pole. The same is true at the South Pole when it is tilted toward the Sun. Daylight and darkness at the poles each last six months.

You may have noticed that the Moon is sometimes visible during the day. The Moon can be seen whenever it is on your side of Earth. This is sometimes during daytime and sometimes during nighttime.

1. ✓**Checkpoint** Why does the Sun seem to rise in the eastern sky?
2. **Math in Science** If an object weighs 300 newtons on Earth, about how much would it weigh on the Moon?

Earth's Orbit and Seasons

Like all objects in space, Earth tends to move in a straight line. The force of the Sun's gravity, however, pulls Earth toward the Sun out of a straight-line path. As a result, Earth revolves around the Sun. An **orbit** is the path of an object that revolves around another object. Earth's orbit around the Sun is an ellipse, a slightly flattened circle. A year, about 365 days, is the total amount of time Earth takes to make one orbit around the Sun.

Because Earth's orbit is an ellipse, it is sometimes slightly closer to the Sun than at other times. People often think summer is when Earth is closer to the Sun, but is this really true? To answer this question, think about standing close to a heater so that your face feels warm. If you step just a few centimeters back, the warmth you feel doesn't change. If you turn around, however, your face no longer feels warm.

The Tilt and the Seasons

In a similar way, the slight difference in the distance to the Sun as Earth moves around its orbit has no effect on seasons. In fact, Earth is slightly closer to the Sun when the northern half has winter. Earth's tilt on its axis causes seasons. The Sun warms the side of Earth that tilts toward it more than it does the side tilted away. When the North Pole tilts toward the Sun, the northern half of Earth has summer and the southern half has winter. When the South Pole tilts toward the Sun, the seasons are reversed. In spring and in fall, neither pole tilts toward the Sun. Both the northern and southern halves of Earth have mild temperatures.

The tilt of Earth's axis affects how directly the Sun shines on Earth as it travels in its orbit.

When the North Pole tilts away from the Sun, the Sun's light is very spread out here. The Northern Hemisphere receives the least amount of energy at this time of year. Temperatures drop, and winter sets in.

The Sun's light strikes the Earth more directly south of the equator. The light is concentrated, not spread out. Concentrated energy gives this region warm summer weather.

In summer, the Sun's rays point almost directly toward you at noon. The direct sunlight makes the days very warm. The shadow you make is very small. As each day passes, the Sun's rays strike you at a greater and greater angle—we say the Sun is lower in the sky. With less direct rays from the Sun, the days are not as warm. Your noontime shadow gets longer and longer. You have winter when the part of Earth where you live is tilted away from the Sun. At noon, the angle of the Sun's rays is large, and you make a long shadow. A year can be defined as the time between the days when your shadow is at its shortest.

1. **√ Checkpoint** How does your noontime shadow change throughout the year?
2. **Writing in Science** **Descriptive** Write a paragraph describing seasons if Earth were not tilted on its axis.

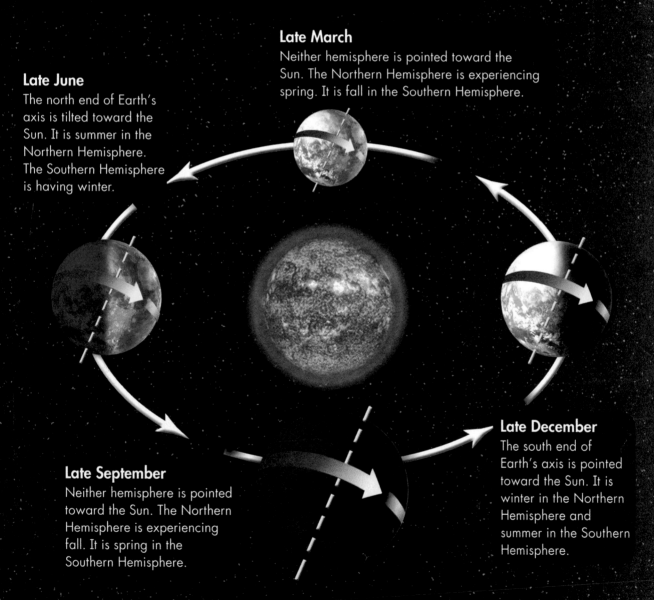

Late March
Neither hemisphere is pointed toward the Sun. The Northern Hemisphere is experiencing spring. It is fall in the Southern Hemisphere.

Late June
The north end of Earth's axis is tilted toward the Sun. It is summer in the Northern Hemisphere. The Southern Hemisphere is having winter.

Late September
Neither hemisphere is pointed toward the Sun. The Northern Hemisphere is experiencing fall. It is spring in the Southern Hemisphere.

Late December
The south end of Earth's axis is pointed toward the Sun. It is winter in the Northern Hemisphere and summer in the Southern Hemisphere.

Solar Eclipses

If you draw a picture of Earth's orbit around the Sun on a piece of paper, you can't draw the Moon's true orbit around Earth on the same paper. The Moon's orbit is tilted slightly at an angle from Earth's orbit. You can see the effect of this during a new moon. If the new moon occurs in daytime, you can see the Sun. The Moon is a little above or below the Sun because of the tilt of its orbit. Sometimes, however, the orbit of the Moon crosses exactly between the Sun and Earth. The Moon eclipses, or covers, the Sun. A **solar eclipse** occurs when the Moon blocks the light of the Sun.

The Moon makes two types of shadows on Earth during an eclipse. The umbra is the darker, inner part of an eclipse shadow. The penumbra is the lighter, outer part of an eclipse shadow. You can see these on the picture at the right. Even though solar eclipses occur several times a year, each place on Earth only experiences one every few hundred years.

During a solar eclipse, a place on Earth may experience a total or partial eclipse of the Sun or no eclipse at all. A total eclipse is when the umbra passes over an area. For several minutes, the Sun is completely blocked from view. The sky darkens, and the stars are visible in daytime. Because the Moon's shadow is so small, only a small part of Earth experiences a total eclipse. Nearby areas that are in the penumbra experience a partial eclipse. A partial eclipse can also occur when the umbra completely misses Earth and only the penumbra passes over.

It's important to remember that you should never look directly at the Sun. A good way to view an eclipse is by using two pieces of white cardboard. Place one piece of cardboard on the ground. Place a pinhole in the center of the other piece. Point the pinhole at the Sun so that you see a round image on the other cardboard. The round spot of light you see on the paper is a pinhole image of the Sun.

Time-lapse photo of a lunar eclipse

Lunar Eclipses

A different kind of eclipse can occur during a full moon, when Earth is between the Sun and the Moon. A **lunar eclipse** happens when the Moon passes through Earth's shadow. You can safely watch a lunar eclipse. During a total eclipse, you might see the Moon passing through Earth's shadow for almost two hours. The time is shorter for partial eclipses. Unlike a solar eclipse, a lunar eclipse can be seen by most parts of Earth where it is nighttime. Lunar and solar eclipses occur about twice a year, but because lunar eclipses are visible from half the Earth, you are much more likely to see one.

Total Solar Eclipse

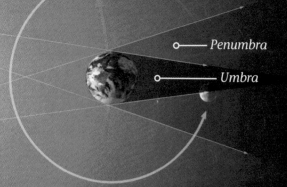

Umbra

Penumbra

Lunar Eclipse

Penumbra

Umbra

✓ **Lesson Checkpoint**

1. What are two ways an area can experience a partial eclipse?
2. 🔄 Write details to support this main idea: During a solar eclipse, the Moon blocks the light of the Sun.
3. **Writing** in Science **Expository** During a total lunar eclipse, the Moon appears slightly red. Research to find the cause of this effect and write a paragraph explaining it.

Investigate How can you make a spectroscope?

Different colors of light are given off by different materials. By studying the light from the Sun, scientists can learn about the materials that make up the Sun. Scientists use a spectroscope to separate light into its different colors. In this activity you will make a spectroscope and compare the color pattern made by "white" light from 3 different sources.

Materials

compact disc

cardboard tube with viewing hole and slit

cardboard circle with slit

masking tape

assorted light sources

What to Do

1 Tape the cardboard circle to one end of the tube.

2 Slide a CD into the slot above the viewing hole. Point the slit at a light source and look through the viewing hole. Look for bands of color.

3 Record your **observations.**

Light Source	Spectroscope Image	Description or Drawing
Fluorescent ceiling light		
Compact fluorescent light bulb		
Incandescent light bulb		

A Point the slit at the light source.

B White light enters the tube through slit.

Process Skills

You can make an **inference** based on your **observations** of the spectra of assorted light sources.

Explain Your Results

1. What did you **observe** when you looked through the viewing hole?

2. Compare and contrast the spectrum from the incandescent light bulb and the spectrum from the fluorescent ceiling light.

3. **Infer** How might a scientist use information about sunlight to learn about the Sun?

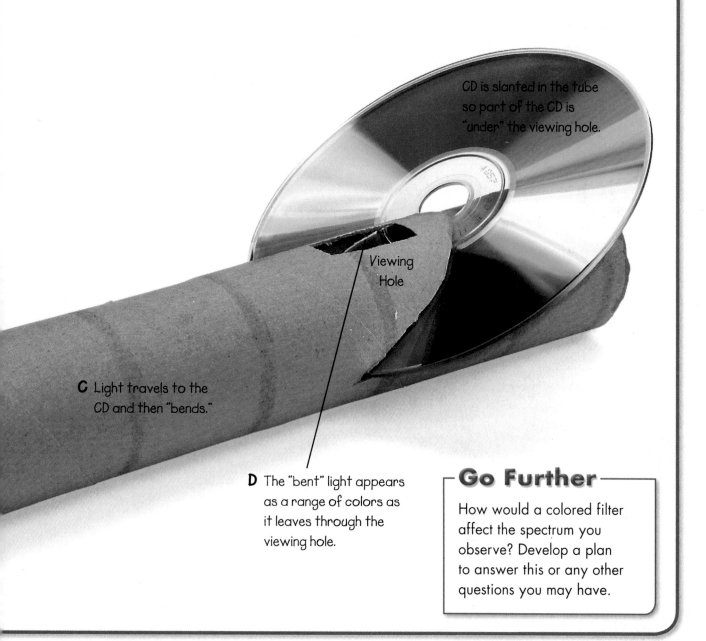

CD is slanted in the tube so part of the CD is "under" the viewing hole.

Viewing Hole

C Light travels to the CD and then "bends."

D The "bent" light appears as a range of colors as it leaves through the viewing hole.

Go Further

How would a colored filter affect the spectrum you observe? Develop a plan to answer this or any other questions you may have.

Math in Science

SPEED IN Space

Objects in space travel great distances at speeds much faster than humans travel on Earth. The Moon travels around the Earth at a speed of about 3700 kilometers per hour!

One of the world's fastest runners set a record in a 100 meter race with an average speed of 10.2 meters per second. Compare this speed with the speed of the Moon given above.

Speed is one type of rate. To compare rates, it is usually necessary to express them using the same units. One way to do this is to analyze the units used for one of the rates and use them to divide and simplify the rate.

To change 10.2 m/s to km/h, first change 10.2 m to km.

$$10.2 \text{ m} \div \frac{1000 \text{ m}}{1 \text{ km}} = \frac{10.2 \text{ m}}{1} \times \frac{1 \text{ km}}{1000 \text{ m}} = \frac{10.2 \text{ km}}{1000} = 0.0102 \text{ km}$$

$$\frac{0.0102 \text{ km}}{1 \text{ s}} \times \frac{60 \text{ s}}{1 \text{ min}} \times \frac{60 \text{ min}}{1 \text{ h}} = \frac{0.0102 \text{ km} \times 60 \times 60}{1 \text{ h}} = 36.72 \text{ km/h}$$

Running 36.72 km/h is very fast for a human, but the Moon travels more than 100 times as fast!

⊡ ⓔ **Tools** Take It to the Net
pearsonsuccessnet.com

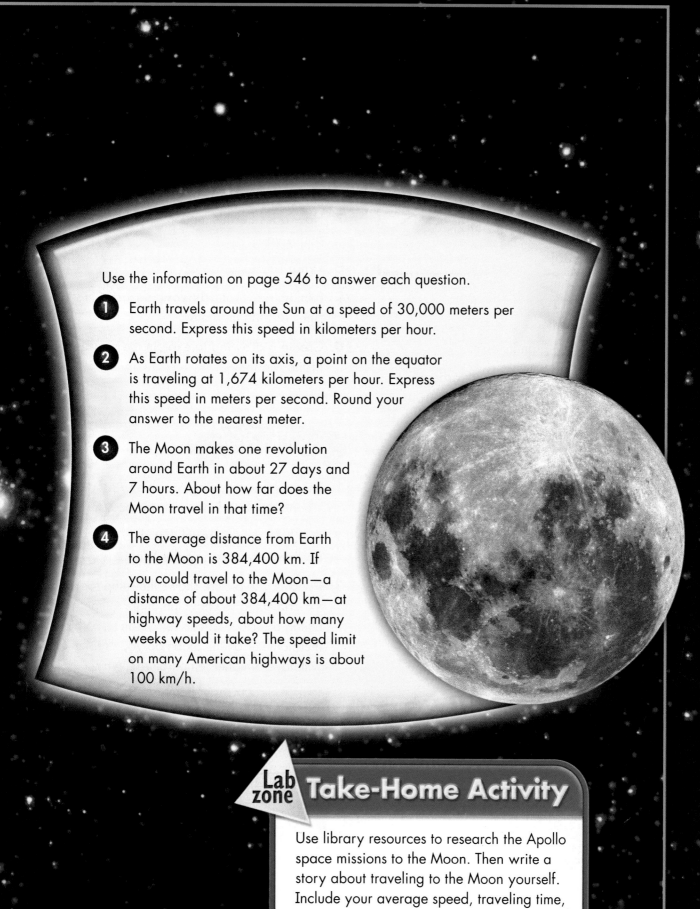

Use the information on page 546 to answer each question.

1. Earth travels around the Sun at a speed of 30,000 meters per second. Express this speed in kilometers per hour.

2. As Earth rotates on its axis, a point on the equator is traveling at 1,674 kilometers per hour. Express this speed in meters per second. Round your answer to the nearest meter.

3. The Moon makes one revolution around Earth in about 27 days and 7 hours. About how far does the Moon travel in that time?

4. The average distance from Earth to the Moon is 384,400 km. If you could travel to the Moon—a distance of about 384,400 km—at highway speeds, about how many weeks would it take? The speed limit on many American highways is about 100 km/h.

Lab zone Take-Home Activity

Use library resources to research the Apollo space missions to the Moon. Then write a story about traveling to the Moon yourself. Include your average speed, traveling time, and length of stay on the Moon.

Use Vocabulary

lunar eclipse (p. 542)	**rotates** (p. 536)
orbit (p. 540)	**solar eclipse** (p. 542)
revolve (p. 536)	

Use the vocabulary term from above that best completes each sentence.

1. The Moon _____ on its axis.

2. The _____ of Earth is its path around the Sun.

3. A(n) _____ occurs when the Moon completely blocks out the Sun's light.

4. The time for Earth to _____ around the Sun once is a year.

5. A(n) _____ occurs when the Moon passes through Earth's shadow.

Explain Concepts

6. Why are you more likely to see a lunar eclipse than a solar eclipse?

7. How does Earth's motion relate to a day and a year?

8. What causes seasons?

9. Explain why your shadow is shorter in summer than in winter.

10. Create a drawing to explain the phases of the Moon.

Process Skills

11. **Infer** Why are scientists able to predict when solar and lunar eclipses occur?

12. **Model** Make a model that shows how Earth revolves around the Sun.

13. **Predict** The picture shows the setup for an experiment to see how the angle of light hitting a surface affects temperature. Which thermometer on the globe do you predict will have a higher temperature? Why?

Main Idea and Details

14. Make a graphic organizer like the one below for each lesson in this chapter. Fill in the main idea and supporting details for each lesson.

Main idea

↗ ↑ ↖

Detail		Detail		Detail

Test Prep

Choose the letter that best completes the statement or answers the question.

15. Which of the following is a reasonable time that a total solar eclipse might take?
 Ⓐ 5 minutes
 Ⓑ 30 minutes
 Ⓒ 1 hour
 Ⓓ 2 hours

16. Which phase can you see when the Moon is waning?
 Ⓕ first quarter moon
 Ⓖ half moon
 Ⓗ new moon
 Ⓘ third quarter moon

17. During which season is the part of Earth where you live tilted toward the Sun?
 Ⓐ fall
 Ⓑ spring
 Ⓒ summer
 Ⓓ winter

18. The Sun is made up of
 Ⓕ solid rock.
 Ⓖ auroras.
 Ⓗ liquids.
 Ⓘ plasma.

19. Explain why the answer you chose for Question 16 is best. For each of the answers you did not choose, give a reason why it is not the best choice.

20. Writing in Science **Narrative** Write a journal entry about a visit to the Sun. Explain what you see and feel on your visit. Remember to include what you see as you look from the Sun and the sky.

Reducing Drag to Save Fuel

When you think about NASA, you probably think of space travel and exploration. However, the work of some NASA scientists has helped improve travel right here on Earth. For example, the shape of some trucks you see on the road has been influenced by NASA technologies.

Until the 1970s, truck cabs were shaped like boxes with sharp corners. These sharp-cornered trucks would pass a NASA aerospace engineer as he rode his bike to and from work every day. The speed and shape of the trucks resulted in very strong and uneven wind gusts that pushed the scientist and his bike toward the side of the road. After the trucks passed, he would get pulled back toward the road. He realized that the forces pushing and pulling him could be costing the truck drivers money—they made the trucks use more fuel.

The force that the scientist experienced was partly the result of drag, a force that works against the motion of moving objects. A truck must use energy to overcome drag. A truck with a box-shaped cab uses a lot of fuel to overcome drag.

Compare NASA's experimental truck cab with the new cab design.

The scientist decided to help trucks glide through air instead of push through it. In the process, the trucks would encounter less drag and become more fuel-efficient. NASA researchers were working on the effects of drag and wind resistance on different kinds of aircraft and the space shuttle. They applied this knowledge to the design of large trucks. The researchers changed the box-shaped cab of the truck by rounding out its corners and edges. Then they observed the changes in drag. Trucks with the new cab design used much less fuel. This new design is now widely used.

Lab zone Take-Home Activity

How would you design a truck's trailer? Trailers still have a box shape for the purpose of storing cargo. Draw a trailer that would limit the force of drag. Write a paragraph that explains your design.

Astronomer

Is there life on other planets? Are there any planets like Earth in distant solar systems? What are particles of the Sun like? What are the farthest objects we can see in space? What lies beyond that?

These are just a few of the many questions that astronomers try to answer. Astronomers use telescopes, computers, space probes, and other complex instruments to explore the universe.

Most astronomers specialize in a certain area of astronomy. For instance, a cosmologist studies how the universe began. A planetologist is most interested in the planets. Some astronomers are experts in how comets and other objects move in space.

Many astronomers teach at universities. Some work for NASA. Still others work at planetariums and help children and adults alike enjoy the wonders of space. In fact, a lot of people use their own telescopes to explore the night sky on a regular basis. These amateur astronomers have made many important discoveries. Becoming a professional astronomer, however, requires a lot of hard work. Math and science, especially physics, are important subjects to study in high school and college.

Lab zone Take-Home Activity

What stars and planets can be seen in your area right now? Find out by looking at the latest issue of astronomy magazines at the library. Then see how many of these objects you can find in the night sky.

Chapter 20

The Universe

You Will Discover

- o what Earth's place is in the universe.
- o what the parts of our solar system are.
- o why planets differ.
- o how stars are born, age, and die.
- o how scientists measure distances in space.

online
Student Edition
pearsonsuccessnet.com

Discovery Channel School
Student DVD
Discovery CHANNEL SCHOOL

Web Games
Take It to the Net
pearsonsuccessnet.com

What is Earth's place in the universe?

galaxy

solar system

astronomical unit

Chapter 20 Vocabulary

constellation

light-year

star

magnitude

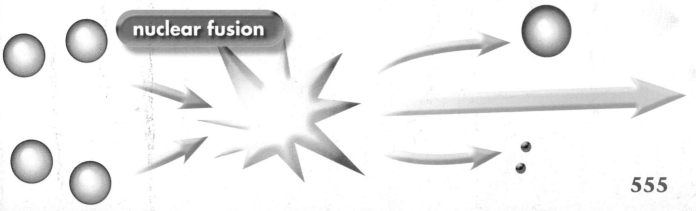

nuclear fusion

Explore How can you find a planet?

In the night sky, both stars and planets can look like points of light. Planets, however, change position or move relative to the stars.

Materials

Sky Pictures

metric ruler

white colored pencil

hand lens

What to Do

1 Look carefully at Sky Picture 1. Which point of light do you think might be the planet Mars?

2 Carefully **observe** Sky Picture 2. Compare it to Sky Picture 1.

3 To help compare the sky pictures, divide each picture into small squares. Then compare the images in corresponding squares one by one.

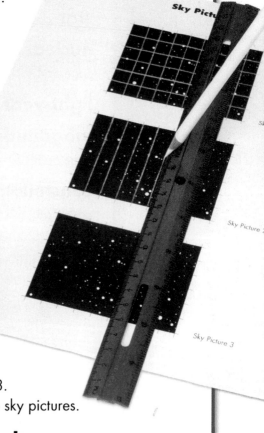

Sky Picture 2

Sky Picture 3

4 Look closely at Sky Picture 3. Compare it to the other two sky pictures.

Explain Your Results

1. How did drawing the grid help you **observe** and compare the 3 pictures?

2. **Infer** Which point of light in the sky pictures do you think is a planet? Explain.

Process Skills

Comparing and contrasting a sequence of sky pictures is one way to carefully **observe** the night sky.

How to Read Science

 Draw Conclusions

When you read, you may form questions that aren't directly answered in the reading passage. In those cases, you often can **infer** ideas from the facts. Then use the facts and your inference to answer the questions by **drawing conclusions.** When you draw a conclusion, you put together facts and ideas to come up with a new idea.

- First, list all the facts.

- Think of a reasonable explanation for the facts.

- Eliminate any conclusions that all the facts do not support.

Read the article below. Look for facts in the article.

Science Article

Seeing the Past

At night when you look at the twinkling stars, the light you see may have taken thousands of years to reach you. The star closest to our Sun is Proxima Centauri. Light given off by this star must travel more than four years to reach Earth. When you look at this star, you are seeing events that took place in the past. How long ago did those events take place?

Apply It!

Make a graphic organizer like this one. List the facts from the science article in your graphic organizer. Write a **conclusion** to answer the question.

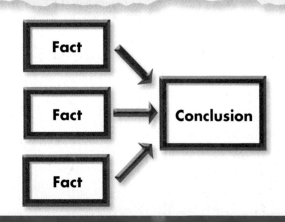

♦))) You Are There!

On a camping trip, you go outside after dark
and look up at the sky. Amazing! Instead of the
misty scattering of light visible in the city, you
see glowing balls of fire in every corner. The Big
Dipper looks as though you could grasp the handle
and pull it down to Earth. What are these brightly
gleaming bodies of light in the sky?

AudioText ♦)))

What is Earth's place in the universe?

The universe contains countless billions of stars grouped in galaxies. One of those stars is our Sun. The Sun and all the planets and other bodies around it make up our solar system.

The Universe

Astronomy—the study of space and the objects in it—is one of the oldest sciences. As far back as 3500 B.C. or more, people have been studying the sky. But it wasn't until 1609 when the Italian scientist Galileo first used a crude telescope to study the sky that scientists could see much more than small dots of light in the sky. His findings changed the way people think about space.

Today scientists use powerful telescopes to look into the universe. They can study all the energy and matter, as well as the empty space, that make up the universe.

The Milky Way Galaxy

We now know that Earth is part of the Milky Way Galaxy. A **galaxy** is a huge grouping of stars. The universe has clusters of billions of galaxies. Each galaxy has billions of stars.

You may have seen part of the Milky Way Galaxy in the night sky. It looks like a pale white stripe or band across the sky. If you were outside of the Milky Way Galaxy and far away from it, you would see that it is shaped like a flat pinwheel. This type of galaxy is called a spiral galaxy. Our Sun, one of the stars in the Milky Way, is in one of the "arms" of the pinwheel. It is just one of at least 100 billion stars in the Milky Way Galaxy. It appears brighter than other stars because it is much closer to Earth.

Spiral galaxies are just one of the three major types of galaxies. Elliptical galaxies are shaped like an oval, or ellipse. Irregular galaxies do not have a regular shape.

The top photo shows the Milky Way Galaxy. Below you can see a closer view of the stars and dust in the center of the galaxy.

1. ✓**Checkpoint** To what galaxy does our solar system belong? What type of galaxy is it?

2. **Technology** in Science Research the major telescopes scientists use today to study the universe. Organize your information into a chart with these headings: Name of telescope, Location, Description, Year developed.

The Planets

The Sun and the cluster of bodies around it make up our **solar system.**
Eight major planets, including Earth, are in our solar system. You can
see the planets below in the order they orbit the Sun. Until 2006, another
object, called Pluto, was called a ninth planet. Now, scientists classify it
as a "dwarf planet." Some other dwarf planets are far beyond Neptune.
Another dwarf planet is in the asteroid belt between Mars and Jupiter.

All the major planets, except Mercury, have almost circular orbits.
Gravity keeps planets orbiting the Sun. Some planets have one or more
moons. Only Mercury and Venus do not have moons.

More than 100,000 asteroids—small bodies made of rock and metal—
also orbit the Sun in our solar system. Comets, which are small icy bodies,
orbit the Sun too. Their orbits are long, narrow ellipses. The far end of a
comet's orbit is deep in space. In part of its orbit, a comet may pass near
the Sun. Then the comet heats up, forming a stream of gas and dust that
trails the comet as it orbits the Sun.

All these objects in our solar system are separated by huge distances.
For that reason, scientists often express distances in our solar system in
astronomical units (AU). An AU is the average distance of Earth from
the Sun—about 149.6 million kilometers.

Mercury
Rocky with craters formed
by meteorites. Extreme
temperatures. Traces of
hydrogen and helium in
atmosphere.

Venus
Mostly rock with craters. Some
volcanoes may be active. Very
hot. Atmosphere made mostly
of carbon dioxide with clouds
of sulfuric acid.

Earth
Mostly water-covered.
Only known planet
with an atmosphere
to support life.

Mars
Covered with red dust. White polar
caps change with seasons. Craters
in southern part. Atmosphere mostly
carbon dioxide. Strong winds blow
red surface dust to create pink sky.

Jupiter
Covered by liquid
hydrogen. Very cold.
Mostly hydrogen with
clouds of ammonia
crystals in atmosphere.

The Inner Planets

	Mercury	Venus	Earth	Mars
Diameter (km)	4,879	12,104	12,756	6,794
Mass (compared to Earth)	0.055	0.82	1.0	0.107
Average distance from the Sun (AU)	0.39	0.72	1	1.52
Time of 1 rotation (Earth days)	58.7	243	1	24.6
Time for 1 revolution (Earth days)	88 days	224.7 days	365.2 days	687 days

The Outer Planets

	Jupiter	Saturn	Uranus	Neptune
Diameter (km)	142,984	120,536	51,118	49,528
Mass (compared to Earth)	318	95	14.5	17.1
Average distance from Sun (AU)	5.2	9.58	19.20	30.05
Time of 1 rotation (Earth hours/days)	9.9 hours	10.7 hours	17.2 hours	16.1 hours
Time for 1 revolution (Earth years)	11.9 years	29.4 years	83.7 years	163.7 years

Saturn
Core of rock and iron surrounded by ice and liquid hydrogen. Very cold. Strong winds and swirling clouds of ammonia in atmosphere.

1. ✓**Checkpoint** How do comets and asteroids differ? How are they alike?

2. ↻ Draw Conclusions Does the size of a planet affect the time it takes for one revolution around the Sun? Use the facts in the charts to support your answer.

Neptune
Possibly covered by liquid hydrogen and helium. Mostly hydrogen, helium, and methane gases in atmosphere. Appears pale blue.

Uranus
Composed mostly of hydrogen, helium, and methane gases. Very cold. Appears green.

A Model of the Solar System

If you took the information about the planets and made a model, it would look something like the one below. The model shows the correct arrangement of planets, but it does not show the relative distances between planets.

The solar system covers very vast distances. On a regular sheet of paper, it would be difficult or impossible to make a drawing of the solar system to scale. The table shows the relative size of and distances between planets if Earth were one millimeter wide at its equator. You can see why showing the planets to scale in this book would be impossible, even if Earth were shrunk to a millimeter.

The Solar System: Relative Distances

Planet	Size (mm)	Distance from Sun (m)
(A) Mercury	0.4	4.5
(B) Venus	1.0	8.5
(C) Earth	1.0	11.7
(D) Mars	0.5	17.9
(E) Jupiter	11.2	61
(F) Saturn	9.5	112
(G) Uranus	4.0	225
(H) Neptune	3.9	352

Mars

Venus

Why Planets Differ

You might think that a planet's distance from the Sun is mostly responsible for its characteristics. It's true that a planet close to the Sun receives more warming sunlight than planets farther out. For example, Mars is about twice as far from the Sun as is Venus. This difference is one reason that temperatures on Venus are warmer than on Mars. But distance is only one reason why planets differ. Other factors also help make each planet unique. Let's look at Venus, Earth, and Mars. These planets were similar when they formed billions of years ago, but they have changed in different ways.

A planet's size affects how strong gravity is at its surface. Larger planets have stronger forces of gravity than smaller planets. Strong gravity holds more gases close to the planet, creating a thicker atmosphere. The gravitational force at the surface of Mars is much less than that on Earth or Venus. Its atmosphere is thin with 200 times less gas than Earth's atmosphere. The thin atmosphere holds in less heat, making Mars even colder than it would otherwise be.

Before planetary space probes began in the 1960s, many people thought that Venus might be very much like Earth. It is about the same size and mass as our planet, and its orbit around the Sun is closer to ours than that of any other planet. However, spacecraft have shown that temperatures there reach 475° C, and atmospheric pressure is about 100 times that of Earth.

Why is Venus so different from Earth? Thick clouds cover Venus, and the planet's atmosphere is mostly carbon dioxide. This gas absorbs heat and reflects it back to the planet's surface.

✓ Lesson Checkpoint

1. What is an astronomical unit? Why do scientists use this unit to measure distances in the solar system?
2. List the planets in order from the Sun.
3. **Writing in Science** **Expository** Choose a planet. Find the latest information that scientists have learned about it. Share the information in the form of a newspaper article.

What do we know about stars?

Through millions or billions of years, stars produce light and other forms of energy in nuclear fusion reactions. In time, stars run out of fuel and experience enormous changes.

What Stars Are

The twinkling bits of light you see in the night sky tell you little about the activity that goes on in each star. A **star** is a huge, hot, glowing ball of gas. Stars shine because processes that go on in them produce huge amounts of energy. The extremely high temperatures and pressure in the center of a star cause the nuclei of atoms there to bump into each other at incredible speeds. Sometimes two nuclei join to form a single, larger nucleus. This process is called **nuclear fusion.** In most stars, hydrogen nuclei join to form helium nuclei during fusion. Large amounts of energy are given off as radiation, some of which is the light we see.

Distances of Stars

Distances in space are enormous—far too large to use the units we use every day to measure distances, such as kilometers. Even the astronomical unit that is used to measure distances in the solar system is too small. When measuring distances in space, scientists use the light-year. A **light-year** is the distance light travels in one year—9 trillion 460 billion kilometers. Light can travel around Earth seven times in one second!

The Sun is the closest star in our galaxy. The next closest star is Proxima Centauri. It is 4.3 light years away. If the star exploded tonight, you wouldn't see the flash for more than four years! Other galaxies and their stars can be millions of light years away. The light you see from them was given off millions of years ago. You are looking back in time!

Hydrogen

Fusion

Small particles

Helium

Energy

Nova

Many stars are paired with a partner star. These systems are called binary (two) stars. If one star is a white dwarf, its gravity attracts gases from the partner star. If enough hot gases collect around the dwarf, it may explode, shining so brightly that to viewers on Earth it looks like a new star. This event is called a nova, from the Latin word for "new."

Black Dwarf

A black dwarf is a dead star. It is still a compact, dense body, but because it has used up all its fuel, it does not shine.

White Dwarf

A red giant gradually loses its outer, gaseous layers into space. What is left is a very hot, dense, compact core known as a white dwarf.

Supernova

After a time, gravity pulls the outer parts of a supergiant toward the dense center. Pressure and temperature increase so much that the star explodes, producing a brilliant supernova. What is left behind becomes a neutron star or, rarely, a black hole.

Supergiant

A supergiant is like a red giant, but on a much bigger scale. Nuclear fusion in the core of a red supergiant creates heavier elements, such as iron. The outer layers expand tremendously, becoming cooler and redder.

1. **✓Checkpoint** What happens to a star when it first begins to run out of fuel?

2. **Social Studies** in Science The Crab Nebula was first seen in China in 1054. Find out more about this supernova and what scientists have learned about it since then. Make a time line of your information.

Constellations

You may have heard people refer to groups of stars with names such as Orion, Leo, Scorpius, and Gemini. These names were first given to groups of stars by the ancient Greeks. The Greeks associated the star patterns with their myths or gods. They named 48 of these star groups, called **constellations.** For example, in Greek mythology, Orion was a handsome hunter who fell in love with the goddess Artemis. Artemis placed Orion in the night sky after accidentally killing him.

Today scientists divide the sky into 88 constellations. Every star is part of a constellation, but stars within a constellation are not necessarily related in any other way.

One of the best-known constellations today is Ursa Major, which means "big bear." The star group called the Big Dipper, which you might be familiar with, is part of Ursa Major. The two stars at the end of the bowl of the Big Dipper always point at the North Star, which is always directly over the North Pole.

If you were able to see both the Sun and stars at the same time, you would notice that the Sun seems to pass through the same ring of constellations each year. The relative position of Earth and the Sun determines where the Sun appears to be among the constellations. This band of stars in which the Sun appears to move is known as the zodiac. Find the zodiac in the picture. How many constellations do you recognize?

The constellation Orion

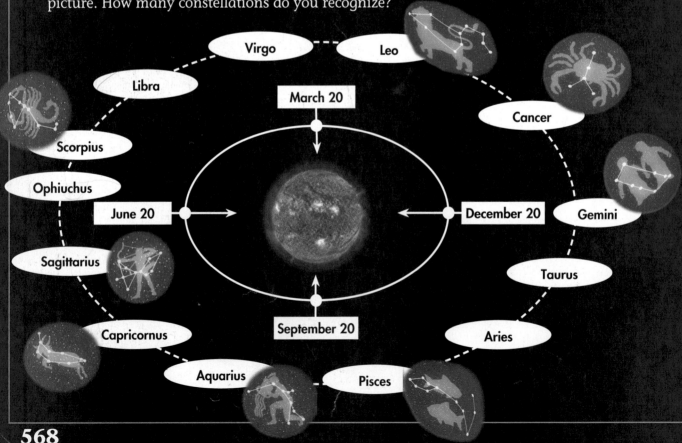

Virgo
Leo
Libra
March 20
Cancer
Scorpius
Ophiuchus
June 20
December 20
Gemini
Sagittarius
Taurus
Capricornus
September 20
Aries
Aquarius
Pisces

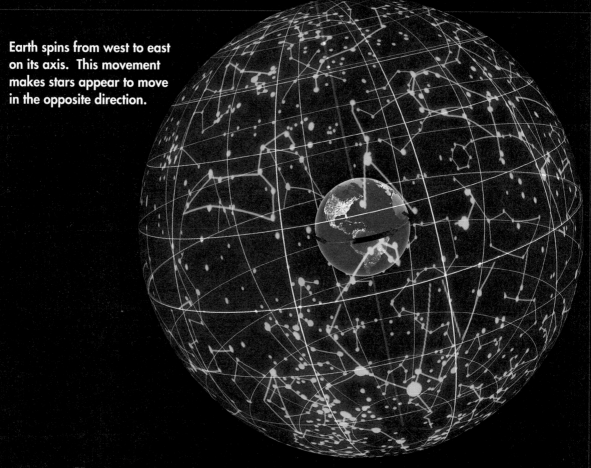

Earth spins from west to east on its axis. This movement makes stars appear to move in the opposite direction.

Constellation Movement

If you are a star watcher, you know that the pattern of the nighttime sky changes from hour to hour. A starry sky looks different early in the evening than it does in the dark morning hours. Star patterns change from season to season too. In the Northern Hemisphere, we see Orion high in the winter sky, but in summer we lose part or all of Orion as it dips below the horizon.

These changes should not surprise you. Like the Sun's movement across the sky during the day, star movements in the night sky are the result of our own Earth's movements. Recall that Earth rotates on its axis and orbits the Sun. These movements affect the star patterns you see.

✓ Lesson Checkpoint

1. Name and explain the process inside a star that produces the star's energy.

2. Explain the difference between apparent magnitude and absolute magnitude.

3. **Draw Conclusions** The star Antares is about 520 light-years from Earth, while the star Betelgeuse is about 430 light-years away. Given this information, can you predict which star appears brighter in the night sky? Why or why not?

Investigate How can you make a model to show the motions of planets?

Planets closer to the Sun orbit the Sun more often than planets farther from the Sun. You can make a model to show this pattern.

Materials

cardboard and drawing compass

colored pencils or markers

white paper

scissors and clear tape

5 round toothpicks

Process Skills

Making and **using a model** of how the planets move can help you form a mental picture of the planets' orbits.

What to Do

1 Draw a circle in the center of the cardboard to represent the Sun. Draw 5 circles around the Sun and make each circle a different color.

Each circle represents an orbit. Actual orbits are not quite circular.

Earth Months Needed for One Orbit

Mercury	3
Venus	7
Earth	12
Mars	23
Jupiter	142

2 Mark 3 evenly spaced dots on the smallest circle. It takes Mercury 3 months to orbit the Sun. In 1 month, it would make $\frac{1}{3}$ of an orbit and would be at the first dot.

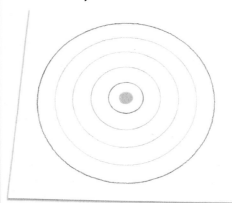

Always place the first dot at the "top" position.

3 Use the data in the chart to complete your **model**. Repeat step 2 for Venus, Earth, and Mars. To save time, for Jupiter simply mark 35 dots in the first $\frac{1}{4}$ of its orbit.

4 Make a planet flag for each orbit. Cut a triangle from white paper. Color it the same color as the planet's orbit. Then tape the triangle to a toothpick.

5 Place each planet flag at the "top" dot of its orbit.

6 Start the planets on their orbits. Move each flag, in turn, counterclockwise by 1 dot. This shows how far each planet would move in 1 month.

7 Move each flag to the second dot in its orbit. Continue to move each flag along dot-by-dot until it has traveled to 12 dots. Record your **observations** in the chart.

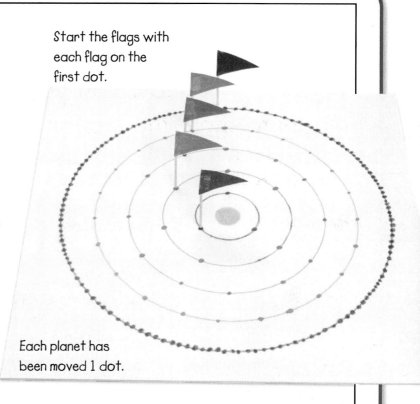

Start the flags with each flag on the first dot.

Each planet has been moved 1 dot.

Movement of Planets in 12 Months

Planets that made more than 1 orbit	
Planet that made exacly 1 orbit	
Planets that made less than 1 orbit	

Explain Your Results

1. Name two ways the orbits in this **model** are like the orbits of actual planets. Name two ways they are different.
2. Neptune takes 1,964 months to orbit the Sun. How fast do you think it appears to move? Why do you think Neptune was discovered later than the inner planets?

Go Further

Extend your model to include all the major planets. Describe the benefits and drawbacks to extending your model.

Math in Science

Scientific Notation and the Planets

You have learned that scientists often use astronomical units to express distances in the solar system. Astronomical units are helpful for comparing distance in space. An AU is the average distance of Earth from the Sun, about 149.6 million kilometers. Written in standard form, the number of kilometers is 149,600,000.

Scientific notation is often used to express very small or very large numbers, like the one above. Scientific notation shows a number as the product of two factors. The first factor is always a number greater than 1 but less than 10. The second factor is always a power of 10.

$$149,600,000 = 1.496 \times 10^8$$

If you multiply 1.496×10^8, the decimal point would move 8 places to the right, so the product would be 149,600,000.

AVERAGE DISTANCE FROM THE SUN							
INNER PLANETS				OUTER PLANETS			
Mercury	Venus	Earth	Mars	Jupiter	Saturn	Uranus	Neptune
0.39 AU	0.72 AU	1 AU	1.52 AU	5.2 AU	9.58 AU	19.20 AU	30.05 AU

What is Venus's average distance from the Sun in kilometers? The table tells us that Venus is 0.72 AU from the Sun.

$$1 \text{ AU} = 1.496 \times 10^8 \text{ km}$$

$$0.72 \times 1.496 \times 10^8 = 1.07712 \times 10^8$$
$$= 107,712,000$$

Multiplying a decimal number by 10^8 will move the decimal point 8 places to the right.

Venus's average distance from the Sun is 107,712,000 km or rounded to the nearest million as 108,000,000 km.

e Tools Take It to the Net
pearsonsuccessnet.com

Use the chart on page 572 to answer the questions. For Questions 1–4, give each answer in scientific notation and in standard form.

Find each planet's average distance from the Sun in kilometers.

1. Mercury

2. Jupiter

3. Saturn

4. Which planets are more than 10 times as far from the Sun as Earth is? Find the average distance of each of these planets from the Sun, in kilometers.

5. What is the average distance of Mars from the Sun, in astronomical units? Use this data to write a statement comparing the distance of Mars from the Sun with the distance of Earth from the Sun.

Lab zone **Take-Home Activity**

Use library resources to find data about five stars. Find the distance of each star from Earth in light years. Put the data for five stars in a chart. Then write each distance in kilometers using scientific notation.

Use Vocabulary

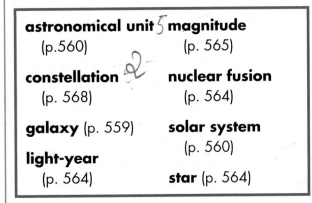

astronomical unit (p.560)	**magnitude** (p. 565)
constellation (p. 568)	**nuclear fusion** (p. 564)
galaxy (p. 559)	**solar system** (p. 560)
light-year (p. 564)	**star** (p. 564)

Use the vocabulary term from above that best completes each sentence.

1. The process that powers stars is ____.

2. Apparent ____ is how bright a star seems to us.

3. The ____ is a useful unit of distance in deep space.

4. Orion is a ____ in the night sky.

5. Distance in the solar system often is measured in a unit called the _____.

6. The ____ includes the Sun, planets, and moons.

7. Our Sun is in the ____ known as the Milky Way.

8. A ____ is a huge ball of glowing gases.

Explain Concepts

9. How is star color related to star temperature and its life cycle?

10. Describe the Milky Way Galaxy and Earth's place in it.

11. Explain the process that causes an aging star to swell up into a red giant.

Process Skills

12. **Classify** Suppose you make a chart of the stars in a large constellation. You want to group stars within subsections of the chart. How might you group them in a scientifically meaningful way?

13. **Predict** Suppose a supergiant star collapses. What probably will happen next? Give reasons for your prediction.

14. **Model** Make a scale model of the solar system, using a large sheet of butcher paper or poster paper. Use the distance units from the chart on page 562 to set up your scale. Careful! To position the outer planets on your paper, you will need to space the inner planets closely. Show your scale in a key.

 Draw Conclusions

15. Make a graphic organizer like the one shown below. Use factors from the chapter to draw a conclusion about which star—A or B—is closer to Earth. Star A and Star B have the same apparent magnitude in the night sky. The absolute magnitude of Star B is greater than Star A.

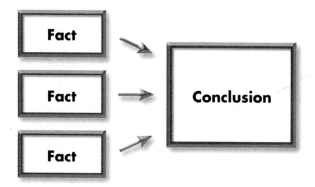

Test Prep

Choose the letter that best completes the statement or answers the question.

16. An astronomical unit (AU) is defined as
- Ⓐ the distance between the Sun and Mercury.
- Ⓑ the distance between the Earth and its moon.
- Ⓒ the distance light travels in one minute.
- Ⓓ the distance between the Sun and the Earth.

17. Our Sun is classified as a
- Ⓕ nova.
- Ⓖ mid-sized star.
- Ⓗ white dwarf.
- Ⓘ red giant.

18. Which statement about constellations is true?
- Ⓐ Stars move so fast that constellations march across the night sky.
- Ⓑ Every constellation represents a particular galaxy.
- Ⓒ People in the Northern and the Southern Hemispheres see the very same constellations.
- Ⓓ The apparent movement of constellations is the result of Earth's movements.

19. Explain why the answer you chose for Question 18 is best. For each of the answers you did not choose, give a reason why it is not the best choice.

20. Writing in Science **Expository**
An analogy compares unlike things to explain a relationship. Think of an analogy to explain the difference between apparent and absolute magnitude of stars. For example, you could use the analogy of viewing skyscrapers in a city skyline. Buildings close to you would look bigger than they really are, while very tall buildings at some distance would look smaller. Write your explanation in a paragraph or two.

PTOLEMY

Ptolemy was a Greek astronomer who lived in Egypt in the second century A.D. He wondered why the planets moved as they did. Each planet seemed to move eastward against the star-studded sky. But sometimes the planet backed up and moved westward for a few months. Then it would continue moving east again.

Ptolemy developed a model to explain the planets' motion. His model included the accepted idea that Earth was the center of the universe. Earth didn't move. The Moon, Sun, and planets revolved around Earth, each in its own orbit. Beyond the farthest planet were all the stars, also revolving around Earth.

Ptolemy said that each planet made smaller orbits as it traveled along its larger orbit. You can show this motion by making small curlicues, or spirals, with your finger as you move your hand through the air. Ptolemy's model explained almost all of the motions in the sky. The Sun and Moon moved across the sky because they were revolving around Earth. This idea made so much sense that it went unchallenged for 13 centuries.

Today we know that the planets move around the Sun, and they don't move in a curlicue fashion. But Ptolemy was a good scientist—he used knowledge available at the time to develop a model that explained his observations. He also gave future scientists something to build upon.

Ptolemy's model

Take-Home Activity

Make a drawing that compares Ptolemy's model of the solar system to the current model of the solar system.

Chapter 21
Technology

online
Student Edition
pearsonsuccessnet.com

You Will Discover

- what robots are.
- how robots help humans every day.
- what nanotechnology is.
- the advantages and disadvantages of nanotechnology.

How can robots help us now and in the future?

robot

robotics

autonomous robot

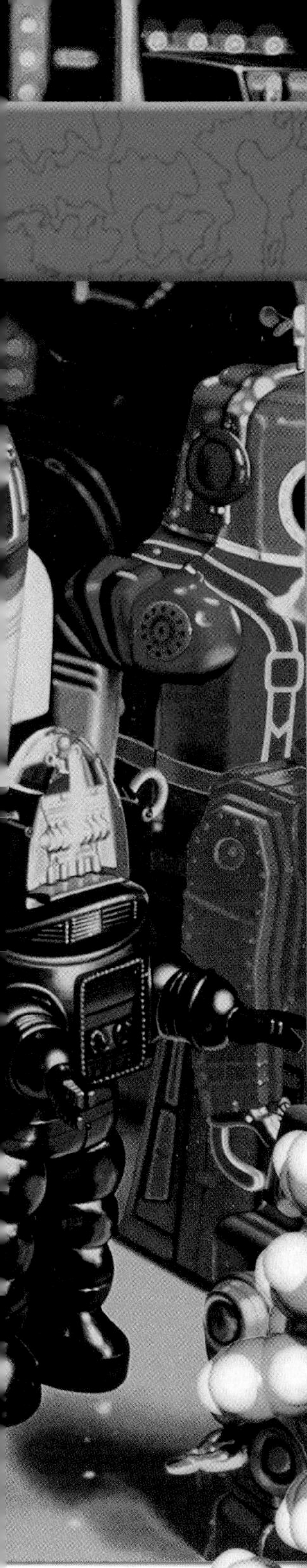

Chapter 21 Vocabulary

industrial robot

nanotechnology

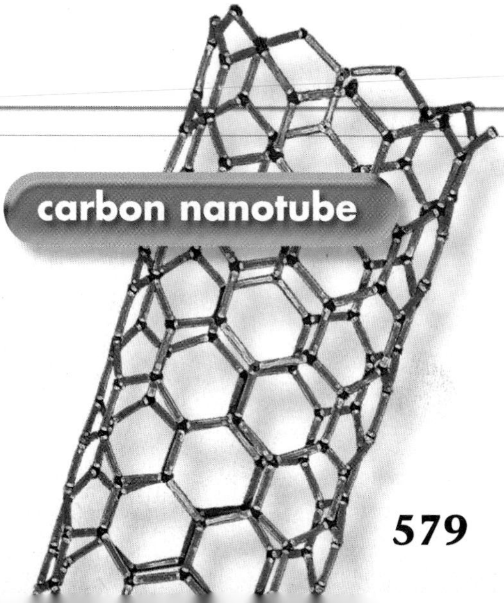

carbon nanotube

579

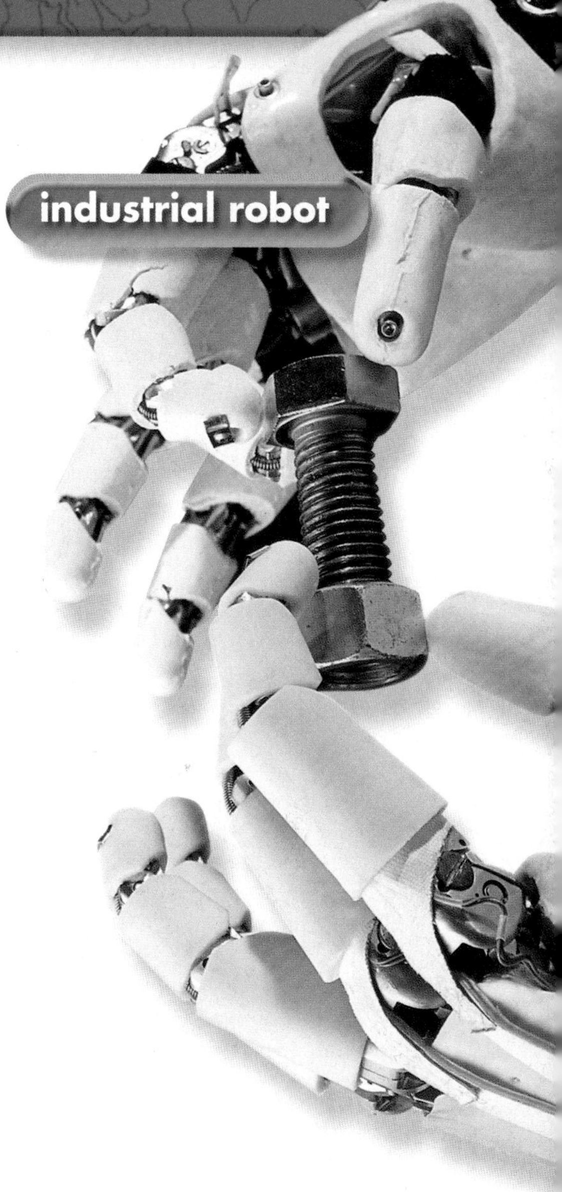

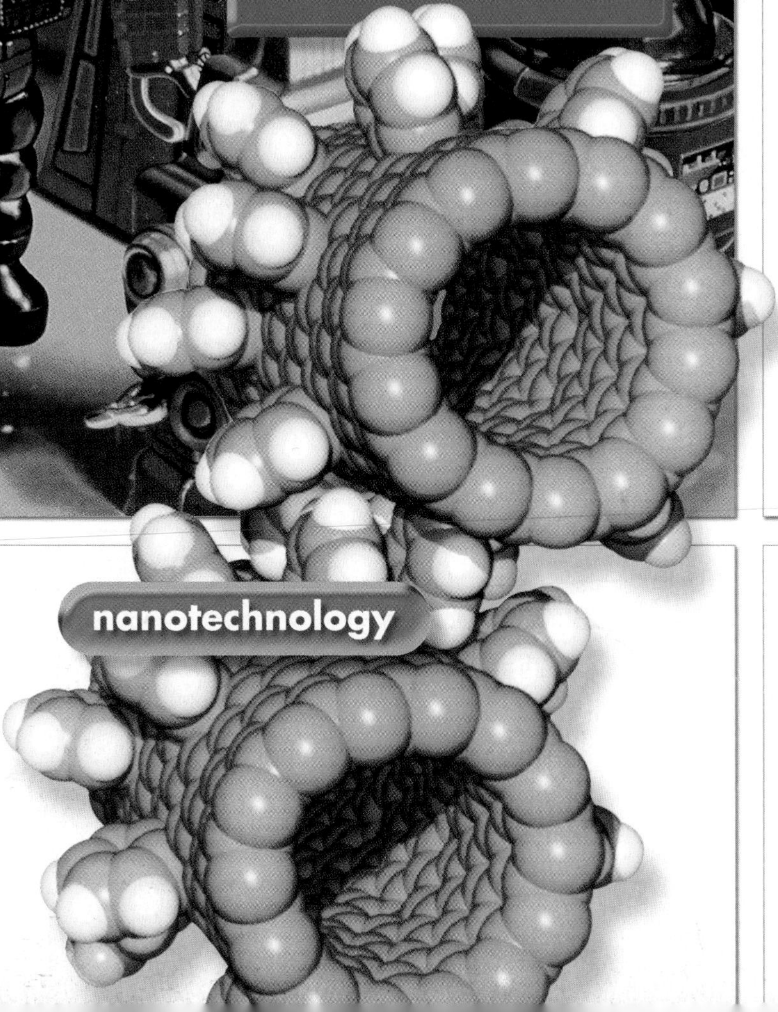

Explore How can a robot tie a shoe?

Few robots are designed to do simple human tasks. Tying a shoe might be a difficult task for a robot. You can learn why as you try this activity.

Materials

shoe with laces

timer

2 plastic bags

2 clothespins

4 craft sticks

masking tape

What to Do

1 Record how long it takes you to tie a shoe.

2 Repeat but limit the feedback and information you get from your senses. Allow only 5 minutes for each try.
- Tie a shoe with your eyes closed.
- Tie a shoe with plastic bags on your hands.

3 Use a clothespin as a **model** of a robot's hand. Tie a shoe using clothespins for hands. Record your time.

4 Act as a model of a robot with few moving joints. Tape craft sticks to your thumbs and forefingers. Tie a shoe. Record your time.

Process Skills

Using a model can help you understand why some activities might be difficult for a robot.

Explain Your Results

1. What could you do that your **model** of a robot could not do?

2. Write a main idea statement that tells what you learned in this activity. Give details to support your statement.

How to Read Science

Main Idea and Details

Sometimes the **main idea** of a reading passage is not directly stated. In those cases, the author gives **details** or key ideas that lead you to the main idea. You must put these ideas together and infer the main idea.

- Identify important details and key ideas.

- Put the ideas together into a general statement about the ideas.

Science Article

Robot Revolution

Robots may someday be the only workers in a factory. Robots can work 24 hours a day without tiring. They can do tedious jobs that would bore the humans they replace. In places that might be dangerous for humans, robots can work without being harmed. Robots can go places that humans can't, including distant planets.

Apply It!

Make a graphic organizer like this one. List the **details** from the article. Then write a sentence that **communicates** the **main idea.**

Main idea

Details	Details	Details

You Are There!

You stare in amazement. You had no idea that there could be so many different robots! Some are so tiny that they can fit in the palm of your hand. Others are tall—almost as tall as you are. Yet all look like humans in some way. Each has its own style of legs, arms, and head. Do all robots look like this?

AudioText

Lesson 1

What is a robot?

A robot is a machine that is able to get information from its surroundings and do physical work. Today robots are used in industry and medicine, for exploration, and at home. Robots have become more complex over time.

Robots and Robotics

You may immediately recognize the figures on these pages as robots, but what about the thousands of other robots that work for us? Many look far different than these robots. Often they do jobs too dangerous, repetitive, boring, or delicate for humans to do. There are robots working 24 hours, 7 days a week to assemble automobile body panels and then weld them together. Other robots have a real sweet job—they draw chocolate stripes on cookies. In some hospitals, robot hands help human doctors complete surgeries too precise and sensitive for human hands alone. And what about robots working for homemakers? Homemakers can use a robot to clean floors or mow lawns.

The wide variety of robots makes forming an exact definition difficult. However, most scientists agree that a **robot** is a machine that is able to get information from its surroundings and do physical work, such as moving or manipulating objects. Often when people talk about robots, they also mention **robotics,** the technology dealing with the design, construction, and operation of robots.

1. ✔**Checkpoint** What two requirements must a machine meet to be a robot?
2. 🔵 **Main Idea and Details** Give three details to support this statement: Robots can help humans perform tasks more efficiently.

Robot Development

Say the word *robot,* and most people think of the robots they have seen on television or in movies. For decades, these imaginary machines shaped our ideas about what robots should look like and what they should be able to do. Long before we had the technology needed to build robots, the fictional robots inspired us. They produced interest in designing and building real robots, pushing us to see how far our imagination and creativity could take us.

Although the term *robot* is less than 100 years old, people have dreamed about robots and how they might be used for thousands of years. In ancient Greece, Aristotle thought that one day machines might do work for humans by obeying directions. Two thousand years later, we find robots working in nearly every aspect of our lives.

In addition to our imagination, robot development has depended in large part on the development of other technologies, such as computers. As computer systems became more capable, computers smaller, sensors more sensitive, and computer programs more precise, robots have become able to do more complex tasks.

Robot designers work to increase a robot's ability to solve problems. The goal is to design a robot that can survey its environment, analyze data, make a judgment, and then take appropriate action. In turn, improved robot design opens new technologies. For example, a robot capable of moving a mere 0.0000001 centimeter at a time will allow us to manufacture a single molecule, one atom at a time.

1921
Czech playwright Karel Capek introduces the word *robot* in the play *Rossum's Universal Robots. Robot* comes from the Czech word *robota,* meaning "drudgery."

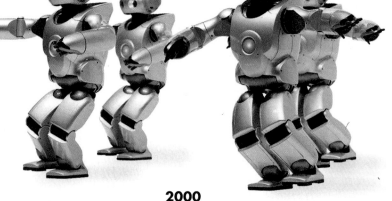

2000
The latest robots that resemble humans appear. They can perform tasks much like humans, including climbing stairs.

1. ✓**Checkpoint** Compare and contrast Capek's 1921 robot shown on the timeline with the 2000 robots.

2. **Art** in Science Draw a robot you would like to have in your home. Show what task you would want it to do. Then trade drawings with a partner. Evaluate your partner's robot design.

584

~270 B.C.
Greek engineer Ctesibus builds organs and water clocks with movable figures.

1739
Jacques Vaucanson, a French engineer, creates an automatic duck that can drink, eat, and perform other functions.

1801
Joseph-Marie Jacquard, a French weaver, invents a method of controlling looms using cards with holes punched in them.

1939–1940
A mechanical man and dog appear at the New York World's Fair.

1951
The first remote-operated, jointed arm handles radioactive materials for the Atomic Energy Commission.

1961
The first industrial robot begins work in an automobile factory.

1970
Shakey, the first mobile robot with vision, figures out how to move around obstacles.

1985
The first robot-aided surgery is performed.

1994
Dante II, a six-legged walking robot, explores Mt. Spurr volcano in Alaska and collects samples of volcanic gases.

2001
The *Space Station Remote Manipulator System (SSRMS)* begins to complete assembly of the International Space Station.

1997
NASA's *Pathfinder* lands on Mars and sends the *Sojourner* rover to explore the Martian landscape.

2002
Researchers develop a robotic assistant for the elderly.

2004
NASA Mars rovers *Spirit* and *Opportunity* land on the red planet.

Robots in Industry

Nearly 90 percent of today's robots work in factories, more than half of them in automobile factories. Robot arms weld, paint, iron, assemble, pack, inspect, and test manufactured parts. An automatically controlled **industrial robot** can handle several products or items at a time and can be programmed to complete several different tasks.

The most common kind of industrial robot is the robotic arm, which is controlled by a computer. Many industrial robots have "joints" that are very similar to a human arm. You can see in the picture below that a robotic arm has a shoulder, elbow and forearm. A human arm can pivot in seven different ways. This kind of robotic arm can pivot in six different ways.

Different parts attached to the robotic arm enable it to perform specific tasks. For example, the robotic hands shown to the right can be attached to a robotic arm to turn a screwdriver or a bolt. Other attachments might be drills, spray painters, or welding tools.

A robot assigned to weld has three arm movements and three wrist movements. It also has position sensors, making it possible to "teach" the robot how to weld. A human operator leads the robot through the motions necessary to weld a specific location. Sensors on the robot's joints record the twists, turns, and other motions. The robot's computer saves the information, allowing the robot arm to repeat the motions exactly.

Similar directions guide robots to place silicon chips onto circuit boards and then solder them. In fact, the same type of information can direct a robot to pick up a delicate muffin from one moving conveyor belt, turn the muffin in the right direction, and finally place it in a box on a second moving conveyor belt.

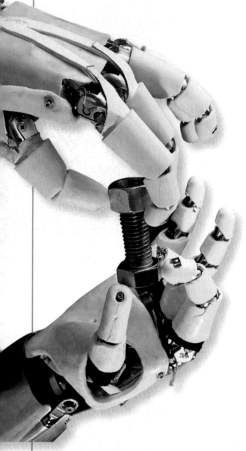

The elbow of this welding robot allows the welding torch to be handled in almost the same ways in which a human would handle it.

This robotic hand is made of metal pieces that are moved by tiny motors.

A Mechanical Arm

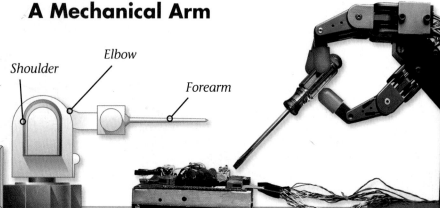

Shoulder

Elbow

Forearm

Base

Exploring with Robots

While industry leads the way in robot use, many robots work in exploration. Robots that are used to explore can be placed into one of two categories. One category includes the remotely operated vehicle (ROV or rover). NASA's Mars missions have used rovers *Sojourner*, *Spirit*, and *Opportunity*. A human operator decided in which direction and how fast each rover should move. The operator then sent signals to the rover describing each move to make.

Rovers search sewers, pipes, collapsed mineshafts, and heating and cooling ducts—places humans cannot go. Rovers investigate and defuse bombs and examine areas contaminated by radioactive materials—jobs far too dangerous for humans.

The second category of exploring robot is an **autonomous robot.** This type of robot acts without direct supervision. It can "decide" whether to travel over a rock or around it. One autonomous robot being developed at NASA is the Personal Satellite Assistant, or PSA. The robot is about the size of a softball. It has sensors for monitoring conditions in a spacecraft, such as the amounts of oxygen, carbon dioxide, and other gases. It can monitor the amount of bacterial growth in the spacecraft too. Sensors also keep tabs on air temperature and air pressure. The camera can be used to video conference. Navigation sensors and other parts enable the robot to move by itself throughout the spacecraft. According to NASA, the robots will function as another set of "eyes, ears, and nose" for the crew.

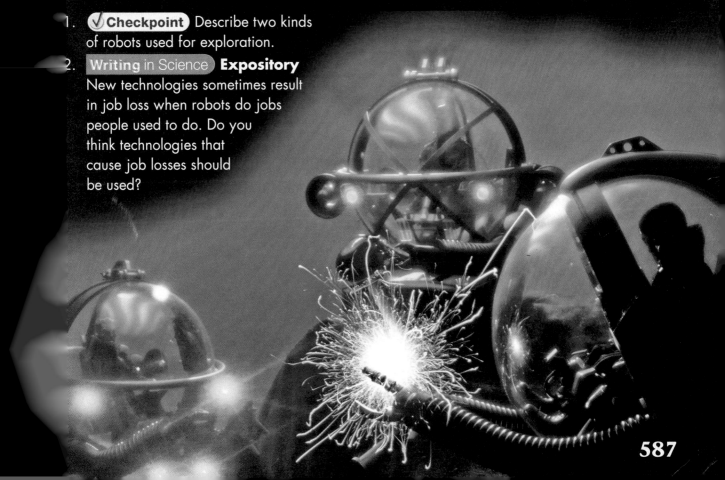

NASA's Personal Satellite Assistant, or PSA

1. ✓ **Checkpoint** Describe two kinds of robots used for exploration.

2. Writing in Science **Expository** New technologies sometimes result in job loss when robots do jobs people used to do. Do you think technologies that cause job losses should be used?

587

Robots in Medicine

Sending robots to explore space and other locations led to another robot function—using them to routinely travel between locations. Hospitals employ these messenger robots to carry supplies, equipment, and medications from one location to another.

Messenger robots are not the only robots in a hospital. Robotic surgeons—robotic hands moved by a human surgeon's hands—are now being used in hospitals around the world. Doctors can control the robots by mechanical devices or voice activation. In many operations, human hands cannot be as precise as robotic hands. Robot-assisted surgery results in smaller scars, less pain, and shorter hospital stays.

In one robotic system, the doctor sits at a control center, which is a few feet from the patient. A camera placed inside the patient sends 3-D images of the operation area and the surgical instruments to the doctor at the control center. The doctor controls the surgical instruments by moving the controls in much the same way a person moves a joystick.

In another use, robots act as patients for medical students. The robots are programmed to show a set of symptoms and then respond to treatment, including surgery and medication. Some robots are programmed to "die" if they receive improper or inadequate treatment.

Robots are tackling another problem—helping doctors check on their patients when they can't actually visit them. The robot contains a video screen on which the doctor's face appears. A video camera acts as the robot's eyes and ears. Doctors can interact with their patients via the robot using a live computer-video hookup. The goal is not to replace human doctors but instead to enable doctors to interact with their patients no matter where the doctor is.

The hands of the surgical robot are capable of more precise movements than a human surgeon's hands.

Human hands guide the hands of a robotic surgical system during precision surgery.

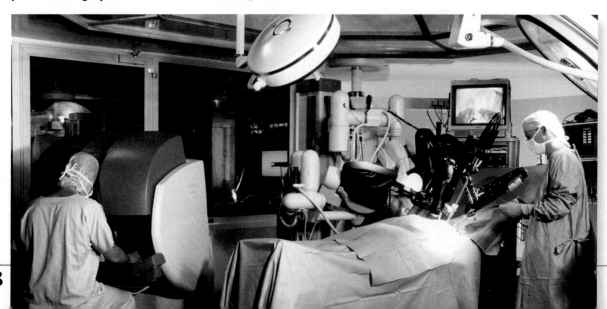

588

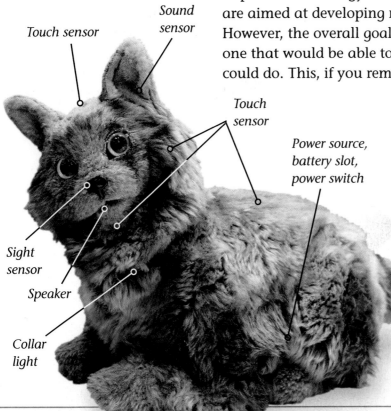

Game robots, like rovers, are remote controlled. However, information gained while working and playing with these robots can help develop completely robotic players for other games or sports.

Robots at Home

You don't have to visit a factory, Mars, or a hospital to see robots in action. In your own home, you can watch popular television programs in which home-built robots challenge one another in an arena. Toy makers offer robot kits that encourage the construction of dozens of interesting robot creations. You may be familiar with the cute, furry robots and the robotic dogs that are made just for entertainment. Given the success of these robots, researchers are working on making a doll-like robot able to perform dozens of movements on its own.

Some companies want to develop a robot that will act as a household companion. This robot would be able to move about the home easily. It would be available to help with tasks, such as giving medication and taking out the garbage. Perhaps such a robot could be programmed to provide care for an elderly or less able person. It could monitor the person's time spent in the kitchen or bathroom, watching television or napping. If any actions seemed out of the ordinary, the robot would dial an emergency number and alert an attendant.

It's clear that robots are here to stay. Each new robot generation will perform new and more complex tasks with less hands-on direction. Large universities, research corporations, and government agencies will rely on improved technology to build these robots. Today's efforts are aimed at developing robots to perform specific tasks. However, the overall goal is to make a universal robot—one that would be able to do almost everything a human could do. This, if you remember, was Aristotle's prediction.

A Robotic Pet

Sound sensor

Touch sensor

Touch sensor

Power source, battery slot, power switch

Sight sensor

Speaker

Collar light

✔ Lesson Checkpoint

1. What kinds of jobs do robots do that humans cannot do?

2. 🎯 **Main Idea and Details** Explain how an autonomous robot solves problems.

3. **Writing** in Science
Expository What are some human needs that you think robots could not provide solutions for? Explain your answers in a paragraph.

Lesson 2

What is nanotechnology?

Nanotechnology deals with materials and machines that are measured in nanometers.

Very, Very Small Technology

People dreamed of robots and what they might do long before they were actually developed. Sometimes scientists accidentally stumble into technologies that offer possibilities beyond our wildest dreams. One of the newest technologies, nanotechnology, seems to offer just such possibilities. **Nanotechnology** is the very small-scale technology that deals with materials and processes on a scale best measured in nanometers. A nanometer is a measure of length that is one billionth the length of a meter.

Atom-by-Atom

Researchers claim that nanotechnology will allow us to build the materials we want, atom by atom. They hope to do this by lining atoms up in a specific arrangement until they form the desired shape. Does handling atoms one at a time sound too fantastic? As you can see in the picture below, scientists have already done it!

In addition to getting each atom in the correct location, this new technology should allow scientists to make almost any material—as long as its construction follows the laws of physics.

Two challenges must be met before nanotechnology succeeds. First, scientists have to find a way to move an atom so that it is placed precisely. Scientists know that robots can be precise, so they might look to a nano-sized robotic arm to pick and position each atom.

The second challenge scientists face is finding a way to pick and position billions and billions of atoms. If they are building something atom-by-atom, they will need a lot of robotic arms to put together nano-sized parts into larger parts. More robots will put together the larger parts into still larger parts, eventually forming a product we can actually see.

Scientists hope to build nanogears such as this.

In 1990, researchers moved 35 xenon atoms, one at a time, arranging them to form letters.

590

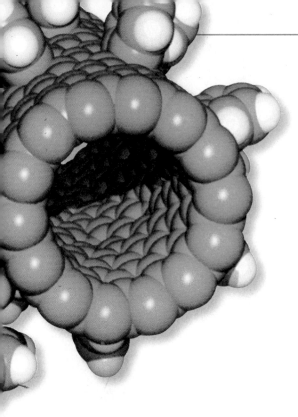

Nanotechnology Applications

Scientists have not yet been able to build many things atom-by-atom. But they have had success changing some existing materials. Researchers have found that they can change certain molecules, called nanopores, to meet their needs. For example, nanopore material can act like a sponge, absorbing mercury or lead from polluted water supplies.

Nanoshells may be the future's best way to fight cancer. Nanoshells are about 120 nanometers in size—that's 1,500 times smaller than a human hair. The shells are injected into a tumor. Then the tumor area is heated. Temperatures inside the tumor become high enough to damage the cancer cells. But they don't damage normal cells in the same area. Nanoshells may be used to deliver cancer drugs to specific parts of the body. Many cancer drugs are harmful not to just cancer cells, but to normal body cells as well. Using nanoshells would limit the body's exposure to harmful substances in the drugs.

Another medical application involves nanocrystals that give off specific colors of light. Researchers can tag chromosomes with these crystals. When the patient's blood sample is exposed to a specific type of light, the nanocrystals glow in response. Researchers can use results from the process to get information about a person's susceptibility to lung cancer.

Scientists are developing procedures to use nanopores to sequence DNA.

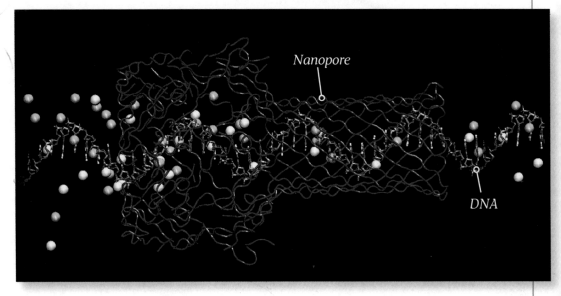

Nanopore

DNA

1. ✓**Checkpoint** What is nanotechnology?
2. Describe two applications of nanotechnology.

Carbon Nanotubes

For hundreds of years people have known that the element carbon exists in three different forms—diamond, graphite, and "amorphous" carbon. In 1985, scientists discovered a fourth form of carbon with individual molecules that are made up of 60 carbon atoms. These molecules are called buckyballs. Study the pictures below to compare the arrangement of atoms in these forms of carbon.

Then in 1991, researchers found a fifth type of carbon molecule. In this molecule, carbon atoms in six-sided rings arrange themselves in the shape of a tube. The size of the molecule is about a nanometer. This form of carbon is called a **carbon nanotube.**

The properties of diamonds are very different from those of graphite. Recent studies show that carbon nanotubes have properties that are different from both graphite or diamond. For example, carbon nanotubes are exceptionally stiff and can be one hundred times tougher than steel at one-sixth the weight.

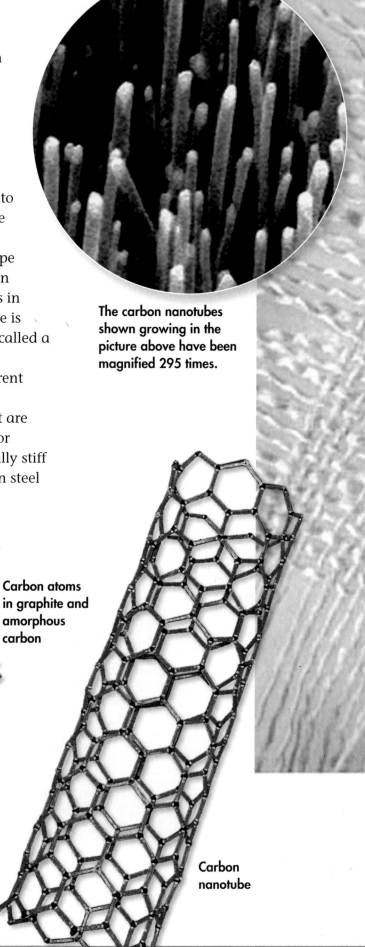

The carbon nanotubes shown growing in the picture above have been magnified 295 times.

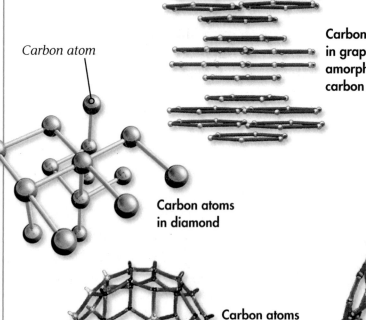

Carbon atom

Carbon atoms in graphite and amorphous carbon

Carbon atoms in diamond

Carbon atoms in a buckyball

Carbon nanotube

The carbon nanotube's electrical properties are astounding. Merely twisting a carbon nanotube can change it from an electrical conductor as efficient as copper to a less efficient conductor similar to silicon. In addition, carbon nanotubes conduct heat better than silicon. Silicon is used in making computers and transistors for electronic equipment. These properties of nanotubes lead researchers to think that it may be possible to produce ultra-small transistors and other electrical devices. These devices might be ten times smaller than those in use today.

Benefits and Risks

At this time, nanotechnology promises enormous benefits—from custom-designed materials to ultra-small computers. But what are the risks? As scientists take advantage of custom molecules, they will need to find out whether the molecules will harm the environment. Ultra-small computers will help design better microphones, cameras, and tracking devices. But people will have to decide how to use these inventions for their own security without giving up privacy. Also, society will need to decide how to use nanotechnology to bring better health care, agricultural practices, and manufacturing knowledge to our own country and others.

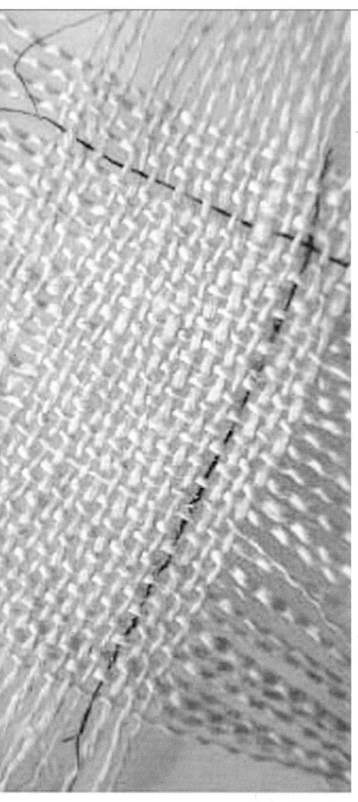

Fibers of carbon nanotubes (black in swatch above) can be woven into fabrics that can store energy, receive radio signals, or act as sensors. These fabrics can track the body movements of athletes, dancers, and soldiers who wear them.

✓ Lesson Checkpoint

1. Name two risks associated with nanotechnology.
2. **Math** in Science What is the size of a nanometer in terms of a centimeter?
3. **Writing** in Science **Persuasive** Write a letter to the editor of your local newspaper explaining whether you think the public ought to have a say in how nanotechnology is used. Explain why.

Investigate How can you make a model of a robot arm?

People who design and build robots to reach, lift, and hold items often use the human arm as a model.

Materials

3 posterboard strips

metric ruler

hole punch

2 fasteners

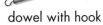

dowel with hook

3 large paper clips

clay and string

rubber band

Process Skills

Making a model of a robot arm can help you form a mental picture of how robots are constructed.

What to Do

1 Use a hole punch to make a hole 2 cm from the ends of each posterboard strip.

2 Use 2 fasteners to join the three strips together.

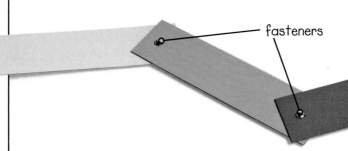

fasteners

3 Put the hook that is on the dowel through the hole in one end of your **model** of a robot arm.

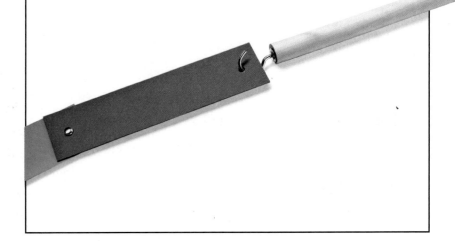

4 Bend a large paper clip into an *S* shape. As shown, put the top part of the *S* into the hole with the hook.

5 Make a clay ball and stick a paper clip into it. Put it on the table along with another paper clip, a rubber band, and a string.

6 Try to pick up each object using the robot arm. Record the number of tries needed to pick up each object.

Stop after ten tries. Record the number of tries you make.

Move the dowel to make the hook move.

This part should not move.

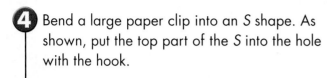

Object	Number of Tries
Clay ball with paper clip	
Paper clip	
Rubber band	
String	

Explain Your Results

1. Which objects were easier to pick up using the robot arm? Why?

2. Name two ways in which this **model** is not like a real robot arm.

Go Further

How could you modify your robot arm so that it could pick up an empty plastic cup? Decide what changes you would make and devise a plan for testing your improved robot arm.

The Mathematics of NANOTECHNOLOGY

You have been learning about nanotechnology, which involves technological developments on a very small scale. The prefix *nano* means "one billionth." So, a nanometer (nm) equals one billionth of a meter, or one millionth of a millimeter. Look at the size of 1 millimeter on a metric ruler. A nanometer is one millionth of that size!

The chart below gives the exponential form of very small numbers.

Word Form	Standard Form	Exponential Form
1 thousandth	0.001	10^{-3}
1 ten-thousandth	0.0001	10^{-4}
1 hundred-thousandth	0.00001	10^{-5}
1 millionth	0.000001	10^{-6}
1 ten-millionth	0.0000001	10^{-7}
1 hundred-millionth	0.00000001	10^{-8}
1 billionth	0.000000001	10^{-9}

Here's another way to think of the size of a nanometer. A millimeter is one thousandth of a meter (0.001 m); a micrometer is one thousandth of a millimeter (0.001 mm) and a nanometer is one thousandth of a micrometer (0.001 μm).

$$0.001 \times 0.001 \times 0.001 = 0.000000001$$
$$10^{-3} \times 10^{-3} \times 10^{-3} = 10^{-9}$$

In nanotechnology, it is important that tiny robots, called nanorobots, be able to make copies of themselves repeatedly. This is called exponential assembly.

@ Tools Take It to the Net pearsonsuccessnet.com

For example, in one process starting with one nanorobot, each nanorobot makes three copies of itself in a day and then stops working. How many nanorobots will be made on Day 4?

The number of nanorobots will increase by powers of 3.

Day	0	1	2	3	4
Power of 3	3^0	3^1	3^2	3^3	3^4
Number	1	3	9	27	81

Use what you've learned to answer each question.

1. You have read that a nanoshell is about 120 nanometers in size. Write this measure in meters, using standard form. Show how you found your answer.

2. A process starts with one nanorobot that makes three copies of itself in a day and then stops working. How many nanorobots will be made on Day 8? Day 10? Copy and extend the chart above to help you find your answer.

3. In the first step of one assembly process, a great number of very small parts are assembled into larger parts. Then these parts are assembled into larger parts, and the step is repeated over and over. If the size of the parts doubles for each step, how many steps would be needed to go from a part that is 1 nanometer in size to a part that is at least 1 millimeter in size? Use a calculator or copy and continue the chart until you find the answer. (Remember: 1 mm = 1,000,000 nm)

Step	0	1	2	3	4
Power of 2	2^0	2^1	2^2	2^3	2^4
Number	1	2	4	8	16

Lab zone Take-Home Activity

Use library resources to find more information about nanotechnology. Make a poster or write a story about the possible benefits of nanotechnology in the future. Use your imagination together with the facts you have found.

Use Vocabulary

autonomous robot (p. 587)	**nanotechnology** (p. 590)
carbon nanotube (p. 592)	**robot** (p. 583)
	robotics (p. 583)
industrial robot (p. 586)	

Use the term from the list above that best completes each sentence.

1. The technology dealing with robots is called _____.

2. A machine able to get information from its surroundings and do physical work is a(n) _____.

3. A robot that can act without direct human supervision is a(n) _____.

4. If a robot is automatically controlled, can handle several products at once, and can be programmed to complete several different tasks, it is a(n) _____.

5. The technology that deals with the materials and processes in terms of one-billionth of a meter is _____.

6. The most recently discovered form of carbon with properties far different from those of diamonds and graphite is a(n) _____.

Explaining Concepts

7. Explain why robots are better at some jobs than human workers are.

8. What must a true robot be able to do without human direction?

9. What problems must scientists solve before nanotechnology can provide the benefits it seems to promise?

10. Explain how technology such as computers has influenced the development of robots.

11. Describe the structure of a buckyball.

12. How are Mars rovers *Spirit* and *Opportunity* different from autonomous robots?

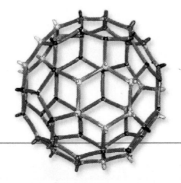

13. Forming Questions and Hypotheses
What question do you have about robots that could be answered by doing an experiment? Write your question as a statement that can be tested by an experiment.

14. Infer Why might a surgeon suggest that the operation you need is best performed with the aid of a robot?

Main Idea and Details

15. Make a graphic organizer like the one shown below. Fill in details about the main idea.

Robots can perform human tasks.

Detail	Detail	Detail

 Test Prep

Choose the letter that best completes the statement or answers the question.

16. Today most robots work in
Ⓐ hospitals.
Ⓑ space exploration.
Ⓒ industry.
Ⓓ home entertainment.

17. Carbon atoms arranged in six-sided rings to form tubes are
Ⓕ buckyballs.
Ⓖ graphite.
Ⓗ carbon nanotubes.
Ⓘ diamonds.

18. Which is a property of carbon nanotubes that might make it possible for them to replace silicon in electronic equipment?
Ⓐ They're poor conductors of heat.
Ⓑ They glow when hit by a light.
Ⓒ They can change from an efficient electrical conductor to a poor one.
Ⓓ They can assemble themselves.

19. Explain why the answer you chose for Question 17 is best. For each of the answers you did not choose, give a reason why it is not the best choice.

20. Writing in Science **Narrative**
Write a short story in which a robot is a hero because it saved people from one of the dangers of nanotechnology.

David Pieri
VOLCANOLOGIST

How could a love for geology take you to the plains of Mars? And from Mars, how do you arrive on the slopes of a Hawaiian volcano? Ask David Pieri.

Pieri's first job after studying geology in college was with NASA. He joined the Jet Propulsion Laboratory in California in 1979. One of his projects was working with the robots that examined the surface of planet Mars. With other scientists, Pieri studied the images of Mars that the robots took. He used his experience with Earth's geology to try to understand how Mars came to look as it does.

More recently, Pieri has concentrated on volcanoes. He has studied volcanoes from Europe to Hawaii. His experiments concentrate on explosive volcanic eruptions in the northern region of the Pacific Ocean. Pieri flies robot airplanes around the volcanoes to gather information about the volcanoes. Because the clouds of ash from a volcano are very dangerous for an airplane, Pieri's team flies robot aircraft through the ash that volcanoes eject.

Ash from volcanoes also can be dangerous for commercial airplanes. Pieri's project goal is to learn how ash spreads from an exploding volcano so that flying can be made safer for everyone.

Lab zone Take-Home Activity

Design a robot to study an erupting volcano. What would a robot be used to study? Why would scientists need this information?

Unit D Test Talk

Write Your Answer

Short-answer test questions require you to write your answer. Write down your thoughts in complete sentences.

Earth's axis is tilted compared to its orbit around the Sun. As Earth **revolves,** sometimes its Northern Hemisphere leans toward the Sun. Other times, it is leaning away from the Sun. This causes the seasons of the year.

When the North Pole is leaning toward the Sun, it is summer in the Northern Hemisphere. Summer is warmer than other seasons, because sunlight hits the Northern Hemisphere more directly at that time. At the same time, the South Pole is tilted away from the Sun, so sunlight there hits Earth at a greater angle. Temperatures are colder, and the southern Hemisphere is having winter.

At times as Earth moves around the Sun, it is tilted neither toward or away from the Sun. Instead it is tilted in the direction it is traveling. We know these seasons as spring and fall.

Regions of Earth near the **equator** do not have these seasonal differences. The regions receive direct sunlight all year.

When answering test questions, write down what you know. Do not leave an answer blank. Even if you do not know the entire answer, you might earn some points for what you write down.

Use What You Know

1. How does the angle at which sunlight hits Earth differ as Earth travels around the Sun?

2. Why are winter temperatures colder than the temperatures in summer?

3. In the passage, what does the word *revolve* mean?

4. Why don't areas near the equator experience winter and summer? Explain.

Unit D Wrap-Up

Chapter 19

What are the effects of the movement of Earth and the Moon?
- The movement of the Moon around Earth causes the Moon's phases.
- Earth's tilt and orbit around the Sun cause seasons.
- The positions of the Sun, Earth and Moon can cause eclipses.

Chapter 20

What is Earth's place in the universe?
- Earth's Sun is only one of many stars in the universe.
- Earth's solar system is part of the Milky Way Galaxy.
- Earth is the third planet from the Sun.

Chapter 21

How can robots help us now and in the future?
- Robots help people in industry, exploration, and medicine and at home by gathering information and doing work.
- Scientists are working on making robots from individual atoms.

Performance Assessment

Moon Phases

What causes phases of the Moon? Make a model of the Sun, Earth, and its Moon. Use a flashlight, a lump of clay, a straw, and two plastic foam balls—one four times larger than the other. Label the smaller ball *Moon.* Label the larger one *Earth.* The flashlight can be the Sun. Place the straw in the Earth ball, and attach it to a table with the clay. Shine the flashlight on Earth as you move the Moon around Earth in its orbit. What happens to the Moon as it orbits Earth?

Read More About Space and Technology

Look for books like these in the library.

Experiment How does a sunscreen's SPF relate to its effectiveness?

While the ozone layer surrounding Earth acts as a barrier to ultraviolet (UV) radiation, some still reaches Earth's surface. UV radiation can cause sunburn, tanning, and aging of the skin. It also increases the risk of skin cancer.

Materials

4 small paper plates

sunscreen lotion

aluminum foil

UV sensitive beads

4 black squares

timer

Process Skills

You **control variables** when you change only one thing in an **experiment**.

Ask a question.

How does the sun protection factor (called SPF) of a sunscreen affect the amount of protection from UV radiation?

no sunscreen / no sun

UV beads are beads that react to UV radiation by changing color.

State a hypothesis.

If UV beads are coated with sunscreens with different SPFs, will the beads coated with a sunscreen that has higher SPF show a smaller color change than UV beads coated with a sunscreen that has a lower SPF? Write your **hypothesis**.

Identify and control variables.

The SPF is the variable that you change. The variable you observe is the amount of color change that will occur in 30 seconds.

Test your hypothesis.

1 Write "no sunscreen, no sunlight" on one plate. Write "no sunscreen, full sunlight" on another paper plate. Label the other two plates with the SPF values of the sunscreens you will test, for example, "SPF 15/full sunlight" and "SPF 45/full sunlight."

SPF 45 / full sunlight

SPF 15 / full sunlight

no sunscreen / full sunlight

2 Place a small dab of sunscreen on a square of aluminum foil. Coat 4 beads with the sunscreen. Put the beads on the plate with the matching label.

3 Repeat with the other sunscreen. Use the same amount of sunscreen.

4 Place 4 uncoated beads on the "no sunscreen/no sunlight" plate and 4 uncoated beads on the "no sunscreen/full sunlight" plate.

SPF 15 / full sunlight

Wash your hands after handling sunscreen lotion.

5 Put black paper over each plate to keep out sunlight. Wait 5 minutes.

no sunscreen / no sunlight

6 Put the plates in direct sunlight. Remove the black paper from every plate except the "no sunscreen/no sunlight" plate.

7 **Observe** the beads after 30 seconds. Record the amount of color change.

Collect and record your data.

Use a chart like the one shown to record your data.

UV Beads (description)	Amount of Color Change after 30 seconds (none, a little, some, a lot)
no sunscreen/ no sunlight	
no sunscreen/ full sunlight	
SPF 15/ full sunlight	
SPF 45/ full sunlight	

Interpret your data.

Think about the SPF of the sunscreens and the amount of color change to the UV beads. Describe the relationship.

State your conclusion.

Draw a conclusion from your data. Does your conclusion agree with your hypothesis? Explain. **Communicate** your conclusions.

Go Further

How might water affect the amount of UV protection provided by a sunscreen? Design and carry out a plan to investigate this or other questions you may have.

Science Fair Projects

Solar Time

The earliest clocks used the Sun and shadows to tell the time of day.

Idea: Build a sundial and demonstrate how it works.

Robotic Arms

A robotic arm can have few parts, or it can have many.

Idea: Design an experiment to see whether more parts make a robotic arm better.

Crater Creations

When you look at Earth and the Moon, you can see evidence of craters.

Idea: Using sand and rocks, demonstrate how meteors form craters.

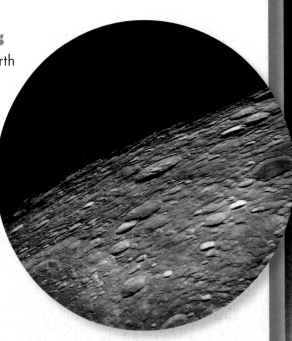

Full Inquiry

Using Scientific Methods

1. Ask a question.
2. State a hypothesis.
3. Identify and control variables.
4. Test your hypothesis.
5. Collect and record your data.
6. Interpret your data.
7. State your conclusions.
8. Go further.

EC CRU 10 9 8 7 6 5 4 3 2

Metric and Customary Measurement

The metric system is the measurement system most commonly used in science. Metric units are sometimes called SI units. SI stands for International System because these units are used around the world.

These prefixes are used in the metric system:

kilo- means *thousand*
1 kilometer equals 1,000 meters

milli means *one thousandth*
1,000 millimeters equals 1 meter

centi means *one hundredth*
100 centimeters equals 1 meter

Length and Distance

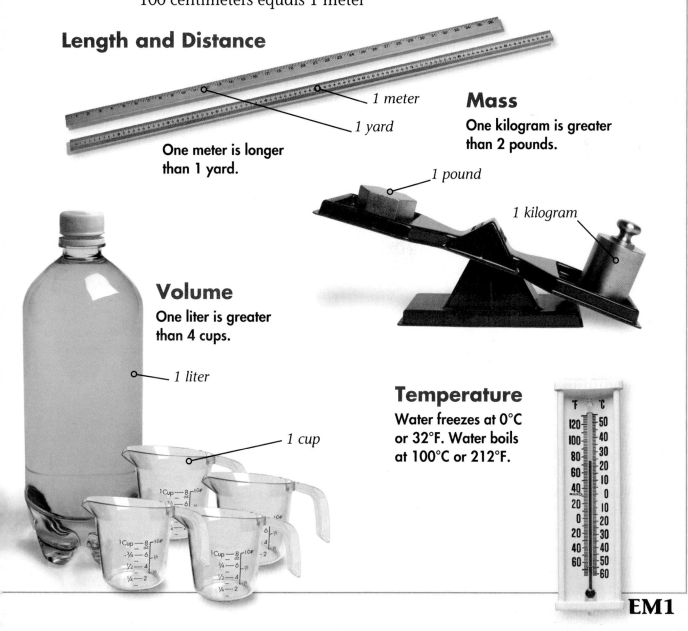

1 meter

1 yard

One meter is longer than 1 yard.

Mass

One kilogram is greater than 2 pounds.

1 pound

1 kilogram

Volume

One liter is greater than 4 cups.

1 liter

1 cup

Temperature

Water freezes at 0°C or 32°F. Water boils at 100°C or 212°F.

Glossary

The glossary uses letters and signs to show how words are pronounced. The mark ′ is placed after a syllable with a primary or heavy accent. The mark ′ is placed after a syllable with a secondary or lighter accent.

To hear these words pronounced, listen to the AudioText CD.

A

abiotic factor (ā′ bī ′ot ik fak′tər) a nonliving part of an ecosystem (page 146)

acceleration (ak sel′ ə rā′shən) the rate at which velocity changes (page 435)

acid precipitation (as′id pri si′ pə tā′shən) rain or snow that is more acidic than normal precipitation (page 307)

adaptation (a′d ap tā′shən) a characteristic that enables an organism to survive and reproduce in its environment (page 8)

air mass (âr mas) a very large body of air that has a similar temperature and humidity throughout (page 336)

air pressure (âr presh′ ər) the measure of force with which air particles push on matter (page 328)

alveoli (al vē′ō lī) tiny sacs in the lungs at the end of bronchioles (page 101)

antibody (an′ti bo′d ē) chemicals produced by white blood cells that kill specific pathogens (page 103)

asexual reproduction (ā sek′shü əl rē′prə duk′shen) production of offspring by a single parent (page 56)

astronomical unit (as′trə nä mi kəl yü′nit) the average distance of Earth from the Sun, about 149.6 million kilometers (page 560)

atmosphere (at′mə sfir) the blanket of gases that surrounds a planet (page 327)

autonomous robot (ȯ ton′ə məs rō′bot) a type of robot that acts without direct supervision (page 587)

B

bacteria (bak tir′ē ə) single-celled organisms that do not have a nucleus (page 12)

biome (bī′ōm) a large group of ecosystems with similar climates and organisms (page 148)

biosphere (bī′ə sfir) part of the Earth that can support living things (page 7)

biotic factor (bī o′t ik fak′tər) a living organism in an ecosystem (page 146)

C

carbon nanotube (kär′bən nan′ō tüb) carbon atoms in six-sided rings that are arranged in the shape of a tube (page 592)

cause (kȯz) the reason something happens (page 85)

cellular respiration (sel′yə lər res′pə rā′shən) the process by which cells combine glucose with oxygen for the release of energy (page 124)

chemical change (ke′mi kəl chānj) the changing of a substance into a completely new substance with different properties (page 376)

chemical property (ke′mi kəl pro′p ər tē) a characteristic that determines how a substance reacts with other substances (page 371)

chemical weathering (ke′mi kəl we′ᴛʜ ər ing) a change in minerals as they react with substances in the environment, such as water or oxygen (page 272)

chromosome (krō′mə sōm) coiled structure in a cell nucleus that carries information controlling the cell's activities (page 39)

classification (kla′sə fə kā′shən) a grouping of things according to their similarities (page 11)

climate (klī′mit) a pattern of weather that occurs in an area over a long period (page 342)

coal (kōl) a solid fossil fuel (page 306)

community (kə myü′nə tē) a group of populations that interact with one another in a particular area (page 144)

compare (kəm pâr′) to show how things are alike (page 5)

competition (kom′pə tis′hən) the struggle among organisms to survive in a habitat with limited resources (page 176)

compound (kom′pound) a substance composed of two or more elements that are chemically combined to form a new substance (page 400)

compound machine (kom′pound mə shēn′) a machine made up of one or more simple machines (page 456)

concentration (kon′sən trā′shən) a measure of the amount of solute dissolved in a solvent (page 405)

conclusion (kən klü′zhən) a decision reached after thinking about facts and details (page 213)

condensation (kon′den sā′shən) the change of state from a gas to a liquid (page 375)

conduction (kən duk′shən) heat transfer between two objects that touch (page 505)

conductor (kən duk′tər) a material through which electricity or heat is easily transfered (page 508)

constellation (kon′stə lā shən) a part of the sky containing a certain group of stars (page 568)

continental drift (kon′tə nen′tl drift) the theory stating that continents are continually moving (page 220)

contrast (kən trast′) to show how things are different (page 5)

convection (kən vek′shən) the transfer of thermal energy by the movement of a liquid or a gas (page 506)

core (kôr) the innermost layer of Earth (page 216)

crust (krust) the outermost solid layer of Earth (page 216)

crystal (kris′tl) a regular, repeating pattern in which particles of minerals are arranged (page 247)

decomposer (dē′kəm pō′zər) an organism that breaks down dead organisms and returns materials to the environment (page 171)

density (den′sə tē) the amount of mass in a certain volume of matter (page 368)

deposition (dep′ə zi′sh ən) the process of dropping sediments onto a new place after being carried away from another place (page 274)

detail (di′tāl or dē′tāl) a piece of information that supports a main idea (page 141)

diffusion (di fyü′shən) the movement of a substance from an area of higher concentration to an area of lower concentration (page 36)

DNA a material in a cell's nucleus that stores coded information about how an organism will grow and develop (page 39)

dwarf planet (dwôrf plan′it) small, spherical object that orbits the Sun (page 560)

ecosystem (ē′kō sis′təm or ek′ō sis′təm) an area in which living things and nonliving parts of the environment interact (page 145)

effect (i fekt′) what happens as the result of a cause (page 85)

effort force (e′fərt fôrs) a force applied to the end of a lever to lift a load (page 458)

egg cell (eg sel) sex cell of the female parent (page 62)

electric circuit (i lek′trik sėr′kit) a closed path along which current can flow (page 483)

electric current (i lek′trik kėr′rənt) a flow of electric charge in a material (page 483)

electric motor (i lek′trik mō′tər) a device that changes electrical energy to kinetic energy (page 487)

electromagnetic wave (i lek′trō mag neti′k wāv) light and other forms of energy that travel through space (page 511)

element (el′ə mənt) a substance made of only one kind of atom (page 394)

endocrine gland (en′dō krən or en′dō krin gland) an organ that releases hormones directly into the blood (page 96)

endoplasmic reticulum (en′dō plaz′mic ri tik′yə ləm) a network of folded membranes that serves as the cell's transportation system (page 34)

energy (e′nər jē) the ability to cause change or to do work (page 479)

energy pyramid (e′nər jē pir′ə mid) a model that shows the amount of energy available at each level of an ecosystem (page 175)

environment (en vī′rən mənt) all the conditions that surround a living thing (page 144)

enzyme (en′zīm) a chemical that helps break down food into nutrients during digestion (page 98)

epidermis (e′pə dėr′mis) the thin outer layer of plant cells through which water and minerals from the soil enter the root (page 119)

erosion (i rō′zhən) the process by which soil and sediments are transferred from one location to another, usually by wind, water, ice, and gravity (page 273)

fault (fôlt) a break in the Earth's crust at the boundaries where plates slide past each other (page 226)

fertilization (fėr′tl ə zā′shən) the joining of male and female cells in sexual reproduction (page 62)

force (fôrs) a push or pull (page 423)

fossil fuels (fos′əl fyü′əlz) energy sources made from the remains of organisms (page 304)

friction (frik′shən) the force that resists the movement of one surface past another (page 426)

front (frunt) the boundary that forms between air masses (page 336)

fulcrum (ful′krəm) a support on which a lever rests while moving or lifting an object (page 458)

fungi (fung′gī or fung′jī) members of a kingdom of mostly many-celled organisms, some of which break down other organisms; includes mushrooms, yeasts, and molds (page 12)

galaxy (gal′ək sē) a huge grouping of stars (page 559)

gene (jēn) sections of DNA that control the substances the cell makes and when it makes them (page 59)

generator (jen′ə rāt′tər) a device that changes mechanical energy into electrical energy (page 488)

geothermal energy (jē′ō thėr′məl en′ər jē) energy of the heat inside the Earth (page 304)

gland (gland) an organ in the endocrine system that produces a chemical (page 96)

gravitational force (grav′ə tā′shən al fôrs) the force of attraction between objects in the universe (page 428)

guard cell (gärd sel) one of a pair of cells that work together to open and close a leaf's stoma (page 121)

heat (hēt) thermal energy that moves from one substance to another (page 504)

heredity (hə red′ə tē) the passing of traits from parents to their offspring (page 55)

hormone (hôr′mōn) a substance released by an endocrine gland that controls some of the body's functions (page 96)

host (hōst) an organism that is harmed in symbiosis (page 180)

humidity (hyü mid′ə tē) the amount of water vapor in the air (page 332)

humus (hyü′məs) the organic part of soil (page 255)

igneous rock (ig′nē əs rok′) rock formed from lava that has cooled and hardened (page 250)

impulse (im′puls) a message that travels across a neuron and from one neuron to another (page 95)

industrial robot (in dəs′trē əl rō′bot) automatically controlled robot that can handle several products or items at a time and be programmed to complete several tasks (page 586)

inertia (in ėr′shə) the tendency of an object to remain at rest or in constant motion unless a force acts on it (page 437)

inference (in′fər əns) a conclusion reached after thinking about a topic (page 29)

instantaneous speed (in′stən tā′nē əs spēd) an object's speed at any moment (page 434)

insulator (in′sə lā′tər) a material through which heat or electricity is not easily transferred (page 508)

kinetic energy (ki net′ik en′ər jē) the energy of a moving object (page 479)

light-year (līt′yir′) the distance light travels in one year: 9 trillion, 460 billion kilometers (page 564)

lithosphere (lith′ə sfir) the Earth's crust and the solid part of the mantle (page 218)

load (lōd) force of an object on a lever (page 458)

lunar eclipse (lü′nər i klips′) the movement of the Moon into Earth's shadow (page 542)

machine (mə shēn′) any device that helps people do work (page 456)

magnetic domain (mag ne′tik dō mān′) a large number of atoms with their magnetic fields pointing in the same direction (page 484)

magnetic field (mag net′ik fēld) the space around a magnet in which the magnet can exert a force (page 484)

magnitude (mag′nə tüd) the brightness of a star (page 565)

main idea (mān i dē′ə) the most important idea of a reading selection (page 141)

mantle (man′tl) a thick layer of Earth just between the crust and the core that contains most of Earth's mass (page 216)

mass (mas) the amount of matter in an object (page 367)

mechanical weathering (mə kan′ə kəl weᴛн′ər ing) breaking down of rock by wind, water, and ice (page 272)

meiosis (mī ō′sis) the process of cell division by which sex cells are formed (page 62)

metamorphic rock (me′tə môr′fik rok′) rock formed when heat, pressure, or chemical reactions change one type of rock into another type of rock (page 250)

meteorologist (mē′tē ə rol′ə jist) a scientist who studies weather (page 336)

mineral (min′ rəl or mi′nərəl) a natural, nonliving solid with a definite chemical structure (page 247)

mitochondria (mī′tə kon′drē ə) parts of cells that convert chemical energy of food into a form that the cell can use (page 34)

mitosis (mī tō′sis) the process in which a cell nucleus divides (page 39)

mixture (miks′chər) a combination of substances in which the atoms of the substances are not chemically combined (page 402)

momentum (mō men′təm) a measure of the force needed to stop a moving object (page 441)

moon (mün) a natural body that orbits a planet (page 560)

nanotechnology (nan′ō tek nol′ə jē) technology that deals with materials and processes on a very small scale (page 590)

natural gas (nach′ər əl or na′ cha rəl gas) a fossil fuel that is a mixture of gases (page 306)

neuron (nür′on) nerve cell that passes messages throughout the body (page 95)

nonrenewable resource (non′ ri nü′ə bəl ri sôrs′ or rē′sôrs) a resource that cannot be replaced as fast as it is used (page 295)

nonvascular plant (non vas′kyə lər plant) a low-growing plant that does not have tubes to carry materials (page 14)

nuclear fusion (nü′klē ər fyü′zhən) the process in which the nuclei of two or more atoms join to form a single, larger nucleus (page 564)

orbit (ôr′bit) the path of an object that revolves around another object (page 540)

organelle (ôr′gə nel′) a structure that performs specific functions within a cell (page 34)

organic matter (ôr ga′nik ma′tər) any substance that is made of living things or the remains of living things (page 255)

osmosis (oz mō′sis) the diffusion of water across the cell membrane (page 37)

parasite (par′ə sīt) an organism that benefits from symbiosis (page 180)

pathogen (path′ə jən) an organism that causes disease (page 102)

periodic table (pir′ē o′dik tā′bəl) a chart in which all the elements are arranged according to the repeating pattern of their properties (page 396)

petroleum (pə trō′lē əm) a liquid fossil fuel (page 306)

phloem (flō′əm) part of a plant's vascular system that carries sugars throughout the plant (page 119)

photosynthesis (fō′tō sin′thə sis) the process in which plants use energy from light to make glucose and release oxygen (page 122)

physical change (fiz′ə kəl chānj) the change in the appearance of a substance while its properties stay the same (page 376)

physical property (fi′zə kəl pro′pər tē) properties of matter that can be seen or measured without changing the substance into something else (page 370)

planet (plan′it) a large, spherical object that orbits the Sun and has cleared other objects from its orbit (page 560)

plate boundary (plāt boun′dər ē) an area where plates meet (page 226)

plate tectonics (plāt tek ton′iks) the theory that the Earth's lithosphere is broken into about 20 moving plates (page 224)

population (pop′yə lā′shən) a group of individuals that belong to the same species and live in the same area (page 144)

potential energy (pə ten′shəl en′ər jē) the energy an object has due to its position (page 479)

predict (pri dikt′) to make a statement about what might happen next (page 165)

radiation (rā′dē ā′shən) the transfer of energy in the form of waves (page 506)

reflection (ri flek′shən) the bouncing of light rays off the surface of a material (page 513)

refraction (ri frak′shən) the bending of light as it passes from one material to another (page 512)

relative humidity (rel′ə tiv hyü mid′ə tē) the amount of water vapor the air actually contains compared with the amount it could hold at a given temperature (page 332)

renewable resource (ri nü′ə bəl ri sôrs′ or rē′sors) a resource that can be replaced through natural processes almost as fast as it can be used (page 295)

revolve (ri volv′) to move on a path around an object (page 536)

ribosome (ri′bə sōm) a structure in the endoplasmic reticulum that begins the process of making proteins (page 34)

robot (rō′bot) a machine that is able to get information from its surroundings and do work (page 583)

robotics (rō bo′tiks) the technology dealing with the design, construction, and operation of robots (page 583)

rock (rok) a solid, natural material made up of one or more minerals (page 250)

rotate (rō′tāt) to spin around an axis (page 536)

sediment (sə′də mənt) solid particles carried from one place and dropped onto another place (page 271)

sedimentary rock (sə′də men′tə rē rok′) rock formed from layers of sediment that have been cemented together (page 250)

selective breeding (si lek′tiv brē′ding) the process of selecting a few organisms with desired traits to serve as parents of offspring (page 72)

sequence (sē′kwəns) the step-by-step ordering of events (pages 53)

sexual reproduction (sek′shü əl rē′prə duk′shən) reproduction by two parents (page 62)

simple machine (sim′pəl mə shēn) a tool made up of one or two parts (page 456)

solar eclipse (sō′lər i klips′) an alignment of the Sun, Moon, and Earth in which the Moon blocks the Sun from Earth's view (page 542)

solar system (sō′lər sis′təm) the Sun and the cluster of bodies that travel around it (page 560)

solubility (sol′yə bil′ə tē) the maximum amount of solute that can be dissolved in a solvent at a particular temperature, usually expressed in grams of solute per milliliter of solvent (page 405)

solute (sol′yüt or sō′lüt) a substance that has been dissolved (page 404)

solution (sə lü′shən) one substance dissolved in another (page 404)

solvent (sol′vənt) a substance in which a solute is dissolved (page 404)

species (spē′shēz) a group of very similar organisms whose members can mate with one another and produce offspring that are able to produce offspring (page 8)

speed (spēd) a measure of how fast an object is moving (page 434)

sperm cell (spėrm sel) sex cell of the male parent (page 62)

star (stär) a huge, hot, glowing ball of gas in the sky (page 564)

stoma (stō′mə) a small hole in the epidermis of a leaf through which water and gases pass in and out of the plant (page 121)

succession (sək səs′hən) a series of predictable changes that occur in an ecosystem over time (page 187)

symbiosis (sim′bē ō′sis) a close, long-term relationship between organisms that benefits at least one of the organisms (page 180)

thermal energy (thėr′məl e′n ər jē) the total kinetic and potential energy of the particles in a substance (page 503)

transpiration (tran′spi rā′shən) the loss of water from a leaf (page 121)

tropism (trō′pi′zəm) plant behavior caused by growth toward or away from something in the environment (page 129)

vascular plant (vas′kya lər plant) a plant that has tubes for carrying water and nutrients throughout the organism (page 14)

velocity (və los′ə tē) the speed of an object in a particular direction (page 435)

volume (vol′yəm) the amount of space that something takes up (page 367)

weather (we′ŦHər) the condition of the atmosphere at a particular time and place (page 336)

weathering (we′ŦHər ing) the process of breaking down rock into smaller pieces (page 272)

weight (wāt) a measure of the pull of gravity on an object (page 368)

work (wėrk) to use force in order to move an object a certain distance (page 455)

xylem (zī′ləm) a layer of plant cells that moves water and minerals from the roots to other parts of the plant (page 119)

Index

This index lists the pages on which topics appear in this book. Page numbers after a *p* refer to a photograph or drawing. Page numbers after a *c* refer to a chart, graph, or diagram.

Glucose, *c*13, 170
  biofeedback loop for, 97, *c*97
  in leaves, 121, *c*121
  photosynthesis and, 122,
    *c*122, *c*123
  in plants, 119, 122, 124
Gneiss, *p*251
GOES (weather satellite), 341,
  *p*341
Gold, 246, 247, *p*394
Gorilla, *c*17, *c*59
GPS. *See* Global Positioning
  System (GPS)
Grand Canyon (Arizona), 215,
  252
Granite, 245, *p*252
Graph and graphing, 183
  changes in states of matter,
    *c*380, 380–381
  of Earth's crust, *c*216
Graphic Organizer, *c*5, *c*15,
  *c*53, *c*65, *c*79, *c*85, *c*117,
  *c*141, *c*165, *c*213, *c*245,
  *c*269, *c*293, *c*325, *c*365,
  *c*389, *c*421, *c*453, *c*477,
  *c*501, *c*533, *c*549, *c*557,
  *c*575, *c*581
Graphite, 592, *c*592
Grass, 120
Grasshopper, *p*152
Grassland, *c*148, 152, *p*152
Gravitational force, 418, *p*428,
  428–429
Gravitational pull
  of Earth, Sun, and Moon, 539
Gravitropism, *c*129
Gravity, 423, 428
  gases in atmosphere and, 327
  Moon's mass and, 536
  orbit of planets and Sun's,
    560
  of planets, 562–563
  star life cycle and, 566
  universe and, 430
  water flow and, 276
  weight and, 368
Gray fox, 167, *p*167, *c*167
Great Lakes, 271
Great Plains of North America,
  271
Green algae, 31, *p*31
Green Belt Movement, 200
Greenhouse effect, 307, 507
Greenhouse gases, 307
Green object, *c*513
Group, periodic table, 399

Growth
  in plant, 128
Guard cell, 115, 121, *c*121
Guided Inquiry Investigate,
  18–19, 42–43, 74–75, 106–
  107, 130–131, 154–155,
  192–193, 234–235, 258–
  259, 282–283, 314–315,
  344–345, 378–379, 408–
  409, 442–443, 466–477,
  490–491, 514–515, 544–
  545, 570–571, 594–595
Guinea pig, *p*68, 68–69, *p*69
Gulf of Mexico, 277, 338
Gulf Stream, *p*342
GWh (1 billion watt-hours), 492
Gymnosperm, 14, *c*15, 127,
  *p*127
Gypsum, *p*248

H

Habitat, 297
Habitat destruction, *p*188
  species extinction and, 169
Hail, 334
Hair cell, *c*105
Hardness of mineral, 248
Hawaii
  surfing waves in, *p*278
  volcanoes in, *c*230
Hazardous material, 188
Health
  habits for staying healthy,
    *c*105
  of muscles and bones, 93,
    *p*93
Health in Science, 57, 87, 89,
  171, 395, 429, 459
Heart, 88, *c*88–*c*89
  cardiac muscle in, 92
  in circulatory system, 100
Heart muscle cell, *c*88
Heart rate equations, *c*108,
  108–109
Heart tissue, *c*105
Heat, 479, 498, 504, *p*504
  conduction and, 505, *c*505
  conductors and, 508
  convection and, 506, *c*506
  from friction, 457, 480
  insulators and, 508, *p*508,
    509, *p*509
  radiation and, 507, *p*507
  from Sun, 535

Heisenberg, Werner, *c*393
Helicopter, *p*457
Helium, *c*397
Helm (sailboat), *c*465
Helsinki, Finland, *c*156
Hematite, *p*248
Herbaceous plant, 120, *c*120
Heredity, 50, 55, *p*55
  modeling, *c*74, 74–75, *c*75
Hess, Harry, 222
Hibernation, 168, *p*168, *c*194,
  194–195
High tide, 431
Himalayan Mountains, *p*227
Hinge joint, 91, *p*91, *c*92
Holmes, Arthur, 222
Home building
  insulation and, 509, *p*509
Home robot, *p*589
Hooke, Robert, *c*32, 33
Horizon, 539
Hormone, 82, 96
  control of glucose in blood
    and, 97, *c*97
Horse, *p*8–*p*9
Horsetail, 14, *c*15, *c*59
Host, 162, 180
Hot spot (volcano), *c*230
Hot spring, *c*13
Household chemicals
  elements and compounds in,
    401
Houseplant, 141
How to Read Science. *See also*
  Target Reading Skills
  Cause and Effect, 85, 91, 97,
    105, 111, 325, 327, 335,
    343, 349, 391, 453, 471
  Compare and Contrast, 5, 13,
    16, 23, 117, 119, 125,
    127, 129, 135, 245, 251,
    253, 257, 389, 392, 399,
    401, 403, 405, 413, 457,
    461, 501, 509, 511, 513
  Draw Conclusions, 213, 217,
    225, 227, 233, 239, 269,
    273, 279, 281, 287, 557,
    561, 569, 575
  Main Idea and Details, 141,
    147, 152, 159, 293, 295,
    297, 305, 307, 319, 533,
    535, 543, 549, 581, 583,
    589, 599
  Make Inferences, 29, 35, 39,
    47

Credits

Illustrations

8-16, 120-134 Sharon & Joel Harris; 32-40 Paulette Dennis AOCA, BScBMC, CMI; 34-40 Robert Ulrich; 38 Bob Kayganich; 50, 66, 168-190, 210-222, 230-233 David Preiss; 51-72 Robert Fenn; 57, 70, 129, 242-255, 593 Tony Randazzo; 82-83, 88-103 Jeff Mangiat; 132, 316, 399, 516 Big Sesh Studios; 139, 149 Adam Benton; 144-152 David Schweitzer; 176, 182-185, 216-232 Precision Graphics; 181, 267, 272-280, 424-440 Clint Hansen; 296-341, 461-464, 536-540. 560-569 Peter Bollinger; 368-376, 403, 505-512 Patrick Gnan

Photographs

Every effort has been made to secure permission and provide appropriate credit for photographic material. The publisher deeply regrets any omission and pledges to correct errors called to its attention in subsequent editions.

Unless otherwise acknowledged, all photographs are the property of Scott Foresman, a division of Pearson Education.

Photo locators denoted as follows: Top (T), Center (C), Bottom (B), Left (L), Right (R), Background (Bkgd).

Cover:

©Planet Earth/Getty Images, ©Gerry Ellis/Minden Pictures, ©Konrad Wothe/ Minden Pictures

Front Matter:

v ©DK Images; xi ©DK Images; xii Getty Images; xiiii ©DK Images; xviii ©Michael & Patricia Fogden/Corbis, (Bkgd) ©T. Allofs/Zefa/Masterfile Corporation, (BR) ©Michael & Patricia Fogden/Minden Pictures; xxv (Bkgd) ©Norbert Wu/Minden Pictures, ©Gloria H. Chomica/Masterfile Corporation, Courtesy of Vision Research, Inc.; xxix (BL) Getty Images, (TL) Courtesy of Vision Research, Inc.; xxx (TR) ©Leonard Lessin/Peter Arnold, Inc.

Unit A:

Chapter 1: 1 ©Wolfgang Kaehler/Corbis; 2 (T) ©1992 John Cancalosi/DRK Photo, (BL) ©Jeffrey Rotman/Photo Researchers, Inc., (BR) ©DK Images, (T) ©Eric Soder/NHPA Limited; 3 (BR) ©Eye of Science/Photo Researchers, Inc., (BL) ©Chinch Gryniewicz/Ecoscene/Corbis, (CR) ©Wolfgang Baumeister/Photo Researchers, Inc., (TR) ©DK Images; 5 (CR) ©Clouds Hill Imaging, Ltd./Corbis, (Bkgd) ©1992 John Cancalosi/DRK Photo; 6 ©1992 John Cancalosi/DRK Photo; 7 (TL) ©Eric Soder/NHPA Limited, (CR) ©George Bernard/OSF/Animals Animals/Earth Scenes, ©David Fleetham/Getty Images; 8 (TL) ©Gerry Ellis/ Minden Pictures, (BL) ©Jeffrey Rotman/Photo Researchers, Inc., (CL) ©Kennan Ward/Corbis; 9 ©J. Eastcott/Y. Eastcott Film/NGS Image Collection; 10 (TR) ©DK Images, (TL, CL) Jerry Young/©DK Images, (TC) Getty Images, (CR) ©George Grall/NGS Image Collection, (BL) Natural History Museum /©DK Images; 12 (BL) ©SciMAT/Photo Researchers, Inc., (CL) ©Clouds Hill Imaging, Ltd./Corbis; 13 ©Wolfgang Baumeister/Photo Researchers, Inc., (CL) ©Andrew Syred/Photo Researchers, Inc., (TC) ©Eye of Science/Photo Researchers, Inc., ©DK Images, (B) ©Martin Harvey/Peter Arnold, Inc.; 14 ©DK Images; 15 (CR) ©DK Images, (C) ©Mary Rhodes/Animals Animals/ Earth Scenes, (CL) ©Chinch Gryniewicz/Ecoscene/Corbis; 16 (CR, BL) ©DK Images, (TL) Andreas von Einsiedel/©DK Images; 17 (B, C) ©DK Images, (TR) ©Norbert Wu/Minden Pictures, (BR) ©Fred Bavendam/Minden Pictures, (TL) ©Franklin Viola/Animals Animals/Earth Scenes; 18 (TR) ©Robert Landau/ Corbis, (C, BR) ©DK Images, (CR) Jerry Young/©DK Images, (BC) ©Kevin & Betty Collins/Visuals Unlimited; 20 (Bkgd) ©David Samuel Robbins/Corbis, (L) ©Brian A. Wikander/Corbis, (BR) ©Dennis Blachut/Corbis, (R) ©David Cayless/ Oxford Scientific Films; 21 (CR) ©Gavriel Jecan/Corbis, (BL) ©Terry Whittaker/ Frank Lane Picture Agency/Corbis; 24 (TR) California Academy of Sciences, (Bkgd) ©Rubberball Productions/Getty Images; 25 (Bkgd) ©Eye of Science/ Photo Researchers, Inc., (BR) ©David Becker/Photo Researchers, Inc.; Chapter 2: 29 (CR) Science Museum, London/DK Images; 30 ©Janet Foster/Masterfile Corporation; 31 (TL) Hilda Canter-Lund/Freshwater Biological Association, (L) ©Dr. David Patterson/Photo Researchers, Inc., (B) ©Eric Grave/Science Photo Library/Photo Researchers, Inc.; 32 (CL) ©Bettmann/Corbis, (BL) Science & Society Picture Library, (BR) Science Museum, London/DK Images, (C) ©K. R. Porter/Photo Researchers, Inc., (BR) Photo Researchers, Inc.; 33 (BL) ©Oliver Meckes/Photo Researchers, Inc., (BL) ©Bettmann/Corbis, (TL) ©DK Images; 35 ©DK Images; 37 (BL) ©Nigel Cattlin/Photo Researchers, Inc., (TR) ©Michael Abbey/Photo Researchers, Inc., (CR) ©Runk/Schoenberger/Grant Heilman Photography; 39 ©Andrew Syred/Photo Researchers, Inc.; 40 ©Runk/ Schoenberger/Grant Heilman Photography; 41 (TR, BR) ©Lester V. Bergman/ Corbis; 42 ©Carolina Biological/Visuals Unlimited; 44 (Bkgd) Custom Medical Stock Photo, (C) ©Reuters/Corbis, (CR) ©Robert Pickett/Corbis, (BR) ©Carolina Biological/Visuals Unlimited; (B) ©Lester V. Bergman/Corbis, (BL) ©Sinclair Stammers/Photo Researchers, Inc.; 45 (BL) ©Carolina Biological/Visuals Unlimited, (Bkgd) ©COLOR-PIC/Animals Animals/Earth Scenes, ©Jim Zipp/ Photo Researchers, Inc.; 48 (Bkgd) Getty Images, (BL) Photo Researchers, Inc.;

49 ©E. R. Degginger/Photo Researchers, Inc., ©Biophoto Associates/Photo Researchers, Inc.; Chapter 3: 50 ©American Images Inc./Getty Images; 51 (TR) ©CNRI/Photo Researchers, Inc., (CR) ©Frans Lanting/Minden Pictures, (BR) Tracy Morgan/©DK Images; 54 ©Gavriel Jecan/Getty Images; 55 ©Gavriel Jecan/Getty Images, (BR) ©DK Images; 56 (CL) ©Carolina Biological Supply Company/Phototake, (TL) ©CNRI/Photo Researchers, Inc., (BL) Getty Images; 57 (BR) ©DK Images, (TR) ©Andrew J. Martinez/Photo Researchers, Inc.; 58 ©Andrew Syred/Photo Researchers, Inc.; 59 (TR) ©Gerry Ellis/Minden Pictures, (BR) ©DK Images, (CR) Jerry Young/©DK Images; 60 ©Gerry Ellis/Minden Pictures; 61 ©James King-Holmes/Photo Researchers, Inc.; 62 (BL) ©Frans Lanting/Minden Pictures, (TL) ©David M. Phillips/Photo Researchers, Inc.; 64 (TL) ©David M. Phillips/Photo Researchers, Inc., (T) ©SciMAT/Photo Researchers, Inc.; 65 (TR) ©Fred Bavendam/Minden Pictures, (BR) ©Bill Bachman/Photo Researchers, Inc.; 66 ©American Images Inc./Getty Images; 67 ©M. I. Walker/Photo Researchers, Inc.; 70 ©J. C. Carton/Bruce Coleman Inc.; 72 ©DK Images; 73 (TL, R) Tracy Morgan/©DK Images; 74 ©Scott T. Smith/Corbis; 76 (Bkgd) ©The Image Bank/Getty Images, (TC) ©Dmitriy Margolin/Acclaim Images, (C, BC) ©ThinkStock/SuperStock; 77 ©ThinkStock/ SuperStock; 79 ©CNRI/Photo Researchers, Inc.; 80 JSC/NASA; 81 ©Lester Lefkowitz/Corbis; 82 ©CNRI/Photo Researchers, Inc.; 86 ©Jay Dickman/Corbis; 88 (BL) ©Science Photo Library/Photo Researchers, Inc., (BC) ©VVG/Photo Researchers, Inc.; 89 (TR) ©A. Syred/Photo Researchers, Inc., (C) ©SIU/Visuals Unlimited; 90 (BR) ©SPL/Photo Researchers, Inc., (CL) ©Dee Breger/Photo Researchers, Inc.; 91 ©P. Motta/Photo Researchers, Inc.; 94 (CR) ©Science Pictures Limited/Photo Researchers, Inc., (CL) ©CNRI/Photo Researchers, Inc.; 99 (TR) ©Omikron/Photo Researchers, Inc., (CR) ©SPL/Photo Researchers, Inc., (BR) ©Eye of Science/Photo Researchers, Inc.; 100 (BL) ©Dr. Richard Kessel & Dr. Randy Kardon/Tissues & Organs/Visuals Unlimited, (C) ©Science Photo Library/Photo Researchers, Inc.; 104 ©RNT Productions/ Corbis; 105 (T) ©Kenneth Eward/Photo Researchers, Inc., (TR) ©Asa Thoresen/ Photo Researchers, Inc., (CR) ©David M. Phillips/Photo Researchers, Inc., (BR) ©Dr. Richard Kessel & Dr. Randy Kardon/Tissues & Organs/Visuals Unlimited; 106 ©Dr. David M. Phillips/Visuals Unlimited; 108 ©Lester Lefkowitz/Corbis; 109 ©The Image Bank/Getty Images; 112 (Bkgd) ©Stem Jems/Photo Researchers, Inc., (BL) ©Lester Lefkowitz/Corbis, (TR) NASA; 113 ©Steve Satushek/Getty Images, (TR) ©Ted Kinsman/Photo Researchers, Inc.; Chapter 5: 114 (T) ©DK Images, (BL) ©Runk/Schoenberger/Grant Heilman Photography; 115 (BL) ©Ed Reschke/Peter Arnold, Inc., (BR) ©Dr. Jeremy Burgess/Photo Researchers, Inc.; 117 (TR) Brand X Pictures, (Bkgd) ©Dan Suzio/Photo Researchers, Inc., (CR) ©A. Riedmiller/Peter Arnold, Inc.; 118 ©Dan Suzio/ Photo Researchers, Inc.; 119 ©Runk/Schoenberger/Grant Heilman Photography; 120 ©Runk/Schoenberger/Grant Heilman Photography, (R) ©DK Images; 121 ©Dr. Jeremy Burgess/Photo Researchers, Inc., ©DK Images; 122 ©DK Images, (BR) ©Dr. Jeremy Burgess/Photo Researchers, Inc.; 124 ©P. Motta & T. Naguro/Photo Researchers, Inc.; 125 (T) ©Bill Brooks/Masterfile Corporation, (TR) ©DK Images; 126 ©Michael Mahovlich/Masterfile Corporation, (TR) ©DK Images; 127 (L) ©Francesc Muntada/Corbis, (TR) ©DK Images; 128 Getty Images; 129 (TL) ©Ed Reschke/Peter Arnold, Inc., (TC) ©Robert Calentine/Visuals Unlimited, (TR) ©Adam Jones/Visuals Unlimited; 130 ©Bryan F. Peterson/Corbis; 136 (Bkgd) ©Stone/Getty Images, (CR) ©Photographer's Choice/Getty Images, (BL) ©John Miller/Bridgeman Art Library; 137 (Bkgd, CR) ©Larry Williams/Corbis; Chapter 6: 138 (BL) ©Jose Fuste Raga/eStock Photo, (BR) ©Steve Kaufman/Corbis, (BC) ©Gray Hardel/ Corbis; 139 ©David Paynter/Age Fotostock; 142 ©Ron Thomas/Getty Images; 143 (CR) ©Gerald L. Kooyman/Animals Animals/Earth Scenes, (BL) ©DK Images; 144 ©David Paynter/Age Fotostock; 146 (BL) ©Steve Kaufman/Corbis, (R) ©Jose Fuste Raga/eStock Photo; 147 (TR) Jerry Young/©DK Images, (L) ©Roger Leo/Index Stock Imagery; 150 (BL) ©G. K. & Vikki Hart/Getty Images, (TR) ©Cornelia Doerr/Age Fotostock, (BR) ©Brian Sytnyk/Masterfile Corporation; 151 ©Michael Sewell/Peter Arnold, Inc.; 152 (TR) ©Charlie Ott Photography/Photo Researchers, Inc., (BR) ©Tom Bean/DRK Photo, (CL) ©Paul A. Souders/Corbis, (BL) ©Frank Greenaway/DK Images; 153 (TL) ©Don Pitcher/Stock Boston, (BL) ©Doug Sokell/Visuals Unlimited, (TR) ©Joseph Van Os/Getty Images, (CR) ©DK Images; 154 ©Bill Bachmann/PhotoEdit; 156 (T) ©Heikki Nikki/Oxford Scientific Films, (BC) ©Sally A. Morgan; Ecoscene/ Corbis, (B) ©O. Alamany & E. Vicens/Corbis; 157 (TL) ©Royalty-Free/Corbis, (TC) ©Joel W. Rogers/Corbis, (TR) ©Jose Fuste Raga/Corbis; 160 (Bkgd) ©The Image Bank/Getty Images, (R) ©Paul A. Souders/Corbis, (CR) Getty Images, (TL) ©Brand X Pictures/Getty Images; 161 (Bkgd) ©Tui De Roy/Minden Pictures, (TR) ©Mitsuhiko Imamori/Minden Pictures; Chapter 7: 162 (T) ©Renee Lynn/ Corbis, (BR) ©Mike Severns/Getty Images, (BR) ©Michael Fogden/Animals Animals/Earth Scenes; 163 (BR) ©DK Images, (BL) ©1999/Gary Braasch; 165 (Bkgd) ©Frans Lemmens/Getty Images, (CR) ©Sally Brown/Index Stock Imagery; 166 (BR) ©DK Images, (Bkgd) ©Frans Lemmens/Getty Images; 167 (TL) ©Royalty-Free/Corbis, (CL) ©Charles Melton/Visuals Unlimited; 168 (L) ©James Balog/Getty Images, (T) ©DK Images, (CL) ©Michael Fogden/DRK Photo, (TL) ©Royalty-Free/Corbis; 169 ©Johnny Johnson/Animals Animals/Earth Scenes; 170 ©DK Images; 171 (BL) ©Patrick Johns/Corbis, (BR) ©DK Images, (TR) ©B. Murton/Southhampton Oceanography Centre/Photo Researchers, Inc.; 172 (L, BL, TC, C, CL, B, TR, CR, R) ©DK Images, (BR) ©H. Taylor/OSF/Animals Animals/Earth Scenes, (T) Frank Greenaway/©DK Images; 173 (C, CL, BC, TR, CR, BR, B) ©DK Images, (BL) ©Harold Taylor/OSF Limited; 174 (T, B, CL) ©DK Images, (CR) Kim Taylor and Jane Burton/©DK Images, (CR) Frank Greenaway/ ©DK Images; 175 (R, CR) ©DK Images, (CL) Dave King/©DK Images; 176 ©Renee Lynn/Corbis; 178 (TL, CL) ©DK Images; 179 (C, BR) ©Michael & Patricia Fogden/Minden Pictures, (T) AP/Wide World Photos, (CR) ©Norbert

EC CRU 10 9 8 7 6 5 4 3 2 1